Charles Walbridge

D1020260

The New Men's Studies

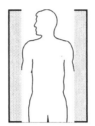

The New Men's Studies

A Selected and Annotated Interdisciplinary Bibliography

Second Edition

Eugene R. August

Alumni Chair in the Humanities
University of Dayton

1994

Libraries Unlimited, Inc.

Englewood, Colorado

To the memory of my father,
Joseph L. August
and my mother,
Florence C. August

Copyright © 1994 Eugene R. August
All Rights Reserved
Printed in the United States of America

No part of this publication may be reproduced, stored in a
retrieval system, or transmitted, in any form or by any means,
electronic, mechanical, photocopying, recording, or otherwise,
without the prior written permission of the publisher.

LIBRARIES UNLIMITED, INC.
P.O. Box 6633
Englewood, CO 80155-6633
1-800-237-6124

Project Editor: Kevin W. Perizzolo
Copy Editor: Jason Cook
Interior Book Design and Typesetting: Judy Gay Matthews
Indexer: D. Aviva Rothschild

Library of Congress Cataloging-in-Publication Data

August, Eugene R., 1935-
   The new men's studies : a selected and annotated interdisciplinary
bibliography / Eugene R. August. -- 2nd ed.
   xx, 440 p. 17x25 cm.
   Includes bibliographical references and index.
   ISBN 1-56308-084-2
   1. Men--Bibliography. 2. Men's studies--Bibliography. I. Title.
Z7164.M49A84 1994
[HQ1090]
016.30531--dc20   94-32454
                                                        CIP

Contents

Acknowledgments

In compiling this bibliography, I have incurred debts of thanks to many people, only some of whom can be acknowledged here:

The University of Dayton Research Council, for a summer grant that enabled me to work full-time on this project;

The staff of the Roesch Library at the University of Dayton, especially Robert L. Leach and Mary Ann Middendorp of the interlibrary loan department; Dr. Nicoletta C. Hary, associate director of technical services; and Jacqueline J. Johnston, acquisitions assistant;

Dr. Paul J. Morman, dean of the College of Arts and Sciences;

Dr. James P. Farrelly, chair of the Department of English, for numerous acts of encouragement and help during the course of this project;

The students in my "Modern Men: Images and Realities" classes during the past 11 years, for insights and bibliographic help;

James R. Rettig of the Earl Gregg Swem Library at the College of William and Mary, for his expertise and friendship;

Carolyn A. Ludwig, for expert secretarial help;

Kevin W. Perizzolo, my project editor at Libraries Unlimited, and Jason Cook, my copy editor, for expert editorial skills;

Barbara August, my wife of 30 wonderful years, and our sons, Robert and James, for unfailing support.

Introduction

Growth of the New Men's Studies

"An excellent case might be made, in short, for the establishment
of gentlemen's studies programs at major universities."
—Alexander Welsh, book review in
Victorian Studies 26 (1982): 85

Even while Alexander Welsh was making his whimsical sugges-
tion about "gentlemen's studies" in 1982, a whole new kind of men's
studies was already taking shape in the academic world. Since that
time, this new men's studies has slowly but surely taken its place in
universities throughout the United States, Canada, Europe, and elsewhere. Neither a fad nor a backlash, the new men's studies is the logical
complement to women's studies and a necessary component of any
balanced gender-related scholarship.

Since the first edition of this bibliography appeared in 1985, the
growth in men's studies has been steady and dramatic. The growth can
be seen in the increasing number of men's studies courses offered at
U.S. universities. From 1984 to 1993, the number of men's studies
courses expanded from 30 to approximately 300. These courses are
offered by various departments, usually sociology, psychology, history,
and literature, but many of the new courses are interdisciplinary. At
some universities, professors in women's studies have begun to include
segments on men in their established courses. At this writing, no
full-scale men's studies program is yet in place, but efforts to formulate
such programs have begun on several campuses. Berkeley, California,
now has a Center for Men's Studies, and a handful of U.S. universities
appear to be making plans to create similar centers.

Additional evidence comes from Canadian and European universities. Both McGill University in Montreal and the University of Windsor,
for example, have created men's studies courses. Also, several universities
in Great Britain offer men's courses, Finland's University of Tempere
presents an introductory course in men's studies, and the Netherlands has
a National Society for Men's Studies. In brief, the new men's studies is a
growing presence on many North American and European campuses.

Elsewhere in the academic world, the new men's studies is making
itself felt. Panels and papers on men's studies have become regular features
at many educational conferences, and special issues of academic journals
devoted to men's studies have appeared. Abandoning the tendency to

devote gender-conscious research to women only, more and more scholars are beginning to study men under the rubric of "gender." A professional organization, the American Men's Studies Association, has been formed and has begun holding annual meetings. At least two journals are now devoted exclusively to men's studies: *Journal of Men's Studies* and *Masculinities* offer scholarly articles, reviews, bibliographies, as well as course and conference information.

The most dramatic growth in men's studies can be seen primarily in the torrent of men's books that has been pouring forth from publishers since 1990. Before that time, the prevailing wisdom in publishing houses decreed that books about women would sell while those about men would not. However, when Robert Bly's *Iron John* stayed on best seller lists for nearly a year, the publishing logjam was broken. Other books like Sam Keen's *Fire in the Belly* and Robert Moore and Douglas Gillette's *King Warrior Magician Lover* also achieved best seller status, thereby confirming publishers' suspicions that the market for men's books was a healthy one. Since then the stream of scholarly and popular books about men has not slowed.

Scope of the Present Bibliography

"Books about men are not books about men as men."
—Michael S. Kimmel,
"How is it that men have no history?"
Chronicle of Higher Education 8 December 1993: B5

This comparative abundance of men's books has dictated a major difference between the present edition of this bibliography and the first one. Whereas the first edition included nearly all men's studies books available in 1985, the sheer number of men's books presently available has required a more rigorous selection of titles. To include all the available titles would have doubled the size of the present bibliography. Titles have been selected by using the following criteria:

1. All contributions to men's studies judged to be truly significant or noteworthy have been included. Inevitably, however, some worthy books have been missed, but every effort was made to reduce their number to a minimum.

2. A representative sampling of works from all major academic disciplines has been made.

3. Selections have been chosen to illustrate a range of philosophical and political viewpoints on men and men's issues.

4. Although works of a more advanced or scholarly nature were given preference in the selection process, many books aimed at more general audiences have been included to indicate trends in nonacademic views of males.

5. Although most entries from the earlier bibliography were brought over into the present edition, some dated items have been deleted, and all previous annotations have been revised when appropriate.

As in the previous edition, *The New Men's Studies* includes only books written in English or available in English translation. In addition, books were required to meet one or more of the following criteria:

1. The book must be primarily about males as males. That is, it must not be primarily about another topic (such as the Vietnam War or the labor movement), however closely related that subject might be to men's lives.

2. The book must exhibit an awareness of the masculine gender role or roles. It should not contain unquestioned assumptions about the nature of masculinity.

3. The book must demonstrate an awareness of other works in men's studies and women's studies. Its contents should not assume that nothing of value has been written on males as a gendered subject.

4. The book must make some effort to transcend stereotypes of males and to present them as human beings in all their complexity and contradictions, with their triumphs and failures given equitable treatment. (See Political Content and "Misandry" below.)

5. The book must contribute significant insights into current conditions shaping men's lives, into the universal experience of being male, or into the question of whether or not such universals exist.

6. The book must explore topics or issues of importance to males as males, such as men's rights, men's health, or fatherhood. It must exhibit an understanding of differing views on the topic when disagreement exists.

In a few cases I have ignored some of the criteria rather than omit a book noteworthy for other reasons. Still, nearly all the books published after 1985 included in *The New Men's Studies* meet most of the above criteria. This fact marks another significant difference between this bibliography and the earlier edition in which many books met only one or two of the criteria. Clearly, an increasing number of writers are now conscious of men as a gendered subject, of men's issues, and of men's studies as a branch of academic inquiry. To a great extent, recent books about men *are* books about men as men.

Rationales for Men's Studies

"Compared with what we know about the identity problems of women, we know relatively little about the American man's struggle with his identity."

—Joe L. Dubbert,
A Man's Place: Masculinity in Transition (1979), 2

The rationales for women's studies are clear and compelling. As women entered the academic world in increasing numbers during the 1960s and 1970s, they discovered the need for a more gender-conscious and gender-inclusive scholarship. It was obvious that traditional studies contained glaring omissions and distortions about women. Women's studies courses and programs emerged to correct this imbalance and to explore new areas of knowledge about women that had been untouched by standard disciplines.

Women's studies educators pioneered the idea of a gender-conscious scholarship that questioned and qualified knowledge formulated largely by male scholars. They also introduced the concept of gender as a major academic and political consideration. Despite disagreements and controversies, few people in education nowadays would deny the necessity for and the importance of women's studies; few would deny the contribution of women's studies scholars to the concept of gendered knowledge.

But an increasing number of scholars have questioned an assumption that underlay early rationales for women's studies. This is the assumption that traditional studies were already men's studies. Over time, many educators have recognized that the same traditional studies which contained omissions and distortions about women also contained omissions and distortions about men. Scholars in the past had been very selective about *which* males they studied and *what* they studied about them. Traditional scholarship studied a few things about a few men.

Traditional historians, for example, reported the public lives of a small minority of males at the top of the social scale—the princes, politicians, popes, presidents, generals, and so on. In standard historical accounts, the lives of the vast majority of males in any given society remained as much of a blank as the lives of nearly all women. As Peter N.

Stearns has remarked in *Be a Man! Males in Modern Society*: "Feminist historians rightly point out that until recently most history dealt with men. But it did not deal with ordinary men, nor with the private spheres of male existence, with masculinity and its standards as focal concepts" (1990, 7).

Similar problems existed in psychology. While Helene Deutsch's *Psychology of Women* was written over forty years ago, Herbert S. Strean in the introduction to Reuben Fine's *The Forgotten Man* notes that "it took psychoanalysts many more years to come up with a book on the psychology of men" (1987, xi). Many earlier theorists, although male, ignored many dimensions of the male psyche in both their theory and clinical practice.

In sociological studies before the 1980s, many researchers equated "mother" with "parent" and gleaned most of their information about fathers through interviews with mothers. The widespread ignorance about fathers (now being corrected) was one of the clearest cases demonstrating the need for a new kind of men's studies.

Moreover, traditional studies were not gender-conscious studies. Earlier scholars usually had little idea that "masculine" and "feminine" were anything but biological givens. In the foreword to Richard L. Meth and Robert S. Pasick's *Men in Therapy*, Ann Hartman notes that, "although psychological writing has been androcentric, it has also been gender blind. It has assumed a male perspective but has not really explored what it means to be a man any more than what it means to be a woman" (1990, vii).

More recent scholars have recognized "masculine" and "feminine" as social scripts assigned to biological males and females. Such a view does not deny a biological role in the shaping of human behavior. In *Constructing Brotherhood*, Mary Ann Clawson wisely remarks: "To say that gender and class are socially constructed is not to say that they are randomly devised and infinitely variable" (1989, 245). But even if differing masculinities represent variations on a biological theme, gender-conscious scholars no longer accept any one cultural variation as a universal norm. Furthermore, many educators now critique gender scripts in the light of numerous other concerns, including the temperament of the individual, the needs of the society at large, and long-term considerations of individual health and personal growth. In short, the presence of gender-conscious content marks an essential difference between traditional studies and the new men's studies.

Finally, if traditional studies really represented men's studies, it would be easy to construct a men's studies program from already existing courses in any university's curriculum. Anyone who attempts such a task, however, soon discovers that the result is a patchwork of courses focusing primarily on males in a gender-unconscious way. The traditional "History of Western Civilization" course, for example, will feature more male names than female names, but it is unlikely to represent a gender-conscious examination of the private lives or inner experiences of most Western males. A collection of traditional courses passed off as a men's studies program would return educators to the very point the new men's scholars are leaving behind to attain fuller understanding of males as human beings.

In short, the notion that traditional studies were men's studies, in any currently significant sense, is untenable.

Moreover, the time has now passed when colleges and universities could justify the presence on campus of women's studies programs without comparable men's studies programs. Male students pay the same tuition as female students. They deserve equal access to courses that examine—critically and compassionately—the personal, social, and political aspects of men's lives.

Political Content and Misandry

"There has been a veritable blitzkrieg on the male gender, what amounts to an outright demonization of men and a slander against masculinity."

—Robert Moore and Douglas Gillette,
King Warrior Magician Lover (1990), 156

When appropriate, the annotations in this bibliography note, and sometimes comment on, political content in the books.

In general, the annotations follow the political classifications in Kenneth Clatterbaugh's *Contemporary Perspectives on Masculinity* (1990), reordered as follows:

1. **Conservatives** hold to traditional forms of masculinity. **Moral conservatives** assess masculine behavior according to a universal, natural law. **Biological conservatives** (e.g., sociobiologists) locate masculine behaviors primarily in biology (16-36).

2. **Mythopoetic** or **mythopoeic men,** seek a spiritual redefinition of masculinity based on myths, archetypes, and, in some cases, mainstream religious beliefs (85-103).

3. **Men's rights activists** focus on legal discrimination against men and unfair social treatment of males (61-83).

4. **Minority men** focus on the special interests of groups such as black men or gay men (127-50).

5. **Pro-feminist men,** or **anti-sexist men,** accept one or another feminist critique of *patriarchy,* which is usually defined as "male-dominated society." **Liberal pro-feminist men** espouse an agenda of equal rights and responsibilities for males and females. **Radical pro-feminist men** regard males as an oppressor class that derives power from patriarchy (37-60).

6. **Socialist men** seek human improvement by way of changing social structures. **Marxist socialists** focus on class differences, **feminist socialists** on gender differences (105-125).

When appropriate, annotations also note the presence of misandry or anti-male sexism in the books listed. *Misandry* is defined by Patrick M. Arnold in *Wildmen, Warriors, and Kings* (1992, 52):

Mis·an·dry (mis'-an'-drē) *n.* hatred of men. **1:** the attribution of negative qualities to the entire male gender. **2:** the claim that masculinity is the source of human vices such as domination, violence, oppression, and racism. **3:** a sexist assumption that (a) male genes, hormones, or physiology, or (b) male cultural nurturing produces war, rape, and physical abuse. **4:** the assignment of blame solely to men for humanity's historic evils without including women's responsibility or giving men credit for civilization's achievements. **5:** the assumption that any male person is probably dominating, oppressive, violent, sexually abusive, and spiritually immature.

A related term is *androphobia,* an irrational fear and loathing of men. Adjective forms are *misandric* and *androphobic.*

Increasingly, writers are distinguishing between 1) legitimate criticisms of masculinity's negative aspects and 2) misandric portraits of males as inherently evil and of masculinity as entirely corrupt. Nevertheless, misandry and androphobia continue to be such acceptable forms of sexism in large segments of modern society that they often go unnoticed and unprotested. In the present annotations, misandry and androphobia are neither ignored nor tolerated.

A Word About Words

"Because traditional scholarship and theology made men into pseudo-universal generic human beings, it excluded from consideration whatever was specific to men *as men.*"
—James B. Nelson,
The Intimate Connection: Male Sexuality,
Masculine Spirituality (1988), 18

In addition to *misandry,* a few other words require comment.

In recent times, heightened awareness of language's political implications has complicated the business of word choice. In the annotations, words have been selected for clarity, sensitivity, and wide acceptance. A sampling of some problematic terms and a brief rationale for the use of each follows.

Feminism and related terms like *feminist, women's liberation,* and *the women's movement* cover a range of opinions and attitudes, as do *masculinist, the men's movement,* and *men's liberation.* Even those who recognize a common core of belief in these terms usually recognize a diversity amid the unity. Although every effort has been made to use such terms precisely, readers should be aware of the leeway of meaning in them.

Gay is used interchangeably with *homosexual.* Although some activists prefer *queer, gay* appears to be more generally acceptable.

Homophobic refers to an irrational fear and loathing of homosexual people. Its complement is *heterophobic,* an irrational fear and hatred of heterosexual people.

Masculinities, the plural form, is sometimes used to indicate the widespread conviction that gender roles are constructed, at least in part, by cultures. Thus, there is no one masculinity but a series of masculinities that vary according to culture, time, place, class, religion, and other factors. Even those who affirm universal or ubiquitous elements of masculinity often acknowledge that these elements are shaped somewhat differently by different cultures, thereby creating masculinities in the sense of "variations of masculinity."

Mythopoetic describes a branch of the men's movement that combines myth and poetry in a search for archetypal patterns of masculinity. Sometimes, *mythopoeic* (myth-making) is applied to this segment of the men's movement. The annotations generally use the more common form *mythopoetic.*

Patriarchy is a word of many meanings, often carrying within it an entire world-view. In recent times, the term has become laden with negative overtones that suggest male oppression. In this usage, *patriarchy* is synonymous with "male-dominated society," a concept that depicts the history of the sexes as the class warfare of the sexes. This use often conveys misandric stereotypes of males as an oppressor class of evil woman-haters. In contrast, the older sense of *patriarchy* as "father-involved or father-protected society" carries more favorable connotations and fosters an ideal of males as loving, responsible fathers. This sense of *patriarchy* is still in use, and an increasing number of writers are employing it as (to use Richard Louv's term) "political fatherlove."

United States and *U.S.* are usually not used synonymously with *America* or *American* to signify a growing awareness that *America* and *American* refer more accurately to all the Americas—North, Central, and South.

In all vocabulary choices, an effort has been made to select terms that are precise and widely acceptable.

Categories and Annotations

"Women's studies does more than question the female role—it tells women they have rights to what was the traditional male role. Nothing tells men they have rights to what was the traditional female role—rights to stay home full-time or part-time with the children while his wife supports him."

—Warren Farrell,
The Myth of Male Power: Why Men Are the Disposable Sex (1993), 15

The present selection has been made from a list of nearly two thousand items gathered through several methods. Searches of bibliographies in periodicals such as the *Journal of Men's Studies* were the easiest and most rewarding method. Library subject headings and computer databases were searched. Searches of bibliographies in men's studies books were also helpful in providing additional titles.

The classifications used in this bibliography are designed to create categories that are useful and manageable for scholars and general audiences. Often, the names of recognized academic disciplines have been used, such as history, literature, and psychology. Other categories reflect areas of interest as indicated by publishing trends of the past two decades, such as archetypal spirituality, awareness of men's issues and topics, and victimization and violence.

Entries in *The New Men's Studies* follow *The Chicago Manual of Style*, 14th ed. (Chicago and London: The University of Chicago Press, 1993). The author's last name—or, in the case of edited anthologies, the editor's last name—is used to list items alphabetically. The author's name is followed by the book's full title and subtitle, translator or editor, place of publication, publisher, publisher's subdivision, date of publication, and page numbers to the last relevant page. If the book has been reprinted, the place of publication, publisher, and date are given. If the book is available in paperback, the abbreviation "pa." is used.

To provide researchers with access to a wider selection of books about men, each entry in *The New Men's Studies* indicates whether the cited book contains a bibliography. If so, the entry includes its page numbers.

Considerable effort has been made to locate all reprintings of a book, although it is likely that some omissions occur. Price information for books has been omitted because, given the rapid fluctuations in prices, the entry would most likely consist of price misinformation. The ISBN has also been omitted because, with the information provided here, it will be readily accessible to those who wish it.

The citations note illustrations, appendixes, bibliographies, notes, and indexes. The page numbers of bibliographies are included as a research tool: in this way *The New Men's Studies* offers valuable openings into a much larger literature about men than is included here.

Any classification of knowledge is necessarily a human construct. Categorizing works in men's studies is particularly difficult owing to the interdisciplinary nature of the area. For example, the burgeoning mythopoetic writings defy easy classification. Should they be listed as psychology, religion, autobiography, history, or cultural studies? Many mythopoetic writings combine most or all of these categories. Also, so much writing about males is now gender-conscious of masculinity that it is often difficult to determine how a given book should be classified. For example, the annotation for Peter N. Stearns's *Be a Man! Males in Modern Society* might have been included in the chapter on masculinity rather than in the chapter on history. To help readers cope with these ambiguities, cross-references have been provided at the end of each chapter.

1

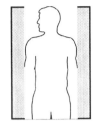

Anthropology, Sociology:
Cultural and Cross-Cultural Studies

1. Allen, M. R. **Male Cults and Secret Initiations in Melanesia.** Melbourne: Melbourne University Press, 1967. 140p. illus. bibliography, 123-36. index. Reprint, London and New York: Cambridge University Press, 1967.

Citing numerous studies, Allen provides an overview of male initiation rites in a wide variety of Melanesian societies. He connects the degree of sexual polarity in these societies to the varying kin-based social structures, and he links their rites to sexual antagonism and social arrangements. Allen also assesses several leading anthropological and psychological theories concerning the male rites, including theories of male envy of females, oedipal rivalry between fathers and sons, and male fears of female contamination.

2. Bettelheim, Bruno. **Symbolic Wounds: Puberty Rites and the Envious Male.** Glencoe, IL: Free Press, 1954. Rev. ed., New York: Collier, 1962. 194p. appendixes. index. pa.

Questioning prevailing psychological and anthropological explanations of puberty rites, Bettelheim suggests that they represent an attempt by males to imitate female powers of procreation. Each sex envies the powers of the other sex to some extent; some puberty rituals spring from male awe of the female's ability to bear children. These rituals represent the male's attempt to assimilate her powers into himself; thus, the bleeding penis that results from circumcision resembles the menstruating vagina. Although myths suggest that circumcision is imposed and desired by women, Bettelheim warns against an oversimplified view of its origins. He examines numerous practices and ceremonies, including circumcision, self-mutilation, subincision, couvade, transvestism, and female mutilation. The author argues that the secrecy surrounding many of these rites derives from the men's need to suggest that their "business" is as important as the women's. Bettelheim concludes that less pressure on males "to fight and to strut" and greater freedom to express their creative and nurturing abilities would lessen vagina envy, would help males achieve greater closeness to females and to other males, and would heighten their positive wish to create life rather than destroy it. The appendixes discuss infant circumcision in the Hebrew scriptures and puberty rites in Australia.

3. Blotnick, Srully. **Ambitious Men: Their Drives, Dreams, and Delusions.** New York: Viking, 1987. 338p. appendix. index.

In this study based on responses from 6,000 white-collar and blue-collar workers, Blotnick defines ambitious men as those who 1) want more than they have, 2) are wealthy, 3) are in a hurry to succeed, 4) have an open-ended quest that cannot be satisfied, and 5) are somewhat ruthless. Utilizing fictional characters, he constructs four composite types who are representative of ambitious white-collar men: 1) the Dreiser-like financier who wants money first, 2) the Gatsby type who seeks social success, 3) the self-reliant Hemingwayesque man, and 4) the more creative type who, like the novelist, can be reclusive and artistic. Blotnick follows his four composite males, finding that their ambitions can take a toll on themselves and their marriages. The best hope is for an ambitious man to become a "hybrid" type who, in the face of failure, can adopt a different and more successful coping strategy. Many readers will find the most intriguing parts of the book those that focus on younger women in business as the primary initiators of affairs, and the reasons why many working men have refused to take on a larger share of housework. The appendix describes the study's methodology.

4. Brandes, Stanley. **Metaphors of Masculinity: Sex and Status in Andalusian Folklore.** Philadelphia: University of Pennsylvania Press, 1980. x, 236p. illus. bibliography, 215-17. index. pa.

Brandes describes a rapidly disappearing culture in southern Spain where the sexes are still rigidly separated and where the males adopt an aggressive-defensive stance about their masculinity. Folklore—including public celebrations, speech, customs, jokes, pranks, riddles, skits, and religious devotion—define a male's place in the social order and his relationship to females. Brandes points out both the disadvantages of these gender roles and the enriching aspects of the folklore that defines them.

5. Cohen, Albert K. **Delinquent Boys: The Culture of the Gang.** Glencoe, IL: Free Press, 1955. 198p. notes. index. Reprint, London: Routledge and Kegan Paul, 1956.

In this study, Cohen explores social class and sex role strain as contributing factors to male juvenile delinquency. He also specifies what the juvenile gang offers the boy that mainstream culture does not.

6. Dann, Graham. **The Barbadian Male: Sexual Attitudes and Practice.** London: Macmillan Caribbean, 1987. x, 228p. appendixes. bibliography, 172-83. index. pa.

Much research has been done on Caribbean women but little has been done on men. This study, commissioned by the International Planned Parenthood Federation, seeks to correct the imbalance and to question negative stereotypes of Caribbean males. Findings are based on 185 in-depth interviews with 18- to 40-year-old men. An estimated 75 percent of Barbadian males are born to unwed parents; 25 percent are raised by teen mothers. Father absence is common. Many boys receive minimal help from church, school, and home. Premarital sex is extensive. Most interviewed men were tolerant of women's liberation but not of homosexuality. Although they frowned on marital infidelity, affairs were frequent. The study examines fertility, the men's knowledge and use of family planning, and their awareness of overpopulation. The book closes with a chapter on trends and policy issues in family planning. Four appendixes contain information on methodology used in the study.

7. Gilmore, David D. **Manhood in the Making: Cultural Concepts of Masculinity.** New Haven, CT, and London: Yale University Press, 1990. xiii, 258p. bibliography, 233-48. index. pa.

In this enormously influential study, Gilmore examines concepts of masculinity in numerous societies and discovers recurring (but not universal) motifs of a masculine ideal that is socially useful. These motifs are created both psychogenetically and culturally. Almost all manhood ideologies involve some testing as a way of subduing the child or boy within. They are neither practices to oppress women (as Marxist feminists argue) nor a compensation for castration fears (as Freudians argue). Rather, they are ways of ending the boy's childhood dependency on the mother and of differentiating the male from the feminine. Examining Mediterranean cultures, Gilmore discovers a masculine ideal that involves four characteristics: potency with a woman, providing for family, protecting the family, and a certain freedom or risk-taking quality. Males are also "foregrounded," that is, pushed into public performance of one sort or another. Gilmore then turns to Truk, where he finds similar patterns: males fight each other to win female attention and approval, and the machismo is socially useful because it leads the male to strive for economic rewards that support the family. Focusing next on the Mehinaku Indians of Brazil, Gilmore finds the foregrounding of males in public wrestling matches and a pressure on males to resist childish helplessness and feminine inwardness. Among the Samburu of Africa, manhood is achieved only after a 12-year initiation period involving circumcision, cattle stealing (incited by girls), and being a provider of meat and wealth. After an extended analysis of the Sambia, Gilmore devotes more general surveys to China, India, and Japan, with similar results. In contrast to all these societies, however, the author finds two societies—in Tahiti and in Semai (Malaysia)—where machismo is relatively unknown and where (significantly) women, children, and men are frequently victimized by outsiders. Gilmore concludes that machismo behaviors have been cultivated by most societies because they are beneficial to those societies.

8. Godelier, Maurice. **The Making of Great Men: Male Dominance and Power among the New Guinea Baruya.** Translated by Rupert Swyer. Cambridge: Cambridge University Press; Paris: Editions de la Maison des Sciences de l'homme, 1986. xv, 251p. illus. bibliography, 239-41. index. pa. Original publication, as *La production des grands hommes*, Paris: Librairie Arthème Fayard, 1982.

Godelier depicts the "classless" Baruya society of New Guinea as male-dominated and female-subjugated, although most males are also subject to "great men" who gain their status either through inheritance or performance. To create great men, the society puts boys through a grueling 10-year initiation that at one time included fellatio. By comparison, women's initiation ceremonies are brief, though hardly painless. The author traces four kinds of great men: warriors, shamans, cassowary hunters, and salt makers. Godelier's depiction of the Baruya is rich in detail, but his shrill sermons on the evils of male power reduce the complexity of Baruya culture to misandric clichés. Denigrating the Baruya men with politically correct condescension, Godelier betrays the trust they placed in him when they gave him their secrets.

9. Gold, Martin. **Status Forces in Delinquent Boys.** Ann Arbor: Institute for Social Research, University of Michigan, 1963. xv, 229p. illustrations. appendixes. bibliography, 221-24. index.

This social-psychological study examines why sons of lower-class families are more frequently delinquent than those of higher-class families. The author reviews the literature on delinquency and reports results of a study conducted in Flint, Michigan. He concludes tentatively, as a partial answer, that there are weaker family ties and greater provocations to delinquency among lower-status boys.

10. Herdt, Gilbert H. **Guardians of the Flutes: Idioms of Masculinity.** New York: McGraw-Hill, 1981. xviii, 382p. illus. appendixes. bibliography, 355-68. notes. name and subject indexes. Reprint, New York: Morningside Books, Columbia University Press, 1987. pa.

This anthropological study examines the lives of males among the Sambia (a pseudonym) people of the East Highlands of Papua New Guinea. Because of intertribal raids, this society requires a warrior class capable of meeting surprise attacks. To turn boys into fighting men, a long-term and sometimes brutal initiation process separates young males from females. In secret, fellatio is practiced in the belief that oral insemination of boys provides them with needed manhood. Surprisingly (at least to many Westerners), such homoerotic activity does not produce homosexuals in later life. Once a male is married and has fathered a child, he is expected to become fully heterosexual. Nearly all males do. Unsurprisingly, such a warrior culture prizes hypermasculine styles, inducts young males forcibly into its rites, despises femininity, and fosters hostility between the sexes. A myth of male parthenogenesis insists that males alone are responsible for creation, but is also evidence of the male's fear of femininity within himself. In a thought-provoking final chapter, Herdt stresses the society's crucial need to convert mother-suckled infants into fierce warriors through a process of masculinization that leaves all the males literally scarred. He also indicates the significance of the study to understanding men in other societies, including the United States.

11. Herdt, Gilbert H., ed. **Rituals of Manhood: Male Initiation in Papua New Guinea.** Berkeley: University of California Press, 1982. xxvi, 367p. illus. bibliography after each chapter. notes.

This collection of eight scholarly essays by 10 authors (plus an editor's preface) stresses repeatedly how some people of New Guinea regard female growth as automatic while believing that the process of "growing" a man must comprise often violent social "hardening." Among the Bimin-Kuskusmin, a systematic brutalization of boys occurs. The Awa male initiations include beatings, nose bleedings, penis cuttings, and induced vomiting. Among the Sambia, boys are coerced into fellatio as a way to make them into men. The *bau,* a ceremonial hunting lodge, is an alternative to initiation, but, among its rituals, anal insemination of boys is used to ensure male growth. The ritualized violence of the Ilahita Arapesh uses terror tactics to heighten the boys' ordeal. Although the Chambri ceremonies are decidedly more playful, even these include scarification of the male's body. Hostility toward women is often either explicit or implicit in these rituals, even though the women frequently collude in them. Terence E. Hays and Patricia H. Hays emphasize, in their account of men's and women's ceremonies among the Ndumba, that women's antagonism toward men is as great as that of men toward women. In the book's introduction, Roger M. Keesing raises important questions about the difficulty of rising above partial views of these rituals to a fuller one. In the final essay, Donald F. Tuzin questions what the response of anthropologists to the ceremonies should be. Significantly, he points out feelings of guilt, present in the initiators because of their participation in ritualized violence against those whom they love. The essays provide often shocking evidence of how boys are tortured into "manhood"; inevitably, they raise questions in the reader's mind about similarities elsewhere.

12. Herdt, Gilbert. **The Sambia: Ritual and Gender in New Guinea.** New York: Holt, Rinehart and Winston, 1987. 227p. illus. bibliography, 217-22. index. pa.

Herdt's most recent and most personal account of the Sambia recapitulates and updates the author's earlier studies, supplying fuller details on matters such as initiation rituals. Children are initially indulged by the adults until around age seven, when the boys are roughly separated from the women and begin a 10- to 15-year ordeal of becoming a man. Beatings, nose bleedings, and fellatio are used to harden the boys into warrior men. The study suggests that the process of creating soldiers damages many of the males and fosters antagonism between the sexes.

13. Herzfeld, Michael. **The Poetics of Manhood: Contest and Identity in a Cretan Mountain village.** Princeton, NJ: Princeton University Press, 1985. xviii, 313p. illus. appendix. index. bibliography, 293-99. notes. pa.

In the Cretan mountain village of Glendi (a fictitious name), the men engage in the "poetics" of manhood; that is, they act out a social drama—a performance of selfhood—that establishes their male identity. The villagers respect a man who is "good at being a man." This drama involves considerable contest: the men engage in drinking, dancing, card playing, politics, and animal theft. Their risk taking expresses *eghoismos*, or aggressive self-regard, and adds *simasia,* or "meaning," to life. Glendi and other villages are organized around "patrigroups" whose agonistic pattern of interaction can be seen at the Glendi coffeehouses, which are male-only preserves. These patrigroups are quick to feud and to reconcile, and they have their own rituals of peacemaking. Paradoxically, among the shepherds of Glendi, animal theft is often a way of establishing friendship. Male contest is expressed in discourse (e.g., *mandinadhes,* or competitive couplets, in which one tries to top one's opponent). Gender differentiation is extensive in the village, and the patrigroups serve to keep the women in line. Politics often means disrespect for officialdom. Herzfeld notes that change is coming to the mountain village, with television, high school careers, and the decline of animal theft, which is now sometimes seen as a thing of the past.

14. Hewlett, Barry S. **Intimate Fathers: The Nature and Context of Aka Pygmy Paternal Infant Care.** Ann Arbor: University of Michigan Press, 1991. ix, 201p. illus. bibliography, 177-94. index.

The result of a 15-year study, this book challenges long-held assumptions about fathers and infants. Among the Aka Pygmy hunter-gatherers of central Africa, fathers spend more time in infant caregiving than in any other known society. On average, men spend almost half of their day holding, caring for, or within reach of infants. Their interaction with infants is gentle; their interaction with wives exhibits great reciprocity. Aka paternal behavior contradicts Western theories that males do not become interested in children younger than three or four years and that fathers always play more roughly with children than mothers do. Above all, Hewlett's findings contradict stereotypes that fathers are incapable of or inadequate at infant caregiving. Hewlett theorizes that, during 120,000 years of human evolution, greater reciprocity between males and females led to father-infant bonding. Drawing conclusions for modern Western parents, Hewlett argues that "quantity" time with children is extremely important and that males in father-involved families are less likely to seek dominance over females or to derogate femininity.

15. Hogbin, [Herbert] Ian. **The Island of Menstruating Men: Religion in Wogeo, New Guinea.** Scranton, PA: Chandler, 1970. xiv, 203p. illus. bibliography, 197-98. index.

The author describes a society in which gashing the penis is used to produce "artificial menstruation," an act of purification. In this culture, the sexes exist in "balanced opposition," and adult males use elaborate secret rituals to separate boys from mothers and to enable them to grow into men.

16. Kaye, Lenard W., and Jeffrey S. Applegate. **Men as Caregivers to the Elderly: Understanding and Aiding Unrecognized Family Support.** Lexington, MA: Lexington Books, D. C. Heath, 1990. xxv, 202p. appendixes. bibliography, 187-94. index.

Traditionally, women have been the caregivers to the elderly, but increasingly more men are performing this function. At least one-fourth (up to one-third in some settings) of the caregivers are now males. The authors describe why the patterns of caregiving are changing. Drawing upon a national survey that they formulated, they describe the typical male caregiver (white, over 60, married, and living with spouse), the patients these men care for (usually white, female, over 60), the tasks they perform well and those they feel uncomfortable with, and the handicaps that they face. Caregiving support groups can help men, but the female orientation of such groups and the concept of self-sufficient masculinity block many men from participating. In the final chapter, the authors make suggestions to help the men, who are often burdened with full-time employment, strained finances, and unfamiliarity with "hands on" caregiving tasks. Of the three appendixes, two are concerned with statistical aspects of the study. The third (appendix B) provides practical recommendations for helping men to become involved with caregiver support groups; it also lists resources, guidebooks, and support organizations.

17. Komarovsky, Mirra. **Dilemmas of Masculinity: A Study of College Youth.** New York: W. W. Norton, 1976. xi, 274p. bibliography, 259-66. index. pa.

An early example of gender-conscious men's studies, *Dilemmas of Masculinity* is distinguished by "its explicit focus upon those strains that the male experiences precisely because he is a male and not a female, living in a particular social milieu." Using a case-study method combining sociological and psychological perspectives, Komarovsky studied 62 seniors in an eastern Ivy League men's college. Because the interviews were held from 1969 to 1970, an attempt was made to update the findings with more recent literature. Also, because the book focuses on role strain, the author warns against seeing the men as being more conflicted than they actually are. Findings include such matters as the men's attitudes toward masculinity and femininity (many men accepted as masculine several traits once labeled as feminine), and the discrepancy between some of the men's theoretical acceptance of women's equal participation in the work force and their own preference for more domestically oriented partners—apparently because the men sense the difficulties involved in a two-career family. Some men were uncomfortable with academically competitive or sexually aggressive women. The sexual revolution has left men more ashamed of being virgins than of being sexually experienced. Many of the men felt emotionally distant from their fathers, although conflict with their mothers was likely to produce more serious psychological effects upon them. The study found that, despite the alleged advantages of being male, nearly 50 percent of the men were anxious about their capability to play the masculine role. The penultimate chapter ("A Theoretical Summary") investigates six modes of sex role strain, illustrating each with reference to the study. The final chapter ("Afterword: The Author's Envoy") argues that the tendency of students to blame themselves rather than social structures for role strain does not bode well for the social reforms needed to facilitate role changes. Despite the authoritativeness of the study, some readers may be disappointed by the smallness and unrepresentativeness of the sample, by the dated nature of the evidence, and by a commentary that often shows greater sensitivity toward the dilemmas of femininity than those of masculinity.

18. Lee, Richard B., and Irven DeVore, with Jill Nash-Mitchell, eds. **Man the Hunter.** Chicago: Aldine, 1968. xvi, 415p. illus. bibliography, 353-92. notes. index.

Originally presented at a 1966 University of Chicago symposium, the 30 papers (plus six discussion sessions) printed here examine present and past hunting societies, with occasional focus on how hunting shapes male behavior. The scholarly, anthropological essays explore such matters as ecology and economics in present-day hunting societies, social and territorial organization, marriage in Australia, demography and population, prehistoric hunter-gatherers, and the effect of hunting upon human evolution.

19. Leemon, Thomas A. **The Rites of Passage in a Student Culture: A Study of the Dynamics of Transition.** New York and London: Teachers College Press, Columbia University, 1972. xi, 215p. (Anthropology and Education Series.) illus, appendixes. bibliography, 203.

Drawing upon Arnold van Gennep's concept of rites of passage, Leemon recounts the process by which a U.S. college fraternity in the spring of 1963 initiated a group of pledges into membership. As a privileged observer of the fraternity, the author traces the three stages of passage—separation, transition, and incorporation—in the rituals, harassments, raids, celebrations, and interactions of members and pledges.

20. Lidz, Theodore, and Ruth Wilmanns Lidz. **Oedipus in the Stone Age: A Psychoanalytic Study of Masculinization in Papua New Guinea.** Madison, CT: International Universities Press, 1989. ix, 228p. bibliography, 201-2. illus. name and subject indexes.

The authors review the literature about male initiation rites in various tribes in Papua New Guinea and Irian Jaya, contrasting the practices with those in Amazon tribes. The rites demonstrate the universal or near-universal awareness of the need to separate boys from mothers in order to make the boys into adult men. Using psychoanalytic theory, the authors suggest that bleeding is often a way of cleansing the boy of the mother's blood. In cultures where the mother's possession of the boy is prolonged and where the father is mostly absent, the rites of masculinization can be extreme and brutal, reflecting the tribe's awareness of the mother's power over the boy. In such cultures, misogyny among the men is likely to be high. In many tribes, however, the women cooperate with the men's take-over of the boys. In some cases, ritual fellatio and homosexual intercourse provide the boys with the semen that is believed necessary for them to become men. This semen becomes a substitute mother's milk to make the boys grow into adult males. The authors conclude that Freud's account of the boy's oedipal fear of castration is but one of many cultural scripts designed to deal with the break from the mother and the identification with the father. In the final chapter, the authors suggest that the increase of single-mother families and absent fathers in the West may produce more severe rituals to meet the need of separating sons from mothers.

21. Malinowski, Bronislaw. **The Father in Primitive Psychology.** New York: W. W. Norton, 1927. vii, 95p. Reprint, 1966. pa.

Studying the Trobriand Islanders, Malinowski uncovers a condition common among early societies: a belief that the mother is the sole parent of the child and that no connection exists between sexual intercourse and pregnancy. Children, it is believed, are returned spirits of the dead who are introduced into the mother's body during sleep by controlling spirits. Thus, the islanders have constructed what amounts to a "fatherless" society. Nevertheless, the father—or, more exactly, the husband of the child's mother—has an important role in the society as provider, protector, and caretaker of children. So important is his role that the islanders consider it disgraceful for an unmarried woman to become pregnant: she has no husband to provide for her and the child. As the child grows older, the paternal role is taken over to some extent by other males, usually the mother's brother. Nevertheless, Malinowski presents intriguing evidence that the concept of fathering may precede even the awareness of paternity.

22. McClelland, David C., William N. Davis, Rudolf Kalin, and Eric Wanner. **The Drinking Man.** New York: Free Press, 1972. xiv, 402p. illus. appendixes. bibliography, 379-86. index.

Most of this book describes experiments conducted over 10 years to determine motives for men's heavy drinking. Cross-cultural research is added to studies done on college campuses and in working-men's bars. Although general readers will be put off by the sociological jargon throughout most of the volume, the authors happily revert to plain English for its crucial sections. Readers should not miss parts of chapter 13 (pp. 303-5, 309-15) and the final chapter. "Men drink primarily to feel stronger," McClelland concludes. The origins of excessive drinking are in the role that society assigns to men. Strong demands are made for male assertiveness, but society offers low support for the male role and provides few socialized outlets for exercising power and assertiveness. Among the solutions offered are for men and society to reduce the need for male power display, for men to find ways of acting out their aggression or to satisfy the power drive vicariously, for society to socialize the male power drive, and for men to succeed at their work. Readers may suspect that the authors have discovered the dynamics underlying not only excessive drinking by males but also many other destructive male behaviors.

23. McGill, Michael E. **The McGill Report on Male Intimacy.** New York: Holt, Rinehart and Winston, 1985. xvii, 300p. appendix. index.

Drawing upon a questionnaire to which 1,383 people responded (737 men, 646 women), and interviews, this popularly written account tries to unravel the question of why males are not more intimate with women. Equating verbal disclosure with intimacy, McGill finds most men lacking in intimacy and most women craving it. Men have a narrow view of sex as intimacy; women have richer concepts of sex and intimacy. Sometimes men are more intimate with "other women" (e.g., mistresses, sisters, friends) than with wives. As husbands and fathers, however, many men are absent as far as intimacy-disclosure is concerned. Few U.S. men have close male friends. McGill locates the principal problem in competition and men's desire to retain power. Because mystery equals mastery, disclosure is weakening. Extolling the values of intimacy-disclosure, McGill offers advice on how men can achieve it more fully and how women can pressure men into it. The appendix reprints the questionnaire and discusses interviews. Some readers may resent McGill's patronizing attitude toward men (e.g., he dismisses the reasons men give for not being open as "excuses," though some of the reasons are valid). Too often, the book seems less interested in helping men than in telling female readers how superior women are.

24. Raphael, Ray. **The Men from the Boys: Rites of Passage in Male America.** Lincoln and London: University of Nebraska Press, 1988. xvii, 228p. notes. pa.

Examining the importance of male rites of passage found in nearly all earlier societies, Raphael argues that initiation rites both dramatize and facilitate the transition of boy to man. Because American society lacks such rites and an agreed-upon concept of masculinity, it poses special problems for males. In the absence of communal rites of passage, males create reasonable facsimiles for themselves. Such makeshift rites include military training, personally created challenges, sexual experiences, fraternity hazing, sports, and playing Super Dad. Drawing upon interviews with 150 men, Raphael describes these substitute rituals in detail. His final two chapters critique makeshift rites. If the aim of the rite is to help most or all males into adult roles, competitiveness (e.g., in sports) may create too many losers. The improvised rites may be so individualistic as to provide no re-entry for the male into the community. Such rites often lack a spiritual basis for designating manhood, and they may narrow greatly the male's repertory of behaviors. Raphael presents a picture of American males winging it on their own to achieve an acceptable concept of masculinity, with more-or-less success.

25. Sanday, Peggy Reeves. **Female Power and Male Dominance: On the Origins of Sexual Inequality.** Cambridge: Cambridge University Press, 1981. xvii, 295p. appendixes. bibliography, 275-83. notes. index. pa.

Neither male dominance nor female subordination is a constance throughout history in different societies. Using cross-cultural research, Sanday surveys numerous cultures that represent a range in the distribution of power between the sexes. Attempting to answer why these variables occur, Sanday traces social scripts for female power and for male power. Factors affecting the balance of power include the connection made between gender and the gods, division of labor, whether the environment is seen as friend or a foe, beliefs that menstrual blood and sexual intercourse are dangerous, and whether the culture has a primarily inner or outer orientation. Male dominance, Sanday concludes, is a solution for confronting various forms of cultural stress, such as adaptation to environment, social conflict, invasion, migration, and food crises. In Western societies, Judeo-Christian beliefs are highly male-oriented and thus foster male dominance, even in secular societies.

26. Scott, George Ryley. **Phallic Worship.** London: Luxor Press, 1966. xii, 234p. illus. appendix. bibliography, 221-26. index. Reprint, London: Panther Books, 1970. pa.

Described as "a history of sex and sex rites in relation to the religions of all races from antiquity to present day," Scott's work surveys, in part 1, the emergence of phallic sun gods with the awareness of the male role in reproduction. He discusses sacred harlotry and male prostitution, serpent worship, and phallicism as part of witchcraft. Part 2 present a historical, geographic review of phallicism among early tribes, during biblical times, in ancient Greece and Rome, in Eastern and Western cultures, and (despite official disapproval) in Christian symbolism.

27. **Sexual Symbolism: A History of Phallic Worship.** Vol. 1: Richard Payne Knight, **A Discourse on the Worship of Priapus (1786).** Vol. 2: Thomas Wright, **The Worship of the Generative Powers (1866).** New York: Julian Press, 2 vols. in one. 1957. vii, 217, 196p. illus.

With an introduction by Ashley Montagu, this volume brings together two early studies of fertility worship, complete with original illustrations. When Knight's book on phallic worship was published in eighteenth-century England, public outrage forced him to withdraw it. A man ahead of his time, Knight examines with great acumen the sacred phallus in ancient societies, using a wide range of images—amulets, sculptures, and so on. Wright provides something of a sequel to Knight's book, expanding the topic to include female generative worship. Focusing mainly on medieval folk traditions in Europe, Wright discusses sexual monuments, images, rituals, figurines, secret ceremonies, witchcraft, festivals, and so on. As Montagu writes of the two books, "To have them made once more available is a great boon to scholars and to students."

28. Stewart, Samuel M. **Bad Boys and Tough Tattoos: A Social History of the Tattoo with Gangs, Sailors and Street-Corner Punks, 1950-1965.** New York: Harrington Park Press, 1990. 204p. appendixes. index. pa.

Getting tattooed has often been regarded as an assertion of masculine status. In this highly personal account, Stewart tells how he left a dead-end teaching job to become a tattoo artist in Chicago. When Alfred Kinsey suggested to Stewart that he keep a journal for exploring the sexual motivations for being tattooed, Stewart began collecting the data used in this account. He lists 29 motivations for being tattooed, ranging from herd instinct, narcissism, and exhibitionism to manhood initiation rite, an existential act, celebration, and guilt and punishment. Stewart tells plenty of tales about his clientele over the years, and he examines the history and art of tattooing, as well as literature on the subject.

29. Strage, Mark. **The Durable Fig Leaf: A Historical, Cultural, Medical, Social, Literary, and Iconographic Account of Man's Relations with His Penis.** New York: William Morrow, 1980. 317p. illus. notes. index. pa.

Some of the earliest known cave paintings contain representations of the phallus, an indication that humanity's fascination with the penis has a long history. Strage surveys several aspects of this fascination, beginning with the connection made by some animals and humans between the erect penis and dominance. Dysfunctioning of the penis, however, leads to male concerns about penis size, fears of insatiable women, and (according to some theorists) homosexuality. Strage describes the mechanism of erection and such matters as "premature ejaculation," "retarded ejaculation," impotence, aphrodisiacs, and the effects of drugs on the libido. Efforts to "improve" on nature include circumcision, subincision, and insertions. (Strage points to evidence that in recent times circumcision is most often encouraged by mothers, perhaps influenced by articles in women's magazines; fathers seem indifferent to the alleged benefits of circumcision.) Strage's consideration of the penis in visual arts ranges from prehistory, through the classical and medieval periods, and into the Renaissance and modern ages, with special emphasis on such figures as Aubrey Beardsley and Pablo Picasso. Reviewing the literature of the penis, Strage begins with Boccaccio and concludes with such twentieth-century writers as D. H. Lawrence and Norman Mailer. Strage's concluding chapter, "Not Very Hopeful," may be unduly pessimistic: his book contains abundant evidence that man's fascination with his penis has

Using data from studies of 54 societies, Young, in this advanced anthropological treatise, weighs the evidence for seeing male initiation ceremonies as a dramatization of sex-role recognition and male solidarity. Female initiation rites within the context of the family are also discussed.

Cross-References

See chapter 13, "Male Midlife Transition," chapter 15, "Masculinity," and chapter 18, "Minority Males, Multicultural Studies."

849. Anderson, Nels. **The Hobo: The Sociology of the Homeless Man.**

155. Bahr, Howard M., ed. **Disaffiliated Men: Essays and Bibliography on Skid Row, Vagrancy, and Outsiders.**

581. Beer, William R. **Househusbands: Men and Housework in American Families.**

476. Benson, Leonard. **Fatherhood: A Sociological Perspective.**

477. Biller, Henry B. **Fathers and Families: Paternal Factors in Child Development.**

906. Blumenthal, Monica D., Robert L. Kahn, Frank M. Andrews, and Kendra B. Head. **Justifying Violence: Attitudes of American Men.**

596. Bowl, Ric. **Changing the Nature of Masculinity: A Task for Social Work?**

781. Delph, Edward William. **The Silent Community: Public Homosexual Encounters.**

910. Drew, Dennis, and Jonathan Drake. **Boys for Sale: A Sociological Study of Boy Prostitution.**

653. Duneier, Mitchell. **Slim's Table: Race, Respectability, and Masculinity.**

93. Editors of *Look*. **The Decline of the American Male.**

865. Eliade, Mircea. **Rites and Symbols of Initiation: The Mysteries of Birth and Rebirth.**

176. Fine, Gary Alan. **With the Boys: Little League Baseball and Preadolescent Culture.**

602. Franklin, Clyde W., II. **The Changing Definition of Masculinity.**

654. Gary, Lawrence, ed. **Black Men.**

793. Greenberg, David F. **The Construction of Homosexuality.**

564. Greif, Geoffrey. **The Daddy Track and the Single Father.**

565. Greif, Geoffrey L. **Single Fathers.**

701. Hall, Nor. **Broodmales: A Psychological Essay on Men in Childbirth.** Introducing **The Custom of Couvade** (1929) by Warren R. Dawson.

1033. Halle, David. **America's Working Man: Work, Home, and Politics among Blue-Collar Property Owners.**

1034. Halper, Jan. **Quiet Desperation: The Truth About Successful Men.**

502. Hanson, Shirley M.H., and Frederick W. Bozett, eds. **Dimensions of Fatherhood.**

746. Janus, Sam, Barbara Bess, and Carol Saltus. **A Sexual Profile of Men in Power.**

1035. Komarovsky, Mirra. **The Unemployed Man and His Family: The Effect of Unemployment upon the Status of the Man in Fifty-nine Families.**

511. Lamb, Michael E., ed. **The Father's Role: Applied Perspectives.**

512. Lamb, Michael E., ed. **The Father's Role: Cross-Cultural Perspectives.**

513. Lamb. Michael, ed. **The Role of the Father in Child Development.**

514. Lamb, Michael E., and Abraham Sagi, eds. **Fatherhood and Family Policy.**

1037. LeMasters, E. E. **Blue-Collar Aristocrats: Life-Styles at a Working-Class Tavern.**

806. Levine, Martin P., ed. **Gay Men: The Sociology of Male Homosexuality.**

519. Lewis, Charles, and Margaret O'Brien, eds. **Reassessing Fatherhood: New Observations on Fathers and the Modern Family.**

464. Lewis, Charlie. **Becoming a Father.**

521. Lewis, Robert A., and Robert E. Salt, eds. **Men in Families**.

659. Liebow, Elliot. **Tally's Corner: A Study of Negro Streetcorner Men.**

920. Lloyd, Robin. **For Money or Love: Boy Prostitution in America.**

525. Lynn, David B. **The Father: His Role in Child Development.**

526. Mackey, Wade C. **Fathering Behaviors: The Dynamics of the Man-Child Bond.**

1038. Matthiessen, Peter. **Men's Lives.**

528. McKee, Lorna, and Margaret O'Brien, eds. **The Father Figure.**

609. Mead, Margaret. **Male and Female: A Study of the Sexes in a Changing World.**

817. Mendola, Mary. **The Mendola Report: A New Look at Gay Couples.**

820. Murray, Stephen O., ed. **Male Homosexuality in Central and South America.**

611. Ong, Walter J. **Fighting for Life: Contest, Sexuality, and Consciousness.**

532. Ostrovsky, Everett S. **Children Without Men.**

574. Pannor, Reuben, Fred Massarik, and Byron Evans. **The Unmarried Father: New Approaches for Helping Unmarried Young Parents.**

1041. Parnes, Herbert S., and others. **Retirement Among American Men.**

535. Pedersen, Frank A., ed. **The Father-Infant Relationship: Observational Studies in the Family Setting.**

2

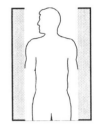

Autobiographical and Biographical Accounts

36. Bouton, Jim. **Ball Four, Plus Ball Five.** Rev. ed. New York: Stein and Day, 1981. xix, 457p. illus. appendixes. pa. Original publication, as *Ball Four* (edited by Leonard Schecter), 1970.

Perhaps because of its unflattering look at baseball machismo, this book aroused hostility around the big leagues in 1970. In this account, baseball "heroes" are depicted, warts and all, in an ironic narrative that often stresses their puerility. The latest edition of *Ball Four* contains information about Bouton's former teammates, the death of his editor and friend Leonard Schecter, Bouton's comeback in baseball, and his divorce and remarriage.

37. Brown, Claude. **Manchild in the Promised Land.** New York: Macmillan, 1965. 415p. Reprint, New York: New American Library, Signet, 1971. pa.

Brown's harsh account of growing up in Harlem contains numerous insights into African-American machismo and what it does to both males and females. Throughout this story of fistfights, paternal beatings, crime, drugs, prostitution, and correctional institutions, Brown weaves the theme of the black boy's need to be seen as a "bad nigger." To be a man, a boy must fight; even his parents will force him to. In correctional facilities, the boys suspected of being gay must be consistently vicious or be degraded. On the streets, males are required to fight over money, women, and manhood. Especially in chapter 10, Brown outlines the code of black masculinity that could lead males to be cruel to women, to each other, and to themselves.

38. Clary, Mike. **Daddy's Home.** 1982. 2d ed. Miami, FL: Pickering Press, 1989. 255p. pa.

When reporter Mike Clary and his wife Lillian Buchanan (a Ph.D. in counseling) had their first child, they did a role reversal. As "housespouse," Clary raised their daughter during her first two years. In *Daddy's Home*, Clary recounts his life as a "mother," complete with the feeling of being an outsider among men who worked and women who mothered. Nurturing his infant daughter, however, was an experience Clary would regret having missed. He says, to a class of sociology students, that "as long as men are denied the chance to be househusbands—because it's considered unmasculine—they are being discriminated against as surely as are women refused entry to the top levels of business." In the second edition, Clary provides a preface updating his and his family's adjustments to his househusbanding.

39. Covington, Jim. **Confessions of a Single Father.** New York: Pilgrim Press, 1982. viii, 181p.

In a compelling narrative, Covington recalls his alcoholic father and dominating mother, his preparation for the ministry, his marriage, and the births of his daughter and son. Then came the social upheaval of the sixties. Covington's religious faith evaporated, his marriage disintegrated, and he found himself a single parent with custody of two children. The troubles and triumphs of this new role are interspersed with reflections on manhood in recent years.

40. Diamond, Jed. **Inside Out: Becoming My Own Man.** San Rafael, CA: Fifth Wave Press, 1983. 184p. illus. bibliography, 182-83.

Set amid California's swinging scene, Diamond's vivid and frank autobiographical account depicts his father-absent childhood and his dependence upon media definitions of manhood. He describes disconcerting experiences with an open marriage, women liberationists, encounter groups, Synanon, Transactional Analysis, and LSD. Divorce, the breakup of other relationships, his role as a single parent, help from men's groups and men's awareness writings (particularly Herb Goldberg's), coming to terms with his parents, and a new relationship mark Diamond's odyssey to discover himself as a man.

41. Firestone, Ross, ed. **The Man in Me: Versions of the Male Experience.** New York: HarperPerennial, 1992. 370p. index. pa. Original publication, as *A Book of Men: Visions of the Male Experience,* New York: Stonehill, 1975.

This collection contains over 100 brief excerpts, poems, and observations from famous twentieth-century men, mostly creative artists. "Each selection," the editor explains, "resonates with me with some sort of truth about what it means to be male." Items are divided into four categories: sons, lovers, husbands, and fathers. The men represented include C. G. Jung, Jack Kerouac, Havelock Ellis, Franz Kafka, Huey P. Newton, August Strindberg, Lenny Bruce, Bertrand Russell, and Dalton Trumbo.

42. Gibson, E. Lawrence. **Get Off My Ship: Ensign Berg vs. the U.S. Navy.** New York: Avon Books, 1978. x, 385p. illus. appendixes. bibliography, 369-77. index. pa.

Closely following the hearings in which Ensign Vernon E. Berg II contested his discharge from the Navy as a homosexual, this book provides insights into the workings of military justice and into military thinking about homosexuality. The illustrations of various participants in the hearings, including the author, are by Berg himself, and five appendixes provide additional information. Amid the tangle of legal issues looms the fact that, as one district court judge lamented, "the U.S. Supreme Court has been reversing any court that suggested that the Constitution applied to servicemen."

43. Greenburg, Dan. **Scoring: A Sexual Memoir.** Garden City, NY: Doubleday, 1972. 223p.

Frank and funny, Greenburg recounts his sexual misadventures as a young man driven by the imperative to score.

44. Houston, James D. **The Men in My Life and Other More or Less True Recollections of Kinship.** Berkeley, CA: Creative Arts, 1987. 163p. notes.

With humor and poignancy, Houston portrays men who have affected his life at crucial moments and thereby revealed something of the complexity, sadness, and resilience of male existence. The 13 vignettes include a hilariously feckless uncle and a expatriate German, a deserter from the Nazi army who mourns his brother killed in World War II. The crucial "moments" include Houston's discovery that football and fraternity life were not for him and his rediscovery of his father through country music.

45. Hoyland, John, ed. **Fathers and Sons.** London: Serpent's Tail, 1992. 207p. pa.

Eight male writers provide deeply moving accounts of their fathers in this collection. In the introduction, Hoyland notes the pattern that seems to unify the sons' diverse recollections: The father is a teacher (about manhood and life), and his gigantic stature must be outgrown by the sons, who eventually rediscover a father they only partly knew. There are eight splendid writers—Paul Atkinson, David Epstein, John Fowles, John Hoyland, Francis King, John McVicar, Christopher Rawlence, and David Simon—whose memoirs of their fathers combine the vividness of well-crafted narrative with that of a child's memory.

46. Kafka, Franz. **Letter to His Father/Brief an Der Vater.** Translated by Ernest Kaiser and Eithne Wilkins. New York: Schocken Books, 1953. 127p. pa.

Written in November 1919, this angry and anguished letter to his father from the 36 year-old Kafka crystallizes in vivid detail a classic antagonism between father and son. "You asked me recently why I maintain that I am afraid of you," is the famous opening sentence, and the rest of the letter explains why—in terms of the father's insensitivity, his sarcastic belittling of his son, his oppressive intellectual and physical presence, his boasting, his crudeness, his displays of temper, and his aversion to the son's writings. Kafka also laments his "saintly" mother's failure to side sufficiently with him against the father, the roles of his sisters in the family conflicts, and the warping of his experiences of Judaism because of the father's behavior. As a result of this antagonism in the home, Kafka insists he has been rendered incapable of career or marriage. Characteristically, in the penultimate paragraph, Kafka imagines his father's "reply" to the letter—and a disconcertingly convincing reply it is. The Schocken edition includes both German text and English translation, as well as a brief publisher's note providing background.

47. Kantrowitz, Arnie. **Under the Rainbow: Growing Up Gay.** New York: William Morrow, 1977. 255p.

Kantrowitz's family was a "Freudian classic," complete with castrating Jewish mother and hapless father. His head filled with film fantasies, Kantrowitz goes off to college in Newark, discovers his gayness, becomes a college teacher, comes out, and evolves into a gay activist in Greenwich Village. Told with humor and verve, Kantrowitz's story carries the reader through the gay awakening of the seventies.

48. Klein, Edward, and Don Erickson, eds. **About Men: Reflections on the Male Experience.** New York: Poseidon Press, 1987. 319p.

When the *New York Times* began a regular Sunday feature called "About Men" on 5 June 1983, no one anticipated the outpouring of responses that it would engender. Eventually, the column developed into a sounding board for male experiences, evidently supplying a long-felt need among men to write about their inner lives. The editors of this volume have selected essays from 69 contributors, grouping the essays into 10 categories: family, love and marriage, children, men without women, friendship, work, play, war, the meaning of manhood, and aging. The essays are brief, and many are deeply moving. The "male experience" of the book's subtitle turns out to be a kaleidoscope of experiences. Essays include Paul Theroux's memorable denunciation of growing up male in America, Samuel G. Freedman' elegy to his mother, and Philip Taubman's second thoughts about being in the delivery room. A reading of this book will dispel forever any lingering stereotypes of men as an unfeeling, inexpressive sex.

49. Kopay, David, and Perry Deane Young. **The David Kopay Story: An Extraordinary Self-Revelation.** New York: Arbor House, 1977. xii, 247p. illus. Reprint, New York: Bantam Books, 1977. pa.

A professional football player, Kopay created shockwaves in 1975 by publicly revealing his homosexuality. His story includes such details as the sexual repressiveness of his Catholic upbringing, his initial awareness of being homosexual, and the anguish of being a closet gay in a sport that prides itself on hypermasculinity. The book contains numerous insights into the relationship between sports and sexual identity.

50. Lee, John H. **The Flying Boy: Healing the Wounded Man.** Deerfield Beach, FL: Health Communications, 1987, 1989. 111p. pa.

When Lee discovered that he was a "flying boy" (i.e., a man who flew from one relationship to another), he attempted to uncover the roots of his malaise. An encounter with Robert Bly convinced him that he was a "soft male" who had rejected his masculinity and overvalued the feminine. Lee also had to confront his father, who had been alcoholic and abusive, as well as his manipulative mother. Throughout the story, Lee has difficulty committing to Laural, and this part of the story ends with their separation and Lee's continuing efforts to come to terms with his life.

51. Lee, John. **The Flying Boy, Book II: The Journey Continues.** 2d ed. Deerfield Beach, FL: Health Communications, 1991. x, 132p. pa. Original publication, as *I Don't Want to Be Alone: For Men and Women Who Want to Heal Addictive Relationships,* 1990.

Lee updates his story by flashing back to an earlier relationship with Lucy, a "flying girl" who could not commit to the relationship. Through Lucy, Lee explores those who enter into addictive relationships that they can neither end nor stabilize. Lee eventually realizes that he must let go of Lucy and begin healing. In the book's postscript, Lee notes that his relationship with Laural has not recommenced, but he looks forward to a future in which he will not be alone and will be able to love more fully.

52. Leiris, Michel. **Manhood: A Journey from Childhood into the Fierce Order of Virility.** Translated by Richard Howard. San Francisco: North Point Press, 1984. ix, 166p. appendix. bibliography, 165. notes. pa. Original publication, as *L'Âge d'homme,* Paris: Librairie Gallimard, 1946.

Beginning life as a shy, sensitive boy, Leiris records how he found himself in the grip of a fierce sexuality that allowed him no respite. Attached to his fond mother and slightly hostile to his bourgeois father, Leiris grew up in a world of art, especially opera. Soon his own volcanic sexuality began to mirror opera's high-powered emotions. Gradually his fantasies coalesced around two female figures painted by Lucas Cranach—Lucrece, the victim-suicide, and Judith, the murdering-castrating femme fatale. Leiris's fantasy plays numerous variations on these two figures, eventually blending them into the figure of Cleopatra. The author recounts his dreams and traces his anxieties about castration, masturbation, impotence, and homosexuality. He also chronicles his sexual initiation, his doomed marriage to a woman named Kay, and his later sexual life. In the appendix, Leiris describes himself as a torero facing annihilation or mutilation in the bullring.

53. Martin, Albert. **One Man, Hurt.** New York: Macmillan, 1975. 278p. Reprint, New York: Ballantine Books, 1976. pa.

This pain-filled retelling of a marital breakup reads like a powerful novel. At age 43, Albert Martin (a pseudonym) is a successful provider, a caring father of four sons, an enlightened Catholic, and a loving husband—right up to the moment on February 5, 1972, when his wife Jean tells him that she no longer loves him and wants a divorce. After months of painful marriage counseling and negotiations, Albert (and probably Jean too) only partly understands her reasons for wanting to leave. Although vaguely involved with a local minister and belatedly rebelling against her perfectionist mother, Jean seems rather to be motivated principally by the current adulation of self-fulfillment. According to Martin, marriage counseling itself, which exalts finding the self above salvaging the marriage, is part of the problem. Eventually, the divorce proceedings are less agonizing than the marital rift that preceded them and the emotional void that follows them. The story of marital collapse may be a familiar one these days, but Martin records a husband's experience of the ordeal with unusual eloquence and drama.

54. Mathias, Frank F. **G.I. Jive: An Army Bandsman in World War II.** Lexington: University Press of Kentucky, 1982. xii, 227p. illus. index.

In this well-written memoir, Mathias combines his skills as an historian with his memories and letters written home during World War II. A small-town boy from Kentucky, Mathias experienced boot camp at Fort Benning and was then swept into the war of the Pacific and the bloody struggle for the Philippines. "I did not think of myself as cannon fodder," Mathias writes, "but that is exactly what I was." What saved his life, most likely, was his ability to play sax. Assigned to an army band, he was able to view the war from a slightly less dangerous and slightly more detached vantage point. As historian, Mathias provides the big picture of the Pacific war, but his G.I. view of events also presents "the war as it was, not as highly placed civilian and military officials believed it to be."

55. McGrady, Mike. **The Kitchen Sink Papers: My Life as a Househusband.** Garden City, NY: Doubleday, 1975. 185p. Reprint, New York: New American Library, Signet, 1975. pa.

At age 40, newspaper columnist Mike McGrady reversed roles for a year with his wife Corinne, who was starting her own business. He became the homemaker and full-time parent to their three children; she became responsible for paying the bills. With an eye for comic details and a knack for hilarious narrative, McGrady charts the reactions of friends and relatives, his successes and failures as a househusband, and his wife's exhilarations and exhaustions as a business person. At year's end, the McGradys became a two-career family, complete with a family contract for sharing household chores and bill-paying responsibilities.

56. McKuen, Rod. **Finding My Father: One Man's Search for Identity.** New York: Coward, McCann, and Geoghegan; Los Angeles: Cheval Books, 1976. 253p. illus. appendixes.

This moving autobiography by the well-known actor-composer-poet is haunted by his search for the father he never knew.

57. Meggyesy, Dave. **Out of Their League.** Berkeley, CA: Ramparts Press, 1970. 263p. illus.

Meggyesy depicts his life as a football player with emphasis on negative aspects of the game, including its dehumanizing impact, brutality, injuries, fraud, under-the-table payments, painkillers, drugs, racism, and sexism.

58. Michaelis, David. **The Best of Friends: Profiles of Extraordinary Friendships.** New York: William Morrow, 1983. 317p. illus.

Miller describes seven male-male friendships that were not homosexual and were as important in shaping the individuals' lives as male-female love. The friendships described include those of businessmen Donold B. Lourie and George H. Love; the Japanese-American Isamu Noguchi and the New England Brahmin Buckminster Fuller; yachtsmen Duncan Spencer and George Cadwalader; John F. Kennedy and his closest friend K. LeMoyne Billings; mountaineers Dave Knowles and Rob Taylor; naval commanders Leonard F. Picotte and Michael B. Edwards; and actors John Belushi and Dan Aykroyd. As Michaelis indicates, close male friendships like those he describes are difficult in the twentieth century: "Rarely do we gauge a man in terms of his success as a friend."

59. Nichols, Beverley. **Father Figure.** New York: Simon and Schuster, 1972. 215p. illus. Reprint, New York: Pocket Books, 1973. pa.

This memoir at times approaches hysteria as it describes how Nichols on three occasions plotted to murder his maddening, alcoholic father. The scene is Edwardian and postwar England; the principal characters are Nichols's domineering and drunken father, his long-suffering mother, and Nichols himself—sensitive, precocious, and leaning toward homosexuality. Although Nichols's hatred of his father permeates the book, the memoir may have the reverse effect of increasing readers' sympathies for the elder Nichols. The son's self-pity is extravagant, the "saintly" mother often appears to be a whining nonentity, and the fact that immediately after her death the father gave up drinking speaks volumes.

60. Painter, Hal. **Mark, I Love You.** New York: Simon and Schuster, 1967. 224p. illus. appendix.

When his wife and daughter were killed in an automobile accident, Hal Painter left his son Mark temporarily in the custody of his in-laws, Dwight and Margaret Bannister of Iowa. A little more than a year later when Hal was about to remarry, he tried to reclaim his son. The rigidly conventional Bannisters, however, loathed Hal's mildly unconventional lifestyle and refused to yield Mark. Those who believe that a father has a legal right to custody of his child need to read on. The Iowa Supreme Court reversed a lower court decision to return Mark to his father, exhibiting fears that the Painter household "would be unstable, unconventional, arty, Bohemian, and probably intellectually stimulating." (The appendix contains the full text of the court's ruling.) Despite a nationwide storm of protest, the U.S. Supreme Court refused to consider the case. At the close of this moving account of frustration and love, Painter had lost custody of his son.

61. Richards, Renée, with John Ames. **Second Serve: The Renée Richards Story.** New York: Stein and Day, 1983. 373p. illus.

This frank autobiography recounts the transformation of Richard Raskind into Renée Richards, the well-known tennis player and doctor. Fraught with perils to a young boy's sexual identity, the Raskind household included a domineering and man-hating mother, an ineffectual and absent father, and an older sister who alternated between attacking Richard and dressing him in her clothing. Eventually, Richard discovered a female personality (whom he named Renée) emerging within himself. This explicit narrative follows the struggle between Richard and Renée for ascendancy, the sex change operation that settled the matter, and Renée's trials and triumphs on the tennis courts. Aside from other interests, the book offers a textbook case of how *not* to raise a male child.

62. Roth, Philip. **Patrimony: A True Story.** New York: Simon and Schuster, 1991. 238p. illus. pa.

In this moving record of his father's last year of life, Roth allows readers to experience the sadness and spunk of Herman Roth as he copes with a brain tumor that slowly short circuits his physical and mental capacities. The son's reactions to his father's "patrimony" of being human form an important part of this poignant document.

63. Rubin, Michael, comp. **Men Without Masks: Writings from the Journals of Modern Men.** Reading, MA: Addison-Wesley, 1980. xx, 312p. pa.

This anthology contains samplings from the diaries of 30 men of the late nineteenth and twentieth centuries. Selections are divided into six categories: sons; idealists; lovers, husbands, and fathers; working men; explorers; and aging, old, and dying men. A gold mine of insights into modern men's experiences, selections range from the journals of anguished sons (e.g., Richard Meinhertzhagen, Franz Kafka, and editor Rubin) to those of idealistic World War I soldiers killed in their youth (Otto Braun and Alan Seeger). Readers can glimpse the love lives of photographer Edward Weston and musician Ned Rorem, as well as the joys and trials of fatherhood as experienced by David Steinberg and Josh Greenfield. Other selections portray the triumphs and trials of work—as well as the costs of unemployment. Explorers include those like Richard E. Byrd and Tobias Schneebaum, who explore new lands, and those like Thomas Merton and Howard Nemerov, who explore unchartered regions of the soul. Interior exploration has not been considered "masculine," Rubin notes in the introduction, praising those who look behind the mask of masculinity to the human reality. "Though the women's movement has done much to break down myths and stereotypes about women in the interests of their complexity," he writes, "it does not often recognize a similar complexity in men."

64. Seabrook, Jeremy. **Mother and Son.** New York: Pantheon Books, 1980. 191p. Original publication, London: Victor Gollancz, 1980.

"This book is about the haunted and obsessive relationship with my mother which, for more than thirty years, was the most total and only real experience of my life." Thus begins Seabrook's account of growing up during the forties in Great Britain with a dominating, man-hating mother, a twin brother who seemed more of an opposite than a sibling, and a father who was alienated, ostracized, disliked, and belittled—and who eventually deserted the family. Seabrook notes the psychosexual damage he sustained. An episode of transvestism and crushes on other boys hint of impending homosexuality, but the book ends abruptly with nothing certain determined.

65. Sifford, Darrell. **Father and Son.** Philadelphia: Westminster Press, Bridgebooks, 1982. 270p.

A newspaper columnist, Sifford describes his midlife crisis, his decision to divorce his wife of 22 years, and the ensuing estrangement from his two sons. Despite some near tragedies, Sifford reconstructs a new life, remarries, and slowly achieves reconciliation with his sons.

66. Stafford, Linley M. **One Man's Family: A Single Father and His Children.** New York: Random House, 1978. 181p.

Stafford recounts how he came to have custody of a teenage son and daughter. His ex-wife had custody of the children originally, but at age 11 the son begged Stafford tearfully to let him move into the father's cramped Manhattan apartment. Despite misgivings and the disastrous first weeks together, father and son became a two-party family. The process began anew, however, when Stafford's daughter also requested to live with her father and brother. Re-creating his experiences for the reader, Stafford provides a narrative that is as vivid and poignant as a good novel. Accompanying the story are his pithy comments on contemporary society, especially its attitudes toward fathers.

67. Steinberg, David. **fatherjournal: Five Years of Awakening to Fatherhood.** Albion, CA: Times Change Press, 1977. 91p. illus. pa. Reprint, New York: Monthly Review Press, 1977. pa.

Dedicated "to all fathers who have been taught to turn away from their children, and the growing number of others who are turning back," this series of diary entries begins with the birth of David and Susan's child, Dylan Joshua, on April 1, 1971. Steinberg records his responses to fathering as he and Susan both work part-time, as he becomes a full-time worker and she becomes a full-time parent, and then as they reverse roles—she works full-time and he becomes a househusband. In poems, songs, and photographs, Steinberg records his deep love for Dylan, but other entries record his moments of anger, frustration, and burnout. "Fathering is something I do well after all," Steinberg writes. "It's not a marketable skill, it's an important one to me."

68. Waller, Leslie. **Hide in Plain Sight.** New York: Delacorte Press, 1976. 275p. Reprint, New York: Dell, 1980. pa.

Can U.S. government bureaucrats kidnap a father's children and keep their whereabouts unknown to him for eight years? Of course they can, as this fascinating retelling of the Tom Leonhard case demonstrates. When law enforcement agents in Buffalo wanted to convict some Mafia bosses, they offered mobster Paddy Calabrese protection, including a new life and identity, for his testimony against Mafia kingpins. The offer extended to Paddy's wife, Rochelle, and her four children. The problem was, however, that Rochelle's two oldest children were from a previous marriage. When she and Paddy disappeared with them, her ex-husband Tom Leonhard had no idea where they had gone. All he knew was that they were in the company of a man whose life was in danger from the Mafia. But none of the law enforcement people apparently gave a thought to Leonhard's plight; in their zeal to convict some Mafia kingpins, robbing a father of his children was a mere triviality. For eight years, Leonhard and his new wife fought a legal battle to recover knowledge of his children's whereabouts. Eventually, he won his case, but at the close of this account he had not yet received an adequate apology from the U.S. government. The author notes that similar cases of separating fathers from their children have already occurred.

69. Wright, Richard. **Black Boy: A Record of Childhood and Youth.** New York and Evanston, IL: Harper & Row, 1945. 285p. pa.

Wright's wrenching account of his early years in the South reveals how poverty and racism can foster a cruel, embittered concept of masculinity in the humiliated, black "boy." Wright's childhood was warped by many things, including the absence of strong male role models and the superabundance of domineering female authority figures. Threatened also by a white world that denied his status as a man, Wright as "black boy" had to battle and connive relentlessly to maintain a modicum of masculine integrity.

70. X, Malcolm, with Alex Haley. **The Autobiography of Malcolm X.** New York: Ballantine Books, 1965. xiv, 460p. pa.

This world-famous autobiography of the charismatic, influential Afro-American activist depicts a search for black male pride. The son of a Baptist preacher and a mother who eventually lost touch with reality, Malcolm Little seemed destined to be a victim of racism, crime, drug abuse, and prison. His enemy was "the white man" who he perceived had denied his own manhood. While serving time, however, Little was converted to the disciplined messianic beliefs of Elijah Muhammad, a conversion that sparked his own intellectual, spiritual, and gender development as Malcolm X. Even while his rise to national fame created fissures within the Nation of Islam, Malcolm X discovered positive masculinity as husband, father, and leader of black people. His own pilgrimage to Mecca and the Middle East brought another phase of spiritual growth that tempered his black separatism and his blanket hatred of white people. This phase of renewal was tragically ended by his assassination on 21 February 1965. As a portrait of an ever striving, ever expanding life, *The Autobiography of Malcolm X* constitutes a memorable tribute to the Afro-American male's struggle to achieve manhood.

Cross-References

171. Abbott, Franklin, ed. **Boyhood, Growing Up Male: A Multicultural Anthology.**

71. Abbott, Franklin, ed. **Men and Intimacy: Personal Accounts Exploring the Dilemmas of Modern Male Sexuality.**

684. Baraff, Alvin. **Men Talk: How Men Really Feel About Women, Sex, Relationships, and Themselves.**

81. Bell, Donald H. **Being a Man: The Paradox of Masculinity.**

860. Black Elk. **Black Elk Speaks: Being the Life Story of a Holy Man of the Oglala Sioux.**

779. Cowan, Thomas. **Gay Men and Women Who Enriched the World.**

3

Awareness: General Discussions of Men's Issues and Topics, and Men's Awareness and Consciousness Raising

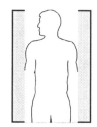

71. Abbott, Franklin, ed. **Men and Intimacy: Personal Accounts Exploring the Dilemmas of Modern Male Sexuality.** Freedom, CA: Crossing Press, 1990. 247p. illus. bibliography, 245-47. pa.

This anthology collects 32 articles and four poems, plus an editor's introduction. Selections are grouped into three sections. Part 1 contains accounts from male victims of various forms of violence, including gay bashing, child sexual abuse, prison rape, circumcision, and racism. Writers often focus on how violence has affected men's ability to be intimate with others. Discussions of erotica and pornography present pro and con viewpoints. Essays in part 2 deal primarily with healing the aftereffects of violence. Topics include bisexual husbands, a father's awareness of his son's dawning sexuality, and several articles on gay relationships. In part 3, writers attempt to change what they regard as harmful social attitudes. Authors represented in the volume include Tom Cahill on prison rape, Robert Staples on black men, and Arthur Levine on the difficulties of gay dating.

72. Abbott, Franklin, ed. **New Men, New Minds: Breaking Male Tradition: How Today's Men Are Changing the Traditional Roles of Masculinity.** Freedom, CA: Crossing Press, 1987. 220p. bibliography, 219-20. pa.

This collection of brief personal recollections, reflections, and poems examines ways in which many men are re-evaluating their lives and concepts of masculinity. The 49 brief selections are divided into four sections: "Fathers," "Stories" (i.e., autobiographical accounts), "Issues," and "Spirit and Soul." The opening essay, Joseph Pleck's poignant memoir of his overworked father sets the tone for much of the volume. The "stories" include accounts from gay men, a victim of male rape, and a retired man. Among the issues are homophobia, circumcision, and war veterans. The final section explores men's spirituality. Noteworthy selections include Robert E. Price's account of becoming a black "instant father" when he married the mother of two children, Ken Fremont-Smith's report of how scars resulting from a childhood burn accident affected his life, Sam Julty's look at the poor state of men's health in the United States, and Keith Thompson's landmark interview with Robert Bly on the meaning of the Iron John story.

72a. Adams, Kathleen. **Mightier Than the Sword: The Journal as a Path to Men's Self-Discovery.** New York: Warner Books, 1994. xvi, 237p. bibliography, 231-35. pa.

Adams makes a convincing case for journal writing as a means of breaking through the inexpressiveness that has been bred into many men. She lists fourteen reasons for using journal writing as a teaching and therapeutic device. Among the reasons: journals help men to read their own minds, clarify and explore their feelings, focus and define their desires, retrieve and heal the past, and explore their spirituality. Providing examples from men's journals, Adams explains techniques that can facilitate and enrich men's journal keeping. To get men to lay down the sword of their anger and grief, Adams suggests they take up the pen of journal writing to explore such matters as their masculine identity, their wounds, their values, the meaning of fatherhood, the difference between positive and negative anger, and their dreams. Journal keeping can be a meditative art that deepens men's spirituality. The final section of the book contains guidelines for journal groups and a bibliography. Adams expounds an important therapeutic technique that can be also a powerful teaching device in men's studies courses.

73. Amneus, Daniel. **The Garbage Generation: The Consequences of the Destruction of the Two-Parent Family and the Need to Stabilize It By Strengthening Its Weakest Link, the Father's Role.** Alhambra, CA: Primrose Press, 1990. ix, 298p. notes. index. pa.

A moral conservative, Amneus argues that the single-parent family is by and large dysfunctional, causing social and individual problems. Primarily, the lack of fathers causes these dysfunctional families. Taking issue with those feminists who exalt matriarchal prehistory as the golden age, Amneus sees female-controlled families as the source of numerous problems. Such families marginalize the father, and female promiscuity undercuts the male obligation to the family. A stable society requires people to resist those feminists who call for female sexual freedom but who simultaneously demand a continuation of male obligations. The patriarchal system puts male energy and sexuality to work for the good of the family, but it also requires female fidelity to ensure that the male will work for her and their children. Amneus distinguishes between "Sleeping Beauty" feminism (women are bored and unchallenged) and "Slaughtered Saints" feminism (women are the victims of male brutality). The latter feminism is largely a ploy to seize tax money to pay for female promiscuity and other "freedoms." The patriarchal family provides the greatest security for women and children. Current divorce and custody practices, however, create mostly dysfunctional, female-headed households that subsist on money from either alienated ex-husbands or taxpayers. Granting custody to fathers would help solve the problem. Amneus differs with George Gilder's idea that women civilize men; rather, it is men who have had to regulate female promiscuity. Social engineering to achieve sexual equality ignores "hypergamy": economically, women marry up, while men marry down. Fathers must continue to struggle for custody and other forms of father-rights.

74. Astrachan, Anthony. **How Men Feel: Their Responses to Women's Demands for Equality and Power.** Garden City, NY: Anchor Press/Doubleday, 1986. xi, 444p. notes. index.

Using interviews and published research, Astrachan finds that many men are feeling more pain than satisfaction from the latest wave of the women's movement. Beginning with the job discrimination faced by his ex-wife as a reporter for the *Washington Post*, Astrachan examines the problems that some women face in the job market, the military, blue-collar work, service industries, and the professions. He notes that male nurses and secretaries can face similar difficulties. Turning to the personal front, he finds gender warfare taking its toll on marriage, fatherhood, and sexuality. Astrachan examines the men's movement, dividing it into three segments: the feminist wing, the "no-guilt" movement, and the divorce-and-custody activists. He examines current novels, poetry, plays, comic strips, and ads for evidence of men's reactions to feminism. He discusses "backlash" to abortion rights and comparable worth schemes. Although the women's movement is encountering obstacles, the author concludes that it will continue to shape American lives.

Some of Astrachan's interpretations of the book's wealth of information may be problematic. The discussion too-easily assumes a uniformity of belief among women, too-readily equates "feminist" with "women." Taking a pro-feminist stance, Astrachan asserts that men as a class exercise power over women, while at the same time insisting that most men do not have much power at all. Thus, he ends up insisting that men must share with women a power that most men do not possess.

75. Avedon, Burt. **Ah, Men! What Do Men Want? A Panorama of the Male in Crisis—His Past Problems, Present Uncertainties, Future Goals.** New York: A and W, 1980. 213p. illus. notes.

For this potpourri of opinions on men in crisis, Avedon interviewed well-known people—seventeen men (e.g., Art Buchwald, Bruce Jenner, Ashley Montague, Gore Vidal) and three women (Helen Gurley Brown, Gael Greene, Elizabeth Janeway). Their views appear in chapters on gender roles, sports, work, sex, feelings, homophobia, men's liberation, and related topics.

76. Baber, Asa. **Naked at Gender Gap: A Man's View of the War Between the Sexes.** New York: Birch Lane Press/Carol, 1992. xvi, 247p.

Containing 73 essays originally published in Baber's widely read "Men" column in *Playboy*, this collection offers feisty views on such matters as male bashing in U.S. society, the alliance of fundamentalists and feminists that denigrates male sexuality, the absence of men's studies on college campuses, the discrimination against fathers in the awarding of custody, and the importance of hanging tough as a divorced father whose ex-wife makes visitation difficult. Above all, Baber stresses the importance of strong fathers. An early essay, "Calling All Blysters," sets the tone for the volume: Baber commends the followers of Robert Bly for clearing the air for a discussion of men's issues, but he faults them for avoiding controversy and ignoring the sexual politics of "feminazis." In contrast, Baber revels in controversy, skewering misandry with zest and wit.

77. Baker, Mark, ed. **What Men *Really* Think: About Women, Love, Sex, Themselves.** New York: Simon and Schuster, 1992. 317p.

Working from interviews with 100 men, Baker distills their comments on women, men, sex, love, physical education, homophobia, abortion, and dads. Promised anonymity, the men provided outspoken, multifaceted responses and stories. From the interview excerpts, one senses that the battle of the sexes has reached an uneasy truce at best, that homophobia still thrives, and that father-hunger is widespread. Abortion seems to cause both men and women an unexpected sorrow. Above all, the men are angry about what U.S. society is doing to men. "If we're really in charge," snaps one man, "how come we got such a lousy job description?"

78. Barbeau, Clayton. **Delivering the Male: Out of the Tough-Guy Trap into a Better Marriage.** Minneapolis, MN: Winston Press, 1982. 136p. bibliography, 133-36. notes. pa. Reprint, New York: Harper & Row, 1982. pa.

A readable and sympathetic attempt to extricate men from the pitfalls of outmoded masculine roles, this book opens with praise of the author's late wife Myra, who helped his liberation. A psychologist with a Catholic-Christian perspective, Barbeau argues that many men are in a more acute identity crisis than women are. Part of the problem is that older masculine roles no longer deliver on their promises. Citing writers like Marc Fasteau (entry 96) and Herb Goldberg (entry 103), Barbeau enumerates the penalties of more traditional male lifestyles. Pointing to the dehumanization that careers often inflict upon men, the author praises those men with the courage to choose simpler, more satisfying lives. A final chapter warns against the widespread passivity among U.S. men and urges a more passionate approach to growth through gender-role modification.

79. Baumli, Francis, ed. **Men Freeing Men: Exploding the Myth of the Traditional Male.** Jersey City, NJ: New Atlantis Press, 1985. xiv, 337p. index. pa.

This rich collection of essays, stories, and poems is unique in presenting an intensive men's rights perspective on gender matters. Selections are divided into 14 sections: "The Process of Reclaiming Ourselves," "About Our Sexuality," "The Game of Dating," "Women in Our Lives," "Men with Men," "Work: Fulfillment or Desperation," "Finding Our Fathers," "Parenting: The Greatest Discovery," "When Daddy Can't Be Daddy Any More" (on divorce and custody), "Violence and the Male Victim," "The Sexist Draft," "Reclaiming the Body," "Men and Women's Issues," and "Making Changes." The anthology devotes space to an extensive range of men's rights issues, including the imbalance of power in dating situations, the joys and pitfalls of male-female relationships, male friendships, gay relationships, challenges and frustrations of the workplace, a range of fatherhood issues involving parenting and divorce, battered and murdered husbands, violence against males as entertainment, the male-only military obligation, men's health and related medical issues, the contradictions in many feminist agendas, getting men's issues out into the open, and the history of the men's movement. The male authors in this volume represent an unusually wide spectrum of experiences and backgrounds; a few female authors also contribute to the discussion. Many of the authors are remarkably outspoken, expressing male insights and anger that are too often censored by the mainstream media.

80. Bednarik, Karl. **The Male in Crisis.** Translated by Helen Sebba. New York: Alfred A. Knopf, 1970. xi, 194, xivp. notes. index. Reprint, Westport, CT: Greenwood Press, 1981. Original publication, as *Die Krise des Mannes,* Vienna: Fritz Molden Verlag, 1968.

Bednarik sees males in crisis because modern bureaucratic and technological society prevents their being naturally active and autonomous. Evidence of crisis can be found in the "impotent anger" of alienated male violence and in the "absurdist revolt" of beats, hippies, hooligans, and other disaffected males. Although favoring equal rights for men, Bednarik sees women's roles as fundamentally different from men's. Men are, he feels, women's natural defenders and protectors. The crisis of modern eros results from commercialization, and hence depersonalization, of sex, a process that allows aggression to contaminate sexual relations. Because male aggressiveness can no longer find legitimate expression in warfare (modern war has made heroism impossible and would result in catastrophic annihilation), conscious control must continually rechannel aggression into constructive or relatively harmless outlets. Because the state has undermined the authority of the father, the male need for exercising authority and autonomy can be recovered only by democratic processes that work upwards from the grassroots.

81. Bell, Donald H. **Being a Man: The Paradox of Masculinity.** Lexington, MA: Lewis, 1982. ix, 158p. notes. Reprint, New York: Harcourt Brace Jovanovich, 1984. pa.

Drawing upon his own experiences and those of men whom he interviewed, Bell explores the paradox of modern masculinity, caught between older traditions and newer lifestyles. In the first three chapters, Bell and his interviewees—all upper-middle-class white men—describe their relationships with their fathers, their lack of close male friends beyond the school years, and their teen boy-girl relationships. The men tell how their marriages became casualties of the gender conflict of the seventies, and how they coped with "beginning again" after divorce. One chapter is devoted to work experiences, including unemployment and the tensions arising between a working wife and a nonworking husband. The experiences of fatherhood—including being present at birth, and being a divorced father—are also explored. The final chapter draws conclusions about the present and raises question about what lies ahead for men.

82. Berkowitz, Bob, with Roger Gittines. **What Men Won't Tell You: But What Women Need to Know.** New York: William Morrow, 1990. 203p.

An NBC correspondent, Berkowitz's informal style may give the impression that he is just kidding around. Actually, he has some perceptive information and practical advice for women trying to figure out men. Like Deborah Tannen (entry 429), Berkowitz understands that men and women sometimes seem to speak a different language; he interprets men's language (both verbal and behavioral) for bewildered women. Chapters in this book discuss such areas as sports, jobs, dating, the difference between flirting and dangerous teasing, sex, and commitment. Berkowitz's commentary is readable, friendly, and refreshingly candid.

83. Bradley, Mike, Lonnie Danchik, Marty Fager, and Tom Wodetzki. **Unbecoming Men: A Men's Consciousness-Raising Group Writes on Oppression and Themselves.** Washington, NJ: Times Change Press, 1971. 64p. illus. pa.

This collection of 12 brief, personal essays was compiled by four members of a men's consciousness-raising group. The unsigned articles recall episodes (mostly painful) illustrating what growing up male in the white middle-class United States can be like. The final essay, written collectively by the four men, describes their consciousness-raising group, warts and all.

84. Brenton, Myron. **The American Male.** New York: Cowan-McCann, 1966. 252p. notes. index. Reprint, Greenwich, CT: Fawcett Crest Books, Fawcett Publications, 1967. pa.

One of the earliest, fullest, and most discerning analyses of the strains in modern masculinity, Brenton's book has retained its relevance well beyond the sixties. "At the present time in history, the American male is subject to an unprecedented number of pressures and tensions," the author writes, underlining his thesis: "Their effect is needlessly deleterious, because he's still trapped by the beliefs and value systems of the past." Brenton states and explores most of the themes that later writers on men's awareness would reiterate, including the attention given to women's concerns and the inattention to men's concerns; the seemingly active man who uses activity to mask his passivity in decision making and leadership; the new demands placed upon men to be emotionally closer, to interchange roles with women, and to be sexual superstars; the binds in which traditional roles place today's men; the "myth" of the good old days of patriarchy when men ruled supreme (Brenton argues convincingly that women privately had great resources for wielding power in so-called patriarchal societies); the father absence that results when males are unprepared by society to assume parental roles; and the "momism" and permissiveness that result from father absence.

Brenton closes with a chapter pointing out new ways to manliness. He warns men to avoid the breadwinner trap, the overspecialization that renders a man vulnerable to adversity and change, and the "myth" that women are morally superior and that real men are destructively aggressive. Conversely, men need to recognize that masculinity can be expressed in personally and socially constructive ways. Especially welcome is Brenton's ability to discuss gender issues candidly without hostility towards either men or women.

85. Bucher, Glenn R., ed. **Straight/White/Male.** Philadelphia: Fortress Press, 1976. x, 149p. notes. pa.
This collection of 10 essays and dialogues by six authors castigates straight white males for oppression of blacks, women, and homosexuals. While Bucher laments the insensitivity of heterosexual white male oppressors, other contributors manage to lay most of the world's evils at their door. Readers are advised to expect not an equitable assessment of men's lives and experiences, but an inundation of heated accusations, sweeping generalizations, and racist and sexist stereotyping of white males.

86. Byers, Kenneth F. **Man in Transition: ... the roles he plays as father, son, friend and lover.** La Mesa, CA: Journeys Together, 1989, 1990. iii, 161p. illus. bibliography, 160-61. pa.
The discovery that his son had a serious drug problem triggered a major rethinking of life by Byers. Today's male experience, he believes, is totally different from anything in history. In a series of short essay on men's lives, Byers reflects on such matters as the roles of father, husband, and son. He also discusses "tools," or techniques for human growth, such as communication, unconditioned love, defining maleness, meditation, forgiveness, and surrender. Byers's meditations are colored by his life in the U.S. Southwest.

87. Cardelle, Frank D. **Journey to Brotherhood: Awakening, Healing, and Connecting Men's Hearts.** New York: Gardner Press, 1990. xxii, 299p. bibliography, 288-98. pa.
A therapist, Cardelle addresses the need for men to move from older, more rigid concepts of masculinity to fuller, more affirming ones. He argues that societies program males for aggression, filling them with bottled-up anger that can explode into violence. Men need to reject the concept of "supra men," face their fears and feelings, and cultivate brotherhood with each other. Using case histories, personal experiences, and cultural history, Cardelle offers self-help strategies to enable men to transform themselves. He envisions a new society of men and women as allies.

88. Connell, R. W. **Gender and Power: Society, the Person and Sexual Politics.** Stanford, CA: Stanford University Press, 1987. xvii, 334p. bibliography, 294-316. notes. index. pa.
This readable work of theory examines the strands of thought and practice that shape gender roles in modern society. Connell does not see men "equally oppressed" as women, although he admits that some men pay a high price for male social advantages. Gay men in particular have suffered considerable disadvantages. Connell surveys the historical and theoretical roots of current gender relations, examining numerous agents that shape gender, such as the family, the state, "the street," and so on. Discussing femininity and masculinity, he explores basic perspectives from sociology and psychology. In the final chapters, Connell considers sexual politics and future social developments. Although the discussion

usually avoids narrow ideology, Connell can occasionally stoop, as when he accuses an author of gender insensitivity for using *Man Makes Himself* as a book title—in 1936. Readers may want to consult Warren Farrell's *The Myth of Male Power* (entry 96), which, in effect, represents a massive critique of Connell's view of gender and power.

89. Cooke, Chris, and others, eds. **The Men's Survival Resource Book: On Being a Man in Today's World.** Minneapolis, MN: M.S.R.B. Press, 1978. xii, 195p. illus. bibliographies after several chapters. pa.
   A potpourri of articles, self-evaluation quizzes, and lists of resources (mostly in the Minneapolis-St. Paul area), this handbook contains chapters dealing with a variety of men's topics, including career and play, health, birth control, sexuality, fathers and parenting, education and personal growth, circumcision, the prostate gland, venereal disease, and assertiveness training for nontraditional males.

90. Craig, Steve, ed. **Men, Masculinity, and the Media.** Newbury Park, CA: Sage Publications, 1992. xii, 271p. (Research on Men and Masculinities Series, no. 1). bibliography, 233-54. notes. author and subject indexes. pa.
   Fifteen articles, plus a foreword by Michael Kimmel, examine images of masculinity in the media. Articles are grouped into five sections: past study of men and the media; case studies of media and masculinities; representations of men's relationships; men, media, and the gender order; and how men "read" media images of masculinity. Representative selections include Stan Denski and David Sholle's discussion of hypermasculinity in heavy metal rock, Norma Pecora's analysis of sexist and racist elements in Superman comics, and David Croteau and William Hoynes's argument that the news media are male dominated. The essays depict masculinities as socially constructed and the media as instruments reinforcing "masculinist hegemony" in "patriarchal capitalism." The radical pro-feminist agenda of the essays leaves several questions unaddressed. Most notably, one is left wondering why—if the media are agents of male power—is male bashing so common in the media?

91. Dolan, Edward F. **Be Your Own Man: A Step-by-Step Guide to Thinking and Acting Independently.** Englewood Cliffs, NJ: Prentice-Hall, 1984. ix, 146p. index. pa.
   This self-help guide, aimed at male readers, touches on such matters as achieving independence, working and the family, guilt, judgments, and interpersonal relationships.

92. Druck, Ken, with James C. Simmons. **The Secrets Men Keep.** Garden City, NY: Doubleday, 1985. 216p.
   A clinical psychologist who conducts *Alive and Male* seminars, Druck offers insights and exercises to help men to break "the silence barrier," that is, to talk about the secrets they harbor. After exploring men's difficulties with expressing their feelings, Druck examines the need for men to contact their fathers and to resolve differences with them. Later chapters deal with male friendship, work stress, mother-son relationships, and life partners.

93. Editors of *Look.* **The Decline of the American Male.** New York: Random House, 1958. 66p. illus.
   This exercise in pop sociology represents the kind of criticism and advice that the U.S. man heard in the fifties. The three essays in the book depict him

as henpecked, passive, tired, anxious, and impotent; the Robert Osborn cartoons caricature him as ludicrous. J. Robert Moskin, in "Why Do Women Dominate Him?" blames women: as wives, they place too many demands on husbands and drive them to early graves. George B. Leonard, Jr., in "Why Is He Afraid to Be Different?" depicts the U.S. male as obsessed with conformity to group standards. In "Why Does He Work So Hard?" William Attwood answers: the puritan ethic, the social expectation that men always be busy, the pressure of public opinion, the need to keep up a standard of living, the pushing by wives, the love of action for its own sake, and ambition. The book's view of men makes it easier to understand such subsequent phenomena as dropouts of the sixties, countercultures, the alleged male flight from commitment, and more recent discontents with traditional masculine gender roles.

94. Emerson, Gloria. **Some American Men.** New York: Simon and Schuster, 1985. 317p. pa.

In this winner of the National Book Award, Emerson writes: "It seems now as if all men were strangers until my late thirties when, as a *New York Times* reporter covering the war in Vietnam at its oldest, I saw huge numbers of American men as few women do: in unimaginable misery and peril." Clearly impatient with the cartoon figures of males perpetuated by U.S. media, Emerson sets out to draw portraits of several American men, in all their complexity, nobility, and weaknesses. With remarkable verbal skills, she depicts such men as entertainment magnate Peter Godoff, reporter Carey Winfrey, a heroic Dr. Gilbert Hunn working among the Cambodian killing fields, unemployed Ohio workers like Barry Whitfield and Michael Paslawski, Vietnam veteran Dan Loney whose daughter suffered the aftereffects of his exposure to Agent Orange, black Fitzroy Herbert who has survived persistent racism, and numerous others. Emerson's observations challenge current misandric clichés about men. Noting the pain experienced by unemployed women, Emerson also notes a differences between them and unemployed men: "The difference was that they did not see themselves as ruined women, suspect as females, people now exposed as profoundly defective." Her insights are captured with often breathtaking verbal precision.

95. Farrell, Warren. **The Liberated Man: Beyond Masculinity; Freeing Men and Their Relationships with Women.** New York: Random House, 1974. Rev. ed. New York: Berkley Books, 1993. xxiv, 350p. appendix. bibliography, 327-28. notes. index. pa.

When it first appeared in 1974, *The Liberated Man* established Farrell as one of the leading commentators on men's issues, a position he has maintained over the years. This new edition contains nearly all of the 1974 text, plus Farrell's reflections on his own growth since then. Part 1 of the 1974 text argues the case for men's liberation by citing the constrictive nature of masculine gender roles and the violence against men that is built into them. Part 2 cites 22 ways in which women's liberation abets men's liberation. Part 3 includes exchanges from consciousness-raising groups and points the way toward human education. In "Introduction 1993," Farrell notes how his earlier, liberal pro-feminist stance included misunderstandings of men. Over the years, he has evolved a more sympathetic insight into why men are the way they are. Acknowledging the many benefits bestowed on women and men by the women's movement, he laments its shadow side—its exiling of men as the enemy through woman-as-victim and man-as-perpetrator stereotyping. In a new introduction to part 3, Farrell provides suggestions for starting a men's group. This new edition provides an intriguing glimpse at the roots of Farrell's thought and its development over the years.

96. Farrell, Warren. **The Myth of Male Power: Why Men Are the Disposable Sex.** New York: Simon and Schuster, 1993. 446p. illus. bibliography, 426-28. notes. index.

In this important analysis of gender issues, Farrell targets the belief in male power as the central distorting myth of modern times. The myth of male power has long poisoned male-female relationships. It now blocks women from assuming roles of responsible equality, and it deadens modern societies to the terrible inhumanities they routinely inflict upon males. Humanity is in transition from Stage I, where males assumed the role of the savior-servant who protected females, to Stage II, where both sexes must exercise equal rights and responsibilities. In part 1 of the book, Farrell argues that concepts like "power," "patriarchy," "male dominance," and "sexism" are actually code words for male sacrifice and disposability. Part 2 supports this argument with detailed analyses of such matters as enforced male military service, the disproportionate number of male suicides, shortened male life spans, greater instances of psychological disorders among males, males as the primary victims of violent crimes, and social indifference about what is happening to males. Part 3 discusses the government as substitute husband, how in recent times the state has enacted double-standard laws that protect female criminal behavior while criminalizing male behavior, how sexual harassment laws essentially harass males, and how male victims of domestic violence and rape are ignored by the "protector" government-husband. Farrell concludes that the sexes can work out of the current spiral of gender antagonism by insisting upon female responsibility and by becoming more sensitive to the unrecognized violence done to males.

97. Farrell, Warren. **Why Men Are the Way They Are: The Male-Female Dynamic.** New York: McGraw-Hill, 1986. xxvii, 404p. illus. bibliography, 382-84. notes. indexes. Reprint, New York: Berkley Books, 1988. pa.

Farrell debunks current clichés about males and proposes a more complex reality. Men are the way they are, he argues, largely because our society makes them that way. Attacking the assumption that "men have all the power," he notes the widespread tendency to ignore evidence of men's powerlessness and women's power. Focusing on one overlooked area of evidence, Farrell surveys ads in popular women's magazines that contain subtexts urging women to use "beauty power" to seduce men. In the process, the ads encourage women to send mixed signals to men and thus to create rape situations. Significantly, the disguised nature of the strategy blinds women to their responsibility for helping to create these circumstances. Elaborating upon this theme, Farrell dissects "The New Sexism," the fashionable male bashing that encourages women to blame men and to deny their own culpability for the way things are. This sexism blocks women's self-understanding and hinders their ability to relate to men. Farrell argues that the sexual revolution came and went so fast because elements of U.S. society blocked it by demonizing men as worthless jerks and dangerous rapists. The current rift between men and women is benefiting neither sex, Farrell argues, and he offers advice for closing it. Throughout the book, Farrell challenges current shibboleths about men with insights that have made him an enormously influential writer on men's issues.

98. Fasteau, Marc Feigen. **The Male Machine.** New York: McGraw-Hill, 1975. xv, 227p. notes. Reprint, New York: Dell, Delta, 1975. pa.

In this widely read critique influenced by feminist thought, Fasteau touches upon nearly all the major dissatisfactions with the traditional masculine role: the stereotyped ideal of the male as a cool and efficient machine, the lack of friendships among adult men, the confusion of sex and violence, the obsession with sexual technique, the denigration of women as inferiors, the failure of fathers as caring parents, sports as a training ground for competition, the cutthroat nature of success-oriented careers, and the mystique of violence. Fasteau also explores how the cult of toughness affected U.S. foreign policy and the Watergate imbroglio. A final chapter offers the ideal of androgyny, which Fasteau sees as creating not a unisex sameness but a greater range of behaviors for both men and women. The book contains an introduction by Gloria Steinem.

99. Filene, Peter, ed. **Men in the Middle: Coping with the Problems of Work and Family in the Lives of Middle-Aged Men.** Englewood Cliffs, NJ: Prentice-Hall, 1981. xi, 193p. illus. notes. pa.

In this collection of autobiographical essays, eight men try to answer the questions, "Where Do We Come From, Who Are We, Where Are We Going?"—to borrow the title of a Gauguin painting that fascinates one of the men. The contributors are "men in the middle," that is, from the middle class, at midlife. Having imbibed the work ethic as youths, they all struggle to balance career and family. Bright, well educated, radicalized by the civil rights movement of the sixties, sensitized by the women's movement of the seventies, they await fuller men's liberation. "Why should women be allowed to shuck the feminine roles," Filene wonders in his essay, "and men be forced to stay with the masculine roles?" Filene's introduction tells how the book took shape and comments on its themes. In a concluding chapter, he constructs a "conversation" from the contributors' most recent letters updating their stories and commenting on the others' essays.

100. Garfinkel, Perry. **In a Man's World: Father, Son, Brother, Friend, and Other Roles Men Play.** New York: New American Library, Mentor, 1985. xv, 208p. bibliography, 188-93. notes. index. pa. Reprint, Berkeley, CA: Ten Speed Press, 1993. pa.

Drawing upon interviews, research, reading, and observation, Garfinkel surveys the changing landscape of masculinity. He finds that fathers and sons are usually locked in a tension-filled love relationship, but the importance of fathers for sons is very great. Fathers alone, however, cannot shape adult males; grandfathers and mentors often play formative roles for boys and young men. Brothers, frequently locked in a bond that includes rivalry, can bring both painful competition and needed support to each other. Men also find male relationships in organizations, from Boy Scouts to male-only clubs and groups. Garfinkel surveys the changing images of heroic males in films and videos, arguing that older macho roles are yielding to more sensitive heroes. Male friendships are marked by scarcity and distance, and Garfinkel finds homophobia to be a blight on all men's lives. In the final chapter, Garfinkel concludes that males need each other, that they need to cherish one another, and that they must break down the barriers that separate them from other men.

101. Gerson, Kathleen. **No Man's Land: Men's Changing Commitments to Family and Work.** New York: Basic Books, HarperCollins, 1993. xvi, 366p. appendix. bibliography, 329-55. notes. index.

"Suddenly men are a hot topic," Gerson notes at the start of this examination of men's current choices in career and family. Surveying current changes in masculine gender roles, the author notes that many men were and are ambivalent about the role of breadwinner. Often the birth of a child pushes a man into the role or drives him away from it. Drawing upon interviews with

138 men between the ages of 28 and 45, Gerson traces the lives of men who took on breadwinning and those who made different choices, including individual autonomy, getting off the fast track, and committing to a nondomestic woman. Gerson examines the dilemmas of balancing autonomy and breadwinning and the dilemmas of fatherhood, especially after divorce. The last two chapters survey the historical reasons for current changes in gender roles and the politics of equality. Although Gerson is sometimes fixated on the alleged powers and privileges of men as a class, she often recognizes that not all men are powerful and some men are disadvantaged.

102. Gilder, George. **Men and Marriage.** Gretna, LA: Pelican, 1986. xix, 219p. notes. Original publication, as *Sexual Suicide,* New York: Quadrangle/New York Times, 1973. Reprint, New York: Bantam Books, 1975. pa.
    The new preface of this updated and expanded version of *Sexual Suicide* describes how plans to print a revised edition of the book were initially sabotaged by feminist editors and how the book's predictions about the decline of marriage and family have since materialized. An opening parable of the Princess and the Barbarian outlines Gilder's conservative view of the sexes: civilization exists only because males, whose sexual needs are briefly satisfied, have adapted to the long-term rhythms of women's sexuality, procreativity, and child nurturing. Most individuals achieve their fullest humanity within carefully defined sex roles, which are neither infinitely malleable nor immune from careless social and political tampering. Gilder castigates sexual liberals for ignorantly disrupting the harmonious interplay of male and female sex roles in monogamous marriage. The feminist drive for workplace careers creates a competitive situation in which young women and successful older men are the winners, but older women and young men are the losers. In all cases, marriage and children suffer. Among the disadvantaged, the breakdown of family leads to "ghetto revenge" in which the young men band together in gangs to terrorize society. Gilder also believes advocacy of gay lifestyles can easily seduce young men who fear they cannot meet the demands of adult masculinity. Gilder castigates coed schools, socialist "reforms" that have undermined marriage (in countries like Sweden), and advocates of women in combat. An afterword defends capitalism for reinforcing a social system that encourages the nuclear family.

103. Goldberg, Herb. **The Hazards of Being Male: Surviving the Myth of Masculine Privilege.** Plainview, NY: Nash, 1976. 200p. notes. index. Reprint, New York: New American Library, 1977. 2d ed., New York: New American Library, Signet, 1987. pa.
    This landmark book debunks the idea that males are a favored sex, "a notion that is clung to despite the fact that every critical statistic in the area of longevity, disease, suicide, crime, accidents, childhood emotional disorders, alcoholism, and drug addiction shows a disproportionately higher male rate." Starting from the premise that U.S. men must unlock themselves from older, destructive patterns of life, Goldberg explores the negative aspects of being male in the United States. He argues that most men live in harness, drudging out their lives at onerous jobs and struggling to reconcile the conflicting demands of their roles as breadwinners, husbands, and fathers. Most men's roles begin and end in a series of impossible binds. Although sympathetic to the women's movement, he warns men against expecting it to liberate them; without undue intellectualization, men themselves must cultivate spontaneity, close male friendships, and the ability to regard women as equals. Significantly, he rejects guilt as a means of motivating men to change; he deplores

the stereotyping in some feminist writings of men as oppressors. Supported by the author's experiences as a clinical psychologist and by his researches into the male condition, *The Hazards of Being Male* has been a seminal book of men's awareness. The 10th anniversary edition contains Goldberg's foreword reflecting on the book's impact upon men, his disappointment with the hostile reactions of many feminist writers, and his concern that male-female relationships are more fragile than ever.

104. Goldberg, Herb. **The Inner Male: Overcoming Roadblocks to Intimacy.** New York and Scarborough, Canada: New American Library, NAL Books, 1987. xiii, 296p. notes. Reprint, New York: New American Library, Signet, 1988. pa.

Goldberg caustically analyzes the post-liberation scene before providing some suggestions for positive change. After a decade of liberation, many men and women find themselves in fragile, hostile relationships. The "magic lady," for example, is often a wounded bird who is paying back men for hurts in her past. Goldberg questions "the commitment obsession" and argues that the partner who leaves a dying relationship has done the necessary dirty work for two. Women "who love too much" are usually vengeance-seeking women who do not love at all. Goldberg praises impotence when it signals the man's deep awareness that his present relationship is wrong. He describes numerous types of men and women who, under the guise of liberation, are trapped in behaviors that guarantee relationship failure. Many "liberated" women are ice queens who despise and blame men, and many "liberated" men are macho types disguised as the rescuing white knight. Men must rethink the business of expressing their emotions, avoid quick-fix "how to" solutions to problems, and find a middle ground that allows them to move forward with women toward more fulfilling relationships.

105. Goldberg, Herb. **The New Male: From Self-Destruction to Self-Care.** New York: William Morrow, 1979. 321p. notes. index. Reprint, New York: New American Library, Signet, 1980. pa.

In this energetic exhortation, Goldberg sees the modern male in crisis, and offers advice on how to replace his self-destructive tendencies with positive changes that will include self-care, spontaneity, and personal fulfillment. The book's first section, analyzing the present male dilemma, depicts the modern U.S. male as a cardboard Goliath, compulsively proving his masculinity, running from failure, and facing midlife burnout. In section 2, Goldberg explores how different kinds of women can place men in difficult binds. Particularly interesting is his account of the Actor-Reactor syndrome in which the male's role as initiating and responsible partner inevitably leads to accusations that he is an oppressor and exploiter, while the woman appears as an innocent victim. Conversely, Goldberg also analyzes how men's conflicting demands upon women can place women in similarly difficult binds. In section 3, he explores how men's timid reactions to the women's movement can result in their getting the worst of both sides of the liberation crunch. He castigates the willingness of present society to accept and perpetuate negative, sexist stereotypes of men; he advises men that the women's movement can save their lives—but only if they stop reacting with guilt-laden accommodation and start refashioning their lives to meet their own needs. The final section offers advice to help men emerge from the restrictions of past gender roles. It urges men to become aware of anti-male sexist vocabulary, to learn to feed themselves, to cultivate "buddyships," to avoid "earth mother" women, and to "custom make" their own lives.

106. Goodman, Andrew, and Patricia Walby. **A Book About Men.** London: Quartet Books, 1975. 167p. notes.

"The thesis of this book is that men need liberating as well as women," Goodman and Walby write in their introduction. The authors, each writing alternate chapters, touch informally on a variety of topics, including male bonding, the macho mystique, sex fantasies, and the "daily crucifixion" of work for most men. At times, the authors depict men as privileged oppressors, at other times, as victims of a malevolent social order. "The subject matter is extensive," the authors write, "and we are aware that we have made too many generalizations and skated over large areas of controversy, but the subject is in its infancy and hitherto undefined."

107. Greene, Thayer A. **Modern Man in Search of Manhood.** New York: Association Press, 1967. 128p. illus. notes.

"Being a man has never been easy," Thayer begins, adding that the job is more difficult now than ever before. A college chaplain, parish minister, and psychotherapist, Greene notes that, although much has been written about men, less has been written for them or to them. Addressing himself primarily to young men between the ages of 18 and 30, he explores the changing roles of men in modern society. Although both biology and culture contribute to sexual identity, menstruation provides definite and regular affirmation of femininity. In contrast, males must constantly prove their masculine identity. Exploring conflicting images of masculinity contained in our culture, Greene believes that men can be easily trapped between roles and their real selves. Homophobia and the need to repress feelings—even anger and aggression, which are "inappropriate" for Christian gentlemen—hamper men in their efforts to discover and nurture their "feminine" qualities. The penultimate chapter stresses the need for men to find the authentic self in solitude; the final chapter summarizes the book concisely.

108. Herzig, Alison Cragin, and Jane Lawrence Mali. **Oh, Boy! Babies!** Boston: Little, Brown, 1980. 106p. illus. pa.

In 1978 an urban boys' school offered an elective minicourse in infant care that would include real infants. Ten boys signed up for the class. In this hilarious and heartwarming book, the text and the photographs (by Katrina Thomas) show the boys learning to handle, dress, diaper, feed, bathe, and play safely with the infants. At first unsure of themselves, the boys quickly gained confidence and eagerly awaited the babies' appearance each Wednesday. Enthusiastic and resourceful, the boys ingeniously coped with a roomful of squalling, crawling babies. They also became greatly attached to the infants and to the idea of caring for them. The book, as Dr. Benjamin Spock writes, "reveals in touching form ... how human beings eventually turn into parents."

109. Hoch, Paul. **White Hero, Black Beast: Racism, Sexism, and the Mask of Masculinity.** London: Pluto Press, 1979. 191p. notes. index. pa.

This examination of masculinity goes beyond the narrower limits suggested by its title. Part 1, a critique of feminists and male liberationists, notes their failure to ask *why* men behave as they do: males, as well as females, are shaped by historical and cultural forces beyond their control. Examining different facets of masculinity, Hoch explores theories of manhood as a social ritual and as a defense mechanism against impotence and homosexuality. A fascinating chapter containing allusions to folk art from classical myth to *Star Wars* outlines the myth of the white hero and the black beast. In this myth, heroic males must conquer a monster who represents some savage aspect of themselves. The racial implications of this account of white-black confrontation are significant. Drawing upon Freud's *Totem and Taboo*, Hoch also examines masculinity as a mask hiding patricidal impulses and incestuous desires. Part 2 explores the "fall" from classless to class-structured society. It also traces alternating ideals of Puritan and Playboy through Western history from Roman times to the present, culminating in the rise of manly individualism in a society of production and consumption. Despite the book's "pious hope" ending that promises vague renewal through a new socialist order, Hoch's observations repeatedly point to areas of needed investigation in men's studies. Equally important, his spirit of inquiry—neither guilt-ridden nor chauvinistic—represents a refreshing and vitalizing approach to men's studies.

110. Hodson, Phillip. **Men ... : An Investigation into the Emotional Male.** London: Ariel Books, British Broadcasting, 1984. 143p. bibliography, 143. pa.

A British marriage counselor, Hodson sees modern males in crisis. Males are the fragile sex, they are emotionally blocked and incommunicative, and they are killing themselves with workaholism. They cannot enjoy sex because of performance pressures, and they need to control their aggressiveness. Good fathers are badly needed but are in short supply. The frequent citing of Dr. Joyce Brothers as an authority on modern men indicates the book's level of sophistication and may help to account for its predominantly patronizing view of males.

111. Hornstein, Harvey A. **A Knight in Shining Armor: Understanding Men's Romantic Illusions.** New York: William Morrow, 1991. 176p. bibliography, 161-67. index.

The counterpart of "The Cinderella Complex" described by Colette Dowling, "The Prince Charming Complex" afflicts many men. These men assume they must ensure that the damsel they have "rescued" lives happily ever after. Relationships suffering from the "manservant syndrome" go through a three-act scenario: the man serves the woman, seeking to make her every wish come true; they both experience disillusionment; and, finally, they end up with oppression and rage. The man is left frustrated; the woman feels controlled. Hornstein describes three kinds of "knights": ministers, educators, and "Lancelots" who dazzle women. Parents and society encourage boys to be girls' problem-solvers; consequently, capable women appear to men to block their road to masculine achievement. Hornstein's advice to men is to be a man, but don't act like one. In particular, men need to talk to other men and to women about their difficulties. Hornstein's treatment of the subject is light and popular; the topic may deserve a more thorough, scholarly examination.

112. Hunter, Mark. **The Passions of Men: Work and Love in the Age of Stress.** New York: G. P. Putnam's Sons, 1988. 320p. index.

A journalist with a capacity for seeing through media clichés about men, Hunter explores the painful paradoxes facing modern men. Work is killing men, he argues, and yet men without work often lose their direction. Drawing upon interviews and extensive reading, Hunter also utilizes his own experiences to offer stunning observations on the contemporary scene. Having lived through youthful radicalism and a relationship with a feminist woman, Hunter has developed into a shrewd observer of the work and gender scenes. Refusing to indulge in fashionable father bashing, Hunter, instead, deplores what younger people have done to their fathers and to patriarchy. Father hunger is less real than father hatred, he proclaims. The proof that the women's movement has succeeded can be found in the general unhappiness of both women and men. Radical feminism has degenerated from a struggle for gender equality into arrogant lesbian separatism. Males are still suffering from the Sidney Carton complex, the wish to sacrifice themselves for women whom they regard as their spiritual superiors. The personal can never be simply the political, Hunter argues, because the personal is concerned with individuals and the political with people in groups. Eminently readable, Hunter sounds a clarion wake-up call for men and women.

113. Karsk, Roger, and Bill Thomas. **Working with Men's Groups: Exploration in Awareness.** Columbia, MD: New Community Press, 1979. ix, 126p. appendix. bibliography after each chapter. pa.

A useful tool for leaders or facilitators of men's groups, this book is aimed at men seeking to enhance personal awareness about alternatives for growth and change. The authors are not interested in examining men's alleged sexism or guilt; instead, they focus on the great unexplored territory of men's feelings about themselves, the sources of men's anger, male sexuality, and parenting. Formats for group sessions are provided, including materials needed, the amount of time to be allotted, desirable group size, objectives of the session, and procedures. Suggestions for outside reading and audiovisual materials are also included. An appendix lists national, specialized, and local support groups for men.

114. Kauth, Bill. **A Circle of Men: The Original Manual for Men's Support Groups.** New York: St. Martin's Press, 1992. xvi, 141p. illus. bibliography, 132-39. pa.

The cofounder of the New Warrior Training Adventure, Kauth offers a systematic program for starting several kinds of new men's groups and for sustaining existing ones. For the group organizer, Kauth offers a program for addressing questions about how to decide what the group's purpose is, how and where to find potential members, and how to choose members. In clear, direct prose, he offers extensive advice on how to run the initial eight meetings, how to introduce men and encourage speaking and listening, how to handle hassles, and how to move on to larger activities and challenges. Dealing with group dynamics, Kauth addresses such matters as using ritual, touching, and handling problems within the group. The book closes with three articles (by Kauth, Danaan Parry, and Gabriel Heilig) on pressing aspects of current masculinity. Information on the New Warrior Training Adventure men's weekend is followed by an annotated bibliography of books and tapes.

115. Kay, Harvey. **Male Survival: Masculinity Without Myth.** New York: Grosset and Dunlap, 1974. 213p. index.

Writing in popular style, Kay examines the crisis of modern masculinity. A practicing psychiatrist and psychoanalyst, he discusses genially and forthrightly various aspects of the masculine mystique—the Superman syndrome, the Neanderthal ideal, the sexual athlete, the heroic imperative, the achiever complex, the playboy in paradise, the dominance drive, and the myth of male superiority. After explaining the biological, psychological, and societal components of masculinity, Kaye delves into the workaday world of the average man. He discusses the performance pressures put on heterosexual men, and he views with some reservation the homosexual "alternative" now being offered to them. Reviewing attacks upon the family and the demands for success placed upon men, Kaye offers a modest critique of the more extreme views of some women's liberationists. Changing male roles will not be easy, Kaye believes, but the possibility of improving conditions for many men makes the effort worthwhile.

116. Kilgore, James E. **The Intimate Man**. Nashville, TN: Abingdon Press, 1984. 144p. pa.

Within a Christian context, Kilgore explores the value of intimacy for men in modern times. Noting a male fear of intimacy as "feminine," he examines the male need for self-acceptance and sharing. Stressing the importance of male closeness with wives and children, he discusses his concept of God as loving father, and a boy's need for male models who verbalize their love. He argues that male chauvinism is often the result of mothers who teach their sons that other women want to lean on them. Discussing the continuing need for intimacy throughout the life cycle, Kilgore advises men not to repress their little-boy spontaneity.

117. Kriegel, Leonard. **On Men and Manhood**. New York: Hawthorn Books, 1979. x, 206p. bibliography, 201-6. notes.

Crippled by disease when he was a boy, Kriegel learned early the positive virtues of courage and endurance. In this prose poem of recollections and observations, he hymns the positive values of old-fashioned masculinity as embodied in U.S. literature (especially Hemingway), sports, and certain screen images (John Wayne in *Stagecoach,* Marlon Brando in *The Men*). Kriegel has little patience with male liberationists who denigrate this masculinity or with the exaltation of androgyny, which he equates with unisexuality. Kriegel also discusses the gay rights movement and the new black masculinity. Knowing that his views are not trendy, he concludes with a chapter entitled "Waiting."

118. Kupers, Terry A. **Revisioning Men's Lives: Gender, Intimacy, and Power**. New York and London: Guilford Press, 1993. viii, 200p. bibliography, 185-97. index. pa.

Men need to redefine their gender role to include power but not sexism, equality but not weakness. In this process of redefinition, men bucking the tide of traditional masculinity will find little support from men or women. But present-day masculinity is problematic: Men experience "pathological arrhythmicity," or periodic disruptions in their lives. Homophobia, which Kupers attributes to latent homosexuality, provokes men's discomfort with new masculine roles. For men and women, equitable roles, not identical ones, are preferable. Kupers finds pornography a stumbling block to male-female equality, and he notes that father-son relationships are particularly conflicted. Men are reluctant to enter therapy, and they have few friends for support. Kupers divides the men's movement into two groups: the mythopoetic movement, which he finds laced with misogyny, and the pro-feminist wing, which he believes disregards men's suffering. Kupers concludes that men need to cultivate tolerance for different kinds of masculinities.

119. Lyon, Harold C., Jr., with Gabriel Saul Heilig. **Tenderness Is Strength: From Machismo to Manhood**. New York: Harper & Row, 1977. xii, 270p. index.

"This book is a statement in behalf of men's liberation," Lyon writes. Concerned that women's liberation will exalt the macho hardness that has been a male ideal, he concludes: "The best thing that could happen to women's liberation would be men's liberation." Toughness may have been a virtue at one time in history when most men had to be protectors and enduring laborers, but now it presents a block to self-growth and a lethal trap for many men and some women. Lyon sees tenderness and strength less as opposites than as complements or as a continuum. He gathers up numerous strands of thought upon such matters as hypermasculinity, homophobia, diet, meditation, the courage to fear, laughter, fatherhood, brotherhood, and the need for tenderness at birth and at death. He occasionally refers to his experiences as a wartime child (told by his soldier father to be the man of the house), a West Point cadet, a Ranger-paratrooper Army officer, government official, teacher, university administrator, divorced and remarried husband-father, and therapist. Gabriel Saul Heilig contributes a chapter on his spiritual odyssey from confused striving to inner enlightenment. The foreword is by John Denver.

120 Maas, James. **Speaking of Friends: The Variety of Man-to-Man Friendships.** Berkely, CA: Shameless Hussy Press, 1985. xi, 143p. illus. pa.
 In this touching book, Maas interviews 28 San Francisco Bay Area men about friendships. The responses vary widely: some men see no need for male friendships, others find deep joy in them. In the introduction, Maas explains the need for male friends that led him to conduct the interviews. In the epilogue he reflects on the men's responses. The book features photographs by Sam Julty.

121. Mailer, Norman. **The Prisoner of Sex.** Boston: Little, Brown, 1971. 240p. notes. Reprint, New York: New American Library, Signet, 1971. pa.
 Oddly reminiscent of Virginia Woolf's *A Room of One's Own,* with its third-person ruminations, Mailer's *The Prisoner of Sex* reflects upon radical feminism in general and Kate Millett's *Sexual Politics* (entry 680) in particular. In an extended, meandering essay laced with sly wit, Mailer is perhaps at his best dissecting Millett's misreadings of Henry Miller and D. H. Lawrence. As usual, Mailer is provocatively outrageous: in the end, he endorses women's liberation—so that women can be free to find the right man.

122. Men Against Patriarchy. **Off Their Backs ... and on Our Own Two Feet.** Philadelphia: New Society, 1983. 29p. pa.
 This publication consists of three pro-feminist essays by men. In "More Power Than We Want: Masculine Sexuality and Violence," Bruce Kokopeli and George Lakey trace a sinister connection between "patriarchal" society and violence, suggesting androgyny as the solution. Peter Blood, Alan Tuttle, and George Lakey, in "Understanding and Fighting Sexism: A Call to Men," describe how sexism works against both sexes, how male guilt is not the answer, and how change can be effected. Among the solutions are a change from capitalist to socialist economy and communal childrearing instead of the nuclear family. "Overcoming Masculine Oppression in Mixed Groups," by Bill Moyer and Alan Tuttle, lists suggestions for replacing confrontational tactics with cooperative ones.

123. Miller, Stuart. **Men and Friendship.** Boston: Houghton Mifflin, 1983. xvii, 206p. bibliography, 199-206. Reprint, Los Angeles: J. P. Tarcher, 1992. pa.
 Rejecting a "cold" study of a much-neglected topic, Miller presents a "warm" view, using his own search for male friends as a springboard for larger considerations. Finding himself at midlife with a need for friends, Miller consciously set out to cultivate them, but with only partial success. Among the diary entries and personal letters, the author defines friendship as involving intimacy and "complicity," that is, a you-and-me-against-the-world understanding. He distinguishes between male bonding involving a group of men and friendship involving two individuals. Miller notes that many men put such a low priority on friendship that it has little chance to flourish in their lives.

The closest friendships, Miller found, were often between gay men who were not lovers. Of the massive pressures allied against male friendship, the greatest is homophobia, which has reached extraordinary intensity in the twentieth century. In lieu of a conclusion, Miller offers some advice on achieving friendship despite the odds.

124. Moore, John H. **But What About Men? After Women's Lib.** Bath, England: Ashgrove Press, 1989. 243p. notes. index. pa.
"Men badly need to liberate in themselves a new vision of themselves if they are to avoid obsolescence," writes the British author of this book. Women's liberation has altered the age-old pattern of gender roles, and males must discard the older roles of fighter and economic strongman. Population growth and environmental damage have rendered obsolete male roles as "hunter, warrior, and predatory lover. The brain/mind is differentiated into a "feminine" left side and a "masculine" right side, but feminism has led many women to access the traditionally masculine side of the brain. The traditional dominance of male brain/mind is evident in "patriarchal," or male-dominated, religion. Only a new spiritual rebirth can rectify the imbalance. At present, marriage is on the rocks and the traditional hero is increasingly outmoded. Only a reconciliation between the conflicting masculine and feminine can produce further human spiritual growth. Moore's reflections alternate between the superficial and the perceptive. Overgeneralizations about men and women fly fast and thick in these ruminations, and Moore seems unaware of the mythopoetic and archetypal elements in recent men's spiritual writings. Still, he issues a compelling call for men to "start seriously reflecting on their image of themselves—not in the eyes of women, but in their own."

125. Murphey, Cecil. **Mantalk: Resources for Exploring Male Issues.** Louisville, KY: Presbyterian, 1991. iv, 81p. illus. bibliographies after each chapter. notes. pa.
This attractive handbook was sponsored by nine Christian ministry groups, including seven groups that minister specifically to men. The 20 brief chapters provide an overview of men's issues, including concepts of masculinity, growing up male, men at midlife, aging, sexuality, violence against women, child abuse, fathers and fathering, male friendships, employment, spirituality, and God language. The discussion is clear and sympathetic to men, although some oversimplification occurs. The author believes only men rape, quotes sensational child abuse statistics uncritically, and ignores the spiritual dimension of the mythopoetic men's movement. But, for anyone ministering to men's physical, psychological, social, and spiritual needs, Murphey's guide is a valuable primary source. The artwork is superb.

126. Naifeh, Steven, and Gregory White Smith. **Why Can't Men Open Up? Overcoming Men's Fear of Intimacy.** New York: Clarkson N. Potter, 1984. xii, 193p. bibliography, 181-93. index.
Summarizing current views of men's difficulties in feeling and expressing their emotions, the authors explore the dimensions and causes of the problem. In the latter half of this popularly written book, they offer advice for the woman trying to reach intimacy with a closed man. After sketching in their own experiences, the authors stress the cultural roadblocks to male expressiveness, indicating that most males have been carefully taught to hold back emotionally and are penalized when they do not. Hormones are not the problem; fathers who teach male inexpressiveness often are. Many women also send mixed signals to men: some women who say they want their man to open up are

frightened or repelled when he does. The mystique of the strong, silent male still flourishes in the post-John Wayne era. Men alone either cannot or will not transform themselves; women (who are better versed in expressiveness) will have to help them. Practical suggestions for women are provided, a casebook of closed male types is presented, and the authors conclude with personal reflections on what they have learned from their researches and interviews.

127. Nardi, Peter M., ed. **Men's Friendships.** Newbury Park, CA: Sage Publications, 1992. viii, 246p. (Research on Men and Masculinities Series, no. 2). bibliography after each chapter. notes. index. pa.
    Several of the 12 essays in this volume reach similar conclusions: male-male friendships are often inhibited by current masculine gender roles; in other times and places, male friendships were often more expressive than they are now; marriage and family often replace male friends in a man's life; and male friendships must not be judged by feminine standards. Other essays discuss male-female friendships and gay male friendships. In an essay on American Indians and Asians, Walter L. Williams concludes that homophobia's first victim is male friendship. Discussing black men, Clyde W. Franklin II observes that underclass male friendships are often strong and supportive, but among upwardly mobile black men, friendship is often weaker. Nearly all the essays question stereotypes of males as devoid or incapable of same-sex friendships.

128. Nichols, Jack. **Men's Liberation: A New Definition of Masculinity.** 1975. Rev. ed., New York: Penguin Books, 1978, 1980. 333p. notes. pa.
    "In future decades," Nichols writes, "today's male role will be remembered as a straitjacket." Pinpointing the over-reliance upon rationalistic thought as the source of men's problems, Nichols extols Eastern philosophy, denigrates Western religion and thought, and urges men towards an androgyny that will incorporate both "masculine" and "feminine" mental abilities. Chapters explore such topics as the loss of playfulness among men, the exaltation of "masculine" competition and violence, and the deadening effect upon men of a lifetime of failure in the workplace. The author praises liberated women, deplores manipulative ladies, and argues that the nuclear family, which restricts men sexually and emotionally, will be radically changed. The term "father," he says, has become synonymous with "financial functionary." Stressing the need for close male friendships and for expunging homophobia, Nichols sees in Walt Whitman's *Leaves of Grass* (entry 336) the noblest expression of American men's liberation.

129. Olson, Ken. **Hey, Man! Open Up and Live!** New York: Fawcett Gold Medal, 1978. 251p. notes. pa.
    In upbeat style, Olson describes why men need to break out of their conditioning. He touches upon such matters as work, emotions, success and failure, the crisis of middle age, retiring, love and sex, and fathering.

129a. Ornstein, Yevrah, ed. **From the Hearts of Men.** Woodacre, CA: Harmonia, 1991. ix, 330p. notes. Reprint, New York: Fawcett Columbine, 1992. pa.
    Founding publisher of *The Men's Journal*, Ornstein has collected a wealth of essays, reflections, poems, interviews, stories, and excerpts from longer works. The controlling perspective of this anthology is that of the mythopoetic men's movement. Selections are divided into 15 chapters: "Fathers and sons"; "Sports"; "Men supporting men"; "The ills of macho man";

"Competition"; "Bonding, loving, touching, sex"; "Beliefs, revelations, forgiveness"; "Mothers and sons"; "Steps along the path"; "Men and women"; "Music of the soul"; "Anger and violence"; "War"; "The new fathers"; and "Rites of passage." A number of the selections are by Ornstein himself. Also included is the complete text of Keith Thompson's seminal interview with Robert Bly, "What Men Really Want"; excerpts from Pat Conroy's *The Prince of Tides* (entry 339); a conversation with Bob Trowbridge; Jed Diamond on the myth of the dangerous dad; and John Macchietto's powerful account of the emotional scars of war. The collections closes with Starhawk's description of the horned god, presented here as an ideal image of masculinity.

130. Pace, Nathaniel. **The Excess Male.** Norfolk, VA: Donning, 1982. vii, 102p. bibliography, 101. pa.

One presumes that this book is a satire in the vein of Jonathan Swift's "A Modest Proposal." Arguing that most human evils are the result of the roughly 50-50 male-female birth rate, the author modestly proposes that "an artificial control of male births be imposed, to insure that of every ten births, only one would be male." (Exactly how this control would be exercised is not made clear.) The author then explains that most of the world's woes are due to "excess" males. Within geographic locales, there are three classes: the privileged (women and children), the preferential males (leaders, executives, etc.), and the excess males (nine-tenths of the male population). These excess males struggle to become preferential males but do not succeed; they cause all sorts of problems fighting for the available women. The author praises (ironically, one presumes) war, alcoholism, and crime as great eliminators of excess males. He extols Stalin and the Ayatollah Khomeini but criticizes Hitler for eliminating women and children instead of just young men, as a good tyrant should. Despite its deadpan seriousness, *The Excess Male* may be a blistering satire on the modern habit of blaming all the world's evils on men and on the widespread acceptance of abuses visited by society upon them. The author is either insane or insanely comic. Readers should have a jolly time deciding for themselves.

131. Playboy Enterprises. **The Playboy Report on American Men.** Chicago: Playboy Enterprises, 1979. 59p. pa.

This survey explores the values, attitudes, and goals of 1,990 men who were interviewed extensively between December 6, 1976, and January 12, 1977. The survey discloses a rich diversity of male opinions, divided fairly evenly among four groups: traditionalists, conventionals, contemporaries, and innovators. Areas touched on include basic values, family, love and sex, marriage, and children, the outer man's appearance, religion and psychotherapy, attitudes toward drugs, money and possessions, work, politics, and leisure. Most of the men interviewed were hardly playboys: nearly 85 percent rated family life as very important for a satisfying life, while only 49 percent rated sex as similarly important. The Playboy survey offers sometimes surprising statistical information about U.S. men in the late seventies.

132. Reynaud, Emmanuel. **Holy Virility: The Social Construction of Masculinity.** Translated by Ros Schwartz. London: Pluto Press, 1983. vi, 119p. notes. pa. Original publication, as *La Sainte Virilité,* Paris: Editions Syros, 1981.

A French male feminist, Reynaud explores familiar themes: men are a class of powerful oppressors (although they pay dearly for their alleged power), women are an oppressed class whose roles are shaped for them entirely by men

(Reynaud never examines women's part in socializing children), and men use sex to confirm their power over women (although Reynaud has some interesting stories about females raping males). Some readers will find the book a stirring piece of consciousness raising, others a ludicrous collection of sexist clichés about men.

133. Roberts, Yvonne. **Man Enough: Men of Thirty-five Speak Out.** London: Chatto and Windus, Hogarth Press, 1984. 308p. pa.

From interviews, Roberts constructs vignettes of 22 British men at ages 34 and 35. A feminist concerned that feminists have been unable to communicate effectively with men, Roberts selected her interviewees for sameness (age 35) and differences (the men range from a gay entertainer to a foulmouthed car salesman). At 35, the men are old enough to have been affected by the gender role tensions of recent times. Roberts constructs each man's portrait, relying heavily on the man's words. The result is a quilt of extraordinary diversity in which it is difficult to find common denominators that apply to all men. Roberts believes that feminism can liberate men, although a few of the interviewees had been badly hurt by feminists.

134. Ruitenbeek, Henrik M. **The Male Myth.** New York: Dell, 1967. 233p. illus. notes. pa.

In 1967, Ruitenbeek was analyzing the crisis of U.S. men in terms that will strike many readers as still pertinent. The author sees men as being in an identity crisis, needing to evolve a new definition of masculinity in the face of economic and social changes. While modern technology has created a world in which men as providers are no longer essential and in which men are often alienated from their jobs, seeking masculine identity through work is perilous. Emancipated women, moreover, can support themselves if necessary. But, Ruitenbeek argues, the father's family role is crucial; absence of a father can hamper the development of both boys and girls. The increasing abdication of males from families may be due to an awareness that home life costs them more than it offers in satisfactions. Widespread homophobia hampers father-son relationships. The demands that men provide sexual satisfaction to women may be causing an increase in impotency (or the reporting of it). This impotency, in some cases, may be an expression of hostility toward an aggressive woman by humiliating her and refusing to satisfy her. Widespread passivity and homosexuality may also be negative reactions to hostility between the sexes. "For the future," Ruitenbeek writes, "the male faces this final question: Can he develop a new concept of his social role and adequate psychological support to confirm him in his conviction of his identity as a male?" While offering some modest suggestions (e.g., men must resist depersonalization, must accept family responsibilities, and must insist upon integration into family life), Ruitenbeek concludes, "We must not fool ourselves that the problems of contemporary American men can be solved by prescription; they only can be solved ultimately in the renewal of man and the rediscovery of his sense of dignity."

135. Sadker, David. **Being a Man: A Unit of Instructional Activities on Male Role Stereotyping.** Resource Center on Sex Roles in Education, National Department of Health, Education, and Welfare, 1977. v, 64p. illus. bibliography, 63-64. pa.

High school teachers and others may find this publication useful for consciousness raising. "With so many women now striving for political, economic, and psychological equality with men," Sadker writes, "one might conclude that men enjoy a special and privileged place in our society, and that their roles and behaviors should be emulated. Such an assumption would be both misleading and simplistic." Section 1, "Background for Teachers," enumerates five "lessons" of the male stereotype: stifle it (repress emotions), choose your occupation (from the following list only), money makes the man, winning at any cost, and acting tough. Then, eight "costs" of living out this stereotype are discussed: early pressures on boys, barriers between men, barriers between men and women, the separation of fathers from families, being locked into a job, being locked out of leisure activities and a satisfying retirement, physical disability and early death, and social and political machismo that endangers everyone. Section 2 presents a series of learning activities designed to counteract stereotyped ideas about male behavior and attitudes. Sadker avoids come controversial issues that might well interest students: whether a male-only military obligation is sexist, who pays for dates, and so on. The bibliography lists works on female role stereotyping. The publication is offered for sale by the Superintendent of Documents, U.S. Government Printing Office, Washington DC 20402; stock number 017-080-01777-6.

136. Schenk, Roy U. **The Other Side of the Coin: Causes and Consequences of Men's Oppression.** Madison, WI: Bioenergetics Press, 1982. 256p. appendixes. notes. pa.

Arguing that men as well as women suffer oppression in modern society, Schenk locates the source of men's anger in socialization that depicts women as spiritually superior to men. Often fostered by mothers and female teachers, the idea of male moral inferiority is internalized by males and leads them to accept roles as cannon fodder in wartime, lifetime providers for families, and pursuers of females for sex. By encouraging male guilt to benefit females, women promote male anger against them. Schenk has little patience with pro-feminist males who perpetuate male guilt or with the stereotype of males as oppressors. He attacks the selective equality of militant feminists. To reduce male anger and violence against females will require reducing female violence against men's psyches. Finding evidence of the belief in female superiority in U.S. laws and customs, Schenk sees little hope for genuine sex equality until males are equally recognized as victims of gender oppression.

137. Seidler, Victor J., ed. **The Achilles Heel Reader: Men, Sexual Politics and Socialism.** London and New York: Routledge, 1991. xiv, 216p. (Male Orders series). illus. notes. index. pa.

Taken from material published between 1978 and 1984 in the British left-wing journal *Achilles Heel*, this collection of essays and poems reflects socialist, pro-feminist concerns of the time. Published by a working collective of socialist men, the journal responds to the radical feminist and gay movements by examining men's power, sexism, and oppression. Although the language is sometimes overburdened with Marxist jargon ("As men we oppress women, but this doesn't mean that we aren't ourselves oppressed, living within patriarchal capitalist society"), the writers more often attempt to speak personally about such matters as raising a child, the tensions of being gay, and the toll that the workplace takes on a man's life. The final essay, by Paul Atkinson, suggests that G. B. Shaw's attitude toward women in *Candida* may be less advanced than some have thought. In a postscript, Seidler suggests that, although the gender wars have moved on to new battlefields, the material from *Achilles Heel* still has value.

138. Shostak, Arthur B., and Gary McLouth, with Lynn Seng. **Men and Abortion: Lessons, Losses, and Love.** New York: Praeger, 1984. xx, 334p. appendixes. notes. name and subject indexes.

Each year, approximately 1,360,000 men are involved in an abortion experience, with 600,000 of them designated as "waiting room men" in abortion clinics. Moved by their personal experiences and dismayed by the lack of information about men in abortion situations, the authors have generated a study based upon responses from 1,000 "waiting room men," extended interviews, and research. Written for the general reader, *Men and Abortion* demonstrates that, contrary to popular belief, many men are profoundly affected by abortion—indeed, they are haunted by it. Contrary to the fears of militant feminists, most men do not seek to dominate abortion decision making. Many men feel, however, that women are in control of contraception and that men are not therefore responsible for it. On the day of the abortion, men at clinics are usually ignored by an overworked staff and are left to face their stress alone. The authors explore the views of "waiting room men" who regard abortion as immoral, of repeaters (men who have been through more than one abortion), black males, pro-choice and anti-abortion activists, and counselors of males in abortion clinics. The legal implications of abortion are starkly depicted: the man has no rights at all in this matter, yet he is still obliged to support a child born to him—even though he wishes to have the fetus aborted and agrees to pay for the procedure. The pros and cons of spousal prenotification laws are reviewed. The final chapter provides suggestions for preventing or easing the trauma of abortion—before conception, on "clinic day," and afterwards. The eight appendixes include such matters as an evaluation of the study's methodology by Joan Z. Spade, a look at men whose wives have undergone mastectomy, a copy of the questionnaire, and a list of the 30 cooperating clinics.

139. Skjei, Eric, and Richard Rabkin. **The Male Ordeal: Role Crisis in a Changing World.** New York: G. P. Putnam's Sons, 1981. 247p. bibliography, 246-47. notes.

This book explores the negative effects on men of recent changes in women's roles. Focusing on men's difficulties as modern concepts of masculinity shift, the book draws upon interviews with 31 people (27 males, 4 females). Skjei and Rabkin found that men, far from being gender imperialists, were often sensitive and vulnerable to women's changes, and that men were often needlessly hurt by "the new misandry" or anti-male hostility of some feminists. The authors accuse these ideologies of a "repressive radicalization" that attempts to defeat men as an enemy rather than enlist men as allies in the women's cause. This "reverse sexism," which seeks to punish men for alleged oppression of women, threatens to alienate the sexes at a time when each sex must include the other in its quest for selfhood. In speaking with interviewees, the authors found that men were more committed to monogamy than is usually believed, that they were neither gypsies nor tyrants in family life, and that they believed firmly in the value of being actively involved parents. The authors conclude that men need "to reclaim a sense of masculine dignity and pride, but to do so without making assumptions of any kind about women and their roles."

140. Snodgrass, Jon, ed. **For Men Against Sexism: A Book of Readings.** Albion, CA: Times Change Press, 1977. 238p. bibliography, 234-38. notes. pa.

This collection of 32 radical items draws heavily upon Marxist feminism. Essays in part 1, "Women's Oppression," adhere to the party line that all men are oppressors and, thus, a humane consideration of men's concerns and issues is an impertinence. Male victims in modern society get short shrift in these discussions: the existence of male rape victims, for example, is denied when rape is defined as "a crime of violence against women." Leonard Schein argues that "All Men Are Misogynists," and John Stoltenberg calls for *"a total repudiation of masculinity"* (his emphasis). While writers exalt homosexual relationships, they excoriate heterosexual male bonding as a conspiracy of the "oppressors." Likewise, they denounce the men's liberation movement for focusing on the "oppressor's" problems. The short part 2, "Gay, Class, and Racial Oppressions," explores issues of homosexuals, blue-collar workers, and third-world men. Polemics throughout this androphobic volume resound with vituperation, finger-pointing, revolutionary rhetoric, and wholesale denunciations of capitalism, patriarchy, and men.

141. Steinmann, Anne, and David J. Fox. **The Male Dilemma: How to Survive the Sexual Revolution.** New York: Jason Aronson, 1974. xv, 324p. appendixes. notes. index.

Assessing the conflict between men and women in the late sixties and early seventies, the authors attempt to redress the imbalance of writings that stress women's issues and changes with a view that includes men's needs and changes. Addressed to general readers, the book seeks to provide greater understanding that will effect positive changes. In their research, the authors find contradictions of what men want for themselves and what they believe women want from them. Women exhibit similar conflicts. Moreover, communication between the sexes is often limited and thus misunderstood. Modern men are being asked to surrender privileges without a clear-cut idea of the gains such surrender would bring. Women, however, are uncertain whether or not they want "to have it all." The resulting confusions and hostilities often strain marriages and leave children conflicted. Surveying the biological and cultural sources of differences between the sexes, Steinmann and Fox conclude that only toward the end of human life does equality become a more easily achievable goal. Nevertheless, social norms are too restrictive for both males and females. Without advocating unisex child rearing, the authors suggest social changes to lessen misunderstanding and antagonism between men and women. The appendixes provide details of the authors' research inventories of masculine and feminine behavior.

142. Sutherland, Alistair, and Patrick Anderson, eds. **Eros: An Anthology of Male Friendship.** London: Anthony Blount, 1961. 433p. Reprint, New York: Citadel Press, 1963.

The selections in this anthology illustrate the range of male friendships, from the nonsexual to the homoerotic to the homosexual. To illustrate the graduated spectrum in male-male friendships, the editors have deliberately cast a wide net. Historically, selections cover biblical times, ancient Greece and Rome, the Dark and Middle Ages in Europe, and the Renaissance through modern times. A chapter of accounts from "exotic" lands and a chapter of selections describing life at English boys' schools close the book. The authors include Plato, Virgil, Petronius, Michelangelo, Montaigne, Shakespeare, Tennyson, Verlaine, Gide, Proust, and D. H. Lawrence.

143. Thomas, David. **Not Guilty: The Case in Defense of Men.** New York: William Morrow, 1993. 255p. bibliography, 252-55.

A British journalist, Thomas examines the wave of misandry currently sweeping the United States and Great Britain. The belief that men are an oppressor class has become a fundamentalist orthodoxy that fosters numerous legal and social injustices against men. The fiction of male power and female victimization needs to be modified by a clearer look at the whole of gender issues. With a sharp eye for spotting rigged statistics, Thomas debunks reports of rape epidemics on U.S. campuses. Examining manipulated logic and language, he explores skewed treatment of sexual harassment in the workplace as a male-only crime. Thomas presents convincing evidence both of the widespread existence of women's domestic violence and of the extraordinary efforts by some feminists and public figures to deny this evidence. Looking at the issue of child abuse, Thomas finds similar denial of women's perpetration of this abuse. Researchers seem eager to pursue an issue as long as they assume males are the villains, but they avoid exploring women as perpetrators. Thomas claims that, in the United States, man hating has become a source of big money and that judges and politicians are afraid to oppose misandric but well financed interest groups. Thomas is neither a misogynist nor an extremist; his occasional errors ("all rapists are men") are not in men's favor, and his writing is marked by friendly goodwill. The virulence and pervasiveness of modern misandry, however, lead him to conclude that men must form themselves into political action groups; otherwise, they will continue to be wronged with impunity.

144. Thompson, Keith, ed. **To Be a Man: In Search of the Deep Masculine.** Los Angeles: Jeremy P. Tarcher, 1991. xxi, 294p. notes. pa.

The mythopoetic men's movement was most likely engendered by Keith Thompson's seminal interview with Robert Bly published in the May 1982 issue of *New Age*. Three excerpts from that interview are published in this anthology, announcing themes that have since preoccupied men's awareness. The soft male, father hunger, and the myth of Iron John appear in early formulation in the Bly-Thompson interview. *To Be a Man* also shows how far the men's movement has come since 1982. Its rich selection of material ranges from the introspective to the political. In the introduction, Thompson argues that, even if all masculinities share some common ground, there is no single masculinity. His selections often illustrate differing views of masculinities. Cooper Thompson's attack on traditional masculinity is followed by Warren Farrell's defense of traditional masculinity, Chris Brazier's argument that men should embrace feminism is followed by Richard Haddad's argument that men should reject feminism, and Ernest Hemingway's celebration of bullfighting as masculine ritual is followed by Christopher Matthews's rejection of bullfighting as an unmanly slaughter. Nearly 90 selections—essays, short stories, poems—are grouped into nine sections: identity, male initiation, the male wound, body and sexuality, encounters with women and the feminine, father, work, male company, and aging. Contributors include big names of the men's movement: Bly, Farrell, Haddad, Aaron R. Kipnis, Michael Meade, Robert Moore and Douglas Gillette, Frederic Hayward, Shepherd Bliss, Samuel Osherson, James Hillman, Sam Keen, and others. Famous authors also appear: Ernest Hemingway, Pablo Neruda, Franz Kafka, D. H. Lawrence, C. G. Jung, Henry Miller, William Butler Yeats, Hermann Hesse, Raymond Chandler, Norman Mailer, Malcolm Muggeridge, James Dickey, Wendell Berry, Edmund Wilson, and Robert Frost. Selections also include excerpts from the works of respected men's studies scholars, including Ray Raphael, Stephen Grubman-Black, John S. Weltner, Eugene Monick, Robert S. Weiss, J. Glenn Gray, and Daniel J. Levinson.

145. Thornburg, Hershel D. **Punt, Pop: A Male Sex Role Manual.** Tucson, AZ: H.E.L.P. Books, 1977. 156p. illus. notes. index. pa.

Emphasizing the need for men to change their attitudes, Thornburg has designed a self-help manual for male consciousness raising. Complete with quizzes to chart the reader's views, the book examines such matters as the breadwinner role, discrimination against women in employment, images of women in advertising, sex stereotyping in sports, and fathering. Some readers may find the book a helpful exercise in nonsexist training; others may regard it as simplistic and condescending to men.

146. Tolson, Andrew. **The Limits of Masculinity: Male Identity and the Liberated Woman.** New York: Harper & Row, 1979. 158p. bibliography, 147-52. index. pa. Original publication, London: Tavistock, 1977.

Tolson provides a view of men's awareness in Britain as shaped by feminist and socialist thought. After tracing the influence of the women's liberation movement upon men, Tolson explores the socialization of boys by family, school, and peer group. Chapter 3 examines men at work in capitalist-patriarchal society. Employing excerpts from interviews, Tolson stresses the alienating effect of labor on working-class men, the frustrations involved in middle-class masculinity, and the contradictions of "progressive" men trying to reconcile their liberalism with traditional notions of masculinity. A final chapter recounts the experiences of Tolson's male consciousness-raising group: having accepted the ideas that men are a class of oppressors and that patriarchal society always works to men's advantage, the group had reached a dead end that rendered it politically impotent. Readers will have to decide whether Tolson's Marxist-feminist perspective clarifies or clouds his view of men and masculinity.

146a. Towery, Twyman L. **Male Code: Rules Men Live and Love By.** Lakewood, CO: Glenbridge, 1992. xiii, 233p. notes.

Men's lives are tightly constricted by the male code of cool performance, inexpressiveness, and solitariness. The code takes its toll on men, Towery argues, saddling them with a shortened life span and emotional desiccation. In popular style aimed at a general audience of male and female readers, Towery discusses topics such as men's lack of friends, the hazards of growing up male, male-female miscommunications, men's money and parenting problems, and the pitfalls that men and women encounter when trying to age gracefully.

147. Vilar, Esther. **The Manipulated Male.** Rev. ed. Translated by Eva Borneman and Ursula Bender. New York: Farrar, Straus & Giroux, 1972. 184p. Original publication, as *Der dressiert Mann* (N.p.: Abelard-Schuman, 1972).

Standing militant feminism on its head, Vilar argues that women have conspired successfully to enslave men: "Women let men work for them, think for them, and take on their responsibilities—in fact, they exploit them." From infancy, males are trained by women to believe that supporting a woman is "masculine," that being taken care of is "feminine." Women have successfully used sex as a reward to manipulate males into supporting females; most women, according to Vilar, are not primarily interested in men sexually or personally but, rather, financially. Deliberately outrageous, Vilar's book is designed to provoke strong and divergent responses. Is it a hilarious put-on? a refreshing corrective? a misogynist diatribe? an eye-opening piece of consciousness raising? a cynical exposé of women's parasitism? an ironic exposé of men's gullibility? In this never-a-dull-moment polemic, the penultimate chapter—in which Vilar dissects the U.S. women's liberation movement—makes for especially heady reading.

Cross-References

See chapter 15, "Masculinity," chapter 17, "Men's Studies," and chapter 23, "Spirituality."

861. Bly, Robert. **Iron John: A Book About Men.**

640. David, Deborah S., and Robert Brannon, eds. **The Forty-nine Percent Majority: The Male Sex Role.**

40. Diamond, Jed. **Inside Out: Becoming My Own Man.**

641. Doyle, James A. **The Male Experience.**

601. Fanning, Patrick, and Matthew McKay. **Being a Man: A Guide to the New Masculinity.**

603. Gaylin, Willard. **The Male Ego.**

604. Gerzon, Mark. **A Choice of Heroes: The Changing Faces of American Manhood.**

992. Jeffers, Susan. **Opening Our Hearts to Men.**

993. Kammer, Jack. **Good Will Toward Men: Women Talk About Fairness and Respect as a Two-Way Street.**

645. Kimmel, Michael S., and Michael A. Messner, eds. **Men's Lives.**

997. Kingma, Daphne Rose. **The Men We Never Knew: Women's Role in the Evolution of a Gender.**

997a. Kipnis, Aaron R., and Elizabeth Herron. **Gender War, Gender Peace: The Quest for Love and Justice Between Women and Men.**

869. Kipnis, Aaron R. **Knights Without Armor: A Practical Guide for Men in Quest of Masculine Soul.**

48. Klein, Edward, and Don Erickson, eds. **About Men: Reflections on the Male Experience.**

960. Klein, Robert. **Wounded Men, Broken Promises.**

226. Levine, Judith. **My Enemy, My Love: Man-Hating and Ambivalence in Women's Lives.**

310. Mead, Shepherd. **Free the Male Man! The Manifesto of the Men's Liberation Movement ...**

615. Pleck, Joseph H., and Jack Sawyer, eds. **Men and Masculinity.**

63. Rubin, Michael, ed. **Men Without Masks: Writings from the Journals of Modern Men.**

548. Shapiro, Jerrold Lee. **The Measure of a Man: Becoming the Father You Wish Your Father Had Been.**

620. Shapiro, Stephen A. **Manhood: A New Definition.**

724. Skovholt, Thomas M., Paul G. Schauble, and Richard Davis, eds. **Counseling Men.**

725. Solomon, Kenneth, and Norman B. Levy, eds. **Men in Transition: Theory and Therapy.**

622. Stoltenberg, John. **The End of Manhood: A Book for Men of Conscience.**

623. Stoltenberg, John. **Refusing to be a Man: Essays on Sex and Justice.**

188. Thompson, Doug. **As Boys Become Men: Learning New Male Roles.**

696. Uhl, Michael, and Tod Ensign. **GI Guinea Pigs: How the Pentagon Exposed Our Troops to Dangers More Deadly than War: Agent Orange and Atomic Radiation.**

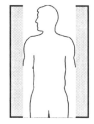

4

Bibliographies

A. Men's Studies Bibliographies

Emphasizing the interdisciplinary nature of men's studies, bibliographies in this section survey a range of men's studies in several academic disciplines.

148. American Association of Counseling and Development, Committee on Men. **Men's Issues: A Bibliography.** Alexandria, VA: American Association of Counseling and Development, 1987. 86p. pa.

Both books and articles are included in this unannotated, unnumbered bibliography. Items are grouped into 38 categories. Sample categories include black men, burnout and stress, changing roles of men, divorce and parenting, gender differences in counseling, grieving, homosexuality, love and sexuality, male clients, mother-son relationships, stereotypes, substance abuse, and working.

149. August, Eugene R., comp. **Men's Studies: A Selected and Annotated Interdisciplinary Bibliography.** Littleton, CO: Libraries Unlimited, 1985. xvii, 215p. author and title indexes.

The first edition of the present bibliography lists 591 books and is divided into 21 sections: bibliographies, anthologies, men's awareness, autobiographical and biographical accounts, men's rights, divorce and custody, war and peace, women and men, masculinity, psychology, sexuality, homosexuality, men in families, single men, male midlife transition, literature, images of men, minorities, religion, and humor. Some sections are subdivided: for example, the section about men in families contains information on fathers, expectant fathers, divorced and single fathers, and other family roles.

150. Flood, Michael, comp. **The Men's Bibliography: A Comprehensive Bibliography of Writing on Men and Masculinity.** 2d ed. Canberra ACT, Australia: privately printed, 1993. 93p. index. pa.

Compiled by an editor of *XY: men, sex, politics* magazine, this ring-bound bibliography lists over 1,000 entries, both books and articles. Items are listed in 38 categories, including race and ethnicity, men's studies and men in academia, growing up male, histories of masculinity, men's bodies and biology, pornography, power and gender politics, fatherhood and parenting, law, child custody, men and feminism, men and the left, spirituality and mythopoetic writing, health, reproductive issues and technology, sport and leisure, masculinity in culture, and friendship. Some items are repeated in several categories. Items are not annotated, and some entries lack complete information. The perspective of the editor is pro-feminist: The "Men's Rights" category is co-titled "Backlash," and nearly all the entries in "The Best Reading on Men and Masculinity" have a radical pro-feminist slant. The bibliography's place of origin ensures inclusion of many Australian and British publications. Current information indicates that copies of the bibliography can be obtained by mailing $15 to *The Men's Bibliography*, P.O. Box 26, Ainslie ACT, 2602, AUSTRALIA. Fax [06] 247 9227.

151. Ford, David, and Jeff Hearn, comps. **Studying Men and Masculinity: A Sourcebook of Literature and Materials.** Bradford, England: University of Bradford, 1988. 39p. (University of Bradford Applied Social Science, Publication 1). pa.

Emphasizing British publications that focus on masculinity as a social construction, this unannotated bibliography of books and articles is divided into 18 sections: general bibliographic sources; sexuality, health, and emotions; violence and competition; boys, childcare, and fatherhood; personality, socialization, and education; paid work; power, politics, and patriarchy; history; imaginative writing; religion and spirituality; anti-sexist and men against sexism literature; anti-sexist magazines and journals; anti-sexist education and other work with boys and men; other books and resources for play and learning; films; studying men and masculinity; anti-sexist men's studies and the critique of men; and other academic contacts. The brief introductions to each section reflect Marxist and feminist socialist viewpoints.

152. Grady, Kathleen E., Robert Brannon, and Joseph H. Pleck, comps. **The Male Sex Role: A Selected and Annotated Bibliography.** Washington, DC: U.S. Department of Health, Education, and Welfare; Rockville, MD: National Institute for Mental Health, 1979; sold by Superintendent of Documents, U.S. Government Printing Office, Washington, DC 20402. x, 196p. author index. pa.

This guide to more than 250 items, which are mostly from the social sciences, groups entries into 14 major divisions: general; attitudes about men and masculinity; the socialization of masculinity; paid employment; marriage; fatherhood; relationships with other men; antisocial behavior; some other traits associated with the male role; mental and physical health and the male role; physical and physiological factors in male behavior; male issues in institutions (military service, athletics); and subcultural, cross-cultural, and historical comparisons. Items are annotated: "hard" research items are given a regular pattern (subjects, method, findings, comments), while a looser essay approach is used for more theoretical writings.

B. Bibliographies in Related Areas

Bibliographies in this section focus on one or more aspects of interdisciplinary men's studies.

153. Anderson, Martin, and Valerie Bloom, comps. **Conscription: A Select and Annotated Bibliography.** Stanford, CA: Hoover Institution Press, Stanford University, 1976. xvii, 453p. title and author indexes.

This precisely annotated bibliography lists approximately 1,385 items concerned with the military draft. Books, unpublished manuscripts, articles, pamphlets, reprints, speeches, and government documents have separate categories.

The following subject headings are used: U.S. history; general history; general works (i.e., more comprehensive works dealing with conscription); all-volunteer armed forces; selective service; universal military training (i.e., conscription applying to all males); National Guard and Reserves; universal national service (i.e., a diversified form of conscription that would require both men and women to perform a variety of public service jobs); economics; law and the Constitution; philosophy (i.e., whether conscription is moral or immoral); conscientious objection; race; England; other foreign countries; miscellanea; and bibliographies.

154. Astin, Helen S., Allison Parelman, and Anne Fisher, comps. **Sex Roles: A Research Bibliography.** Washington, DC: Center for Human Services; Rockville, MD: National Institute of Mental Health, 1975. viii, 362p. author and subject indexes. pa.

This fully annotated bibliography of 456 items is divided into five sections: observations and measurement of sex differences, origins of sex differences and sex roles (biological, sociological, attitudes toward sex roles), manifestation of sex roles in institutional settings (e.g., family, work, law, politics), cross-cultural overviews and historical accounts of the sexes, and general reviews and position papers on socialization and the development of sex roles. As might be expected, more material on women than on men appears.

155. Bahr, Howard M., ed. **Disaffiliated Men: Essays and Bibliography on Skid Row, Vagrancy, and Outsiders.** Toronto: University of Toronto Press, 1970. xiv, 428p. name and subject indexes.

Focusing on men who have hit rock bottom, this bibliography has two principal purposes: first, to provide easy access to an extensive literature from several disciplines on men who are homeless or who suffer from chronic inebriation and other forms of disaffiliation; second, to enable researchers to relate this literature to the study of general social problems and processes. The bibliography is preceded by five essays exploring different areas of disaffiliation: "Sociology and the Homeless Man," by Theodore Caplow; "Societal Forces and the Unattached Male: An Historical Review," by James F. Rooney; "Homelessness, Disaffiliation, and Retreatism," by Howard M. Bahr; "Survivorship and Social Isolation: The Case of the Aged Widower," by Felix M. Berardo; and "Dimensions of Religious Defection," by Armand L. Mauss. The bibliography, annotated but unnumbered, is divided into 12 sections: skid row and its men; taverns and bars; the law; treatment, punishment, and rehabilitation for homelessness; treatment, punishment, and rehabilitation for alcoholism; drink and alcoholism; etiology and patterns; transiency among young persons; journalistic and literary accounts; employment and unemployment; voluntary associations; aging and disaffiliation; and anomie, isolation, and marginality.

156. Bowker, Lee H., comp. **Prisons and Prisoners: A Bibliographic Guide.** San Francisco: R and E, 1978. vii, 93p. pa.

This bibliography is divided into four sections: books and articles on prison subcultures among incarcerated men, publications on female correctional subcultures, publications on correctional subcultures in institutions for boys, and background materials for the study of prisons and prisoners (this final section is coauthored by Joy Pollack). Each section is preceded by an introductory overview. Items are unannotated and unnumbered.

157. Bullough, Vern L., W. Dorr Legg, Barrett W. Elcano, and James Kepner, comps. **An Annotated Bibliography of Homosexuality.** 2 vols. New York:

Garland, 1976. xxxvii, 405p. (Garland Reference Library of Social Science, vol. 22). appendixes. author indexes.

These two volumes contain more than 12,794 items relating to homosexuality. Despite the title, annotations are nonexistent or minimal. In volume 1, the categories are bibliography; general studies; behavioral sciences (anthropology, history, psychology, sociology); education and children; medicine and biology; psychiatry; law and its enforcement; court cases; military; and religion and ethics. In volume 2, the categories are biography and autobiography; the homophile movement; periodicals (movement and other); and transvestism and transsexualism. Because so much writing about homosexuality has been done under pseudonyms, a list at the end of volume 2 that matches pen names to authors (if known) is most useful. (A similar listing in volume 1 is less clear and less complete.) Volume 1 contains an appendix of legal code indexing; volume 2 includes a brief history of the homophile movement, from 1948 to 1960, by Salvatore J. Licata.

158. Dynes, Wayne R., comp. **Homosexuality: A Research Guide.** New York and London: Garland, 1987. xviii, 853p. (Garland Reference Library of Social Science, vol. 313). subject and name indexes.

This bibliography contains 4,858 annotated entries describing books and articles concerned with homosexuality. Entries are collected into 24 categories: general, women's studies, history and area studies, anthropology, travel, humanities, philosophy and religion, language, lifestyles, economics, education, politics, military, sociology, social work, psychology, psychiatry, family, boundary crossing, law, law enforcement, violence, medical, and biology. Each of these categories is further subdivided: "The AIDS crisis," for example, is listed under the main medical category. Entries include materials in languages other than English, as well as classic and historic works.

159. Franklin, H. Bruce, comp. **American Prisoners and Ex-Prisoners: Their Writings: An Annotated Bibliography of Published Works, 1798-1981.** Westport, CT: Lawrence Hill, 1982. vii, 53p. pa.

This is a bibliography of prison narratives, autobiographical novels, poems, and political writings. The entries are unnumbered, and most are briefly annotated.

160. Horner, Tom, comp. **Homosexuality and the Judeo-Christian Tradition: An Annotated Bibliography.** Metuchen, NJ, and London: American Theological Library Association, Scarecrow Press, 1981. ix, 131p. (ATLA Bibliography Series, no. 5).

Spreading a wider net than its title might suggest, this bibliography collects 459 items—books, articles and essays, pamphlets and papers, and bibliographies. Even works that make only a minor connection between homosexuality and the Judeo-Christian tradition are included. Nearly all items are annotated. The appendixes list biblical references to homosexuality and periodical publications of gay religious organizations.

161. Johnson, Carolyn, John Ferry, and Marjorie Kravitz, comps. **Spouse Abuse: A Selected Bibliography.** Washington, DC: U.S. Department of Justice, Law Enforcement Assistance Administration, National Institute of Law Enforcement and Criminal Justice, 1978. ix, 61p. (National Criminal Justice Reference Service). appendixes. index. pa.

This bibliography contains 91 annotated items, a few of which deal with battered husbands. According to one study, three women are battered for every male; the battered husband, however, remains largely ignored in the literature and by the social agencies. The appendixes include a list of sources and a list of resource agencies.

162. Loeb, Catherine R., Susan E. Searing, and Esther Stineman, comps., with Meredith J. Ross. **Women's Studies: A Recommended Core Bibliography, 1980-1985.** Littleton, CO: Libraries Unlimited, 1987. xvi, 538p. appendix. author, title, and subject indexes.

With 1,211 fully annotated entries, this bibliography updates Esther Stineman's 1979 bibliography of women's studies. Entries are divided into 19 categories, arranged alphabetically: anthropology, cross-cultural surveys, and international studies; art and material culture; autobiography, biography, diaries, memoirs, and letters; business, economics, and labor; education and pedagogy; history; law; literature; medicine, health, sexuality, and biology; politics and political theory; psychology; reference; religion and philosophy; science, mathematics, and technology; sociology and social issues; sports; women's movement and feminist theory; and periodicals. Entries sometimes refer to additional, unlisted works. Many items are of interest to men's studies scholars. As champions of feminism, the annotators are sometimes defensive about conservative women, men's rights advocates, and others who challenge feminist perspectives.

163. Parker, William, comp. **Homosexuality: A Selective Bibliography of Over 3,000 Items.** Metuchen, NJ: Scarecrow Press, 1971. viii, 323p. appendix. subject and author indexes.

Parker's unannotated bibliography is divided into 14 sections: books, pamphlets, theses and dissertations, articles in books, newspaper articles, articles in popular magazines, articles in religious journals, articles in legal journals, court cases involving consenting adults, articles in medical and scientific journals, articles in other specialized journals, articles in homophile publications, literary works, and miscellaneous works—movies, television programs, and phonograph records. An appendix lists state laws applicable to homosexual acts by consenting adults.

164. Parker, William, comp. **Homosexuality Bibliography: Supplement, 1970-1975.** Metuchen, NJ: Scarecrow Press, 1977. v, 337p. appendixes. author and subject indexes.

A supplement to Parker's 1971 bibliography, this listing of 3,136 items follows the same outline and format as its predecessor. The appendixes contain lists of motion pictures and television shows with a homosexual theme, audiovisual materials, and U.S. laws, as of 1 January 1976, applicable to homosexual acts by consenting adults. Parker has also published *Homosexuality: Second Supplement, 1976-1982* (Metuchen, NJ: Scarecrow Press, 1985).

165. Schlesinger, Benjamin. **The One-Parent Family: Perspectives and Annotated Bibliography**. 4th ed. Toronto: University of Toronto Press, 1978. x, 224p. appendixes. author index.

Sections of this book are extremely valuable for students of men's studies. Six essays by Schlesinger precede the bibliography. The first essay ("Motherless Families: A Review") points to over 1 million U.S. single-parent families headed by fathers, explores research done on motherless families in several countries, and comments on common themes, social policies, and needed research. The other essays are "Fatherless Separated Families," "Divorce and Children: A Review of the Literature," "The Crisis of Widowhood in the Family Circle," "The Unmarried Mother Who Keeps Her Child," and "Single-Parent Adoptions: A Review." The bibliography itself contains 750 annotated items divided into three period sections: 1930-1969, 1970-1974, and 1975-1978. All three sections are subdivided into subject categories. "One Parent Families" appears in all three sections; "Motherless Families" appears only in the third. Especially valuable is appendix 1 which contains a selected and annotated bibliography, prepared by Parents Without Partners, of 62 books for children and teens on single-parent families, death of a parent, divorce, and so on. Books portraying positive father-child relations are keyed. Appendix 2 contains a list of publishers' addresses.

166. Sell, Kenneth D., comp. **Divorce in the 70s: A Subject Bibliography.** Phoenix, AZ: Oryx Press, 1981. viii, 191p. author, geographical, and subject indexes.

   Among the pertinent subjects in this bibliography of 4,760 items are alimony and maintenance, child custody, father absence, one-parent families, father custody, stepfathers, male alimony, and joint custody.

167. Stineman, Esther, comp., with Catherine Loeb. **Women's Studies: A Recommended Core Bibliography.** Littleton, CO: Libraries Unlimited, 1979. 670p. author, title, and subject indexes.

   Although now superseded by the 1987 bibliography *Women's Studies,* compiled by Catherine R. Loeb and others (entry 162), this 1979 bibliography still contains valuable information in its 1,748 annotated items, many of which will interest scholars in men's studies.

168. Suvak, Daniel, comp. **Memoirs of American Prisons: An Annotated Bibliography.** Metuchen, NJ: Scarecrow Press, 1979. viii, 227p. name-title and prison indexes.

   This bibliography, containing nearly 800 annotated items, includes memoirs from criminals, prisoners of conscience, and military prisoners. The vast majority of the writers are male.

169. Weinberg, Martin S., and Alan P. Bell, comps. **Homosexuality: An Annotated Bibliography.** New York: Harper & Row, 1972. xiii, 550p. author and subject indexes.

   In this fully annotated guide to 1,265 items on homosexuality, which are mostly from the social sciences, items are grouped as follows: physiological considerations (etiology, treatments), psychological considerations (etiology, assessments, treatments), and sociological considerations, which include the homosexual community in its social and demographic aspects; homosexuality in history, non-Western societies, and special settings; societal attitudes towards homosexuality; and homosexuality and the law. Other bibliographies and dictionaries are listed in a final section. The bibliography excludes belles lettres (biographies, autobiographies, literary works) and items from popular magazines and newspapers.

170. Young, Ian, comp. **The Male Homosexual in Literature: A Bibliography.** 2d ed. Metuchen, NJ: Scarecrow Press, 1982. x, 350p. appendixes. title index and title index of gay literary anthologies.

In addition to listing more than 4,282 works of fiction, drama, poetry, and autobiography in which male homosexuality is a theme or in which male homosexual characters appear, this bibliography contains five essays: a short history of the gay novel, the poetry of male love, some notes on gay publishing (all by the compiler), homosexuality in drama (by Graham Jackson), and gay literature and censorship (by Rictor Norton).

Cross-References

569. McCormick, Mona. **Stepfathers: What the Literature Reveals: A Literature Review and Annotated Bibliography.**

125. Murphey, Cecil. **Mantalk: Resources for Exploring Male Issues.**

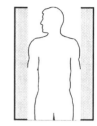

5

Boys: Education
and Socialization of Males

171. Abbott, Franklin, ed. **Boyhood, Growing Up Male: A Multicultural Anthology.** Freedom, CA: Crossing Press, 1993. 297p. appendix. pa.

Abbott has collected 45 reminiscences (memoirs and poems) that recall boyhood in a diversity of cultures. Many of the accounts, like Terry A. Kupers's "Schoolyard Fights," tell painful episodes of boys being molded into uncongenial roles. Others, like Shepherd Bliss's "My War Story," tell of youthful rebellion and adult reconciliation. Several of the writers, like John Silva in "Iyay," recall memorable adults who shaped their lives. Troubles with fathers recur in a number of entries, like Robert Bly's poem "Snow Geese." Abbott has chosen multicultural accounts from Brazil, Africa, Sri Lanka, Malta, the Philippines, Nigeria, India, as well as the United States. Writers represent various religious and ethnic groups (e.g., Jews, Native Americans, Catholics). A few gay men are also included in the collection. The accounts are often powerfully moving snapshots of the hazards of growing up male.

172. Askew, Sue, and Carol Ross. **Boys Don't Cry: Boys and Sexism in Education.** Milton Keynes, England, and Philadelphia: Open University Press, 1988. xvi, 234p. (Gender and Education Series). name and subject indexes. bibliography, 221-28. pa.

The authors amass considerable evidence showing that boys and girls learn and behave differently at school. They focus on aggressive boys' behavior that intimidates girls and quieter boys. In all-boys schools, the aggressive atmosphere may result in harassment of women teachers. In general, boys are more competitive and physical, and the authors believe that society encourages the more brutalizing aspects of this behavior. Using a "non-sexist" approach to the situation, the authors devise exercises to offset the boys' more violent propensities and social stereotypes of girls as passive nonachievers. Although the authors' goals are praiseworthy, the book contains disturbing signs of underlying misandry. The authors' ideology creates its own problems of sexism: committed to a radical feminist concept of males as an oppressor class and females as a victimized class, they perpetuate stereotypes of boys as nasty imitators of what the authors see as the prevailing gender-class oppression. Askew and Ross see masculinity in entirely negative terms; they have little sympathy for boys' friendly rough-and-tumble play. Their ideology does not permit them to notice that girls frequently humiliate insufficiently "masculine" boys, that girls sometimes encourage boys to engage in aggressively violent behavior, or that some girls can be cruel to other girls. In this study, girls are always "nice" victims. The authors' classroom exercises seem designed to create "nice" boys who are ashamed of their masculinity.

173. Carlson, Dale. **Boys Have Feelings Too: Growing Up Male for Boys.** New York: Atheneum, 1980. 167p. illus. bibliography, 167.

In language addressed to teenage boys, Carlson warns that the "privilege" of being male in the United States carries a price tag: males must repress feelings, constantly prove their masculinity, never say "no" to pressures, enter areas of study that lead to money-making jobs, be responsible for supporting their wives and children, and die early as a result of these demands. Discussing what happens to males in the parental home, in school, after high school, and on the job, the author does not blink at the radical implications of her message. Males must reject pressures to succeed, for such pressures only make men into society's scapegoat, that is, someone to be blamed for everyone else's problems. Carlson also reviews religious and historical views of males, the use of men as cannon fodder in wars, and the rise of a men's movement in the United States. "The truth is that male liberation is a very simple idea," Carlson concludes. "A man can be a man without being treated like a work slave, a replaceable robot with no human rights or feelings, a sacrifice on the altars of economic security, or an animal on a battlefield."

174. Chandos, John. **Boys Together: English Public Schools, 1800-1864.** New Haven, CT, and London: Yale University Press, 1984. 412p. illus. appendix. bibliography, 370-90. notes. index.

This extensively researched account of early-Victorian British public schools (read "private schools" in American English) draws largely negative conclusions about them. Focusing principally on Eton, Harrow, and Westminster schools, Chandos reports on the shock the boys felt coming to schools governed by heavy-handed masters and ruled by bullying older boys. The fagging system amounted to slavery. Drinking and violence to weaker boys were commonplace. Learning consisted mostly of construing classical verses. Flogging was frequent and severe. At times, the schoolboys rebelled aggressively. The moral reforms of Thomas Arnold, according to Chandos, only increased priggishness in the schools. Even the new order that changed the schools brought losses as well as gains. Chandos's study demonstrates once again that the privileges of education extended to boys were often a grueling ordeal of initiation into masculinity. "You're not at a girl's school," remarked the fierce Dr. Keate to a terrorized student. Most parents accepted the brutalization of their sons on the grounds that it prepared them for manhood.

175. Eastman, Charles A. **Indian Boyhood.** New York: McClure, Phillips, 1902. Reprint, New York: Dover, 1971. 247p. illus. pa.

Probably no other record of male Native American childhood and youth is as full as Eastman's account. Born a Lakota (Sioux) Indian, Eastman spent the first 15 years of his life, during the 1870s and 1880s, with his tribe. At first called by the name Hakadah (the pitiful last), because his mother died shortly after his birth, Eastman was rescued from neglect by his paternal grandmother. At four, he was renamed Ohiyesa (winner). Although Eastman's boyhood had its idyllic aspects, it was unmistakably a systematic training of the boy to be a warrior. Aside from skirmishes with white people, the Sioux were constantly raiding and being raided by neighboring tribes. Elders and peers of both sexes required boys to endure pain stoically. It was understood by the tribe that no young man would dare to seek a maiden in marriage until he had proven himself on the war path. At the age of 15, Eastman was reclaimed by his father, who had been imprisoned for his part in a raid on white people. During those years, the father had converted to Christianity. When he takes Ohiyesa away from the tribe at the end of this account, one has a sense of loss and gain: the boy has been removed from a world of natural innocence but one where violence probably would have taken his life early.

176. Fine, Gary Alan. **With the Boys: Little League Baseball and Preado-lescent Culture.** Chicago and London: University of Chicago Press, 1987. xiii, 289p. appendixes. bibliography, 271-86. index. pa.

In this sociological study, Fine reports on Little League teams in four cities, the involvement of adults in the teams, and the effects upon the boys. Little League baseball combines both work and play; indeed, it is a form of "dis-play" or public performance that foregrounds the boys, preparing them for adult masculine roles. Often a conscious effort is made to teach the boys certain behaviors, such as sportsmanship, appropriate emotional displays, toughness, self-control (especially control of anger), avoidance of crying or moping, handling pain, desire to win, looking professional, taking the game seriously, and being "hot and cool." Usually, the boys accept the task of being men and are eager to adopt a masculine gender role. Sexual and aggressive themes appear in the boys' behavior, including the insulting of peers, concern about sexual "reputation," racism, and gay-bashing talk. Preadolescent subcultures often have their own slang. The appendixes elaborate more personally on the study. In appendix 1, Fine concludes that, overall, Little League baseball has positive effects on the boys, providing athletic exercise, leadership skills, increased popularity, and greater father-son contact. Criticisms of Little League remain "not proven" (i.e., problems surface in individual cases but not in general). In appendix 2, Fine describes how he reconciled two roles: observing the boys and interacting with the boys. Appendix 3 describes the settings and sources of the study.

177. Green, Richard. **The "Sissy Boy Syndrome" and the Development of Homosexuality.** New Haven, CT, and London: Yale University Press, 1987. x, 416p. illus. bibliography, 399-409. notes. index. pa.

This book is based upon a 15-year study of two groups of boys: 66 "feminine" boys and 56 "masculine" boys. (The author cautions that *feminine* and *masculine* are slippery and problematic terms.) Distinguishing anatomic identity from gender role behavior and from sexual orientation, Green further distinguishes among homosexuals, transsexuals, and transvestites. He identifies the elements of the sissy boy syndrome (a major characteristic is alienation from other males) and argues that "childhood gender nonconformity" is closely related to adult homosexuality. After considering numerous scenarios and variables, the author is cautious about drawing cause-effect conclusions. A "good enough" mother and a father involved in caregiving, together, seem to reduce the likelihood of the sissy boy syndrome but do not appear to guarantee heterosexuality in boys. Father involvement has significant but not always predictable effects upon boys' development. Psychotherapy does little or nothing to alter sexual development. A study of twins indicates that the biological factor cannot completely explain the development of adult sexuality; socialization is important. The study suggests numerous possibilities about the development of male homosexuality but confirms few of them as isolated causes.

178. Hawley, Richard A. **Boys Will Be Men: Masculinity in Troubled Times.** Middlebury, VT: Paul S. Eriksson, 1993. xx, 188p. bibliography, 181-82. notes. index.

Ron Powers's introduction presents Hawley as a man who has served for many years in a boys' preparatory school. Taking a dark view of current gender controversies, Hawley believes that innate sexual differences determine most gender differences. He critiques the oedipal obsessions of Freud and Horney for reducing masculinity to an overcompensation against femininity. The mythopoetic men are too self-conscious to create genuine male bonding. He retells the story of Percival as a myth of the boy formulating masculine identity through quest. The biblical story of David shows the golden boy becoming the flawed man, but a greatness shines through both his successes and his sins. The heart of this book, however, lies in Hawley's stories about his most memorable students. A gifted storyteller, Hawley tells of funny boys, helpless boys, evil boys, unworldly boys, boys who died young, and inspiring boys. The final chapter reaffirms the essence of masculinity in solitary questing.

179. Honey, J. R. de S. **Tom Brown's Universe: The Development of the English Public School in the Nineteenth Century.** New York: Quadrangle/New York Times, 1977. xv, 416p. bibliography, 408-10. notes. index. Original publication, London: Millington Books, 1977.

This scholarly study of the nineteenth-century British public school (read "private school" in American English) indicates that even boys from the privileged classes enjoyed a decidedly mixed blessing in being sent to such a school, usually around eight years of age. Honey details the grinding studies, the bullying, the unsanitary conditions, the sexual immorality and exploitation, and the ruthless punishments—especially the ritual of the flogging block. Particularly interesting is the author's speculation that complacent parents knowingly sent their sons into these torments with the belief that they would "harden" the boys and thus prepare them for assuming the male role in society.

180. Kempler, Susan, Doreen Rappaport, and Michele Spirn. **A Man Can Be ....** New York: Human Sciences Press, 1981. 27p. illus. pa.

This book is designed to show boys aged three to seven some of the possibilities of adult manhood. The photographs by Russell Dian show a white father and son in diverse moods and settings. At a playground, they meet a black father and son. With a light touch, the simple text depicts a range of male behaviors and emotions. The book affirms father-son role modeling.

181. Mahony, Pat. **Schools for the Boys? Co-education Reassessed.** London: Hutchinson, in association with the Explorations in Feminism Collective, 1985. 118p. illus. appendixes. bibliography, 113-18. notes. pa.

The title is misleading. This short book is actually a hatred-filled, radical feminist diatribe arguing for separate schools for girls. The author contends that boys inhibit and harass girls, and (horrors!) that boys are sexually interested in girls. Mahony's loathing of boys, especially of their sexuality, borders on the pathological. The author is unwilling to consider that most girls are also sexually interested in boys and that some girls can be quite aggressive in pursuing them. The book's demand for girls-only schools seems to mask a lesbian separatist agenda. A graduate of the Dale Spender school of special pleading (entries 427, 647, 981), Mahony musters page after page of dubious arguments ending with the conclusion that patriarchy and capitalism are to blame for practically everything. There may be good arguments for single-sex schools, but this boy-hating tract does not contain them.

182. Miedzian, Myriam. **Boys Will Be Boys: Breaking the Link Between Masculinity and Violence.** New York: Doubleday, Anchor Books, 1991. xxviii, 355p. bibliography, 235-45. notes. index. pa.

Recognizing that "the masculine mystique" of violence must not be confused with masculinity itself, Miedzian points out that males are the chief victims of violence. Drawing upon a wide range of research, she argues that biology is not destiny. Because more males than females are predisposed to aggressiveness, it is crucial for society to steer boys away from violent behavior. Distinguishing between aggression and violence, Miedzian argues that U.S. society encourages many boys to convert their predisposition for aggressiveness into violent behavior. A primary problem in the United States is father absence, which allows boys to indulge violent tendencies and diminishes examples of nurturant masculinity. Widespread anti-father attitudes only make the problem worse. Forcing boys into narrow, violent masculine roles encourages some boys to define themselves as homosexual. Miedzian examines school programs that encourage concepts of responsible fatherhood among boys, provide alternatives to fistfights and bullying, and take the glory out of war. She vigorously protests against the violence marketed by the entertainment industry, arguing that it pushes boys toward antisocial behavior. Although Miedzian at times minimizes the extent of female violence and downplays the involvement of women in war, her book is marked by an evenhandedness that usually avoids male shaming and exhibits a genuine desire to help boys.

183. Nerburn, Kent. **Letters to My Son: Reflections on Becoming a Man.** San Rafael, CA: New World Library, 1993. xviii, 212p.

"We are born male. We must learn to be men," writes the author. To a son born at the father's midlife, Nerburn offers reflections on becoming a man. Knowing that if he does not offer guidance, others will, Nerburn urges his son not to confuse maleness with manhood. Maleness without moral courage is destructive, he says. Because work still significantly defines a man's sense of his manhood, he urges his son not to accept a job but to find a vocation, a worthy calling in life. Possessions, Nerburn says, finally possess us. Giving is the most satisfying part of having. Particularly interesting are Nerburn's reflections on war: Governments do not give men the choice of deciding whether a war is just or unjust. Total pacifism or compulsory military service are the only two choices. Nerburn urges his son to decide for himself whether or not to participate in a war, and then to stand by his conviction. Nerburn urges his son to seek greater respect for and equality with women. Sex must combine the earthy and the spiritual; otherwise, it becomes debased or atrophied. How people treat elders is a touchstone of morality, Nerburn says. Throughout the volume, the author exhibits a wisdom and serenity that many fathers will envy.

184. Paley, Vivian Gussin. **Boys and Girls: Superheroes in the Doll Corner.** Chicago and London: University of Chicago Press, 1984. xii, 116p. pa.

Understandably, this delightful book about kindergarten has become something of a classic. Recording a year of her pupils' activities, Paley notes, "Kindergarten is a triumph of sexual self-stereotyping." Allowing for minor lapses, the boys and girls relentlessly define themselves as separate. The boys fantasize superhero play in the building-block corner of the classroom, and the girls play at fairy tales in the doll corner. In general, the boys have more momentum; they seem forever in motion. The girls have greater coordination and are better at table play and finger painting. The boys are fascinated by Darth Vader, the girls by Barbie. "I have come to an unavoidable conclusion," Paley writes. "My curriculum has suited girls better than boys." Although initially more comfortable with the girls' more ordered play, Paley eventually develops an understanding of and a liking for the boys' more boisterous activities. "The boys and girls look at one another without rancor," she notes. "I, the teacher ... need not act as if the superheroes will pull down the classroom walls. Let the boys be robbers, then, or tough guys in space. It is the natural, universal, and essential play of little boys." Written with warmth, Paley's record is often hilarious in its depiction of the wonderful wackiness and wisdom of childhood.

185. Pomeroy, Wardell B. **Boys and Sex.** 3d ed. New York: Delacorte Press, 1991. xi, 205p. bibliography, 189-91. index.
    An updated edition of Pomeroy's concise, readable guide, this book provides boys with essential knowledge about sexual matters. A colleague of Kinsey, Pomeroy explains the book's purpose thusly: "For boys approaching or entering adolescence, I hope it will be a guide to what is happening or about to happen to them, and I hope, too, it dispels their guilt and fear about sexual behavior, leading them toward a well-adjusted sexual life as adults." After an introduction for parents and brief statement that all boys have a sex life, subsequent chapters consider the anatomy and physiology of sex, sex play before adolescence, masturbation, homosexuality, dating, petting, intercourse, and consequences of sex. Following a chapter of questions and answers, a brief afterword reiterates principal themes in the book. Whether readers find Pomeroy's attitude toward sexual behavior too permissive, sufficiently cautious, or too inhibiting, most are likely to find his explanations frank and clear.

186. Sexton, Patricia Cayo. **The Feminized Male: Classrooms, White Collars and the Decline of Manliness.** New York: Random House, 1969. 214p. appendix. notes. Reprint, New York: Random House, Vintage, 1970. pa.
    This controversial book argues that U.S. schools are inimical to boys and masculinity. The female presence in the classrooms, especially in the lower grades, is stifling in its pervasiveness, schools reward feminine behavior and proscribe masculine behavior, and the least masculine boys are most likely to succeed in school. These conclusions are based on a survey of school children from a fictionally named town and corrected by findings from a national survey. Sexton's solution to over-feminized schools is to move more men and masculine attitudes into the schools while moving more women and feminine attitudes into the power structure of society—in effect, to balance out the presence of the sexes throughout the social system. "Only as the strength of women in other institutions increases, will their stranglehold on home and school weaken," Sexton argues. "Men may then be removed as targets of female resentment."

187. Standing Bear, Luther. **My Indian Boyhood.** Boston: Houghton-Mifflin, 1931. Reprint, Lincoln and London: University of Nebraska Press, Bison Books, 1988. 190p. illus. pa.
    Written for white children, this memoir recalls Standing Bear's boyhood among the Lakota (Sioux) Indians in the present-day Dakotas. The boys' play trained them for hunting, trapping, and war parties. As the author reports, "To be a coward was unforgivable." Accepting fear and pain was mandatory. When Standing Bear cried after a nasty fall, a stepmother admonished him, "Be brave, son. You are not a girl." Later, his father told him, "Son, I am proud of you that you did not cry like a woman." Differentiating from the feminine was obligatory for boys. Fighting among indian tribes was common: the author's Indian name, "Plenty Kill," refers to his father's exploits on the warpath. For the most part, however, Standing Bear's account is idyllic. The memoir ends with the boy's first buffalo hunt. Soon after, Standing Bear was swept off to school among the whites—and to a far different life.

188. Thompson, Doug. **As Boys Become Men: Learning New Male Roles.** Denver, CO: Institute for Equality in Education, University of Denver, 1980. vii, 72p. appendixes. bibliography, 55-58. pa.

This curriculum guide for junior high school and high school classes presents classroom exercises for addressing male issues. In the preface, Thompson argues that sex equality is itself a male issue; living up to some standards of masculinity can be harmful for some boys. Each of the book's sections includes student objectives and background information for the teacher. The eight sections are: gender role stereotypes, masculine role stereotypes, media definitions of the masculine role, language, career and work choice preference, competitive athletics, fatherhood, and emotions and relationships. The appendixes include a bibliography, a listing of damaging effects of sex stereotyping on boys and men, a discussion of the masculine role stereotype, and an excerpt from Warren's Farrell's *The Liberated Man* (entry 95) on the gender significance of Super Bowl Sunday. Although some of the book's material is now dated (and some would say wrong-headed), teachers may still find it a useful stimulus to raising male issues in the classroom.

189. Weiner, Bernard, with Tom Baker, David Edeli, Heide M. Lindsmayer, Jim Thurston, Erik Weiner. **Boy into Man: A Father's Guide to Initiation of Teenage Sons.** San Francisco: Transformation Press, 1992. 70p. illus. pa.

Concerned about the lack of initiation rituals that allow boys to experience a rite of passage into positive masculine adulthood, Weiner found himself creating a ceremony with help from neighbors and friends who recognized a similar gap in modern society. As plans progressed, the question of whether or not women (i.e., mothers) should participate in the ceremony created a temporary roadblock. But a compromise that allowed the women to participate from afar won acceptance. The 13- to 14-year-old boys looked forward to the ceremony with anticipation, but they also felt some uncertainty. Weiner describes how the men "summoned" the boys from schools and mothers, and how the weekend in the woods involved them in lessons of responsible manhood and good fellowship. The views of others involved in the experience (including those of some of the boys) are included in this book, which can be used as a guide to create similar ceremonies.

Cross-References

See chapter 14, "Males in Families," and chapter 15, "Masculinity."

580. Arcana, Judith. **Every Mother's Son.**

381. Aymar, Brandt. **The Young Male Figure: In Paintings, Sculptures, and Drawings from Ancient Egypt to the Present.**

903. Bartollas, Clemens, Stuart J. Miller, and Simon Dinitz. **Juvenile Victimization: The Institutionalization Paradox.**

904. Biller, Henry B. **Fathers and Families: Paternal Factors in Child Development.**

905. Biller, Henry B., and Richard S. Solomon. **Child Maltreatment and Paternal Deprivation: A Manifesto for Research, Prevention, and Treatment.**

907. Bolton, Frank G., Jr., Larry A. Morris, and Ann E. MacEachron. **Males at Risk: The Other Side of Sexual Abuse.**

37. Brown, Claude. **Manchild in the Promised Land.**

5. Cohen, Albert K. **Delinquent Boys: The Culture of the Gang.**

910. Drew, Dennis, and Jonathan Drake. **Boys for Sale: A Sociological Study of Boy Prostitution.**

1032. Glasstone, Richard. **Dancing as a Career for Men.**

9. Gold, Martin. **Status Force in Delinquent Boys.**

349. Golding, William. **Lord of the Flies.**

914. Grubman-Black, Stephen D. **Broken Boys/Mending Men: Recovery from Childhood Sexual Abuse.**

356. Hemingway, Ernest. **The Nick Adams Stories.**

10. Herdt, Gilbert H. **Guardians of the Flutes: Idioms of Masculinity.**

11. Herdt, Gilbert H., ed. **Rituals of Manhood: Male Initiation in Papua New Guinea.**

12. Herdt, Gilbert. **The Sambia: Ritual and Gender in New Guinea.**

108. Herzig, Alison Cragin, and Jane Lawrence Mali. **Oh, Boy! Babies!**

583. Herzog, Elizabeth, and Cecelia E. Sudia. **Boys in Fatherless Families.**

916. Hunter, Mic. **Abused Boys: The Neglected Victims of Sexual Abuse.**

405. Johnson, Wendell Stacy. **Sons and Fathers: The Generational Link in Literature, 1780-1980.**

280. Kett, Joseph F. **Rites of Passage: Adolescence in America, 1790 to the Present.**

507. Keyes, Ralph, ed. **Sons on Fathers: A Book of Men's Writing.**

585. Klein, Carole. **Mothers and Sons.**

919. Lew, Mike. **Victims No Longer: Men Recovering from Incest and Other Sexual Child Abuse.**

20. Lidz, Theodore, and Ruth Wilmanns Lidz. **Oedipus in the Stone Age: A Psychoanalytic Study of Masculinization in Papua New Guinea.**

920. Lloyd, Robin. **For Money or Love: Boy Prostitution in America.**

286. Macleod, David I. **Building Character in the American Boy: The Boy Scouts, YMCA, and Their Forerunners, 1870-1920.**

921. Miles, Rosalind. **Love, Sex, Death and the Making of the Male.**

587. Olsen, Paul. **Sons and Mothers: Why Men Behave As They Do.**

664. Poinsett, Alex. **Young Black Males in Jeopardy: Risk Factors and Intervention Strategies.**

922. Porter, Eugene. **Treating the Young Male Victim of Sexual Assault: Issues and Intervention.**

420. Quigly, Isabel. **The Heirs of Tom Brown: The English School Story.**

24. Raphael, Ray. **The Men from the Boys: Rites of Passage in Male America.**

292. Rosenthal, Michael. **The Character Factory: Baden-Powell and the Origins of the Boy Scout Movement.**

135. Sadker, David. **Being a Man: A Unit of Instructional Activities on Male Role Stereotyping.**

929. Sonkin, Daniel Jay. **Wounded Boys, Heroic Men: A Man's Guide to Recovering from Child Abuse.**

378. White, Edmund. **A Boy's Own Story.**

34. Wilmott, Peter. **Adolescent Boys of East London.**

69. Wright, Richard. **Black Boy: A Record of Childhood and Youth.**

6

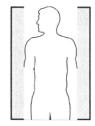

Divorce and Custody

190. Athearn, Forden. **How to Divorce Your Wife: The Man's Side of Divorce.** Garden City, NY: Doubleday, 1976. 167p. appendixes. index.

Like its title, the book is abrupt and direct. Athearn, a West Coast attorney, provides a how-to guide to the legal and emotional pitfalls of divorce, including such topics as what to do *before* telling your wife you want a divorce, the foolish and destructive reactions of some men whose wives file for divorce, the grounds for divorce, the trial, alimony, custody, child support, visitation, property division, and handling lawyers. Appendix A contains divorce information by state; appendix B is a glossary of legal terms.

191. Cassidy, Robert. **What Every Man Should Know About Divorce.** Washington, DC: New Republic Books, 1977. ix, 247p. appendixes. bibliography, 190-96. index.

A veteran of the divorce wars, Cassidy offers advice to avoid the pitfalls of marital separation and to encourage growth amid the pain. He focuses upon the emotional turmoil that the divorcing man will face. Horror stories about what divorce courts have done lead into Cassidy's advice about fighting back. He offers information about finding an attorney, how the courts work, custody, visitation, children's reactions, and starting a new life. The appendixes include a guide to divorce laws by state, and a listing of divorce reform groups. The foreword is by Mel Krantzler.

192. Doppler, George. **America Needs Total Divorce Reform—Now!** New York: Vantage Press, 1973. 125p.

This denunciation of the American judicial system's handling of divorce focuses on men's concerns. Dealing primarily with divorce and custody proceedings in Pennsylvania, Doppler points to abuses in other states and issues a call for reform. He touches upon such matters as discrimination against men in the courts, how the law rewards wives for ending a marriage, how attorneys profit from marital breakups but not from reconciliation, the inequities involved in child support, how alimony and separate maintenance are forms of legalized extortion, the abuse of fathers' visitation rights by ex-wives, and the inequities of property settlements. The author argues for mandatory counseling for separating couples, includes a petition to the United Nations for equal rights for fathers, and lists men's divorce organizations around the country. Doppler writes not as a dispassionate observer but as a militant reformer.

193. Epstein, Joseph. **Divorced in America: Marriage in an Age of Possibility.** New York: E. P. Dutton, 1974. 339p. Reprint, New York: Penguin Books, 1981. pa.

Epstein regards divorce as a painful joke, as this ironic narrative reveals. Interspersed with ghastly scenes from a divorce, the book reviews the tolls taken upon marriage by sexual liberation, female emancipation, and "growth" philosophies. Epstein provides a quick history of divorce and delves into the improbabilities of alimony. He concludes that divorce brings at least as much bondage as a bad marriage, that those who boost "creative divorce" are full of hot air, and that the nuclear family is really the only option for men and women. Throughout the book, Epstein provides a vivid account of divorce from a male viewpoint.

194. Franks, Maurice R. **How to Avoid Alimony.** New York: Saturday Review Press/E. P. Dutton, 1975. xiv, 173p. notes. index. Reprint, New York: New American Library, Signet, 1976. pa.

Gleefully dedicated to the author's ex-wife and her attorney (who failed to get Franks to pay alimony), this book offers strategies for avoiding wife maintenance after divorce. Franks's principal tactic is to move the divorce case from the state courts, which regularly discriminate against males, to the federal courts, where such issues as equal rights and slavery can be raised. Franks cites constitutional and legal support for his belief that wife support is sexist and a form of male peonage, especially in this day of working wives. He opposes no-fault divorce as a means of allowing the wife who is at fault to soak her husband for property and maintenance. In snappy prose, Franks offers suggestions about how to find the right lawyer, how to lower unreasonable child support payments, what to do if your ex-wife has a live-in lover, and why premarital contracts are expedient.

195. Franks, Maurice R. **Winning Custody.** Englewood Cliffs, NJ: Prentice-Hall, 1983. 192p. notes. index. pa.

In this "no-holds barred guide for fathers," Franks provides jargon-free advice on the problems and strategies of winning custody. He estimates costs, offers suggestions for finding a good lawyer, and warns fathers to prepare for war. He discusses means of impressing judges favorably, and he explains the legal factors that will influence a custody decision. After attacking no-fault divorce and the "tender years" mentality, Franks goes beyond courtroom practice to discuss the possibilities of tape-recording telephone conversations and of hiring detectives. He provides advice for fathers seeking to change custody or to enforce visitation rights, and he provides formulas for figuring child support. Suing malpracticing lawyers and removing bad judges are also explored. The penultimate chapter contains Franks's suggestions for what divorce and custody law ought to be, and the final chapter offers advice to divorced fathers who are thinking of remarrying.

196. Goldstein, Joseph, Anna Freud, and Albert J. Solnit. **Beyond the Best Interests of the Child.** Rev. ed. New York: Free Press, 1979. xiv, 203p. notes. index. pa.

First published in 1973, this controversial book attempts to apply psychoanalytic theory to law cases in order to find "the least detrimental alternative" in placing a child after a family breakup. The authors argue that the child, whose sense of time is different from an adult's, needs continuity with a "psychological" parent; therefore, long delays in settling cases, joint custody, and disruptive visitations from a noncustodial parent are harmful to the child. In legal matters, the child—not just the parents—should be legally represented. In an epilogue added to the latest edition, the authors attempt to answer objections raised by the first publication. The book's most controversial suggestions still involve visitation from a noncustodial parent: the authors argue that the custodial parent, not the courts, should determine whether or not visitation is beneficial to the child. Because most noncustodial parents are fathers, the book's guidelines seem especially inimical to them. The authors' discussion ignores the question of whether or not noncustodial parents without visitation rights must provide child support, and critics of the book argue that the authors have underestimated the value to the child of having contact with two parents, even when the parents are separated and somewhat hostile to each other.

196a. Horgan, Timothy J. **Winning Your Divorce: A Man's Survival Guide.** New York: Dutton, 1994. xi, 196p. appendixes. glossary, index.

"Popular mythology and the feminist movement contend that the American legal system favors men," Horgan writes. "Nothing could be further from the truth." The divorce system is "out of control," and males are its principle victims. In this up-to-date guide to divorce and custody battles, Horgan employs clear, direct prose to guide men from the moment a divorce is imminent to recovering from its aftermath. He warns that the divorce process will be financially and emotionally draining. Men must be forever vigilant and must take an active role in everything from closing joint accounts to selecting a lawyer. They must be wary of divorce mediation, motions for temporary relief, and settlement conferences. Because prejudice against fathers still permeates the system, a man's bid for custody and visitation are likely to involve an uphill struggle. False accusations of child molestation should be expected. Horgan discusses alimony, the trial, and its aftereffects. The three appendixes contain a glossary of legal terms, a short list of fathers' rights organizations in the U.S., and a state-by-state summary of residency requirements and divorce grounds.

197. Kerpelman, Leonard. **Divorce: A Guide for Men.** South Bend, IN: Icarus Press, 1983. xi, 292p. index.

Convinced that the judicial system is prejudiced against males in divorce cases, attorney Kerpelman provides hard-nosed advice for men contemplating divorce. Speaking bluntly, he says that anything less than militancy in conducing his case will ensure the man's defeat. Kerpelman has a low opinion of most lawyers' willingness and ability to handle the man's case. Judges are even worse: most are "male chauvinists," that is, they believe that women should be protected and supported by males and that women are automatically more suited for parenting than men. Kerpelman tells male readers that they will need the support of a competent and active fathers' group; if the man cannot find such a group, he had better start one. Drawing upon the experiences of a Maryland Fathers' United for Equal Rights group, the author tells of its founding and of how it evolved tactics to pressure judges who regularly handed down blatantly anti-male decisions. "Mr. Nice Guy" will invariably lose, Kerpelman argues, advising men to be tough, angry, and militant—but never violent—throughout the divorce experience.

198. Kiefer, Louis. **How to Win Custody.** New York: Simon and Schuster, Cornerstone Library, 1982. xi, 308p. appendixes. index. pa.

A divorced attorney who obtained custody of his children "not because of the legal system but in spite of it," Kiefer writes primarily for fathers (the traditional underdogs in custody cases), although his advice is useful for either parent (the book includes a chapter for the noncustodial mother). Kiefer's legal knowledge provides an unusually detailed account of the custodial tug-of-war, his courtroom experiences enable him to cite numerous (often hair-raising) cases, and his writing skills produce clear, jargon-free prose. Kiefer has few illusions about the legal system, his advice is both practical and blunt ("trust no one"), and his thorough coverage explores both the usual topics (how to locate a good lawyer) and the less familiar ones (how to nullify your spouse's "dirty tricks," making phone taps and taping conversations, the legalities of absconding with children, and how to locate "kidnapped" children). The six appendixes include a sample joint custody agreement, a list of deposition questions, questions for cross-examining a psychiatrist, and the texts of the Uniform Child Custody Jurisdiction Act and the Parental Kidnapping Prevention Act of 1980.

199. Metz, Charles V. **Divorce and Custody for Men: A Guide and Primer Designed Exclusively to Help Men Win Just Settlements.** Garden City, NY: Doubleday, 1968. xvii, 147p.

Metz, a pioneer in justice for divorced fathers, designed this primer to jolt about-to-be-divorced men out of their complacency; they must be prepared to fight viciously if they hope to win even the semblance of a just settlement. Loss of income, property, and children is among the prices that men pay for their ignorance of divorce law and practice, which are strongly biased in women's favor. Get mad, be prepared, file first, and fight to win, Metz advises. He takes a dim view of alimony, social workers, judges, attorneys, and visitation practices, arguing that men must organize to effect changes in divorce law and procedures. While some readers will see Metz's book as dated, others will note how little has changed since 1968.

200. Morgenbesser, Mel, and Nadine Nehls. **Joint Custody: An Alternative for Divorcing Families.** Chicago: Nelson-Hall, 1981. vii, 168p. illus. bibliography, 151-61. index.

Calmly and equitably, the authors provide a history of child custody and a definition of current joint custody. After describing the effects of divorce upon children, they argue the benefits—and potential drawbacks—of joint custody. Also included are suggestions on how to achieve joint custody, sample joint-custody agreements, interviews with parents sharing custody, and an overview of research on the topic.

201. Myers, Michael F. **Men and Divorce.** New York: Guilford Press, 1989. xv, 286p. bibliography, 271-78. index.

A Canadian therapist, Myers surveys, in part 1, the history of divorce, the clinical research on divorce, and the theories of why people marry and divorce. In part 2, he examines eight aspects of men and divorce: the not-yet-separated man, the newly separated man, divorce at various ages in the male life cycle, the phenomenon of divorcing men who take up with younger women, abandoned husbands, previously divorced men, gay men who are coming out through divorce, and divorced fathers and their children. Part 3 examines therapeutic interventions, discusses common themes in treatment (e.g., anger, dependency, sexuality, and grief), and explains patient-to-therapist transference of feelings and therapist-to-patient countertransference. The final chapter surveys the future of men and divorce. Throughout the discussion, Myers's pro-feminist perspective creates a disturbing pattern of husband blaming and wife exonerating. Nearly every case history cited in the book depicts the divorce as due to the husband's "problems" that persist despite the wife's long-suffering endurance. Because the author has difficulty recognizing a dark side to some women's actions, his attitude toward male patients is often patronizing.

202. Ricci, Isolina. **Mom's House/Dad's House: Making Shared Custody
Work.** New York: Macmillan, 1980. xv, 270p. illus. appendixes. bibliography
throughout notes and 264-66. notes. index. pa.

Indicating that single-parent custody often does not work well, Ricci
offers an extensive list of suggestions for separated couples to turn two houses
into two homes for their children. She considers myriad complications that can
arise, offers practical solutions, and, in the process, makes a case for shared
custody as often being preferable to single-parent custody.

203. Roman, Mel, and William Haddad, with Susan Manso. **The Disposable
Parent: The Case for Joint Custody.** New York: Holt, Rinehart and Winston, 1978. 215p. notes. index. Reprint, New York: Penguin Books, 1979. pa.

In this classic fathers' rights text, Roman and Haddad argue that the
disposable parent is usually the father. With divorce, child custody goes to the
mother in over 90 percent of contemporary cases. After an introduction describing their own divorces and those of other men, the authors explore, in chapter
1, the legal history of custody, concentrating upon the reversal in England and
the United States from nineteenth-century practice (which regularly awarded
custody to the father) to twentieth-century practice (which does just the
opposite). In chapter 2, the authors argue that the present method of splitting
the family between custodial and noncustodial parents does not work. Chapter
3 is devoted to what is known about fathers and fathering as well as the
stereotypes that underlie many studies. Chapters 4 and 5 reply to arguments
against joint custody and cite evidence for its feasibility. In chapter 6, the
authors show why joint custody is seldom considered. In particular, they point
to feminist ambivalence on the subject: while recognizing that single parenthood places heavy burden on women, some feminists have been reluctant to
abandon the principal stronghold of female power, and some are guilty of
misandric sexism, believing that men do not care about or cannot handle
parenting. In the final chapter, the authors make suggestions for creating a
social climate in which joint custody can work better.

204. Vail, Lauren O. **Divorce: The Man's Complete Guide to Winning.**
New York: Simon and Schuster, Sovereign Books, 1979. viii, 280p. appendixes.
bibliography, 246-51. notes. index.

"Definitely pro men," but not "against women," Vail's book takes a dim
view of the legal system of domestic relations in the United States. Vail sees
men victimized by their ignorance of the law, the bias against men in the
courts, and the nice-guy psychology that makes men vulnerable to manipulation. Arguing that men must pursue their cases aggressively. Vail offers
hard-nosed advice on such matters as preliminary do's and don'ts of divorce;
finding a good lawyer; the grounds and proofs needed for divorce; what to
expect of the legal system; support, property, and custody agreements; preparing for trial; and how to survive psychologically during and after the divorce.
A clinical psychologist (but not a lawyer), Vail avoids legal jargon. The four
appendixes contain advice on how to do your own legal research, a list of helpful
readings, a list of men's rights organizations, and a glossary of legal terms.

205. Victor, Ira, and Win Ann Winkler. **Fathers and Custody.** New York:
Hawthorn Books, 1977. xiii, 209p. appendixes. bibliography, 193-201. notes.
index.

"There is overwhelming evidence," the authors write, "that prejudice
exists against fathers in a custody situation." This book considers the growing
phenomenon of fathers with child custody, the difficulties they encounter in

obtaining it, and the problems they face once they have it. After presenting case histories to demonstrate that a representative "father" does not exist, the authors explain why more men are seeking custody now than in the past. One reason is that the "feminine" bride who valued motherhood sometimes becomes the "feminist" wife who deplores it. Discussing women who "drop out" of marriage and fathers who "cop out" of custody hassles, the authors observe that the principal victims in these situations are often the children. Despite changing attitudes, fathers seeking custody have an uphill battle. In discussing the ambiguous impact of the 1970s men's movement, the authors review division in its ranks between militants pushing for men's equal rights and pro-feminist males reiterating radical feminist accusations against men. The hostility of the women's movement toward awarding custody to fathers, except when the mother agrees to give it up, is also noted. The authors examine the increase of kidnapping among divorced parents, help for fathers with custody, and visitation problems. Despite the doomsaying of some authorities, the authors argue that joint custody and full custody for fathers can—and often does—work. In concluding chapters, they look briefly at dating, remarriage, and step-parenting, as well as a new emerging parental consciousness. The appendixes list divorced fathers groups, single-parent and child-help groups, and legal advice referral groups.

206. Warshak, Richard A. **The Custody Revolution: The Father Factor and the Motherhood Mystique.** New York: Poseidon Press, 1992. 272p. appendix. notes. index.

Custody decisions in twentieth-century America have been distorted by the "motherhood mystique," that is, the belief that women, because of their nature, make better parents than men, and mothers are more important to children than fathers. This mystique overburdens mothers, exiles fathers, and shortchanges children. Warshak surveys recent scholarship that demonstrates the impact of the father on the child's infancy development, intelligence, academic achievement, motivation, maturity, moral development and self control, empathy and caring, and responsibility. Delinquency is closely linked with father absence. He notes the existence of single fathers who cope successfully with children. Mothers who give up custody are socially stigmatized for doing so. Many feminists, who would be expected to support equal parenting, have a double standard after divorce because of their reluctance to relinquish a traditional stronghold of women's power. The present single-parent mode of custody is hurting children, especially boys, who often lose their father after divorce. Warshak cites studies indicating that, after divorce—on balance— boys do better with fathers and girls do better with mothers. Thus, he argues that gender should be one factor to consider when custody is being decided. Exploring various forms of joint and split custody, he concludes that the pros of such custody arrangements usually outweigh the cons. He is critical of the "primary caregiver" criterion for granting custody, because the primary caregiver is not necessarily the better parent or the more important parent for the child to be with. Warshak urges a custody revolution because the present system is irreparably damaging many children.

207. Woody, Robert Henley. **Getting Custody: Winning the Last Battle of the Marital War.** New York: Macmillan, 1978. xii, 179p. appendixes. bibliography, 172-73. index.

A clinical psychologist specializing in marriage problems, Woody offers legal suggestions and psychological advice (mostly for men) for waging and surviving custodial battles.

Cross-References

See chapter 14, "Males in Families: C. Divorced and Single Fathers, Stepfathers," and chapter 16, "Men's Rights."

340. Corman, Avery. **Kramer Versus Kramer.**

39. Covington, Jim. **Confessions of a Single Father.**

350. Goldman, William. **Father's Day.**

53. Martin, Albert. **One Man, Hurt.**

60. Painter, Hal. **Mark, I Love You.**

166. Sell, Kenneth D., comp. **Divorce in the 70s: A Subject Bibliography.**

66. Stafford, Linley M. **One Man's Family: A Single Father and His Family.**

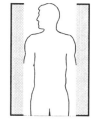

7

Erotica and Pornography

208. Christensen, F. M. **Pornography: The Other Side.** New York: Praeger, 1990. viii, 189p. bibliography, 177-83. notes. index.

Christensen argues that pornography is not the problem; sexual repression is. He distinguishes among different kinds of "pornography," ranging from erotica to violent porn. He argues that most males are predisposed by biology to respond to erotic visual cues. In contrast, females tend to be more interested in "romance" and long-term commitments. What is called pornography, Christensen argues, is a legitimate way to meet a healthy, predominantly male need. Antisexual attitudes in Western society have been encouraged by Christianity and Islam, but these biases are neither innate nor healthy. Common charges against pornography are without merit. In a compelling chapter, "Pornography and Women," Christensen attacks the argument that explicit depictions of sex debase women, and he argues that some feminist attacks on pornography carry strong overtones of misandry. Focusing on violent porn, Christensen notes that such materials represent a small percentage of all pornography and that critics of violent porn generally are concerned only when females are victimized; these critics usually ignore violence done to men in standard entertainments. Those who regard sexual content as inherently degrading most often regard sex itself as degrading. The alleged ill effects of pornography have not been demonstrated; indeed, legalizing pornographic materials in countries like Denmark has lowered the number of sex crimes. The alleged link between pornography and rape is spurious, and legal efforts to repress pornography create more problems than they solve. Christensen offers intriguing reasons for considering "the other side" of pornography.

209. Dworkin, Andrea. **Pornography: Men Possessing Women.** New York: E. P. Dutton, 1989. xl, 300p. bibliography, 239-85. notes. index. pa. Reprint, New York: Plume, 1989. pa.

Pornography harms women, Dworkin argues, citing cases in which the use of pornography led to crimes against women. She defines pornography as anything that depicts women as sexual objects or as subordinate to men. Not content with denouncing pornography and its producers and consumers, however, Dworkin sees pornography as part of a universal conspiracy of male power against females. Having made this dubious leap of logic, Dworkin goes on a rhetorical rampage condemning the entire male sex as unspeakably evil and masculinity as irretrievably corrupt. With this thesis, Dworkin is quick to interpret everything in terms of male brutalization of women. The penis is a weapon of oppression, and sexual intercourse is an act of violence. When boys transfer their gender identification from mother to father, they degrade the feminine. There is no distinction between erotica and pornography; both are manifestations of male power. The Marquis de Sade is a representative man whose fantasies are typical of male bestiality. Men regard women simply as sexual objects, and male use of force in sexual relations is the norm. Here and there, Dworkin acknowledges that some pornography is degrading to males, but as this idea does not fit her thesis of male omnipotence over women, it is given short shrift. "Male perceptions of women are askew, wild, inept," Dworkin writes, and the same might be said of her perceptions of males. If pornography consists of dehumanizing a class of people, Dworkin has written a pornographic book.

210. Kimmel, Michael S., ed. **Men Confront Pornography.** New York: Crown Publishers, Inc., 1990. xi, 340p. notes.

Noting that the radical feminist attack on pornography has been met with silence from men, Kimmel presents 31 discussions of pornography from male writers, representing differing reactions to the topic. In the introduction, Kimmel summarizes differing feminist responses to pornography: radical feminists see it as an assault upon women that reasserts male power, liberal feminists see it as a celebration of sexuality that women should encourage. Essays are divided into six sections: pornography and the construction of male sexuality; the politicization of pornography; the psychology of pornography; social science research on pornography; gay male pornography; and questions about what is to be done concerning pornography. Some writers (like David Steinberg) defend pornography as a needed response to sexual scarcity, to men's desire to be desired, and to the demeaning of male sexuality that permeates the society. Other writers (like John Stoltenberg) see pornography warping sexuality with notions of male supremacy. Writers explore connections (or lack of connections) between pornography and rape, pornography as addiction, how blacks respond to the pornography debate (not a major issue, according to Robert Staples), pornography as therapy, and how gay male pornography raises some questions about feminist analyses of pornography. Authors include Phillip Lopate, Timothy Beneke, Philip Weiss, Harry Brod, Scott Tucker, and Bernie Zilbergeld.

211. Melton, J. Gordon, with Gary L. Ward. **The Churches Speak On: Pornography: Official Statements from Religious Bodies and Ecumenical Organizations.** Detroit: Gale Research, 1989. xxv, 267p. index. pa.

Melton has collected documents issued by more than 30 religious organizations and denominations concerning pornography. The documents date from the 1930s through the 1980s. Catholic, Protestant, and Jewish groups are represented, as well as Shi'a and Sunni Islam and the Unitarian Universalist Association. Most documents condemn "pornography" (which is almost always defined in terms of male-oriented materials, rarely in terms of female-oriented, gay-oriented, or couple-oriented materials). The religious groups are especially concerned about pornography's negative impact upon women and children; they seldom express concern for its impact on males. Some of the documents deplore the censorship that the war on pornography often entails.

212. Mura, David. **A Male Grief: Notes on Pornography and Addiction.** Minneapolis, MN: Thistle Series, Milkweed Editions, 1987. 24p. pa.

This brief monograph consists of a series of reflections on pornography as a male addiction. (Mura does not consider female addiction to romance pornography.) The reflections often consist of questionable generalizations; for example: "Like all addicts, the addict to pornography dreams then of ultimate power and control." Maybe yes, maybe no.

Cross-References

See chapter 21, "Sexuality."

71. Abbott, Franklin, ed. **Men and Intimacy: Personal Accounts Exploring the Dilemmas of Modern Male Sexuality.**

8

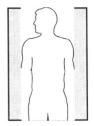

Feminism: Feminisms, Critiques of Feminism, Feminist Critiques

213. Brown, Wendy. **Manhood and Politics: A Feminist Reading in Political Theory.** Totowa, NJ: Rowman and Littlefield, 1988. xiii, 231p. (New Feminist Perspectives Series). bibliography, 215-23. notes. index. pa.

In this thoughtful analysis, Brown argues that politics has borne a masculine identity throughout history. Seeking freedom from constraint, masculinist politics tends to produce fetters. The bulk of Brown's study is devoted to three major figures of Western political theory. Rejecting Hannah Arendt's analysis of Aristotle as enthusiastic but flawed, Brown sees Aristotle's thought producing alienation of ruler from ruled and mind (male) from body (female). In Machiavelli, politics becomes a way for men to achieve manhood through ambition; yet the struggle of manly *virtù* to conquer feminine *fortuna* creates a man-made jungle. Max Weber's account of politics arising from warrior consociations ends in politics stifling the life it supposedly protects. In the final chapters on "post masculinist" politics, Brown faults feminist thinkers for oversimplified notions of power and for demonizing men. "Not maleness but [some?] institutionalized ideals of manhood are the problem." Brown challenges feminists (and men?) to discover a new politic that will sustain life.

214. Collard, Andrée, with Joyce Contrucci. **Rape of the Wild: Man's Violence against Animals and the Earth.** Bloomington and Indianapolis: Indiana University Press, 1989. xvii, 187p. notes. index. pa.

An example of radical ecofeminist writing, Collard's polemic is laced with sensitivity for women, animals, and plants, but with a toxic hatred for men. All sins against the ecosystem, in Collard's view, have been committed by men and their creations—patriarchy, capitalism, science, Western civilization, and Judeo-Christian religion. Special pleading pervades the book. Discussing the hunting and trapping of animals, Collard writes as if women in earlier cultures never trapped animals, never wore fur clothing, and never ate meat. Discussing the use of laboratory animals, she writes as if no women biologists or laboratory assistants ever experimented on animals. Men are to blame for everything. Do some women love fur coats? That is because male advertisers have brainwashed them. Better yet, male advertisers have convinced men to give fur coats to women (and the men presumably force the women to wear them). Predictably, Collard waxes poetic over the mythical golden age of prehistoric matriarchal societies when mothers ruled over non-hierarchical communes. The introduction by Mary Daly seethes with her usual vitriolic misandry. The epilogue by Joyce Contrucci profiles the life of Collard, who died in 1986.

215. Davidson, Nicholas. **The Failure of Feminism.** Buffalo, NY: Prometheus Books, 1988. 392p. appendix. bibliography, 349-50. notes. index.

This extensive analysis of U.S. feminism finds it fatally flawed by messianic ideology and naive assumptions. Although recognizing the need to redress social wrongs suffered by women as well as the positive victories achieved by feminism, Davidson finds the movement maimed by its hatred of men and masculinity, its paradoxical devaluing of the feminine, and its commitment to unisexism (i.e., a belief that the sexes are fundamentally the same). Davidson locates the origins of the current wave of U.S. feminism in the turbulence of the sixties, and he documents its depreciation of feminine values and roles in such works as *The Feminine Mystique, Sexual Politics* (entry 680), and *The Female Eunuch*. The Feminist Era, which he dates from 1969 to 1984, was punctuated by a series of failures. Ideologically, feminism narrowed itself to a belief that men have caused all the world's evils through "patriarchy" while women have remained an innocent, subjugated class. Feminism forced both women and men into inauthentic "New Woman" and "New Man" roles. Part 2 of the book argues that, by politicizing sex as power politics, feminists robbed heterosexual love of its joy and spontaneity. In public politics, feminists virtually ensured the defeat of the ERA, anti-pornography laws, day-care and comparable worth schemes, and the candidacy of Geraldine Ferraro. In part 3, Davidson locates the failures of feminist theory in cultural determinism that ignores biosocial gender differences. Part 4 looks beyond current feminism to new recognition of gender distinctiveness, the validation of feminine and masculine behaviors, and the abandonment of unisexism. In "An Open Letter to American Men," Davidson urges men to defend themselves from misandric attacks, champion authentic masculinity, and listen carefully to the feminine voice of women. The appendix offers advice on how to counter typical rhetorical tactics of messianic feminists.

216. Davidson, Nicholas, ed. **Gender Sanity.** Lanham, MD: University Press of America, 1989. ix, 260p. bibliography, 245-48. notes. index.

The 17 essays in this volume present a conservative critique of feminist ideology and practice. The crux of the argument is found in three essays in part 4: Davidson's own attack on cultural determinism, Steven Goldberg's argument that biology predetermines patriarchal and male dominant social structures, and Yves Christen's essay on "Sex Differences in the Human Brain." Other writers attack the negative effects of feminist ideology on women (in part 1), on men (in part 2), and on children (in part 3). The essays on men include Jack Kammer's observations on the ubiquitousness of male bashing, Jane Young and John Rossler's assessment of America's devaluation of fatherhood, and Frank Zepezauer's analysis of the trashing of masculinity in the arts. In part 5, five articles assail feminist distortions of truth. R. L. McNeely and Gloria Robinson-Simpson address domestic violence as a falsely framed issue, Carol Iannone examines distortions in feminist scholarship, and Margarita Levin surveys some peculiar feminist responses to "male" science. In the final essay, George Gilder decries "the myth of role revolution." As Davidson points out in his preface, the viewpoints expressed here have often been suppressed by the "lace curtain" of feminist censorship in publishing.

217. Fordham, Jim, with Andrea Fordham. **The Assault on the Sexes.** New Rochelle, NY: Arlington House, 1977. 480p. illus. bibliography, 469-74. index.

From a conservative perspective, the Fordhams take on feminist activists, "sexperts," the media, and others who assault traditional sex roles and the family. They deplore the trendy denigration of housewives and resent the assumption of some feminists that they speak for all women. The authors question the media's love affair with fiery feminist rhetoric and the obligatory daily quota of "feminist news." They question some feminist scholarship, in particular that in Betty Friedan's *The Feminine Mystique* and in Jessie Bernard's *The Future of Marriage*. They argue that feminist language (e.g., "sexism," "male chauvinist") does not describe reality but is used to manipulate unthinking responses. The authors insist that the push for "equality" and "options" will actually enforce unisex standards and behaviors. The Fordhams support special privileges for women and reject equal military obligations for both sexes. They say they support equal pay for equal work but argue that men are paid more because they are legally responsible for supporting wives and families, a situation the authors presumably do not wish to see remedied.

218. Franks, Helen. **Goodbye Tarzan: Men After Feminism.** London: George Allen and Unwin, 1984. 231p. bibliography, 223-27. index.
Interviewing 70 British men, ages 19-59, as well as groups of adolescent boys 15-18, Franks constructs a mosaic of male reactions to feminism. Actually, Franks uses snippets from the interviews to present her feminist views on matters such as masculinity, male bonding and homophobia, the constrictions of the breadwinner role, the "deprived father" after divorce, fatherhood, sons of feminist mothers, men's health, women at work, the men's movement, and future gender roles. Some readers may wish that Franks had let the men speak more than she does, and that she had generalized less about men and women. Her efforts to depict Warren Farrell's *The Liberated Man* (entry 95) and Herb Goldberg's *Hazards of Being Male* (entry 103) as anti-feminist tracts do not inspire confidence.

219. Freedman, C. H. **Manhood Redux: Standing up to Feminism.** Brooklyn, NY: Samson, 1985. viii, 294p. notes. pa.
A conservative journalist, Freedman levels a host of charges at radical feminists. He accuses them of censorship in academia and in the publishing industry, of fostering hostility between the sexes, of intolerance toward non-feminist women, and of ignoring inherent sex differences in their quest for a spurious equality. Freedman deplores the forced hiring of less qualified female police officers and the lowering of firefighter requirements in order to accommodate feminist demands. He feels that women cannot meet standards for combat soldiers. In a section devoted to men as the "oppressed" sex, he denounces such matters as the male-only military obligation, job discrimination against men, the inequities of divorce settlements, the justice system's discrimination against males, and the legal scams by which women who kill men are exonerated. To muster resistance to radical feminism's hegemony, Freedman calls for abolition of women's professional sports (so that women athletes will have to compete with male athletes), support for women like Phyllis Schlafly (who engineered the stunning defeat of the ERA), and rejection of male feminists, who are despised by the female feminists they support.

220. Friedman, Scarlet, and Elizabeth Sarah, eds. **On the Problem of Men: Two Feminist Conferences.** London: Women's Press, 1982. ix, 262p. bibliographies at the end of some chapters. notes. pa.
This collection of 20 radical feminist papers from two British conferences contains essays on such matters as family, sex, pornography, rape, fathers, male feminists, the men's movement, and raising sons. Whatever the topic, relations between the sexes are invariably reduced to Marxist formulations of male "oppression" and female "struggle."

221. Gittelson, Natalie. **Dominus: A Woman Looks at Men's Lives.** New York: Farrar, Straus & Giroux, 1978. ix, 291p. Reprint, New York: Harcourt Brace Jovanovich, 1979. pa.

Casting a skeptical eye on the women's liberation movement of the seventies and on male reaction to it, Gittelson draws upon "hundreds" of interviews in the United States and Europe to argue that "the so-called feminist revolution has transformed the consciousness of American men more dramatically, more decisively—and perhaps more dangerously—than the consciousness of women." Denied the opportunity to exercise *dominus* (masterly leadership), U.S. men have developed questionable substitutes, including "vaginal men" who disparage masculinity, nice guys who have attempted to placate militant feminists and who have become male chauvinists in the process, and callous macho types who overreact to the women's challenge. Nostalgic for men who can exercise *dominus* gracefully, Gittelson locates modern decadence in the narcissistic lives of materialistic singles, in the guilt mongering of some pro-feminist men, and in the relationships between supermen and wonder women in which caring means losing and freedom means loneliness. She sees black men as reveling in *dominus* at the very time when white men are jettisoning it; she notes the hostility that underlies some men's support for women's rights (for these men, equality is the best revenge). After exploring the status of European gender relationships and the battle of the sexes in corporate life, Gittelson writes movingly of male blue-collar workers facing angry wives and single parenthood. She is critical of gay liberation's attempt to become gay imperialism and of the antics of sexual liberation gurus. Acidly suave and eminently quotable, Gittelson presents a stimulating case for men to rethink their rejection of *dominus*.

222. Gordon, John. **The Myth of the Monstrous Male, and Other Feminist Fables.** New York: Playboy Press, 1982. xv, 253p. bibliography, 251-53.

In this lively polemic, Gordon takes issue with some current trends of militant feminism. Describing himself as a feminist who supports equal rights and opportunities, Gordon goes on to offer a riposte to feminist tracts such as Susan Brownmiller's *Against Our Will* (entry 908), Marilyn French's *The Women's Room,* Kate Millett's *Sexual Politics* (entry 680), Adrienne Rich's *Of Woman Born,* Mary Daly's *Gyn/Ecology,* and Ashley Montagu's *The Natural Superiority of Women.* He contends that the women's liberation movement has become sexually repressive, linking itself to the antisexual elements of earlier women's movements. He regards the men-are-oppressors stereotypes of some modern feminists as a variant of men-are-sexual-beasts stereotypes of older feminists. In the past, he argues, women pretended to be asexual creatures; they granted sex to the hungry male only in exchange for marriage, which included the male's commitment to lifetime financial support. The recent women's movement, which initially promised to liberate women from hypocritical bargaining, is now becoming reluctant to surrender the power that such bargaining confers on them. "As for men," Gordon concludes, "their need right now is not for the much-vaunted right to cry, but simply to get very damned angry at what is being said about them as a sex, and at the everywhere-manifest consequences of the propaganda."

223. Hagan, Kay Leigh, ed. **Women Respond to the Men's Movement: A Feminist Collection.** New York: Pandora, HarperCollins, 1992. xiv, 176p. illus. pa.

The women of the title are radical feminists such as Margo Adair, Phyllis Chesler, and Starhawk. Their responses are contained in 18 short essays, plus an introduction by Gloria Steinem, a short story by Ursula K. Le Guin, and three cartoons by Nicole Hollander. The men's movement of the title is the mythopoetic movement, with Robert Bly's *Iron John* (entry 861) as the central text. Overwhelmingly, the responses are hostile and defensive. Criticism is directed against several aspects of the mythopoetic movement, including its belief in innate sexual differences, its injunction that boys break with the Mother and bond with the Father (most of the essays are hostile to fathers, fatherhood, and patriarchy), and its use of "warrior" imagery (several writers believe it encourages male violence against women). Because the writers regard males as a powerful, privileged class of oppressors, they feel threatened by what they fear is a return of male power. Several authors favor a men's movement, but only if it espouses radical feminism. Some essays are man-hating (e.g., Jane Caputi and Gordene O. MacKenzie's diatribe against "cockocratic power"; Phyllis Chesler's harangue against fathers' rights). A few essays offer helpful suggestions (e.g., Zsuzsanna Emese Budapest contributes alternative rituals of male initiation; Myriam Miedzian provides practical suggestions for engaging fathers more closely in child rearing).

224. Jardine, Alice, and Paul Smith, eds. **Men in Feminism.** New York and London: Methuen, 1987. ix, 288p. notes. pa.
    This collection of 24 contributions grew out of a pair of conference seminars. Because female feminists in academia tend to regard males as an oppressor class and because they regard feminism as woman-centered activity, the question of where pro-feminist male academics fit into the movement is awkward. In the opening essay, Stephen Heath argues that men do not belong in feminism at all; their only proper response is admiration. Paul Smith, however, argues that pro-feminist males can support the cause and even contribute insights. Female feminist responses to such suggestions alternate between amusement and anger. Often, male feminists are suspected of trying to beat women at their own game, to be better feminists than women are. Elaine Showalter, for example, finds the film *Tootsie* to be sexist for just this reason: a male character assumes female guise and shows the women how to be good feminists. Showalter also berates Jonathan Culler for presuming to "read like a woman" and Terry Eagleton for trying to appropriate feminism for his own Marxist purposes. Nancy K. Miller berates Denis Donoghue for raising questions of excellence about women's writings. (Donoghue is not a male feminist, and his contribution, "A Criticism of One's Own," is printed in a different type to underline its outcast status.) Rosi Braidotti believes men wish to appropriate the glory of women's status as victims. Much of the critical theory discussed in the volume is French: the names of Roland Barthes, Hélène Cixous, Michel Foucault, Luce Irigaray, and Jacques Lacan are frequently invoked, and an edited seminar with Jacques Derrida is included. In the final selection, the transcript of a dialogue, Jardine and Smith reflect on issues raised in the collection. For a discussion of male feminist criticism, readers should see entry 392.

225. Levin, Michael. **Feminism and Freedom.** New Brunswick, NJ, and Oxford, England: Transaction Books, 1987. xi, 336p. bibliography, 307-23. notes. index. pa.
    In this wholesale assault, Levin portrays feminism as a totalitarian belief system that uses government coercion to restrict people's freedoms. Denying biological innateness, feminism uses state power to enforce sexual "equality." Thus, "affirmative action" is state-sanctioned discrimination against white males, while "comparable worth" schemes are efforts to manipulate peoples' incomes through government intervention. In state-supported elementary

education, feminist indoctrination distorts reality to fit a political agenda, while in the universities, feminist scholarship falsely designates women as a class and replaces an objective search for truth with political ends. With the help of the government, feminists have reduced academic freedom and have legitimized discrimination against males. Equal opportunity in sports programs discriminates against male athletes in order to create artificial victories for female athletes. Coercive manipulation of language stems from a feminist conviction that language creates reality rather than reflects it. Putting women into combat, Levin argues, disregards traditional practices that stem from innate sexual differences. At war with the family, feminism fosters divorce and the impoverishment of ex-wives, encourages abortion, and aligns itself with homosexuality. Levin concludes that feminist rage has developed from inadequate fathering, and that men—having lost touch with their masculinity—have been tongue-tied in the face of feminist accusations.

226. Levine, Judith. **My Enemy, My Love: Man-Hating and Ambivalence in Women's Lives.** New York: Doubleday, 1992. xii, 416p. bibliography, 399-402. notes. index.

A committed feminist, Levine is troubled by the amount and intensity of man hating among U.S. feminists, and among women in general. Virulent misandry is everywhere (except in the many dictionaries that either do not contain the word *misandry* or define it weakly as "dislike of men"). Misandry is a cultural phenomenon that tears women apart: they are often close to men (as fathers, brothers, lovers, husbands, sons, friends, coworkers, and so on), but they have learned to despise men as a class. Levine surveys the various stereotypes by which U.S. women now caricature men (e.g., the baby, the bumbler, the betrayer, the beast, etc.). While acknowledging some justice in some of these portraits, Levine is contemptuous of male-bashers: Jackie Collins, the author of numerous man-hating romances; conservative women like Phyllis Schlafly who distrust men too greatly to grant them legal freedoms; Phyllis Chesler, whose misandric manipulation of the facts is evident in *Mothers on Trial*; the "femi-Nazis" who rallied to the defense of Mary Beth Whitehead and characterized fathers as "sperm donors"; Susan Brownmiller, whose justification for the murder of Emmett Till in *Against Our Will* (entry 908) reeks of racism; and Catharine MacKinnon and Andrea Dworkin, whose anti-pornography ordinances barely mask their anti-male sexism. Levine traces misandry in the women's movement of the 1960s and 1970s, and she argues that man hating is born of father absence. In the final chapters, Levine provides close-ups of women coping with the split in their lives induced by the ubiquitous misandry of U.S. society.

227. Lyndon, Neil. **No More Sex War: The Failures of Feminism.** London: Sinclair-Stevenson, 1992. 250p.

The publication of this book caused a stir in Great Britain as feminists rushed to defend the faith against Lyndon's attacks. A child of the sixties, Lyndon depicts current feminism as a backlash against the freedoms and the benefits that both sexes stood to gain by events of the sixties. Although the pill and abortion provided women and men with an opportunity for greater sexual freedom, feminists could not handle the social change and retreated into man-hating puritanism. In the process, they betrayed the social reforms that men and women were striving for. Lyndon traces the roots of this misandry to misapplied Marx, Engels, and Freud. In the writings of current feminists like Germaine Greer and Rosalind Miles (entry 921), Lyndon finds examples of Nazi attitudes towards men as well as phony statistical evidence. He sees the mass of this misandry directed against the father, whom feminists are determined to drive out of the family. He disavows any men's movement, however, arguing that society needs gender unity, not a male version of the feminist sex war. Although Lyndon makes no distinction among different feminist ideologies and does not always have his facts straight, his outspoken critique of some feminist attitudes and practices will strike a chord with many readers.

228. Marine, Gene. **A Male Guide to Women's Liberation.** New York: Holt, Rinehart and Winston, 1972. vi, 312p. bibliography, 275-303. notes. index. Reprint, New York: Avon-Discus, 1974. pa.

For the confused male, Marine attempts to explain what the women's liberation movement of the late sixties and early seventies is all about. Although recognizing the excesses of some militant feminists, he regards the feminist cause as eminently just and reasonable.

229. Parturier, Françoise. **Open Letter to Men.** Translated by Joseph M. Bernstein. New York: Heineman, 1968. 173p. (Open Letter Series). pa.

Radical French feminism, 1960s style, presents itself in a dialogue between the author and a fictional male persona, who presumably speaks for the entire male sex. Parturier is convinced that males devalue women's minds and have conspired throughout history to oppress them. Some changes in perspective from the 1960s are evident: the idea that women think differently from men, now a staple of some feminist scholarship, is denounced by Parturier as part of the male plot against women. Bombarded by the author's seemingly endless accusations about men's evil intentions, some male readers may note that Parturier makes equally hostile generalizations about gay males and lesbians.

230. Porter, David, ed. **Between Men and Feminism.** London and New York: Routledge, 1992. xiv, 186p. bibliographies and notes after some chapters. pa.

Another entry in the ongoing skirmish over how pro-feminist males can relate to the dominant radical feminism of academia, this collection consists of an introduction and nine essays. In the introduction, Porter argues that, although men do not belong *in* feminism, they can occupy a space between feminism and current concepts of masculinity. This theme is reiterated in the opening essay by Joseph A. Boone. In the following essay, Naomi Segal raises a series of questions about "good" versus "sexy" men, and how both sexes are presently confused by social changes that neither sex can fully assimilate. Andrea Spurling discusses the different styles of classroom behavior exhibited by Cambridge males and females. Joseph Bristow offers critiques of two canonical feminist texts, Kate Millett's *Sexual Politics* (entry 680) and Eve Kosofsky Sedgwick's *Between Men* (entry 425). From a gay male perspective, Gregory W. Bredbeck critiques leading ideas of French feminists Hélène Cixous and Luce Irigaray. John Forrester wonders about sexual perversion actually representing male normalcy. Other essays recount the formation and evolution of the Cambridge Men's Group, Martin Humphries's experiences as a gay male with the Achilles Heel anti-sexist collective, and Jeff Hearn's Marxist update of gender politics in the personal, political, and theoretical realms.

230a. Roiphe, Katie. **The Morning After: Sex, Fear, and Feminism on Campus.** Boston: Little, Brown, 1993. xii, 180p. notes.

The feminism that Roiphe learned at her mother's knee was all about women's liberation. The feminism that Roiphe encountered at Harvard and Princeton was about a nonexistent rape crisis, extravagant accusations of sexual harassment, and women as shrinking victims of male power and lust. A feminist herself, Roiphe deplores the bunker mentality of Take Back the Night rallies, the mixed messages of feminist students who dress to get men's attention and then denounce the attention as sexist, and the puritanical fervor of Catharine MacKinnon, whose antipornography crusade has all the earmarks of a modern day witch hunt. Dismayed by the pro-feminist men who have internalized radical feminist visions of males as beasts, Roiphe sees some forms of feminism as detrimental to women's advancement and as rooted in misandry.

231. Rowan, John. **The Horned God: Feminism and Men as Wounding and Healing.** London and New York: Routledge and Kegan Paul, 1987. xi, 155p. illus. bibliography, 143-50. index.

In the first four chapters of this book, Rowan describes his wounded efforts to respond to the challenges of British radical feminism during the 1970s and 1980s. Because radical feminists had proclaimed men as the enemy and patriarchy as entirely oppressive to women, not even the most well-intentioned male feminist could do much that was not suspect to the sisterhood. While struggling against patriarchy, Rowan estranged his wife and neglected his children (an irony that, it seems, he does not fully appreciate). After numerous conferences, position papers, therapy sessions, and a divorce, Rowan discovered masculine spirituality. Healing began when he discovered that, in addition to "the bad penis" and "the nicey-nicey penis," there is "the good penis," that is, masculinity that might be acceptable to radical feminists. Rowan advocates Goddess worship in which men assume the role of the Horned God, consort and servant to the Goddess. Dionysus and Robin Goodfellow are familiar versions of the Horned God. Rowan rejects Robert Bly's wildman as insufficiently connected to women, and he describes initiation rites that may introduce men to the Horned God. Describing his new relationship with Sue Mickleburgh, Rowan celebrates *hieros gamos*, the sacred marriage of the Goddess and her priest.

231a. Sommers, Christina Hoff. **Who Stole Feminism? How Women Have Betrayed Women.** New York: Simon and Schuster, 1994. 320p. notes. index.

Describing herself as a classical liberal feminist, Sommers laments the highjacking of the feminist movement by "gender feminists." Big name gender feminists include Gloria Steinem, Susan Faludi, Patricia Ireland, Marilyn French, and Catharine MacKinnon. While pretending to speak for all women, gender feminists are deeply alienated from most women. Gender feminists believe that they are at war with patriarchy, which they see as a political system that empowers men and victimizes women. In this gender war, the enemy is men, and the first casualty is truth. Sommers debunks the findings of several widely and uncritically reported "studies" that wildly exaggerated statistics of rape and domestic violence. Another piece of "advocacy research" "proved" that U.S. schools are shortchanging girls. (If anything, the evidence indicates that schools are shortchanging boys, Sommers argues.) Taking advantage of academic tolerance, gender feminists have infiltrated higher education where they now terrorize anyone who disagrees with them. At the base of gender feminism lies a deep-seated misandry, which has been challenged only sporadically by academic administrators and professors. Sommers believes that neither women nor liberal, mainstream feminism benefits from the lies and misandry that gender feminists perpetuate.

Cross-References

See chapter 19, "Patriarchy, Patriarchal Society," and chapter 26, "Women and Men."

74. Astrachan, Anthony. **How Men Feel: Their Responses to Women's Demands for Equality and Power.**

76. Baber, Asa. **Naked at Gender Gap: A Man's View of the War Between the Sexes.**

389. Balbert, Peter. **D. H. Lawrence and the Phallic Imagination: Essays on Sexual Identity and Feminist Misreading.**

884. Bianchi, Eugene C., and Rosemary R. Reuther. **From Machismo to Mutuality: Essays on Sexism and Woman-Man Liberation.**

885. Bloesch, Donald G. **Is the Bible Sexist? Beyond Feminism and Patriarchalism.**

392. Boone, Joseph, and Michael Cadden, eds. **Engendering Men: The Question of Male Feminist Criticism.**

598. Chapman, Rowena, and Jonathan Rutherford, eds. **Male Order: Unwrapping Masculinity.**

396. Claridge, Laura, and Elizabeth Langland, eds. **Out of Bounds: Male Writers and Gender(ed) Criticism.**

981. Cline, Sally, and Dale Spender. **Reflecting Men at Twice Their Natural Size.**

1031. Cockburn, Cynthia. **In the Way of Women: Men's Resistance to Sex Equality in Organizations**.

889. Eller, Vernard. **The Language of Canaan and the Grammar of Feminism.**

945. Elshtain, Jean Bethke. **Women and War.**

95. Farrell, Warren. **The Liberated Man.**

96. Farrell, Warren. **The Myth of Male Power: Why Men Are the Disposable Sex.**

98. Fasteau, Marc Feigen. **The Male Machine.**

102. Gilder, George. **Men and Marriage.**

498. Green, Maureen. **Fathering.**

956. Jeffords, Susan. **The Remasculinization of America: Gender and the Vietnam War.**

993. Kammer, Jack. **Good Will Toward Men: Women Talk About Fairness and Respect as a Two-Way Street.**

407. Kiberd, Declan. **Men and Feminism in Modern Literature.**

282. Kimmel, Michael S., and Thomas E. Mosmiller, eds. **Against the Tide: Pro-feminist Men in the United States, 1776-1990: A Documentary History.**

997. Kingma, Daphne Rose. **The Men We Never Knew: Women's Role in the Evolution of a Gender.**

121. Mailer, Norman. **The Prisoner of Sex.**

1045. Messner, Michael A., and Donald F. Sabo, eds. **Sport, Men, and the Gender Order: Critical Feminist Perspectives.**

680. Millett, Kate. **Sexual Politics.**

124. Moore, John H. **But What About Men? After Women's Lib.**

369. Reed, Ishmael. **Reckless Eyeballing.**

133. Roberts, Yvonne. **Man Enough: Men of Thirty-five Speak Out.**

927. Schechter, Susan. **Women and Male Violence: The Visions and Struggles of the Battered Women's Movement.**

618. Segal, Lynne. **Slow Motion: Changing Masculinities, Changing Men.**

928. Shupe, Anson, William A. Stacy, and Lonnie R. Hazlewood. **Violent Men, Violent Couples: The Dynamics of Domestic Violence.**

139. Skjei, Eric, and Richard Rabkin. **The Male Ordeal: Role Crisis in a Changing World.**

140. Snodgrass, Jon, ed. **For Men Against Sexism: A Book of Readings.**

647. Spender, Dale, ed. **Men's Studies Modified: The Impact of Feminism on the Academic Disciplines.**

667. Staples, Robert. **Black Masculinity: The Black Man's Role in American Society.**

623. Stoltenberg, John. **Refusing to Be a Man: Essays on Sex and Justice.**

295. Strauss, Sylvia. **"Traitors to the Masculine Cause": The Men's Campaign for Women's Rights.**

900. Tennis, Diane. **Is God the Only Reliable Father?**

143. Thomas, David. **Not Guilty: The Case in Defense of Men.**

146. Tolson, Andrew. **The Limits of Masculinity: Male Identity and the Liberated Woman.**

147. Vilar, Esther. **The Manipulated Male.**

1027. Walczak, Yvette. **He and She: Men in the Eighties.**

296. White, Kevin. **The First Sexual Revolution: The Emergence of Male Heterosexuality in Modern America.**

9

Health and Related Topics

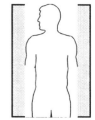

A. AIDS

With males as its primary victims, AIDS requires attention in a men's studies bibliography. From the enormous amount of AIDS literature published during the last decade, this section lists a few books with special interest for men.

232. Coyle, Susan L., Robert F. Boruch, and Charles F. Turner, eds. **Evaluating AIDS Prevention Programs.** Expanded ed. Washington, DC: National Academy Press, 1991. xii, 376p. appendixes. bibliography after each chapter. index. pa.

The product of a panel of scholars, this book examines a series of AIDS information and prevention programs asking three questions about them: what interventions were actually delivered? does the intervention make a difference? and what interventions or variations work better? Half of the volume is devoted to six appendixes examining methodologies and other matters.

233. Ford, Michael Thomas. **100 Questions and Answers About AIDS: A Guide for Young People.** New York: New Discovery Books, Macmillan, 1992. 202p. (An Open Door Book). illus. glossary. index.

In clear prose, Ford answers 100 questions about the nature of HIV and AIDS, facts and falsehoods concerning the disease, keeping safe from the disease, and testing and treatment for AIDS. Four interviews with people who contracted AIDS mark the four sections of the text. A resource guide of agencies and hotlines is included, as well as a glossary of terms.

234. Froman, Paul Kent. **Pathways to Wellness: Strategies for Self-Empowerment in the Age of AIDS.** New York: Penguin Books, Plume Book, 1990. 282p. bibliography, 281-82. pa.

Aimed primarily (but not exclusively) at an audience of gay men, Froman offers advice on how to cope with the age of AIDS. For both those who have tested HIV positive and those who have not, he urges a strategy of wellness as opposed to destructive, victim thinking. Empowerment requires a victim-ectomy, that is, a release of negative emotions, self-hate, and helplessness. Forgiving, healing, positive thinking, loving others—all are coping strategies. Froman offers tools for creating wellness, for stress reduction, for problem solving, and for other life-affirming actions.

235. Fumento, Michael. **The Myth of Heterosexual AIDS.** New York: Basic Books, A New Republic Book, 1989. xv, 411p. appendix. notes. index.

In the late 1980s, the notion arose that U.S. society would exhibit sufficient interest in AIDS only if people no longer thought of the virus as only a gay disease. Hence, some activists, journalists, and politicians began to push the idea of an imminent AIDS plague among heterosexuals. Fumento records how the scare stories spread nationwide, fueled by left- and right-wing over-reactions, Hollywood, and media hype. The misinformation damaged the credibility of responsible AIDS awareness activists, did a great disservice to gays and drug users who were at high risk from AIDS, and created racist fears about the peoples of Africa and Haiti as the originators of an AIDS plague. Fumento provides evidence of the dismal mishandling of the AIDS problem.

236. Melton, J. Gordon. **The Churches Speak On: AIDS: Official Statements from Religious Bodies and Ecumenical Organizations.** Detroit: Gale Research, 1989. xxiii, 203p. index. pa.

Melton has collected over 50 official statements about AIDS from the Roman Catholic Church, Protestant and Eastern Orthodox Churches, and Jewish Groups, as well as Buddhist, Mormon, Islamic, Unitarian-Universalist, Neo-Paganism and New Age organizations. Although mainstream Christian and Jewish groups question such matters as sexual promiscuity and the use of condoms to prevent sexual diseases, nearly all express compassion for AIDS sufferers, and they call for dedication to ending the scourge. Nearly all reject the notion that AIDS is a plague from God, and they caution believers about cold-hearted responses to AIDS sufferers.

237. Shilts, Randy. **And the Band Played On: Politics, People, and the AIDS Epidemic.** New York: St. Martin's Press, 1987. xxiii, 630p. notes. index. Reprint, New York: Penguin Books, 1988. pa.

When the first victims of AIDS appeared in the mid-1970s, the disease was simply baffling. By the early 1980s, however, it was clear to many people that a major epidemic was brewing. Swift and compassionate action might have contained the situation, but those in power preferred to ignore what many thought of as "gay cancer." After Rock Hudson died in October 1985, the United States was at last fully aware of AIDS as a killer disease. But by then it was too late. In this moving and panoramic nonfiction narrative of the delayed response to AIDS, Shilts presents the tragedy in personal and political terms.

238. Turner, Charles F., Heather G. Miller, and Lincoln E. Moses, eds. **AIDS: Sexual Behavior and Intravenous Drug Use.** Washington, DC: National Academy Press, 1989. xiii, 589p. appendixes. bibliography after each chapter. index. pa.

Compiled by a national panel convened to study AIDS, this scholarly and clearly written book contains a wealth of information about the nature of HIV infection and its spread across the United States. In addition, the authors make recommendations to contain the AIDS epidemic, and they examine the barriers to future research and intervention. One appendix consolidates all the authors' recommendations into a single unit; the second provides supplementary data and tables about AIDS. The book also includes six background papers. Particularly interesting is Tom W. Smith's critique of the methodology used by Shere Hite in her 1987 study *Women and Love*: those who suspected Hite's accuracy will find their suspicions confirmed here.

B. Men's Health, Circumcision, the Prostate, and Related Topics

For additional materials on male sexual or reproductive health, readers should consult chapter 21, "Sexuality: A. Heterosexuality."

239. American Medical Association. **Men: How to Understand Your Symptoms.** Edited by Charles B. Clayman and Jeffrey R.M. Kunz. New York: Random House, 1986. 128p. illus. index. pa.

In clear prose, this book describes symptoms and treatments of common male ailments. The discussion is organized around "pain sites" in the head, brain, eyes, ears, mouth, muscles, skin, heart, abdominal area, genitals, and so on. Drawings convey important information visually. The text provides a medication guide, with warnings about possible side-effects. The final section of the book is devoted to sexual and fertility problems.

240. Cant, Gilbert. **Male Trouble: A New Focus on the Prostate.** New York: Praeger, 1976. xiv, 146p. (A Frank E. Taylor Book). illus. index.

Cant's book has four objectives: to acquaint lay readers with basic information about prostatic health and disease, to encourage men to seek medical attention at the first signs of disorder, to recommend routine rectal examinations earlier in life, and to indicate that, despite much surrounding mystery, prostatic troubles can often be treated effectively. Cant describes the urogenital system, the disorders that can involve the prostate, and the different treatments for them. He describes the effects of prostatic troubles on men and looks to future research for additional solutions.

241. Diagram Group. **Man's Body: An Owner's Manual.** New York: Paddington Press, 1976. (unpaged) ca. 250p. illus. index. Reprint, New York: Bantam Books, 1977. pa.

This compendium of information and statistics about men's bodies contains over 1,000 drawings, diagrams, and charts. The 12 sections of the book cover essential information about such matters as the development of the male body from conception to old age; life expectancy for males, including principal causes of death; illnesses; body care, especially of skin, hair, and teeth; the mind and body connection; physical fitness and exercise; food, including gaining and losing weight; drugs, alcohol, and smoking; male sex organs, potency, and sterility; sexuality, intercourse, contraception, homosexuality; and aging. The final section briefly describes the woman's body. The attractive format makes basic information about men's bodies available to a wide range of readers.

242. Editors of *Men's Health Magazine*. **How a Man Stays Young.** Emmaus, PA: Rodale Press, 1993. xiv, 300p. illus. index. pa.

In clear, crisp prose, the authors offer upbeat advice on maintaining physical and mental health. They discuss such matters as diet, healthful recreations, male-male activities, and learning to argue therapeutically. Men are different from women, the editors insist unapologetically, and men need to pursue their well-being in manly ways. They praise the value of frequent sex, an aspirin every other day, and regular medical exams. They advise men to avoid excessive amounts of sun, alcohol, and high-cholesterol foods. Numerous other topics are covered, including sleep, grooming, exercise, and work habits. The final chapter provides answers to the most frequently asked questions received by *Men's Health*.

243. Friedman, Meyer, and Ray H. Rosenman. **Type A Behavior and Your Heart.** New York: Alfred A. Knopf, 1974. x, 274, xp. illus. index. Reprint, Greenwich, CT: Fawcett, 1978. pa.

Heart disease respects neither class nor race, but in the past it has preyed particularly on U.S. men. Considering the sure and possible causes of this killer, the authors of this popular study focus on "Type A behavior," a pattern marked by stress, hurrying, and noncommunication. Other contributing causes are investigated, including cholesterol, diabetes mellitus, diet, and smoking. Exercise is no cure-all and may sometimes be contributory. In the closing chapters, Friedman and Rosenman provide guidelines for modifying Type A behavior. Although the connection between U.S. masculine gender roles and coronary disease is touched upon, readers may wish it had been probed more deeply.

244. Julty, Sam. **Men's Bodies, Men's Selves.** New York: Dell, Delta, 1979. 453p. illus. bibliography after each chapter. notes. pa.

Described as "the complete guide to the health and well-being of men's bodies, minds, and spirits," Julty's book is aimed at men seeking to liberate themselves from the binds inherent in traditional masculinity. The 13 chapters include discussions of work, relationships with women, marriage and divorce, homosexuality, physical health, mental health, fathering, aging, sexuality, male genitalia, birth control and abortion, venereal disease, and rape. A storehouse of information, illustrated liberally with photographs and drawings, the text of this book is punctuated with editorials, autobiographical accounts, documents, definitions of unfamiliar terms, and other useful materials. Each chapter closes with an annotated list of suggested readings compiled by James Creane and a helpful listing of resources (e.g., newsletters, organizations, films, government agencies) compiled by Paul Siudzinski.

245. Pesmen, Curtis, and the Editors of *Esquire*. **How a Man Ages.** New York: Ballantine Books, Ballantine/Esquire Press Book, 1984. xiii, 226p. illus. bibliography, 215-17. notes. index. pa.

In clear, concise style, Pesmen describes the aging process in males and suggests ways to minimize its deleterious effects. Chapters are devoted to skin, hair, eyes, hearing, the mouth, bones and muscles, sexuality and sex organs, the heart, lungs and kidneys, the brain and memory, stamina and fitness, and nutrition and weight control.

246. Rous, Stephen N. **The Prostate Book: Sound Advice on Symptoms and Treatment.** Rev. ed. New York: W. W. Norton, 1988. 273p. illus. glossary.

Written for lay readers, this book describes the prostate and its normal function, the range of methods for diagnosing prostate problems, and infections and inflammations of the prostate. Separate chapters are devoted to prostate enlargement and prostatic cancer. Rous describes surgical and radiation therapy, telling what the patient can expect during each step of the treatment. A final chapter describes complications of prostate surgery. The book contains a glossary of medical terms.

247. Rowan, Robert L., and Paul J. Gillette. **Your Prostate: What It Is, What It Does, and the Diseases That Affect It.** Garden City, NY: Doubleday and Co., 1973. xv, 147p. illus. appendix. index.

For lay readers, the authors describe the male urogenital system and the prostate's part in it. They discuss disorders of the prostate (and disorders connected with it), as well as possible treatments of them. Topics include inflammation, growths, prostatitis, benign prostatic hypertrophy, cancer, trichomonas vaginalis, and premature ejaculation (which is sometimes related to problems in the prostate). A glossary of terms is included.

248. Siegel, Mary-Ellen. **Dr. Greenberger's What Every Man Should Know About His Prostate.** Rev. ed. New York: Walker, 1988. xvii, 186p. illus. appendixes. glossary. bibliography, 175-77.

This updated version of the late Monroe E. Greenberger's *What Every Man Should Know About His Prostate* (1983) was written by Greenberger's daughter. In readable prose, Siegel describes the normal prostate and various methods of urological examination. She surveys infectious and non-infectious prostatitis. Three chapters discuss prostate enlargement, cancer, and treatments. A separate chapter is devoted to the beneficial influence of zinc and other vitamins on the prostate. The final chapter discusses social and sexual activity after prostate surgery. Four appendixes provide information on when to see a urologist, questions to ask the urologist, complicating drugs, and a reference guide to further information. A glossary of medical terms in included.

249. Ursin, Holger, Eivind Baade, and Seymour Levine, eds. **Psychobiology of Stress: A Study of Coping Men.** New York: Academic Press, 1978. xv, 236p. bibliography after each chapter. index.

From 72 investigations of young men in the Norwegian Army Parachute School in 1974, 21 contributors to this study assess physiological and psychological effects upon males coping with stress.

250. Wagenvoord, James, ed. **The Man's Book: A Complete Manual of Style.** New York: Avon Books, 1978. 320p. illus. bibliography, 310-11. index. pa.

This compendium of information and advice attractively treats care of the male body and mind (including such matters as exercising, handling stress, medications, diet, skin and hair care), clothing, and social life (including jobs, money, entertaining, travel, and love and sex). The readable text is interspersed with illustrations, charts, and humorous drawings.

251. Wallerstein, Edward. **Circumcision: An American Health Fallacy.** New York: Springer, 1980. xix, 281p. illus. appendixes. notes. subject and author indexes. (Focus on Men Series, no. 1). pa.

Calling circumcision "a solution in search of a problem," Wallerstein raises important questions about the U.S. obsession with routine circumcision. About 85 percent of all U.S. male children are circumcised. While other Western countries have abandoned routine circumcision, only the United States continues the practice. He debunks past and present rationales for the operation, arguing that circumcision does not prevent masturbation, venereal disease, premature ejaculation, or anything else. The foreskin, he argues, serves as a useful protective shield and has an erotic function. Moreover, the circumcision operation can lead to complications, and the pain and trauma of infant circumcision (usually performed without anesthetic) may have unknown harmful effects upon the male psyche. For entirely irrational reasons, the practice of routine circumcision lingers on in the United States, long after the medical profession should have discouraged it. Three appendixes cover the details of the surgery, its frequency in U.S. history, and an almost unknown statement against routine circumcision issued in 1975 by the American College of Obstetricians and Gynecologists.

252. Young, Frank R. **Yoga for Men Only.** West Nyack, NY: Parker, 1969. x, 214p. illus. index.

Revealing "well guarded Yoga secrets," Young describes how yoga exercises can overcome the "four Horsemen of the Mastabah" (the early grave): constant pull of gravity, faulty posture, weight-bearing, and ground resistance. The author makes extraordinary claims for Yoga, promising, among other things, greater sex appeal, self-mastery, personal energy, powerful muscles, and popularity. The book is punctuated with success stories (e.g., "How 49-Year-Old Alfred, Who Was Avoided Generally, Swept People Off Their Feet By Relieving His Subchronic Aches and Pains"). Readers will have to decide for themselves whether Young's approach represents Oriental wisdom or a snake-oil pitch.

C. Vasectomy, Male Fertility, Contraception

253. Carson, Rubin. **The Coward's Guide to Vasectomy.** Marina del Rey, CA: Schmidt and Hill, 1973. xiv, 174p. illus. appendix. Reprint, New York: Pinnacle Books, 1982. pa.

Providing facts and fun for the fainthearted, Carson attempts to dispel male misgivings about vasectomy. He also devotes a chapter to female cowards considering their own sterilization. The appendix lists Planned Parenthood Centers, Zero Population Growth chapters, and information concerning the Association for Voluntary Sterilization. The text is abetted by Michael Bedard's comic illustrations.

254. Fleishman, Norman, and Peter L. Dixon. **Vasectomy, Sex and Parenthood.** Garden City, NY: Doubleday, 1973. xv, 128p. appendixes. bibliography, 126-28.

Stressing the need for population control, this book for lay readers includes a personal account of what it is like to undergo vasectomy, answers frequently asked questions about the operation, and raises questions that men should ask before having it. One chapter contains Diane Fleishman's account of the positive marital effects of her husband's vasectomy. The appendixes list vasectomy clinics in the United States, organizations concerned with vasectomy, and sperm banks.

255. Fried, John J. **Vasectomy: The Truth and Consequences of the Newest Form of Birth Control—Male Sterilization**. New York: Saturday Review Press, 1972. 148p. bibliography, 144-48.

In contrast to cheerleaders for vasectomy, Fried raises questions about it. He discusses possible complications from the operation, as well as its possible effects upon the body's immune system. He stresses the irreversibility of vasectomy and its negative psychological consequences, especially when it is performed to save a rocky marriage or when the man's masculine identity is shaky. Readers will have to decide whether Fried is alarmist or soundly cautious.

256. Gillette, Paul J. **Vasectomy: The Male Sterilization Operation.** New York: Paperback Library, 1972. 235p. illus. appendixes. bibliography, 229-35. pa. Reprint as, *The Vasectomy Information Manual,* New York: Outerbridge and Lazard, 1972.

A popular information guide, this book examines the need for population control, the question of what kind of men should consider vasectomy, an explanation of how conception occurs, and a description of a vasectomy operation. Aside from sterilization, vasectomy usually has either positive or nonexistent effects upon male sexuality. Gillette examines the legal implications and religious responses to vasectomy, medical views of the operation, and the methods of attempting to reverse it. A chapter is devoted to salpingectomy, the female sterilization operation. A question-and-answer section, personal accounts, and endorsements for the operation conclude the book.

257. Greenfield, Michael, and William M. Burrus. **The Complete Reference Book on Vasectomy.** New York: Avon Books, 1973. 253p. illus. appendixes. bibliography, 173-253. pa.

Part 1 of this book answers questions raised by those considering vasectomy. Topics include a brief history of vasectomy, men who might not be good candidates for the operation, what the operation consists of, whether or not it is reversible ("don't count on it"), and whether or not it will affect masculinity ("it won't"). Part 2 consists of a married couple's accounts of how the husband's vasectomy improved their lives. In part 3, the authors provide information for men seeking a vasectomy, including questions raised by candidates for the operation. About half of the book consists of appendixes and a bibliography. The three appendixes list vasectomy clinics, genetic counseling facilities, and insurance information. An extensive annotated bibliography covers worldwide research on vasectomy.

258. Kasirsky, Gilbert. **Vasectomy, Manhood and Sex.** New York: Springer, 1972. 128p. illus. appendixes. bibliography after each chapter. pa.

This popularly written book answers principal questions about vasectomy, explains the reasons for having the operation, describes the surgical procedures, discusses its aftereffects and the possibilities of reversing the operation, and lists the ethical responses of major religious organizations. A chapter by Elaine Kasirsky presents her positive assessment of the operation, and the foreword by Helen Edey discusses the book's value for doctors and for men contemplating vasectomy. The appendixes show the instruments used in the operation and sample consent forms, discuss vasectomy around the world, and list places in the United States where men can obtain a vasectomy.

259. Lader, Lawrence, ed. **Foolproof Birth Control: Male and Female Sterilization**. Boston: Beacon Press, 1972. viii, 286p. illus. appendixes. index.

This collection of forty-two brief essays on male and female sterilization considers such topics as reasons for having a vasectomy, accounts of the operation, its effects upon men's physical and mental health, the difficulty of reversing vasectomy, frozen-semen banks, costs, and overcoming obstructions to voluntary sterilization. Of the four appendixes, one lists vasectomy clinics in the United States.

260. Mancini, R. E., and L. Martini, eds. **Male Fertility and Sterility.** London and New York: Academic Press, 1974. xvi, 588p. (Proceedings of the Serono Symposia, vol. 5). illus. bibliographies after each chapter. author index.

Fifty percent of sterility in couples is due to male infertility. The 32 scholarly studies in this volume examine the various facets of andrology—the morphology, physiology, pathology, and clinical aspects of the male genital tract—with major emphasis on understanding and treating male infertility.

261. Raspé, Gerhard, ed. **Schering Workshop on Contraception: The Masculine Gender (Berlin, November 29 to December 2, 1972).** Oxford: Pergamon Press; Braunschweig: Vieweg, 1973. vii, 332p. (Advances in the Biosciences, 10). illus. bibliography after each chapter. index.

This collection of 24 papers from a workshop on male contraception consists primarily of reports and speculations on biological and biochemical research with implication for development of additional forms of male contraception. Lay readers may be most interested in Alfred Jost's paper "Becoming a Male" ("becoming a male is a prolonged, uneasy, and risky venture: it is a kind of struggle against inherent trends toward femaleness"); Brigitta Linnér's feminist call for equality in society, in family, and in bed; and (above all) Caroline Merula Days and David Malcolm Potts's essay "Condoms and Things," which deals with worldwide male involvement in contraception. Days and Potts argue that family planning programs are geared for female contraception when "male methods of contraception have been and remain numerically the most important in nearly all countries." These male methods include coitus interruptus, condoms, and vasectomy. In addition, males often take responsibility for female birth control (e.g., seeing that the woman has a supply of birth control pills and takes them regularly). Days and Potts conclude: "Men are in the majority of family-planning users in nearly all countries." The book closes with a manifesto of desiderata for new forms of male contraception.

262. Rosenfeld, Louis J., and Marvin Grosswirth. **The Truth About Vasectomy.** Englewood Cliffs, NJ: Prentice-Hall, 1972. 156p. appendixes. notes. index.

In language easily comprehensible to the layperson, the authors discuss the facts of vasectomy, weighing its pros and cons. After a brief question-and-answer chapter, the book quickly surveys the history of contraception, explains the male reproductive system, and describes a vasectomy operation. The authors discuss the doctor's role in advising couples, the problems that a machismo-oriented man may encounter when considering a vasectomy, women's views of vasectomy, the usually positive aftereffects of the operation, and what can (and cannot) be done if the man changes his mind afterward. Among the options are surgery, semen banks, and adoption. The appendixes contain a sample vasectomy release form, a list of vasectomy clinics and hospitals in which vasectomy is performed as an outpatient procedure, and a short list of semen banks.

263. Troen, Philip, and Howard R. Nankin, eds. **The Testis in Normal and Infertile Men.** New York: Raven Press, 1977. xiv, 578p. illus. bibliography after each chapter. notes. index.

This collection consists of 45 scholarly, technical papers, plus discussions from a 1976 conference in Pittsburgh.

264. Zorgniotti, Adrian W., ed. **Temperature and Environmental Effects on the Testis.** New York and London: Plenum Press, 1991. xi, 335p. illus. appendixes. notes. index. list of participants.

The 33 scholarly papers in this anthology represent the proceedings of a conference on temperature and environmental factors and the testis, held in December 1989, at the New York University School of Medicine. In the preface, Zorgniotti stresses that evidence presented at the conference demonstrates the centrality of temperature to testicular function and male fertility.

Cross-References

See chapter 21, "Sexuality: A. Heterosexuality."

592. Bahr, Robert. **The Virility Factor: Masculinity Through Testosterone, the Male Sex Hormone.**

601. Fanning, Patrick, and Matthew McKay. **Being a Man: A Guide to the New Masculinity.**

278. Haley, Bruce. **The Healthy Body and Victorian Culture.**

50. Lee, John H. **The Flying Boy: Healing the Wounded Man.**

51. Lee, John H. **The Flying Boy, Book II: The Journey Continues.**

707. Lenfest, David. **Men Speak Out: In the Heart of the Men's Recovery: Six Dialogues for, by and About Conscious Men.**

714. Nowinski, Joseph. **Hungry Hearts: On Men, Intimacy, Self-Esteem, and Addiction.**

969. Uhl, Michael, and Tod Ensign. **GI Guinea Pigs: How the Pentagon Exposed Our Troops to Dangers More Deadly than War: Agent Orange and Atomic Radiation.**

10

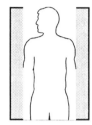

History: Historical Studies, Social History, History of Ideas

265. Barker-Benfield, G. J. **The Horrors of the Half-Known Life: Male Attitudes Toward Women and Sexuality in Nineteenth-Century America.** New York: Harper & Row, 1976. xiv, 352p. notes. index.

Examining nineteenth-century attitudes of white, U.S. males, Barker-Benfield finds male pathology expressing itself toward women and sexuality in a conspiracy of subjugation and mutilation. A rigid division of sex roles on the frontier resulted in male energy and female endurance. Moreover, U.S. women had little choice but to marry; their "freedom" was merely a compulsion to accept bondage to men. Barker-Benfield discusses the displacement of midwives by male gynecologists as part of men's war against women. The gynecological surgery of J. Marion Sims is presented as typical of a male mania for ghoulish assaults on women's genitalia. Barker-Benfield examines the anti-masturbatory fulminations of the Rev. John Todd and the vaginal operations of Dr. Augustus Kinsley Gardner. Generalizing from Todd and Gardner, the author concludes that all U.S. men were Nazis in their view of women. Barker-Benfield's research is filtered through a highly misandric lens. Card stacking is frequent. Gardner's account of the dissection of a live horse, for example, is interpreted (first) as an anti-female fantasy in which the horse represents women and (second) as a masochistic fantasy in which the horse represents Gardner. The book leaves one wondering whether some nineteenth-century views of women were any more grotesque than some twentieth-century views of men.

266. Brander, Michael. **The Victorian Gentleman.** London: Gordon Cremonesi, 1975. 215p. illus. bibliography, 206-11. index.

In this richly illustrated book, Brander examines the life of the British Victorian gentleman from birth to adulthood. Separate chapters are devoted to childhood, schooling, and university life. Adult life is covered in chapters examining taste and manners, morality and sex, sensational trials and wartime experiences, travel at home and abroad, India and empire, and sports and pastimes. Brander writes with sympathetic understanding of the masculine gender role. The text contains numerous photographs and illustrations, some in color.

267. Cady, Edwin Harrison. **The Gentleman in America: A Literary Study in American Culture.** Syracuse, NY: Syracuse University Press, 1949. 232p. notes. index. Reprint, Westport, CT: Greenwood Press, 1969.

This readable, scholarly study traces the concept of the gentleman in American life and letters. Noting that gentlemanliness is as old as history, Cady explores the eighteenth-century British contrast between the rake and the Christian gentleman. In America, a similar distinction contrasted the "fine" gentleman and the religious one, as well as the born gentleman of class and the natural gentleman of democracy. A spectacular natural gentleman, John Adams had trouble reconciling his puritan pessimism with his democratic idealism. Exalting an *aristoi* of virtue and talent, Thomas Jefferson looked to education to bring it into existence. James Fenimore Cooper held up the ideal of the agrarian gentleman, although his most memorable fictional gentlemen are noble American Indians and the natural gentleman, Natty Bumpo. While Oliver Wendell Holmes praised the gentlemanliness of proper Bostonians, Ralph Waldo Emerson championed the self-reliance of the natural gentleman who was also something of a social activist. Influenced by Leo Tolstoy's writings, William Dean Howells exalted the gentleman as socialist. In a concluding chapter, Cady sees the shift to feminism as making chivalry irrelevant; the new goal for the gentleman, he says, is discovering a self-validating way of life and thought.

268. Carnes, Mark C., and Clyde Griffen, eds. **Meanings for Manhood: Constructions of Masculinity in Victorian America.** Chicago and London: The University of Chicago Press, 1990. vi, 281p. notes. index. pa.

Twelve essays—all solidly researched and thoughtful—make up this anthology of gender history in nineteenth-century America. The essays focus only on white, middle-class males, a shortcoming that the editors readily acknowledge. The discussion of constructions of masculinity is divided into four sections: boyhood to adulthood, friendship and marriage, work and the workplace, and future research in men's history. The introduction and many of the essays indicate that men's history has already reached the point where revision of earlier work is in order. The editors criticize the tendency of some previous men's historians to over-generalize about males. Essays examine "boy culture," fraternal rituals, gender-defined forms of madness, the age's masculine social gospel, fraternal love among male abolitionists, grounds for divorce as a means of defining masculinity, and the remasculinization of printers' work. In the penultimate essay, Clyde Griffen provides a fascinating synthesis that links the previous essays, questions earlier speculation about men's history, and points forward to needed future research.

269. Castronovo, David. **The English Gentleman: Images and Ideals in Literature and Society.** New York: Ungar, 1987. x, 171p. illus. bibliography, 149-57. notes. index.

In this concise social and literary history, Castronovo surveys different types of British gentlemen as they appeared in history and in literature. Although the concept of the gentleman goes back to medieval times, Castronovo focuses primarily on the flowering of the ideal in the nineteenth century, stressing both its positive and negative aspects. He examines a wide range of authors, including Dickens, J. H. Newman, Thackeray, and Dinah Mulock. In the twentieth century, gentlemanly values and privileges have come under fire (as a look at the novels of E. M. Forster and D. H. Lawrence reveals), but they are by no means dead. Although informed, Castronovo's discussion of the British gentleman is not a gender-conscious one.

270. Cawelti, John G. **Apostles of the Self-Made Man.** Chicago: University of Chicago Press, 1965. xiv, 279p. illus. bibliography, 259-71. notes. index.

Tracing the cult of the self-made man through nineteenth- and twentieth-century America, Cawelti focuses upon three main sources of the myth: major figures like Benjamin Franklin, Thomas Jefferson, and Horatio Alger; success manuals and guides; and novels for adults and stories for children (almost always boys) in which the self-made man is a central figure. Contrasting with nineteenth-century celebrations of success in fiction and philosophy is twentieth-century ambivalence about success as a rat race rather than a dream. In addition to well-known authors like Twain, Howells, Dreiser, Fitzgerald, and Henry James, Cawelti examines the thought of John Dewey and of such popular advice givers as Norman Vincent Peale, Dale Carnegie, and Napoleon Hill. The connection between success and American masculinity, however, is not Cawelti's topic and must be inferred by the reader.

271. Clawson, Mary Ann. **Constructing Brotherhood: Class, Gender, and Fraternalism.** Princeton, NJ: Princeton University Press, 1989. ix, 270p. notes. index.

Clawson traces the rise of U.S. fraternal orders from their European origins to their peak in the early twentieth century. Fraternalism, she notes, is a social and cultural form marked by idiom, ritual, proprietorship, and masculinity. The origins of U.S. fraternalism can be found in such early modern European organizations as guilds, journeymen's societies, and confraternities. A most powerful influence was the emergence of freemasonry in England during the seventeenth and eighteen centuries. Although U.S. workingmen joined fraternal orders, the mixed blue- and white-collar membership at first prevented them from becoming workers' organizations. Fraternal orders heightened gender separation. Many women, however, endorsed the idea of separate spheres, and the fraternal orders reinforced male-provider and female-beneficiary ideology. The presence of women's auxiliaries and lodges somewhat qualified the separatism of male lodges. The fraternal orders also excluded blacks and some immigrant groups. In the twentieth century, the decrease in gender separatism and other factors led to the decline of fraternal organizations, which are now (according to Clawson) anachronisms.

271a. Darmon, Pierre. **Damning the Innocent: A History of the Persecution of the Impotent in pre-Revolutionary France**. Translated by Paul Keegan. New York: Viking Penguin, 1986. 234p. bibliography, 231-34. Original publication, as *Le Tribunal de l'Impuissance* (Paris: Editions du Seuil, 1979).

If a man could be convicted of impotence in seventeenth- and eighteenth-century France, his marriage could be annulled and the legitimacy of his offspring could be questioned. This legal situation created a series of grotesque trials involving men who were impotent, hermaphroditic, or simply falsely accused. Efforts to establish a man's virility could be equally grotesque. As an example of legal and social requirements placed by past societies upon men, the trials have an inherent interest. The trouble with this account of them, however, is that Darmon's narrative is suffused with an intrusive anger that often seems misdirected. It is as if Darmon keeps posing in front of his material, asking the reader to notice what a righteously indignant soul he is. Someone else needs to reassess more coolly the sensational materials that Darmon presents here.

272. Dubbert, Joe L. **A Man's Place: Masculinity in Transition.** Englewood Cliffs, NJ: Prentice-Hall, 1979. xi, 323p. essay on sources, 307-15. notes. index. pa.

Dubbert traces the evolution of masculinity in the United States from the early 1800s to the present, using a rich assortment of historic and literary documents. The introduction states the case for studying men and masculinity: "Compared with what we know about the identity problems of women, we know relatively little about the American male's struggle with his identity." The American masculine gender role is traced in detail, almost decade-by-decade, as it was shaped by the frontier, capitalism, the changing nature of work, religion, family roles, wars, the women's movement, sports, and numerous other factors. In the epilogue, Dubbert writes: "It has been my intention to suggest that men too have been trapped, that the identity and roles many men have assumed throughout American history have caused certain problems unique to male identity and fulfillment." The extensive notes contain a gold mine of primary materials for elucidating American masculinity.

273. Dudley, Edward, and Maximillian E. Novak, eds. **The Wild Man Within: An Image in Western Thought from the Renaissance to Romanticism.** Pittsburgh, PA: University of Pittsburgh Press, 1972. xi, 333p. illus. notes. index.

For anyone who thought that Robert Bly had invented the wild man (entry 861), this 1972 book will come as a revelation. The 11 scholarly essays describe the wild man image from ancient times through the Middle Ages and into the European discovery of the Americas, early U.S. colonial days, the Age of Reason, and the Romantic Age. Traditionally, the wild man has been raised by wolves or bears, lives in isolation, and has great physical strength and sexual appetite. He has haunted the Western imagination for centuries, appearing in various guises, from ancient mythical figures (like the cyclops) to King Kong, from Caliban in *The Tempest* to Cardenio in *Don Quixote*, from Papageno in *The Magic Flute* to the Yahoos in *Gulliver's Travels,* and from the noble savage of the Romantics to the Hunchback of Notre Dame. The editors indicate that the wild man often represents freedom from civilized control, the triumph of nature over art, and passion over abstract reasoning. This book details the rich heritage from which the current mythopoetic movement has drawn for the latest incarnation of the wild man as image of the deep masculine. For more on the wild man, see Timothy Husband, *The Wild Man: Medieval Myth and Symbolism* (entry 384).

274. Ferguson, Charles W. **The Male Attitude.** Boston: Little, Brown, 1966. xiv, 365p. notes. index.

Miffed by books like Philip Wylie's *Generation of Vipers,* which blamed America's ills on Mom, Ferguson gallantly sets out to defend womanhood by denigrating manhood. The result is a debunking of U.S. history and culture in which nearly everything that went wrong (and apparently nearly everything did) is blamed on men. Sweeping generalizations about male evil and ineptness are used to reduce history to a tale of men's inhumanity to women and other men.

274a. Filene, Peter G. **Him/Her/Self: Sex Roles in Modern America.** 2d ed. Baltimore and London: Johns Hopkins University Press, 1986. xvi, 323p. appendixes. bibliography, 239-51. notes. index. pa.

Braiding together an account of masculine and feminine gender roles, Filene surveys U.S. history from the late Victorian era to the 1980s. Filene's narrative begins at the end of the Victorian era (1890-1919) with the "new women" (who rejected Victorian womanhood) and with the suffragists. In this latest edition of his book, Filene gives a fuller hearing to those who opposed women's new roles as disruptive to family and society. The temperance movement and "the purity movement" in part were expressions of women's resentment against the double standard that apparently gave men more freedom. World War I helped to solve a crisis in masculinity by defining military virtues as manly. In the Modern Era (1920-1985) the liberated flapper disappeared from the scene during the depression of the 1930s. Feminism was a luxury as men and women coped with economic hardships, with the crises of World War II, and with the war-delayed establishment of families during the fifties. In the sixties, however, gender discontents reappeared, as women became troubled by "the feminine mystique." The movement of large numbers of women into the work force spawned a new wave of the women's movement and a smaller men's movement to cope with the stresses of gender role changes. The children of the women's movement are now toting up their losses and gains. The book closes with excerpts from Paul Cowan and Rachel Brown in which they record their attempts to handle the conflicting demands of parenthood and career in the 1980s.

275. Fraser, John. **America and the Patterns of Chivalry.** Cambridge: Cambridge University Press, 1982. x, 301p. notes. index.

   With dazzling erudition, Fraser traces the influence of chivalric ideals and practices upon numerous aspects of nineteenth- and twentieth-century American life. He examines such areas as U.S. politics, militarism, social life, literature, art, pop culture, radicalism, and education. In this study, however, the light thrown upon the U.S. masculine gender role is usually oblique.

276. Girouard, Mark. **The Return to Camelot: Chivalry and the English Gentleman.** New Haven, CT, and London: Yale University Press, 1981. 312p. illus. notes. index.

   Although it is now officially dead, the chivalric ideal has been an important shaper of modern masculinity, and a residue of chivalric behavior is still expected from men. Girouard traces the rise and fall of the cult of chivalry in Victorian and Edwardian England, including its origins and its influence on manners, sports, politics, love, and war. Extensively illustrated, *The Return to Camelot* focuses (necessarily) on the upper classes but also examines how chivalry affected the middle-class ideal of the gentleman, the curricula of British public (i.e., private) schools, and the manly virtues of the Boy Scout movement. In the early twentieth century, however, the concept of heroic combat trapped men in a rising tide of militarism that led them directly into the horrors of World War I trench warfare. Girouard depicts the absurdity, the nobility, and—finally—the tragedy of the neochivalric ideal.

277. Griswold, Robert L. **Fatherhood in America: A History.** New York: Basic Books, 1993. xi, 356p. notes. index. pa.

   The basic change in twentieth-century U.S. fatherhood has been from the breadwinner role to the "daddy track" caregiver. Nineteenth-century fatherhood was defined by breadwinning, according to Griswold. Marginalized workers and black fathers were vulnerable to unemployment and thus to psychic emasculation. Beginning with the later nineteenth century, the state took over many of the father's roles (e.g., educator). Immigrant fathers often saw a generation gap open up between them and their Americanized children. From 1920 to 1940, U.S. society called for a new fatherhood that was more companionable, but men's continuing breadwinner responsibilities often made such a role difficult to achieve. The economic depression of the 1930s devastated many fathers, and World War II took many of them away from homes. The suburban, white, middle-class father throve in the 1950s; but, since 1965, family roles have been under renegotiation as wives went out to work, husbands resisted housework and childcare, and increasing divorce separated many fathers from children. In a final chapter, Griswold surveys the current politics of father-hood, including fathers' rights organizations, the "deadbeat dad" problem, the anger of some feminists, wildmen training, and the defense of the traditional family by conservatives. The major problem confronting U.S. families today is how to accommodate working mothers and caregiving fathers.

278. Haley, Bruce. **The Healthy Body and Victorian Culture.** Cambridge: Harvard University Press, 1978. 296p. notes. index.

Haley demonstrates how British Victorian society linked healthiness with manliness until intellectuals pressed for fuller concepts of both terms. Among the eminent Victorians discussed in depth are Carlyle, Spencer, New-man, Kingsley, the Arnolds (father and son), Thomas Hughes, George Eliot, and George Meredith.

279. Hearn, Jeff. **Men in the Public Eye: The Construction and Decon-struction of Public Men and Public Patriarchies.** London and New York: Routledge, 1992. xii, 292p. (Critical Studies on Men and Masculinities Series, no. 4). bibliography, 254-75. notes. subject and name indexes. pa.

Hearn examines "public patriarchies" in recent history, focusing on late-nineteenth- and early-twentieth-century Britain. Public patriarchies are male-dominated political and social structures, which Hearn believes are uniformly harmful. Hearn's elaborate Marxist-based theorizing leads into an extensive review of turn-of-the-century British history. Among the topics explored are the blurring of public and private spheres, the different concepts of patriarchy, and the rise of British feminism. Hearn concludes that all men's organizations, even pro-feminist ones, are suspect (men being the oppressors they are) and that the running of the world is best relegated to left-wing feminist organizations.

280. Kett, Joseph F. **Rites of Passage: Adolescence in America, 1790 to the Present.** New York: Basic Books, 1977. xiii, 327p. illus. notes. index.

Kett has written a social history of adolescence in the United States, in particular of white, male adolescents. He divides American history into three periods. In part 1, the author explores the early republic, 1790-1840. He notes the contemporary indefiniteness about age and age groups, the fact that adolescent sons were expected to work, the movement of young people from the farms to the chaotic new cities, the roles of schools and religious conversions in shaping young lives, and the mixture of oppression and freedom faced by youths. Part 2, 1840-1900, describes how Americans defined adolescence first in girls, then in boys. Kett examines youthful resistance to dead-end jobs, the emergence of formal professional education, the cults of physical fitness and muscular Christianity, and organizations like the YMCA. Part 3, 1900 to the present, depicts the "invention" of adolescence and the growth of institutions geared to molding it. Kett's study is based upon a wealth of primary sources listed in the copious notes.

281. Keuls, Eva C. **The Reign of the Phallus: Sexual Politics in Ancient Athens.** New York: Harper and Row, 1985. 452p. illus. bibliography, 421-34. notes. index. pa.

In this thoroughly documented and profusely illustrated study, Keuls argues that ancient Athenian society was unique in its public display of the phallus, not as an emblem of male generation but of male power. Although

Keuls recognizes the remarkable achievements of ancient Athens, she insists that another side of the city has not been explored. Male citizens sequestered their wives and daughters, minimized the female role in reproduction, erected phallic monuments everywhere in the city, sponsored houses of male and female prostitution, emphasized rape in mythology, and were notorious war-mongers. Using evidence drawn from texts, vase paintings, statuary, and many other sources, Keuls reconstructs the roles of men and women, citizens and slaves, in fifth-century Athens. Keuls explores a multitude of topics, such as the barren goddess Athena as patron of the city, depictions of the penis in vase paintings, women's isolation at home and their participation in frenzied public rituals, the division of women into mothers and whores, the role of the concubine, pederasty (or boy love) among Athenian men, the war against the Amazons as an image of the male defeat of female power, and Greek tragedy as a dramatization of the war between the sexes. Concerning the never-solved mystery of who mutilated the city's phallic herms in 415 B.C., just before Athenians launched an ill-advised military expedition against Syracuse, Keuls argues that the women, disgusted with war, were the vandals. The book closes with a discussion of the Philoxenos' famous Alexander mosaic as an anti-war representation. Even for one remaining unconvinced, Keuls's analysis of the mosaic—like everything else in this book—is fascinating and thought provoking.

282. Kimmel, Michael S., and Thomas E. Mosmiller, eds. **Against the Tide: Pro-feminist Men in the United States, 1776-1990: A Documentary History**. Boston: Beacon Press, 1992. xxxi, 521p. illus. bibliography, 481-518.

The editors write, "What this book documents ... is a history of men who have supported women's struggles since the founding of the nation." Rejecting the notion that all men have opposed women's rights movements, Kimmel and Mosmiller have assembled more than 130 selections from U.S. men who enlisted themselves in various feminist causes. (The extensive bibliography lists many more writings not included in the volume; the editors gathered over 1,000 pro-feminist documents by U.S. men.) The book's organization is both historical and thematic. Divided into three historical periods (1775-1848, 1850-1960, and 1961-1990), the selections are also grouped according to such concerns as education for women, economic independence, women in the trades, women in the professions, political equality, suffrage, social equality, marriage and divorce reform, "sex rights," birth control, and women's studies. The introduction by Kimmel surveys the history of pro-feminist men. While celebrating men sensitive to women's rights, Kimmel is dismissive of men sensitive to men's rights. Moreover, the discussion never confronts the paradox that many men's pro-feminism was rooted in old-fashioned chivalry, a product of the patriarchal society that is alleged to have been so anti-female.

283. Kinmonth, Earl H. **The Self-Made Man in Meiji Japanese Thought: From Samurai to Salary Man.** Berkeley: University of California Press, 1981. xi, 385p. illus. bibliography, 357-71. notes. index.

Based upon three years of research in Japan, this hefty study uses a wealth of primary materials to trace the rise of the self-help ethic in late-nineteenth-century Japan. This ethic helped to convert Japan into a nation of male overachievers. Kinmonth demonstrates how the notion of a self-made man was imported from late-Victorian England. The major text was Samuel Smiles's *Self-Help*. Meshing neatly with Confucian samurai tradition, the notion of self-help fostered a generation of success-driven young men. With *success* defined as earning money, education was skewed to produce young men of "lofty ambition." Although some youths rebelled against the pressures of "rising in the world," self-help took on a patriotic tinge around the turn of the century and was used to support Japanese expansionism. Later, American influence was paramount: Andrew Carnegie became a heroic figure for young men to emulate, Orison Swett Marden's *Pushing to the Front* achieved great influence, and a journal named *Success* defined the male imperative. The dreams of most Japanese males, however, were frustrated because only a few men could achieve great wealth. Most men ended up as lowly "salary men." Although Kinmonth's study is not especially gender-conscious, it offers a fascinating glimpse of modern Japanese masculinity in the making.

284. Kirshner, Alan M. **Masculinity in an Historical Perspective: Readings and Discussions.** Washington, DC: University Press of America, 1977. iii, 173p. illus. pa.

This book derives from the author's "A History of Masculinity" course at Ohlone College. Materials include lectures, edited discussions, and course reading materials on such topics as popular and scientific views of "cave men" masculinity, masculinity in the classical world, Judeo-Christian views of manliness, chivalry and courtly love, puritan and Victorian masculinity, Latin-American machismo, middle-class American masculinity, and new roles for men.

285. Kriegel, Leonard, ed. **The Myth of American Manhood.** New York: Dell, Laurel Editions, 1978. 412p. pa.

This collection of 21 selections—essays, short stories, excerpts from longer works—provides views of U.S. masculinity from Cotton Mather's idealized portrait of William Bradford to Pete Hamill's 1976 essay "Farewell to Machismo." Kriegel's introduction provides historical and cultural perspectives, indicating that traditional masculinity is no longer fashionable and will change irretrievably. Nineteenth-century selections include writings of Melville, Twain, and Crane, as well as Grant's account of Lee's surrender. Twentieth-century selections include essays on boxing and baseball, Mailer's "The Time of Her Life" and "The White Negro," and Kriegel's essay on being handicapped, "Uncle Tom and Tiny Tim."

286. Macleod, David I. **Building Character in the American Boy: The Boy Scouts, YMCA, and Their Forerunners, 1870-1920.** Madison: University of Wisconsin Press, 1983. xx, 404p. notes. index.

This massive social history argues that character-building organizations for middle-class boys arose from middle-class concerns about transmitting values. Macleod acknowledges social worries about masculinity, the feminization of schools, masturbation, and women's changing roles, but he concludes that reaction to urban life was the primary impetus behind the creation of the YMCA boys departments, the Boy Scouts, and other groups. The notes reflect extensive research in primary sources.

287. Mangan, J. A., and James Walvin, eds. **Manliness and Morality: Middle-Class Masculinity in Britain and America, 1800-1940.** Manchester, England: Manchester University Press, 1987. x, 278p. illus. bibliography, 261-65. notes. index. Reprint, New York: St. Martin's Press, 1991. pa.

"Nearly everything we know about human behaviour in the past concerns men," writes E. Anthony Rotundo in this collection, "and yet it is equally—and ironically—true that we know far more about womanhood and the female role than we know about masculinity or the man's role." The 12 scholarly essays in this anthology alternate between Britain and the United States, examining aspects of middle-class masculinity. Among the essays are Rotundo's definition of three U.S. masculine ideal types (the achiever, the Christian gentleman, and the primitive), Roberta J. Park's study of the biological view of the mind-body relationship and the resultant emphasis upon sports, and Jeffrey Richards's packed essay on close male friendships. Other essays examine Social Darwinism, the heroic ideal at Yale, Baden Powell and scouting, and the U.S. military and the cult of manliness. Contributors include John Springhall (on British attempts to export Christian manliness to working-class boys), Peter N. Stearns (on male anger), and John M. MacKenzie (on late-Victorian masculinity and imperialism). Period drawings and photographs illustrate the text.

288. Pleck, Elizabeth H., and Joseph H. Pleck, eds. **The American Man.** Englewood Cliffs, NJ: Prentice-Hall, 1980. xii, 433p. notes. pa.

This anthology consists of 16 previously printed essays on aspects of masculinity in American history. The editors' introduction stresses the need to review what is known about men and to place this information in a new, gender-conscious light. Dividing American history into four periods—agrarian patriarchy (1630-1820), the commercial age (1820-1860), the strenuous life (1861-1919), and companionate providing (1920-1965)—the editors provide an overview of each period, preparing the way for the more narrowly focused essays that follow. These studies range from Robert Oaks's account of sodomy and buggery in seventeenth-century New England to Joseph H. Pleck's analysis of the men's movement. The contributors include Eugene D. Genovese on slave husbands and fathers, Jeffrey P. Hantover on the significance of the Boy Scout movement, Joe L. Dubbert on Progressivism and the masculinity crisis, Peter Gabriel Filene on men in World War I, Mirra Komarovsky on unemployed husbands during the depression of the 1930s, and Marc Fasteau on toughness in American foreign policy. Of special interest also are Blanche Glassman Hersh's account of nineteenth-century feminist marriages (which were not always made in heaven); Charles E. Rosenberg's wide-ranging assessment of sexuality, class, and role in nineteenth-century America; and Jon M. Kingsdale's view of the saloon as the "poor man's club."

289. Pugh, David G. **Sons of Liberty: The Masculine Mind in Nineteenth-Century America.** Westport, CT: Greenwòod Press, 1983. xxii, 186p.(Contributions in American Studies, 68). bibliography, 171-78. notes. index.

Combining psychological, cultural, and historical insights, Pugh traces the American cult of masculinity from Jacksonian democracy, through the Gilded Age, and into the he-man literature of popular twentieth-century magazines. A chapter devoted to "the female foil" concludes that not all women were the passive victims depicted in some current assessments.

290. Rischin, Moses, ed. **The American Gospel of Success: Individualism and Beyond.** Chicago: Quadrangle Books, 1965. x, 431p.

Rischin performs a valuable service by collecting 48 documents that define and proclaim the American gospel of success (for males). Although it is rarely spelled out in the texts themselves, the relation between the documents and the American man's gender role is obvious. Selections include a sermon by Cotton Mather, an excerpt from Benjamin Franklin's *Poor Richard's Almanac*, P. T. Barnum on the art of "money-getting," an abridged tale by Horatio Alger, and advice from Andrew Carnegie. The editor also includes a selection of scholarly works examining the gospel's effects upon big business, as well as writings depicting the fates of outsiders (e.g., minorities, the poor, the nonbelievers in the gospel). Other writings explore the means of excluding nonconformists from becoming members of the economic elect, the fate of the gospel in modern times, and the uneasy rapprochement between Christianity and the gospel of success.

291. Roper, Michael, and John Tosh, eds. **Manful Assertions: Masculinities in Britain Since 1800.** London and New York: Routledge, 1991. x, 221p. illus. bibliography, 212-13. index. pa.

Nine essays explore key moments in British masculinities since the early Victorian age. The introduction by Roper and Tosh argues that masculinities are relational constructs that change over time. Social power, especially men's power over women, is an organizing principle of past masculinities. Just when it seems that Roper and Tosh are merely parroting the standard socialist-feminist views of men's power, they qualify those views significantly. Masculinity, they argue, cannot be equated with a proclivity for male dominance, and patriarchy is a troublesome term when used as shorthand for male oppression. The essays in the volume examine matters such as the corrosively strenuous masculinity of Thomas Carlyle, how the paternal strictness of Edward White Benson may have contributed to the homosexual leanings of his wife and sons, and the ideas of masculinity among artisans and in the Salvation Army. Other essays explore the psychosexual troubles of Lawrence of Arabia as colonial masculinity confronted postcolonial times, the concept of manliness in boys' story papers, and the British company man from 1945 to 1985. Peter M. Lewis's moving autobiographical account of the missing feminine in male institutions closes with these important words: "To change destructive male behaviour is a hard, but urgent task. Equally hard is to find a way of encouraging and celebrating the good in men."

292. Rosenthal, Michael. **The Character Factory: Baden-Powell and the Origins of the Boy Scout Movement.** New York: Pantheon Books, 1986. x, 335p. illus. bibliography, 318-29. notes. index.

Rosenthal presents a cultural reading of Robert Baden-Powell's life and the youth movement in turn-of-the-century England. Viewing scouting as a response to the needs of an imperial nation, Rosenthal argues that scouting's efforts to cultivate moral and physical health among boys really served upper-class interests. Although the racist and anti-Semitic elements in Baden-Powell's ideology are convincingly demonstrated, Rosenthal strains to find sinister class interest behind Baden-Powell's every idea. One suspects Baden-Powell deserves better than this Lytton Strachey-like debunking. The author does not focus on gender concerns, although scouting was clearly an attempt to fulfill a social need to initiate boys into adult masculinity.

293. Rotundo, E. Anthony. **American Manhood: Transformations in Masculinity from the Revolution to the Modern Era.** New York: Basic Books, 1993. xii, 382p. appendix. notes. index.

Working on the premise that manhood has a history, Rotundo surveys concepts of masculinity among middle-class, New England white males during the nineteenth century. He contrasts Victorian males with their puritan and eighteenth-century forebears who exalted a "communal manhood" that stressed patriarchal duties and authority. In a major cultural change, this social masculinity gave way to a more self-assertive model during the nineteenth century. Following a life-cycle pattern, Rotundo describes boy culture as a time of differentiating from the feminine, a youth culture that stressed control of impulses, romantic friendships between young males, the protector-servant relationships that developed between brothers and sisters, young men's conflicting views of young women as angels or devils, and love and courtship (the young man had to take most of the emotional risks and he could not marry until he could support a family). Marriage led to the couple's subsequent intimacy or alienation. For men, work outside the home defined male identity and provided male companionship. Late in the nineteenth century, another major cultural shift favored a "passionate manhood" marked by physical fitness, sports, muscular Christianity, the military ideal, and a return to nature and the primitive. This masculinity exalted Social Darwinism, retention of boyhood qualities, and dislike of effeminate men. The epilogue is the book's most controversial and perhaps least satisfactory chapter: Rotundo attempts to survey twentieth-century U.S. masculinity, link the present-day mythopoetic men's movement with turn-of-the-century primitivism, and settle questions of male power and victimization. The appendix presents Rotundo's reasons for limiting the scope of his history.

294. Stearns, Peter N. **Be a Man! Males in Modern Society.** 2d ed. New York: Holmes and Meier, 1990. x, 300p. illus. bibliography, 291-95. notes. index. pa.

Starting with a discussion of manhood as a social construct, *Be a Man!* (first published in 1979) surveys changes in the masculine gender role in Western Europe and North America from the industrial revolution to the present. Noting the dearth of literature on men in society, Stearns conducts a quick review of history from hunting and agricultural society to the preindustrial world of eighteenth-century Europe and America. Focusing on his principal subject, Stearns argues that industrialism fundamentally changed the traditional concepts of masculinity by changing the nature of labor and property and by moving work outside the home, thereby dividing labor more radically between the sexes. Working-class men were separated from their families, with the home becoming women's province. Middle-class men were split between the demands of work and family life, between the roles of aggressive competitor and nurturing husband-father. As the family's enforced breadwinner, a man was sometimes overwhelmed attempting to support a growing family. Stearns's account of manhood in the twentieth century reviews the impacts on men of World War I and the women's movement; he argues, however, that the feminist movement has not significantly affected most men, although the anti-male hostility of some feminists threatens to deflect men from making changes that were already in progress. In the second edition, Stearns continues the story through the 1980s, addressing the reaction against androgyny and the reaffirmation of more traditional masculine styles. Still, important gender innovations have occurred, especially the discovery (or rediscovery) of nurturant fatherhood. Stearns indicates that, along with greater sexual equality, an updated paternalism and fuller concepts of masculinity are needed and are perhaps evolving.

295. Strauss, Sylvia. **"Traitors to the Masculine Cause": The Men's Campaign for Women's Rights.** Westport, CT: Greenwood Press, 1982. xix, 292p. (Contributions in Women's Studies, no. 35). illus. bibliography, 273-79. index.

Tracing the history of the Fathers of Feminism, Strauss provides a connected account of the most important men who aided the women's movement in nineteenth-century England and America. After exploring the roots of male feminism in eighteenth-century radicalism, Strauss focuses on such major figures as John Stuart Mill, George Bernard Shaw, and Frederick Pethick-Lawrence, whose devotion to the cause led to his imprisonment,

financial ruin, and eventual ostracism by Emmeline and Christabel Pankhurst. The book also devotes considerable space to a host of other men,
including William Godwin, Francis Place, William Thompson, Robert Owen,
Charles Bradlaugh, John Humphrey Noyes, W. T. Stead, George Meredith,
Richard Pankhurst, Henry Fawcett, Jacob Bright, Charles Dilke, Keir Hardie,
and Floyd Dell. Organizations like the Men's Political Union for Women's
Suffrage and the Men's League for Women's Suffrage are also studied. Strauss
divides the male partisans into two camps: the domestic feminists who saw a
woman's lot as tied to the home and who tried to ameliorate her situation there,
and the philosophical feminists who worked for women's equal participation
in public life as well. The latter group, believing that femininity was more
democratic and compassionate than masculinity, hoped that including women
in the political process would help humanize it. Strauss's narrative closes after
World War I and the granting of suffrage, although she briefly traces some
developments to the present and also comments on the ambiguous success of
the recent women's liberation movement. Despite its subject, the book accords
no positive traits to masculinity: terms like *masculine* and *masculinity* carry
negative connotations and are identified with exploitive capitalism, power
politics, and militarism.

296. White, Kevin. **The First Sexual Revolution: The Emergence of Male
Heterosexuality in Modern America.** New York and London: New York
University Press, 1992. xii, 263p. (The American Social Experience Series, no.
27). bibliography, 235-49. pa. notes. index.

We know much about the New Woman "flapper" of the early twentieth-century, but what about her boyfriend? White attempts to describe how primarily
young, white, middle-class men responded to the breakup of Victorian codes. The
"male flapper" actually inherited much of the respectful Christian gentleman ideal
of late Victorianism, while the "underworld primitive" went in for manly sports
and body building. But the outing of male heterosexuality soon commercialized
sex itself and led to less desirable results. The New Woman was no longer protected
by the moral control that Victorianism exercised over men. In working-class,
dance-hall culture, women could be brutalized. In the middle class, young men
were sexually liberated but clueless about how to handle dating and other new
freedoms; they turned increasingly to films and popular literature for help.
Resentment against women could flair as men felt harassed by pressures and
inequality; the term *gold digger* points to men's anger at having to foot the bills
for women who were supposedly equal. Feminist egalitarian marriages usually
foundered, although several notable exceptions are on record. In the concluding
chapter, White glances gloomily at the 1970s through the 1990s. He sees some
feminists engaging in a futile campaign against men and male sexuality, he
suspects that the wild man is a throwback to Teddy Roosevelt primitivism, and
he argues that the commercialization of sex and the loss of Victorian "character"
has brought out the worst in both sexes.

297. Wilkinson, Rupert. **American Tough: The Tough-Guy Tradition and
American Character.** Westport, CT: Greenwood Press, 1984. Rev. ed. New
York: Perennial Library, Harper & Row, 1986. xiv, 221p. illus. notes. index.
pa.

In this encyclopedic survey of U.S. social history, Wilkinson depicts an
almost infinite variety of the U.S. macho ideal in writings, films, illustrations,
public figures, business people, and so on. The analysis is organized around
three themes. First, U.S. "toughness" is contradictory. For example, aggressiveness and control, mind and muscle, and realism and moralism vie with

each other as characteristics of U.S. toughness. Sometimes the tough guy represents the upper classes, sometimes the lower classes. Second, in U.S. capitalism, the economic tough guy is contrasted with the soft consumer. Third, Americans often frame the conflict between conformism and individuality as a tough-guy matter. Wilkinson compares and contrasts U.S. toughness with forms of masculinity from other cultures (e.g., Mexico, Canada, and Australia). The revised edition contains a new foreword and numerous illustrations emphasizing that some women (e.g., Calamity Jane and Mother Jones) exemplify U.S. toughness as ably as some men do.

298. Wyllie, Irvin G. **The Self-Made Man in America: The Myth of Rags to Riches.** New Brunswick, NJ: Rutgers University Press, 1954. ix, 210p. illus. bibliography, 197-205. notes. index. Reprint, New York: Free Press, 1966. pa.

Few U.S. men can have escaped the influence of the gospel of success that flourished in the nineteenth century; despite its lingering decline in the twentieth century, it still flavors U.S. life. In this cult of the self-made man, the causes of triumph or failure were believed to lie in the man rather than in the environment. Thus, the rags-to-riches myth supposedly put a man's manhood to the test, a test that most men were destined to fail or to pass only modestly. In this readable survey, Wyllie traces the gospel of self-reliance from early American exemplars like Benjamin Franklin, through the rise of such major figures as Andrew Carnegie, to the gospel's gradual diminution during the twentieth century. The anti-idleness doctrine, which spurred many men to work hard—a badge of manliness—was preached far and wide by Protestant clergymen, journalists, authors, lecturers, and educators. Wyllie finds that Social Darwinism had less influence in the U.S. than is usually believed. He shows how the self-help gospel was attacked from the right by those who exalted aristocratic culture and from the left by those who argued that social conditions, not personal attributes, determined financial success.

Cross-References

See chapter 15, "Masculinity."

768. Altman, Dennis. **The Homosexualization of America: The Americanization of the Homosexual.**

771. Bérubé, Allan. **Coming Out Under Fire: The History of Gay Men and Women in World War II.**

773. Boswell, John. **Christianity, Social Tolerance, and Homosexuality: Gay People in Western Europe from the Beginning of the Christian Era to the Fourteenth Century.**

394. Bristow, Joseph. **Empire Boys: Adventures in a Man's World.**

776. Bullough, Vern L. **Homosexuality: A History.**

777. Burg, B. R. **Sodomy and the Perception of Evil: English Sea Rovers in the Seventeenth-Century Caribbean.**

174. Chandos, John. **Boys Together: English Public Schools, 1800-1864.**

778. Chester, Lewis, David Leitch, and Colin Simpson. **The Cleveland Street Affair.**

782. D'Emilio, John. **Sexual Politics, Sexual Communities: The Making of a Homosexual Minority in the United States, 1940-1970.**

784. Dover, K. J. **Greek Homosexuality.**

785. Duberman, Martin, Martha Vicinus, and George Chauncey, Jr., eds. **Hidden from History: Reclaiming the Gay and Lesbian Past.**

982. Ehrenreich, Barbara. **The Hearts of Men: American Dreams and the Flight from Commitment.**

692. Etheredge, Lloyd S. **A World of Men: The Private Sources of American Foreign Policy.**

946. Fields, Rick. **The Code of the Warrior: In History, Myth, and Everyday Life.**

947. Friedman, Leon. **The Wise Minority.**

790. Goodich, Michael. **The Unmentionable Vice: Homosexuality in the Later Medieval Period.**

1043. Gorn, Elliott J. **The Manly Art: Bare-Knuckle Prize Fighting in America.**

403. Green, Martin. **The Adventurous Male: Chapters in the History of the White Male Mind.**

793. Greenberg, David F. **The Construction of Homosexuality.**

794. Halperin, David M. **One Hundred Years of Homosexuality, and Other Essays on Greek Love.**

954. Hicken, Victor. **The American Fighting Man.**

797. Hinsch, Bret. **Passions of the Cut Sleeve: The Male Homosexual Tradition in China.**

179. Honey, J. R. de S. **Tom Brown's Universe: The Development of the English Public School in the Nineteenth Century.**

657. Howe, Irving, with Kenneth Libo. **World of Our Fathers.**

802. Katz, Jonathan. **Gay American History: Lesbians and Gay Men in the U.S.A.**

959. Keegan, John. **The Face of Battle.**

962. Laffin, John. **Americans in Battle.**

414. Leverenz, David. **Manhood and the American Renaissance.**

808. Licata, Salvatore J., and Robert P. Petersen, eds. **Historical Perspectives on Homosexuality.**

415. Lynn, Kenneth S. **The Dream of Success: A Study of the Modern American Imagination.**

809. Marotta, Toby. **The Politics of Homosexuality.**

681. Mount, Ferdinand. **The Subversive Family: An Alternate History of Love and Marriage.**

964. O'Sullivan, John, and Alan M. Meckler. **The Draft and Its Enemies: A Documentary History.**

824. Plant, Richard. **The Pink Triangle: The Nazi War Against Homosexuals.**

420. Quigly, Isabel. **The Heirs of Tom Brown: The English School Story.**

828. Rector, Frank. **The Nazi Extermination of Homosexuals.**

833. Rowse, A. L. **Homosexuals in History: A Study of Ambivalence in Society, Literature and the Arts.**

666. Sochen, June, ed. **The Black Man and the American Dream: Negro Aspirations in America, 1900-1930.**

1042. Swados, Harvey, ed. **The American Writer and the Great Depression.**

971. Young, Peter. **The Fighting Man: From Alexander the Great's Army to the Present Day.**

11

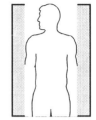

Humor

299. Berman, Edgar. **The Compleat Chauvinist: A Survival Guide for the Bedeviled Male.** New York: Macmillan, 1982. x, 219p.

In prose laced with quips and puns, Berman twits militant feminists on such matters as work outside the home, menstruation, spouse battering, women in sports, affirmative action, and the ERA (which Berman enthusiastically supports as a boon to male chauvinists). Insisting that he is only anti-feminist and not misogynist, Berman (an M.D.) believes that hormones are destiny, and he praises the "feminine" woman. Readers will have to decide for themselves whether Berman's book represents an exercise in witty wisdom or ridiculous reactionism.

300. Burkett, Michael. **The Dad Zone: Reports from the Tender, Bewildering, and Hilarious World of Fatherhood.** New York: Simon and Schuster, 1993. 223p. illus.

As the father of a boy and a girl, Burkett seems to have seen it all. He reports his derailings from the daddy track in warm and wildly funny essays. Not to be missed are the dead goldfish that Jesus swiped, nighttime conversations, translations from "child-speak," and how to get food inside a baby in 23 easy steps.

301. Chapple, Steve. **Conversations with Mr. Baby: A Celebration of New Life.** New York: Arcade, 1992. ix, 177p. illus.

Look who's talking now. Chapple holds imaginary conversations with his unborn/newborn son, who responds with some precocious retorts. The conversations are a way of working around the fears and frustrations of parenthood and childhood, and a way of emphasizing the joys and wonder of life. Illustrations are by Skip Morrow.

302. Cosby, Bill. **Fatherhood.** Garden City, NY: Doubleday, Dolphin Book, 1986. vi, 178p. pa.

In real life, America's favorite television father is the father of five children—and he has the zany anecdotes to prove it. The famous Cosby wit ripples through these adventures in fathering, recalling children whose only lines of conversation were "I don't know" and "Mine! Mine! Mine!" The book is a jubilant hymn to the perplexities and joys of fatherhood. In both the introduction and the afterword, Dr. Alvin F. Poussaint cites the importance of good fathering and offers some advice for achieving it.

303. Everitt, David, and Harold Schechter. **The Manly Handbook.** New York: Berkley Books, 1982. 134p. illus. pa.
    Written so a "real man" can understand it, the text of this hilarious spoof of U.S. machismo is supplemented by wickedly funny photographs featuring the likes of Humphrey Bogart, John Wayne, and (of course) George C. Scott as General Patton.

304. Feirstein, Bruce. **Real Men Don't Eat Quiche.** New York; Pocket Books, 1982. 93p. pa.
    A bestseller that spawned numerous spin-offs, this "guidebook to all that is truly masculine" parodies the macho pose, both working-class and corporate style. Cartoons by Lee Lorenz punctuate brief chapters on such matters as the Real Man's vocabulary, great moments in Real Men's history, and so on. Like many parodies, *Real Men* hovers between ridicule of and affection for its subject.

305. Friedman, Bruce. **The Lonely Guy's Book of Life.** New York: McGraw-Hill Book, 1978. xiv, 206p. illus.
    The walking wounded of modern life, the lonely guys are here provided with whimsical advice on such matters as apartment living, cooking, grooming ("clothes left overnight in Woolite tend to rot away when you're wearing them at parties"), running, eating alone in restaurants, illness, psychiatric counseling, and sex. Victor Juhasz supplies the comic illustrations.

306. Gannon, Frank. **All About Man.** Atlanta: Longstreet Press, 1993. 131p. illus.
    Gannon retells the history of MAN (which he insists upon capitalizing), from his origins to his extinction. Along the way, we learn about early MAN, sex (Gannon assures male readers that they should not feel diminished if they have not had sex with 20,000 women, as Wilt Chamberlain declared), mythology, language, Iron Men (who complain about their wounds while beating drums in the woods), Real Men, and Cool Men. In the final chapter, Gannon contemplates his own death, realizing that MAN is mortal.

307. Gingold, Alfred. **Fire in the John.** New York: St. Martin's Press, Cader Books, a Thomas Dunne book, 1991. 160p. illus. appendix. pa.
    Billed as a book about and for "the Manly Man in the Age of Sissification," this send-up of drum-and-chant masculinity makes merriment with the mythopoetic journeys charted by Captain Bly. Part 1 deplores the current glorification in some circles of "soft men." Part 2 takes the reader through 12 steps to true manhood. Part 3 celebrates the "brave new guy" of trendy myths. The appendix retells a lost tale of the Brothers Grimm. Many of the book's photographs have wickedly funny cutlines.

308. Jones, Julia Runk, and Milo Trump. **Livingston's Field Guide to North American Males.** Garden City, NY: Doubleday, Dolphin Books, 1984. 124p. illus. notes. index. pa.
    In this daffy guide to North American males, the authors provide species and subspecies descriptions, including accounts of plumage (clothing), feathering (hairstyles), songs (identifying comments), habitat, range, nests, courtship and mating practices, and tracks ("little tell-tale signs males leave behind, such as cigarette butts, beer cans, business cards and dandruff"). Species include The Machoman (homo hardhat), The Good Ol' Boy (homo buddy), The

Slob (homo porkus), The Jock (homo sweatsocks), The Golden Throated Tanner (homo coke), and The Sweet Young Thing (homo cookie). The comical photographs of the species "in their natural habitats" are by Alan Rabold. Not to be overlooked are the zany footnotes.

309. King, Florence. **He: An Irreverent Look at the American Male.** New York: Stein and Day, 1978. x, 204p.

King describes herself as being neither a Total Woman nor a women's liberationist. (The most readable section of *Ms* magazine, she notes, is the "No Comment" department.) With a sharp eye and ear, King skewers the foibles of U.S. males—and females. After regaling readers with salty recollections of her teenage sexual experiments in the fifties, King goes on to characterize various types of males in the seventies. Not to be missed is her send-up of the male feminist, whom she dubs Jonathan Stuart Mill. Ever trendy, Jonathan has lost interest in black causes and is now (he says with a straight face) "into women." King also exposes the literary sins of recent male writers, and she portrays the new misogynists, who got that way (she confesses) partly from too many encounters with strident feminists. Although she professes a passion for polished Alistair Cooke types, one suspects that in reality they would be too tepid for her. Despite her "irreverent look at the American male," King clearly enjoys him, foibles and all.

310. Mead, Shepherd. **Free the Male Man! The Manifesto of the Men's Liberation Movement, Examining the Urgent Need to Free Malekind and Re-establish the Equality, Both Economic and Sexual, of the Two Sexes, Containing Explicit Sexual Instructions, Diagrams, and Battle Plans for the Coming Masculist Revolution.** New York: Simon and Schuster, 1972. 155p. illus.

Examining the comic side of the hazards of being male, Mead provides a laughable, consciousness-raising book about men's issues. John Huehnergarth's cartoons add to the fun.

311. Myer, Andy. **The Liberated Father's Handbook.** New York: St. Martin's Press, 1983. vii, 87p. illus. pa.

Myer provides the text and the illustrations—both are hilarious—for this comic guide for the pregnant father. Chapters cover such topics as visiting the gynecologist ("No Man's Land"), surviving the baby shower, assembling the crib, handling labor and delivery, late-night feedings, the diaper dilemma ("Winning the Poo"), and traveling with baby ("The Longest Mile").

312. O'Neill, Hugh. **Daddy Cool: How to Ride a Seesaw with Dignity, Wear a Donald Duck Hat with Style, and Sing "Bingo Was His Name-O" with Panache.** New York: Warner Books, 1988. iv, 133p. illus. pa.

For dads who are attempting to maintain a modicum of Clint Eastwood cool amid family mayhem, O'Neill offers advice on keeping things under control. Beneath the comedy lies some valuable advice on how to be a good father. The illustrations by Peters Day show Dad chilling out in raincoat and sunglasses even in the most compromising situations.

313. Schoenberg, Fred. **Middle Age Rage ... and Other Male Indignities.** New York: Simon and Schuster, 1987. 128p. illus.

Schoenberg makes merry with the debacle of middle age. He tells men how to recognize the symptoms and what not to do about them. Forget exercise and diet, for instance. There is positive advice: get new glasses, make sure your fly is zippered, and don't get caught staring at younger women. Remember to keep the Sabbath holy: pro-football and a few beers bring a man closer to God and restore his health. The comic illustrations are by Rob Edwards.

314. Schoenstein, Ralph. **Yes, My Darling Daughters: Adventures in Fathering.** New York: Farrar, Straus & Giroux, 1976. 133p. Reprint, New York: Avon Books, 1977. pa.

In comic style that will remind some readers of Jean Kerr's early family writings, Schoenstein recounts his wacky adventures as the father of two daughters.

315. Stewart, D. L. **Father Knows Best—Sometimes.** New York: Warner Books, 1986. 212p. illus. pa.

Fatherhood isn't anything like what the Robert Young television series led us to believe, Stewart reports. In wonderfully wacky fashion, Stewart tells how, as the father of four in suburban Ohio, he tries to cope with such crises as sending off a nubile daughter to college, being hounded by a son who has just reached driving age, and attending parent-teacher conferences. The deliciously comic stories are accompanied by Ted Pitts's illustrations.

316. Stewart, D. L. **Fathers Are People Too.** Dayton, OH: Journal Herald, 1980. 122p. illus. Reprint, Indianapolis, IN: Bobbs-Merrill, 1983. pa.

Stewart, perhaps America's funniest writer on fatherhood, recounts fourteen of his hilarious misadventures as the father of four. Lovers of laughter should not miss Stewart's accounts of chaperoning a cub scout troop around New York City, taking a son fishing (and actually catching a fish), a night with the kids at a roller-skating rink, and the ordeal of having a teen party in the basement. Illustrations are by Ted Pitts.

317. Stewart, D. L. **Stepfathers Are People Too.** Dayton, OH: Dayton Daily News, 1991. 195p. illus. pa.

Stepfathers are the relief pitchers of family life, Stewart notes. Divorced and remarried, Stewart finds himself the stepfather of two as well as the father of four. Without missing a beat, he retells side-splitting stories of a "blended" family that is more like a tag-team wrestling match among siblings. Not to be missed are Stewart's run-ins with his fiendishly clever stepcat. The book's comedy is modified by a touching tribute to one of Stewart's stepsons who died in an accident, and by Stewart's admiration for all those who conscientiously take on the duties of step-parenting. Illustrations are by Frank Pauer.

318. Stuart, Jan. **Guide to Being a Man in a Woman's World: How to be "Macho" Without Offending Anyone.** New York: Shapolsky Publishers, 1989. xvii, 171p. illus.

It seems that somebody was uneasy about this book. In addition to its rather colorless title, it is prefaced with a warning that "this book was not written to offend *anyone*." While not politically correct, Stuart's comedy is not mean-spirited either. Instead, it takes a savvy and evenhanded look at growing up male in today's world. A representative chapter title is "Why Dating Is the Worst Experience of Your Life." Because Stuart is an authority on men's skin care, several straight chapters on that topic are inserted, somewhat incongruously, near the end.

Cross-References

494. Gilbert, Sara D. **What's A Father For? A Father's Guide to the Pleasures and Problems of Parenthood with Advice from the Experts.**

853. Gordon, William J., and Steven D. Price. **The Second-Time Single Man's Survival Handbook.**

43. Greenburg, Dan. **Scoring: A Sexual Memoir.**

44. Houston, James D. **The Men in My Life and Other More or Less True Recollections of Kinship.**

55. McGrady, Mike. **The Kitchen Sink Papers: My Life as a Househusband.**

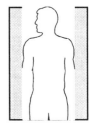

12

Literature and the Arts: Primary Works and Critical Commentary

A. Classic Literature: Pre-1900

319. Apuleius. **The Golden Ass.** Translated by Jack Lindsay. Bloomington, IN: Indiana University Press, 1960. 255p. notes. pa.

    Dating from the second century A.D., *The Golden Ass* tells the adventures of young Lucius, who is accidentally transformed into an ass when a witch's magic spell goes awry. Stolen by thieves, Lucius embarks on a series of tribulations that, on a symbolic level, mark his initiation into full manhood. Interspersed with Lucius' story are several tales, including the enduring story of Psyche and Amor (Cupid). Angered by Psyche's beauty, the goddess Venus seeks revenge against Psyche, whose search for her true love, Cupid-Amor, is a variant of Lucius' quest to discover human masculinity. Eventually, Lucius is redeemed by the goddess Isis and achieves adult manhood. The tale can be interpreted as an extended version of what Robert Bly in *Iron John* (entry 861) calls "the descent to ashes" aspect of male initiation. A comprehensive Jungian reading of the tale can be found in Marie-Louise von Franz's *The Golden Ass of Apuleius: The Liberation of the Feminine in Man* (entry 729). Clearly, the tale contains a gold mine of archetypal material depicting male individuation.

320. Besant, Walter. **The Revolt of Man**. Edinburgh and London: William Blackwood and Sons, 1882. 358p.

    Besant's half-comic, half-serious novel deserves to be better known than it is, especially for its prophetic depiction of England after the Great Transition. Women exercise political and social dominance, the monarchy has been abolished, the state is a matriarchal theocracy worshipping The Perfect Woman, and the men are kept in guilty subjection by such devices as public hysteria over wife beating. At last, a young nobleman, coached by his female professor of ancient and modern history, leads a revolt of the men. Despite some late-Victorian outlandishness, the novel manages to be both pertinent and perceptive.

321. Conrad, Joseph. **Heart of Darkness.** 1899, 1902. Reprint (3d ed.), edited by Robert Kimbrough. New York: W. W. Norton, Norton Critical Editions, 1988. xvii, 420p. illus. appendixes. notes. bibliography, 419-20. pa.

The basis for the film *Apocalypse Now*, Conrad's tale of a journey up the Congo river in the late nineteenth century offers a glimpse into the corrupt nature of men. The literal story concerns Marlow, the story's principal narrator, who leaves England and Belgium to captain a steamboat in the Belgian Congo. Once in Africa, Marlow witnesses the Europeans' brutal treatment of natives, their murderous intrigues, and their greed. He heads upriver to rescue Kurtz, an agent who has been left at an inland post, and discovers in Kurtz a terrifying mirror image of the male heart of darkness. At one level, Conrad's short novel presents a sordid picture of European colonialism at its worst. At another level, it suggests that beneath the veneer of civilization lies a "horror" of male barbarism. The men in the novel are savages at heart; the women (like Marlow's aunt and Kurtz's fiancée) are simplemindedly naive. The Norton edition contains plentiful materials on biography, historical backgrounds, critical commentaries, and interpretations.

322. Crane, Stephen. **The Red Badge of Courage.** 1895. Reprint (2d ed.), edited by Sculley Bradley, Richmond Croom Beatty, E. Hudson Long, and Donald Pizer, New York: W. W. Norton, Norton Critical Editions, 1976. viii, 364p. appendixes. bibliography, 361-64. notes. pa.
Vividly depicting a young soldier's first taste of battle during the American Civil War, *The Red Badge of Courage* shows how Henry Fleming's growing sense of valor is linked with his growing sense of manhood. Having fled in combat and having abandoned a soldier in distress, Henry returns to the war, fiercely engages in battle, and even becomes a "heroic" standard-bearer. At the end, he is able to beat down his shameful memories and quietly bask in his newfound masculinity: "He felt a quiet manhood, nonassertive but of sturdy and strong blood.... He was a man." But Crane's pervasive irony has left some readers wondering whether Henry has achieved genuine manhood or tragically internalized a destructive definition of masculinity. The Norton edition includes textual notes, background materials, and critical essays.

323. Dickens, Charles. **Dombey and Son.** 1848. Reprint, edited by Peter Fairclough, New York: Penguin Books, 1970. 992p. illus. appendix. bibliography, 37. notes. pa.
Perhaps the most profound of Dickens's portraits of fatherhood corrupted by monetary concerns, *Dombey and Son* is—ironically—the name of a business "house" rather than a description of a father-son relationship. A wealthy businessman, Mr. Dombey regards his daughter Florence as insignificant because she cannot succeed to the firm. He regards his fragile son Paul more as a business successor and a bid for immortality. When Paul dies, the novel suggests that lack of paternal love is partly responsible. The widowed Mr. Dombey then "buys" a new wife, Edith, from the marriage market. Repelled by what she has done, Edith proceeds to make life miserable for Mr. Dombey, herself, and young Florence. When his financial world collapses, Mr. Dombey at last awakens to the "feminine" qualities of love and care embodied in his daughter. In this novel, the most attractive father figure is the warm-hearted Captain Cuttles, and he—significantly—has no business acumen whatsoever. Another kindly father, Mr. Toodles, is a poor workingman. In dramatic terms, *Dombey and Son* depicts the incompatibility of cutthroat capitalism and loving fatherhood. The Penguin edition contains the original illustrations of the novel by Hablot K. Brown (known as "Phiz") and an introduction by Raymond Williams.

324. Dostoevsky, Fyodor. **The Brothers Karamazov.** 1879-1880. Reprint, translated by Constance Garnett, revised by Ralph E. Matlaw, New York: W. W. Norton, 1976. xiii, 887p. appendixes. bibliography, 887. notes. pa.

Dostoevsky's crowning achievement as a novelist, this work is, among other things, a psychological thriller that explores the heart of darkness—and light—in fathers and in sons. When the depraved Fyodor Karamazov is murdered, the killer could be any one of his four sons: the passionate Dmitri, who has been locked in an oedipal struggle with his father for the attentions of the earth-mother Grushenka; the intellectual Ivan, who has come to the conclusion that God has disappeared and that therefore "all is permitted"; the Christ-like Alyosha, whose steps are haunted by a dark "double" named Rakitin; or the diabolical Smerdyakov, who is apparently the son of Fyodor and a retarded woman whom he has wronged. While the sensual Fyodor and the saintly Father Zosima represent opposite extremes of father figures, the four brothers are volatile compounds of passion, intellect, mystical love, and demonic hate. The women in the novel are equally tempestuous, especially the hot-blooded Grushenka and the highly strung Katerina. Perhaps no other novel has portrayed so vividly the range of men's spiritual possibilities and the fury of their hidden torments. The Norton edition includes backgrounds and sources of the novel, as well as essays by such authors as Harry Slochower on the book's incest theme, D. H. Lawrence and Albert Camus on the Grand Inquisitor section, and Ralph E. Matlaw on the novel's religious myth and symbol.

325. **Epic of Gilgamesh, The.** Rev. ed. Translated and edited by N. K. Sandars. New York: Penguin Books, 1972. 128p. illus. appendixes. glossary. notes. pa.

One of the oldest of recorded narratives, *The Epic of Gilgamesh* is cited increasingly by men's studies scholars in a variety of contexts. Dating back to the third millennium B.C. and recorded on clay tablets found in the Middle East, *The Epic of Gilgamesh* tells of the legendary king of Uruk whose arrogance threatens his people and offends the gods. The Babylonian deities fashion a double of Gilgamesh, a wild man named Enkidu. After a fearsome struggle, the two men become intimate friends, and together they defeat the giant, Humbaba. When the goddess Ishtar makes sexual overtures to Gilgamesh and is rejected, she afflicts Enkidu with a fatal illness. Grieving for his dead friend, Gilgamesh sets out to find Utnapishtim, a Babylonian Noah who had survived the great flood and who holds the secret of immortal life. On Gilgamesh's return journey from Utnapishtim, a snake steals the flower of immortality from him, and Gilgamesh returns in sorrow to Uruk to await death. This plot outline only hints at the story's richness. Some scholars see in Enkidu the first wild man. The relationship between Gilgamesh and Enkidu has become the subject of endless speculation. Gilgamesh's rejection of Ishtar may represent patriarchal rejection of mother-goddess supremacy. Because Sandar's translation retells the story as an uninterrupted narrative, most lay readers will find it easily accessible. Sandars also provides a 60-page introduction to the epic, a map of the Middle East, a glossary of names, and an appendix listing sources of the story. Those seeking a translation closer to the fragmentary story contained on the tablets should consult *The Epic of Gilgamesh*, translated by Maureen Gallery Kovacs (Stanford, CA: Stanford University Press, 1985).

326. Hardy, Thomas. **Jude the Obscure.** 1896. Reprint, edited by C. H. Sisson, New York: Penguin Books, 1978. 511p. illus. glossary of dialect and unfamiliar words. notes. pa.

Hardy's last and bleakest novel, *Jude the Obscure* tells the tale of a poor boy whose dreams of attending Christminster University (i.e., Oxford University) are cruelly shattered by class prejudice and his own sexual needs. Those who imagine that, in the past, universities were closed only to women will be in for a rude awakening: only a small minority of males was eligible for higher education in Jude Fawley's day. To make matters worse, Jude finds himself trapped between the sexually frigid Sue Bridehead, who is all nervous intellect and restless liberation, and the sensual Arabella Donn, who is all amoral earthiness. The two female characters may represent Hardy's grim view of modern women. As D. H. Lawrence noted, the plot of *Jude the Obscure* is that of *Tess of the D'Urbervilles* with the genders of the main characters changed. While numerous critics have insisted that *Tess* depicts the oppression of women, few have had the courage to suggest that *Jude* depicts the tragic fate of modern men.

327. Homer. **The Iliad.** Translated by Robert Fitzgerald. Garden City, NY: Anchor Press/Doubleday, 1974. 595p. illus. notes. pa.

This grim and glorious epic represents perhaps the earliest and most electrifying account of combat warfare and its effect upon men. Retelling an episode from the legendary Trojan War, the poem focuses on the Akhaian warrior Akhilleus (Achilles) whose quarrel with King Agamemnon leads to Akhilleus' angry withdrawal from battle. During his absence, his friend Patroklos is killed by the Trojan hero Hektor, an act that sends an infuriated Akhilleus back into battle. His mania for revenge knows no bounds, even after he has killed Hektor. Only when Hektor's father, the pathetic King Priam, quietly asks Akhilleus for the return of his son's body does the hero's fury subside into a tragic sense of men's lot. Although *The Iliad* is crowded with vivid characters both human and divine, Akhilleus is at its center. Is he a macho soldier-killer obsessed with military slaughter and triumph? Is he a deluded young man who has taken the only path to masculine glory that his culture exalts? Is he a tragic figure who comes to realize the futility of the male hero's way of life? After nearly 3,000 years, *The Iliad* still raises these and other disturbing questions about the nature of war and male identity, about freedom and necessity in human fate, and about the relationship between combat and men's behaviors. The Robert Fitzgerald translation has received numerous accolades for its vigor, clarity, and ingenuity. The more recent translation by Robert Fagles (New York: Viking Penguin, 1991) has also been acclaimed widely.

328. Homer. **The Odyssey.** Translated by Robert Fitzgerald. Garden City, NY: Doubleday, 1961. 474p. illus. appendix. Reprint, Garden City, NY: Doubleday-Anchor, 1963. pa. Reprint, New York: Random House-Vintage, 1990. pa.

This epic of perilous journey and homecoming has enthralled the Western mind for nearly 3,000 years. Having spent 10 years fighting the Trojan War, Odysseus incurs the wrath of the sea god Poseidon, who prevents his return to his homeland of Ithaka for another 10 years. Wandering the Mediterranean Sea, Odysseus encounters numerous adventures before facing a final challenge—a group of lawless suitors who have invaded his household. These young men are pressuring his wife Penelope to marry, and they have murderous designs on her son by Odysseus, Telemakhos. Aided by the goddess Athene, Odysseus slays the suitors and reestablishes himself within his family and his kingdom. In doing so, he forges a new masculine identity by reclaiming his roles as husband, father, son, and king. Although Odysseus' fabulous voyages are exciting and memorable, the poem also celebrates the stability of the two-parent family and responsible fatherhood. In this way, *The Odyssey* can be seen as the epic of patriarchy (defined as father-involved society). Modern readers may also see the tale as a parable of a man's midlife search for meaning. A far different kind of hero than Akhilleus, Odysseus speaks from the heart when he says that "the best thing in the world [is] a strong house held in serenity / where man and wife agree." Robert Fitzgerald's lively verse translation has been praised greatly by scholars and general readers alike.

329. Ihara Saikaku. **The Great Mirror of Male Love.** Translated by Paul Gordon Schalow. Stanford, CA: Stanford University Press, 1990. ix, 371p. illus. notes. bibliography, 357-61. index. pa.

This collection of 44 short stories represents a complete translation of *Nanshoku ōkagami* (1687) by Ihara Saikaku (1642-1693). Schalow, in the introduction, describes love between adult males and adolescent boys in seventeenth-century Japan. The first group of stories, dealing with samurai warriors, usually involves intense relationships, violence, bloodshed, misogyny, and tragic results. The second group, dealing with kabuki actors, is more sentimental. Many of the stories are tinged with a sadness at the fleeting nature of beauty. The illustrations resemble those of Yoshida Hambi (fl. 1660-1700).

330. **Pearl: A New Verse Translation.** Translated by Marie Borroff. New York: W. W. Norton, 1977. xxii, 40p. pa.

Dating from late-fourteenth-century England, this exquisite poem is many things, including a father's lament for his dead daughter. It thus refutes those who assert that before modern times, parents—especially fathers—were emotionally detached from their young children and regarded them as hardly human. The poem shows that fathers can deeply mourn the death of a young child. Readers who prefer to tackle the poem in the original Middle English should see *Pearl*, edited by E. V. Gordon (New York: Oxford University Press, 1953).

331. Shakespeare, William. **As You Like It: With Reader's Guide.** Edited by Frank S. Zepezauer. New York: Amsco School Publications, 1991. 287p. notes. pa.

Shakespeare's gender-bender comedy features a young woman who assumes a male disguise and then begins instructing her male lover on how to court a woman. Rosalind, one of Shakespeare's most appealing heroines, also finds that her male disguise has made her the object of another woman's affections. But the tangled love affairs get sorted out in the end. Although aimed at highschool audiences, this edition of the play features such clear print and commentary that general readers also will find them helpful. Predictably, Rosalind has been a favorite with some feminist critics who argue that men need a woman to clean up their act. But Zepezauer's commentary is notably evenhanded: "In her disguise as a man, Rosalind has been able to poke fun at men. But she has also used it as a means by which she could be candid about the less attractive inclinations of her own sex." And what man can resist an inward cheer when Rosalind reprimands the haughty Phebe for slighting her honest lover, Silvius: "Down on your knees, / And thank heaven, fasting, for a good man's love."

332. Shaw, George Bernard. **Arms and the Man: A Pleasant Play.** 1884. Reprint, New York: Penguin Books, 1955. 78p. pa.

The sparkling wit of Shaw's dialogue is deadly serious about several matters, including how men are socialized to become soldiers, how men and women manipulate each other into playing frustrating gender roles, how society associates masculinity with combat aggressiveness, and how people glamorize war. This improbable, antiromantic comedy concerns a young Bulgarian woman who rescues a fleeing Swiss mercenary by hiding him in her bedroom. But that is just the start of the zany plot twists that Shaw uses to puncture cultural balloons about sex roles, war, and honor.

333. Strindberg, August. **The Father.** 1887. Reprint, in *Pre-Inferno Plays: The Father, Lady Julie, Creditors, The Stronger, The Bond.* Translated by Walter Johnson, Seattle: University of Washington Press, 1970. x, 243p. illus. bibliography, 237-40. notes. Reprint, New York: W. W. Norton, 1976. pa.

Strindberg is the grandfather of men's awareness. His 1887 drama *The Father* depicts a struggle between the Captain and his wife Laura over the future of their daughter. Representative of the older paternal order, the Captain seems strong but is really vulnerable to his dependency upon women, his little-boy need for mothering, his chivalry, his overdependence on reason, and his willingness to believe suggestions that deny his paternity. In a stunning echo of Shylock's famous speech in *The Merchant of Venice*, the Captain denounces misandry as a form of bigotry on the same order as anti-Semitism and racism. Walter Johnson's translations are both readable and actable. Among the other plays in this collection, *The Bond* (1892) dramatizes a furious custody battle that makes *Kramer Versus Kramer* look like a tea party.

334. Strindberg, August. **Getting Married.** 1884, 1886. Reprint, translated by Mary Sandbach, New York: Viking Press, 1972. 384p. notes.

The publication in 1884 of part 1 of *Getting Married* gave such offense to Swedish feminists and right-wing pietists that Strindberg found himself facing prosecution for blasphemy. The whole improbable story of Strindberg's ordeal is recounted in Sandbach's introduction to this translation of 30 short stories embellished with polemical prefaces. A favorite target of part 1 is Ibsen's play *A Doll's House*, which Strindberg dissects as a sham in his preface and assaults further in a short story titled "A Doll's House." Other stories in part 1 deal with the hazards faced by men in marriage. Typical of Strindberg's views, in "Love and the Price of Grain" the hapless young hero finds that he must pay and pay and pay again for the privilege of being married. Part 2, published in 1886 after Strindberg had been acquitted of blasphemy charges, shows him defiantly unrepentant. After declaring in the preface that women ruthlessly manipulate men, he dramatizes the point unflinchingly in such stories as "The Bread-Winner." Whether one regards Strindberg as an outrageous misogynist or as the grandfather of men's liberation, it is difficult to disagree with Sandbach's conclusion that "he alone among contemporary Swedish writers refused to be castrated or muzzled."

335. Twain, Mark [Samuel Langhorne Clemens]. **The Adventures of Huckleberry Finn.** 1884. Reprint, (2d ed.) edited by Sculley Bradley, Richmond Croom Beatty, E. Hudson Long, and Thomas Cooley, New York: W. W. Norton, Norton Critical Editions, 1977. xi, 452p. appendixes. bibliography, 451-52. notes. pa.

One of the great reads of American literature, *The Adventures of Huckleberry Finn* is also a hymn to male bonding, to the friendship between man and boy in a hostile world, and to the goodwill that can exist between black and white males. Persecuted by his brutal father, Huck Finn flees downriver on a raft with an escaped slave, Jim. As their adventures multiply, Huck becomes increasingly aware of Jim's compassionate humanity, and, in one of the book's most memorable scenes, he decides to violate his "conscience" and to help Jim become a free man. Although some readers have misinterpreted the story as racist and others are disappointed with the last quarter of the novel when Tom Sawyer steals the spotlight from Huck and Jim, most readers are deeply moved by the eloquence and humor of the novel's great middle section: Huck and Jim drift down the Mississippi, discovering their brotherhood. Like other Norton Critical Editions, this one contains useful background materials and critical essays.

336. Whitman, Walt. **Leaves of Grass.** 1855-1891. Reprint (rev. ed.), edited by Sculley Bradley and Harold W. Blodgett, New York: W. W. Norton, Norton Critical Editions, 1973. lx, 1008p. appendixes. illus. bibliography, 995-97. notes. index of titles. pa.
    Whitman's hymn to life is regarded by some critics as the great American poem of male liberation. In particular, the "Calamus" and "Drum-Taps" sections contain celebrations of male comradeship that anticipate modern efforts to reestablish male emotional closeness. This edition contains textual variants, Whitman's critical writings, and modern literary studies.

B. Modern Literature: Twentieth Century

337. Bly, Robert, James Hillman, and Michael Meade, eds. **The Rag and Bone Shop of the Heart: Poems for Men.** New York: HarperCollins, 1992. xxi, 536p. index of poets and first lines. pa.
    Americans live in a "poetically underdeveloped nation," the editors note in the introduction to this large, spirit-enriching collection of poems from around the world. The anthology reflects the editors' social and personal agendas. Sections include "Approach to Wildness" (celebrations of the wild man in men); "Fathers' Prayers for Sons and Daughters"; "War"; "I Know the Earth, and I Am Sad" (poems celebrating the earth and lamenting its desecration); "The House of Fathers and Titans"; "Language"; "Making a Hole in Denial" (poems acknowledging the shadow side of reality); "Loving the Community and Work"; "The Naïve Male" (the male who is intoxicated with the feminine and believes he can take over women's sufferings); "The Second Layer: Anger, Hatred, Outrage" (poems that express rage); "Earthly Love"; "The Cultivated Heart" (the ideal of masculinity); "Mother and Great Mother" (poems about mother as person and myth); "The Spindrift Gaze Toward Paradise" (poems of heavenly vision); "Zaniness"; and "Loving the World Anyway." Brief introductions to each section provide a context for reading the poems. A wide range of authors are represented (e.g., Robert Frost, Gerard Manley Hopkins, D. H. Lawrence, Rainer Maria Rilke, César Vallejo, William Butler Yeats). The selections crystallize male experience with an intensity that only great poetry can achieve.

338. Butler, Samuel. **The Way of All Flesh.** London: Grant Richards, 1903. Reprint, as *Ernest Pontifex, or The Way of All Flesh: A Story of English Domestic Life,* edited by Daniel F. Howard, Boston: Houghton Mifflin, Riverside Editions, 1964. xxviii, 365p. appendixes. bibliography, xxv-xxvi. notes. pa.
    This savagely ironic novel exposes the chasm that widened between British middle-class fathers and sons in late-Victorian England. In Theobald Pontifex, Butler drew a memorable caricature of the authoritarian clergyman

father whose son Ernest is predictably warped and rebellious. Howard uses Butler's manuscript for the text of this edition.

339. Conroy, Pat. **The Prince of Tides.** Boston: Houghton Mifflin, 1986. 567p. Reprint, New York: Bantam Books, 1987. pa.

Conroy's novel focuses on Tom Wingo, the troubled product of a troubled family. A native of South Carolina, Wingo flies to New York City to help psychiatrist Susan Lowenstein unravel the secrets that led to his sister Savannah's latest attempted suicide. In the process, Tom's past also unravels. Among the revelations is Tom's inability to face his being raped as a child. "I did not know a boy could be raped," Tom says. His mother is a purveyor of denial, misinformation, and southern-belle misandry; his father is a frequently absent, abusive misogynist. Left with numerous gender problems to sort out, Tom becomes entangled in the life of Dr. Lowenstein, who has her own share of family problems. Tom Wingo speaks for many men when he says, "There's only one thing difficult about being a man, Doctor. Only one thing. They don't teach us how to love."

340. Corman, Avery. **Kramer Versus Kramer.** New York: Random House, 1977. Reprint, New York: New American Library, Signet, 1978. 234p. illus. pa. Reprint, New York: Ivy Books, 1988. 247p. pa.

This novel—and the Academy Award-winning film based on it—deeply touched a large segment of the U.S. public and thus became something of a cultural landmark indicating an altered attitude toward divorced fathers. From one point of view, the novel can be seen as a modern continuation of Henrik Ibsen's *A Doll's House* which closes with the middle-class wife walking out on husband and children. *Kramer Versus Kramer* centers upon Ted Kramer, a hustling advertising salesman, whose wife Joanna walks out on him and their four-year-old son Billy. In the process of coping with the situation, Ted and Billy forge closer emotional bonds than would have been possible otherwise. But after 18 months, Joanna returns, seeking custody of Billy. Following a wrenching trial, she wins custody because of traditional court prejudice favoring the mother as primary parent. The novel's ending, in which Joanna decides to relinquish Billy to Ted, may strike some readers as wishful thinking.

341. Dickey, James. **Deliverance.** Boston: Houghton Mifflin, 1970. 278p. Reprint, New York: Dell, 1971. pa.

When four suburban men escape from their tacky, banal lives for a weekend of white-water canoeing and hunting in the wilds, the outing becomes a journey into the heart of male darkness. Set upon by two depraved mountain men, the four are swept into a maelstrom of violence that includes male rape and killings. Disturbingly, the novel suggests that some men, secretly bored with "feminized" civilization, yearn to light out for a wilder territory where they can engage in savage male-only rituals of challenge, death, and survival.

342. Dreiser, Theodore. **An American Tragedy.** 2 vols. New York: Boni and Liveright, 1925. 429, 406p. Reprint, New York: New American Library, 1973. pa.

In this large, richly detailed novel, the U.S. male's dream of success becomes his downfall. Arriving in a small, upstate New York town after a brush with the law in Kansas, poor boy Clyde Griffiths becomes caught between two women: the gentle factory worker, Roberta Alden, who shares his dreams of rising in the social scale, and the shallow socialite, Sondra Finchley, who personifies all the empty glamour that Clyde worships. Roberta becomes pregnant just as Clyde seems about to win Sondra. In his desperation he contemplates murdering Roberta, but when their boat overturns on a lake, her drowning is partly contrived and partly accidental. Nevertheless, Clyde is convicted of murdering her, and he dies in the electric chair. Instead of a Horatio Alger success story, Dreiser depicts a young man destroyed by the American dream.

343. Duberman, Martin. **Male Armor: Selected Plays, 1968-1974.** New York: E. P. Dutton, 1975. xv, 352p. pa.

This collection contains seven plays: *Metaphors, The Colonial Dudes, The Guttman Ordinary Scale, The Recorder, The Electric Map, Payments*, and *Elagabalus*. As Duberman explains in the introduction, the plays reverberate with the question, "What does it mean to be a 'man'?" and with the concept of male armor, that is, the rigid shell of masculinity that some men construct to confront the world.

343a. Ellison, Ralph. **Invisible Man.** New York: Random House, 1947. Reprint, 1992. xviii, 572p.

A richly textured novel that has achieved the status of modern classic, *Invisible Man* records the journey of a black Everyman in twentieth-century U.S. society. In the South, the unnamed narrator as a youth is brutalized and patronized by white men before he is sent off to a black college, where he is betrayed by the college president. As he heads north to Harlem, it begins to dawn on the narrator that he is an invisible man because no one—white or black—wants to see him as a unique individual. In Harlem he continues to run afoul of people and organizations that are blind to his "visibility." During an urban riot, he confronts his violent alter ego, a black revolutionary named Ras the Destroyer. At the end of the action, the narrator has become a "running man," fleeing from destructive forces but clutching his selfhood like the briefcase he carries. Significantly, the narrator avoids the castration he dreams about: At the end of the novel, he is running, but he is a running *man*.

344. Fitzgerald, F. Scott. **The Great Gatsby.** New York: Charles Scribner's Sons, 1925. 182p. pa.

For many readers, Fitzgerald's enormously successful novel dramatizes how the U.S. male has been destroyed by the American dream of success. Unlike Willy Loman in *Death of a Salesman* (entry 366), Gatsby attains great wealth, but only to discover how hollow this success is. Believing in all the Horatio Alger myths, young Jimmy Gatz transforms himself into wealthy Jay Gatsby and wins his dream woman, Daisy Buchanan. But Daisy is as shallow as Gatsby's dream of success. In the end, she returns to her husband Tom and his "old money," leaving Gatsby to be destroyed by the catastrophe that she and Tom have created.

345. Fitzgerald, F. Scott. **Tender Is the Night.** New York: Charles Scribner's Sons, 1933. 315p. pa. Reprint (rev. ed.), in *Three Novels of F. Scott Fitzgerald*, edited by Malcolm Cowley and Edmund Wilson, New York: Charles Scribner's Sons, 1953. appendix. notes. pa.

This Fitzgerald novel traces the rise and fall of Dick Diver, a likable and promising psychiatrist whose character and career are eroded by the emptiness of life among the wealthy in Europe. Like Gatsby, Diver is broken by a misguided attraction for glamorous wealth, represented in this novel by the beautiful but mentally unstable Nicole Warren. Diver's story can also be read as an account of a man unsuccessfully negotiating a midlife crisis. It is punctuated by insights into such matters as the ephemeral attraction between younger women and older men, midlife awareness of death, the harmful nature of many modern male-female relationships, and the greater survival skills of women. The 1953 edition incorporates Fitzgerald's considerable revisions of the earlier text.

346. Forster, E. M. **A Passage to India.** 1924. Reprint, New York: Harcourt Brace Jovanovich/Harvest, 1984. 316p. pa.

Forster's brilliantly complex novel is set during the British occupation of India, early in the twentieth century. In the presence of prejudice and distrust, the male friendship between the Indian, Dr. Aziz, and the British schoolmaster, Cyril Fielding, holds out the possibility of brotherhood between East and West. The bond is cruelly tested, however, when Dr. Aziz is accused of sexually molesting a British woman, Adela Quested, while they are visiting the mysterious Marabar Caves. The friendship is eventually healed, although the novel ends with the two friends' separating—a hint that the times are not yet ripe for full rapprochement between Eastern and Western men. For the most part, literary critics have been too timid to explore the significance of the false rape charge in the novel's overall structure, but Forster vividly depicts the vulnerability of males, especially minority males, to accusations of sexual impropriety.

347. García Márquez, Gabriel. **Chronicle of a Death Foretold.** Translated by Gregory Rabassa. New York: Alfred A. Knopf, 1982. Reprint, New York: Ballantine Books, 1984. 145p. illus. pa. Original publication, as *Crónica de una muerte anunciada* (Bogotá, Columbia: Editorial La Oveja Negra., 1981).

Few stories capture the dark side of Latin American machismo as memorably as this superbly ironic tale set in a small Caribbean town. When Angela Vicario is rejected by her new bridegroom because she is not a virgin, the male code of honor requires her twin brothers, Pedro and Pablo, to revenge the family honor by murdering her alleged lover, Santiago Nasar. Nearly everyone in town knows that Nasar's murder is imminent, but no one prevents it. The brothers want to be stopped, but community silence forces them to act. If they do not, they will no longer be considered men. Thus, the entire society imposes machismo upon men, even those men who loathe its violent requirements.

348. Gold, Herbert. **Fathers: A Novel in the Form of a Memoir.** New York: Random House, 1966. 309p. Reprint, New York: Random House, 1968. Reprint, Berkeley, CA: Creative Arts, 1980. pa. Reprint, New York: Arbor House, 1983. pa.

This novel tells the story of Sam Gold, a Jew who left Russia as a boy during Czarist persecutions and who came to the United States early in the twentieth century. Gold not only dramatizes his father's experiences but also tells a representative story about many men's struggle to succeed in the new land. When the novel ends in the mid-1960s, Sam is a vigorous 80-year-old survivor. As the divorced father of two daughters, his son Herb has a deepened appreciation of Sam's achievement. The novel closes with an "Epilogue and a Beginning" that recalls the figure of The Crippler. To prevent their sons from being conscripted into the brutalities of the Czarist armies, nineteenth-century Russian Jews had them deliberately maimed by a "crippler." This story—and the novel-memoir itself—are parables of the price males must often pay to survive.

349. Golding, William. **Lord of the Flies.** New York: Coward, McCann and Geoghegan, 1955. 243p. Reprint, New York: G. P. Putnam's Sons, Capricorn Books, 1959. pa. Reprint, New York: Coward, McCann and Geoghegan, 1962. pa.

When a group of British boys is marooned on a tropical island, the scene seems to be set for an idyllic adventure story. Instead, the situation becomes a nightmare as the boys degenerate into brutal savagery. Golding's terrifying suspense novel is also an electrifying parable of unchecked male aggression destroying civilized values and creating the threat of total annihilation. That no girls are present on the island may suggest that evil lurks in the hearts of males only. The 1959 reprint contains a biographical and critical note by E. L. Epstein. The 1962 reprint contains an introduction by E. M. Forster.

350. Goldman, William. **Father's Day.** New York: Harcourt Brace Jovanovich, 1971. 215p.

In this funny-sad novel, a divorced father (whose Walter Mitty-like imagination works overtime) attempts to reach out to his vulnerable, six-year-old daughter, only to leave her scarred, literally and figuratively, by their encounter.

351. Gosse, Edmund. **Father and Son: A Study of Two Temperaments.** London: Heinemann, 1907. vi, 373p. Reprint, edited by William Irvine, Boston: Houghton Mifflin, Riverside Editions, 1965. pa.

In this famous autobiographical novel, Gosse crystallizes the plight of the mid-Victorian father who rejects science when he cannot reconcile it with religious faith, and the late-Victorian son who rejects his father's faith when he cannot reconcile it with life. Exacerbated by the conflict between Darwinian agnosticism and evangelical piety, the estrangement between well-meaning father and dutiful son is raised by Gosse's art to a representative and poignant tale of generational incompatibility.

352. Guest, Judith. **Ordinary People.** New York: Viking Press, 1976. 263p. Reprint, New York: Ballantine Books, 1977. pa.

With an extraordinary ability to get inside her male characters, Guest writes a hymn to father-son bonding in this novel that served as the basis for a splendid film directed by Robert Redford. For young Conrad Jarrett, the usual teenage problems are compounded by his older brother's accidental drowning and by his own attempted suicide. His parents reverse the usual role expectations: his mother Beth has locked herself away from feelings because they are too painful to cope with, while his father Calvin has begun to break out of the provider's usual detachment to establish emotional connections with those around him. Also influencing Conrad is a memorably frank and understanding psychiatrist named Berger. Guest's narrative conveys a vivid sense of "felt life" right up to what was once one of the most unusual and moving climactic love scenes in modern fiction, a scene in which father and son manage to say to each other "I love you."

353. Gurian, Michael. **The Odyssey of Telemachus: A Novel in Prose and Poetry.** San Francisco: Swallow Song Press, 1990. 87p. appendix. pa.

Convinced that an important episode has been lost from *The Odyssey* (entry 328), Gurian sets out to close the gap. This episode describes how Odysseus' son Telemachus discovers his identity as an adult male. Told in prose and verse, the story becomes a vision quest, "a journey which mirrors, revises, expands and modernizes Homer's, especially in its appeal to gender influences on Telemachus." The young man's masculine maturity is shaped by Athena, the goddess of wisdom, as much as by the men whom Telemachus encounters, including his father. Gurian's idea is intriguing, but Homer is a tough act to follow poetically. (See entry 866.)

354. Heller, Joseph. **Something Happened.** New York: Alfred A. Knopf, 1974. 565p. Reprint, New York: Ballantine Books, 1975. pa.

In a lengthy interior monologue, Bob Slocum explores the messy emotional upheavals of his midlife crisis. At work he is clawing his way through the corporate jungle. At home he is alienated from his wife (who drinks during the day) and his teenage daughter (who alternately hates and loves him). One son is hopelessly retarded; the other is lovable and distressingly vulnerable. Slocum makes it through his various crises, but only at the cost of destroying the little boy within himself, an act dramatized when he smothers his vulnerable son to end the boy's suffering. Drawing together Slocum's memories, his fantasies, and his participation in the callous pettiness of the office and in the emotional sparring at home, the novel provides lightning glimpses into the lives of many modern men.

355. Hemingway, Ernest. **Men Without Women.** New York: Charles Scribner's Sons, 1927. 232p. pa.

According to Leslie Fiedler, all of Hemingway's fiction concerns men without women. In this collection of 14 short stories, the Hemingway heroes struggle to affirm positive masculine values in the face of almost inevitable defeat. In addition to several Nick Adams stories, the selection includes "The Undefeated," "White Elephants," and "Fifty Grand."

356. Hemingway, Ernest. **The Nick Adams Stories.** New York: Charles Scribner's Sons, 1972. 268p. pa. Reprint, New York: Bantam Books, 1973. pa.

Philip Young notes that the somewhat autobiographical Nick Adams "*is* the Hemingway hero, the first one." This collection brings together 24 short stories, including eight previously unpublished sketches, recounting Nick's early life. Nick is first seen as a frightened boy fishing with his father in the Michigan woods, then as a youth tramping around the country. Later, he is seen as a young soldier wounded amid the carnage of World War I, as a shattered veteran returning home, as a young writer perfecting his art, and finally as a father guiding his own son in the ways of men. Many of the earlier stories are initiation episodes in which Nick encounters the violence inherent in birth and death. Like many Hemingway heroes, the wounded Nick becomes a lonely hero, stoically sensitive, serious, honest, courageous in his own way, and strangely vulnerable. He also remains alienated from mainstream society and from most women. He validates his manhood by capably performing such tasks as fishing, hunting, and (above all) writing honestly. This collection includes "The Killers," "Big Two-Hearted River," and "Fathers and Sons."

357. Hemingway, Ernest. **The Old Man and the Sea.** New York: Charles Scribner's Sons, 1952. 140p. pa.

In this hymn to manly courage and endurance, Hemingway exalts his philosophy of manhood to the status of religion. The story's protagonist is an aging Cuban fisherman engaged in a life-and-death struggle with a marlin longer than the old man's fishing skiff. Battling his failing bodily powers as dauntlessly as he battles the marlin and the sharks that appear on the scene, the old man states the book's theme thusly: "A man can be destroyed but not defeated."

358. Kopit, Arthur. **Oh Dad, Poor Dad, Mamma's Hung You in the Closet and I'm Feeling So Sad: A Pseudoclassical Tragifarce in a Bastard French Tradition.** New York: Hill and Wang, 1960. 89p. illus. Reprint, New York: Pocket Books, 1966. pa.

This bizarre tragifarce features the quintessential castrating mother, Madame Rosepettle, who travels about with the stuffed corpse of her late husband whom she did to death. Also included in her entourage are two Venus-flytraps, a piranha, and her 17-year-old son Jonathan, whom she has so smothered with her "love" that he remains a stuttering child. When Jonathan literally smothers a young woman who tries to make love to him, the mother-son legacy becomes all too apparent. As the title indicates, the play caricatures the plight of the U.S. father and son as victims of an all-powerful Mom.

359. Lawrence, D. H. **Lady Chatterley's Lover.** Florence, Italy: Giuseppe Orioli, 1928. Reprint, New York: Grove Press, 1957. 384p. pa.

Lawrence's hymn to phallic tenderness still drives some people into a frenzy. For decades the novel was banned as obscene; now some academics denounce it as politically incorrect. The story centers upon Lady Connie Chatterley, whose husband, Sir Clifford, has been rendered impotent by a World War I wound. Symbolically, Sir Clifford represents the impotent British aristocracy and the sterility of much twentieth-century masculinity. Lady Chatterley finds herself surrounded by men who treat women "as equals" but who do not really like them, much less respond to them with full human sexuality. The women are not much better, if Mrs. Ivy Bolton, Sir Clifford's nurse, is any indication: while mothering men, she despises them and seeks power over them. Connie's life changes when she begins an affair with Oliver Mellors, the gamekeeper of her husband's estate. Hedged in by England's industrial blight and an embittered ex-wife, Mellors retains enough primal manliness to rouse Connie Chatterley to sexual love. Despite the worst that law and custom can do to them, the couple, at the end of the novel, are determined to find a new life together. Although many modern readers will hold the few brief scenes of lovemaking to be lyrical, the episodes were once condemned as pornographic and are now denounced as phallocentric. Far from degrading sexual love, however, Lawrence exalts it as something sacred. Far from degrading women or men, he rejects a sexless view of people as an insult to their humanity. The famous Grove Press edition contains an introduction by Mark Schorer and extracts from the 1959 legal decision that allowed the novel to be distributed in the United States.

360. Lawrence, D. H. **Sons and Lovers.** London: Duckworth, 1913. vii, 423p. Reprint, as *Sons and Lovers: Text, Background, and Criticism*, edited by Julian Moynahan, Viking Critical Library, New York: Viking Press, Penguin, 1968. xiii, 622p. illus. appendixes. bibliography, 619-22. pa.

Set in a nineteenth-century Nottinghamshire mining town, this some-what autobiographical novel dramatizes important insights into the plight of workingmen in industrial countries and into the psychosexual binds of young men who grow up in a mother-dominated household. In part 1, the drudgery of working in the mines transforms the joyously spontaneous Walter Morel into an irritable, drink-soaked authoritarian who is alienated from his family yet pitifully dependent on wife and home. Part 2 concentrates upon the son, Paul Morel, as he tries to break away from his mother's possessive love. His task is complicated by his inability to identify with his father and by his prolonged yet sexually inadequate affair with the daughter of a neighboring farm family. Paul drifts into another affair with Clara Dawes, an older and more dominating woman (like his mother), but he eventually relinquishes her to her estranged husband (who resembles Paul's father). Even though Paul has symbolically resolved his oedipal tensions and even though his mother dies, the question of whether Paul will ever be free of her domination is left unresolved at the novel's end. The Viking critical edition includes a wealth of autobiographical and social background material, literary assessments, and psychoanalytical studies, including Freud's "The Most Prevalent Form of Degradation in Erotic Life."

361. Lawrence, D. H. **Women in Love.** New York: privately printed for subscribers only, 1920. 356p. Reprint, London: M. Secker, 1921. Reprint, New York: Penguin Books, 1976. pa.

This novel, which Lawrence considered his best, is "about" many things, including men in love—with women and with other men. In the relationship between Rupert Birkin and Gerald Crich, Lawrence vividly portrays men's hunger for—and resistance to—close male friendships that are not homosexual but that are a form of love.

362. Lopate, Phillip. **Bachelorhood: Tales of the Metropolis.** Boston: Little, Brown, 1981. xvi, 286p.

This polished collection of personal essays, reminiscences, poems, anecdotes, and vignettes reflects numerous aspects of the author's bachelor life in New York City. Writing as a bachelor observer of life, Lopate offers wry and poignant "tales of the metropolis," including accounts of relationships that did not work out, reflections on bachelorhood as a state of life, a poetic look at an extrovert couple making the most of a second marriage, a brief portrait of a gay couple, an assessment of pornography and the men who patronize the 42-Street establishments, and an essay on the literature of bachelorhood.

363. Mailer, Norman. **An American Dream.** New York: Dial Press, 1965. 271p. Reprint, Garden City, NY: Doubleday, 1983. pa.

In this outrageous pop classic, tough-guy Steve Rojack murders his rich wife, seduces the German maid, eludes police investigators, makes it with a singer named Cherry, faces off with a black pimp named Shago Martin, defeats his tycoon father-in-law, and escapes various forms of mayhem. Whatever it means, the novel seems quintessentially Maileresque, touching on familiar themes, including the macho mystique, the blending of sex and violence, and black-and-white love-hate.

364. Mamet, David. **Oleanna.** New York: Vintage Books, Random House, 1993. ix, 80p. pa.

Mamet's controversial play features a male college professor whose ambition and glib cynicism about his profession leave him an easy target for a female student. The student, Carol, seems to have learned nothing in college except how to misinterpret everything as sexism, harassment, and a display of male power. Their disjointed discussion of her grades in act 1 spirals out of control in act 2 and culminates in an accusation of rape. John, the professor, is a classic example of the distracted male who has no idea how pervasive and corrosive modern misandry has become. Carol is a chilling depiction of the budding "femi-Nazi" moving in for the kill.

365. Maugham, W. Somerset. **The Moon and Sixpence.** New York: George H. Doran, 1919. 314p. Reprint, New York: Penguin Books, 1944. pa.

Written in 1918 and 1919 when Maugham was 44 and 45 years old, this novel draws upon its author's stormy passage through midlife. It is also based somewhat loosely upon the life of Paul Gauguin. The protagonist, Charles Strickland, at age 40 suddenly breaks away from his stuffy life as a London businessman and runs off to Paris to be a painter. Refusing to feel guilt for deserting his wife and children, Strickland relentlessly pursues his new vocation, regardless of whom he hurts. Eventually, he finds in Tahiti an environment more congenial to his art and self, but there he is consumed by leprosy, a disease as implacable as his monomania to create art. However one reacts to Strickland, Maugham has drawn a powerful portrait of a man driven by midlife passions.

366. Miller, Arthur. **Death of a Salesman: Certain Private Conversations in Two Acts and a Requiem.** New York: Viking Press, 1949. 139p. Reprint, New York: Penguin Books, 1976. pa.

Since its first performances in 1949, Miller's *Death of a Salesman* has continued to move audiences strongly, and it promises to become an enduring fixture of the American stage. Among other things, the play depicts a representative little man (a low man) whose lot mirrors that of other ordinary U.S. men. Its pitiful protagonist, Willy Loman, is typical in having once harbored Horatio Alger-like dreams of success. These dreams are presented in imagined conversations between Willy and his older brother Ben who made his fortune in the jungles of ruthless business enterprise. But Willy has been unable to attain such success, and near the end of his career, in his early sixties, he feels himself a failure as a man. Although Willy has anxiously tried to raise his two sons with the proper formula for male success, his own work and his values have deeply estranged him from both of them. When his older son Biff discovers his father's affair with The Woman (possibly representing the Bitch Goddess of Success), the break between father and son is irrevocable. Willy's wife Linda loves him deeply, but feeds his dreams and is powerless to prevent his impending catastrophe. Having been used and cast aside by his employer, Willy concludes that he is worth more dead than alive, and he commits suicide in a last desperate effort to win an opportunity for his son Biff. In brief, Willy kills himself trying to fulfill the masculine role of the provider who raises his family's social status. In the poignant Requiem that closes the play, Biff sadly concludes that Willy had all the wrong dreams and that "he never knew who he was."

367. Moramarco, Fred, and Al Zolynas, eds. **Men of Our Time: An Anthology of Male Poetry in Contemporary America.** Athens and London: University of Georgia Press, 1992. xxxviii, 408p. appendix. indexes of poets, titles, and first lines. pa.

This handsomely printed, generous selection of poetry reveals the inner lives of contemporary males in language that is both forceful and memorable. The editors believe that men have undergone enormous changes in recent years and that the most powerful record of those changes can be seen in men's poetry. "A quiet revolution has been taking place in men's poetry over the past few decades, as men have been chronicling the 'history of their hearts' and have been examining those relationships central to their being in the world: their connections to their fathers and mothers; their own sense of fatherhood and of being sons and brothers; their marriages, divorces, and other aspects of their love lives; as well as the ways they conceive of maleness and femaleness."

Poems are gathered into nine sections: boys becoming men; sons seeing fathers; sons and their mothers; fathers and their sons; fathers and their daughters; men and women; brothers, friends, lovers, and others; men at war; and the hearts of men. Poets include Robert Bly, Ishmael Reed, Richard Wilbur, David Citino, Barton Sutter, and Patrick O'Leary.

368. Perlman, Jim, ed. **Brother Songs: A Male Anthology of Poetry.** Minneapolis, MN: Holy Cow! Press, 1979. xi, 118p. illus. appendix.

Perlman has collected poems from 55 modern poets, arranged into sections about fathers, sons, brothers, and friends and lovers. The appendix contains information about the contributors. Graphics are by Randall W. Scholes.

369. Reed, Ishmael. **Reckless Eyeballing.** New York: St. Martin's Press, 1986. 148p.

In this wickedly funny, something-to-offend-everyone novel set in New York City, the Flower Phantom is shaving the heads of black female writers whose works have portrayed black men as oversexed savages, exactly the sort of image that white racists have been purveying for decades. Apparently, the Phantom's motive is to brand the women just as French people after World War II marked female Nazi collaborators. Among the Phantom's victims is feminist playwright Tremonisha Smarts (does she owe something to Alice Walker?), whose successful play *Wrong Headed Man* featured numerous black, male brutes. Meanwhile, black playwright Ian Ball is so at odds with trendy notions of sexism that he cannot get anything produced. Indeed, producer Becky French (does the last name link her with Marilyn French?) is pouring all her money and energy into a play demonstrating that Eva Braun was the victim of male chauvinism. Ball's play, *Reckless Eyeballing*, concerns a black man lynched by white men because he looked at a white woman. To get the play produced, however, Ball has to agree to have it rewritten by Smarts; it comes out as an all-female play justifying the lynching because any man guilty of recklessly eyeballing any woman is a rapist. (Shades of Susan Brownmiller in *Against Our Will,* entry 908, justifying the murder of Emmett Till!) The reworked play's new political correctness guarantees its success. Reed's novel, however, is so deliciously incorrect that one wonders how it ever got into print.

370. Remarque, Erich Maria. **All Quiet on the Western Front.** Translated by A. W. Wheen. Boston: Little, Brown, 1929. Reprint, New York: Fawcett Crest Books, 1979. 297p. pa. Original publication, as *Im Westen Nichts Neues* (N.p.: Ullstein A. G., 1928).

Perhaps more than any other novel, *All Quiet on the Western Front* captures the devastating effects upon men of the horror and futility of modern combat. Moved by the patriotic slogans of his teachers and the pressure from family and friends, young Paul Baumer enlists in the German army, only to be progressively dehumanized by military training and the nightmare of trench warfare. Although Baumer is the central figure, the novel follows in some detail the grim plights of several other soldiers, as well as prisoners and civilians. As the senseless carnage of battle continues, Paul's comrades are wounded or killed, and his own humanity is so irreversibly ravaged by warfare that his death is likely to be perceived by the reader as a blessing and a release.

371. Roth, Philip. **My Life as a Man.** New York: Holt, Rinehart and Winston, 1974. 330p. Reprint, New York: Penguin Books, 1985. pa.

Trying to achieve manhood, author Peter Tarnopol involves himself in a wildly disastrous marriage from which he may never recover. The first part of this novel consists of two Tarnopol stories in which he tries to exorcise his marital nightmare through fiction; in the longer second part of the book, he attempts to tell his "true story." Growing up in the fifties, Peter is told by society that it is "unmanly" and "immature" not to marry; it is men's duty to rescue women through marriage. "I wanted to be humanish: manly, a man," Peter reports—and so he succumbs to "the Prince Charming phenomenon." He marries Maureen, only to find himself in a cage with a wildcat. Peter discovers that in the sixties he cannot divorce his wife without her consent, that the judge at the separation hearings regards women as victims and men as oppressors who ought to pay for their "misdeeds," and that alimony payments are rigged against him. After the separation, Peter begins an affair with Susan, who has her own emotional problems. After Maureen's death in a car accident, Peter must face the challenge of living with his and Susan's battered psyches. In this novel, life as a man is nothing short of earthly damnation.

372. Roth, Philip. **Portnoy's Complaint.** New York: Random House, 1969. iii, 274p. Reprint. New York: Bantam Books, 1972. pa.

Portnoy's complaint is a familiar disorder—a messed-up sex life traced primarily to a smothering mother-son relationship. With a schlemiel father and a guilt mongering "Jewish mother," Alex Portnoy finds his only relief in incessant masturbation and (later) kinky sex. When he finds a liberated but not-too-bright sex partner whom he calls The Monkey, Portnoy has trouble relating to her except in bed. The novel, consisting of Portnoy's primal-scream monologue to his psychotherapist, is by turns horrifying and hilarious.

373. Schultz, Susan Polis, ed. **I Love You, Dad: A Collection of Poems.** Boulder, CO: Blue Mountain Press, 1983. 63p. illus. pa.

Forty-five affectionate tributes to father from as many poets are attractively printed along with stylized color illustrations.

374. Shepard, Sam. **Seven Plays.** New York: Bantam Books, 1981. xxvii, 336p. pa.

Shepard's *True West* dramatizes the struggle of men who envy other men for "the road not taken." Two brothers, Lee and Austin, have chosen opposite lifestyles: Lee is a drifter on intimate terms with the desert, Austin is a successful Los Angeles screenwriter. Sibling rivalry pushes them into an almost fatal role reversal, and the play's ending may suggest that the differences between the brothers can never be resolved. This volume also contains *Buried Child, Curse of the Starving Class, The Tooth of Crime, La Turista, Tongues,* and *Savage Love,* the latter two plays written in collaboration with Joseph Chaikin.

375. Sherman, Martin, **Bent.** New York: Avon Books, Bard, 1979. 80p. appendix. pa.

Depicting Nazi extermination of homosexuals, Sherman's play provides a metaphor for all persecution of gays.

376. Trumbo, Dalton. **Johnny Got His Gun.** Philadelphia: J. B. Lippincott, 1939. 309p. Reprint, New York: Lyle Stuart, 1959, 1970. pa. Reprint, New York: Bantam Books, 1970. pa.

This unsparing novel consists of the tortured ruminations of a World War I soldier whose wounds have left him a quadruple amputee, blind, deaf, speechless, and faceless. As such, Joe Bonham represents the millions of men who have died or been hideously wounded in battle. Bonham also imagines himself speaking for all the "little guys" of history who have been exploited, enslaved, tortured, or killed. Learning that the authorities prefer to ignore him in his present grotesque condition, Bonham envisions a time when victimized people will discover who their true enemies are and will turn their weapons on warmongering leaders.

377. Updike, John. **Rabbit, Run.** New York: Alfred A. Knopf, 1960, 1970. 309p. Reprint, New York: Fawcett World Crest, 1962. pa. Reprint, New York: Ballantine Books, 1981. pa.

The plight of Harry (Rabbit) Angstrom has hit a nerve with many U.S. men. After his high school years of basketball glory, Rabbit at 26 has settled into a life of thoroughgoing banality that includes a second-rate marriage to Janice (complete with son Nelson and a baby on the way) and a deadening job as a five-and-dime salesman in a drab small town. Unable to dispel the feeling that "somewhere there was something better for him than listening to babies cry and cheating people in used-car lots," Rabbit instinctively takes to flight—first into the arms of a prostitute, Ruth, then back to Janice when she gives birth to their child, and then away from her again after she accidentally drowns the baby in the bathtub during a bout of daytime drinking. A final, futile attempt to reunite with Ruth ends in another of Rabbit's flights. Perhaps, in Rabbit Angstrom, many U.S. men have found the fictional representative of their feelings of being trapped in early adulthood, of their need for something more than meaningless jobs and empty marriages, and of their desire for flight from such life-sapping institutions.

378. White, Edmund. **A Boy's Own Story.** New York: E. P. Dutton, 1982. 218p. Reprint, New York: New American Library, Plume Books, 1983. pa.

This novel about growing up homosexual in America is laced with ironies, insights, and cynicism.

379. Wilson, August. **Fences.** New York: Penguin-Plume, 1986. xviii, 101p. pa.

Troy Maxson's final days become a retrospective of his life, a life familiar to many twentieth-century black males. Troy recapitulates his impoverished childhood, his move to the city where desperation led him to crime, his prison time, the discrimination he faced as a black baseball player, his bouts with alcohol, and other handicaps in the game of life. He has found some blessings, however, especially in his marriage to Rose. But Troy's later years are complicated by his infidelity, his troubles on the job (significantly, he is a garbage collector), his rivalry with one of his sons, and his concern to fence out Death. When Death comes for Troy, the play's concluding scene suggests that, despite his flaws, his courage in batting what life pitched to him has won him salvation. As a black counterpart of *Death of a Salesman* (entry 366), *Fences* eloquently dramatizes African-American male experience and the process of healing the wounded father.

380. Wulbert, Roland, and Larry Laraby, eds. **A Good Crew: An Alaskan Men's Anthology.** Fairbanks, AL: Fireweed Press, 1986. iv, 78p. pa.

Alaska is already a place in the imagination, the editors point out in their introduction. This collection of 29 short stories and poems by male authors features primarily male characters. Several of the entries record rites of passage; a number employ Alaskan fishing as a setting.

C. The Arts: Film, Painting, Photography

381. Aymar, Brandt. **The Young Male Figure: In Paintings, Sculptures, and Drawings from Ancient Egypt to the Present.** New York: Crown, 1970. vii, 247p. illus. bibliography, 245-47. index.

With the aid of numerous black-and-white photographs, Aymar traces the depiction of the young male body in classical antiquity, in the Renaissance and mannerist periods, in European art of the seventeenth through the twentieth centuries, and in more exotic art.

382. Gloeden, Wilhelm, Baron von. **Photographs of the Classic Male Nude.** New York: Camera/Graphic Press, 1977. 105p. illus. Original publication, as *Taormina debut du siecle* (Paris: Editions du Chêne, 1975).

Living in Taormina in the early twentieth century, Baron von Gloeden photographed nude Sicilian youths, attempting to evoke a homoerotic Arcadia. Although the preface by Jean-Claude Lemagny stresses their datedness, others may see the photographs reproduced in this volume as a hymn to the young male body.

383. Hayes, Dannielle B., ed. **Women Photograph Men.** New York: William Morrow, 1977. unpaged. illus. pa.

Hayes brings together 118 photographs of males by 71 artists, including Dawn Mitchell Tress, Kathryn Abbe, Dianora Niccolini, Patt Blue, Arlene Alda, Ruth Breil, Karen Tweedy-Holmes, and Carolee Campbell. Happily, the photographers look at men as humans first, avoiding idealizations and caricatures. Although a few celebrities (e.g., Richard Burton) and a few pretty faces appear, the majority of males are remarkable for their ordinary humanity—a Vietnamese boy with a pained smile and a missing leg, a pair of muddy oil riggers engaging in a ballet of work with their gear, and an elderly roustabout wearily propped against a circus tent pole. Although some nudes are included, the photographers seem most fascinated by the men's hands and hairiness. Unfortunately, the introduction by Molly Haskell comes freighted with all the clichés about men that the photographers have avoided so splendidly.

384. Husband, Timothy, with Gloria Gilmore-House. **The Wild Man: Medieval Myth and Symbolism.** New York: Metropolitan Museum of Art, 1980. xii, 220p. illus. appendixes. bibliography, 205-15. notes. index.

This book grew out of an exhibit on the medieval wild man presented at The Cloisters in New York City. Superbly illustrated with dozens of black-and-white and color illustrations, the book discusses the repeated appearances of the wild man in medieval iconography. This book is the place to trace Iron John's family tree. (See entry 861.) For more on the wild man, see *The Wild Man Within* (entry 273).

385. Keyes, Roger S. **The Male Journey in Japanese Prints.** Berkeley: University of California Press, 1989. xxx, 189p. illus. index.

With 255 color and black-and-white reproductions of Japanese woodblock prints, this oversized volume presents the male journey of life in visual images of *ukiyo-e*, pictures of the everyday changing world. Most of the pictures are examples of *surimono*, or pictures with verses. The male journey begins with growing up in the presence of mother and other women. Pictures of fathers and children are comparatively few. After childhood comes youth, with pictures of boy prostitutes and young heroes. Maturity brings a wealth of situations portrayed in the prints, including love and sex, work, hardships, leisure, conflict, and battle. Old age can bring serenity, mastery, and detachment. Death and survival close the journey. Keyes's commentary links people and events depicted in the prints to the particulars of Japanese life and to the universals of men's lives.

386. Reich, Hanns, comp. **Children and Their Fathers.** Text by Eugen Roth. New York: Hill and Wang, 1962. 11, 74p. illus. Original publication, Munich: Hanns Reich Verlag, 1960.
    Containing a splendid collection of photographs depicting fathers and children from around the world, this is a book to cherish.

387. Scavullo, Francesco, with Bob Colacello and Séan Byrnes. **Scavullo on Men.** New York: Random House, 1977. 186p. illus.
    This collection of photographs and interviews features 50 famous men. Scavullo quizzes the men on such topics as health, food, fatherhood, careers, drugs, and the women's movement. Memorable photographic images include William F. Buckley, Jr., with finger to pursed lips, Truman Capote grinning like a possessed imp, Bruce Jenner and Christopher Reeve in barechested splendor, the serenity in Arthur Ashe's face and the intensity in Julian Bond's, the pain in Norman Mailer's eyes and the humane twinkle in Arthur Miller's, and the radiant smile and open arms of operatic tenor Luciano Pavarotti.

D. Critical Commentary on the Arts, Language, Literature

388. Absher, Tom. **Men and the Goddess: Feminine Archetypes in Western Literature.** Rochester, VT: Park Street Press, 1990. xv, 157p. bibliography, 147-52. notes. index. pa.
    Far from being hostile to feminine qualities and women, the classics of Western literature often show the male hero as growing in humanity because he accepts the Goddess or the Feminine. Whether the male hero successfully incorporates the Feminine often decides his growth or decline as a human being. Absher demonstrates this thesis by examining *The Epic of Gilgamesh* (entry 325), *Death of a Salesman* (entry 366), *The Odyssey* (entry 328), *The Adventures of Huckleberry Finn* (entry 335), *Macbeth, A Midsummer Night's Dream, Sir Gawain and the Green Knight, The Death of Ivan Ilyich, The Bear,* and *To the Lighthouse.* By defining patriarchy as "male-dominated" rather than "father-involved" society, Absher stacks the deck against it, but he argues convincingly that many literary classics, even those written by dead, white males, are pro-feminine.

389. Balbert, Peter. **D. H. Lawrence and the Phallic Imagination: Essays on Sexual Identity and Feminist Misreading.** New York: St. Martin's Press, 1989. xi, 190p. notes. index.

Mincing no words, Balbert savages the politicized misreadings of D. H. Lawrence's works by feminist critics, both female and male. Long canonized in academia, these misreadings do not deal honestly with Lawrence's texts. In *Sexual Politics* (entry 680), Kate Millett altered passages from Lawrence's writings, and Robert Scholes parroted feminist critiques without citing textual evidence. Balbert praises feminists like Anaïs Nin for more reliable assessments of Lawrence, and he offers extended, revisionist analyses of *Sons and Lovers* (entry 360), *The Rainbow*, *Women in Love* (entry 361), "The Woman Who Rode Away," and *Lady Chatterley's Lover* (entry 359). Like Lawrence, Norman Mailer, and Ernest Hemingway, Balbert celebrates the phallic imagination, which, he argues, does not demean women but accepts women and men as sexual human beings. Balbert's critique makes for lively reading and offers a refreshing alternative to radical feminist assessments of Lawrence's work.

390. Bamber, Linda. **Comic Women, Tragic Men: A Study of Gender and Genre in Shakespeare.** Stanford, CA: Stanford University Press, 1982. 211p. notes. index.

In contrast to critics who see Shakespeare as androgynous, Bamber argues that he often writes from a masculine viewpoint and sees women as "the other." Such a stance does not necessarily mean that Shakespeare is a male chauvinist; the acceptance of "the other" may be positive. Bamber traces the Shakespearean heroine in the comedies, as well as in *Antony and Cleopatra*, *Hamlet*, *Macbeth*, and *Coriolanus*. In the final comedies, the "return of the feminine" can be seen as positive, although in *The Tempest* the mood is saddened by the failure of this return.

391. Bloch, R. Howard, and Frances Ferguson, eds. **Misogyny, Misandry, and Misanthropy.** Berkeley: University of California Press, 1989. xvii, 235p. illus. notes. index. pa.

This collection of eight essays focuses on misogyny in the arts. Despite the title, equal consideration is not always given to misandry. At their best, the essays examine the complexities of defining misogyny. Frances Ferguson's essay, for example, looks at how the complexities of rape accusations affect readings of novels like Richardson's *Clarissa*. In an intriguing analysis of slasher films, Carol J. Clover argues that males in the audience often do identify with the "Final Girl" who destroys the (usually male) slasher. At their worst, the essays exhibit misandry. Naomi Schor's essay on French women's writings about men both flaunts and attempts to justify its anti-male sexism. Other essays present R. Howard Bloch on medieval misogyny, Joel Fineman on Shakespeare's *Rape of Lucrece*, Jacqueline Lichtenstein on women and make-up in seventeenth-century France, Gillian Brown on agoraphobia and Melville's "Bartleby the Scrivener," and Charles Bernheimer on Degas's brothel drawings.

392. Boone, Joseph, and Michael Cadden, eds. **Engendering Men: The Question of Male Feminist Criticism.** New York and London: Routledge, 1990. 333p. illus. bibliography, 324-26. notes. index. pa.

After the gender sniping in *Men in Feminism* (entry 224), the editors of this book decided to handle the question of male feminist criticism in a less acrimonious way. The result is a collection of 17 essays that discuss divergent topics, most of them centered on gay sensibilities. Essays focus on familiar literary figures such as the influential, closet gay critic F. O. Matthiessen, Wallace Stevens, Nathaniel Hawthorne, Oscar Wilde, Emily Dickinson, and Sylvia Townsend Warner. Topics include such subjects as the homosexual overtones of American Puritan religious poetry, homoerotics in the *Bonanza* television series, and gay subtexts in the films *Rebel Without a Cause* and *Nightmare on Elm Street 2: Freddy's Revenge*. Individual discussions are interesting, but coherence is not the collection's strong suit. Likewise, the book leaves one feeling that the work of male and gay critics improves when they branch out from radical feminist categories and ideologies.

393. Boose, Lynda E., and Betty S. Flowers, eds. **Daughters and Fathers.** Baltimore, MD, and London: Johns Hopkins University Press, 1989. 453p. illus. bibliography, 431-50. pa.
    The daughter-father relationship has been all but overlooked in literary and social criticism, according to the editors. In this collection of 18 articles, the authors examine daughters and fathers, usually in literary texts. Hawthorne, Yeats, Plath, Christina Rossetti, Dickinson, Woolf, and Thackeray are among the authors examined. Other essays discuss Freudian theory, Mexican-American culture, and Henry VIII's daughters.

394. Bristow, Joseph. **Empire Boys: Adventures in a Man's World.** London: HarperCollins *Academic*, 1991. 233p. (Reading Popular Fiction series). illus. bibliography after each chapter. pa.
    This readable study attempts to link popular boys literature in England from 1860 to 1928 with British political aims, indicating how this literature shaped an "imperialistic" definition of manhood. Bristow examines periodicals such as *Boy's Own Paper* and fiction such as *Tom Brown's School Days*, *Treasure Island*, *She*, *Kim*, and *Tarzan of the Apes*. Combining social history and literary analysis, the study sometimes strains to condemn "dominant, or hegemonic, masculinity."

395. Butters, Ronald R., John M. Clum, and Michael Moon, eds. **Displacing Homophobia: Gay Male Perspectives in Literature and Culture.** Durham, NC, and London, England: Duke University Press, 1989. 314p. notes. index. pa.
    The 12 essays in this anthology discuss a range of literary and cultural phenomena from a gay male perspective. Topics include the use of boys to play women's parts on the English Renaissance stage, depiction of gays on American television, considerations of gayness in Willa Cather's "Paul's Case," the homoerotics of Lawrence Durrell's *Alexandrian Quartet*, implications of gayness in Spenser's *Shepheardes Calender*, Mercutio as "gay" character in *Romeo and Juliet*, homophobic discourse in Tennessee William's life and work, a survey of British "sodomy" laws, a reading of Oscar Wilde's *Portrait of Mr. W.H.*, Whitman's reactions to realistic fiction, U.S. Supreme Court rulings on crimes of gay sexuality and fictions like *The Talking Room* and *The Story of Harold*, and the interconnections between AIDS, politics, and literary theory. Contributors include Stephen Orgel, Joseph A. Boone, and Joseph A. Porter.

396. Claridge, Laura, and Elizabeth Langland, eds. **Out of Bounds: Male Writers and Gender(ed) Criticism.** Amherst: University of Massachusetts Press, 1990. xii, 344p. illus. notes after each essay. pa.
    This collection of 15 essays, plus an introduction, attempts to move gender literary criticism beyond the polarity of male-evil, female-good that has

characterized much feminist criticism. In the introduction, the editors argue that male authors can be as ill at ease in patriarchy as female writers can be. The term "patriarchy" cannot be equated with "male": not all males are patriarchs, nor do they all subscribe to patriarchal ideology. (The editors' desire to transcend polarized stereotypes, however, is undercut by their inability to see anything positive in patriarchy.) The re-visioning quality of the volume is evident in Joseph Wittreich's lead-off essay on John Milton as less of a misogynist than many feminist critics claim. Later essays focus on such "canonical" authors as Sterne, Blake, Percy Shelley, Keats, Thackeray, Robert Browning, Whitman, Wilkie Collins, Hardy, James, Forster, Frost, Faulkner, and Durrell.

397. Crompton, Louis. **Byron and Greek Love: Homophobia in 19th-Century England.** Berkeley: University of California Press, 1985. xiii, 419p. appendix. notes. index.

Homophobia led Lord Byron to conceal his bisexuality during his lifetime and led to a cover-up by Byron's contemporaries and later biographers. Although much evidence was destroyed during and after Byron's lifetime, Crompton carefully pieces together what is known of Byron's homosexual and pederastic affairs. He portrays the temper of the times and traces Byron's life in England and abroad. He locates the reflections of Byron's affairs in his poetry (often in passages that never saw print) and letters. Crompton also examines the sexual attitudes of several contemporaries, especially Jeremy Bentham and Percy Shelley. Byron's death while fighting for Greek independence has sexual as well as political implications.

398. Davis, Robert Con, ed. **The Fictional Father: Lacanian Readings of the Text.** Amherst: University of Massachusetts Press, 1981. 206p. notes. index.

Literary criticism, as well as the social sciences, has discovered the father. Utilizing the thought of Jacques Lacan (whose theories were fathered by Freud), the critics represented in this collection search for literary fathers in such texts as *The Odyssey* (entry 328), and Dickens's *Bleak House*, and in Faulkner's novels.

399. Easthope, Antony. **What A Man's Gotta Do: The Masculine Myth in Popular Culture.** London: Paladin Grafton Books, 1986. vii, 184p. illus. bibliography, 180-81. index. Reprint, Boston: Unwin Hyman, 1990. pa.

Easthope examines "the masculine myth" in diverse items of popular culture, films like *Red River, The Deer Hunter, North Dallas Forty*, and *Butch Cassidy and the Sundance Kid*, as well as Michelangelo's *David,* beer and cigarette ads, newspaper items, pop novels, and much else. Although Easthope has some interesting insights into the artifacts he examines, the book's overall thesis is murky. Apparently, Easthope has visions of destroying patriarchy by exposing the "myth" that masculinity does not represent all of humanity, an insight he regards as revolutionary. Easthope's Marxist-feminist brew is flavored with pinches of Freud and Lacan. The overall effect is somewhat incoherent, misandric, and heterophobic.

400. Federico, Annette. **Masculine Identity in Hardy and Gissing.** Rutherford, NJ: Fairleigh Dickinson Press, 1991; London and Toronto: Associated University Presses, 1991. 148p. bibliography, 143-46. notes. index.

Although the female characters in the novels of Thomas Hardy and George Gissing have received much attention, their male characters have been largely ignored by gender-conscious critics. Federico finds these male characters torn between male identity and masculine roles. The men are also under stress from the demands of traditional gender roles, new women, and internal pressures. To add to the confusion, the socially accepted idea of male superiority conflicts with the equally accepted idea that "boys are nasty." Federico discusses numerous novels including *Far From the Madding Crowd*, *Jude the Obscure* (entry 326), and *The Odd Women*.

401. Fone, Byrne R.S. **Masculine Landscapes: Walt Whitman and the Homoerotic Text.** Carbondale and Edwardsville: Southern Illinois University Press, 1992. xiv, 306p. bibliography, 295-300. notes. index.

Rejecting hesitancy on the question of Walt Whitman's sexual orientation, Fone argues that a homosexual subtext with homoerotic pleasures permeates Whitman's writings, including his early fiction, drafts of poems, and *Leaves of Grass* (entry 336).

402. Franklin, H. Bruce. **Prison Literature in America: The Victim as Criminal and Artist.** 1978. Expanded ed., New York: Oxford University Press, 1989. xxxii, 352p. bibliography, 293-341. notes. index. pa. Original publication, as *The Victim as Criminal and Artist: Literature from the American Prison* (1978).

In this updated version of a study published earlier in 1978 and 1982, Franklin surveys slave and prison literature in America, devoting separate chapters to slave narratives, Melville (the ship as prison), literature by prison inmates (with special attention to works by Malcolm Braly and Chester Himes), and contemporary prison literature from Malcolm X (entry 70) to the present. An especially full bibliography of prison writings is included. The introductions argue convincingly that current concepts of "American literature" need to be expanded, although the heated denunciation of past scholars as purveyors of race and class bias is often unfair. Franklin notes, for example, the omission of American Indian literature from past literary anthologies, without mentioning the enormous difficulties faced by scholars who try to study this literature. Franklin also insists that the disproportionate number of blacks in prison demonstrates the racism in U.S. society, but he fails to confront the radical corollary of this argument: the disproportionate number of males in prison demonstrates the sexism in U.S. society.

403. Green, Martin. **The Adventurous Male: Chapters in the History of the White Male Mind.** University Park, PA: The Pennsylvania State University Press, 1993. 245p. bibliography, 229-33. index.

Although "adventure" in life and art is popular, Green argues that it has seldom received serious critical attention. He also argues that the masculine is closely linked with adventure that combines *eros* (the erotic) and *potestas* (power). For this reason, some feminists frown on adventure as concept and art. Green defines adventure as a series of episodes in which the normal rules of civilized life are broken to attain some desirable end; the central virtue of the adventure hero is courage. Adventure has both positive and negative aspects: it can represent a quest for the unknown or the seemingly unattainable, but it can also involve domination. Although the primary texts of adventure derive from late-nineteenth-century British literature (with its imperialistic overtones), Green's discussion of adventure ranges through an extraordinarily wide range of art, history, and literature. He considers, for example, travel and exploration, sports and holidays, the founding of Israel, the history of Scotland's rebellion against England, philosophy and metaphysics, science and the social sciences, and caste and empire. Throughout the discussion, Green maintains a balanced view of adventure, weighing its pluses and minuses.

404. Hornback, Bert G. **Great Expectations: A Novel of Friendship.** Boston: Twayne, 1987. xiv, 152p. (Twayne Masterwork Studies, no. 6). illus. bibliography, 147-49. notes. index. pa.

Hornback gives a full analysis of Dickens's novel, connecting its many elements to the overriding theme of male friendship as the source of ultimate value. Starting with *A Tale of Two Cities* (1859), Hornback notes, Dickens's heroes do not end by marrying but by learning friendship and the freedom it can bring. In *Great Expectations* (1860-61), young Pip's dreams of becoming a wealthy, idle "gentleman" are realized, but when crises occur, Pip is saved not by his class status but by his friendships with the simple blacksmith Joe Gargery and the ingenuous Herbert Pocket.

404a. Houston, Jean. **The Hero and the Goddess:** *The Odyssey* **as Mystery and Initiation.** New York: Ballantine Books, 1992. xvi, 424p. Book I: Transforming Myth series. illus. appendixes. bibliography, 401-6. notes. index. pa.

Not a traditional literary critic, Houston uses *The Odyssey* (entry 328) as a mythic text for a soul journey that explores initiation and transformation. She provides instructions and exercises for solo and group readers, along with commentary on the action and characters of Homer's epic. Drawing on such sources as Joseph Campbell's *The Hero with a Thousand Faces* (entry 862), Houston encourages readers to participate in the myth in which the hero Odysseus is transformed by accessing the goddess Athena.

405. Johnson, Wendell Stacy. **Sons and Fathers: The Generational Link in Literature, 1780-1980.** New York: Peter Lang, 1985. vii, 237p. (Studies in Romantic and Modern Literature, no. 1). notes. index.

Taking their cue from Christian theology that identifies the Son and the Father, Western writers in the nineteenth and twentieth centuries have been exploring the "generational link" between sons and fathers. In Wordsworth's poetry, the child within is a crucial force, but this child is lost in the work of Coleridge and Byron. In the Victorian era, Thomas Carlyle and Dickens focus on the child as orphan. In the writings of John Ruskin, J. S. Mill, and Matthew Arnold, the estranged child is paramount. Johnson traces father-son patterns in W. B. Yeats, James Joyce, and William Faulkner, concluding with an assessment of the father within who appears in twentieth-century literature.

406. Kahn, Coppélia. **Man's Estate: Masculine Identity in Shakespeare.** Berkeley: University of California Press, 1981. xiii, 238p. notes. index.

In this scholarly blend of psychology and literary criticism, Kahn explores the recurring theme of masculine identity in Shakespearean drama. She focuses on the difficulties that various male characters have in achieving gender identity in a culture that provides them with social dominance over females and yet makes them vulnerable to females for their masculine identity. Rather than a chronological study, the author examines different themes as they appear in groups of works. In *Venus and Adonis,* the young hero's refusal to grow to sexual maturity reverses the adolescent rite of passage and causes his loss of identity. The history plays are fiercely masculine, concentrating on male-male tensions that almost exclude women. *Romeo and Juliet* shows adolescents trying to grow up but thwarted by adult enmity, while in *The Taming of the Shrew,* Petruchio's conquest of Kate is qualified by the covert recognition that his identity depends upon her actions. Kahn traces the theme of cuckoldry through several plays, including *Hamlet* and *Othello,* and she sees in Macbeth and Coriolanus two half-grown men who are fatally dependent on wife and mother. The final chapter examines male characters in the context of family, especially fathers who lose and then recover the feminine in daughter and wife. In *The Tempest,* however, Prospero does not rejoin with the feminine but surrenders his daughter to her groom and proceeds to his own solitary life. Kahn believes that Shakespeare questioned cultural definitions of manhood and knew how tenuous masculine identity could be.

407. Kiberd, Declan. **Men and Feminism in Modern Literature.** New York: St. Martin's Press, 1985. xii, 250p.

Examining how men reacted to the emergence of turn-of-the-century feminism, Kiberd scrutinizes some leading male authors of the time. Resisting the temptation to dismiss August Strindberg as a misogynist, Kiberd offers intriguing readings of *Miss Julie* and *Comrades.* In Thomas Hardy's *Jude the Obscure* (entry 326) and in D. H. Lawrence's *Women in Love* (entry 361) Kiberd finds the worst aspects of the "new woman" in Sue Bridehead and Gudrun Brangwen. He also examines the poetry of W.B. Yeats, the plays of Henrik Ibsen, and James Joyce's novel *Ulysses.* Unfortunately, when Kiberd shifts from literary analysis to social history in the final chapter, the discussion becomes unconvincingly mushy, especially when socialism is introduced as the cure-all for humanity's ills.

408. Kirchhoff, Frederick. **William Morris: The Construction of a Male Self, 1856-1872.** Athens: Ohio University Press, 1990. xv, 248p. bibliography, 239-43. index.

Critics and biographers often find Morris to be one of the most enigmatic of the Victorians. Kirchhoff argues that Morris rejected the male power system and women's role in it. In the process, he constructed a new male self that baffles many of his later biographers. This kinder, gentler male self helps to explain Morris's socialism and his apparent acceptance of his wife's affairs. Kirchhoff provides close readings of Morris's major writings between 1856 and 1872 to support his analysis of Morris's new male self.

409. Klotman, Phyllis Rauch. **Another Man Gone: The Black Runner in Contemporary Afro-American Literature.** Port Washington, NY: Kennikat Press, 1977. 160p. (National University Publications, Literary Criticism Series). bibliographic essay, 149-157. notes. index.

Klotman identifies the running man as a recurring figure in Western literary narratives from the earliest times. The tradition extends from Odysseus and Orestes to Natty Bumppo and Huckleberry Finn, and beyond. Within this larger framework, Klotman locates U.S. black writers, beginning with slave narratives depicting the run from slavery to freedom. Discussing a wide range of authors, she focuses on such major figures as Richard Wright (entry 69), James Baldwin, Ralph Ellison (entry 343a), Claude Brown (entry 37), and Imamu Amiri Baraka.

410. Knox, Bernard. **The Oldest Dead White European Males, and Other Reflections on the Classics.** New York: W. W. Norton, 1993. 144p. notes.

In the title essay of this collection, a leading classical scholar answers critics who argue that the canon of Greek classics represents an aristocratic, male-chauvinist plot to tyrannize the masses. Although fifth-century B.C. Athens was a slave society that gave women no public role, the classic works of the time are precious precisely because they transcend the class and gender limitations of their age. It is impossible to argue convincingly that works like Euripides' *Medea* reinforce "male structures of authority," and few historical works are as multicultural as Herodotus' history. Rather than being instruments of reactionism, the Greek classics throughout Western history have been instruments of social change, human progress, and (at times) revolution. The Greek classics—such as the works of Plato and Aristotle, Aeschylus and Sophocles, Xenophon and Thucydides—are not the products of male narrowness but of male inclusive genius. These works have survived the ages not because male tyrants imposed them upon oppressed populations but because active human minds treasured their intellectual and artistic excellence.

411. Koestenbaum, Wayne. **Double Talk: The Erotics of Male Literary Collaboration.** New York: Routledge, 1989. x, 214p. bibliography, 199-208. notes. index. pa.

Koestenbaum unearths a good deal of homoerotic "double talk" in works created by male collaborators. He examines Josef Breuer's and Sigmund Freud's *Studies in Hysteria* (1895), Havelock Ellis and John Addington Symonds's *Sexual Inversion* (1897), William Wordsworth and Samuel Taylor Coleridge's *Lyrical Ballads* (1798), T. S. Eliot and Ezra Pound's *The Waste Land* (1922), and a number of late-Victorian and Edwardian "romances," including works by Robert Louis Stevenson, H. Rider Haggard, and Joseph Conrad. In all these works, Koestenbaum finds "homotextuality." Many of the textual readings in this study are persuasively perceptive, but when Koestenbaum leaps from texts to psychobiography, he often seems to be indulging in free association.

412. Krutnik, Frank. **In a Lonely Street:** *Film Noir*, **Genre, Masculinity.** London and New York: Routledge, 1991. xiv, 268p. appendixes. notes. index. pa.

Krutnik explores the Hollywood *films noir* of the 1940s, comparing and contrasting them with classical Hollywood films. The *noir* films popularized psychoanalysis, and Krutnik analyzes them in terms of Freudian theory as filtered through Jacques Lacan and feminist critics. He examines the dramatization of tough-guy masculinity threatened by the phallic woman, destabilized masculinity, and other dangers. Krutnik discusses the tough investigative thriller, the tough suspense thriller, and the criminal-adventure thriller. Such films as *The Maltese Falcon*, *The Dark Corner*, and *Dead Reckoning* are examined in detail. Sometimes the politicized Freudian analyses lead to simplistic results: for example, a negatively portrayed female character (like the female lead in *The Maltese Falcon*) means that the film is "misogynist." The appendixes contain a filmography of hard-boiled Hollywood films of the 1940s and a list of 1940s crime-film cycles.

413. Lee, M. Owen. **Fathers and Sons in Virgil's** *Aeneid*: **Tum Genitor Natum.** Albany: State University of New York Press, 1979. xi, 200p. notes. index. pa.

This reading of Virgil's epic locates its prevailing sadness in the repeated failure of father-son relationships. Such failures are the touchstones of a tragic vision that is political, personal, and cosmic.

414. Leverenz, David. **Manhood and the American Renaissance.** Ithaca and London: Cornell University Press, 1989. x, 372p. notes. index. pa.

Assessing American literature of the mid-nineteenth century, Leverenz finds that the most important male writers (e.g., Emerson, Thoreau, Whitman, Hawthorne, Melville) feel that they are deviant from the acquisitive norm of masculinity that prevails in the society. The authors' struggle to create a more viable concept of masculinity lies at the heart of such works as "Self-Reliance," *The Blithedale Romance, The Scarlet Letter,* and *Moby Dick.* Leverenz's study is complex, involving examination of race and class attitudes, textual ambiguities, and a range of authors that also includes Frederick Douglass, Richard Henry Dana, Francis Parkman, and Harriet Beecher Stowe.

415. Lynn, Kenneth S. **The Dream of Success: A Study of the Modern American Imagination.** Boston: Little, Brown, 1955. 269p. notes. index.

Lynn traces the theme of the American success dream for men as found in writers like Theodore Dreiser (entry 342), Jack London, David Graham Phillips, Frank Norris, and Robert Herrick.

416. Margolies, Edward. **Native Sons: A Critical Study of Twentieth-Century Negro American Writers.** Philadelphia and New York: J. B. Lippincott, 1968. 210p. bibliography, 201-2.

This critical survey, written in the late sixties, assesses twentieth-century black authors, almost all of them male, focusing on such figures as Richard Wright (entry 69), James Baldwin, Malcolm X (entry 70), Chester Himes, and LeRoi Jones (Imamu Amiri Baraka).

417. Massey, Daniel. **Doing Time in American Prisons: A Study of Modern Novels.** New York: Greenwood Press, 1989. x, 246p. (Contributions in Criminology and Penology, no. 24). bibliography, 233-41. notes. index.

This study examines characteristics of the prison-novel "world," devoting separate chapters to the writings of Chester Himes, Malcolm Braly, Edward Bunker, and Nathan C. Heard.

418. Mellen, Joan. **Big Bad Wolves: Masculinity in the American Film.** New York: Pantheon Books, 1977. xvi, 367p. illus. index.

Hollywood has not been kind to men, Mellen argues in this study of masculine images in U.S. films. By manufacturing outsized screen images of males, Hollywood has made the ordinary male viewer feel insignificant, while women have been made to feel inadequate: "An abiding malaise results in the male, victimized by this comparison between himself and the physical splendor of the hero with whom he has so passionately identified." Mellen's examples are not the comedians or the musical stars but the "leading men" who have embodied cinema fantasies of masculinity. The book's introduction explains how Hollywood manufactures its supermales on the screen, how U.S. films have fostered competition between men and hostility toward women, and how the average working-class man has been virtually ignored by Hollywood's escapism. Politically, U.S. films have encouraged men to support the status quo, fostering conformism, anti-intellectualism, and passive patriotism among men. Later chapters provide a decade-by-decade survey of U.S. films, fitting in accounts of such stars as Tom Mix, Rudolph Valentino, Douglas Fairbanks, Gary Cooper, Clark Gable, Cary Grant, Humphrey Bogart, James Dean, and Marlon Brando. Mellen's severest strictures are reserved for John Wayne, Clint Eastwood as Dirty Harry, Sean Connery as James Bond, Charles Bronson, and other heroes of tight-lipped violence. The relationship between Humphrey Bogart and Katharine Hepburn in *The African Queen* comes nearest to being Hollywood's depiction of male-female equality. Mellen is suspicious of male-bonding films, finding them laced with misogyny; she is impressed neither by Paul Newman's liberal facade nor Robert Redford's good looks. The author examines the image of black men in films, and she has positive words for the documentary *Men's Lives* by Josh Hanig and Will Roberts.

419. Merriam, Sharan B. **Coping with Male Mid-Life: A Systematic Analysis Using Literature as a Data Source.** Washington, DC: University Press of America, 1980. vii, 129p. bibliography, 118-25. index. pa.

Using 12 fictional works from twentieth-century American literature, Merriam explores their insights into male midlife transition, comparing her findings with psychosocial research. Midlife is marked by an awareness of aging, a search for meaning, a generation squeeze as the man finds himself neither young nor old, career malaise, and efforts at ego rejuvenation. Among the works examined are F. Scott Fitzgerald's *Tender Is the Night* (entry 345), Arthur Miller's *Death of a Salesman* (entry 366), Tennessee Williams's *Night of the Iguana*, Saul Bellow's *Herzog*, and Joseph Heller's *Something Happened* (entry 354). "This study confirmed my belief," Merriam writes, "that literature offers the potential for uncovering significant insights into the process of adult development and aging."

420. Quigly, Isabel. **The Heirs of Tom Brown: The English School Story.** London: Chatto and Windus, 1982. 296p. illus. bibliography, 284-87. notes. index.

In this well-documented study, Quigly examines how boys' experiences in nineteenth-century British schools were transformed into fiction. The most influential text was Thomas Hughes's *Tom Brown's Schooldays*, which set the standard for numerous, less familiar fictions, including *Eric or Little by Little*, Rudyard Kipling's *Stalky & Co.*, and some novels by P. G. Wodehouse. Quigly also devotes chapters to girls' school fiction, the *Boy's Own Paper*, *Vice Versa* (an unfavorable account of boys' schooling), and the homoerotic and homosexual overtones of schoolboy romances. Separate chapters also cover the novels as documentary, as allegory, and as novels of character. Quigly examines the impact of World War I on schoolboy fiction, twentieth-century versions of school fiction (including *Goodbye, Mr. Chips*), and the decline and fall of the genre. Despite some boys' negative experiences, most of the fiction remains upbeat.

421. Ruderman, Judith. **D. H. Lawrence and the Devouring Mother: The Search for a Patriarchal Ideal of Leadership.** Durham, NC: Duke University Press, 1984. xi, 211p. notes. index.

In a study that is a model of scholarly writing, Ruderman argues that Lawrence never abandoned his desire for an ideal of patriarchal leadership. This ideal required the destruction of the devouring mother. Combining biography, psychology, and literary analysis, Ruderman traces this motif through such "secondary" Lawrence works as *The Lost Girl*, *The Fox*, *The Ladybird*, *Aaron's Rod*, *Kangaroo*, *The Boy in the Bush*, "The Woman Who Rode Away," *Lady Chatterley's Lover* (entry 359), and *Apocalypse*. Even in his excesses, Lawrence's rage against women can be seen as the symbolic murder of the devouring mother, and his worship of the dark gods proclaims his recognition of the father's importance in the individual's journey toward an autonomous self.

422. Sadoff, Dianne F. **Monsters of Affection: Dickens, Eliot, and Brontë on Fatherhood.** Baltimore, MD: Johns Hopkins University Press, 1982. vii, 193p. notes. index.

In this scholarly blend of Freudian, Lacanian, and feminist literary criticism, Sadoff traces the search for the father who engenders the action in Dickens's novels, the father-daughter seduction in George Eliot's novels, and the symbolic castration in Charlotte Brontë's novels.

423. Savran, David. **Communists, Cowboys, and Queers: The Politics of Masculinity in the Work of Arthur Miller and Tennessee Williams.** Minneapolis and London: University of Minnesota Press, 1992. xi, 205p. notes. index. pa.

A child of the sixties in rebellion against the fifties (including the family and heterosexuality), Savran uses literary analysis as a means of deconstructing "heterosexualized masculinity" represented by the image of the cowboy. He depicts the fifties as paranoid about communists and homosexuals. Because Savran can see only negative value in heterosexual masculinity, his discussions of Miller and Williams tend to be exercises in textual male bashing. In Arthur Miller's plays and in the film *The Misfits*, Savran finds much negative criticism of masculinity, although Miller stops short of abandoning it altogether. In Williams's plays and films, Savran finds a movement toward increasingly radicalized gay sensibility. The readings of Williams's texts resonate more convincingly than those of Miller's.

424. Schwenger, Peter. **Phallic Critiques: Masculinity and Twentieth-Century Literature.** London: Routledge and Kegan Paul, 1984. 172p. notes. index.

Some feminist critics have discerned a feminine style of writing. Arguing that there is a corresponding masculine style, Schwenger proceeds to define it by examining members of "the new virility school" of writing. In Norman Mailer's prose, for example, Schwenger finds a tough-guy style marked by obscenity, vigor, and license. Hemingway depicts the manly restraint of emotion through an emotionally restrained style. In Yukio Mishima, style is like a well-developed male body that finds fulfillment in self-destruction. Some writers (e.g., Alberto Moravia, D. H. Lawrence, and Philip Roth) carry on conversations with the willful phallus. Robert Kroetsch constructs novels that resemble "dirty" male jokes, while novels like *Deliverance* (entry 341), *Why Are We in Vietnam?*, and *Blood Sport* use hunting as the central metaphor of the struggle for masculine identity. Michel Leiris's *Manhood* (entry 52) and Roth's *My Life as a Man* (entry 371) also exemplify aspects of the new virility style. Schwenger is unapologetic about macho writing, and he is optimistic that a men's movement will liberate male writers from a debilitating self-consciousness about masculinity.

425. Sedgwick, Eve Kosofsky. **Between Men: English Literature and Male Homosocial Desire.** New York: Columbia University Press, 1985. x, 244p. bibliography, 229-39. notes. index.

The major premises of this study seem to be that male bonding ("male homosocial desire") is reprehensible because it involves the "exchange" of women as a "counter" to cement bonds between men, and that male bonding turns nasty when men do not admit the homoerotic or homosexual components in it. Sedgwick attempts to locate these ideological-gender themes in an array of literary texts, including Shakespeare's sonnets, Wycherley's *The Country Wife*, Sterne's *A Sentimental Journey*, a number of Gothic novels, Hogg's

Confessions of a Justified Sinner, George Eliot's *Adam Bede*, Thackeray's *Henry Esmond*, Tennyson's *The Princess*, and Dickens's *Our Mutual Friend* and *The Mystery of Edwin Drood*. Although male-male-female triangles in literature clearly deserve attention, the reader-unfriendly prose of this study makes comprehension an uphill struggle. Vocabulary is stretched considerably. "Male homosocial desire" includes cuckoldry and murder. The "exchange" of women includes the rivalry between Shakespeare's "dark lady" and "the poet" for the "fair youth" of the sonnets. Facts are similarly stretched: Emily Tennyson, it is hinted, was engaged to Arthur Hallam solely to cement bonds between him and her brother, Alfred. The book's Marxist-feminist and gay-activist misandry reveals itself in such things as gratuitous sneers at heterosexual middle-class men. Apparently, heterosexual males are irredeemably corrupt, and female association with them is misguided. Thus, Lizzie Hexam of *Our Mutual Friend*, who nurtures her father and marries a middle-class man, is a "reactionary." Such skewing converts a potentially illuminating literary study into an elitist exercise in male bashing.

426. Smith, Timothy d'Arch. **Love in Earnest: Some Notes on the Lives and Writings of English "Uranian" Poets from 1889-1930.** London: Routledge and Kegan Paul, 1970. xxiii, 280p. illus. appendixes. bibliography, 256-68. notes. index.
      This literary history surveys a group of British "Uranian" poets who hymned boy-love. Beginning with such precursors as William Johnson Cory, John Addington Symonds, and Edward Carpenter, the study focuses on such figures as John Gambril Nicholson, F. W. Rolfe (alias Baron Corvo), Charles Sayle, and Charles Kains Jackson.

427. Spender, Dale. **Man Made Language.** London: Routledge and Kegan Paul, 1980. xi, 250p. bibliography, 236-45. index. pa.
      Spender believes that men have imposed a myth of male superiority upon women, using language as a tool of oppression. Language is entirely man-made, according to Spender, and thus it is laden with anti-female messages. Many words denigrate women, and throughout history men have conspired to silence women. In this study, polemics override scholarship. Trying to support the idea that men regard females as secondary to males, e.g., Spender claims—incorrectly—that the word *female* was derived from the word *male*. The study entirely ignores language that denigrates males. Spender's premise that males alone create and control language is dubious, and the argument that males "silence" females is challenged by works like Deborah Tannen's *You Just Don't Understand* (entry 429). Spender's glee when reporting how her consciousness-raising sessions succeeded in breaking up heterosexual couples suggests a lesbian separatist agenda. In this book, language study is a thin veneer for misandry and gender divisiveness.

428. Spoto, David. **Camerado: Hollywood and the American Male.** New York: New American Library, Plume Books, 1978. xi, 238p. illus. index. pa.
      With the aid of numerous stills, Spoto describes dominant images of men in American films, including the Ordinary Guy, the sex symbols, the comedians, the heroes of suspense, and the strong men.

429. Tannen, Deborah. **You Just Don't Understand: Women and Men in Conversation.** New York: William Morrow, 1990. bibliography, 310-19. notes. index. Reprint, New York: Ballantine Books, 1990. pa.
      Written by a professor of linguistics, this best-seller explains to general audiences how women and men can miscommunicate in discourse. According

to Tannen, most males and females are speaking from entirely different perspectives. Males grow up in a world of contest and problem solving in which "report talk" predominates. Females find themselves in a world of contact through discourse in which "rapport talk" predominates. Tannen refutes the idea that males dominate (or even intend to dominate) females in conversation through such techniques as interruption. Noting that many ethnic peoples (e.g., Jews, African-Americans, Italians) also engage in highly interruptive discourse that has no relation to dominance, Tannen distinguishes between "high involvement" and "high consideration" styles of conversation. She refuses to blame either women or men for their different conversational techniques. Tannen seeks to bring the sexes together by aiding them to understand each other's modes of conversation.

430. Tayler, Irene. **Holy Ghosts: The Male Muses of Emily and Charlotte Brontë.** New York: Columbia University Press, 1990. viii, 342p. bibliography, 325-29. notes. index.
Just as male authors have traditionally invoked a female muse to inspire their work, so the Brontë sisters invoked male muses to inspirit their art. Tayler provides close readings of the Brontës' poems and fictions, tracing the ambivalent feelings that each artist had for the "male" element in herself and her writings.

431. Todd, Janet, ed. **Men by Women.** New York: Holmes and Meier, 1981. 251p. (Women and Literature, vol. 2 (new series)). illus. notes. pa.
This collection of 15 essays examines male characters and images of men created by female authors. The contributors examine such topics as men in the eighteenth-century novel, male characters in female authors' nineteenth-century British industrial novels, and the distinction between penis and phallus in the critical theories of Jacques Lacan. Individual essays are devoted to such concerns as the portrayal of men in Jane Austen's novels, the "feminization" of male characters in George Eliot's fiction, Emily Brontë's Heathcliff, Charlotte Brontë's Rochester, Emily Dickinson's poetry, the "spectacular spinelessness" of men in Dorothy Arzner's films, the biographical implications of Sylvia Plath's short fiction, and Iris Murdoch's male narrators.

432. Tuss, Alex J. **The Inward Revolution: Troubled Young Men in Victorian Fiction, 1850-1880.** New York: Peter Lang, 1992. 198p. (Series IV, English Language and Literature Series, vol. 152). bibliography, 189-98.
In this eminently readable study, Tuss links shifting concepts of masculinity in nineteenth-century Britain to a wealth of fiction and poetry, paying special attention to *Lady Audley's Secret, Bleak House, A Tale of Two Cities, Our Mutual Friend, Daniel Deronda,* and *The Picture of Dorian Gray.* Tuss illuminates the spirit of the age by examining such figures as Carlyle, Mill, and Arnold, as well as recent writers like Carol Gilligan. The troubled young man who emerges in many guises in the literature often seems a forerunner of modern men searching for more rewarding forms of masculinity.

433. von Franz, Marie-Louise. **The Golden Ass of Apuleius: The Liberation of the Feminine in Man.** 1970. Rev. ed. Boston and London: Shambhala, 1992. vii, 246p. illus. bibliography, 241-46. notes. pa.
A distinguished Jungian analyst, von Franz here offers a reading of Apuleius' Roman novel *The Golden Ass* (entry 319). The interpretation combines psychological, historical, cultural, and literary analyses. In Apuleius'

tale of a young man, Lucius, who is turned into an ass, von Franz sees the universal struggles of young men to free themselves from the negative mother complex, to get in touch with the earthy masculine (the wild man of current mythopoetic analyses), and to liberate the feminine within themselves. She devotes three chapters to the Psyche-Cupid story contained within *The Golden Ass*, depicting Psyche as the female counterpart of Lucius. In the final two chapters, von Franz analyzes Egyptian mystery religions to interpret Lucius' redemption by the goddess Isis.

434. Walters, Margaret. **The Nude Male: A New Perspective.** New York and London: Paddington Press, 1978. 352p. illus. bibliography, 339. notes. index. Reprint, New York: Penguin Books, 1979. pa.

Calling the male nude "a forgotten subject," Walters surveys its history from classical Greece to modern pinups, focusing primarily on recognized paintings, sculptures, and other art forms. In contrast to the perfected glory of Greek nudes, Christian art used nudity to convey pathos and shame. Separate chapters are devoted to the Renaissance nude, Michelangelo, and each century from the sixteenth through the twentieth. After the "disappearing" male nudes of nineteenth-century art and the "disembodied" nudes of twentieth-century works, the newsstand pinup and the nude males depicted by women artists represent new departures in seeing men's bodies.

435. Welch, Julie, and Louise Brody. **Leading Men.** New York: Villard Books, 1985. 224p. illus. index. Rev. ed. London: Conran Octopus, 1993.

Generously illustrated with studio photographs, this book surveys 125 romantic male film stars from the silent era to modern times, from Rudolph Valentino to Sean Penn. Extended attention is given to Gary Cooper, Clark Gable, Cary Grant, James Dean, Marlon Brando, Paul Newman, and Robert Redford. The text is by Welch, the design by Brody. The 1993 edition features a foreword by Jane Russell.

436. Wisse, Ruth. **The Schlemiel as Modern Hero.** Chicago and London: University of Chicago Press, 1971. xi, 134p. appendix. bibliography, 127-30. notes. index. Reprint, Chicago and London: University of Chicago Press, Phoenix Books, 1980. pa.

The wise fool of Jewish folklore and fiction, the schlemiel has emerged as the prototypical modern male hero, a preeminently weak man facing a hostile world. This perceptive and lucidly written study traces the history of the schlemiel, analyzes his humor, and follows his fortunes in such works as Sholom Aleichem's stories, Saul Bellow's *Herzog*, and Philip Roth's *Portnoy's Complaint* (entry 372). Wisse goes beyond literary studies to suggest the relevance of the schlemiel to the lot of modern man.

437. Woodcock, Bruce. **Male Mythologies: John Fowles and Masculinity.** Sussex, England: The Harvester Press; Totowa, NJ: Barnes and Noble, 1984. 192p. bibliography, 176-82. notes. name and subject indexes.

Woodcock argues that British novelist John Fowles's negative view of masculinity and positive view of femininity are embodied in his novels, *The Collector, The Magus, The French Lieutenant's Woman, Daniel Martin,* and *Mantissa.* An ardent feminist, Woodcock is nevertheless unhappy with Fowles and constantly berates him for not seeing masculinity as sufficiently corrupt. Woodcock's analysis lacks any positive concept of masculinity and deals in oversimplifications of Marxist-feminist doctrine. *Male Mythologies* offers the spectacle of a male critic, having internalized a misandric mythology of male evil, relentlessly flagellating himself and other men.

438. Wren, Brian. **What Language Shall I Borrow? God-Talk in Worship: A Male Response to Feminist Theology.** New York: Crossroad, 1990. xi, 264p. notes. pa.

The male response of British minister Brian Wren to feminist theology is to accept it uncritically. Echoing radical feminists, Wren recites a familiar litany of misandric accusations: patriarchy is a male-dominated society (not a father-involved one), men seek to control women and everything else, men despise the feminine, men are addicted to rational thought, and so on. Wren believes that Jesus was a feminist who sought to undermine patriarchy. Wren's text is interspersed with his inclusive-language lyrics for hymns. Arguing that traditional masculine imagery for God focuses too exclusively on such metaphors as father and ruler, Wren seeks a wider range of names for the Almighty. Among the new names that Wren suggests are "Bag Lady God" (to link the divine with the lowly) and "Old, aching God" (to include the elderly in God-talk). There are no hymns to "deep masculine God" or "wildman God," because Wren evidently believes that masculinity can be enriched only by adding the feminine.

439. Yaeger, Patricia, and Beth Kowaleski-Wallace, eds. **Refiguring the Father: New Feminist Readings of Patriarchy.** Carbondale and Edwardsville: Southern Illinois University Press, 1989. xxiii, 319p. notes.

This collection of 15 articles focuses primarily on the figure of the father in literature. Although several authors warn that "The Father" of patriarchal society should not be confused with an individual father, a number of the authors have difficulty sorting out "The Father" from "my father." Nearly all the authors regard patriarchy as evil, and several are suspicious of fathers. Kowaleski-Wallace, however, argues that demonizing the father as oppressor serves only to empower him. Among the works discussed are Euripides' *Phaedra*, Fanny Burney's *Evelina*, and Toni Morrison's *The Bluest Eye*. The essays vary in quality. At the top of the list is Adrienne Auslander Munich's perceptive analysis of fatherhood in *The Aeneid* and *The Idylls of the King*. At the bottom is Susan Fraiman's foolish attempt to persuade readers that Elizabeth Bennet is being humiliated when, at the end of *Pride and Prejudice*, she marries rich, young, handsome, and newly sensitized Fitzwilliam Darcy.

Cross-References

767. Adams, Stephen. **The Homosexual as Hero in Contemporary Fiction.**

594. Betcher, R. William, and William S. Pollack. **In a Time of Fallen Heroes: The Re-creation of Masculinity.**

269. Castrovono, David. **The English Gentleman: Images and Ideals in Literature and Society.**

270. Cawelti, John G. **Apostles of the Self-Made Man.**

90. Craig, Steve, ed. **Men, Masculinity, and the Media.**

946. Fields, Rick. **The Code of the Warrior: In History, Myth, and Everyday Life.**

159. Franklin, H. Bruce, comp. **American Prisoners and Ex-Prisoners: Their Writings: An Annotated Bibliography of Published Works, 1798-1981.**

789. Galloway, David, and Christian Sabisch, eds. **Calamus: Male Homosexuality in Twentieth-Century Literature: An International Anthology.**

702a. Hudson, Liam, and Bernadine Jacot. **The Way Men Think: Intellect, Intimacy and the Erotic Imagination.**

45. Hoyland, John, ed. **Fathers and Sons.**

956. Jeffords. Susan. **The Remasculinization of America: Gender and the Vietnam War.**

46. Kafka, Franz. **Letter to His Father/Brief an Der Vater.**

507. Keyes, Ralph, ed. **Sons on Fathers: A Book of Men's Writing.**

121. Mailer, Norman. **The Prisoner of Sex.**

713. Mullahy, Patrick. **Oedipus, Myth and Complex: A Review of Psychoanalytic Theory.**

718. Pedersen, Loren E. **Sixteen Men: Understanding Masculine Personality Types.**

719. Rochlin, Gregory. **The Masculine Dilemma: A Psychology of Masculinity.**

835. Sarotte, Georges-Michel. **Like a Brother, Like a Lover: Male Homosexuality in the American Novel and Theater from Herman Melville to James Baldwin.**

619. Seidler, Victor J. **Rediscovering Masculinity: Reason, Language and Sexuality.**

29. Strage, Mark. **The Durable Fig Leaf: A Historical, Cultural, Medical, Social, Literary, and Iconographic Account of Man's Relations with His Penis.**

1042. Swados, Harvey, ed. **The American Writer and the Great Depression.**

729. von Franz, Marie-Louise. **The Problem of the Puer Aeternus.**

170. Young, Ian, comp. **The Male Homosexual in Literature: A Bibliography.**

13

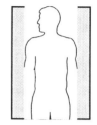

Male Midlife Transition

440. Bergler, Edmund. **The Revolt of the Middle-Aged Man.** 2d ed. New York: Hill and Wang, 1957. xiii, 312p.

One of the earliest assessments of male midlife crisis, Bergler's study depicts the middle-aged man as rebelling and yet wanting his rebellion to fail. Through extensive accounts of interviews with patients, the psychiatrist and author argues that midlife rebellion is doomed to failure; at best, it can be survived and converted into personal growth. Bergler depicts the younger women with whom such men sometimes become involved as neurotic; he advises wives to hang on to their marriages, for the husband's midlife storm will pass. Biological changes are not the source of male midlife changes, and divorce is not the solution because it does not provide the needed therapy. Bergler views middle-aged men as suffering from psychic masochism, and his views of patients, wives, and "other women" are sometimes severely judgmental.

441. Bowskill, Derek, and Anthea Linacre. **The Male Menopause.** Los Angeles: Brooke House, 1977. 195p. appendix. bibliography, 195.

Despite the infelicitous title (and the authors had ample warning about it from those they interviewed), this book offers vivid, firsthand accounts of male midlife crises from Great Britain. The authors present extended extracts concerning midlife problems from husbands, wives, and medical practitioners. If organic evidence of midlife changes is uncertain, the psychological and emotional evidence seldom is. Midlife symptoms include disillusionment with success or disappointment at not having achieved it, awareness of physical decline, the desire to be attractive to women, impotence, extramarital affairs, dissatisfaction with work, personality changes, and a feeling that no one cares. "As there is minimal or no sanction for a man to grieve in our society," remarks one man, "there is also neither one for him to grow old." The authors review some of the remedies for midlife anxiety, suggesting that the solution lies in two difficult achievements: fixing a new midlife identity and facing death squarely. An extensive appendix contains extracts reviewing organic evidence for midlife changes, their emotional implications, and female menopause.

442. Chew, Peter. **The Inner World of the Middle-Aged Man.** New York: Macmillan, 1976. xix, 278p. notes. index. Reprint, Boston: Houghton Mifflin, 1977. pa.

This popular account of midlife crisis draws upon the work of Daniel J. Levinson (entry 445), Elliott Jaques, and others. A journalist, Chew uses interviews and a wide range of readings to explore such midlife concerns as stocktaking, extramarital affairs, impotence, work, leisure, and age discrimination.

443. Farrell, Michael P., and Stanley D. Rosenberg. **Men at Midlife.** Boston: Auburn House, 1981. xix, 242p. illus. appendixes. bibliography, 227-35. notes. index. pa.

Begun in 1971, this study combines a wide sample of 450 men with more detailed study of 20 selected subjects. Instead of a single pattern of predictable male midlife crisis, the authors discovered four distinct paths through midlife: that of the antihero or dissenter who exhibits alienation, identity struggle, and orientation towards his own ego; that of the transcendental-generative male who thrives during this period and is marked by openness to feelings; that of the pseudo-developed man who cultivates a facade of satisfaction but is actually undergoing a midlife crisis; and that of the punitive-disenchanted or authoritarian man who is highly dissatisfied and often in conflict with his children. Farrell and Rosenberg stress that male midlife transition must be seen in the larger context of family relationships. Class also influences the experience: wealthy or educated middle-class males are more likely to weather the period positively. The authors explore husband-wife relationships ("middle age represents the doldrums of marriage in our culture"), parent-child relationships, extended family relationships, and male friendship groups during midlife. Of the four paths through midlife, only one is described positively. The authors conclude that because "most men strive to conform to a limited range of cultural stereotypes of masculinity," their lives "become increasingly burdensome, particularly in relation to work and family."

444. Hallberg, Edmond C. **The Grey Itch.** N.p.: Ombudsman Press, 1977. Reprint (Rev. ed.), as *The Gray Itch: The Male Metapause Syndrome.* New York: Stein and Day, 1978. ix, 228p. bibliography, 209-22. notes. index. Reprint, New York: Warner Books, 1980. pa.

Writing for corporate and professional white men, Hallberg spells out the ingredients of male *metapause*, a word signifying a midlife pause in the man's life changes. Part 1 explores the life stages and the symptoms of male metapause, including dissatisfaction with work, marital boredom, memory slips, distaste for the role of family money machine, and (above all) an identity crisis. Part 2 examines in greater detail problem areas of men at midlife. Part 3 offers suggestions for coping and changing in these problem areas. The final chapter deals with "emansumation," a term and a concept combining *man, sum,* and *emancipation.*

445. Levinson, Daniel J., and Charlotte N. Darrow, Edward B. Klein, Maria H. Levinson, and Braxton McKee. **The Seasons of a Man's Life.** New York: Alfred A. Knopf, 1978. xiv, 367p. illustrations. notes. index. Reprint, New York: Ballantine Books, 1979. pa.

An extremely influential book, this study has affected both scholarly and popular conceptions of the male life cycle. Building upon the work of Jung and Erikson, Levinson presents a developmental perspective on men in adulthood, based upon in-depth biographical interviews with 40 men, ages 35 to 45, in four occupations: hourly workers in industry, business executives, university biologists, and novelists. In addition, Levinson refers to a secondary sampling of famous men and fictional characters. The study concludes that male adult development proceeds through a series of eras, each of which occurs at an average or most frequent age: 17-22 (Early Adult Development), 22-28 (Entering the Adult World), 28-33 (Age Thirty Transition), 33-40 (Settling Down), 40-45 (Midlife Transition), 45-50 (Entering Middle Adulthood), 55-60 (Culmination of Middle Adulthood), 60-65 (Late Adult Transition), 65 and beyond (Late Adulthood). At each era, the man must perform certain developmental tasks or risk impeding his individuation process. Usually at age 40, the man enters a midlife transition in which he must reappraise the past, modify his life structure, continue individuation, and reconcile four polarities: young/old, destruction/creation, masculine/feminine, and attachment/separation. Levinson describes five different pathways through midlife transition: advancement within a stable life structure, serious failure or decline, breaking out to a new life structure, advancement that produces a change in life structure, and unstable life structure. Humane and literate, *The Seasons of a Man's Life* is both moving and thought provoking.

446. Mayer, Nancy. **The Male Mid-Life Crisis: Fresh Starts After Forty.** Garden City, NY: Doubleday, 1978. xv, 295p. bibliography, 275-83. notes. index. Reprint, New York: New American Library, Signet, 1979. pa.

In readable style, Mayer examines sympathetically what is known about the male midlife crisis and offers advice about how it can be directed positively. Supplementing her researches with interviews, Mayer surveys the thought of Freud, Jung, and Erikson, as well as the more recent findings of Daniel J. Levinson (entry 445) and others. She explores the traditional masculine gender role and its liabilities (e.g., workaholism, disillusionment with "success," exploitation in the marketplace, impacted emotions, early death), as well as the symptoms of midlife transition (e.g., penis angst, the quaking marriage, the pressure of unwanted responsibilities). Nevertheless, Mayer's outlook is essentially optimistic as she details the possibilities for growth and renewal that midlife transition can offer.

447. McGill, Michael E. **The 40- to 60-Year-Old Male: A Guide for Men—And the Women in Their Lives—To See Them Through the Crises of the Male Middle Years.** New York: Simon and Schuster, Fireside, 1980. 299p. appendix. pa.

McGill argues that insufficient research has been done on male midlife transition, that too many studies focus on its negative aspects, and that good advice for dealing with it has been lacking. McGill's own study is based upon a four-year research effort involving 500 questionnaires completed by men and women, as well as 200 interviews. Keeping an eye on the women, children, friends, employers, and others involved with the midlife male, the author reviews seven possible causes of the crisis. To cope with midlife trauma, McGill suggests five steps for the male; these steps include recognition that there is a problem, a deliberate decision to change in a certain way, and integration of the change into the man's personality. The common denominator of male midlife crisis is a threat to the man's identity; thus, men who define themselves too narrowly will be more prone to the crisis. "Men and women, all of us," McGill concludes, "need to encourage men as individuals to explore who they are as whole men."

448. McMorrow, Fred. **Midolescence: The Dangerous Years.** New York: Quadrangle/New York Times, A Strawberry Hill Book, 1974. xiv, 366p.

"This book is not a sociological or psychoanalytical study," the publishers note. "It makes no pretensions. There is nothing scientific about it in conception or execution." The author presents, usually verbatim, question-and-answer dialogue from interviews concerning midlife crises. Those interviewed are seven experts (e.g., a psychiatrist, a psychoanalyst and sociologist, and a labor-relations lawyer), seven midlife men, and seven women involved with midlife men. Three concluding chapters survey the midlife crisis in history, in literature, and in headline stories; midolescence and awakening homosexuality; and what lies in the years beyond midolescence.

449. Osherson, Samuel D. **Holding On or Letting Go: Men and Career Change at Midlife.** New York: Free Press, 1980. xii, 258p. appendix. bibliography, 250-54. notes. index.

In this study, Osherson reviews the literature on male midlife crisis and interviews 20 men who made radical career changes at midlife by exchanging their professional careers for work in arts and crafts. The author places the midlife years between 35 and 50; he uses a free-association interview procedure described in the appendix. Focusing on six men in the group, Osherson finds a prechange period that often precedes the actual crisis, which is characterized by a sense of loss. The self is called into question, and the man seeks to reconstitute a new self. At midlife, a man may discover the inadequacy of the career choice he made in young adulthood, forcing him to decide whether to "hold on" or "let go." Osherson contrasts premature decisions with more fully "sculpted" ones that are more integrative. He discusses the impact upon sons of the "strong mother-unavailable father" family pattern. In his conclusion, Osherson points to the wisdom of adaptively holding on and letting go, that is, the wise integration of the old and the new.

450. Ruebsaat, Helmut J., and Raymond Hull. **The Male Climacteric.** New York: Hawthorn Books, 1975. xviii, 190p. illus. appendix. glossary. index.

Ruebsaat (an M.D.) and Hull (a writer) explain to lay readers the nature of the male climacteric that usually occurs between the ages of 41 and 50. The introduction contains Hull's personal account of his climacteric experiences. Part 1 enumerates the physical and emotional symptoms of midlife climacteric. Alluding to famous men of the past—Dickens, Tolstoy, Shakespeare, Napoleon, Mussolini—the authors explore the climacteric's social dimensions. Contrasting male climacteric with female menopause, the authors reject the term *male menopause.* Part 2 traces the causes of the climacteric, indicating an interrelationship of physical, psychological, and social contributing factors. In part 3 the authors offer advice to midlife men and to those dealing with them in personal relationships or in public life. A glossary of terms is included.

451. Sharp, Daryl. **The Survival Papers: Anatomy of a Midlife Crisis.** Toronto: Inner City Books, 1988. 157p. (Studies in Jungian Psychology by Jungian Analysts, no. 35). index. pa.

In this unusual study, a drama develops involving the book's rather controlled analyst-narrator, a midlife patient named Norman whose marriage to Nancy is headed for the rocks, the narrator's own analyst-mentor Arnold, and his anima, whom he calls Rachel. As Norman's story unfolds in the analyst's office, the narrator uses it to illustrate Jungian concepts of midlife crisis. Jung, for example, differed with Freud and regarded neurosis as an opportunity for greater individuation. The narrator expounds on numerous matters, such as serpent dream imagery and the four stages of the anima, which he labels Eve, Helen, Mary, and Sophia. He links Norman's travails with the hero's journey described by Joseph Campbell (entry 862). At the end of the book, it appears that the characters in the psychodrama may be aspects of the author's self. In any event, they have been presented primarily to illustrate Jungian interpretations of midlife transition.

452. Still, Henry. **Surviving the Male Mid-Life Crisis.** New York: Thomas Y. Crowell, 1977. xi, 240p. bibliography, 227-28. notes. index.

In the first section of this popular account of male midlife crisis, Still characterizes the physical and emotional changes in men between the ages of 40 and 45. The lost dreams, awareness of mortality, the death of one's parents, and the empty nest—all can combine with the rigid gender role of U.S. masculinity to precipitate a crisis in many men's lives. In the second section, Still explores the personal equation of midlife crisis—physical decline, tired marriage, sagging sexuality, and the inability to express feelings or to explore different modes of loving. The book's final section deals with professional reckonings (i.e., work dissatisfaction and burnout, the discovery by some men that they have sacrificed their lives in careers they never really wanted, and the problems of retirement). Especially interesting are Still's idea of granting sabbaticals to midlife men to allow them breathing space to recover and his chapter on the need for lifetime learning. Despite the book's grim portrait of middle age, Still believes that "the midlife crisis of the American male ... is an opportunity for new growth and directions."

453. Tamir, Lois M. **Men in Their Forties: The Transition to Middle Age.** New York: Springer, 1982. x, 150p. (Focus on Men series, no. 2). appendixes. bibliography, 144-48. index. pa.

A sociologist and lifespan developmental psychologist, Tamir has tapped a national survey conducted in 1976 by the University of Michigan in order to draw a picture of men in midlife transition. "Ages 40 to 49 years in the life of the adult male," she finds, "comprise a major transitional period that is reflected in the quality of life experience, with repercussions in the world of work, family, and social relationships." In her study, Tamir includes only men in their forties who are both married and parents; she uses an educational control, distinguishing college-educated men from non-college-educated men. As for quality of life, middle-aged college-educated men displayed a lack of zest, indicating possible psychological distress, while the other group suffered from low self-esteem. For both groups, satisfaction with marriage and parenthood dropped, although, toward the end of the decade, marriage satisfaction began to increase again. Self-respect became a dominant value for both groups of men. Although job satisfaction increased (particularly among college-educated men), this satisfaction was no longer linked with personal well-being: appar- ently, midlife men disengage from work as a source of personal fulfillment. For college-educated men, marriage became a more important source of personal satisfaction, although heightened awareness or marital problems also surfaced at this time. Increasingly, the men sought social relationships, perhaps to share midlife troubles with others. Despite the evident difficulties of midlife transition, Tamir cautions against seeing it too bleakly and points to its rewards and opportunities. She concludes with suggestions for future research.

454. Vaillant, George E. **Adaptation to Life.** Boston: Little, Brown, 1977. xvii, 396p. appendixes. notes.

Ninety-five men from an elite private college are followed through 35 years of development in this study. Most of the men were predictably "success- ful," but success did not mean trouble-free lives. Vaillant studies in detail the men's methods of adapting to reality. Their midlife years were troubled by what Erik Erikson designates as a search for "generativity," a desire for socially creative achievement. Midlife crises, however, were neither universal nor chronologically regular among the men. One appendix contains a glossary of defense mechanisms; the other two concern methodology.

Cross-References

99. Filene, Peter, ed. **Men in the Middle: Coping with the Problems of Work and Family in the Lives of Middle-Aged Men.**

345. Fitzgerald, F. Scott. **Tender Is the Night.**

354. Heller, Joseph. **Something Happened.**

328. Homer. **The Odyssey.**

365. Maugham, W. Somerset. **The Moon and Sixpence.**

419. Merriam, Sharan B. **Coping with Male Mid-Life: A Systematic Analysis Using Literature as a Data Source.**

313. Schoenberg, Fred. **Middle Age Rage ... And Other Male Indignities.**

65. Sifford, Darrell. **Father and Son.**

14

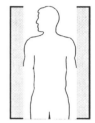

Males in Families

A. Expectant Fathers, New Fathers

455. Alliance for Perinatal Research and Services: Rae Grad, Debora Bash, Ruth Guyer, Zoila Acevedo, Mary Anne Trause, Diane Reukauf. **The Father Book: Pregnancy and Beyond.** Washington, DC: Acropolis Books, 1981. 263p. illus. appendixes. bibliography, 255-59. notes. index. pa.

In this informative and lucid guide, the six authors explore the choices available to fathers in such matters as preparing for childbirth, pregnancy, childbirth classes, father participation in child delivery, unexpected events (e.g., multiple births, stillborn child), the postpartum period, living with an infant, interactions and exercises (a chapter by Jan Shaffer), and recent trends in fathering. Appendix 1 offers information and advice about how to cope with hospital personnel and policies concerning father participation in labor and birth. Appendix 2 lists organizations interested in childbirth.

456. Bittman, Sam, and Sue Rosenberg Zalk. **Expectant Fathers.** New York: Hawthorn Books, 1978. xxv, 291p. illus. appendixes. glossary. bibliography, 278-83. notes. index. pa. Reprint, New York: Ballantine Books, 1980. pa.

A full-scale look at expectant fathers, this book uses current literature, 47 interviews, and 162 questionnaire responses. Although expectant fathers often undergo difficult emotional experiences, modern sex roles discourage their expression, and society tends to ignore these feelings. The authors examine the couvade syndrome in primitive and modern societies; they trace the father's emotional and physical changes during the trimesters of pregnancy. A separate chapter is devoted to sexual relations during pregnancy. The authors describe the stages of labor and birth with the participating fathers' roles during each stage. They warn fathers of infants about men's postpartum depression and urge fathers to resist being pushed aside by well-meaning mothers, relatives, or friends. Despite some negative aspects, involved fatherhood has more than sufficient rewards; the new father is urged to enjoy this deepening human experience. The text is illustrated by F. X. Tobin's drawings. The appendixes list questionnaire findings, home birth agencies, contraindications for home birth, and medical emergencies during home birth. A glossary of terms is also included.

457. Bradley, Robert A. **Husband-Coached Childbirth.** 3d ed. New York: Harper Row, 1981. xiii, 238p. illus. index.

This pioneering book, first published in 1965, recounts how Bradley (an M.D.) first became an advocate of natural childbirth and only later recognized the importance of involving the father in pregnancy, labor, and birthing. (Bradley uses "birthing" to describe natural childbirth, as opposed to *delivery* by a doctor using medication while the father is pacing in the waiting room.) Chapter 4, "Where Do Fathers Fit In?" is necessary reading for any man thinking of becoming a father. Other chapters instruct the man on the part he can play in helping his pregnant partner with physical and mental well-being, his role during the various stages of labor, and his function in the birthing process. Bradley also discusses postpartum family relations and the husband's role in breastfeeding. As an advocate of natural childbirth, Bradley discourages the use of chemical substances by prospective parents. Obstacles to the father's presence in the birthing room have diminished considerably since the first edition of this book, but Bradley warns against recalcitrant doctors, medical personnel, parents, and friends. The book closes with two chapters on problems during pregnancy. *Contra* Bradley, Ashley Montagu, in the foreword, advocates home birthing; he agrees with Bradley on everything else. This book makes a strong case for the man's presence during birth as a part of the natural bonding of man and woman—and child.

458. Burton, Jerome, and Milt Rosen. **The Fatherhood Formula.** Chatsworth, CA: Major Books, 1976. 187p. index. pa.

Dismayed by the lack of information about such matters ("men know less than women"), the authors use a question-and-answer format and a sense of humor to elucidate topics every father-to-be should know about. Contents include the male reproductive system, impregnation, the male responses to pregnancy, the development of the fetus, delivery (the authors believe the father should be present), Cesarean sections, treatment of infants (Burton recommends circumcision), and the newborn at home.

459. Greenberg, Martin. **The Birth of a Father.** New York: Continuum, 1985. xii, 198p. notes. Reprint, New York: Avon, 1986. pa.

"Engrossment" is the term coined by Greenberg to describe the bonding attachment of father to newborn child. Drawing upon his experiences with his son, interviews with other fathers, and scholarly studies, Greenberg describes for a general audience the characteristics of engrossment. Because hospital staffs vary in their encouragement of father participation in child delivery, the new father must be firm about asserting his right to be near his wife and child. Greenberg discusses family bonding after the delivery, how to be a working father, coping with baby's crying, jealousy, ways to recharge the parents' batteries, and changing diapers. He especially recommends fatherly walks with infants as a way of bonding. Stressing a positive view of fatherhood, the book offers new fathers encouragement and practical advice.

460. Gresh, Sean. **Becoming a Father: A Handbook for Expectant Fathers.** New York: Butterick, 1980. 144p. appendixes. bibliography, 140-141. index. Reprint, New York: Bantam Books, 1982. pa.

This highly readable book provides fathers-to-be with essential information and suggestions during pregnancy, labor, childbirth, and afterward. Without pressuring men, Gresh outlines the choices available to them. He warns prospective fathers that they will be ignored by professionals and that they will experience anxieties; the rewards of active fatherhood, however, outweigh such drawbacks. Discussing men's fears (about finances, dangers of childbirth, sex, and marital relationships), Gresh stresses the importance to men of talking out these fears and maintaining communication with their partners. Separate chapters are devoted to men's changes during pregnancy (including the phenomenon of couvade); women's changes during each trimester of pregnancy; costs; preparations for childbirth; the man's role during labor (the importance of not separating husbands and wives at this time is stressed); and adjustments to life with a newborn. The foreword by Elizabeth Bing briefly traces how separation of fathers-to-be from childbirth occurred in the nineteenth and twentieth centuries and how the situation is presently being rectified. The appendixes include a list of chapters and groups of the American Society of Psychoprophylaxis in Obstetrics, a listing by state of chapters of the International Childbirth Education Association, and the Pregnant Patient's Bill of Rights and Responsibilities.

461. Heinowitz, Jack. **Pregnant Fathers: How Fathers Can Enjoy and Share the Experiences of Pregnancy and Childbirth.** Englewood Cliffs, NJ: Prentice-Hall, 1982. xiii, 126p. appendix. bibliography, 117-19. notes. index. pa.

Arguing that *couples* get pregnant and that the pregnant father has been almost overlooked, Heinowitz offers information and suggestions to encourage males to become full partners in pregnancy. He debunks the ideas that the father is a secondary parent and that fathers' influence on infants and on growing daughters is minimal. Repeatedly stressing the need for men to express their feelings, he warns that repressed feelings can damage a couple's relationship. Exercises in awareness and listening to one's partner are included. Heinowitz discusses couvade, sympathy symptoms, and numerous other topics. Despite the pitfalls of being an involved pregnant father, the rewards are great. An appendix suggests how childbirth educators and others can make their classes more helpful.

462. Jones, Carl. **Sharing Birth: A Father's Guide to Giving Support During Labor.** New York: Quill, 1985. 195p. illus. appendixes. bibliography, 187-89. notes. index. pa.

In Jones's view, a father at childbirth is more than a coach; he is the sharer in the miracle of birth. Jones describes pregnancy, labor, and birth in detail, providing suggestions on how husbands can share in both events. By providing massages and retaining a positive attitude, the man can foster his partner's maximum physical and emotional well-being. Much of the advice is practical (e.g., lowering the lights during childbirth can soothe the woman, taking off one's shirt and achieving skin contact with the newborn can increase engrossment, and keeping away a swarm of well-wishers may provide the mother with needed rest). Jones includes a chapter on special situations (e.g., Cesarean section) and considers the roles of other family members (including children) at childbirth. Photographs illustrate the text. The appendixes describe subjects to consider before labor begins and a labor record.

463. Kahan, Stuart. **The Expectant Father's Survival Kit.** New York: Monarch, Sovereign, 1978. viii, 181p. index. pa.

With rare good humor, Kahan provides a guide for the expectant father. After exploring men's initial reactions to the news, Kahan takes men through the nine months of pregnancy, with updates on the wife's and the child's changes. Kahan touches upon such matters as figuring costs, finding an obstetrician, the changes men can expect to go through, sex during pregnancy, clothes for the pregnant woman, exercises, and labor and delivery, including instructions for an emergency do-it-yourself delivery. The final chapter covers coping with an infant at home.

464. Lewis, Charlie. **Becoming a Father.** Milton Keynes, England, and Philadelphia: Open University Press, 1986. ix, 222p. appendix. bibliography, 204-16. author and subject indexes. pa.

Research on fathers has been either nonexistent or badly handled, according to Lewis, who takes delight in challenging received wisdom about fatherhood. Drawing upon a study of 100 fathers in England conducted in 1979 and 1980, Lewis finds fathers a more complex, varied group than was suggested by most earlier research. He rejects the idea that the new, nurturant father is really new. Rather, the involved father has been emerging gradually, although powerful social forces (including traditional motherhood and fatherhood) still hinder acceptance of dramatically new roles for most fathers. Lewis finds men closely involved in their wives' pregnancies, and he speculates about the father's presence at delivery as a modern couvade ritual. Not all men do well in the delivery room, Lewis finds. When the baby arrives at home, the father's desire to become an involved parent is often hampered by his marginal status as caregiver. As the infant's first year unfolds, however, the father begins to relate to the child more closely. Significantly, many fathers are more indulgent than mother, and many reject the role of punisher. Many mothers report high father involvement with children, and many fathers have a respect for their role as fathers. However unsettling the presence of the new child may prove, the fathers usually try to be the sturdy oak who weathers crises. Although father's role has become more "nurturant," few parents were motivated by a desire for gender role reversal. The appendix contains the interview format.

465. Mayle, Peter. **How to Be a Pregnant Father: An Illustrated Survival Guide for the First-time Father, Including the Pregnant Father's Cookbook by Len Deighton.** London: Macmillan, 1980, 1993. 54p. illus. pa.

Lighthearted advice from Mayle, a quick-meal cookbook from Deighton, and comical cartoons from Arthur Robbins comprise this upbeat guide for the expectant father. No advice is offered, however, about father participation in childbirth.

466. Phillips, Celeste R., and Joseph T. Anzalone. **Fathering: Participation in Labor and Birth.** 2d ed. Saint Louis: C. V. Mosby, 1982. xv, 168p. illus. glossary. bibliography after each chapter. notes. pa.

Stressing the positive effects of father participation in labor and childbirth, the authors argue that "since fathers tend to be undervalued in our culture ... men may have suffered as much from discrimination as have women—particularly when it comes to pregnancy and birth." Surveying the father's role in history, Phillips and Anzalone find that excluding the father from birthing parallels the father's diminished role in child rearing. The attack on nineteenth-century paternalism unfortunately also diminished fatherhood. Although some hospitals still regard men as excess baggage during labor and birthing, the movement to make men active participants is growing stronger. Without insisting that every man be present at birth, the authors discuss the impact of pregnancy upon men, ways in which the physician gains from father participation, and its positive effects (e.g., father-infant bonding). Such results are movingly dramatized in a series of accounts from fathers, and sometimes mothers, of their experiences during childbirth. Photographs illustrate these accounts. An additional chapter records the memories of men who pioneered father participation. A glossary of medical terms is included.

467. Sasmor, Jeannette L. **What Every Husband Should Know About Having a Baby: The Psychoprophylactic Way.** Chicago: Nelson-Hall, 1972. 232p. illus. appendix. bibliography, 221-22. index.

Sasmor provides a readable guide for husbands to the psychoprophylactic method (PPM). "Prophylaxis," she explains, "is a long, unwieldy name that refers to the prevention (prophylaxis) of mental or emotional (psycho) trauma experienced by most unprepared women during the process of childbearing." In Sasmor's plan, the husband becomes the wife's birthing coach. Without mounting any soapboxes, Sasmor explains the value of the husband's involvement in pregnancy and childbirth. (Readers would be well advised to skip the foreword by Benjamin Segal, which manages to be antagonistic to men in a way that Sasmor never is.) Sasmor surveys the history of "natural childbirth" ideas and outlines the husband's role during pregnancy, delivery, and afterward. As a practicing nurse, Sasmor is able to offer numerous hints for husbands about such matters as breathing and relaxation techniques, what to expect in the delivery room, episiotomy, rooming-in after birth, and taking care of a new baby. Without attempting to usurp the function of husband-coached childbirth classes, Sasmor's book provides a valuable supplement.

468. Schaefer, George. **The Expectant Father.** Rev. ed. New York: Barnes and Noble, 1972. xii, 167p. appendixes. bibliography, 159-62. index. pa.

In concise style, Schaefer surveys the expectant father's role from premarital examination to costs of caring for an infant. He explains such matters as genes, chromosomes, and the Rh factor; he offers information and advice about living with a pregnant wife, education for parenthood, and deciding whether or not to participate in childbirth.

469. Shapiro, Jerrold Lee. **When Men Are Pregnant: Needs and Concerns of Expectant Fathers.** San Luis Obispo, CA: Impact, 1987. ix, 274p. bibliography, 269-70. index. Reprint, New York: Delta, 1993. pa.

Drawing upon interviews with 227 expectant and recent fathers, as well as his personal experiences, Shapiro surveys men's concerns and needs from preconception to postpartum. A professor of counseling psychology, Shapiro writes for a popular audience, providing perceptive insights into situations and issues that other writers often ignore or skim. He looks in depth at how modern life can complicate the decision to have a child, the couvade syndrome, and the strains that pregnancy can place upon couples. He notes differing responses by fathers to similar challenges. Shapiro has misgivings about some medical care during childbirth, and he notes the sexist attitudes toward fathers that persist among some doctors and nurses. Despite the numerous pitfalls depicted in this book, Shapiro remains decidedly upbeat about fatherhood.

470. Spacek, Tim. **Fathers: There at the Birth.** Chicago: Chicago Review Press, 1985. 148p. pa.

Spacek has collected 13 varied accounts of childbirth from fathers who were there—including Spacek himself for two of his children. One father's child was born at home unexpectedly, another had trouble with an imperious hospital staff, and still another was excluded when complications led doctors to perform a Cesarean. Spacek concludes, "There are no 'laws' governing birth, and each story, while similar, is a little different." The accounts provide deeply human perspectives on the impact of birth upon fathers.

471. Weiss, Robert Russell, and Myron Ray Pexton. **Dr. Pexton's Guide for the Expectant Father.** North Quincy, MA: Christopher, 1970. 208p. index.

This popular guide for fathers consists of questions by Weiss and answers by Pexton, an M.D. The topics include birth control, father's presence in the delivery room, Cesarean section, vasectomy, Rh factor, postpartum blues, infant care, and so on. Some readers will find Pexton's responses refreshingly commonsensical; others will find them sometimes dubious and dated. In this book, the father's role is largely a supportive one, a contrast to the more active role recommended by more recent fathers' advocates.

472. Worth, Cecilia. **The Birth of a Father: New Fathers Talk About Pregnancy, Childbirth, and the First Three Months.** New York: McGraw-Hill, A Sun Words Book, 1988. x, 150p. bibliography, 149-50. pa.

A nurse who has taught expectant parents courses for 20 years, Worth offers fathers-to-be clear advice about coping with pregnancy, birth, and the first three months of child care. New fathers go through a major life change, the author argues, and are often ignored by society in general and hospital personnel in particular. Using interviews with new fathers, Worth examines such matters as sex during pregnancy and the male couvade syndrome. Participating in childbirth and caring for a newborn can be scary but rewarding for men. Without omitting negative experiences, the author stresses the positive potential of new fatherhood.

B. Fathers, Fatherhood, Husbands, Married Men

473. Andersen, Christopher P. **Father: The Figure and the Force.** New York: Warner Books, 1983. xi, 256p. bibliography, 255-56.

"Nearly every American adult alive today," Andersen declares, "has been raised in his or her father's absence." Arguing that fathers have been given short shrift by American society, the author presents evidence of fathers' overwhelming importance to children. Writing in popular style, Andersen utilizes interviews with celebrities, experts, friends, and acquaintances, as well as his own experiences as son and father, to construct an informal portrait of fatherhood in modern America. He touches upon such matters as fathers as resident aliens in the family, the effects of father absence upon children, the Oedipus and Electra complexes, and father as mediator of the outside world to the child. Later chapters deal with surrogate fathers and mentors, breaking away from father, and the New Dad—whom Andersen regards as a fraud. Both Dad and Mom, he argues, are defecting from their responsibilities as parents. Despite Andersen's willingness to portray Dad with warts and all, his book is a vigorous defense of fatherhood in a society that he regards as increasingly complacent about parenting.

474. Appleton, William S. **Fathers and Daughters: A Father's Powerful Influence on a Woman's Life.** Garden City, NY: Doubleday, 1981. xv, 198p. Reprint, New York: Berkley Books, 1984. pa.

Although written for daughters, this book makes equally valid reading for fathers. The author, an M.D. with two daughters, writes lucidly of the father's profound effect upon his daughter's life. Rejecting the Freudian model that stresses childhood influences, Appleton argues that the father-daughter relationship occurs over a 30-year period in their separate life cycles. These years he divides into three segments: oasis (when daughter is "daddy's little girl" and when father is building his career), conflict (when daughter is an adolescent and when father is passing through midlife turmoil), and separation (when daughter reaches autonomy and when father sees her as an adult). Although Appleton recognizes that many father-daughter bonds are warm and strengthening, he focuses upon those that adversely affect women's lives in such areas as sex, careers, insecurity, and relationships with men. Making changes in one's life, Appleton points out, requires a process of understanding and an act of will on the woman's part.

475. Barret, Robert L., and Bryan E. Robinson. **Gay Fathers.** Lexington, MA: D. C. Heath, Lexington Books, 1990. xv, 197p. appendix. bibliography after each chapter and in appendix. notes. index.

A minority within a minority, gay fathers face discrimination from society, the legal system, and counselors who reject gay parenthood. The authors seek to dispel a number of misperceptions about homosexual fathers, including the myths that children will "catch" gayness from them and that gay fathers are likely to molest their children. They examine different gay family structures. Because divorce is usually involved, children of gay men often face the pain of family breakup in addition to the stigma of parental gayness. Parents and wives of homosexuals are likely to pass through several stages of reactions to news of the man's homosexuality. The impact of AIDS on gay fathers is explored. Because the little research that is available on gay parenthood is often methodologically flawed, the authors present desiderata for future research. Throughout the book, they offer advice for gay fathers and mental health professionals. The appendix includes resources for gay fathers, such as scholarly and popular literature, organizations, periodicals, and audiovisuals.

476. Benson, Leonard. **Fatherhood: A Sociological Perspective.** New York: Random House, 1968. xii, 371p. bibliography, 325-59. index.

An early (1968) study that has retained its validity, this book provides a systematic account of the sociological literature on fatherhood. Deploring our society's comparative neglect of fathers, Benson notes: "It is apparent that the problems of women *as women* arouse our most anxious concern, while those of men rarely stir our passion for reform." Part 1 puts fatherhood into sociological perspective, examining the link between masculinity and fatherhood, our society's encouragement of instrumental roles for males, the passing of patriarchal styles of fathering, and the emergence of the father-mother team. In part 2 Benson discusses the male as parent, examining the father as "weak link" in the family chain who needs more careful adjustment to marriage and family. The greater discrepancy between the husband-father roles than between the wife-mother roles also increases stress for men in families. Benson traces the various theories of sexual identification and father's roles, the urge to excel instilled by many fathers, and the pressures on male children to assume a masculine role. A discussion of father-child conflict is followed by an account of fatherlessness in families. While any individual father in a household may be expendable, Benson concludes, the institution of fatherhood is not. Part 3 examines conflicts between father's obligations as breadwinner and his role as parent. A final chapter of prognosis indicates that the family has become more important to fathers.

477. Biller, Henry B. **Fathers and Families: Paternal Factors in Child Development.** Westport, CT: Auburn House, 1993. xiii, 327p. bibliography, 275-302. notes. author and subject indexes. pa.

Stressing the benefits of positive "father presence," Biller crystallizes an enormous amount of research to document the value of nurturing fatherhood. Linking biological, psychological, and social interconnections, he notes the overall advantages of the two-parent family in which father and mother are partners in parenting. Fathers need encouragement to bond closely with infants, and their nurturing presence can contribute greatly to the child's gender and identity development. Biology gives children a nudge in a developmental direction, but parents can smooth the way in helping children establish their individuality. In the development of the child's morality, intelligence, and creativity, Biller demonstrates the contributions of positive fathering. In elementary schools, the shortage of male teachers reinforces the father absence in too many children's homes. For several reasons, boys are often badly served by U.S. schools. Fathers can contribute greatly to the independence and assertiveness of daughters as well as sons. In numerous other areas—athletics, fitness, intimacy, sexuality, and social adjustment—the presence of a caring father is of great benefit to the child. Surveying family problems, Biller concludes that many result from absent fathers and overburdened mothers. The hurried pace of modern life hampers close family interaction, to the detriment of both parents and children. Biller's work represents a major summation of evidence indicating the benefits of nurturant fathering.

478. Biller, Henry. **Paternal Deprivation: Family, School, Sexuality, and Society.** D. C. Heath, Lexington Books, 1974. xi, 227p. bibliography, 171-207. author and subject indexes.

"The thesis of this book is that paternal deprivation, including patterns of inadequate fathering as well as father absence, is a highly significant factor in the development of serious psychological and social problems." This sequel to Biller's *Father, Child, and Sex Role* (entry 595) examines numerous aspects of paternal deprivation, including theories of a boy's identification with his father and the resulting development of masculinity, father-infant attachments, the boy's sex role, surrogate models of masculine behavior, the effects of paternal deprivation on the child's personal and social adjustment (including psychopathology), the mother-son relationship caused by paternal deprivation, effects of father-daughter relations on her emotional and interpersonal functioning, the intellectual and academic development of children (including effects of the feminized classroom), ways of coping with paternal deprivation, and suggested solutions for alleviating the problem. Throughout the book, Biller offers impressive evidence of the need for good fathers. The bibliography is unusually full.

479. Biller, Henry, and Dennis Meredith. **Father Power.** New York: David McKay, 1974. 376p. bibliography, 361-68. notes. index. Reprint, Garden City, NY: Doubleday, Anchor, 1975. pa.

"Father power" means the enormous influence that a father exercises over his child's life. To harness this power for positive ends, the authors have written a manifesto and guide for the man striving to transcend older, more rigid concepts of fathering and to give his children secure, personal identities, without locking them into narrow gender roles. Drawing upon research studies, as well as their own work and experiences as fathers, Biller and Meredith offer stimulating advice on such matters as how fathers can overcome stereotyped views of fatherhood, how they can help children develop a fulfilling sense of masculinity or femininity, and how they can encourage positive attitudes towards physical growth, learning, work, and morality. A separate section of the book addresses "special problems" (e.g., divorce, stepfathering, handicapped fathers and children, black fathers, and father absence). The easy-to-read style makes *Father Power* widely accessible to men who want to be more active and nurturing fathers.

480. Bozett, Frederick W., ed. **Gay and Lesbian Parents.** New York: Praeger, 1987. xvi, 247p. bibliography after each chapter and 237-38. notes. index. pa.

Bozett has collected 13 scholarly articles dealing with numerous aspects of gay parenting. Gay men are likely to be most interested in the essays "Gay Fathers" and "Children of Gay Fathers" (both by Bozett), and "Counseling Gay Husbands and Fathers" (by Brian Miller). In the final essay, Bozett considers future perspectives for gay and lesbian parents.

481. Bozett, Frederick W., and Shirley M. H. Hanson, eds. **Fatherhood and Families in Cultural Context.** New York: Springer, 1991. xxiv, 290p. bibliography after each chapter. subject and author indexes.

The 11 articles in this anthology examine fathers and families in a wider cultural context than many earlier studies had done. In an historical perspective of fatherhood from preindustrial to postindustrial times, Peter N. Stearns questions current stereotypes of past fatherhood and cites its positive and negative attributes. Alfredo Mirandé examines differences and similarities among African-American, Latino, Asian, and Native American fatherhood, while Lynda Henley Walters and Stephen F. Chapman alert readers to the danger of our legal system's insensitivity to different cultural concepts of fathering. Teresa Donati Marciano offers a rare study of the impact of religion on fatherhood. Other essays discuss how social class and fatherhood can interact, how "Organizational Culture" can affect fathers, and how positive fathering can be enhanced in family cultures.

482. Bronstein, Phyllis, and Carolyn Pape Cowan, eds. **Fatherhood Today: Men's Changing Role in the Family.** New York: John Wiley, 1988. xix, 347p. bibliography after each chapter. author and subject indexes.

An important collection of 19 articles, plus foreword, *Fatherhood Today* extends the range of fatherhood studies to include cultural variations of paternal behavior, divorced fathers, remarried fathers, stepfathers, gay fathers, grandfathers, as well as white, black, and Latino fathers. The book's major sections explore fathers in developing two-parent families, variations and changes in father and family relationships, prevention and intervention programs for men and boys, and directions for research and social change. Articles include a study of "the fatherhood click" (when men decide the time is right for them to become fathers), the social pressures faced by black fathers, conflicts between gay lifestyle and fathering behaviors, and the need for stepfathers to move slowly in establishing a bond with stepchildren. Special mention should be made of Shirley M. H. Hanson's compassionate discussion of divorced fathers with custody and of James W. Loewen's challenging account of visitation fatherhood. All the articles, however, are models of thoughtful scholarship.

483. Cammarata, Jerry, with Frances Spatz Leighton. **The Fun Book of Fatherhood: Or, How the Animal Kingdom Is Helping to Raise the Wild Kids at Our House.** Los Angeles: Corwin Books, 1978. xiii, 303p. illus. bibliography, 301-3. Reprint, Los Angeles: Pinnacle Books, 1979. pa.

Cammarata attracted headlines by fighting for—and winning—a four-year paternity leave from his job. He wanted the leave not to enable his wife to go out to work (she didn't), but to enable him to be closely involved in raising their two daughters. In frenetically informal prose, Cammarata records his insights into parenting, often by way of zany analogies with animal parents. Using anecdotes from his experiences at home, he touches upon such matters as not pressuring children to succeed, feeding, fighting, telling children about sex, discipline, education, play, and sleeping.

484. Cath, Stanley H., Alan R. Gurwitt, and John Munder Ross, eds. **Father and Child: Developmental and Clinical Perspectives.** Boston: Little, Brown, 1982. xxv, 663p. bibliography, 587-613. name and subject indexes.

Citing the father as the "forgotten parent" and deploring the "relative dearth of reflection on paternity," the editors have collected 36 essays (plus a preface and an afterword) by 39 contributors with impressive credentials. Although geared primarily for clinicians, *Father and Child* covers such a range of topics and is so readable that it invites a wider audience. Divided into five sections, the book begins with reviews of the psychological literature on fathers (understandably, Freud looms large in these surveys). The next two sections trace the development of the male from infancy to old age, emphasizing the father-child relationship. Among the topics discussed are engrossment (bonding between fathers and newborn infants), father hunger (the need for a father's presence, especially to modulate aggressive drive and fantasy), the father's role in establishing the child's gender identity during early childhood, fathers and adolescent sons, expectant fathers, fathers in midlife crises, grand-fatherhood, and the death of the father. Section 4 deals with cultural and historical variations, including the child's representation of God, the patriarchal tradition in Genesis, and a survey of the changing faces of fatherhood in the United States. Exploring clinical problems and applications, section 5 touches upon such matters as divorce, abusive fathers, incest, the relationship between abdicating fathers and homosexual sons, and the importance of involving fathers in clinical treatment of children. An afterword by E. James Anthony examines the internalized early-childhood father by citing the lives of Kafka, J. S. Mill, Gosse, Butler, and Freud. *Father and Child* maintains a continuity and a consistency of excellence seldom found in anthologies.

485. Colman, Arthur, and Libby Colman. **Earth Father/Sky Father: The Changing Concept of Fathering.** Englewood Cliffs, NJ: Prentice-Hall, 1981. xii, 206p. illus. notes. index. pa. Rev. ed., *The Father—Mythology and Changing Roles.* Wilmette, IL: Chiron Publications, 1988. pa.

Before the current wave of mythopoetic studies, the Colmans employed Jungian archetypes to depict five models of the father. Arguing that men need images of the nurturing father to validate their changing roles as fathers, the authors insist upon the importance of both the Sky Father who mediates between family and outside world and the Earth Father who functions within the family itself. Using literature, dreams, and myth, as well as interviews with 15 men and case histories, the Colmans examine the archetype of Father the Creator, arguing that parenting may be a man's most significant act of creation. The archetype of Earth Father can be found in images of male fertility and nurturance: in everyday life, this kind of father is totally involved in raising children. The Sky Father is provider, judge, and protector, but men playing this role nowadays may find it frustrating and difficult. The Royal Father controls children's lives completely: at present the single parent is often forced into this role. The Dyadic Father is half of a pair of creative parents who nevertheless retain their own identities. The authors also trace varying images of the father through the life cycle—from the child's idealization of the father to the adult's reconciliation with the father. In the final section, the Colmans discuss nontraditional fathering, the need for males as earth-father nurturers, and the benefits for children of dyadic parents. The 1988 edition contains a new preface, indicating that the more nurturant father has become more widely accepted, although not universally admired.

486. Corneau, Guy. **Absent Fathers, Lost Sons: The Search for Masculine Identity.** Translated by Larry Shouldice. Boston and London: Shambhala, 1991. x, 186p. bibliography, 183-86. pa.

A Jungian analyst from Canada, Corneau is emphatic about the necessity of fathers in families. During the first two years of life, male children absolutely need a father. "Lacking a father," Corneau writes, "is like lacking a backbone." In the father-absent family, the oedipal triangle can cause trouble for the growing boy. The author points to the near-universal initiation rites that separate the boy from the mother. Arguing that modern fathers do not spend nearly enough time with children, Corneau lists five ways of being an inadequate father, and he cites the inordinate amount of deviant and antisocial behavior exhibited by father-deprived boys. Examining the various roles that father-absent males play, Corneau draws upon Robert Bly's retelling of the Iron Hans (Iron John) story (entry 861) to illustrate the boy's need for directed aggression in contest. Life crises can be helpful for "lost sons" if they push these men to forgive their absent fathers and initiate "self-fathering."

487. Cottle, Thomas J. **Like Fathers, Like Sons: Portraits of Intimacy and Strain.** Norwood, NJ: Ablex, 1981 xvii, 140p. pa.

Utilizing his work in constructing life studies, Cottle provides 10 accounts of fathers and sons. Avoiding "scientific" detachment, he re-creates the people and events impressionistically, thereby conveying the men's experiences of generational stress, love, and legacy. Many readers will find these accounts moving and powerful vignettes of male lives.

488. Daley, Eliot A. **Father Feelings.** York: William Morrow, 1978. 192p. Reprint, New York: Pocket Books, 1979. pa.

Drawing upon his experiences as a father, Daley reflects upon a variety of family and men's concerns, including the emotional costs of today's frantic mobility, his triumphs and pratfalls in dealing with three children, the dubious advice of family "experts," the teaching of values to children, the overcomplicated mechanisms that thwart us as often as they benefit us, and the place of money in one's priorities. In the chapter with the most radical implications, "The Great Juggling Act, or Trying to Do Justice to Both a Career and a Family," Daley writes: "Women may be tired of being culturally regarded as housekeepers and diaper washers; well, I am tired of being culturally regarded as a breadwinner whose primary responsibility to the family is to be a 'good provider' . . . I'd rather be a father."

489. Dobson, James C. **Straight Talk to Men and Their Wives.** Waco, TX: Word, 1980. 222p. illus.

Deploring the erosion of family leadership among men, Dobson invokes the memory of his father to redefine a Christian concept of masculinity. He discusses paternal authority and love, husband-wife relations, and men and work. Later chapters focus on masculine identity, emotions, and religious belief.

490. Dodson, Fitzhugh. **How to Father.** Edited by Jeanne Harris. Los Angeles: Nash, 1974. xviii, 537p. illus. appendixes. bibliography, 503-20. notes. index. Reprint, New York: New American Library, Signet, 1975. pa.

In this guidebook for fathers, Dodson uses psychological stages of child development as a basis for practical advice on how fathers can deal effectively with children as they grow from infancy to young adulthood. Five appendixes contain guides to commercial toys and play equipment, inexpensive toys and play equipment that fathers can make, children's books, children's records, and a "survival kit" of reading materials for fathers.

491. DuBrin, Andrew J. **The New Husbands and How to Become One.** Chicago: Nelson-Hall, 1976. xiv, 213p. notes. index.

In what often reads like once-trendy advice for yuppies, DuBrin distinguishes between old- and new-style husbands. The new husband can have it all—a good-paying job, a feminist wife, and children who are politically correct about gender roles. The book's unquestioning acceptance of unisex child-rearing may be one indication of its datedness.

492. Elster, Arthur B., and Michael E. Lamb, eds. **Adolescent Fatherhood.** Hillsdale, NJ: Lawrence Erlbaum Associates, 1986. xiii, 204p. bibliography after each chapter. author index.

Eleven essays, plus an epilogue, are addressed to various aspects of the adolescent father. In the opening chapter, Raymond Montemayor defines and describes adolescence; in the following essay, Douglas M. Tell and Michael E. Lamb discuss gender role stereotypes and young men's problems in achieving adult masculinity. Freya L. Sonenstein discusses contraceptives, finding that young males use them at about the same rate as young females do. Subsequent essays are devoted to stresses and coping strategies of adolescent fathers, and the greater failure of adolescent fathers to complete high school education. Lamb and Elster note that most studies of adolescent parental behavior have focused exclusively on mothers; fathers seem to share the same higher rate of unsuccessful parenting patterns. In a study by Frank G. Bolton, Jr., and Jay Belsky, however, the predicted higher rates of child maltreatment by adolescent fathers did not materialize. An essay by Belsky and Brent C. Miller argues that the transition to parenthood is more stressful and complicated for adolescent fathers. James S. Kahn and Bolton argue the reasons why clinicians should attend to teen fathers, and Debra G. Klinman and her associates describe the Teen Father Collaboration, an effort to reach adolescent fathers through organizations in several cities. Maris A. Vinovskis paints a dismal picture of U.S. attitudes towards adolescent fathers and of lawmakers focusing on the teen mother while ignoring or castigating the teen father. In the epilogue, the editors list future research priorities for studying adolescent fathers.

493. Fields, Suzanne. **Like Father, Like Daughter: How Father Shapes the Woman His Daughter Becomes.** Boston: Little, Brown, 1983. xii, 299p. bibliography, 291-99. notes.

In this popularly written discussion of father-daughter relationships, Fields blends questionnaire replies, interviews, a review of psychological and sociological literature, and autobiography. Although the impact of father absence upon sons has been studied more thoroughly, Fields finds that a missing father can have devastating effects upon a daughter. The father confirms her lovableness while she romances him and learns how to relate to other males. Although fathers tend to be more affectionate with daughters than with sons, this closeness can have its drawbacks if it fixes the daughter's dependence upon males. Puberty can be troubling for both daughter and father as both awaken to her sexuality. While not discounting the seriousness of father-daughter incest, Fields refuses to blame it on a patriarchal plot against females. When a daughter marries, she sometimes must make the transition from Daddy's Little Girl to Woman-Wife. Just how trying this adjustment can be is illustrated by an account of Field's colorful father, Samuel "Bo" Bregman, and her first years of marriage to Ted Fields. While welcoming the increased interest of many men in being better fathers, Fields is skeptical of men who worship "feminine" values while denigrating "masculine" ones: "When men pursue a feminine sensibility, women inevitably are shortchanged in their own fundamental psychic and sensual needs."

494. Gilbert, Sara D. **What's A Father For? A Father's Guide to the Pleasures and Problems of Parenthood, with Advice from the Experts.** New York: Parents' Magazine Press, 1975. xxiii, 231p. illus. appendix. bibliography, 191-202, 213-18. notes. index. Reprint, New York: Warner Books, 1975. pa.

With humorously informal prose, Gilbert examines a father's roles and offers advice from the experts. She considers such matters as the reasons for wanting to be a father, coping with the demands of fatherhood, a brief history of fathering styles, avoiding sexist stereotyping of boys and girls, new forms of fathering (including dual-career fathers and househusbands), handling smaller children, coping with teens, and launching children into the world. She discusses the special problems of part-time fathers and single fathers ("double-time fathers"). A final chapter examines difficulties of men's roles in modern society and the father's need to develop as a fulfilled human being. "A typical father ... is somebody's husband, somebody's father, *and* somebody's employee," Gilbert notes for the benefit of women envying men's lot. "He can't do what he wants any more than his wife can." Comic cartoons by James Stevenson of *The New Yorker* supplement the text.

495. Golant, Mitch, with Susan Golant. **Finding Time for Fathering.** New York: Fawcett Columbine, 1992. xii, 288p. bibliography, 269-78. index. pa.

For an audience of general readers, the Golants stress the importance of fathers' spending time with children. The demands of the breadwinner role militate against quality time between fathers and children. However, men provide important kinds of nurturing. The authors extol the authoritative father (not to be confused with the authoritarian one) and offer practical advice on how to discipline with love. They suggest ways for fathers to deal with the different stages of childhood, from prebirth to adolescence. Sexuality must be dealt with positively and appropriately. Separate chapters cover how to achieve quality time with children, how to play with children at different ages, and how to introduce children to father's workplace. The authors suggest ways for fathers, especially divorced fathers, to keep in touch during times of absence.

496. Goulter, Barbara, and Joan Minninger. **The Father-Daughter Dance: Insight, Inspiration, and Understanding for Every Woman and Her Father.** New York: G. P. Putnam's Sons, 1993. 256p. bibliography, 237-42. notes. index.

Although the son's need for a father has been stressed in the literature, father hunger affects women too. The authors trace six father-daughter patterns that can adversely affect daughters: lost father and yearning daughter, abusive father and victim daughter, pampering father and spoiled daughter, pygmalion father and companion daughter, ruined father and rescuing daughter, and anguished father and angry daughter. The patterns are illustrated by means of biographies, case histories, fictional characters, and historical figures. Goulter and Minninger argue that "mother-raising" of children glamorizes the absent father and overburdens the mother. They describe "redecision therapy" and other means of healing hurtful father-daughter relationships. The discussion is somewhat undercut by the authors' failure to get storylines straight (e.g., *Die Walküre*), their too-easy acceptance of radical feminist dogmas (e.g., patriarchy devalues women and overvalues males), and their occasional mangling of literature (e.g., *Antigone*). The foreword is by Harville Hendrix.

497. Grant, Wilson Wayne. **The Caring Father.** Nashville, TN: Broadman Press, 1983. 155p. appendix. notes. pa.

In the context of evangelical Christianity, Grant (an M.D.) considers the importance of fathers to children and offers advice on how fathers can maximize the beneficial aspects of their family role. Men need to allot time for fatherhood, stress the positive when relating to children, and handle discipline with love and intelligence. Children need to see their fathers at work, have their fathers involved in family worship, and understand that their fathers love their mothers. In an addendum, Grant considers the future of the family, indicating that reports of its death have been premature.

498. Green, Maureen. **Fathering.** New York: McGraw-Hill, 1976. ix, 230p. bibliography, 219-25. notes. Reprint, *Life without Fathering*, New York: McGraw-Hill, 1977. pa. Published in Great Britain as *Goodbye Father* (London and Henley: Routledge and Kegan Paul, 1976).

In popular style, Green analyzes the crisis of modern fatherhood, arguing that the role must be either reinvented or abandoned. Despite all the evils attributed to patriarchy, Green feels that radical feminist efforts to eliminate fathers from families are a mistake. Fathers are expendable, she warns, but their loss to the family does considerable damage to children, wives, society at large, and men themselves.

499. Hallowell, Christopher. **Father to the Man: A Journal.** New York: William Morrow, 1987. 177p.

Recording a special vacation with his wife and children, Hallowell offers a meditation upon fathers and sons. The family travels to (fictitiously named) "Weenaumet Point" on Cape Cod, a place where Hallowell had spent summers as a boy. Watching his own children, Hallowell recalls his relationship with his father, now dead. The children, Matthew and Maggie, exhibit sharp gender differences at an early age. Hallowell concludes that they are not picking up on parental or social cues; rather, parents and society throughout the ages have shaped gender roles by picking up cues from children. Hallowell's own father was distant, leaving the son filled with father hunger. When the current vacation at Weenaumet ends, Hallowell seems to have made peace, albeit a somewhat regretful one, with his father.

500. Hamilton, Marshall L. **Father's Influence on Children.** Chicago: Nelson-Hall, 1977. x, 230p. bibliography, 173-96. index. pa.

Hamilton surveys research done on fathers up to 1974. Rejecting the stereotype of fathers as uninvolved incompetents, he finds indications of strong paternal involvement with children. He explores the effects of father absence on children, and of fathers' influence upon children's sex roles and development. Thumbnail sketches of people like Lee Harvey Oswald, Ralph Nader, and Indira Gandhi emphasize the father-child relationship. The concluding chapter presents characteristics of an "ideal" father.

501. Hammer, Signe. **Passionate Attachments: Fathers and Daughters in America Today.** New York: Rawson, 1982. xi, 303p. notes. index.

Drawing upon interviews, recollections, and scholarly studies, Hammer discusses uneasy father-daughter relationships in modern U.S. society. Her own father, absent during World War II, returned to dominate and discourage her search for autonomy. Similar problems surface in several accounts in the book: the fathers here seldom prepared their daughters for an independent role in the world. Hammer hypothesizes that some fathers identify their own femininity with their daughters and want to protect and pamper them. The "successful" fathers in this book are the ones whose daughters have made it in the outside "male" world. In a concluding chapter, the author considers how overly dutiful daughters can undo the paralyzing effects of an overbearing father.

502. Hanson, Shirley M. H., and Frederick W. Bozett, eds. **Dimensions of Fatherhood.** Beverly Hills, CA: Sage Publications, 1985. 464p. illus. notes after each chapter. index. pa.

An influential collection of 19 articles written by 27 contributors, *Dimensions of Fatherhood* examines the state of knowledge among social scientists about fathers. It expands the range of earlier studies of fatherhood, and presents a blueprint for the future of fatherhood. Articles follow a similar pattern: an historical perspective on some aspect of fathering, a survey of research, discussion of implications for professional practice, recommended research, and summary and conclusions. Articles are grouped under "Roles Throughout the Life Cycle" and "Variations of Fatherhood." In the former section, essays range from Janice M. Swanson's "Men and Family Planning" to Marc C. Baranowski's "Men as Grandfathers." In the latter section, studies consider topics such as househusbands, stepfathers, fathers in the military, gay men as fathers, single custodial fathers, and widowers as fathers. A final article by Frank A. Pedersen considers "Research and Fathers: Where Do We Go From Here?"

503. Hearn, Jeff. **Birth and Afterbirth: A Materialist Account.** London: Achilles Heel, 1983. 60p. illus. notes. pa.

This brief essay shows the author conflicted by his powerful feelings as a father and his faith in a Marxist ideology that proclaims fatherhood a part of patriarchy's oppression of women. As a true believer, Hearn jettisons his feelings and attempts to understand reproduction in terms of Marxist teachings on labor and production in capitalism. In the end, Hearn proposes a new matriarchy in which mothers control birth and "childwork" while fathers are dutifully subservient. "Most importantly," Hearn concludes, "the notion of fatherhood must be smashed or more precisely dropped bit by bit into the ocean." The essay is likely to raise more questions than it answers. How will the new matriarchy avoid the weaknesses of the old ones (none of which has survived)? Is denying fathers' powerful attachments to their children treating them as less than human? How is a powerless father to intervene when a mother is harming a child? How can humanity expect to socialize males to become caring and responsible fathers when the notion of fatherhood has been discredited? Many readers will wish that Hearn had listened more to his heart and less to his ideology.

504. Heidebrecht, Paul, and Jerry Rohrbach. **Fathering a Son.** Chicago: Moody Press, 1974. 218p. illus. appendix. bibliography, 205-14. pa.

From a biblical, Christian viewpoint, the authors describe how a man can become a loving, encouraging father instead of a domineering, distant one. Arguing that men need to be liberated from false images of masculinity, the authors spell out the father's importance in shaping the son's sex role, his concept of God, his moral values, his ability to deal with society, and his desire to achieve. They examine the boy's development from infancy to teen years, with suggestions on how fathers can foster the son's intellectual and spiritual growth. Additional chapters are devoted to such matters as discipline, school-work, career choices, and fathers and daughters. Interviews with four men provide personal insights into fathering. The appendix lists resources for the active fathers, including an annotated bibliography.

505. Johnson, Spencer. **The One Minute Father: The Quickest Way for You to Help Your Children Learn to Like Themselves and Want to Behave Themselves.** New York: William Morrow, 1983. 112p.

In this brief, easily read book, Johnson describes his "one-minute repri-mand," a technique for showing disapproval of a child's behavior, showing approval of the child, and letting the father's feelings get expressed. The technique leads to other practices such as positive reinforcement of desired behavior.

506. Jones, Evan, ed. **The Father: Letters to Sons and Daughters.** New York: Rinehart, 1960. xx, 268p. index.

This anthology, containing over 100 letters to children from fathers through-out the ages, features, for the most part, famous men (Lorenzo the Magnificent, Lord Chesterfield, Dickens, Theodore Roosevelt, Gandhi), although a few un-knowns are included (an American soldier in World War II writing to his unborn child). Comments before and after the letters provide the necessary context.

507. Keyes, Ralph, ed. **Sons on Fathers: A Book of Men's Writing.** New York: HarperCollins, 1992. xxix, 315p. index.

Love him or hate him, Father has a profound impact on Son's life, as this unusually rich and moving collection of writings indicates. Keyes has assem-bled 80 essays, excerpts, short stories, and poems in which sons recall their fathers. In the introduction, Keyes points to recurring themes amid the diver-sity of the sons' responses to dad: trying to meet the father's expectations, learning not to be too physically affectionate with dad, sharing experiences with dad (playing ball, playing cards, etc.), competing with father, trying to accomplish what father could not, realizing the terrible cost that father paid to be a good provider, realizing one's own mortality after father's death, and coming to terms with memories of dad. Contributors include Robert Bly, John Cheever, James Dickey, Bob Greene, Patrick Hemingway, Bill Moyers, Sam Osherson, and Paul Zweig. The collection closes with Larry L. King's marvelous memoir, "The Old Man."

508. Klein, Ted. **The Father's Book.** New York: William Morrow, 1968. xiii, 393p. illus. index.

This readable handbook from the sixties attempts to provide a Dr. Spock-like guide for fathers. Klein's advice covers such matters as basic information for the father-to-be, understanding childhood development, childhood diseases, father-son and father-daughter relations, absent fathers and divorced fathers, disci-pline, stepfathers and foster fathers, father's role in sex education and in motivating general learning, money management, grandparents, religion, accidents and first aid, and how to get help from experts. Nowadays, some of Klein's advice still rings true ("If you wait *too* long to become involved, you may not fit in with your child's needs and already developed behavior patterns"), while other views are dated ("when the husband is present in the labor room—and even more often, at delivery ... he is the one who usually needs help just when the baby is born").

509. Klinman, Debra G., Rhine Kohl, and The Fatherhood Project at Bank Street College of Education. **Fatherhood U.S.A.: The First National Guide to Programs, Services, and Resources for and about Fathers.** New York: Garland, 1984. xxiv, 323p. illus. appendixes. bibliography, 205-46. indexes. pa.

An invaluable resource book for fathers and men interested in changing male roles, *Fatherhood U.S.A.* is divided into six chapters. Chapter 1 lists programs for expectant and new fathers and for fathers of children with special needs, as well as organizations concerned with male reproductive health. Chapter 2 includes information about nurturant males in the educational system, including child-care classes for school-age boys, programs to encourage male involvement in schools, father-child classes, and college and university courses on fathering and on male roles. In chapter 3 are listed social and supportive services for all kinds of fathers (fathers in general, single fathers, stepfathers, teen fathers, gay fathers, and incarcerated fathers), as well as a listing of men's organizations resource centers and support groups established by men's organizations. Fathers and family law are covered in chapter 4, including a listing of divorce and custody mediation services and of fathers' rights organizations. Chapter 5 is devoted to fathers and work, including information about alternative work schedules, parental leave policies, and education and support programs. The largest section of the book, chapter 6 is devoted to bibliographies and others resources for fathers and "new" men. Books and publications about numerous aspects of fathering are listed, as well as books for children featuring fathers and men in nurturing roles, films and videocassettes about fathers and nurturant males, newsletters of interest to many kinds of fathers, and information about the National Fatherhood Forum Series. The appendixes describe The Fatherhood Project (included is a printed questionnaire). Two indexes of programs and organizations, by alphabet and by geographical location, are followed by a subject index. As this outline suggests, the book's contents go well beyond the limits suggested by the title. This book is testimony to a burgeoning interest in both fatherhood and the changing gender roles of U.S. men. "Ten years ago," James A. Levine writes in the foreword, "this book could not have been written."

510. Kort, Carol, and Ronnie Friedland, eds. **The Fathers' Book: Shared Experiences.** Boston: G. K. Hall, 1986. xviii, 293p. illus. pa.

In this collection of personal essays, poems, and interviews, 70 fathers recount the joys and tribulations of fatherhood. The range of topics is extensive, including expectant fathers, new fathers, fathers and daughters, fathers and sons, fathers and mothers, the tensions between career and fatherhood, new-style fathers, the two-career family, single fathers, stepfathers, teen fathers and fathers of teens, the difficulties faced by gay fathers, infertility, adoption, vasectomy, handicapped and seriously ill children, and miscarriage and death of a child. The essays illustrate the many-faceted aspects of fatherhood, as well as the powerful and sometimes contradictory emotional responses it can elicit in men. The photographs in the book strongly underline the positive faces of fatherhood.

511. Lamb, Michael E., ed. **The Father's Role: Applied Perspectives.** New York: John Wiley/Interscience, 1986. xiv, 461p. illus. bibliography after each chapter. author and subject indexes.

In this first of two volumes (the other is Lamb's *The Father's Role: Cross-Cultural Perspectives*, entry 512) Lamb argues that the father is no longer the forgotten parent and that researchers need to summarize what has come to light about fathers. Sixteen articles examine legal and clinical issues as well as programs and policies concerning fathers. Graeme Russell surveys the factors that lead to greater paternal involvement, and Ross A. Thompson criticizes the "best interests" concept that often influences judicial decisions in custody disputes. The gender and age of the child is often an important factor to consider in these decisions. The importance of involving fathers in family therapy is stressed in several essays, and Donald J. Meyer considers ways of aiding the fathers of children with mental handicaps. In her study of abusive fathers, Ann H. Tyler points to stepfathers as the principal offenders and notes that abusers have often been abused as children. Other essays consider the "overseas father" (who is usually an absent, overachiever father) and the adolescent father (who is often misunderstood). Concerning programs and policies, authors consider the impact of unemployment on fathers, the effects of various employment innovations (e.g., flextime or flexitime) on fathers, and the school as alien turf for many fathers. The volume closes with Frank G. Bolton, Jr.'s stinging critique of the social services system's failure to aid fathers. Having stereotyped the father as villain, social workers refuse to see him as victim.

512. Lamb, Michael E., ed. **The Father's Role: Cross-Cultural Perspectives.** Hillsdale, NJ: Lawrence Erlbaum, 1987. xiv, 377p. illus. bibliography after each chapter. author and subject indexes. pa.

This companion volume to *The Father's Role: Applied Perspectives* (entry 511) reprints the same introduction in which Lamb concludes that the father is no longer the forgotten parent. Rather, the need now is to crystallize what has been learned about fathers. The 13 articles in this collection discuss fatherhood in North America, Western Europe, France, Germany, Sweden, Italy, Ireland, Israel, China, Japan, West Africa, the Central African Republic, and Australia. Perhaps most fascinating are the accounts from Sweden and Israel, where social experiments in gender equality have been only partly successful in eliminating traditional parenting patterns. Conversely, Irish fathers, despite traditionalism, are relatively involved in caregiving. In Italy and China, traditional patterns reign. Japanese fathers seem to be in trouble: their breadwinning, but little else, is respected. Among the Aka pygmies of central Africa, the fathers' holding of children creates intimacy. This volume provides a fascinating look at fathering around the world.

513. Lamb, Michael, ed. **The Role of the Father in Child Development.** 2d ed. New York: John Wiley/Interscience, 1981. xiv, 582p. illus. bibliography at the end of each chapter. author and subject indexes.

In this collection of 14 essays surveying father-child relations, literature on the following topics is surveyed: an overview of fathers and child development (by Michael E. Lamb), the development of Western fatherhood during selected historical periods (by Jonathan Bloom-Feshback), recent developments in psychoanalytic theory of the father (by Veronica J. Mächtlinger), anthropological perspectives on the father's role (by Mary Maxwell Katz and Melvin J. Konner), the role of fathers in the Soviet Union (by Jaan Valsiner), male paternal care among monkeys and apes (by William K. Redican and David M. Taub), the father as a member of the child's social network (by Michael

Lewis, Candice Feiring, and Marsha Weinraub), the influence of fathers viewed in a family context (by Frank A. Pedersen), the father's importance in the child's sex role development (by Henry B. Biller), the father's role in the child's moral internalization (by Martin L. Hoffman), the paternal role in the child's cognitive, academic, and intellectual development (by Norma Radin), the determinants of paternal involvement in caregiving and play with infants (by Ross D. Parke and Barbara R. Tinsley), the development of father-child relationships (by Michael E. Lamb), and the effects of father absence and divorce on the child's personality development (by Henry B. Biller). The bibliographies at the ends of chapters are indispensable for anyone researching father-child relationships.

514. Lamb, Michael E., and Abraham Sagi, eds. **Fatherhood and Family Policy.** Hillsdale, NJ: Lawrence Erlbaum, 1983. xi, 276p. illus. bibliography at the end of each chapter. author and subject indexes.
    The 14 essays in this book examine the effects of public policy on fathers. Lamb's introduction stresses the importance of international and interdisciplinary perspectives on the topic. Highlights of the volume include James A. Levine and Lamb's assessment of how family policy in Sweden has not produced the effects it was supposed to; an account of the aims and undertakings of The Fatherhood Project by Lamb, Levine, and Joseph H. Pleck; Martin Wolin's delightfully irreverent discussion of the gender dilemma in social welfare; Eliezer D. Jaffe's account of fathers as the forgotten clients in welfare services; and Lois Wladis Hoffman's evaluation of the losses and gains for mothers from increased father participation. Lamb, Sagi, and Graeme Russell conclude with a chapter of recommendations for public policy in such areas as employment, law, health, and education.

515. Lee, John. **At My Father's Wedding: Reclaiming Our True Masculinity.** New York: Bantam Books, 1991. xxii, 201p. appendixes. bibliography, 191. pa.
    In short, reflective chapters, Lee addresses the pain of father hunger. Moved by Robert Bly's observations about the lack of fathering, Lee addresses the wound of father absence. Drawing upon his experiences with men's gatherings, he meditates upon such matters as father-induced repression of emotion, the soft male, and the wounded lover. Describing a journey toward healing, he discusses reclaiming the male body and feelings, the freeing of the feminine within men, friends, grieving, and honoring elders. In the book's final section, Lee describes the new man who becomes his own father. Appendixes contain listings of books, magazines, audiocassettes, and men's centers.

516. Leonard, Linda Schierse. **The Wounded Woman: Healing the Father-Daughter Relationship.** Athens, OH: Swallow Press, Ohio University Press, 1982. xx, 186p. notes. pa. Reprint, Boulder, CO, and London: Shambhala, 1983. pa.
    Besides the wounded daughter, the wounded father and the wounded "feminine" in men are also subjects of this book. A Jungian analyst, Leonard discusses how both men and women are spiritually impoverished when the feminine is devalued, whether by narrowly masculine males or by "armored amazon" females. To illustrate her thesis, the author analyzes dreams, case histories, her own experiences with an alcoholic father, plays, films, novels, myths, and fairy tales. Leonard takes a healing approach, not a blaming one.

517. Levant, Ronald, and John Kelly. **Between Father and Child: How to Become the Kind of Father You Want to Be.** New York: Penguin Books, 1989. xii, 236p.

Written for a popular audience, *Between Father and Child* advises fathers on how to communicate more effectively with children. The advice stresses listening skills, hearing the hidden messages, and "reflecting" the child's message. It tells fathers how to negotiate with children to settle arguments and fights. The authors also suggest ways to encourage children's moral development and ways to show them how to say no to alcohol, drugs, and sex. By building children's self-esteem, fathers can help them become achievers. The book addresses problems of divorce, stepfathering, and ways of treating sons and daughters equally. Some readers may find the advice simplistic and aimed solely at middle-class fathers; others may find the advice perceptive and helpful.

518. Levine, James A. **Who Will Raise the Children? New Options for Fathers (and Mothers).** Philadelphia and New York: J. B. Lippincott, 1976. 192p. notes. Reprint, New York: Bantam Books, 1977. pa.

This influential book examines men who have chosen child care in a society that actively discourages any family role for men other than that of breadwinner. Levine examines how, in the past, social scientists have overlooked fathers and how courts have discriminated against them in granting custody. Drawing upon extended interviews, he describes the struggles and triumphs of fathers with sole and joint custody. Noting that full-time jobs do not accommodate the father's role as parent, Levine investigates such alternatives as part-time work, flextime, small businesses operated jointly by wife and husband, joint college teaching appointments for couples, and paternity leave policies. The single male who adopts a child faces special difficulties, including the suspicion that he is homosexual. Because homemaking is not an esteemed career (especially for men), househusbands encounter puzzlement and hostility. Levine's concluding chapter argues that, because gender roles are interdependent, the problem of reconciling family and career is not simply a woman's problem. While much attention has been focused on women's new roles in society, little time and energy have been devoted to redirecting men's roles. Despite the discouraging evidence of widespread prejudice against men in child-caring roles, Levine offers heartening evidence of the human reward reaped by men who undertook them.

519. Lewis, Charles, and Margaret O'Brien, eds. **Reassessing Fatherhood: New Observations on Fathers and the Modern Family.** London and Beverly Hills, CA: Sage Publications, 1987. 270p. index. bibliography and notes after each chapter. pa.

This collection of 15 articles, mostly by British and Canadian authors, continues the study of fathers begun in Lorna McKee and Margaret O'Brien's earlier volume *The Father Figure* (entry 528). Essays are printed under three headings: "Constraints on Fathers," "Attempts to Change Paternal Roles," and "Fathers and Family Crisis." In the introductory essay, Lewis and O'Brien examine the social, ideological, institutional, personal, and economic constraints that hinder fathers from playing paternal roles successfully. Other essays in this section survey British middle-class family life from the late Victorian age to the 1920s, fathers and employment (men with children work more than men without children), a Canadian view of fathers and family participation (the option of being a nonworking father is not available to most men), the negotiation of family responsibilities (women have considerable power in the home), and the experience of grandfatherhood. In section 2, on changing paternal roles, an essay by Michael E. Lamb, Joseph H. Pleck, and James A. Levine finds that, while increasing paternal involvement in the family is not an absolute good, the opportunity to do so should be available to men. Other essays indicate gains and losses in newer family styles: dual-earner households still embody inequities for both husband and wife, which they can often accept; Swedish efforts to increase paternal involvement have had mixed results for women and men; and role-reversal families offer both opportunities and problems for couples. The final section, on fathers and family crisis, considers such matters as the exclusion of fathers from social work with families in crisis, the difficulties of men in marriage counseling, challenges facing the noncustodial father, patterns of kin and friendship among single fathers, and conciliation services for men undergoing divorce.

520. Lewis, Robert A., and Marvin B. Sussman, eds. **Men's Changing Roles in the Family.** New York: Haworth Press, 1986. xvi, 277p. glossary of major terms. bibliography after each article and 229-53. filmography, 255-72. pa.

Compiled from the Winter 1985/86 issue of *Marriage and Family Review*, this anthology consists of 14 articles. Topics range from Shirley M. H. Hanson's discussion of single fathers to John Lewis McAdoo's debunking of stereotypes of black fathers. Other articles include multiple-author studies of why fathers spend less time at home than mothers do and of the effects that paternal involvement has upon fathers and mothers. The political spectrum represented in the articles is also wide, ranging from Teresa Donati Marciano's radical feminist denunciation of patriarchy to Robert E. Salt's vigorous defense of fathers' rights. Even the mythopoetic movement is represented in Kris Jeter's use of myth and Jungian psychology to illuminate the concept of the "honeymoon." The bibliographies after each chapter and "Fatherhood: A Library," a separate 24-page bibliography, are invaluable for anyone researching fatherhood.

521. Lewis, Robert A., and Robert E. Salt, eds. **Men in Families.** Beverly Hills, CA: Sage Publications, 1986. 288p. bibliography after each chapter. pa.

This collection of 16 sociological articles (plus a preface and an introduction) is divided into three sections: "Men as Husbands," "Men as Fathers," and "Men in Family, Kin, and Friendship Networks." Nearly all the articles follow the same pattern: a question is posed, literature on the subject is reviewed, a study is conducted, results are reported, and conclusions are presented. In this way, contributors reassess commonly held views about men in families. Topics examined include why men do (and do not) marry, husbands' involvement in family work, husbands' jealousy, men's decisions on whether or not to have a child, grandfatherhood, male friendships, and identity change in older and younger men. Other articles focus on African-American men, single-parent fathers, and fathers with daughters in college. Articles from The Netherlands and Australia supplement American-based research. Contributors include familiar names such as Jack O. Balswick, Lawrence E. Gary, Michael E. Lamb, James A. Levine, and Joseph H. Pleck.

522. Lockerbie, D. Bruce. **Fatherlove: Learning to Give the Best You've Got.** Garden City, NY: Doubleday, Doubleday-Galilee Original, 1981. 237p.

In gracefully written essays, Lockerbie uses Christian scriptures, personal anecdotes, and the experiences of others to investigate such matters as the importance of the father's role, building character, disciplining with love and wisdom, and integrating faith into family life.

523. Louv, Richard. **FatherLove: What We Need, What We Seek, What We Must Create.** New York: Pocket Books, 1993. x, 276p. notes. bibliography, 263-65. pa.

As a nation and a society, as individuals and as men and women, we need nothing less than a rediscovery of the possibilities of fatherhood. Many public and personal problems are traceable to the loss of a father's love. Instead of marginalizing fathers and denigrating fatherhood, our society needs to reconnect masculinity and fatherhood. Interviewing young people, Louv finds that they miss absent fathers and are harmed by inept ones. Fatherhood has five dimensions: breadwinning, nurturing, community building, finding oneself in time and place, and spirituality. As breadwinners, fathers must find a balance between work and family. Producing nurturing fathers may require our society to teach parenting systematically. Perhaps most interesting are Louv's speculations on fathers as protectors of the community and the need for men to fight for their "village." (Although he does not use the term, what Louv calls "political fatherlove" is a renewed version of *patriarchy*, a term that, sadly, theorists and academics have negativized in recent times.) Fathers must also adjust their fathering to the life cycle, changing with the circumstances—their own and those of others. Finally, fathers must be spiritual leaders with genuine, religious vision. Louv's book constitutes a moving manifesto for the best of fathering.

524. Lucarini, Spartaco. **The Difficult Role of a Father.** Translated by Hugh Moran. Brooklyn, NY: New City Press, 1979. 75p. pa. Original publication, as *Il difficile mestiere di padre* (Rome: Città nuova, 1968).

In a series of informal essays that use interviews with fathers and children, Lucarini stresses children's need for a loving father's presence, examines the generational conflict between fathers and children, and advises fathers to listen carefully to their children and to talk frankly with them about sexuality "before it is too late."

525. Lynn, David B. **The Father: His Role in Child Development.** Monterey, CA: Brooks/Cole, a division of Wadsworth, 1974. xiii, 333p. illus. bibliography, 287-319. author and subject indexes.

Although recognizing that many fundamental questions remain unanswered, Lynn provides an early synthesis of the growing body of research on fathers. Part 1, on fathers and cultures, discusses U.S. fatherhood in transition, paternal behavior in animals and early men, the paternal role in different cultures, cultural experiments in restructuring the family (in the Soviet Union, Sweden, Israeli kibbutzim, and U.S. communes), the changing nature of fatherhood in the Western world, and fathers in the U.S. Part 2, on the father-child relationship, explores theories of the father's role (with focus upon Freud and Parsons), the father-mother relationship, and the influence of fathers upon children's sex role behavior, scholastic aptitude, achievement, vocational choice, creativity, moral development, and mental health. Other chapters deal with the father's approach to child-rearing (with some attention to abusive fathers) and with the effects upon children of father absence. The final chapter draws conclusions about what is known concerning fathers.

526. Mackey, Wade C. **Fathering Behaviors: The Dynamics of the Man-Child Bond.** New York: Plenum Press, 1985. xviii, 203p. bibliography, 185-96. author and subject indexes.

"Men like children" is the first conclusion reached in this study drawn from observations of over 49,000 adult-child dyads from five continents. What motivates men's love of children? This is the question that Mackey sets out to answer in this cross-cultural study laced with dry wit and thought-provoking observations. Human males are far more solicitous of their young than simians are. Because paternal nurturing enhanced survival, Mackey argues females selected males who exhibited potential or actual fathering involvement. Cultural factors also impinged on male behavior: where males were needed as plowmen or protectors, they were socialized to perform these roles. Because societies universally assign females as primary caregivers of young children, "it is the man-child bond which is more the litmus test for societal dynamics." Although U.S. fathers are warmly involved with their children, the public perception of fathers is largely negative. Images of the derelict and incompetent dad may be our society's hidden method of pushing males towards the soldier-protector role. The conflict between individual freedoms and the demands of child rearing has hit women especially hard and calls for imaginative solutions. Mackey believes that two types of families are now battling for supremacy in the United States: the single-mother family versus the mother-father family. Some evidence supports the idea of a fathering instinct: "Men, as a class, are built to protect and provision bonded children."

527. Marone, Nicky. **How to Father a Successful Daughter.** New York: McGraw-Hill, 1988. xiv, 320p. appendixes. bibliography, 310-15. notes. index. Reprint, New York: Ballantine, 1989. pa.

Because fathers generally transmit traditional gender roles, Marone enlists fathers in the effort to encourage a greater diversity among daughters. Traditional feminine roles can hinder the development of many girls, especially gifted ones. Marone offers a checklist of assumptions about femininity and surveys conditions for girls' academic success. What the father does is more important than what he says. Fathers must encourage girls, not pressure them, especially potential high achievers who are not well served by public schools. Fathers must work as a team with mothers to foster positive self-concepts in daughters. Because fathers must spur girls to take unconventional risks, Marone offers strategies for encouraging daughters to achieve. The final two chapters discuss how fathers can best handle a daughter's adolescence and what to do about eating disorders. One appendix provides biographies of "successful" women (the idiosyncratic list includes Belle Starr along with Jane Addams and Margaret Mead); a second appendix lists questions to ask about a gifted-child program. The foreword is by Gilbert Simon. Clearly, Marone's advice is valuable, but it is marred by occasional misandry: she is hostile to boys' rambunctiousness (which she sees as a threat to girls' self-esteem), and she regards the attractions of young men to pretty young women as sexism.

528. McKee, Lorna, and Margaret O'Brien, eds. **The Father Figure.** London and New York: Tavistock Publications, 1982. xii, 239p. bibliography, 207-27. notes. name and subject indexes.

This collection of 13 readable essays by British scholars reverses the mother-focused perspective of past social science studies; in the process, it challenges many cultural stereotypes of men as fathers. In the first essay, the editors explore why fathering has recently become a popular topic for study, although no adequate history of fathering now exists and numerous aspects of fathering are still ignored. They offer a useful critique of the use (and misuse) of the word *patriarchy* in modern feminist writings. Other essays include a survey of the legal status of fathers in Great Britain by Nigel V. Lowe and Trevor Lummis's study of turn-of-the-century fathers, which dispels the myth of the working-class brute. Martin P.M. Richards reflects on needed areas of study involving fathers, and David Owens studies the impact of infertility upon men who had hoped to become fathers. Joel Richman recounts men's reactions to pregnancy and childbirth, and Angela Brown reports on the disharmony between hospital staffs and fathers participating in childbirth. Lorna McKee offers a critique of fathers' participation in infant care, Madeleine Simms and Christopher Smith examine the effects of fatherhood upon younger males, while Charlie Lewis criticizes the methodology used in recent father-infant studies. Tony Hipgrave details the trials of being a "lone" (single) father: "There is, in short, no evidence that lone fathers cannot plan and organize a healthy developmental environment for themselves and their children. There is a good deal of evidence we, the community, make it extremely hard for them to do so." Margaret O'Brien examines the different patterns and experiences of men who became single fathers. The final essay by Jacqueline Burgoyne and David Clark explores the role of the stepfather. All essays exhibit scholarly acumen and a willingness to abandon stereotypes for a fresher view of the father figure. For a more recent anthology that updates themes in this volume, see entry 519.

529. Meister, Robert. **Fathers.** New York: Richard Marek, 1981. 277p. Reprint, New York: Ballantine Books, 1983. pa.

A book about "the subjective *experience* of being a father and having one," this book consists of domestic horror stories gleaned from 213 interviews with fathers and children. After revealing his own sense of failure as a son and as a father, Meister retells a number of chilling case histories, grouping them into accounts of fathers who were distant and silent, seductive, tyrannical and demanding, idealized (usually for the wrong reasons), macho and competitive, and eccentric and bizarre. Capable and caring fathers are in short supply in this book.

530. Miller, Ted, ed. **The Christian Reader Book on Being a Caring Father.** New York: Harper & Row, 1983. 128p. illus. pa.

This anthology of 27 brief, previously published essays presents Christian perspectives on a range of fathering topics. Representative titles include "The Husband Who Leads His Family," by Robert H. Schuller; "Homes Are For Building Christians," by Howard Hendricks; "Dad's Night at Home," by Don Crawford; and "Fathers Can Be Beautiful!" by Marcia Schwartz.

531. Osherson, Samuel. **Finding Our Fathers: The Unfinished Business of Manhood.** New York: Free Press, 1986. xiv, 217p. notes. index. Reprint, as *Finding Our Fathers: How a Man's Life Is Shaped by His Relationship with His Father,* New York: Fawcett Columbine, 1987. pa.

Citing father absence as "one of the great underestimated tragedies of our times," Osherson employs findings from a longitudinal study of 370 men who graduated from Harvard in the mid-1960s. The author notes that boys have the dual task of breaking from mother and identifying and bonding with father. In this lifelong process, males must deal with the "wounded father," the internal image of the father carried by the son. In modern times, numerous difficulties beset the process. Mother and child may conspire to "protect" and isolate the father; the boy may fashion an absent father into a monster. The unfinished business of adult manhood can trigger problems in later life. Because men often regard mentors as father substitutes, the break from the mentor can be stormy. A wife's going out to work, her pregnancy (or rather *their* pregnancy), a couple's inability to have a child, and the birth of a child may all trigger uncertainties in men. Osherson offers advice for healing the wounded father, coping with the stresses of adult manhood, and becoming a functional link in the father-son family chain.

532. Ostrovsky, Everett S. **Children Without Men.** Rev. ed. New York: Collier, 1962. 188p. index. pa. Originally published as *Father to the Child.*

An early and poignant account of how father absence can affect children, Ostrovsky's study uses a case-history approach, drawing upon observations of children at a nursery school. Eight illustrative cases are presented in detail. One girl, whose father is often away on business trips, clings to the male teacher; another, from a divorced home, constantly needs reassurance that the male teacher is not displeased with her. A boy whose father is emotionally distant has trouble expressing his affection for others; another, whose father died a year previously, feels that he was deserted and responds hostilely to grown men. Perhaps most significant is Barbara, a child whose fastidious mother constantly short-circuits her curiosity and spontaneity; closer contact with her more expansive father would help her, but he is necessarily less available to her than her mother is. The case illustrates well Ostrovsky's thesis: the absence or infrequent presence of one parent hinders the child's optimum development. Ostrovsky argues that the missing male distorts sex roles for both girls and boys, misorienting them for the future. Nor can the oedipal conflict be satisfactorily resolved when men are not around. His recommendations include fuller participation of fathers in child care and more male teachers in nursery and grade schools.

532a. Owen, Ursula, ed. **Fathers: Reflections by Daughters.** London: Virago, 1983. Reprint, New York: Pantheon, 1985. xiv, 240p. illus. pa.

Containing twenty-one reflections on fathers by well-known daughters, this collection boasts exquisite writing and vivid memories. Contributors include Doris Lessing, Mary Gordon, Adrienne Rich, Sheila Rowbotham, Alice Walker, and Grace Paley. Love him or hate him, a father leaves an indelible image on his daughter's soul.

533. Parke, Ross D. **Fathers.** Cambridge: Harvard University Press, 1981. 136p. (The Developing Child Series). bibliography, 133. notes. index. pa.

Parke describes his book as "a progress report of what we know today about how fathers act and how they influence their children." Stressing the idea that fathers influence children both directly and indirectly, this compact volume gracefully surveys such topics as the distorting "myths" about fathers (particularly from Freud and Bowlby), expectant fathers, how fathers interact with infants, and how fathers affect children's socialization, particularly their gender roles. The final two chapters explore the effects of custody decisions and of innovations in fathering—including paternity leaves, flexible working hours, work-sharing couples, dual-career couples, and role-sharing families. Parke concludes: "Fathers are no longer, if they ever were, merely a biological necessity—a social accident. . . . Children need their fathers, but fathers need their children, too."

534. Pedersen, Anne, and Peggy O'Mara, eds. **Being a Father: Family, Work, and Self/Mothering Magazine.** Sante Fe, NM: John Muir Publications, 1990. xi, 161p. illus. appendix. notes after some chapters. pa.

Twenty-seven brief, popular articles (plus a foreword) are divided into six sections: "Becoming a Father," "Fathering and Self," "Fathers and Work," "Fathering Alone," "Remembering Our Own Fathers," and "The Fun of Fathering."

Representative articles include Ken Druck's account of how his friend Terry supported Ken and Karen during pregnancy and childbirth, Peter J. Dorsen's analysis of how becoming a father deepens the self, and Karen Hill Anton's memoir of her elderly father functioning as super single parent. Written in clear prose, all of the articles are filled with personal experiences, insights, and practical advice.

535. Pedersen, Frank A., ed. **The Father-Infant Relationship: Observational Studies in the Family Setting.** New York: Praeger, 1980. x, 185p. (Praeger Special Studies). illus. bibliography, 164-79. notes. index.

This collection presents five studies in infant-parent interaction, with special attention to fathers. In the introductory essay, Pedersen discusses the past failure of social sciences to examine the father-infant relationship; he points to the importance of studying that relationship in the context of the family. In the first study, Michael E. Lamb rejects the uniqueness of the mother-child relationship and explores parent-infant attachments during the first two years of life. From the earliest ages, infants are attracted to both parents, and the two parent-child relationships differ qualitatively: "Fathers are not merely occasional mother-substitutes." Ross D. Parke and Douglas B. Swain, assessing the interaction of fathers and infants, as well as parental attitudes, find both similarities and differences in mothers' and fathers' responses; the differences are partly dependent upon the infant's sex. Pedersen, Barbara J. Anderson, and Richard L. Cain, Jr., study parent-infant and husband-wife interactions at five months. Jay Belsky examines how fathers may influence their infant's ability to explore. K. Alison Clarke-Stewart views the father's contribution to cognitive and social development in early childhood; she stresses the importance of father's play and his contribution to the child's social-affective development. In a concluding chapter, Pedersen evaluates the findings and reformulates questions that need to be asked about fathers, infants, and families.

536. Pruett, Kyle D. **The Nurturing Father: Journey Toward the Complete Man.** New York: Warner Books, 1987. 322p. notes. index.

Whether or not fathers can nurture children as well as mothers is the central question posed by this book. Pruett notes that the body of evidence supporting the nurturing abilities of fathers has been kept "underground." He suggests that society wishes to keep men at their traditional roles, that men themselves fear being seen as nurturing parents, and that socialization of boys steers them away from close parenting. Over a five-year period, Pruett tracked 17 families in which the father was initially the primary caregiver. He presents detailed accounts of three families and summarizes findings from the others. Fathers, Pruett discovers, nurture differently than mothers, but just as effectively. Still, formidable forces keep more men from becoming nurturing fathers: schools, media, and parent guidance all discourage the idea; many women—including some feminists—see the caregiving father as invading their turf; divorce separates fathers from children; and rigid workplace rules hinder family flexibility. Still, the struggle to become a nurturing father is a movement toward fuller humanity. Pruett concludes: "What is needed is a call to men to reach out and claim their *own* fatherhood."

537. Rapoport, Rhona, Robert N. Rapoport, and Ziona Strelitz, with Stephen Kew. **Fathers, Mothers and Society: Towards New Alliances.** New York: Basic Books, 1977. ix, 421p. bibliography, 366-405. index. Reprint, as *Fathers, Mothers and Society: Perspectives on Parenting*, New York: Random House, 1980. pa.

This rich survey of literature places men's family roles in the larger context of family studies. Taking issue with the "myth" that "parenting means mothering" and with the child-focused, mother-oriented, expert-guided view of the family prevailing throughout much of the twentieth century, the authors, in chapter 1, spell out their own views of parenting in a series of 12 propositions. The first proposition states that parents, as well as children, are people with needs to be met. In chapter 2, the authors argue that the recognition of parents' needs by the experts has been unsatisfactory. The next six chapters consist of a packed review of and commentary on studies of the family from several disciplines. The timeline of the survey begins before the birth of the first child, continues through the early and middle years of active parenting, and concludes with parenting of adolescent and adult children. A final chapter recapitulates the book's findings and explores new directions in parenting. The discussion has historical, academic, professional, and social implications. The bibliography is extensive.

538. Reynolds, William. **The American Father: A New Approach to Understanding Himself, His Woman, His Child.** New York and London: Paddington Press, distributed by Grosset and Dunlap, 1978. 227p. index. pa.

Somewhat misleadingly titled, this book presents Reynolds's personal and mildly sardonic view of what is happening in the modern-American, upper-middle-class, white family. While recounting the interactions of Father, Mother, Sonny, and Sis, Reynolds flings barbs at what he considers the trendy "experts" on mental health, marriage counseling, and child care.

539. Robinson, Bryan E. **Teenage Fathers**. Lexington, MA: Lexington Books, D. C. Heath, 1988. xvi, 173p. bibliography after each chapter. index. pa.

As Harriette McAdoo points out in the foreword, *Teenage Fathers* fills a void in the literature on fathers. Despite the large population of teen fathers in the United States, Robinson indicates that negative images of young fathers have made them invisible. "Contrary to the stereotype that unwed teenage fathers disappear at the first mention of pregnancy," Robinson writes, "more recent and better designed studies indicate that it is the young fathers who have been abandoned—pushed away by social agencies, peers, and the adolescent mother's family." Using his work with hundreds of teen fathers and in-depth studies of 26 subjects (22 black, 3 white, 1 American Indian), Robinson presents a sympathetic picture of teenage fatherhood. The consequences of early fatherhood can be harsh for fathers, mothers, and children. In chapter 6, written by Robert L. Barret, 10 adult men recall their experiences as teen fathers. Robinson provides suggestions for practitioners, assesses programs to assist teen fathers, and offers a rich listing of resources, including books, special reports, periodicals, programs, and audiovisuals.

540. Robinson, Bryan E., and Robert L. Barret. **The Developing Father: Emerging Roles in Contemporary Society.** New York: Guilford Press, 1986. xv, 224p. bibliography after each chapter. index. pa.

Robinson and Barret have assembled and organized a wealth of information about various aspects of fathering. Divided into six chapters, the book opens with a theoretical overview of fatherhood. The authors examine leading psychological and sociological theories of fatherhood and discuss family-systems theories. The second chapter examines childless men and expectant fathers. Discussing the changing roles of fathers, the authors contrast the traditional father, the androgynous father (who takes on "feminine" roles), and the typical father, who combines elements of both categories. In chapter 4, the tasks of fatherhood, changing over the life cycle, are examined; a section on grandfatherhood is included. The remaining chapters explore different types of fathering experiences: single fathers, stepfathers, gay fathers, and teenage fathers. The final chapter on fathers of disabled children is written by Mary Jane Brotherson, Ann P. Turnbull, Jean Ann Summer, and H. Rutherford Turnbull. Throughout the book, Robinson and Barret summarize what is known about fatherhood with clarity and evenhandedness. Among the major assets of this volume are the bibliographic listings, one after each chapter. In addition to books and articles, the references often include categories such as audiovisuals, organizations, professional resources, programs, and pertinent government legislation. The authors also close each chapter with helpful suggestions for professionals dealing with problems connected with various aspects of fatherhood.

541. Rue, James J., and Louise Shanahan. **Daddy's Girl, Mama's Boy.** Indianapolis, IN, and New York: Bobbs-Merrill, 1978. xvi, 250p. bibliography, 249-50. index. Reprint, New York: New American Library, Signet, 1979. pa.

Because the father-daughter and mother-son relationships can be crucial to child formation, the authors consider both their positive and their negative potentials. (Homosexuality is considered as a negative possibility.) Throughout the book, Rue and Shanahan illustrate their theses by citing case histories and biographies of the famous—including Jacqueline Bouvier and Jack Bouvier, Elizabeth I and Henry VIII, Ella Quinland O'Neill and Eugene O'Neill, and Margaret Carnegie and Andrew Carnegie. Rejecting "avant-garde life styles" (including extramarital affairs, cohabitation, and homosexual relationships), the authors consider at some length, the elements of enduring and happy marriages, and they provide a workbook by which readers can assess themselves as daddy's girls or mama's boys. In this way, the book is intended as a guide to a positive understanding and directing of the self.

542. Russell, Graeme. **The Changing Role of Fathers?** St. Lucia, Queensland, Australia: University of Queensland Press, 1983. x, 250p. appendixes. bibliography, 238-45. index. pa.

Based upon investigation into 145 traditional families and 71 shared-caregiving families, this study describes four types of fathers—uninterested and unavailable, traditional, "good," and nontraditional and highly participant. A mother's employment outside the home had a small but significant impact on a father's participation in child care: it increased the fathers' competence with children. Reviewing the literature and assessing cross-cultural evidence, Russell describes the benefits and costs to parents and children in households with participant fathers.

543. Salk, Lee. **My Father, My Son: Intimate Relationships.** New York: G. P. Putnam's Sons, 1982. 255p. Reprint, New York: Berkley Books, 1983. pa.

Using informal questioning and making no attempt at statistical representativeness, Salk has gathered 28 interviews with fathers and sons. Although some marred relationships are recounted, most of the recollections are upbeat: many men tell of strong affectional ties with their nurturing fathers, and they strive to emulate that behavior with their sons. The importance of loving attention, physical contact, and discipline recurs in the interviews. A few of the interviewees are well known (e.g., talk-show host Mike Douglas). Noting that fathers and sons either have or crave loving relationships, Salk concludes that "the acceptance of males in the nurturant role ... will contribute to the survival of the family as a social unit."

544. Schulenburg, Joy A. **Gay Parenting.** Garden City, NY: Anchor Books, Anchor Press/Doubleday, 1985. 177p. appendixes. bibliography, 160-70. index. pa.

For gay and lesbian parents, Schulenburg provides a readable guide to a number of key issues, including coming out to children, dealing with lovers, married gay people, the fear of AIDS, creating alternate families, lesbian choices, adoption and foster parenting, and custody and visitation. The first appendix lists services, resources, and organizations; the second contains the bibliography.

545. Scull, Charles S., ed. **Fathers, Sons, and Daughters: Exploring Fatherhood, Renewing the Bond.** Los Angeles: Jeremy P. Tarcher, 1992. xvii, 263p. notes. pa.

This unusually judicious selection of 34 essays and three poems explores five principal topics of modern fatherhood: the evolving father who is replacing absence with presence, father-son relationships, father-daughter relationships, the challenges and opportunities of modern fatherhood, and renewing the bond between fathers and children by healing within and without. Scull has selected first-rate material from such authors as Loren Pedersen, Robert Bly, James Hillman, Ram Dass, Maureen Murdock, Betty Carter, Warren Farrell, Perry Garfinkel, Joseph Pleck, Linda Schierse Leonard, Samuel Osherson, and Bill Cosby. Without minimizing the problems and failures of the new fathers, Scull's anthology manages to stress their achievements while providing readers with the most current and perceptive analyses of the importance of fatherhood.

546. Sears, William. **Keys to Becoming a Father.** New York: Barron's Educational Series, 1991. 152p. (Barron's Parenting Keys). glossary. index. pa.

A pediatrician and father of seven children, Sears provides practical advice for fathers, from the mother's pregnancy to the child's adolescence. He considers concisely such matters as taking care of a pregnant wife, being involved in labor and delivery (Sears advises fathers to hire a labor coach, or *doula*), taking charge after delivery, serving the mother, developing nurturing skills (including the "neck nestle"), and getting babies to sleep (Sears advises that couples try sleeping with the baby in their bed). The author covers such matters as father absence, traveling with children, and developing healthy masculinity and femininity in children. He provides play tips and disciplinary techniques for fathers. Although much of Sears's advice echoes that in other manuals, some of it has a personalized twist.

547. Secunda, Victoria. **Women and Their Fathers: The Sexual and Romantic Impact of the First Man in Your Life.** New York: Delacorte Press, 1992. xxv, 483p. notes. bibliography, 465-69. index. pa. Reprint, New York: Delta, 1993. pa.

This large volume, utilizing interviews with 150 daughters and 75 fathers, as well as extensive research, examines the often-neglected topic of father-daughter relationships. The impact of fathers upon daughters' lives, Secunda finds, can be enormous and multifaceted. The author reviews concepts of masculine and feminine gender roles, and she observes that "maternal gatekeeping" can sometimes distance fathers from daughters. Different kinds of fathers include the Good-Enough Father, the Doting Father, the Distant Father, the Demanding Father, the Seductive Father, and the Absent Father. Despite such categorizing, Secunda displays a lively awareness of the exceptions to the rule and the complexities that inform father-daughter relationships. The chapter on the

Seductive Father carefully examines father-daughter incest, but it fails to note widespread false charges of child molestation directed against fathers, especially in custody cases. Each chapter closes with a profile of a particular kind of father. The same pattern is followed in chapters dealing with various kinds of daughters—the Favored Daughter, the Good Daughter, the Competitive Daughter, the Fearful Daughter, and the Maverick Daughter. Even favored, good, and competitive daughters may pay a price, and fearful daughters may turn to lesbianism because their heterosexual impulses have been blocked. Maverick daughters may be rebelling against fathers or rebelling with their fathers' support. The final four chapters deal with adult daughters coming to terms with fathers and with men redefining masculinity and fatherhood. The chapter on the men's movement too-easily blames all men for the evils of patriarchy, which Secunda sees in entirely negative terms. Although she recognizes value in the mythopoetic men's movement, she is critical of its failure to address father-daughter issues.

548. Shapiro, Jerrold Lee. **The Measure of a Man: Becoming the Father You Wish Your Father Had Been.** New York: Delacorte Press, 1993. xv, 364p. bibliography, 357. notes. index.

In this pro-father, pro-male book, Shapiro draws upon interviews with more than 400 fathers and 200 couples, as well as extensive research and experience, to chart a course for the new father. Modern U.S. society does not make fathering easy; it provides plenty of criticism and comparatively little help. (Shapiro vigorously protests the damage done by mindless media male bashing.) Still, there is a movement afoot by fathers to be better fathers than their own fathers were. Because men and women are different, Shapiro insists, fathers parent differently than mothers do—not better or worse, just different. He urges people to respect that difference. Shapiro describes the family pitfalls that the inadequate father creates, as well as the benefits that the good father provides. Men need to learn about their own fathers and reconcile with them if possible. They must try to access the father within. Shapiro describes the life cycle of the father, from dating and mating to grandfathering. Two chapters are devoted to "hard" fathering, for the single father and for the stepfather. A chapter on the need for good fathering is followed by one of questions and answers. The book closes with a letter from the author to his children.

549. Shedd, Charlie. **The Best Dad Is a Good Lover.** Kansas City, KS: Sheed Andrews and McMeel, 1977. 135p. illus.

A father of five, the author of the syndicated column "Strictly for Dads," and a Presbyterian minister, Shedd elaborates upon the thesis that "to love his children well a dad must first love their mother—and show it consistently." Brief chapters contain illustrative stories, letters from correspondents, and practical advice. Shedd's later books include *A Dad Is for Spending Time With* (1978) and *Smart Dads I Know* (1978).

550. Singer, Wenda Goodhart, Stephen Shechtman, and Mark Singer. **Real Men Enjoy Their Kids! How to Spend Quality Time with the Children in Your Life.** Nashville, TN: Abingdon Press, 1983. 176p. illus. appendix. pa.

Written as a practical guide to help men interact positively with children, this upbeat handbook contains numerous suggested activities designed to develop the child's social, emotional, cognitive, physical, and spiritual capacities. Presented in two versions (one for children six and under, the other for children ages seven to twelve), the activities include home life, the working world, leisure time, and crises (new baby, separation or divorce, death). A final section of the book offers additional suggestions for encouraging a deepening relationship between men and children.

551. Stolz, Lois Meek, and others. **Father Relations of War-Born Children: The Effect of Postwar Adjustment of Fathers on the Behavior and Personality of First Children Born While the Fathers Were at War.** 1954. Reprint, New York: Greenwood Press, 1968. viii, 365p. illus. appendixes. bibliography, 361-65. Reprint, Stanford, CA: Stanford University Press, 1975.

This classic study examines the effects of father absence upon children and parents alike.

552. Streiker, Lowell D. **Fathering: Old Game, New Rules: A Look at the Changing Roles of Fathers.** Nashville, TN: Abingdon Press, 1989. 221p. notes. pa.

It's a whole different world out there for fathers, Streiker reports, but fathers are still badly needed, and brave men still stand by their jobs as fathers. After separation from his first wife, Streiker married a divorced woman with two sons. During his lifetime, Streiker has seen it all: the shifting of traditional paternal roles, the working couple, divorce and custody wars, step-parenting, grandfathering, and on and on. With the present-day family in turmoil, fathers make a difference more than ever. They are still needed to serve as role models and teachers, to instill values, to provide discipline, and to negotiate between family and the outside world. The new dad must also adopt more androgynous qualities without becoming feminized. The job description for modern fathers has become dauntingly difficult, but both adults and children benefit greatly when men tackle the job lovingly and courageously.

553. Sullivan, S. Adams. **The Father's Almanac.** Garden City, NY: Doubleday, Dolphin Books, 1980. xvii, 365p. illus. bibliography, 339-42. index.

In this attractive, oversized book, Sullivan offers practical information and advice on such matters as the father's role during pregnancy and childbirth, tending babies, working and fathering, everyday and special family events, child learning, and playing with children.

554. Towle, Alexandra, ed. **Fathers.** New York: Simon and Schuster, 1986. 288p. illus. index.

A blurb on the title page aptly describes this book as a "celebration in prose, poetry, and photography of fathers and fatherhood—fathers loved and fathers feared, famous fathers and fathers obscure, real-life fathers and fathers from fiction." The generous and perceptively selected anthology offers varied insights into the father-child relationship. Some selections are pithy and poignant, such as, E. B. White's observation: "The time not to become a father is eighteen years before a world war." The text is supplemented with a series of attractive photographs.

555. Valentine, Alan, ed. **Fathers to Sons: Advice Without Consent.** Norman: University of Oklahoma Press, 1963. xxxii, 237p. bibliography, 219-26. notes. index.

From the Middle Ages to the twentieth century, fathers have written to sons, exhorting, criticizing, advising, praising, and loving them. The letter writers in this collection (most are well known), range from Edward II to Franklin D. Roosevelt. Valentine's introductions and notes are both witty and helpful.

556. Welch, Don. **Macho Isn't Enough! Family Man in a Liberated World.** Atlanta, GA: John Knox Press, 1985. viii, 100p. pa.

The feminist revolution has changed the way men should behave in the family, according to Welch. Defining *feminist* to mean greater equality between the sexes, Welch argues that the traditional male role is too constrictive and that equal partners in marriage should be the ideal. He offers advice about balancing career and family and about raising non-sexist children. Outside the family, men should challenge sexism, such as gender-exclusive language. The good family man will give priority to family, not work. Although much of Welch's advice makes sense, parts of it resemble an uncritically recycled feminist agenda from the 1970s.

557. Winokur, Jon, ed. **Fathers.** New York: Dutton, 1993. 226p. index.

The excerpts in this anthology range from one-liners to short essays and stories. Fathers, in all their diversity, come leaping out at the reader from the selection—fathers positive and negative, fathers creative and crazy, fathers aggressive and passive, fathers wise and foolish. The more than 200 contributors include Arthur Ashe on his father's resourcefulness, Alissa Wayne on her father's courage in the midst of cancer pain, Patti Davis on her father's ability to defuse tensions with humor, and Itabari Njeri's bittersweet memories of an intellectual, left-wing, and formidable father.

558. Woolfolk, William, with Donna Woolfolk Cross. **Daddy's Little Girl: The Unspoken Bargain Between Fathers and Their Daughters.** Englewood Cliffs, NJ: Prentice-Hall, 1982. 220p. index.

In the love affair of father and daughter, she agrees to worship him, and he agrees to protect her against the world. The danger in this relationship, the authors contend, is that she may never develop her own competencies and he may be unwilling to let her grow up. The authors, father and daughter, provide evidence from their own relationship to support this thesis, and they look for it in the lives of an unspecified number of fathers and daughters whom they interviewed. The book relies on "the idiosyncratic, intuitive, impressionistic method"; it is thus informal and personal rather than rigorously analytic. The authors touch upon such matters as fathers and young daughters, the conflicts created by daughters' awakening sexuality, special situations (e.g., absent fathers, single parenthood, incest, homosexuality, inadequate fathers), and separation between maturing daughters and their fathers.

559. Yablonsky, Lewis. **Fathers and Sons.** New York: Simon and Schuster, 1982. 218p. notes. Reprint, as *Fathers and Sons: The Most Challenging of All Family Relationships.* New York: Gardner Trade Book Press, 1990. pa.

Yablonsky draws upon interviews with more than 100 men, conducted over a four-year period, and questionnaire responses from 564 men. He also draws upon his own, often-troubled relations with his parents, his clinical experiences with men (usually involving a technique known as psychodrama), research, novels, plays, and television. Examining father-son relationships, warts and all, he delineates the sometimes-conflicting dreams and messages from fathers to sons. He enumerates different kinds of father styles and traces three phases of father-son interaction. Looking at family dynamics, Yablonsky sees the mother as a filter between father and son. He also discusses siblings, grandparents, divorce and separation, and teachers and coaches. Among the special situations considered are deviance and emotional disorders, alcohol and drug abuse, homosexuality, and health problems. A final chapter presents problems and solutions for modern fathers.

C. Divorced and Single Fathers, Stepfathers

560. Atkin, Edith, and Estelle Rubin. **Part-Time Father.** New York: Vanguard Press, 1976. 191p. Reprint, New York: New American Library, Signet, 1977. pa.

Drawing upon their experiences as therapists, the authors—each possesses impressive credentials—offer information and advice to divorced fathers for the breaking-up period and afterward. Topics covered include the visiting father, money problems, "bachelor" fathers, remarriage, extended families, and special problems of adolescent children. The authors' advice is calm, concise, and compassionate.

561. Barber, Dulan. **Unmarried Fathers.** London: Hutchinson, 1975. 179p.

Usually ignored, dismissed, or reviled, the unmarried father deserves a closer, more humane look. Although the author of this British study concludes that most unwed fathers are unconcerned, this is not true of all. He provides extracts from interviews with eight unmarried fathers to demonstrate the range of their characteristics. Examining British law, he finds that it discourages the father's involvement with the child; by denying the unwed father nearly all rights, it also discourages his willingness to support the child. New approaches are needed to help unmarried fathers assume their responsibilities. Also, Barber insists that the same social help given to mothers should be given to single-parent fathers caring for children: "A man who chooses domesticity and total daily care for his child is regarded as work-shy, perhaps a malingerer." An increasing number of men, Barber concludes, are demanding the right to be involved, caring fathers—a right often denied them by law and society.

562. Ferrara, Frank. **On Being Father: A Divorced Man Talks about Sharing the New Responsibilities of Parenthood.** Garden City, NY: Doubleday, Dolphin Books, 1986. xiv, 175p. pa.

In easily read prose, Ferrara describes his divorce and the joint custody arrangement that he and his ex-wife worked out for their son Christopher. (Basically, Christopher alternates two-week periods with each parent.) Ferrara offers supportive suggestions for divorcing and divorced fathers. Before the actual divorce, the man needs to minimize the damage to himself and his children by acting with as much sense and restraint as he can muster. Most often, he needs to recreate a new home for the children. Ferrara urges divorced men to cool any hostilities, as much as possible, with their ex-wives, especially in front of the children. He offers suggestions for introducing new women friends to the children and for handling one's job. He advises fathers on how to avoid the weekend-sugar-daddy routine and how to overcome the problems of the long-distance dad. A chapter is devoted to surveying the challenges of different stages of children's development. The final chapter stresses the rewards, for everyone involved, of putting it all together.

563. Gatley, Richard H., and David Koulack. **Single Father's Handbook: A Guide for Separated and Divorced Fathers.** Garden City, NY: Anchor Press/Doubleday, 1979. xvii, 196p. index. pa.

For the separated or divorced father who does not have custody, the authors—both psychologists and both divorced fathers—provide helpful advice on such matters as maintaining a working relationship with the children's mother, handling grandparents and former in-laws, preparing space for the children at the father's new home, "mothering" children (the authors even provide a few favorite recipes), and bringing children together with new women friends. Above all, the authors provide support for the divorced father who must cope with society's view of him as an expendable parent, incompetent when it comes to caring for children.

564. Greif, Geoffrey. **The Daddy Track and the Single Father.** Lexington, MA: Lexington Books, D. C. Heath, 1990. ix, 246p. appendixes. bibliography, 237-39. notes. index.

In this update and expansion of his earlier work, *Single Fathers* (entry 565), Greif argues that single fathers often find themselves on a daddy track that influences all areas of the their lives. Greif's book is based upon a 1988 national survey of over 1,100 single fathers. At that time, the United States had about 1 million single fathers. After a historical survey of custody in the United States, Greif details the differing situations of two single fathers: Dave, whose relationship with his son Jerry seems solidly grounded, and Mark, who is struggling with his ex-wife for custody of their four children. Paternal custody of children is still unusual in the United States: about 10 percent of divorced fathers have custody. When it comes to running a household, most single fathers, like Dustin Hoffman in *Kramer Versus Kramer*, learn how to do it. In raising children, most single fathers seem to do well, perhaps because they made a conscious decision to gain custody and are determined to succeed at the job. Few businesses offer the single father much help, and maintaining a social life is difficult. Most custodial fathers get no child support from their ex-wives. Joint custody can work well, but it requires a high degree of organization and cooperation between ex-spouses. Greif devotes a chapter to widowers, whose sorrowing may be necessary but may also cause family tensions. Another chapter provides a 25-year update on a family headed by a single father. Many chapters in this book conclude with checklists of advice for the single father, and an entire chapter (coauthored by Risa Garon) advises fathers on how to cushion children from the negative effects of divorce. Single fathering is not for every man, nor is it easy. But it can be rewarding. The appendixes present details of the survey and a list of places where single fathers can seek help.

565. Greif, Geoffrey L. **Single Fathers.** Lexington, MA: Lexington Books, D. C. Heath, 1985. xii, 195p. appendix. bibliography, 183-87. notes. index. pa.

Drawing upon an unusually large study of 1,136 fathers with sole custody, Greif is able to paint a much more detailed picture of single fatherhood than was previously possible. In 1983, there were 600,000 single fathers in the United States. Most of the fathers in Greif's study were white, middle-class, Christian men. Greif provides a detailed report on one family, in some ways atypical, after 20 years of single fathering; he finds both gains and losses in the family. Greif then examines larger patterns of families, before and after divorce, and the reasons why fathers had custody. Most often, fathers received custody when the mother agreed to the arrangement. The author devotes separate chapters to housekeeping and child care arrangements, balancing the demands of work and child rearing, and the father's relationship with the children. Most fathers did not have housekeepers but managed on their own. Single fathers cited flextime as their most important need. Adjusting to being single again was painful, and the ex-wife's involvement with the children could be a source of both help and hindrance for the father. Although some fathers had no complaints about the legal system, most felt that it was stacked against fathers. Few of the fathers received child support from their ex-wives. A comparison of 150 custodial mothers revealed both similarities and differences with the fathers. In a chapter coauthored by Kathryn L. Wasserman, Greif recounts the toll exacted upon children of divided parents. The final chapter concludes that, although single fatherhood is difficult, it has its rewards. Despite stereotypical views of fathers as bumbling caregivers, men can be capable and loving single parents. The appendix provides details of methodology and tables of results. Readers should consult Greif's update of this study, *The Daddy Track and the Single Father* (entry 564).

566. Hill, Gerald A. **Divorced Father: Coping with Problems, Creating Solutions.** White Hall, VA: Betterway Publications, 1989. 190p. appendix. bibliography, 181-82. notes. index. pa.

Drawing upon his own experiences with divorce, Hill has fashioned a self-help guide for men. The advice is both personal and public. Hill tells the divorcing man how to ward off depression, how to avoid foolish mistakes, how to find the right lawyer, and how to minimize the damage of such dirty tricks as false charges of child molestation. Hill's own desire to maintain contact with his daughter is the source of a series of chapters on how to handle children lovingly after divorce. The appendix is a short list of action organizations.

567. Jacobs, John W., ed. **Divorce and Fatherhood: The Struggle for Parental Identity.** Washington, DC: American Psychiatric Press, 1986. x, 99p. (The Clinical Insights Monograph Series). bibliography after each chapter. pa.

This collection of five essays examines sympathetically the divorced father, the understudied party in divorce literature. In the opening article, Jacobs reviews the psychiatric literature on fatherhood and divorce, custody and visitation, fatherhood, and treatment of divorced fathers. Frank S. Williams argues that divorce usually results in a "parentectomy," or removal of one parent, usually the father. Social and economic forces encourage the mother to surgically remove the father from the children's lives, and U.S. society has done little to understand or help the discarded father. In the third essay, Jacobs describes the "involuntary child absence syndrome" as an affliction suffered by divorced fathers. Dorothy S. Huntington discusses the father as the forgotten figure in divorce, reviewing a series of topics ranging from California's joint custody law to child kidnapping by divorced parents. In the final article, Mel Roman updates information about joint custody, arguing that forms of shared custody are usually more successful than the present practice of sole custody.

568. Kahan, Stuart. **For Divorced Fathers Only.** New York: Monarch, Sovereign, 1978. 179p. bibliography, 179. pa.

On the premise that divorce is usually a hellish experience, this supportive book offers the divorced father reassurance, suggestions, and information for coping. A divorced father himself, Kahan discusses the man's problems of establishing a new life after divorce, the dynamics of maintaining father-child relationships, and the complications of dating and remarriage. A final chapter provides a quick survey of the financial and legal aspects of divorce. The epilogue raises questions about the ready availability of, and the rapid resort to, divorce in the United States. This readable book is informed by Kahan's belief that "no matter what you may have heard, the chief victim in most divorces is the man."

569. McCormick, Mona. **Stepfathers: What the Literature Reveals: A Literature Review and Annotated Bibliography.** LaJolla, CA: Western Behavioral Sciences Institute, 1974. iv, 76p. bibliography, 42-75. pa.

Deploring the scarcity of information on the stepfather, McCormick provides a survey of literature available in the early 1970s. She cautions stepfathers not to attempt to supplant the biological father entirely. McCormick enumerates factors affecting the stepfather's role and provides practical solutions to problems. She concludes that, despite difficulties, stepfathers and stepchildren can have loving relationships.

570. McFadden, Michael. **Bachelor Fatherhood: How to Raise and Enjoy Your Children as a Single Parent.** New York: Walker, 1974. 158p. bibliography, 155-58.

In upbeat, "can do" style, the author—a divorced father with custody of three children—surveys the basics of handling and enjoying child-rearing as a single parent. McFadden is eager to demonstrate that a single father can succeed as a parent. Skeptical of "happy marriage" and "painless divorce" myths, and aware of fathers' difficulties in gaining custody, the author argues nevertheless that divorce and raising children can be a liberating, fulfilling experience for men. Using interviews with 50 divorced fathers with custody, McFadden offers advice on running a household, loving and living with small children, coping with teenagers, doing the housework, and cooking the meals (a survival handbook of basic recipes is included). A brief afterword suggests that the strong man of the future may not be the warrior but the peacemaker and nurturer.

571. Newman, George. **101 Ways to Be a Long-Distance Super-Dad.** Mountain View, CA: Blossom Valley Press, 1981. 108p. illus. pa.

From creative tape recording to swapping jokes, Newman presents 101 practical suggestions for the long-distance parent who wishes to sustain an imaginative and loving relationship with his or her child.

572. Oakland, Thomas, with Nancy Vogt Wedemeyer, Edwin J. Terry, and Jane Manaster. **Divorced Fathers: Reconstructing a Quality Life.** New York: Human Sciences Press, 1984. 201p. index.

For the man facing divorce, this book offers helpful advice—although in somewhat confusing order. Readers may want to start with chapters 7 through 9 on alternatives to divorce and on legal matters, move on to discussions of child custody (chapter 6), the man's psychological and social changes during divorce (chapter 2), the effects of divorce upon children (chapters 3 through 5), life after divorce (chapter 1), and finish with information on household management and budgeting (chapters 10 and 11).

573. Pannor, Reuben, Fred Massarik, and Byron Evans. **The Unmarried Father: New Approaches for Helping Unmarried Young Parents.** New York: Springer, 1971. xii, 196p. illus. appendix. notes. author and subject indexes.

Usually overlooked by social workers and researchers, the unmarried father is the primary focus of this early 1970s study. The authors note that males are often less prepared for parenthood than females, that the unwed father is usually regarded as little more than a handy scapegoat for an unwanted pregnancy, and that society asks that he either marry the woman, pay support, or disappear from the scene. Seldom are unmarried fathers regarded as human beings with feeling and conflicts. After describing the methodology of their study at the Vista Del Mar Child-Care Services of 96 fathers and 222 mothers, the authors discount stereotypes of unmarried fathers (e.g., the older roué who seduces younger women or the young man who engages in casual affairs). Most of the fathers were emotionally involved with the mothers, most were reachable by the researchers, and most felt more guilt than the mothers did. In drawing a profile of the men, the authors discovered that many had masculine identity problems that were often rooted in unsatisfactory relationships with their own fathers. Also, many of the men came from father-absent or conflicted families without strong religious ties. Such men may be trying to prove their masculinity by fathering a child. The authors list goals that workers should strive for with these fathers, particularly involving them in the pregnancy and decision making. Among the options open to unmarried parents, the opportunity for the father to raise the child with community help—as a mother can—is not listed, nor do the authors comment on that anomaly. They do, however, make a series of suggestions to decrease the number of unmarried fathers. The appendix contains the recording form used in the study.

574. Ritner, Gary. **Fathers' Liberation Ethics: A Holistic Ethical Advocacy for Active Nurturing Fathering.** Lanham, MD: University Press of America, 1992. xviii, 285p. bibliography, 201-73. index. pa.

Taking equality between men and women as the goal of his ethic, Ritner argues that active nurturant fathering (ANF) is the best way to achieve this equality. Traditional parental roles allocate different child care activities to each parent. The absent father creates a disparity between a mother's and a father's caregiving. Ritner advances four moral arguments for ANF, as well as four motivating myths that encourage it. He finds that ANF overcomes fathers' alienation from the reproduction process. He examines the impact upon ANF of employment factors such as part-time work, flextime, parental leave, and women in the workforce. Ritner argues that the father must be brought back into the family, even the divorced and banished father. He critiques the history of child custody decisions and rejects the primacy of mother that is advocated in *Beyond the Best Interests of the Child* (entry 196). He argues the positive value of joint custody. The final chapter contemplates the return of the prodigal father to the family.

575. Rosenthal, Kristine M., and Harry F. Keshet. **Fathers Without Partners: A Study of Fathers and the Family After Marital Separation.** Totowa, NJ: Rowman and Littlefield, 1981. xxiii, 187p. appendixes. bibliography, 167-79. index.

The authors—both are divorced parents—explore the effects of marital breakup upon men and the father-child relationship. Drawing upon interviews with more than 129 divorced fathers, they conclude that parents need children as much as children need parents, that caring for children often stabilizes divorced fathers, and that some fathers are closer to their children after divorce. Rosenthal and Keshet also comment on numerous related matters, ranging from the women's liberation movement through joint custody. The concluding chapter defines the family in terms of parent-child relationships rather than husband-wife relationships. "We learned," Rosenthal writes, "that fathering means many things, that divorce need not mean an inevitable distancing of a father and his children."

576. Rowlands, Peter. **Saturday Parent: A Book for Separated Families.** New York: Continuum, 1980. viii, 143p. bibliography, 143. pa.

A divorced father, Rowlands urges similar Saturday parents to recognize that being involved with their children is crucially important. A psychologist by training, he offers case histories to illustrate problems and possibilities in noncustodial parenting. He offers practical advice on such matters as visits, the father's "new friend," and going to court for visitation rights (not a particularly encouraging chapter). Although most of Rowlands's advice is aimed at fathers, he includes a special chapter for the mother who is a Saturday parent.

577. Shepard, Morris A., and Gerald Goldman. **Divorced Dads: Their Kids, Ex-Wives, and New Lives.** Radnor, PA: Chilton, 1979. xi, 154p. notes. Reprint, New York: Berkley, 1980. pa.

Joint or shared custody is the subject of this book. The authors (both divorced fathers with six preteens between them) decided early on not to become Disneyland Dads or Sunday Heroes. Instead, each worked out a custody arrangement in which the father has the children at least 50 percent of the time. From personal experiences, they offer nuts-and-bolts suggestions about how to make joint custody work, touching on such matters as single parenting, career demands, money problems, and remarriage. Skeptical of the courts, child "experts," and public schools, the authors offer practical advice for coping with each. They report on a Brandeis University study of divorced fathers, and discuss how Sweden's family policy has affected fathers there.

578. Silver, Gerald A., and Myrna Silver. **Weekend Fathers.** Los Angeles: Stratford Press, 1981. xiv, 236p. appendix. bibliography, 231-36.

"If we are going to be a truly equal society," the authors write, "the next major revolution must be men's rights." Within the larger context of inequalities suffered by males, this book focuses upon divorce, custody, property settlements, visitation, support, the plight of second wives and grandparents, and starting over. They find a cultural bias against males that, once divorce occurs, creates a domino effect: the man leaves the house, setting up the process by which the woman will be awarded the children and hence a good deal of the property, spouse support, and so on. Even if the man does not leave the house, judges' outmoded views of gender roles will accomplish the same result. While support payments are rigidly enforced, visitation rights are not. No-fault divorce laws do not improve the male's disadvantage, and language changes (e.g., *alimony* becomes *spouse support*) are merely cosmetic. Despite their expressed goal of sexual equality, some feminists support "selective equality" that benefits women only. The authors, both of whom have suffered through painful divorces, depict and assess the situation of the Disneyland Dads, impact of father absence on children, the needs of divorced men in modern America, the games children play to manipulate divorced parents, the sex bias of many judges and attorneys, and the process of picking up the pieces of one's life after divorce. A final chapter describes the men's rights movement, and the appendix lists divorce reform organizations in the United States.

579. Somervill, Charles, with Herman D. Colomb. **Stepfathers—Struggles and Solutions.** Louisville, KY: Westminster/John Knox Press, 1989. 152p. bibliography, 149-52. pa.

Somervill creates a fictional narrative involving Doug, a divorced man with a teenage son, who marries Beth, a divorced woman with two children. As Doug attempts to establish himself in his new family, his struggles illustrate the difficulties faced by stepfathers. After each episode in Doug's story,

Somervill offers solutions for similar situations. Gradually, Doug and his new family grope their way towards greater coherence and understanding. For his account of stepfathering, Somervill consulted with psychiatrist Herman D. Colomb.

D. Other Family Roles

580. Arcana, Judith. **Every Mother's Son.** Garden City, NY: Anchor Press/Doubleday, 1983. ix, 322p. notes. bibliography, 303-9. index.

A divorced mother and militant feminist, Arcana confronts the problems of raising a non-sexist son. Beginning with diary episodes involving her son, Arcana uses interviews with 60 mothers and sons to explore mother-son relationships. Later chapters examine myths and fairy tales as accounts of patriarchal victories over matriarchy, and discuss sexual politics in modern times. Arcana's total acceptance of ideology about male power and oppression is used throughout the book to justify her extreme hostility toward males, masculinity, and fathers.

581. Beer, William R. **Househusbands: Men and Housework in American Families.** New York: Praeger, J. F. Bergin, 1983. xxi, 153p. (Praeger Special Studies). appendixes. bibliography, 142-48. index.

This vigorously written study is one of the few to deal with men and housework. Beer points out that men have traditionally done some forms of housework, such as, mowing the lawn, painting the house, fixing the car, replacing a broken window, and so on. His study, however, highlights men who do the housework that is traditionally assigned to women. Dividing these men into equal-time and full-time househusbands, Beer describes his own life as an equal-time househusband and parent. Utilizing such literature as there is, as well as information from 46 househusbands in the New York area, he indicates that men are far from the stereotyped monsters who have conspired to foist housework upon women. Among men whose work schedules are flexible, he finds considerable sharing of household tasks. A man's age, a working wife, and available role models can also influence his participation in housework. Few of the men responding to Beer's questionnaire were consciously pioneering new sex roles: the work had to be done, and they did it. Challenging the stereotypical idea that men hate housework, Beer finds that men's attitudes toward it varied in the same way women's did. The men found it dull and repetitive but also rewarding: they could work at their own pace, they saw tangible rewards, and they took pride in workmanship. Those least free to do housework were least enthusiastic about it. Doing housework did not drastically change most men; certainly it did not feminize them. If U.S. society wishes to encourage more men to become househusbands, Beer has some forthright advice. At present, because husbands are legally required to support wives (while wives have no reciprocal obligation to support husbands), being a full-time househusband is actually illegal. Such laws will have to change. So also will social values that denigrate men who do "women's work." Finally, men's work schedules will have to become more flexible. In a summary chapter, Beer argues that housework is "the last bastion of nonalienated work in modern society"; putting houseworkers on salary would reduce them to the level of other alienated wage laborers. The appendixes spell out Beer's methodology and present his questionnaire.

582. Benson, Dan. **The Total Man.** Wheaton, IL: Tyndale House, 1977. 272p. notes. pa.

In a presentation designed for a conservative Christian husband-father in a middle-class marriage with a traditional housewife-mother, Benson offers advice on such matters as the pitfalls of machismo and success-obsession, fitness and diet, being a loving leader of the family, marital infighting, loving and disciplining the children, and putting more spark into marital sex.

583. Herzog, Elizabeth, and Cecelia E. Sudia. **Boys in Fatherless Families.** Washington, DC: U.S. Department of Health, Education, and Welfare, Office of Child Development, Children's Bureau, 1971. iv, 120p. (DHEW Publication No. (OCD) 72-33). bibliography, 99-120.notes. pa.

Although dated, this review of the literature on the effects of father absence upon boys (particularly in terms of juvenile delinquency, intellectual and psychosocial development, and masculine identity) is still useful for pointing out the many pitfalls involved in such research. The authors' conclusions will strike some readers as being no more convincing than those they criticize.

584. Humez, Alexander, and Keith Fitzgerald Stavely. **Family Man.** Chicago: Contemporary Books, 1978. xiv, 262p.

The authors have collected 14 extended interviews with a variety of men who discuss their family roles—as sons, husbands, and fathers.

585. Klein, Carole. **Mothers and Sons.** Boston: Houghton Mifflin, 1984. 272p. bibliography, 251-62. index.

Using responses to questionnaires and interviews, Klein surveys several topics from both the mother's and the son's viewpoints. Above all, she recognizes the difficulties of the son in trying to separate from identification with the mother. She examines the pressures of the masculine role and how these can lead to conflict between mothers and sons. Both parties are likely to feel guilt. Also examined are feminist mothers who resent motherhood, lesbian mothers and homosexual sons, the working mother, troubled sons and successful sons, sons who are pushed too early to become "the man of the house," and mothers' fears of nonaggression in sons. Divorce requires special adjustments for both mothers and sons. Klein's perspective is both equitable and informed.

586. Newman, Joseph, ed. **Teach Your Wife How to Be a Widow.** Washington, DC: U.S. News and World Report Books, 1973. 287p. illus. appendixes. index.

Because women outlive men so decisively, widows need to know about matters such as wills, sale of houses, social security, stocks and bonds, taxes, estates, and so on. While the authors provide much information, they assume it is the husband's responsibility to instruct the wife about these topics. A more current book, one hopes, would be addressed to the wife, thereby relieving the husband of one more burden that is probably driving him to an early grave.

587. Olsen, Paul. **Sons and Mothers: Why Men Behave As They Do.** New York: M. Evans, 1981. 192p. notes. Reprint, New York: Fawcett Books, 1982. pa.

An extended essay rather than a systematic study, this book describes the ultimate power of the mother to shape a son's life. Interspersing his analysis with excerpts from case histories, Olsen sees mothers as primarily responsible for creating active sons and passive daughters. The "good enough" mother provides security, but not too much: she also stirs her son to rebel, and she permits him to be independent. In some cases, she can create a macho male to wreak vengeance upon a male world she hates. The father, in Olsen's view, is an outsider looking in; he must be interpreted to his son by the mother. Because of the close mother-son ties, leaving home is painful to sons, and even death cannot sever a son's link to his mother. Critics may feel that Olsen has overdrawn maternal bonding with sons; other readers may feel he has provided a needed corrective to recent studies blaming the father for perpetuating traditional gender roles in children.

588.   Robertiello, Richard C. **A Man in the Making: Grandfathers, Fathers, Sons.** New York: Richard Marek, 1979. 185p.

In this confessional search for his identity, Robertiello recalls the males who most influenced him, particularly a harsh grandfather who raised him, his father who alternately ignored and competed with him, and his own son with whom he has been only partly successful in establishing a loving relationship. Among the patterns that emerge from these recollections is the idea that men need women so badly because men provide so little love to each other. In a final chapter, Robertiello begins to formulate a psychology of the self that is derived from his experiences.

589.   Shedd, Charlie W. **Letters to Philip: On How to Treat a Woman.** Garden City, NY: Doubleday and Co., 1968. xii, 131p. Reprint, New York: Jove Publications, 1968. pa. Reprint, Old Tappan, NJ: Fleming H. Revell, 1969. pa.

In 29 letters addressed to the young husband, Shedd offers traditional Christian advice on how to treat a young wife. Suggestions include: be a leader but not a tyrant, treat her as a person, and when you disagree, fight fair and constructively.

590.   Vernon, Bob, and C.C. Carlson. **The Married Man.** Old Tappan, NJ: Fleming H. Revell, 1980. 160p.

Formerly an assistant chief of police in Los Angeles, Vernon presents a conservative Christian view of the married man's role. Quoting scripture and recounting events from his police work, Vernon offers advice on such mattes as male leadership in family and society, disciplining children, and the importance of moral conviction. Each chapter is introduced with a few paragraphs from Carole C. Carlson. Some readers will find the book a refreshing endorsement of fundamental concepts of masculinity; others will find it simplistic and authoritarian.

591.   Voth, Harold M. **The Castrated Family.** Kansas City, KS: Sheed Andrews and McMeel, 1977. xvii, 241p. appendix. bibliography, 223-34.

The author, a psychiatrist and psychoanalyst, argues for a return to traditional family roles for men and women. He details the psychological damage that can be sustained by children in nontraditional, or "castrated," households. Skeptical of current trends in sexual and personal liberation, Voth regards homosexuals as "very sick people" and encourages parents to foster strongly differentiated sex roles in their children.

Cross-References

See chapter 5, "Boys," chapter 6, "Divorce and Custody," chapter 19, "Patriarchy, Patriarchal Society," and chapter 22, "Single Men."

683. Allen, Marvin, with Jo Robinson. **In the Company of Men: A New Approach to Healing Husbands, Fathers, and Friends.**

73. Amneus, Daniel. **The Garbage Generation: The Consequences of the Destruction of the Two-Parent Family and the Need to Stabilize It By Strengthening Its Weakest Link, the Father's Role.**

595. Biller, Henry B. **Father, Child, and Sex Role: Paternal Determinants of Personality Development.**

905. Biller, Henry B., and Richard S. Solomon. **Child Maltreatment and Paternal Deprivation: A Manifesto for Research, Prevention, and Treatment.**

393. Boose, Lynda E., and Betty S. Flowers, eds. **Fathers and Daughters.**

300. Burkett, Michael. **The Dad Zone: Reports from the Tender, Bewildering, and Hilarious World of Fatherhood.**

338. Butler, Samuel. **The Way of All Flesh.**

625. Chambers, David L. **Making Fathers Pay: The Enforcement of Child Support.**

301. Chapple, Steve. **Conversations with Mr. Baby: A Celebration of New Life.**

38. Clary, Mike. **Daddy's Home.**

626. Conine, Jon. **Fathers' Rights: The Sourcebook for Dealing with the Child Support System.**

340. Corman, Avery. **Kramer Versus Kramer.**

302. Cosby, Bill. **Fatherhood.**

39. Covington, Jim. **Confessions of a Single Father.**

398. Davis, Robert Con, ed. **The Fictional Father: Lacanian Readings of the Text.**

323. Dickens, Charles. **Dombey and Son.**

689. Dinnerstein, Dorothy. **The Mermaid and the Minotaur: Sexual Arrangements and Human Malaise.**

324. Dostoevsky, Fyodor. **The Brothers Karamazov.**

627. Doyle, R. F. **The Rape of the Male.**

690. Drew, Jane Myers. **Where Were You When I Needed You Dad?: A Guide for Healing Your Father Wound.**

673. Engels, Friedrich. **The Origin of the Family, Private Property and the State.**

100. Garfinkel, Perry. **In a Man's World: Father, Son, Brother, Friend, and Other Roles Men Play.**

101. Gerson, Kathleen. **No Man's Land: Men's Changing Commitments to Family and Work.**

102. Gilder, George. **Men and Marriage.**

348. Gold, Herbert. **Fathers: A Novel in the Form of a Memoir.**

350. Goldman, William. **Father's Day.**

351. Gosse, Edmund. **Father and Son: A Study of Two Temperaments.**

277. Griswold, Robert L. **Fatherhood in America: A History.**

352. Guest, Judith. **Ordinary People.**

866. Gurian, Michael. **The Prince and the King: Healing the Father-Son Wound: A Guided Journey of Initiation.**

701. Hall, Nor. **Broodmales: A Psychological Essay on Men in Childbirth.** Introducing **The Custom of Couvade** (1929) by Warren R. Dawson.

676. Hearn, Jeff. **The Gender of Oppression: Men, Masculinity, and the Critique of Marxism.**

915. Herman, Judith Lewis, with Lisa Hirschman. **Father-Daughter Incest.**

108. Herzig, Alison Cragin, and Jane Lawrence Mali. **Oh, Boy! Babies!**

14. Hewlett, Barry S. **Intimate Fathers: The Nature and Context of Aka Pygmy Paternal Infant Care.**

328. Homer. **The Odyssey.**

45. Hoyland, John, ed. **Fathers and Sons.**

405. Johnson, Wendell Stacy. **Sons and Fathers: The Generational Link in Literature, 1780-1980.**

46. Kafka, Franz. **Letter to His Father/Brief an Der Vater.**

629. Katz, Sanford N., and Monroe L. Inker, eds. **Fathers, Husbands and Lovers: Legal Rights and Responsibilities.**

16. Kaye, Lenard W., and Jeffrey S. Applegate. **Men as Caregivers to the Elderly: Understanding and Aiding Unrecognized Family Support.**

995. Kimball, Gayle. **The 50-50 Marriage.**

996. Kimball, Gayle. **50-50 Parenting: Sharing Family Rewards and Responsibilities.**

358. Kopit, Arthur. **Oh Dad, Poor Dad, Mama's Hung You in the Closet and I'm Feeling so Sad ....**

413. Lee, M. Owen. **Fathers and Sons in Virgil's *Aeneid*: Tum Genitor Natum.**

1002. Maine, Margo. **Father Hunger: Fathers, Daughters and Food.**

21. Malinowski, Bronislaw. **The Father in Primitive Psychology.**

1002. Maine, Margo. **Father Hunger: Fathers, Daughters and Food.**

21. Malinowski, Bronislaw. **The Father in Primitive Psychology.**

56. McKuen, Rod. **Finding My Father: One Man's Search for Identity.**

366. Miller, Arthur. **Death of a Salesman.**

893. Miller, John W. **Biblical Faith and Fathering: Why We Call God "Father."**

711. Mitscherlich, Alexander. **Society Without the Father: A Contribution to Social Psychology.**

1005. Mooney, Elizabeth C. **Men and Marriage: The Changing Role of Husbands.**

681. Mount, Ferdinand. **The Subversive Family: An Alternate History of Love and Marriage.**

311. Myer, Andy. **The Liberated Father's Handbook.**

183. Nerburn, Kent. **Letters to My Son: Reflections on Becoming a Man.**

312. O'Neill, Hugh. **Daddy Cool: How to Ride a Seesaw with Dignity, Wear a Donald Duck Hat with Style, and Sing "Bingo Was His Name-O" with Panache.**

60. Painter, Hal. **Mark, I Love You.**

330. **Pearl: A New Verse Translation.**

878. Perry, John Weir. **Lord of the Four Quarters: Myths of the Royal Father.**

613. Pittman, Frank S., III. **Man Enough: Fathers, Sons, and the Search for Masculinity.**

386. Reich, Hanns, comp. **Children and Their Fathers.**

897. Renich, Fred. **The Christian Husband.**

62. Roth, Philip. **Patrimony: A True Story.**

422. Sadoff, Dianne F. **Monsters of Affection: Dickens, Eliot, and Brontë on Fatherhood.**

165. Schlesinger, Benjamin. **The One-Parent Family: Perspectives and Annotated Bibliography.**

314. Schoenstein, Ralph. **Yes, My Darling Daughters: Adventures in Fathering.**

373. Schultz, Susan Polis, ed. **I Love You Dad: A Collection of Poems.**

64. Seabrook, Jeremy. **Mother and Son.**

166. Sell, Kenneth D., comp. **Divorce in the 70s: A Subject Bibliography.**

65. Sifford, Darrell. **Father and Son.**

898. Smail, Thomas A. **The Forgotten Father.**

66. Stafford, Linley M. **One Man's Family: A Single Father and His Children.**

67. Steinberg, David. **fatherjournal: Five Years of Awakening to Fatherhood.**

315. Stewart, D. L. **Father Knows Best—Sometimes.**

316. Stewart, D. L. **Fathers Are People Too.**

317. Stewart, D. L. **Stepfathers Are People Too.**

333. Strindberg, August. **The Father**.

334. Strindberg, August. **Getting Married.**

900. Tennis, Diane. **Is God the Only Reliable Father?**

68. Waller, Leslie. **Hide in Plain Sight.**

189. Weiner, Bernard, and others. **Boy Into Man: A Father's Guide to Initiation of Teenage Sons.**

636. Weitzman, Leonore J. **The Marriage Contract: Spouses, Lovers, and the Law.**

32. Wheelock, Jane. **Husbands at Home: The Domestic Economy in a Post-Industrial Society.**

881. **Where the Two Came to Their Father: A Navaho War Ceremonial Given by Jeff King.**

637. Wishard, William R., and Laurie Wishard. **Men's Rights: A Handbook for the 80's.**

15

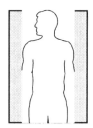

Masculinity: Masculinities,
Masculine Gender Roles,
Male Sex Roles, Biology, Physiology

Books in this chapter 1) examine the origins of masculinity (in physiology or culture or both) or 2) analyze one or more aspects of the masculine gender role. Readers should also see chapter 3, "Awareness," chapter 20, "Psychology," and chapter 23, "Spirituality."

592. Bahr, Robert. **The Virility Factor: Masculinity Through Testosterone, the Male Sex Hormone.** New York: G. P. Putnam's Sons, 1976. x, 212p. appendix. glossary. bibliography, 197-205. index.

A popular scientific account of "the male hormone," this book describes how testosterone is produced and how it functions to create maleness. After reviewing the history of research into testosterone, Bahr describes the hormone's effects upon the male from the embryonic stage to old age. He portrays the effects of too little—and too much—testosterone, how it changes the male's appearance, how homosexuality and prostate trouble may be connected with hormone levels, and how testosterone can be affected by diet and drugs. Along the way, Bahr touches on some controversial matters. He argues that male behavior is strongly affected by the hormone: "If anything, society may actually curb a boy's natural tendency to be his hormonal self." Macho men, however, are out of touch with their biological selves: they overreact to "female" estrogens that are a natural part of maleness. Still, Bahr has nothing good to say about "liberated " men who apologize for maleness. Despite attempts to broaden gender roles, nature has no love for unisex: conditions favor the mating of "men with very high testosterone—i.e., aggressive/sexual compulsion—levels ... [and] passive, submissive, highly estrogenic" women, their offspring being "highly androgenized boys and highly estrogenized girls." The book includes a glossary of terms.

593. Balswick, Jack. **The Inexpressive Male.** Lexington, MA: Lexington Books, D. C. Heath, 1988. xv, 221p. illus. bibliography, 201-16. index.

Inability or unwillingness to express feelings is widespread among males, a condition, Balswick argues, that is unhealthy to men and damaging to male-female and male-male relationships. After examining eight theoretical explanations of inexpressiveness, he concludes that socialization is largely at the root of the matter. Using Joseph Pleck's Sex Role Strain paradigm to indicate the dysfunctional nature of male inexpressiveness, Balswick examines

205

methodology for measuring expressiveness. Drawing upon experiments, question-naires, and interviews, he profiles male inexpressiveness and its consequences for marriage and friendships. The book closes with additional arguments for increasing male ability to both feel and express emotions.

594. Betcher, R. William, and William S. Pollack. **In a Time of Fallen Heroes: The Re-creation of Masculinity**. New York: Atheneum, 1993. xiii, 288p. bibliography, 267-80. index.

Masculinity is in trouble, partly because the women's movement has attempted to redefine masculinity in feminine terms. Angry with men, many feminists have declared that masculinity is defective and needs to be feminized. The authors believe, however, that men need to redefine masculinity in male terms. To clarify their ideas, they use ancient myths, especially those of Oedipus (entry 713), Achilles (entry 327), and Odysseus (entry 328). The story of Oedipus illustrates the male need to be autonomous. Although men need to be free of Mother, they need not be unrelated to the Special Women who animates their lives. Men also need Special Men (e.g., good-enough fathers, mentors, and friends). Achilles helps to define male aggressiveness and assertiveness, as well as male vulnerability. The authors explore work, sports, love and lust, and fathering. They find Odysseus to be an important image of re-created masculinity.

595. Biller, Henry B. **Father, Child, and Sex Role: Paternal Determinants of Personality Development.** Lexington, MA: Heath Lexington Books, D. C. Heath, 1971, xi, 195p. bibliography, 137-80. author and subject indexes.

Biller surveys literature on the connection between the father and the child's sex role development. Distinguishing sex role orientation, preference, and adoption, the author explores the effects of father absence upon the boy's masculine development, noting that such absence apparently has its most severe effects when it occurs during the boy's first four years of life. Biller explores theories of sex role identity, stressing Freud's ideas and derivatives from them. Examining sociocultural and constitutional variables affecting paternal influence, Biller notes that sex role demands are heavier upon boys than upon girls, and that boys do not learn fathering as girls learn mothering. Describing paternal influences upon general personality functioning, he touches upon such matters as cognitive, interpersonal, and conscience development. In separate chapters, Biller analyzes literature on mother-son and father-daughter relationships. A final chapter stresses the importance of effective fathering, charts directions for additional research, and makes suggestions for minimizing the impact of father absence and maximizing the impact of father presence.

596. Bowl, Ric. **Changing the Nature of Masculinity: A Task for Social Work?** Norwich, England: University of East Anglia, 1985. 40p. (Social Work Monograph no. 30). bibliography, 35-40. pa.

Based on an M.A. dissertation, this British monograph raises the question of whether or not social workers should attempt radical action to alter the prevailing concept of masculinity. Influenced by Marxist feminism, Bowl argues that intervention in particular cases is insufficient; the social worker must also be a revolutionist who intervenes to subvert the social order. Bowl describes prevailing masculinity as a prop of capitalist patriarchy, which fosters competition and, thus, violence. In overheated terms, he describes working-class families as pits of domestic violence and misogyny, and working-class masculinity as brutal, emotionally constricted, and sexist. Bowl dismisses arguments that gender role is determined by biology. After the revolutionary buildup, Bowl's actual recommendations are fairly mild. He urges limited intervention to alter negative masculine behaviors. Still, some readers may be infuriated by Bowl's tendency to refer to men as a "problem" that social workers must correct.

597. Brittan, Arthur. **Masculinity and Power.** Oxford and New York: Basil Blackwell, 1989. 218p. bibliography, 205-13. index. pa.
    Brittan surveys mostly left-wing, European theories concerning the nature of masculinities, the linking of masculinity and identity, the political problematics of male sexualities, the question of whether males are a ruling class, the tie between masculinity and aggression, the universalizing of the masculine as the norm, and the current crisis in masculinity. A pro-feminist who emphasizes the shaping power of culture rather than biology, Brittan finds masculinity "dangerous and volatile." His misandry is evident in such tactics as the repeated comparison of masculinity to Nazism and to South African white rule. Being both powerful and flawed, men have created patriarchy, masculinism (an ideology that justifies male dominance), heterosexism, and other evils. Brittan focuses on women's oppression by men, men's fear of women, and male violence against women. (Apparently, he believes that only males commit rape.) All men do not constitute an oppressor class, Brittan argues, but fathers who support their wives and children do: these men "appropriate" and "exploit" the "reproductive labour" of women for male profit and power. Such arguments are likely to leave many readers suspecting that the gap between left-wing theory and reality can yawn wide indeed.

598. Chapman, Rowena, and Jonathan Rutherford, eds. **Male Order: Unwrapping Masculinity.** London: Lawrence and Wishart, 1988. 331p. illus. notes. pa.
    British socialism has fallen on hard times: the labor movement is allegedly dominated by white males whose concern with economic and class issues allows little room for feminist, gay, and minority issues. The only solution, many of the contributors argue, is to construct a more enlightened masculinity. In the opening essay to this collection of 10 articles, Jonathan Rutherford denounces at length the flaws of current masculinity, using popular ads and films as his primary texts. Lynne Segal looks at the angry young men of the fifties, and Kobena Mercer and Isaac Julien examine racism in the gay men's movement and in the larger society, primarily using such texts as Robert Staples' *Black Masculinity* (entry 667) and Robert Mapplethorpe's *Black Males*. In an amusing exposé, Suzanne Moore argues that many fashionable spokesmen of postmodernism—from Prince to Roland Barthes, from Jacques Lacan to Jean Baudrillard—have simply appropriated femininity for their own masculine purposes. A similar fear is shared by Rowena Chapman in her discussion of male fashions and ads. In opposition, Cynthia Cockburn feels that the only salvation for men is to modify their masculinity by appropriating more of the feminine; until they do, Cockburn urges more separatism by socialist feminists.

599. Cherfas, Jeremy, and John Gribbin. **The Redundant Male: Is Sex Irrelevant in the Modern World?** London: Bodley Head, 1984. Reprint, New York: Pantheon Books, 1984. 198p. notes. index. pa. Reprint, London: Triad/Paladin Books, 1985. pa.
    Basically, this book surveys the biological function of sex in evolutionary history, but Cherfas and Gribbin have given the topic a best-seller twist by advancing the sensationalist proposition that males may be biologically unnecessary in the future.

Females are depicted as nurturant and thus essential to human survival, while males are generalized as violent philanderers whose biological contribution is more troublesome than efficient. The thesis seems less an inherent part of the topic than a way to sell books by engaging in fashionable male bashing. The authors speculate that, in the future, females may be able to reproduce themselves through virgin-birth cloning, although they admit that male genetic input helps prevent diseases in offspring. One suspects that the authors were amusing themselves by advancing an outrageously anti-male thesis that panders to current misandric prejudices. Still, many people will be offended by the Nazi-like evaluation of male humans strictly in "biological" terms. Had the book been titled *The Redundant Jew*, for example, its bigotry would have been immediately apparent.

600. Easlea, Brian. **Fathering the Unthinkable: Masculinity, Scientists and the Nuclear Arms Race.** London: Pluto Press, 1983. 230p. (The Politics of Science and Technology Series). notes. index. pa. Reprint, New York: Schocken Books, 1987. pa.

A nuclear physicist who abandoned his career in the 1960s because of moral scruples, Easlea traces the history of nuclear power from the scientific revolution to the development of the hydrogen bomb. He sees both scientific inquiry and the arms race as resulting from irrational masculinity. Men envy women's reproductive power and try to emulate it, usually with disastrous results. (In current academic discourse, it is sexist to suggest that women experience penis envy, but it is acceptable to claim that men suffer from womb envy.) This envy and its consequences are fictionalized in Mary Shelley's novel *Frankenstein*, which Easlea uses as a running commentary on his account of how nuclear weapons were developed. Easlea also examines the sexual metaphors used by men of science. He approvingly quotes Simone de Beauvoir's observation that women are "the sex that brings forth" and men are the sex "which kills." (Easlea writes as if millions of women did not have abortions each year.) To underscore the difference between peaceful female nature and violent male nature, the afterword contrasts a peaceful natural-childbirth scene with the violent aims of male scientists. (Again, had Easlea depicted an abortion clinic, the contrast would not have worked so well.) The end of the Cold War raises questions about Easlea's thesis: could it be that those Western, male, military leaders and scientists actually saved humanity from Soviet tyranny by pursuing the arms race long enough for the Soviet Union to collapse?

601. Fanning, Patrick, and Matthew McKay. **Being a Man: A Guide to the New Masculinity.** Oakland, CA: New Harbinger Publications, 1993. 278p. illus. bibliography, 277-78. pa.

Starting on an upbeat, male-positive note, the authors provide a self-help guide to becoming a more fully human man. The discussion is divided into four sections. Part 1 discusses gender differences and the son's need to relate to the father. Part 2 explores ways of enriching one's inner life, deepening and strengthening masculine values, and finding one's right work. Part 3 deals with male friends, lovers, partners, and children. Part 4 examines men's feelings and how to express them. Each of the book's 13 chapters contains practical advice and self-help exercises, such as journal writing, methods of retaining dreams, and so on. The book is user-friendly, especially its clear, informal prose.

602. Franklin, Clyde W., II. **The Changing Definition of Masculinity.**
New York and London: Plenum Press, 1984. xi, 234p. bibliography, 215-25.
index.

Using writings in men's studies—especially works by Marc Fasteau
(entry 98), Joseph Pleck (entry 614), Jack Nichols (entry 128), and Herb
Goldberg (entry 103)—Franklin conducts an inquiry into changing concepts of
masculinity. Assessing male responses to the women's and the men's movements, gay liberation, and "moral majority" traditionalism, he explores such
topics as the socialization of males, the ways in which racial differences may
shape masculinity, sexual identity, marriage, work, fatherhood, male friendship, and themes in male sexuality. Sensitive to, but occasionally critical of,
feminist views, Franklin's book is designed for college courses on men, especially courses in sociology or psychology. A final chapter attempts to chart
changes in the masculine gender role.

603. Gaylin, Willard. **The Male Ego.** New York: Viking, 1992. xxviii, 276p.
notes. index. Reprint, 1993. pa.

The title may be misleading: Gaylin carefully defines *ego* to mean masculine
identity. Arguing that at present too many males are self-destructive, Gaylin
surveys what current social sciences report about masculinity and how it can
become more socially and personally functional. Although earlier feminists insisted that gender differences were due entirely to culture, Gaylin agrees with
more recent feminists, like Carol Gilligan, who affirm deeper sexual divergence.
Aware of these differences, most societies assign three recurring roles to "real
men": procreator, protector, and provider. Gaylin examines the potentials and
pitfalls in those roles. He describes male sexuality, discusses work as the man's
form of nurturing, and examines the importance of sports in men's lives. The signs
and symbols of "success" are depicted negatively as "male jewelry." Describing
present-day masculinity as faltering, Gaylin says he knows no successful men.
Gaylin's dismissal of the wild man is suspiciously abrupt, and some statements
cry out to be challenged (e.g., a man "cannot be raped by a woman, only seduced
or encouraged"). Nevertheless, *The Male Ego* is largely pro-male: Gaylin believes
that modern society must liberate masculine pride.

604. Gerzon, Mark. **A Choice of Heroes: The Changing Faces of American Manhood.** Rev. ed. Boston: Houghton Mifflin, 1992. xii, 305p. notes. pa.

In an account that is personal and political, historical and contemporary,
Gerzon examines U.S. cultural images of manhood. His descriptions of The
Frontiersman and The Soldier expand into essays on virility and violence, genocide, nuclear warfare, the anti-war movement, and political machismo; the portraits of The Breadwinner and The Expert expand into assessments of boyhood,
manhood, marriage, fatherhood, and male religious images. The "emerging masculinities," or new emblems of heroism toward which some men are beginning to
aspire, are identified as The Healer, The Companion, The Mediator, and The
Colleague. While critical of many masculine stances, Gerzon is sensitive to the
psychological and social structures that create them. He argues that destructive
and repressive conditions are created by men and women acting in collusion with
each other and that the important task now is for the sexes not to blame each
other. Rather, Gerzon concludes, "It is our shared responsibility to break the
pattern." An afterword updates Gerzon's experiences during the 10 years following
the book's original publication. During that time, he has come to value the
masculine more than he did at first. His fear of the masculine originally led him
to label positive qualities as "feminine." But the mythopoetic men's movement

and New Warrior Training have convinced him that the deep masculine is also worthy.

605. Gunther, Max. **Virility 8: A Celebration of the American Male.** Chicago: Playboy Press, 1975. 280p.

Although it is not fashionable these days to be a U.S. male, according to Gunther, his book nevertheless celebrates the American man as mover, maker, and mucker-up. Arguing that, for better or for worse, men still dominate U.S. society, Gunther delineates eight types of modern "virility," ranging from the No-Nonsense Pragmatist who shuns "feminine" frivolity to The Mild Man who effaces himself. In the latter part of the book, Gunther offers 25 tongue-in-cheek rules for acting male, discusses with good-natured humor such current issues as the "new" impotency, and closes with a decidedly optimistic chapter, "Prognosis: OK."

606. Hapgood, Fred. **Why Males Exist: An Inquiry into the Evolution of Sex.** New York: William Morrow, 1979. 213p. bibliography, 189-99. index. Reprint, New York: New American Library, Mentor Books, 1980. pa.

A superb example of readable scientific writing, *Why Males Exist* explores the mysteries of why sexual reproduction arose in the evolutionary process and—more specifically—why males came into existence. Hapgood divides living creatures into four groups. Among the first, consisting of creatures like bacteria, asexual reproduction is standard. Among the second group are "bisexuals" who occasionally resort to sexual reproduction to cope with extreme conditions in their environment. Among the third group, specialization has led to distinct sexual differences and sexual reproduction. At this stage, the female generally controls the reproductive cycle, leaving the males to struggle, demonstrate their fitness, and be rewarded with mating. These animals seldom form couples, mating is quickly achieved, and the female is left to rear the offspring. The fourth group is marked by monogamy among animal couples and by male, as well as female, parenting. Hapgood cites the gains of such an arrangement, including the opportunity to raise more highly developed young, the modification of different sexual tempi in males and females, the disappearance of sex-differentiated roles and tasks, and a mutual dependency of the two-parent animals that allows for closer bonding between them and prepares for the emergence of love in the evolutionary process.

607. Holliday, Laurel. **The Violent Sex: Male Psychobiology and the Evolution of Consciousness.** Guerneville, CA: Bluestocking Books, 1978. 254p. illus. appendixes. notes. pa.

This oddly contradictory book begins as an explanation for the layperson of how males are more psychologically predisposed toward violence than females are, but it ends with a man-hating diatribe that can only be described as violent. The book begins rather dispassionately. A lengthy opening chapter describing brain and hormonal differences in males and females is followed by one arguing that elements in our culture (including mothers) too often encourage violence in males. Chapters 3 and 4—on the evolution of the sexes and on modern males—resort to operatic polemics involving wild generalizations and sexist stereotypes of males as destroyers and females as nurtures. Hunting and meat eating are depicted as the "fall" of humanity, and all the world's problems are credited to men. Readers can be amused or repelled by the contradictions that follow fast and thick in the remaining sections. After pages of warning against poisoning one's body with dubious foods and chemicals, Holliday advises men to use marijuana to lower their testosterone levels. After pages of invective against male interference with the natural order of things, the author provides instructions so that women, by artificial means, can bear only female children—in order not to "burden the world with any more males if you can help it." After lengthy tirades against male insensitivity to life, the author suggests that a pregnant woman who "learns that the fetus is not the sex of her choice ... may decide to have an abortion."

608. Kemper, Theodore D. **Social Structure and Testosterone: Explorations of the Socio-Bio-Social Chain.** New Brunswick, NJ, and London: Rutgers University Press, 1990. x, 271p. bibliography, 231-64. notes. index.

Deploring the hostilities that hinder interdisciplinary work between sociology and biology, Kemper sets out to explore sociopsychoendocrinolgy, focusing primarily on how testosterone affects male behavior. He is anxious to stress that social conditions can affect biology and that biology is not destiny, in any crude sense. His thesis is that a relationship exists between dominance/eminence and testosterone (T). Power and status thus stimulate T levels and make the male more attractive to females. Defeat lowers T levels. Examining sexual activity among males, Kemper concludes that higher T levels energize males to succeed socially and stimulate greater levels of sexual activity. Kemper classifies male sexual infidelities in terms of social conditions and T energy. Higher levels of T give males certain advantages over females, but the women's movement may be stimulating higher T levels in women, thereby enabling them to succeed in public life and to overcome such apparently inherent deficiencies as lesser spatial abilities. The results of this change are mixed: successful women are less likely to reproduce. Kemper speculates that male spectator sports may be a form of vicarious dominance in which a winning team offers male fans a T surge. In the concluding chapter, the author considers several issues, including dominance/eminence and the self, how T may affect men's political opinions, and alternatives for vicarious dominance. An egalitarian liberal eager to avoid conservative conclusions, Kemper argues that the shift away from male dominance/eminence need not be at the expense of T.

609. Mead, Margaret. **Male and Female: A Study of the Sexes in a Changing World.** New York: William Morrow, 1949. vi, 477p. appendixes. bibliographies located in several places in the appendixes. index. pa.

One of the giants of modern anthropology, Mead, in *Male and Female,* crystallizes her mature thinking concerning gender roles. Recapitulating her ground-breaking studies among several South Seas cultures, Mead discusses how sex roles are shaped in diverse societies. She explores, for example, how different cultures offer differing ways for males to respond to the oedipal conflict. Noting that girls in general are surer of their gender identities, Mead argues that "the recurrent problem of civilization is to define the male role satisfactorily enough ... so that the male may in the course of his life reach a solid sense of irreversible achievement." Especially significant for men's studies is Mead's ninth chapter, "Human Fatherhood Is a Social Invention," in which she concludes that societies must teach males to want to beget and cherish children. Societies that fail to do so court disaster. Discussing the sexes in contemporary society, Mead rejects the notion that males have conspired throughout history to oppress women: "It takes considerable effort on the part of both men and women to reorient ourselves to thinking—when we think basically—that this is a world made not by men alone, in which women are unwilling and helpless dupes and fools or else powerful schemers hiding their power under their ruffled petticoats, but a world made by mankind for human beings of both sexes." Such a sweeping rejection of radical feminist ideology has made Mead problematic for many feminists, but it indicates her importance as an antidote to ubiquitous formulations of male oppression and female victimization. Mead concludes her study by exploring how, in the future, both sexes can benefit without denying the differences between them.

610. Money, John, and Patricia Tucker. **Sexual Signatures: On Being a Man or a Woman.** Boston: Little, Brown, 1975. 250p. illus. bibliography, 237-39. index.

Writing for the layperson in clear, readable prose, the authors explain the mysteries of gender identity and role. Gender identity is defined as the inner, private experience of one's sexuality, gender role as the public expression of that experience. The authors use "gender identity/role" to express the continuity and interaction of the two. They explain what creates hermaphrodites, and they define homosexuality, transvestism, and transsexualism. Describing prenatal development, the authors invoke the "Adam principle" to explain why males are at greater risk: something extra is needed to prevent the fetus from developing into a female. They explain chromosomes and hormones, as well as variations that can occur in the standard XX and XY patterning. Discussing the socialization of humans, the authors distinguish between "reannouncement" (announcing that an infant thought to be of one sex is actually of the other) and "reassignment" (a more drastic effort to clarify an uncertain identity or to rectify the condition of a person assigned to the "wrong" sex). Examining childhood and adolescence, the authors recommend greater social flexibility toward roles. Their chapter on the sex revolution is necessary reading for anyone interested in what lies behind the men's movement and other indications of male discontent in the United States.

611. Ong, Walter J. **Fighting for Life: Contest, Sexuality, and Consciousness.** Ithaca, NY: Cornell University Press, 1981. 237p. bibliography, 211-22. index. Reprint, Amherst: University of Massachusetts Press, 1989. pa.

Ong explores the relation between contest and male identity. Arguing that self-consciousness emerges from the biological but is not entirely determined by it, he focuses on contest, or adversativeness as a shaping force of male identity. Whether in animals or humans, males live more at risk, needing to define their sexual identity in a way that females do not. Even as an embryo, the male must differentiate himself through hormonal activity or else develop into a female. Males thus have a built-in resistance to nurture; they exhibit a need to resist the prevailing female environment of existence. Boys must shift their gender identity away from the feminine by proving themselves male; even in intercourse men must perform in order to demonstrate their masculinity. Males thus establish their identity by taking or creating risks. Ong sees irreconcilable differences between the masculine and the feminine. The male is the archetypal quester, at times ridiculous, like Don Quixote. The female is the primary parent, a "Pietà" figure who must lovingly relinquish possession of her child. Masculinity is external; femininity is internal. Males are dispensable; females are not. Surveying current society, Ong notes that women's sports have failed to develop the life-and-death sense of contest—and hence the audience—of men's sports, that the highly agonistic nature of politics and business reflects masculinity, and that the essentially feminine nature of the Roman Catholic Church (Holy Mother Church) is balanced by its male-only clergy. The agonistic nature of academic life has diminished since women entered academia, and narrative art has become more interiorized with the emergence of women authors. Discussing the positive and negative aspects of contest, Ong notes that difficulties are likely to ensue as males have fewer opportunities for creative contest and as females are increasingly subjected to the insecurity that comes with contest.

612. Petras, John W., ed. **Sex: Male/Gender: Masculine: Readings in Male Sexuality.** Port Washington, NY: Alfred, 1975. 256p. bibliographies after some selections. notes. pa.

Twenty-four previously published items examining the physiology of maleness and the cultural roles of masculinity make up this anthology. Part 1 includes essays on the biological imperatives of maleness, nineteenth-century discourse on the allegedly hideous effects of masturbation, and early-twenti-eth-century views of how the "real boy" ought to behave. Part 2 presents the socialization of males. Two comical boyhood memoirs by Julius Lester and Bill Cosby are followed by portraits of both executive and blue-collar working-class men in their homes. Mirra Komarovsky explores contradictions in the mascu-line role as experienced by college students. Part 3 includes Jack O. Balswick and Charles W. Peek on the inexpressive male, Norman Mailer on women's liberation, and Michael Korda on the domestic chauvinist. Part 4, which explores new directions for men, includes Keith Olstad's "basis for discussion" of brave new men, as well as essays on breaking away from mainstream U.S. masculine roles.

613. Pittman, Frank S., III. **Man Enough: Fathers, Sons, and the Search for Masculinity.** New York: G. P. Putnam's Sons, 1993. 287p. bibliography, 271-76. index.

Necessarily, boys learn masculinity from other males, whether fathers, grandfathers, mentors, siblings, peers, or male heroes created by the society. In Part 1 of this book, Pittman argues that many modern men have been hurt because society prevented their fathers from being teachers of masculinity. Consequently, many sons strive for a compulsive display of masculinity. Whether as philanderers, contenders, or controllers, these men are damaged by hypermasculinity. In Part 2, Pittman surveys how boys become men. A sketch of the origins of patriarchy (badly oversimplified because of Pittman's uncritical reliance on skewed sources like Gerda Lerner's *The Creation of Patriarchy*, item 679) is followed by a discussion of the necessity for sons to separate from mothers. Because of widespread homophobia, many men fear the male friendship that they need. In the book's final section, Pittman advises men to stop proving their manhood and start practicing it, as caring fathers, husbands, sons, brothers, and so on.

614. Pleck, Joseph H. **The Myth of Masculinity.** Cambridge: MIT Press, 1981. ix, 229p. appendixes. bibliography, 189-216. notes. name and subject indexes. pa.

Challenging the Male Sex Role Identity (MSRI) paradigm, Pleck calls into question over 40 years of sex role research and some of the most widely held assumptions about masculinity. Pleck lists 11 questionable MSRI propositions, including: sex role identity derives from identification-modeling and (to a lesser extent) from reinforcement and cognitive learning of sex-typed traits, homosexuality reflects a disturbance of sex role identity, exaggerated mascu-line behavior indicates insecurity in some men's sex role identity, problems of sex role identity account for men's negative attitudes and behaviors toward women, and black males are particularly vulnerable to sex role identity prob-lems. Surveying past sex role research, Pleck finds it often based upon inade-quately defined psychological theory, misinterpretations, contradictions, and cultural biases. He questions the validity of sex-typing scales, the idea of identification-modeling, theories of what paternal absence does to children, and arguments that schools feminize male students. In the two concluding chapters, Pleck examines an alternative explanation of male behaviors in the Sex Role Strain (SRS) paradigm, which he formulates in 10 propositions, including: sex roles are contradictory and inconsistent, the proportion of people who violate sex roles is high, violating sex roles has more severe consequences for males than for females, each sex experiences sex role strain in its work and family roles, and historical change causes sex role strain. Appendix A reviews theories that biology is the basis for male aggression; appendix B critiques the idea that biology insures weak paternal involvement. Appendix C contains a valuable list of resources for studying or teaching male roles. The bibliography is extensive.

615. Pleck, Joseph H., and Jack Sawyer, eds. **Men and Masculinity.** Englewood Cliffs, NJ: Prentice-Hall, Spectrum Books, 1974. viii, 184p. bibliography, 175-84. (The Patterns of Social Behavior Series). pa.
This collection of 31 previously published essays is divided into seven sections. Essays in section 1, "Growing Up Male," explore how boys are socialized into learning the masculine role; selections include Brian Allen's disturbing short story "A Visit from Uncle Macho," Ruth E. Hartley's classic essay on the socialization of the male child, and Sidney M. Jourard's study of the lethal aspects of the masculine role. Section 2, "Men and Women," examines relationships between the sexes and sexual problems; Julius Lester's hilarious "Being a Boy" and Sam Julty's discussion of impotence are among the selections. Items in section 3, "Men and Children," include Robert A. Fein's informative essay "Men and Young Children," which examines how men are blocked from the rewards of child nurturing, and Kelvin Seifert's discussion of the problems encountered by men who work in child care centers. The next section, "Men and Men," explores the troubled relationships between men, especially the problem of homophobia as a bar to male friendships. Section 5, "Men and Work," consists of an essay on measuring masculinity by the size of a paycheck (by Robert E. Gould), an essay on executives as human beings (by Fernando Bartolomé), and an autobiographical account of a hip homosexual college teacher attempting to work within the system (by Michael Silverstein). Section 6, "Men and Society," focuses on machismo in the military and in politics. The final section, "Men's Liberation," includes such items as Barbara J. Katz's survey of the men's liberation movement, two accounts of men's groups, Jack Sawyer's brief essay "On Male Liberation," and the Berkeley Men's Center Manifesto. Pleck and Sawyer provide introductions to the volume and to each section.

616. Rose, Frank. **Real Men.** Garden City, NY: Doubleday, Dolphin Books, 1980. viii, 213p. illus. pa.
In this study of "sex and style in an uncertain age," Rose and photographer George Bennet present in-depth portraits of seven men representing highly diverse styles of masculinity: Virginia Military Institute cadet Rick Wetherill, rock star Dee Dee Ramone, gay interior-space designer Norm Rathweg, New York Rangers hockey player Pat Hickey, Youngstown steel worker Carroll Megginson, Dallas stockbroker Billy Bob Harris, and actor Andrew Rubin.

617. Rutherford, Jonathan. **Men's Silences: Predicaments in Masculinity.** London and New York: Routledge, 1992. x, 227p. (Male Orders series). bibliography, 213-21. notes. index. pa.

"Men's silences" refers to the gap between language and men's affective relations. Writing in the wake of British, left-wing feminist anger at left-wing male politics, Rutherford notes the narrowing of the men's anti-sexist movement to accommodate that anger. The Men Against Sexism movement degenerated into anti-pornography fundamentalism, typified by the "demagoguery" of John Stoltenberg's *Refusing To Be a Man* (entry 623). To construct a broader-based theory of masculinity, psychology, and politics, Rutherford conducts a far-ranging theoretical inquiry. Along the way, he examines matters such as Nancy Chodorow on the reproduction of mothering in capitalism, French poststructuralist thought, the writings in the men's pro-feminist journal *Achilles Heel*, the thesis of *The Sexuality of Man* (1985), Wittgenstein on language, the father in Freud and Lacan, and numerous other topics. In contrast to previous oedipal theories that put the mother and the father into opposition, Rutherford postulates a "thirdness," an interrelation between the two parents that can enable the boy to move successfully beyond the oedipal phase. Rutherford offers extended readings of films such as *Alice in the Cities*; *Paris, Texas*; *Dead Poets Society*; and the Rambo films to illustrate the idea. The success of "the good father" in Rutherford's "thirdness" theory is crucial to the development of male affective life.

618. Segal, Lynne. **Slow Motion: Changing Masculinities, Changing Men.** London: Virago Press, 1990. New Brunswick, NJ: Rutgers University Press, 1990. xiii, 396p. bibliography, 361-82. notes. index. pa.

In this thoughtful, carefully researched analysis of changing concepts of masculinity, British psychologist Lynne Segal often challenges conventional wisdom about men. After a survey of masculinities that begins with the angry young men of the 1950s, Segal examines the new fatherhood, one that comparatively few men are opting for and one that, paradoxically, threatens female dominance in the family. She examines contemporary research on gender differences, finding most current theories wanting. With admirable clarity, Segal manages to explicate and assess Jacques Lacan's theories on the phallus as symbolic signifier. Three chapters are devoted to describing competing masculinities in recent times—the historical dominant mode, those of "traitors" to this mode (such as gays), and black masculinities. In discussing sexuality, Segal rejects the radical feminist linking of male sexuality with dominance and violence. Her analyses of pornography and domestic violence discover complexities in both topics. She examines the anti-sexist men's movement in Britain, noting its limited success. Rejecting the misandry of some feminists, Segal believes men can join women in creating social structures that will ensure a more humane future for both sexes. If *Slow Motion* at times is not critical enough (it sometimes parrots Marxist-based pieties about men as a ruling class, and it accepts too easily the bad press that masculinity has been given by some liberals, academics, and feminists), the book always presents Segal's active mind confronting the puzzles of what men want and what men are.

619. Seidler, Victor J. **Rediscovering Masculinity: Reason, Language and Sexuality.** London and New York: Routledge, 1989. xvi, 234p. bibliography, 221-28. notes. name and subject indexes. pa.

In this blend of theory, memoir, and reflection, Seidler argues that males have been affected by a cultural heritage that equates masculinity with reason and progress. The Enlightenment defined reason as masculine and emotion as feminine. By doing so, it shut men away from their emotions and atrophied their identity. Feminism has challenged traditional masculinity, but no replacement model has emerged. Seidler finds little help in Marxist or liberal thought; he argues that rethinking masculinity means rethinking socialism. Disagreeing with Dale Spender's *Man Made Language* (entry 427) on male dominance of language, the author argues that men often use language to mask their emotions. Interwoven with his theoretical critique, Seidler recalls growing up in the fifties, his shame at his Jewishness and sexuality, his life on a Massachusetts commune in the seventies, and his later involvement in an East London socialist organization. He finds a gap between "the institutionalized power of men" and the experiences of individual men, who are, often enough, powerless in the grip of repressed feeling, sexuality, and intimacy.

620. Shapiro, Stephen A. **Manhood: A New Definition.** New York: G. P. Putnam's Sons, 1984. 266p. bibliography, 258-60. notes. index.

Arguing that the concept of manhood is now in shambles, Shapiro sounds a call to recover positive masculinity. In eight exhortatory chapters, he denounces male narcissism, passive-aggressive silence, and father-son tensions as the core of the problem. He urges men to recover a sense of responsible brotherhood for other men, to evolve a sense of purpose during midlife transition, and to reestablish trust between the sexes. Regarding Joseph Campbell and other mythologists as too far removed from the world of everyday needs, Shapiro prods men to recover a concept of practical heroism that distinguishes between violence and sacrifice.

621. Steinberg, Warren. **Masculinity: Identity, Conflict, and Transformation.** Boston and London: Shambhala, 1993. ix, 228p. bibliography, 215-21. notes. index. pa.

In this Jungian analysis of masculinity, Steinberg argues that boys need to establish a gender identity before they can move on to fuller masculinity. "A too-early emphasis on androgyny done at the behest of political correctness," the author writes, "is harmful to masculine development." The father plays a crucial role in aiding the son's comfortable movement away from Mother. Rather than being the fearful castrator of Freudian theory, the loving father can provide the boy with an attractive alternative to the mother. The hostile or absent father can complicate the son's attainment of masculine identity. "The Isaac complex," for example, describes a son who sacrifices his individuality to rebel against Father or to quell his guilt for having done so. Society's insistence upon male achievement and power can leave a man with a fear of failure and of the "feminine." The Shadow and the hairy Wild Man are opposing archetypes that can either warp or aid masculine achievement. Initiation rites are valuable if they lead to rebirth and not to humiliation. However, initiation into traditional masculine roles is but one step toward individuation: the male must incorporate "feminine" qualities in order to become a male human being.

622. Stoltenberg, John. **The End of Manhood: A Book for Men of Conscience.** New York: Dutton, 1993. xviii, 313p.

Stoltenberg urges men to abandon "manhood" for "selfhood." He equates manhood with male dominance and insensitivity; he defines selfhood as an egalitarian humanity. Stoltenberg parodies Robert Bly's Iron John (entry 861) as Deep Bob, a purveyor of slobbering manhood. Men who subscribe to manhood are like Jekyll and Hyde; they can be kind one moment and cruel the next. Such men compete with other men, or they gang up on weaker men or women. Stoltenberg's rambling reflections are interspersed with autobiographical and satiric parables, and they end with a denunciation of pornography (on which manhood allegedly thrives). The discussion apparently has a subtext: Stoltenberg's caricature of manhood appears to be a covert attack on heterosexuality. By equating manhood with a stereotype of machismo, he evidently seeks to elevate a bisexual, polymorphous, or gay "selfhood." Trying to subvert homophobia, he lapses into heterophobia. He misreads Bly's *Iron John* as a call to oppression by straight males. The book's ultimate puzzle is never fully solved: How can one be a *man* of conscience after one's *man*hood has been abandoned?

623. Stoltenberg, John. **Refusing to Be a Man: Essays on Sex and Justice.** Portland, OR: Breitenbush Books, 1989. 225p. bibliography, 211-225. Reprint, New York: Penguin USA, Meridian Books, 1990. pa. Reprint, London: Fontana, 1990. pa.

　　Stoltenberg sees "man" almost entirely as a social-political construct with little biological basis. Thus, "sexual identity," as usually understood, is a fiction. A radical pro-feminist, Stoltenberg argues that the masculinity that has prevailed throughout human history is almost entirely negative and oppressive, but it can be deconstructed and replaced by a more positive gender role. The author focuses on rape and pornography as classic cases of male "objectification" of females. He depicts patriarchy negatively as "father right" and urges its dissolution. Although the point is not explicitly made, Stoltenberg apparently envisions a new matriarchy or "mother right" society. Any claim to fathers' rights, especially in abortion cases, is just another male ploy to gain power over women. Stoltenberg is at his best urging a more humane masculinity; he is at his worst fulminating so wildly against fatherhood and pornography that his arguments wilt in the overheated polemics.

624. Tiger, Lionel. **Men in Groups.** New York: Random House, 1969. xx, 255p. bibliography, 218-45. notes. index. Reprint, New York: Random House, Vintage, 1970. pa. Reprint, New York: Boyars, Marion, 1989. pa.

　　Influential and controversial, Tiger's book argues that male bonding in human societies is not only socially learned but also biologically transmitted. Like the female-offspring relationship and the male-female sexual link, the male-male bond is rooted in an underlying biological predisposition. After discussing male bonding in animal communities, Tiger traces the evolution of modern male associative interaction from generations of male group hunters. A primary function of male bonding is aggressive action to enhance survival of the society, whether through defence against enemies, hunting for food, or other strenuous activities. The critical nature of such tasks leads men to "court" other men, that is, to test and select "fit" males for inclusion in the group, often through symbolic initiation practices. The link between aggressive action and violence, however, indicates that male aggression can become antisocial; hence, managing such behaviors is a primary social concern. Although Tiger favors the inclusion of more women in the public life of modern society, he stresses the difficulty of achieving this goal: Because of the predisposition to assign critical public affairs to males, in times of crisis males tend to reject females as colleagues, and both males and females tend to reject females as leaders. Paradoxically, in social matters, the modern middle-class bias against widespread male bonding may impoverish men's lives by failing to formulate acceptable male-male relationships. Any hope of future progress demands that humanity recognize and deal with its biological-social heritage of male bonding.

Cross-References

See chapter 1, "Anthropology, Sociology," chapter 3, "Awareness," chapter 5, "Boys," chapter 10, "History," chapter 17, "Men's Studies," and chapter 23, "Spirituality."

171. Abbott, Franklin, ed. **Boyhood, Growing Up Male: A Multicultural Anthology.**

72. Abbott, Franklin, ed. **New Men, New Minds: Breaking Male Tradition: How Today's Men Are Changing the Traditional Roles of Masculinity.**

154. Astin, Helen S., Allison Parelman, and Anne Fisher, comps. **Sex Roles: A Research Bibliography.**

390. Bamber, Linda. **Comic Women, Tragic Men: A Study of Gender and Genre in Shakespeare.**

81. Bell, Donald H. **Being a Man: The Paradox of Masculinity.**

477. Biller, Henry B. **Fathers and Families: Paternal Factors in Child Development.**

478. Biller, Henry. **Paternal Deprivation: Family, School, Sexuality, and Society.**

479. Biller, Henry, and Dennis Meredith. **Father Power.**

861. Bly, Robert. **Iron John: A Book About Men.**

4. Brandes, Stanley. **Metaphors of Masculinity: Sex and Status in Andalusian Folklore.**

650. Brod, Harry, ed. **A Mensch Among Men: Explorations in Jewish Masculinity.**

268. Carnes, Mark C., and Clyde Griffen, eds. **Meanings of Manhood: Constructions of Masculinity in Victorian America.**

486. Corneau, Guy. **Absent Fathers, Lost Sons: The Search for Masculine Identity.**

272. Dubbert, Joe L. **A Man's Place: Masculinity in Transition.**

343. Duberman, Martin. **Male Armor: Selected Plays, 1968-1974.**

653. Duneier, Mitchell. **Slim's Table: Race, Respectability, and Masculinity.**

400. Federico, Annette. **Masculine Identity in Hardy and Gissing.**

150. Flood, Michael, comp. **The Men's Bibliography: A Comprehensive Bibliography of Writing on Men and Masculinity.**

151. Ford, David, and Jeff Hearn, comps. **Studying Men and Masculinity: A Sourcebook of Literature and Materials.**

7. Gilmore, David D. **Manhood in the Making: Cultural Concepts of Masculinity.**

103. Goldberg, Herb. **The Hazards of Being Male: Surviving the Myth of Masculine Privilege.**

987. Goldberg, Herb. **The New Male-Female Relationship.**

1043. Gorn, Elliott J. **The Manly Art: Bare-Knuckle Prize Fighting in America.**

152. Grady, Kathleen E., Robert Brannon, and Joseph H. Pleck, comps. **The Male Sex Role: A Selected and Annotated Bibliography.**

178. Hawley, Richard A. **Boys Will Be Men: Masculinity in Troubled Times.**

10. Herdt, Gilbert H. **Guardians of the Flutes: Idioms of Masculinity.**

13. Herzfeld, Michael. **The Poetics of Manhood: Contest and Identity in a Cretan Mountain Village.**

109. Hoch, Paul. **White Hero, Black Beast: Racism, Sexism and the Mask of Masculinity.**

406. Kahn, Coppélia. **Man's Estate: Masculine Identity in Shakespeare.**

115. Kaye, Harvey. **Male Survival: Masculinity Without Myth.**

868. Keen, Sam. **Fire in the Belly: On Being a Man.**

284. Kirshner, Alan M. **Masculinity in an Historical Perspective: Readings and Discussions.**

48. Klein, Edward, and Don Erickson, eds. **About Men: Reflections on the Male Experience.**

17. Komarovsky, Mirra. **Dilemmas of Masculinity: A Study of College Youth.**

412. Krutnik, Frank. **In a Lonely Street:** *Film Noir*, **Genre, Masculinity.**

870. Lawlor, John. **Earth Honoring: The New Male Sexuality.**

515. Lee, John. **At My Father's Wedding: Reclaiming Our True Masculinity.**

52. Leiris, Michel. **Manhood: A Journey from Childhood into the Fierce Order of Virility.**

414. Leverenz, David. **Manhood and the American Renaissance.**

20. Lidz, Theodore, and Ruth Wilmanns Lidz. **Oedipus in the Stone Age: A Psychoanalytic Study of Masculinization in Papua New Guinea.**

661. Majors, Richard, and Janet Mancini Billson. **Cool Pose: The Dilemmas of Black Manhood in America.**

287. Mangan, J. A., and James Walvin, eds. **Manliness and Morality: Middle-Class Masculinity in Britain and America, 1800-1940.**

418. Mellen, Joan. **Big Bad Wolves: Masculinity in the American Film.**

182. Miedzian, Myriam. **Boys Will Be Boys: Breaking the Link Between Masculinity and Violence.**

921. Miles, Rosalind. **Love, Sex, Death and the Making of the Male.**

531. Osherson, Samuel. **Finding Our Fathers: The Unfinished Business of Manhood.**

184. Paley, Vivian Gussin. **Boys and Girls: Superheroes in the Doll Corner.**

663. Paz, Octavio. **The Labyrinth of Solitude ....**

288. Pleck, Elizabeth H., and Joseph H. Pleck, eds. **The American Male.**

289. Pugh, David G. **Sons of Liberty: The Masculine Mind in Nineteenth-Century America.**

291. Roper, Michael, and John Tosh, eds. **Manful Assertions: Masculinities in Britain Since 1800.**

293. Rotundo, E. Anthony. **American Manhood: Transformations in Masculinity from the Revolution to the Modern Era.**

423. Savran, David. **Communists, Cowboys, and Queers: The Politics of Masculinity in the Work of Arthur Miller and Tennessee Williams.**

424. Schwenger, Peter. **Phallic Critiques: Masculinity and Twentieth-Century Literature.**

667. Staples, Robert. **Black Masculinity: The Black Man's Role in American Society.**

668. Teague, Bob. **Letters to a Black Boy.**

143. Thompson, Keith, ed. **To Be a Man: In Search of the Deep Masculine.**

431. Tuss, Alex J., S.M. **The Inward Revolution: Troubled Young Men in Victorian Fiction, 1850-1880.**

556. Welch, Don. **Macho Isn't Enough! Family Man in a Liberated World.**

437. Woodcock, Bruce. **Male Mythologies: John Fowles and Masculinity.**

16

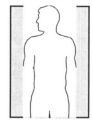

Men's Rights

625. Chambers, David L. **Making Fathers Pay: The Enforcement of Child Support.** Chicago and London: University of Chicago Press, 1979. xiv, 365p. illus. appendix. bibliography, 359-62. notes. index.

Chambers covers the procedures used in three Michigan counties to force divorced fathers to pay alimony and child support. He examines the treatment of men by the courts, a public agency named Friend of the Court, and the jails. Fathers' rights advocates will find plenty to outrage them in what is reported, but the book depicts a situation producing more than enough misery and hardship for everyone involved—fathers, mothers, and children. The methodological appendix is by Terry K. Adams.

626. Conine, Jon. **Fathers' Rights: The Sourcebook for Dealing with the Child Support System.** New York: Walker, 1989. xvi, 220p. appendixes. index.

Fathers are punished by divorce procedures and a child support system that do not—indeed, cannot—work. The man who fails to grapple with the insanities of the system, however, may be destroyed by it. Conine argues that the system often attempts the impossible when it takes children from fathers and then expects fathers to support them willingly. Those who run the system typically blame fathers for its failures and persecute fathers as the villains. In clear prose, Conine spells out the labyrinthine operations of the child support enforcement system, including tracking down fathers, collecting child support, establishing paternity, withholding wages, and enforcing orders. Numerous horror stories of the system out of control punctuate the exposition. Conine encourages fathers to meet their legal support requirements, but he points out the pitfalls confronting even the most cooperative father when dealing with the system. Appendix A lists child support enforcement agencies in each state; appendix B lists fathers' rights organizations.

627. Doyle, R. F. **The Rape of the Male.** St. Paul, MN: Poor Richard's Press, 1976. xi, 286p. illus. bibliography, 279-86. notes. pa.

The founder of Men's Rights Association, Doyle here takes angry aim at favoritism toward women in U.S. society, especially in the divorce courts. Doyle criticizes no-fault divorce laws that permit automatic granting of custody to women and support payments to men, without any real enforcement of non-custodial visitation rights. "Upon dissolution of marriage, men's functions continue to be enforced," Doyle writes, "yet no judge has ever ordered a woman to cook, clean, and sew for her ex-husband; and damned seldom for an existing one." Ex-husbands are jailed if they cannot meet support payments, perhaps the only surviving example of imprisonment for debt. Courts routinely presume males guilty until proven innocent: "'orders to show cause why the accused should *not* be held in contempt of court' are a subterfuge, applied almost exclusively to males." Doyle illustrates his argument with horror stories gleaned from years of counseling divorced men and from his own experiences with the courts. As Doyle notes, "This is not a chivalrous book." Present information indicates that this book can be obtained from the Men's Rights Association, 17854 Lyons St., Forest Lake, MN 55025-8854.

628. Kanowitz, Leo. **Equal Rights: The Male Stake.** Albuquerque: University of New Mexico Press, 1981. viii, 197p. appendix. notes. case and subject indexes. pa.

One purpose of this book is to demonstrate that men as well as women have been historically victimized by social gender discrimination and by sexist legal decisions. "By contrast, a casual glance at the treatment males have received at the hands of the law solely because they are males suggests that they have paid an awesome price for other advantages they have presumably enjoyed over females in our society," Kanowitz writes. "Whether one talks of the male's unique obligation of compulsory military service, his primary duty for spousal and child support, his lack of the same kinds of protective labor legislation that have traditionally been enjoyed by women, or the statutory or judicial preference in child custody disputes that have long been accorded to mothers vis-à-vis fathers of minor children, sex discrimination against males in statutes and judicial decisions has been widespread and severe." Kanowitz argues that men's interests coincide with those of women seeking equal rights under the law; he deplores the anti-male attitude of some feminists. In a series of essays, Kanowitz examines such matters as "benign" sex discrimination (which he finds not so benign at all), Social Security benefits favoring women, alimony decisions, "protective" laws that are not extended to males, equal pay and overtime restrictions, the New Mexico Equal Rights Amendment, the military draft, the national campaign for the ERA during the 1970s, and prospects for future adoption of such an amendment. Particularly disturbing is the evidence presented to demonstrate the almost total inability or unwillingness of the Supreme Court to recognize the extent and effects of anti-male discrimination in the past. Although the book is somewhat disjointed because it is made up in part of materials published over an eight-year period, readers can watch Kanowitz evolve from a pro-feminist male who in 1972 accepted the fashionable idea of men as an oppressor class to a genuine equal rights advocate who in 1980 recognizes the impact of anti-male bias on men. A postscript on recent Supreme Court decisions concerning statutory rape and the male-only draft leaves little doubt that men have a long way to go before achieving equality in the courts.

629. Katz, Sanford N., and Monroe L. Inker, eds. **Fathers, Husbands and Lovers: Legal Rights and Responsibilities.** Chicago: American Bar Association Press, 1982. v, 318p. notes. pa.

Ten essays plus an introduction originally published in *Family Law Quarterly* explore several aspects of law relating to males, including medical tests to determine paternity more accurately (and hence child support obligations), the complications arising from "test tube baby" situations, the impact of *Stanley v. Illinois* on securing the rights of unwed fathers, the impact of *Roe v. Wade* on paternal support (if the woman and her doctor have the right to decide on abortion or birth, why should the father be responsible for supporting a child he may not want?), a historical survey of laws regulating fathers' rights and obligations, laws concerning wife battering (no laws concerning husband battering are discussed), and changing alimony and property decisions. A few writers are sympathetic to men's rights, but others—like the editors—convey the impression that males are a privileged class that deserves to be punished by law.

630. Lynch, Frederick R. **Invisible Victims: White Males and the Crisis of Affirmative Action.** New York: Praeger, 1991. xvii, 237p. appendixes. bibliography, 225-31. notes. index. pa.

Lynch addresses the "forgotten" problem of discrimination suffered by white males as a result of affirmative action quotas and preferential treatment of women and minorities in hiring, promotion, and educational opportunities. Several factors have operated to cover up the issue of anti-male discrimination. Judges and bureaucrats imposed the policies upon the nation from above, preventing open discussion of them. The male sex role inhibited men from complaining about injustices. "Blaming the victim" was widespread as the media and Democratic politicians accused white males of having created racial and gender inequities in the first place. A "spiral of silence" made a minority view favoring quotas appear to be a majority view, and a "new McCarthyism" that denounced opponents of quotas as racist or sexist further squelched resistance. Corporations found it easier to comply with preferential programs than to face lawsuits and public accusations of racism and sexism. Yet, the majority of Americans have always opposed race and gender quotas. Lynch cites in detail the experiences of 34 white, male victims of affirmative action. He notes the media's positive presentation of affirmative action and the corresponding inattention to discrimination against white males. The numerous problems created by preferential quotas, especially in the academic world where they have been actively embraced, have led to a crisis of affirmative action.

631. Rivkin, Robert S. **GI Rights and Army Justice: The Draftee's Guide to Military Life and Law.** New York: Grove Press, 1970. xii, 383p. appendixes. notes. index.

Published during the Vietnam War, this book provides a look at legal rights in the military, then and now. Regarding the draftee or reluctant enlistee as a member of an oppressed minority, Rivkin depicts the realities of power and law in the army as a system of coercion producing a travesty of justice. From the time of induction to discharge, the soldier can expect harassment, low pay, maltreatment, and questionable legal practices. The military mind, the author argues, believes that humiliation plus fear equals obedience, revels in an antidemocratic caste system, glorifies killing, and likes to try its own cases. The ordinary soldier can expect little redress for many abuses he suffers. Exercising First Amendment rights of free speech, for example, can be hazardous for the GI, and rights of privacy can be easily violated. Nevertheless, Rivkin spells out what the soldier's rights are and explains how he can protect himself legally, including methods of filing complaints and bringing charges. The abuse of servicemen in stockades is described, including an account of the Presidio 27. The final chapter debunks a series of military "myths" (e.g., discipline in combat will disappear in the absence of terror in training) and argues for a more humane and equitable system of military justice.

632. Rivkin, Robert S., and Barton F. Stichman. **The Rights of Military Personnel: The Basic ACLU Guide for Military Personnel.** Rev. ed. New York: Avon Books, Discus, 1977. 158p. appendix. notes. pa. Original publication, as *The Rights of Servicemen* (New York: Avon Books, 1972. Reprint, New York: Richard W. Barton, 1973).

"The military services are still unnecessarily oppressive," the authors state, "but no longer are they immune from public scrutiny and civilian court review of their lawless actions." Taking a less than enthusiastic view of military law and practice, the authors review such matters as military law and the court-martial system, Article 15 (which allows a commanding officer to punish any member of his command for minor offenses), the soldier's rights during interrogation, AWOL and desertion, the right to privacy (apparently more honored in the breach than in the observance), First Amendment rights of freedom of expression, conscientious objection, the right to disobey illegal orders, getting out of the military, and filing complaints against military personnel. The appendix includes a worldwide list of agencies that provide various forms of military-legal counseling.

633. Rudovsky, David, Alvin J. Bronstein, and Edward T. Koren. **The Rights of Prisoners: The Basic ACLU Guide to a Prisoner's Rights.** Rev. ed. New York: Bantam Books, 1983. An American Civil Liberties Union Handbook. 145p. appendixes. bibliography, 137-38. notes.

Painting a dismal picture of prisoners' rights, the authors argue that the courts' hands-off policy regarding prisons guarantees almost total control of them by prison officials. In question-and-answer format, they touch briefly upon such matters as due process in prison disciplinary cases, freedom from cruel and unusual punishment, problems of censorship in prison, prisoners' rights to free communication and access to the courts, questions of religious and racial discrimination in prison policies, political rights of prisoners, questions of privacy and personal appearance, and rights to medical care and protection from physical or sexual abuse. The authors also discuss pretrial confinement ("the jails are an unmitigated disgrace"), parole, and procedures for remedies of prisoners' complaints. Prisoners' rights are both scarce and arbitrary: the authors advise the reader that "this guide offers no assurances that your rights will be respected."

634. Sherrill, Robert. **Military Justice Is to Justice as Military Music Is to Music.** Rev. ed. New York: Harper & Row, 1971. 306p. index. pa.

While U.S. women are exempt from compulsory military service, U.S. men can still face the possibility of conscription. Once he is in service, the American man "may anticipate not only the possibility of giving up his life but also the certainty of giving up his liberties." This book indicates what men can expect from military courts because both Congress and the Supreme Court have consistently refused to extend constitutional rights to soldiers. Sherrill intersperses his history of military law with accounts of specific cases of miscarriage of justice, atrocities in military stockades, and cruel and unusual punishments meted out by the military. He concludes: "Justice is too important to be left to the military. If military justice is corrupt—and it is—sooner or later it will corrupt civilian justice."

635. Stoddard, Thomas B., E. Carrington Boggan, Marilyn G. Haft, Charles Lister, and John P. Rupp. **The Rights of Gay People.** Rev. ed. New York: Bantam Books, 1983. xiii, 194p. appendixes. bibliography, 167-70. notes. pa.

Using a question-and-answer format, this book surveys gay rights in such areas as freedom of speech and assembly, employment, armed services, security clearance, immigration and naturalization, and housing and public accommodations. Separate chapters cover the gay family, gays and criminal law, and the rights of transvestites and transsexuals. The appendixes include criminal statues listed by state that relate to consensual homosexual acts between adults; antidiscrimination laws of Minneapolis and East Lansing; executive orders of the governors of California and Pennsylvania concerning sexual minorities; a list of selected gay organizations; and ACLU state affiliates. This book is the revised edition of *The Basic ACLU Guide to a Gay Person's Rights.*

636. Weitzman, Leonore J. **The Marriage Contract: Spouses, Lovers, and the Law.** New York: Free Press, 1981. xxiii, 536p. appendix. notes. index. pa.
In exhaustive detail, Weitzman examines the legal implications of marriage and cohabitation, focusing on traditional obligations (the husband must support the wife, the wife must provide domestic service and child care), as well as the discrepancies between the law's view of marriage and the social reality. Weitzman argues the case of "intimate contracts" between couples to ensure a more equitable distribution of powers and obligations. The author's feminist slant stresses the disadvantages to women in the traditional view of marriage and sometimes downplays or overlooks the disadvantages to men.

637. Wishard, William R., and Laurie Wishard. **Men's Rights: A Handbook for the 80's.** San Francisco: Cragmont Publications, 1980. 264p. appendix. bibliography, 259-60. index.
"This book is pro-men; it is not anti-woman or anti-family," the authors explain. In informal and lively language, the Wishards—father and daughter— begin with the idea that, with the qualified success of women's rights in the courts, the time has come to balance the scales by considering men's rights. Most of their discussion concerns family law: marriage as a blank contract, the legal obligations of cohabitation arrangements, the father's well-defined responsibility to support his children and his less well-defined rights as a parent, the father's lack of rights in abortion cases, and the slightly expanding rights of unmarried fathers. The Wishards devote much space to discussing the legal ins and outs of separation, divorce custody (including the benefits and drawbacks of joint custody), spouse support (as, traditionally, a form of discrimination against men), child support, visitation, and related matters. The authors also discuss the less noticed matter of reverse discrimination in employment opportunities and on the job—how it occurs, what has been done, and what can be done to nullify it. Only a brief mention is made of men's unequal military obligations. The appendix contains a short list of men's rights organizations.

Cross-References

See chapter 6, "Divorce and Custody," and chapter 14, "Males in Families," section C, "Divorced and Single Fathers."

942. Barker, A.J. **Prisoners of War.**

79. Baumli, Francis, ed. **Men Freeing Men: Exploding the Myth of the Traditional Male.**

483. Cammarata, Jerry, with Frances Spatz Leighton. **The Fun Book of Fatherhood ...**

912. Eberle, Paul and Shirley. **The Abuse of Innocence: The McMartin Preschool Trial.**

96. Farrell, Warren. **The Myth of Male Power: Why Men Are the Disposable Sex.**

955. Jacobs, Clyde E., and John F. Gallagher. **The Selective Service Act: A Case Study of the Governmental Process.**

957. Johnson, R. Charles. **Draft, Registration and the Law: A Guidebook.**

514. Lamb, Michael E., and Abraham Sagi, eds. **Fatherhood and Family Policy.**

964. O'Sullivan, John, and Alan M. Meckler. **The Draft and Its Enemies: A Documentary History.**

60. Painter, Hal. **Mark, I Love You.**

136. Schenk, Roy U. **The Other Side of the Coin: Causes and Consequences of Men's Oppression.**

138. Shostak, Arthur B., and Gary McLouth, with Lynn Seng. **Men and Abortion: Lessons, Losses, and Love.**

578. Silver, Gerald A., and Myrna Silver. **Weekend Fathers.**

931. Spiegel, Lawrence D. **A Question of Innocence: A True Story of False Accusation.**

966a. Surrey, David S. **Choice of Conscience: Vietnam Era Military and Draft Resisters in Canada.**

967. Tax, Sol, ed. **The Draft: A Handbook of Facts and Alternatives.**

968. Taylor, L. B., Jr. **The Draft: A Necessary Evil?**

143. Thomas, David. **Not Guilty: The Case in Defense of Men.**

936. Tong, Dean. **Don't Blame Me, Daddy: False Accusations of Child Abuse.**

68. Waller, Leslie. **Hide in Plain Sight.**

937. Webb, Cathleen Crowell, with Marie Chapian. **Forgive Me.**

845. Wolinsky, Marc, and Kenneth Sherrill, eds. **Gays and the Military: Joseph Steffan Versus the United States.**

17

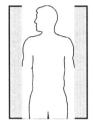

Men's Studies: Interdisciplinary
Collections and Studies

638. Brod, Harry, ed. **The Making of Masculinities: The New Men's Studies.** Boston: Allen and Unwin, 1987. xvi, 346p. notes. index. pa.

An important collection of 14 articles (plus a foreword and an introduction), this book attempts to define men's studies and to demonstrate its practice. In the introduction and in his article "The Case for Men's Studies," Brod defines *men's studies* as "the study of masculinities and male experience as specific and varying social-historical-cultural formulations." Males (or, more exactly, a single concept of masculinity) are to be no longer regarded as "the norm" but as a phenomenon to be examined. Men's studies is "a complement, not a co-optation, of women's studies." More controversial is Brod's attempt to define the politics of men's studies as "pro-feminist" and to locate its goals in vague socialist transformations of society. Most essays in the volume reflect this agenda, thereby suggesting that the new men's studies has a narrower political range than in fact it has. Thus, in this collection, one reads much about the evils of patriarchy, little about fatherhood, and nothing about fathers' rights. Nevertheless, most articles provide solid contributions to men's studies as both an interdisciplinary project and as a fresh perspective on individual disciplines. If "Towards a New Sociology of Masculinity," by Tim Carrigan, Bob Connell, and John Lee, stumbles under the weight of its Marxist-feminist presuppositions, James D. Riemer's "Rereading American Literature from a Men's Studies Perspective: Some Implications" demonstrates thoughtfully how literary criticism can benefit from a fresh masculinist approach. Joseph Pleck continues to raise troubling questions about male sex role research in his article, and Clyde W. Franklin II opens discussion on the decimation of America's black male population. Most refreshing are the articles that come nearest to questioning the volume's political perspective, such as Peter Filene's riposte to those who insist that traditional study of history has been "his-story" and Perry Treadwell's careful defense of a "biosociological" understanding of gender. Dorothy Hammond and Alta Jablow examine the "myth of male friendship" from Gilgamesh (entry 325) to Butch Cassidy, and Louis Crompton discusses "Byron and Male Love: The Classical Tradition." Although the book provides no general bibliography, the notes to each article contain a wealth of resources for additional research in men's studies.

639. Clatterbaugh, Kenneth. **Contemporary Perspectives on Masculinity: Men, Women, and Politics in Modern Society.** Boulder, CO: Westview Press, 1990. ix, 182p. bibliography, 161-73. index. pa.

Sorting out the various strands of the men's movement and elucidating their philosophical foundations, Clatterbaugh provides a valuable service for anyone interested in men's studies. Clatterbaugh finds six major masculinist perspectives: conservative, pro-feminist, men's rights, spiritual, socialist, and group-specific. He examines each perspective in terms of its history and primary sources, its description and explanation of male reality, and its assessment of that reality and its agenda for change. Clatterbaugh then provides a series of criticisms and responses for each perspective, a summary and personal conclusion, and a list of suggested readings. Conservatives, he finds, are divided into moral conservatives (who see protective, breadwinning masculinity as the triumph of civilizing forces) and biosocial conservatives (who see take-charge masculinity as biological destiny). Pro-feminist men are divided into radicals (who see masculinity as a violent and misogynist evil) and liberals (who see masculinity as hurtful to men and others). Similarly, men's rights advocates are divided between those who stress fathers' rights and those seeking a broader agenda of men's rights. The spiritual or mythopoetic movement is divided between "wild men" who seek to initiate males through distinctly masculine archetypes and "horned god" advocates who stress a feminist orientation for men. Socialists are divided into classical Marxists for whom capitalism causes the evils of patriarchy and socialist feminists for whom patriarchal evils are not limited to capitalism. The group-specific perspective focuses mainly on gay men and African-American men. Although Clatterbaugh's own socialist perspective seems set in Marxist concrete, his clear and systematic presentation of the various masculinist perspectives goes far toward reducing the seeming chaos of the men's movements to reasonable order.

640. David, Deborah S., and Robert Brannon, eds. **The Forty-nine Percent Majority: The Male Sex Role.** Reading, MA: Addison-Wesley, 1976. xiv, 338p. bibliographies after several essays and 331-34. notes. pa. Reprint, New York: Random House, 1976. pa.

Widely used in college courses, this anthology contains 38 selections by 36 authors. The extensive introduction by Brannon, "The Male Sex Role: Our Culture's Blueprint of Manhood, and What It's Done for Us Lately," defines four principal components of the role, which are the subjects of the first four chapters. Chapter 1 contains essays on the stigma for males of being characterized as feminine, while those in chapter 2 explore requirements for success and status. Selections in chapter 3 examine the "manly air of toughness, confidence, and self reliance"; those in chapter 4 deal with the masculine "aura of aggression, violence, and daring." Two additional chapters explore learning the male role and changing it. Selections include Gregory K. Lehne's original essay on homophobia among men, Robert Gould's "Measuring Masculinity by the Size of a Paycheck," James Thurber's famous short story "The Secret Life of Walter Mitty," Ruth E. Hartley's classic essay "Sex Role Pressures and the Socialization of the Male Child," Julius Lester's hilarious "Being a Boy," and Andrea S. Hayman's informative "Legal Challenges to Discrimination Against Men." Some items, like Lois Gould's parable "X: A Fabulous Child's Story," may now seem naive and dated.

641. Doyle, James A. **The Male Experience.** 3d ed. Madison, WI, and Dubuque, IA: Brown and Benchmark, 1995. xii, 343p. illus. bibliography after each chapter and 294-327. name and subject indexes. pa.

An expanded and updated edition of Doyle's overview of men's studies, this volume can serve as a college text for a men's studies course or as a primer for general audiences on the interdisciplinary content of men's studies. In section 1, Doyle surveys such matters as the current flux in men's roles, a history of the various men's movements, biological ingredients of maleness, psychological views of masculinity, sociological analyses of male behavior, and anthropological views of differing masculinities. Section 2 examines elements of the male role, including the need to differentiate from the feminine, "success," aggression, and sexuality. Section 3 covers some issues of concern to males, including power and relationships, homosexuality, race, fatherhood, and men's health. The discussion reflects Doyle's "inclusive" model of men's studies, that is, one that presents divergent viewpoints. Although sensitive to feminist concerns, the discussion strives to articulate numerous promasculinist concerns as well. The section on rape acknowledges the existence of male victims of rape; the account of domestic violence recognizes the existence of some violent women and abused men. This edition draws on the latest scholarship in men's studies.

642. Franklin, Clyde W., II. **Men and Society.** Chicago: Nelson-Hall, 1988. vii, 263p. bibliography, 235-53. index. pa.

This survey of men and society opens with four newspaper stories: in the first story is a man who buried his girlfriend alive, in the second is a man who engaged in sex with a two-year-old girl, in the third is a man who slashed a female model's face with razor, and in the fourth is a man who exposed himself in public. All four activities, Franklin argues, are representative of traditional masculinity. The book's opening should prepare the reader for Franklin's extremely negative views of white, heterosexual males and modern U.S. society. The author argues that heterosexual masculinity is an inherently barbarous influence on society, that social structures reinforce the power of evil males, and that only the overthrow of heterosexual and patriarchal society will rescue humanity. In this indictment of men and society, the components of heterosexual masculinity are reduced to misogyny, racism, aggressive violence, power mania, and homophobia. The card stacking of evidence damages the book's credibility and its legitimate protest against current social and private evils.

643. Hearn, Jeff, and David Morgan, eds. **Men, Masculinities and Social Theory.** London: Unwin Hyman, 1990. xvi, 252p. (Critical Studies on Men and Masculinities, no. 2). bibliography, 229-245. author and subject indexes. pa.

The fifteen articles in this collection emerged from a 1988 conference in England on men, masculinity, and social theory. Radical feminist and socialist thought influence most of the articles. In the introduction, Hearn and Morgan point out that awareness of gender and sexual politics has created an awareness of the "malestream" nature of discourse and study. Gender studies allows deconstruction, i.e., the breaking down of artificial unities such as "masculinity" and false dichotomies such as masculine-feminine and gender-sexuality. In part 1, "Power and Domination," the uneasy rapprochement between radical feminism and pro-feminist men's studies becomes explicit in Jalna Hanmer's angry, touchy article insisting upon the unique victimization of women in patriarchy. (Despite the talk of deconstructing false dichotomies, nearly all the contributors to this volume write as if only women were victims of rape and violence and as if only men purchased pornography.) In succeeding articles, John Remy distinguishes between patriarchy (rule of the fathers) and fratriarchy (rule of younger men) as differing forms of male power groups. A similar distinction appears later in Harry Brod's discussion of pornography for male audiences: using Marxist and feminist theory, he argues that pornography alienates male sexuality. Sallie Westwood studies the impact of racism on black working-class men, and Cynthia Cockburn tallies the successes and limitations of equal opportunity efforts in Britain. Part 2, "Sexualities," includes Michael Kimmel's examination of the impact made by gender awareness upon sociology. Part 3, "Identity and Perception," features Barry Richard's reading of Ronald Reagan's oedipal conflicts. Part 4, "Commentaries," contains Joyce E. Canaan and Christine Griffin's concerns about the new men's studies. The concerns include funding (will men's studies drain off funds from women's studies?) and politics (will men's studies develop its own agenda that does not mesh with feminist agendas?). The closing essay by Victor J. Seidler argues for balancing pro-feminism with a respect for some aspects of masculinity. Men can change masculinity, he notes, but they cannot reject it. "In working towards a transformed masculinity," Seidler notes, "we have to recognize the injuries that were done by the idea that men should be guilty *as men*." In this essay, Seidler manages not only to deconstruct but to reconstruct.

644. Kimmel, Michael S., ed. **Changing Men: New Directions in Research on Men and Masculinity.** Newbury Park, CA: Sage Publications, 1987. 320p. bibliography after each chapter. notes. pa.

This anthology contains 19 essays divided into six sections: "Reformulating the Male Role," "Men in Domestic Settings," "Men and Women," "Sexuality," "Race and Gender," and "Toward Men's Studies." Selections include two essays (by Kimmel and by Harry Brod) defining and justifying the new men's studies, as well as Kimmel's account of teaching a men's studies course. A number of disciplines are represented in the collection. Several sociological studies examine the changing roles of men and women at work and in the family. Joseph H. Pleck succinctly surveys the history of U.S. attitudes towards fatherhood from the eighteenth century to the present, and Michael Shiffman recounts the history of the pro-feminist men's movement. Arthur B. Shostak explores negative attitudes towards males in abortion clinics, and Leonore Tiefer critically examines medical attempts to improve men's sexual performance.

645. Kimmel, Michael S., and Michael A. Messner, eds. **Men's Lives.** 2d ed. New York: Macmillan, 1991. xiii, 586p. illus. bibliographies and notes after most chapters. pa.

Selections in this anthology of writings cover various aspects of men's studies and issues. The articles are divided into 10 sections: "Perspectives on Masculinities," "From Boys to Men," "Sports and War: Rites of Passage in Male Institutions," "Men and Work," "Men and Health: Body and Mind," "Men with Women: Intimacy and Power," "Men with Men: Friendship and Fears," "Male Sexualities," "Men in Families," and "Men and the Future." The editors have aimed at an inclusiveness that is wider than usual: among the 56 articles, several are devoted to black, gay, Chicano, Jewish, and Asian men. Selections usually reflect the editors' pro-feminist and gay-affirmative perspective. A number of now-classic essays appear, such as, Gregory K. Lehne's analysis of homophobia and Jack Sawyer's account of the inexpressive male. More recent articles include Richard Major on the "cool pose" of young black males and Leonore Tiefer's intriguing account of how some members of the medical profession promise to provide men with the perfect penis.

646. Lewis, Robert A., ed. **Men in Difficult Times: Masculinity Today and Tomorrow.** Englewood Cliffs, NJ: Prentice-Hall, 1981. xvi, 332p. illus. bibliographies after some items. notes. index. pa.

This unusually rich collection contains 55 items, including essays, research summaries, historical analyses, autobiographical accounts, poems, and songs. The material from numerous contributors is gathered into six sections. In section 1, "The High Costs of Traditional Masculine Roles," items focus on competitiveness, male lack of playfulness, divorce and custody, men in therapy, and midlife decline. In section 2, "Socialization into Male Sex Roles," authors deal with sports, masculinity in comic strips, male chauvinism, and inexpressive males. Section 3, "Feminism and Men Facing Change," includes discussion of social change and the family, women's changing (and sometimes conflicting) expectations, the rise and fall of a men's group, and evolving masculine gender roles and male identities. In section 4, "Nurturance By and for Males," authors tackle the problems of single fathering, grandfatherhood, male teachers and young children, and barriers that make men's closeness with each other so difficult. Section 5, "Resources for Change in Males," includes an analysis of male power and powerlessness, advice for male consciousness-raising groups, explorations of how homophobia can be eliminated, and desiderata for research on African-American males. The final section, "The New Man," includes an essay on shared parenting, suggestions for moving men toward greater intimacy, and an historical survey of the male role from preindustrial to postindustrial times.

647. Spender, Dale, ed. **Men's Studies Modified: The Impact of Feminism on the Academic Disciplines.** Oxford, England: Pergamon Press, 1981. xiii, 248p. bibliography after each chapter. pa.

Despite its title, this collection of 16 articles has nothing to say about the new men's studies. Each of the articles describes the impact of feminist thought on a traditional academic area. The authors note the omissions and distortions concerning females in these studies, but they ignore the omissions and distortions concerning males. In the introduction, Spender equates traditional studies with "men's studies," apparently assuming that earlier male academics knew all there was to know about men and spoke for the entire male sex. All the contributors to this collection take a radical feminist view of men as an oppressor class that despises women and seeks to keep them in their place. They report considerable misogyny on the part of male academics, and in turn they exhibit considerable misandry in their discussions of men.

Cross-References

See chapter 4, "Bibliographies," section A, "Men's Studies Bibliographies."

18

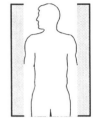

Minority Males,
Multicultural Studies

Books in this section focus primarily on males identified with racial, ethnic, or religious minority groups in the United States.

648. Ali, Shahrazad. **The Blackman's Guide to Understanding the Blackwoman.** Philadelphia: Civilized Publications, 1989. x, 184p. pa.

In this controversial, outspoken polemic, Ali (a Blackwoman) accuses the Blackwoman of undermining respect for the Blackman and thereby harming both him and her, as well as the Black family and Blacks in general. The Blackwoman is out of control, and the Blackman must regain and exercise authority. According to Ali, mothers teach their children disrespect for the Blackman, teenage girls manipulate boys, and adult women are too undisciplined to stay in long-term relationships. The Blackman is a recovering slave whose recovery is often thwarted by the Blackwoman. Ali disapproves of Black-White relationships, and she finds the Blackwoman's behavior exacerbating Black problems. The book's thesis and the author's bluntness practically guarantee strong reactions.

649. Barbeau, Arthur E., and Florette Henri. **The Unknown Soldiers: Black American Troops in World War I.** Philadelphia: Temple University Press, 1974. xvii, 279p. illus. appendix. bibliography, 249-70. notes. index.

In a documented account, the authors vindicate the valor of black U.S. soldiers during World War I. Despite racism, hostility, and humiliation that were all too often officially sanctioned, black troops served their country well. The narrative is enhanced by period photographs, extensive notes, and a bibliography.

650. Bowser, Benjamin P., ed. **Black Male Adolescents: Parenting and Education in Community Context.** Lanham, MD: University Press of America, 1991. 352p. illus. bibliographies after many chapters. name and subject indexes.

Twenty-two contributors address what Bowser calls the most maltreated and underserved segment of the U.S. population—black, male adolescents. The 18 essays are divided into four sections: "Up Against the Odds" (the problems faced by black, male adolescents), "Families and Communities—Parenting," "Education for Survival and Success," and "Development of Cultural Identity." Robert Staples sets the keynote early in the volume by describing the treatment of young black males in the United States as a form of genocide. Walter Stafford shows how these young men are "sorted out" from the opportunities that lead to success. Accusations of racism quickly give way to grappling with solutions. In a rousing biographical account, Loften Mitchell describes how community coparenting can operate effectively to socialize young black men. Robert Fullilove and Mindy Fullilove reach the surprising conclusion that AIDS may save the black community by forcing sexual responsibility on young people. Daphne Muse provides a reading list for young black people, and Peter Harris calls for humane portrayals of black fathers. Bowser's conclusion ingeniously sums up the volume by quoting key passages under two headings: "Crucial Insights," and "What Can Be Done." Many of the contributors tackle the grave difficulties facing young black men with verve, courage, and imagination.

651. Brod, Harry, ed. **A Mensch Among Men: Explorations in Jewish Masculinity.** Freedom, CA: Crossing Press, 1988. xv, 191p. notes. pa.

This is the first book about Jewish men as Jewish men, Brod writes. The 21 essays, according to Brod, examine both gender and ethnicity. The foreword by Letty Cottin Pogrebin tells of her charismatic but distant father who "betrayed" her by remarrying after her mother's death. In the introduction, Brod also tells of his father, a survivor of the Holocaust, who evidently was wounded by his son's movement away from Orthodox Judaism. Both the introduction and the book itself reflect Brod's pro-feminist, gay-affirmative stance. Selections are divided into four sections: Jewish male identities; fathers and sons; anti-Semitism, sexism, and heterosexism; and men's movements and social activism. Essays include Chaim I. Waxman's survey of Jewish fatherhood from the Rabbinic-Talmudic period to the present, and Barry Dov Schwartz's survey of Jewish views of homosexuality. As a Jewish father, Zalman Schacter-Shalomi agonizes over his infant son's circumcision—and then rationalizes it. An emotionally strained article by Andrea Dworkin links the Holocaust with rape, and Bob Gluck's essay on battered Jewish women ignores the topic of battered Jewish men. Two essays consider the fictional Jewish characters of Philip Roth, and a poem by Morris Rosenfeld (1862-1923) describes a working father's wish for shorter hours so that he can enjoy his son. In the final essay, Brod advocates a Jewish male feminism.

652. David, Jay, and Elaine Crane, eds. **The Black Soldier: From the American Revolution to Vietnam.** New York: William Morrow, 1971. 248p.

In the introduction to this anthology, the editors point out that the black soldier has always waged two wars simultaneously—one against the common U.S. enemy and one against U.S. racism. The 18 selections in this book illustrate the point vividly. Selections start with James Roberts's narrative of a black soldier in the Revolutionary War and end with Jon Nordheimer's account of a black Vietnam soldier who won the Congressional Medal of Honor and who died of gunshot wounds in Detroit. Other items include extracts from Thomas Wentworth Higginson's record of a black regiment in the Civil War, William Leckie's report of the Buffalo Soldiers (a black cavalry unit on the Western frontier), Arthur Little's story of black soldiers overseas in World War I, and Sammy Davis, Jr.'s autobiographical account of his encounter with racism in the army during World War II.

653. Duneier, Mitchell. **Slim's Table: Race, Respectability, and Masculinity.** Chicago and London: University of Chicago Press, 1992. 192p. illus. notes. pa.

Neither U.S. journalists nor sociologists have done justice to the diversity and integrity of black males, Duneier argues. To demonstrate the point, he describes the black (and white) males who gather regularly at the Valois Cafeteria, a Greek restaurant in south Chicago. His portraits of the men do not match the stereotypes. The black men show a compassion, integrity, and ability to cope, qualities that seldom find their way into media accounts or academic studies. In their relationships with women, for example, the men do not fit the oppressor stereotype popularized in works like *The Color Purple*. Although sociology has led Americans out of the Dark Ages of prejudiced thinking about black men, it still needs to reassess its images of them as dysfunctional men.

654. Gary, Lawrence, ed. **Black Men.** Newbury Park, CA: Sage Publications, 1981. 295p. bibliography after each chapter. pa.

Sixteen essays, plus an introduction and a conclusion, depict issues of U.S. black men. Essays are divided into four parts. In part 1, two essays by Gary summarize the African-American man's situation in the United States. Problems range from being undercounted by census takers to experiencing higher rates of mortality, fewer educational opportunities, and lower earnings. (To avoid hostility between black men and women, essays in the volume tend to compare black and white males, rather than enumerate black women's gains and black men's losses. The authors do not consider whether they are thus fostering hostility between black and white males.) Part 2, which examines African-American men and their families, opens with two essays indicating strain in black male-female relationships. Other essays discount stereotypes of African-American fathers as uninvolved in family matters, although highly demanding fathers can take a toll by showing little warmth to children. Leo E. Hendricks examines black, unwed fathers and suggests ways of helping them. Part 3, examining psychological and social coping patterns, contains four essays painting a dismal picture of stress, inadequate support systems, alcohol, and suicide among African-American men. The five essays in the final section, on black men and institutions, depict the disadvantages to black men found in education from grade school to college, in prisons and in the judicial system, and in social services. Despite the positive effects of the black church, according to James E. Tinney, it too can affect black men negatively. The volume convincingly portrays African-American men as penalized by both race and gender in U.S. society.

655. Gibbs, Jewelle Taylor, Ann F. Brunswick, Michael E. Connor, Richard Dembo, Tom E. Larson, Rodney J. Reed, and Barbara Solomon. **Young, Black, and Male in America: An Endangered Species.** Dover, MA: Auburn House, 1988. xxxiii, 377p. bibliography after each chapter. index. pa.

The seven authors contribute 10 solid chapters covering numerous aspects of young black males as an endangered species in U.S. society. In the opening chapter, Gibbs outlines the social, economic, political, and educational pitfalls facing young black man. Reed next examines the educational scene in greater detail and recommends changes. In chapter 3, Larson explores employment and unemployment among young black males. In the following chapter, Dembo examines delinquency and victimization among adolescent black males, and Brunswick's chapter is devoted to drug use. Connor examines teenage fatherhood. In two separate chapters, Gibbs analyzes physical and mental health and early male death among blacks. Solomon discusses varying effects of public policy upon young black males, and Gibbs concludes the volume with a series of recommendations.

The consistently high level of scholarship makes this book essential reading for understanding the crisis facing many young black men.

656. Gilder, George. **Visible Man: A True Story of Post-Racist America.** New York: Basic Books, 1978. xiii, 249p.

On one level, Gilder's book recounts the story of Mitchell (Sam) Brewer, a black man accused of raping a white woman in Albany, New York. On another level, it is a conservative's tale of how black masculinity and the black family are being destroyed by welfare in a "post-racist" United States. Gilder depicts life on Clinton Avenue, a region of black women on welfare, idle and often-violent black men, fatherless children, winos, and white women—often welfare mothers and sometimes prostitutes, lesbians, or both. Because their earnings cannot compete with welfare benefits, the men drift from one welfare woman to another, fathering children who will never know them for long as a father in the house. "Unlike virtually all human societies known to anthropologists," Gilder observes, "America does not offer virility rites. This society does not wish to acknowledge that boys have special problems of sexual passage. . . . Without such opportunities, boys all too often resort to the lowest terms of masculinity: sexual violence." When Brewer finds himself facing a rape charge from a white lesbian who apparently supports herself and her lover by occasional prostitution, his trial becomes a *cause célèbre* involving the Albany Rape Crisis Center, lesbian activists, and an overeager female assistant district attorney. Although Brewer is acquitted of the rape charge, his future is hardly bright as he returns to Clinton Avenue to join the ranks of violent male castoffs. "Poor black males," Gilder comments, "do not get brought up by fathers, socialized by marriage, or regulated by breadwinning." Unlike the "invisible" middle-class black males who help to hold families together, these are the "visible men" whose masculinity has been eroded by well-meaning but shortsighted vendors of poverty "aid" and welfare "rights."

657. Howe, Irving, with Kenneth Libo. **World of Our Fathers.** New York and London: Harcourt Brace Jovanovich, 1976. xx, 714p. illus. bibliography, 685-93. notes. index. Reprint, New York: Bantam Books, 1981. pa.

In this massive social and cultural history, Howe charts the journey of 2 million east-European Jews who, starting in the 1880s, migrated to the United States, settled mostly in New York's East Side, established a rich Yiddish culture there, and then dispersed to other locales of the U.S. landscape.

658. Kingston, Maxine Hong. **China Men.** New York: Alfred A. Knopf, 1980. 310p. Reprint, New York: Ballantine Books, 1980. pa. Reprint, New York: Vintage Books, 1989. pa.

In impressionistic prose, Kingston recreates the stories of her male ancestors and other China Men who left their homeland to labor in Hawaiian cane fields, build railroads in the Sierra Nevada mountains, work the gold fields of Alaska, and establish families on the U.S. mainland. From thence, sons issued forth to fight with U.S. troops on World War II battlefields, in Korea, and in Vietnam. Kingston's initial tale of a man painfully transformed into a woman, however, sounds a note of misandry that recurs throughout the book.

659. Liebow, Elliot. **Tally's Corner: A Study of Negro Streetcorner Men.** Boston: Little, Brown, 1967. xvii, 260p. appendix. bibliography, 257-60. pa.

A superbly written study, *Tally's Corner* recounts the activities of a group of black streetcorner men in inner-city Washington, D.C. By looking closely and humanely at their lives, Liebow is able to offer rare glimpses of poor or marginally poor urban, black males—the "losers" in our society. Such men have often been overlooked by scholars and social workers, the author contends, because it is assumed that "able-bodied" males neither need nor deserve social support. Liebow demonstrates the complex connection between men and work: The jobs available to them are sometimes beyond their physical ability, the pay is often too low to support a family, and frequently the work is temporary. The men often lack hope for the future; in time they quit or drift away. The job fails the man, and the man fails the job. Liebow describes the range of father absence and presence in families, noting that fathers who feel they have failed their families drift away from them. Marriages and consensual unions are familiar in this world. Although the men frequently talk against marriage, they consider it a necessary rite of passage into manhood. The breakup of marriages is often attributed by the men to male infidelity, but the man's inability to meet the demands of being head of the family is another likely cause. Similarly, the men talk about themselves as "exploiters" of women, but much of this talk may be crowing to cover up failure. An elaborate and shifting network of friends helps the men cope with the hardships of their lives. In a concluding chapter, the author discusses better employment as one of the needs to upgrade the lot of streetcorner men. The appendix describes how the white author conducted field work among black streetcorner men; like the rest of the book, it is a fascinating human drama.

660. Madhubuti, Haki R. **Black Men: Obsolete, Single, Dangerous? Afrikan American Families in Transition: Essays in Discovery, Solution, and Hope.** Chicago: Third World Press, 1990. ix, 274p. bibliography after each chapter. pa.

Because racism deforms black men in America, Madhubuti rejects the stereotype of them as the clowns-criminals of society. To confirm their greatness, black men must develop a "revolutionary" mentality that espouses self-discipline, integrity, rejection of sexism directed against black women, love of book-learning and education, cultivation of family values, investment in the black community, and a sensitivity towards black art and culture. Madhubuti deplores the scarcity of positive father figures in the black community, as well as the lack of Afrikan initiation rites to induct boys into strong masculine adulthood. These deficiencies create the destructive gangs found in many cities. Because reading is a crucial skill for young black males, he provides an extensive reading list of writings by blacks. He offers advice on how to live responsibly and healthfully, for healing antagonisms between black women and men, and for effective fathering. Madhubuti believes that black men are engaged in a war with white men in which there is no hope of peace or truce, because white males are oppressors by nature. He believes the AIDS epidemic is a human-made conspiracy to eliminate "undesirables." The book reveals some animosity towards Jews as an overly influential minority group. Madhubuti offers tributes to Malcolm X, Hoyt W. Fuller, and Bobby Wright.

661. Majors, Richard, and Janet Mancini Billson. **Cool Pose: The Dilemmas of Black Manhood in America.** New York: Lexington Books, Macmillan, 1992. xvi, 144p. bibliography, 127-35. notes. index. pa.

"It is much more difficult for the black man to enact the traditional male role successfully than it is for the black woman to establish a positive female role," the authors argue. Gender and racism combine to hinder black males from succeeding as providers and protectors. Consequently, black males are disproportionately victims of mental disorders, educational failure, early death, homicide, stress, alcoholism, drug use, and incarceration. As a survival tactic in a society that figuratively castrates black men, some black males resort to "cool," an in-control aloofness. Cool demonstrates the black male's social competence and offers him a form of pride. On the negative side, it can demonize even nondiscriminating white males as the black man's enemy. It can drive a wedge between black men and women, as the man holds himself aloof and seeks to dominate his partner. Cool can also be used as a weapon against "uncool" black males. The authors trace the origins of cool to West African *ewuare* and to the "masking" strategies of black slaves in America. They examine the expressive style of cool, the "cool cat" lifestyle, and the sometimes cruel game of playing the dozens. Majors and Billson present strategies for aiding black males, and they conclude that the new men's studies needs to broaden its scope and examine more closely the complexities of black male experience.

662. Majors, Richard G., and Jacob U. Gordon, eds. **The American Black Male: His Present Status and His Future.** Chicago: Nelson-Hall, 1993. xii, 372p. bibliography, 317-47. notes. name and subject indexes. pa.

The 21 essays in this solid collection explore areas of African-American male experience that have received comparatively little attention in the past. The anthology is divided into 5 sections: historical perspectives, present status of black men, search for empowerment, psychosocial development and coping, and the black male's future. Two essays by Clyde W. Franklin II are especially important for placing the study of black males within the academic framework of men's studies. James B. Stewart critiques neoconservative accounts of black males, e.g., those of George Gilder (entry 656) and Thomas Sowell. William L. Andrews traces the black man in American literature. Other essays critique the NCAA's Proposition 40, discuss AIDS and black men, and examine black male anger. Moving beyond stereotypes of black males, Manning Marable argues that the black man's best ally is the black woman. Although many of the essays are marked by frustrated anger at the widespread damage suffered by African-American males, the writers have positive suggestions for making the future better. Especially noteworthy on this count is Major's concluding article on reasons for hope concerning black males.

663. Paz, Octavio. **The Labyrinth of Solitude, The Other Mexico, Return to the Labyrinth of Solitude, Mexico and the United States, The Philanthropic Ogre.** Translated by Lysander Kemp, Yara Milos, and Rachel Phillips Belash. New York: Evergreen Books, Grove Press, 1985. 398p. pa.

No one has defined Mexican manhood more incisively than the poet and essayist Octavio Paz. In his classic work *The Labyrinth of Solitude* (1961), Paz describes the soul of Mexico, focusing on the men's sense of aloneness, or solitude, the sense of life lived behind a mask. The heart of Paz's account of Mexican males is in the chapter "Sons of La Malinche," where he examines concepts contained in words like *la chingada. Chingón* or *gran chingón* is the *macho*—active, violent, and something of a despoiler. *Chingada* refers to the feminine, the passive, the sufferer. The polarization is related to whether one identifies with the conquistadors or the conquered natives of Mexico. As Paz sees it, Mexican men are defensively *macho* because they are sons of *La Malinche,* the native woman who became Cortez's mistress and was later discarded by him. Yet, modifications of *macho* abound: Mexicans worship Christ as a suffering male, and the Virgin of Guadalupe is not identified with the violated feminine. While capturing the flavor of Mexican *macho,* Paz is also alive to its complexities and contradictions. In addition to *The Labyrinth of Solitude,* this volume contains other essays by Paz, including a retrospective interview (1985) concerning *The Labyrinth.*

664. Poinsett, Alex. **Young Black Males in Jeopardy: Risk Factors and Intervention Strategies.** New York: Carnegie Corporation, 1988. appendixes. 31p. pa.

Described as "Report of a Meeting Held at Carnegie Corporation of New York, February 11, 1988," this brief monograph touches on such matters as the young black male's struggle to define himself, early childhood and elementary school years, ways of expressing racial pride, and examples of effective intervention. The appendixes list the participants and the meeting's agenda.

665. Rogosin, Donn. **Invisible Men: Life in Baseball's Negro Leagues.** New York: Atheneum, 1983. xiii, 284p. illus. appendixes. index.

Rogosin recounts the history of black baseball greats in the days before the major leagues were integrated.

666. Sochen, June, ed. **The Black Man and the American Dream: Negro Aspirations in America, 1900-1930.** Chicago: Quadrangle Books, 1971. ix, 373p.

This collection of more than 70 contributions of nonfiction and fiction, shows how much black men wanted to share in the Horatio Alger dream of success rather than subvert it. On occasion, it also suggests the repercussions to black masculinity of a dream deferred.

667. Staples, Robert. **Black Masculinity: The Black Man's Role in American Society.** San Francisco: Black Scholar Press, 1982. 181p. notes. pa.

Without denying the validity of some women's grievances, Staples argues that "in the black community, it is the men who need attending to." Exploring the reality behind the image of the black male, Staples presents a disturbing picture of black men victimized by a virulent combination of racism and the masculine mystique. Shortchanged educationally and denied opportunities for life-sustaining and family-supporting work, the black man too often becomes the prey of exploitive capitalism, drugs, and suicide. Depicting the black community as an underdeveloped colony within the larger society, Staples explores the causes of high crime rates there and the socialization of young black males into numerous forms of violence. He discusses the "myth" of black sexual superiority, homosexuality, and the changing nature of male-female relations in recent times. The relationship between black men and white women is also reviewed. During the seventies, the promises of the civil rights legislation and black pride were fulfilled more for black women than for black men. "As it was," Staples notes, "the decade's flowering of black manhood turned into a withering away of what little supremacy they had and consigned many black men into a prison of their gender." In the eighties, black men may prove to be the first and only casualty of the women's movement as affirmative action schemes increasingly benefit white women rather than black men. Although sympathetic with many feminist issues, Staples criticizes some black feminists for directing their anger indiscriminately against black men, who are not always the cause of the women's difficulties. In the final chapter, Staples calls for a new unity between black men and women to forge their future together.

668. Teague, Bob. **Letters to a Black Boy.** New York: Walker, 1968. 211p.

In a series of letters to his infant son, Teague captures the mood of black men in the late sixties. Touching upon the militants and the visionaries in the black movement, Teague offers an apologia for his own less-activist stance. He recounts episodes from his life, especially his career in television broadcasting.

Everywhere in the letters—both explicitly and implicitly—is Teague's concept of what black masculinity should be.

669. Wallace, Michele. **Black Macho and the Myth of Superwoman.** New York: Dial Press, 1979. ix, 182p. index. Reprint, New York: Warner Books, 1980. pa. Reprint, London: Verso, 1990. pa.

Wallace addresses what she perceives as an increasing hostility between black men and women. Attempting to assert their manhood in a racist society, black men have embraced a misogynist macho ethic; meanwhile, black women have been stereotyped as superwoman—capable and castrating. These antithetical roles have set black men and women on a collision course.

670. Whyte, William Foote. **Street Corner Society: The Social Structure of an Italian Slum.** 4th ed. Chicago and London: University of Chicago Press, 1993. xx, 398p. illus. appendixes. bibliography, 390-92. pa.

In this classic study, Whyte describes the lives of men in the North Boston Italian community during the late 1930s. He provides a history of the neighborhood, followed by a distinction between "corner boys" and "college boys," as well as an overview of racketeering and politics. Whyte focuses first upon the Nortons, a streetcorner gang of men mostly in their twenties, led by Doc. Next he examines the college boy Chick Morelli and his club, contrasting Chick and Doc as representative of upwardly mobile and nonmobile Italian men. Whyte then describes racketeering and its connection with the Social and Athletic club, depicting the conflict between racketeer Tony Cataldo and corner boy Carlo Tedesco for control of the club. The interlinking of politics and streetcorner social structure is examined, and, in the conclusion, Whyte surveys his findings, offering a vivid reminder of how ethnic prejudice hampered Italians in their efforts to enter the U.S. mainstream. The first editions of *Street Corner Society* appeared in 1943 and 1955. The latest edition includes three appendixes. In the first, Whyte provides a personal account of his adventures while doing field work in North Boston; he describes his later relations with the corner boys and college boys of the study, and he tells of the book's rising and falling fortunes over the years. In the second appendix, Angelo Ralph Orlandella recounts how working with Whyte turned his life around. The third appendix contains a bibliography of Whyte's writings.

671. Wilkinson, Doris Y., and Ronald L. Taylor, eds. **The Black Male in America: Perspectives on His Status in Contemporary Society.** Chicago: Nelson-Hall, 1977. viii, 376p. bibliography, 361-69. notes. author and subject index. pa.

The popular image of the black male as "emasculated" by white society and by his matrifocal upbringing, as immature, and as a poor husband and father is examined in 24 scholarly, readable articles. Contributions are grouped into four sections: socialization to the black male role, stereotyping and stigmatizing of black males, the issue of interracial mating, and the black male's roles in postindustrial society. Highlights include essays by Ronald L. Taylor and Ulf Hannerz on growing up as a black male, Robert Coles on black fathers, William H. Turner's account of "myths" and stereotypes of the African man in America, Harry Edward's discussion of white fears of black athletes, Robert Staples's assault upon the "myth" of black matriarchy, Joan Downs's account of the political overtones of black-white dating, Nathan Caplan's description of the "new" ghetto male, and essays by Charles V. Willie and David A. Schulz on black fathers and black families. Many scholars regard this book as a necessary introduction to any study of black men.

Cross-References

See chapter 1, "Anthropology, Sociology."

171. Abbott, Franklin, ed. **Boyhood, Growing Up Male: A Multicultural Anthology.**

860. Black Elk. **Black Elk Speaks: Being the Life Story of a Holy Man of the Oglala Sioux.**

481. Bozett, Frederick W., and Shirley M.H. Hanson, eds. **Fatherhood and Families in Cultural Context.**

482. Bronstein, Pyllis, and Carolyn Pape Cowan, eds. **Fatherhood Today: Men's Changing Role in the Family.**

37. Brown, Claude. **Manchild in the Promised Land.**

6. Dann, Graham. **The Barbadian Male: Sexual Attitudes and Practice.**

785. Duberman, Martin, Martha Vicinus, and George Chauncey, Jr., eds. **Hidden from History: Reclaiming the Gay and Lesbian Past.**

175. Eastman, Charles A. **Indian Boyhood.**

343a. Ellison, Ralph. **Invisible Man.**

946. Fields, Rick. **The Code of the Warrior: In History, Myth, and Everyday Life.**

346. Forster, E. M. **A Passage to India.**

402. Franklin, H. Bruce. **Prison Literature in America: The Victim as Criminal and Artist.**

789. Galloway, David, and Christian Sabisch, eds. **Calamus: Male Homosexuality in Twentieth-Century Literature: An International Anthology.**

347. García Márquez, Gabriel. **Chronicle of a Death Foretold.**

348. Gold, Herbert. **Fathers: A Novel in the Form of a Memoir.**

795. Harry, Joseph, and Man Singh Das, eds. **Homosexuality in International Perspective.**

797. Hinsch, Bret. **Passions of the Cut Sleeve: The Male Homosexual Tradition in China.**

109. Hoch, Paul. **White Hero, Black Beast: Racism, Sexism and the Mask of Masculinity.**

329. Ihara Saikaku. **The Great Mirror of Male Love.**

47. Kantrowitz, Arnie. **Under the Rainbow: Growing Up Gay.**

385. Keyes, Roger S. **The Male Journey in Japanese Prints.**

645. Kimmel, Michael S., and Michael A. Messner, eds. **Men's Lives.**

283. Kinmouth, Earl H. **The Self-Made Man in Meiji Japanese Thought: From Samurai to Salary Man.**

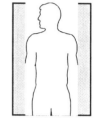

19

Patriarchy, Patriarchal Society

672. Amnéus, Daniel. **Back to Patriarchy.** New Rochelle, NY: Arlington House, 1979. 221p. notes. index.

In this negative response to the latest wave of the women's movement, Amnéus calls for a renewed patriarchalism that will strengthen the family. Widespread divorce has hurt women, children, and men. Custody decisions discriminate glaringly against fathers. Arguing that modern feminism encourages a victimizer-victim mentality, Amnéus scoffs at the "myth" of female oppression. Affirmative Action schemes upset the workplace imbalance caused by men's aggressive quest for financial means to support wife and children. "Free" child care will cost the taxpayers, and gay militants have strong-armed their way to legitimacy with the media and politicians. Amnéus gleefully trashes the myths of idyllic prehistoric matriarchies, and he argues that men's liberation must involve responsible fatherhood.

673. Engels, Friedrich. **The Origin of the Family, Private Property and the State.** 1884. Translated by Alick West. Rev. ed., edited by Michèle Barrett, New York: Penguin Books, 1985. 236p. appendixes. glossary. index. pa.

Engels's *Origin of the Family* remains the grandfather of all attacks on patriarchy and the father-involved family. Although the book can no longer be taken seriously as an anthropological work, its powerful rhetoric has long instigated strong anti-male and anti-father sentiment. Drawing upon and distorting Lewis Morgan's *Ancient Society* (1877) and J. J. Bachofen's *Das Mütterrecht (Mother-Right*, 1861), Engels created a misandric myth disguised as a scientific treatise. According to Engels, early societies were happily communal, promiscuous, and mother-centered. But male greed for surplus property destroyed these edenic societies. To bequeath property to their sons, males/fathers destroyed mother-right and the ancient gens. In their place, men introduced the oppression of women by the means of the patriarchal and monogamous families, slavery, polygyny, prostitution, private property, and the oppressive State to maintain the whole system. In short, class and sexual oppression are simultaneous. Thus, the fall of humanity was due entirely to male greed, the source of all social evils. The book's stirring rhetoric ("The overthrow of mother right was *the world historical defeat of the female sex*") has long fired up Marxist-feminist anger against men, and its stereotyping of father as tyrant anticipates much current anti-monogamy, anti-family rhetoric. Discredited as an historical or scientific text, *The Origin* still exercises great influence as a misandric diatribe.

674. Figes, Eva. **Patriarchal Attitudes: Women in Revolt.** New York: Stein and Day, 1970. 191p. bibliography, 188. notes. index.

Women are shaped by men, Figes argues, reciting a familiar litany of complaints against males as women-hating oppressors from prehistory to the present. Women collude in their own oppression, Figes admits, but she pays little attention to mothers as the primary socializers of children. While frequently citing Margaret Mead, Figes never mentions that, in *Male and Female* (entry 609), Mead explicitly rejects Figes's thesis that men are malicious conspirators and women are helpless dupes.

675. Goldberg, Steven. **Why Men Rule: A Theory of Male Dominance.** Chicago and La Salle, IL: Open Court, 1993. xiii, 254p. appendix. notes. index.

This updated and largely rewritten revision of *The Inevitability of Patriarchy* (1973) argues that physiology gives males an edge in attaining high status positions. As a result, patriarchy is universal throughout human history. Goldberg defines patriarchy as any hierarchical system in which the highest positions are held primarily by males. All societies value male attainment of high status positions, and male dominance or authority is the norm throughout human history. Debunking theories of prehistoric matriarchies, Goldberg argues that matriarchies (societies in which women hold suprafamily authority) have never existed. He insists that he is being purely descriptive not prescriptive, that is, he is merely presenting scientific evidence and drawing no political conclusions. Nevertheless, Goldberg as a biological conservative knows his viewpoint will offend "environmentalists" who regard gender roles as solely the product of social forces. Among the environmentalists are feminists who resist evidence that gender roles follow a physiological lead. Goldberg takes issue with Friedrich Engles (entry 673) and the "vulgarized Marxism" that attempts to treat women and men as separate classes. He argues with John Stuart Mill's *The Subjection of Women* and Kate Millett's *Sexual Politics* (entry 680) for attributing gender roles entirely to social forces while dismissing biological factors. Goldberg argues that sexual difference, however, does not translate into sexual "superiority" and "inferiority." He states that statistical averages do not justify discrimination against those who are exceptions to the norm. He believes that women are at the center of human society, and that males, as protectors of women and children, are marginalized and more expendable. He concludes that those who push women to compete with men on men's terms are pushing women to inevitable failure. Examining alleged exceptions to patriarchy in anthropological literature, Goldberg in the appendix concludes that the studies themselves actually support the universality of patriarchy.

676. Hearn, Jeff. **The Gender of Oppression: Men, Masculinity, and the Critique of Marxism.** New York: St. Martin's Press, 1987. xv, 239p. bibliography, 205-22. notes. author and subject indexes.

Hearn redirects Marxism away from economics and class politics to gender politics, because patriarchy preceded capitalism. Indeed, Hearn faults some Marxist and socialist feminists for not paying sufficient attention to gender as the primary form of oppression. Patriarchy is defined as "father right," and Hearn believes social revolution requires nothing less than the abolition of fatherhood. In Hearn's view, men are an oppressor class, even though individual men may attempt to destabilize patriarchy by revolutionary means. Hearn suggests (apparently seriously) that such means might include men's selling their sexual favors for money. Marx mistakenly focused on production; Hearn argues that the politics of reproduction (conception through child care)

244 / Patriarchy, Patriarchal Society

is paramount. He asserts that males completely control the social organization of reproduction. Moreover, men appropriate the products of women's reproductive labor (i.e., children) without recompense. (Hearn writes as if fathers never paid bills.) The solution is to turn reproductive power entirely over to women by such means as abortion on demand and 24 hour state-provided child care. In brief, capitalistic patriarchy should be replaced by socialist matriarchy. Fathers are undependable parents who can easily shift from nice to nasty. (Hearn writes as if there were no abusive mothers.) Because men are an oppressor class, any men's organizations are inherently threatening. Because fatherhood is oppressive, recent celebrations of its importance are reactionary. Hearn believes that men will become more responsible for children once they have renounced fatherhood. Instead of being fathers, men should seek to become "sons within a possible matriarchy." On the subject of men's studies, Hearn believes that their major task is a critique of men in the light of feminism.

677. Hey, Valerie. **Patriarchy and Pub Culture.** London and New York: Tavistock, 1986. 84p. (Social Sciences Paperback, no. 323). illus. bibliography, 77-78. notes. name and subject indexes. pa.

British pubs are not friendly neighborhood establishments. According to Hey, they are political spaces created by patriarchy in which the battle of the sexes has been raging since Victorian days. Most of the book's "evidence" consists of a heavy use of the passive voice to hint at a male conspiracy and of Hey's ingenuity in misconstruing anything into a patriarchal plot. Simply because a man once made an unwanted pass at Hey in a pub, she concludes that pubs are patriarchal enclaves privileging male desire. Hey's thesis may have merit, but her treatment of it invites disbelief. Although the book is a revised version of an MA dissertation, it is difficult to imagine its methodology passing muster in a high school report.

678. Kaufman, Michael, ed. **Beyond Patriarchy: Essays by Men on Pleasure, Power, and Change.** Toronto and New York: Oxford University Press, 1987. xix, 322p. illus. bibliography, 319. notes. pa.

In this collection of 15 essays, patriarchy is considered only as a social structure of male dominance that must be jettisoned. Kaufman's introduction indicates that the essays seek to balance the ways in which patriarchy hurts both women and men. Essays are divided into two sections. In section 1, "Masculinity, Sexuality, and Society," Kaufman's lead-off essay considers men's violence against women and men. In the only essay to consider the origins of patriarchy, Richard Lee and Richard Daly attempt to demonstrate that earlier societies were more egalitarian by citing evidence from the !Kung. Carmen Schifellite argues against biological determinism, and E. Anthony Rotundo examines patriarchal fatherhood (1620-1800) and modern fatherhood (1800-the present) in the United States. Kaufman and Gad Horowitz consider male sexuality and pornography (female use of pornography is not considered), and two essays by Gary Kinsman and Seymour Kleinberg examine the impact of out-of-the-closet gayness on heterosexuality. The longest essay, by Tim Carrigan, Bob Connell, and John Lee, reviews changing concepts of masculinity in recent years. In section 2, "Men, Work, and Cultural Life," Brian Easlea recounts his own disillusionment with male scientists and the military during the Cold War. Moving from the ivory tower to the shop floor, Stan Gray describes his efforts as a union shop stewart to integrate female workers into a male skilled workforce. Michael Kimmel examines the image of the cowboy in entirely negative terms, and Bruce Kidd sees little but anti-female sexism in sports. Robin Wood examines the homophobic subtext of the film *Raging Bull*, and Andrew Wernick sees narcissism in recent advertising images of men. In the final essay, Peter Fitting examines feminist utopian fiction for clues to the future. Having limited the definition of patriarchy to male-dominant structures, the contributors often seem to be beating a straw dummy. Alternate views of patriarchy (e.g., as social structures adopted to maximize the survival of the society) might have enriched the discussions.

679. Lerner, Gerda. **The Creation of Patriarchy.** New York: Oxford University Press, 1986. xvi, 318p. illus. appendix. bibliography, 283-303. notes. index. pa.

Branching out from her specialty in nineteenth-century history, Lerner attempts to explore the origins of patriarchy in prehistory. She depicts the creation of patriarchy as a process covering 2,500 years from the third millennium to 600 B.C. Relying heavily on Marxist-feminist ideology of male evil and oppression, Lerner's study usually reaches predictable conclusions: males "appropriated" female reproduction and symbol systems to subjugate women. The study uses heavily politicized prose, such as negative stereotyping of men and persistent use of the passive voice to suggest a male conspiracy against females. Special pleading is frequent. For example, Lerner sees sexism against women in the fact that early conquerors enslaved female captives but butchered male captives on the spot, and she mangles *The Odyssey* (entry 328) to fit a men-are-evil motif. Use of selective evidence is frequent: the argument that females suffered more than males from patriarchal societies ignores such considerations as the use of males as cannon fodder throughout history. *The Creation of Patriarchy* seems less an inquiry into prehistory than a political tract tailored to fit a radical feminist belief system.

680. Millett, Kate. **Sexual Politics.** Garden City, NY: Doubleday, 1970. Reprint, New York: Avon Books, 1971. pa. Rev. ed., New York: Simon and Schuster, Touchstone Books, 1990. xiv, 397p. bibliography, 364-77. notes. index. pa.

Controversial and enormously influential, Millett's study has redefined patriarchy for modern audiences. Chapter 2, "Theory of Sexual Politics," acknowledges that not all men hold power but attempts to demonstrate that males nevertheless constitute a powerful class of oppressors. Millett argues that, because most positions of power are held by men, males as a class are empowered. The argument is strained, but Millett (like her mentor, Friedrich Engels) musters powerful rhetorical forces to overwhelm doubts. She argues that the patriarchal conspiracy against women has been so pervasive that almost no one has noticed it. Millett, however, finds the ideology of male superiority to be ubiquitous. Like Engels (entry 673), she locates the root of oppression in the family, an institution whose demise she eagerly awaits. In more recent times, Millett finds a sexual revolution aimed at greater gender equality that extended from 1830 to 1930, only to be followed by a counterrevolution that lasted until 1960. The book closes with extended analyses of writings by D. H. Lawrence, Henry Miller, Norman Mailer, and Jean Genet. A grab bag of history, ideology, psychology, literary misreadings, and much else, *Sexual Politics* is laced with a toxic hatred of men as intrinsically evil beings. The revised edition contains a new introduction describing how the book was written.

681. Mount, Ferdinand. **The Subversive Family: An Alternate History of Love and Marriage.** London: Jonathan Cape, 1982. 282p. appendix. bibliography, 272-76. notes. index. Reprint, New York: Free Press, 1992.

Challenging current beliefs that history reveals a pattern of oppressed women subverting a patriarchal order, Mount argues that men and women together in the family have been the most subversive unit in human history, defying the worst that church and state, feudal lords and feminist zealots, Marxist and other ideologues could do to destroy it. Opponents of the family pass through a six-stage relationship with it. First, they attempt to devalue the family, then they reluctantly recognize its strength, and eventually they abandon efforts to replace it with alternate pseudofamilies. In the fourth stage, they reach a one-sided peace agreement with the family, and then they rewrite history to demonstrate that they were always its friend. Finally, the family imposes its own terms on its opponents. Dismissing "mass-media sociology myths" about the family, Mount contends that the nuclear family, far from being a modern invention, has been the norm throughout history; that romantic marital love existed before the troubadours sang the praises of adultery; and that divorce, no great novelty in the past, has long been an integral part of family law and is an indication of marriage's popularity. Mount insists that, for the most part, the Christian church has been no friend to the family, that the state is usually jealous of the allegiance the family commands and tries to weaken it, that Marxists have tried unsuccessfully to break the power of the family, and that modern feminists who began by attacking the family as a source of oppression are now beginning to perceive its strength and are (sometimes reluctantly) trying to come to terms with it. Because *The Subversive Family* offers such a heady critique of standard theories predicating "patriarchal oppression" by means of the family, its belated publication in the United States (with a new, brief preface) is a welcome event.

682. Walby, Sylvia. **Theorizing Patriarchy.** Cambridge, MA: Basil Blackwell, 1990. viii, 229p. bibliography, 203-22. notes. index.

In opposition to those who reject the concept of patriarchy as ahistorical, Walby argues that only the forms of patriarchy change over time. She defines patriarchy as "a system of social structures and practices in which men dominate, oppress and exploit women." Women are exploited in six "structures": in the family, in the labor market, in the state (which is capitalist, racist, and anti-female), in male violence against women, in "compulsory heterosexuality" with its sexual double standard, and in cultural institutions. In separate chapters, Walby examines feminist theorizing about patriarchy in these structures. She concludes that (in Britain at least) the change from private to public patriarchy has liberated women from domestic tyranny but left them free to be tyrannized in the larger world. The discussion makes large assumptions. Walby takes the dark side of patriarchy as the whole of it. She accepts uncritically the conviction that a power struggle is the most salient feature of gender relations. Selective attention to evidence is apparent. Walby asks why some men molest children but does not ask why some women molest children. (Does she believe that only men molest children?) Her analysis of feminist theory is clearly written and well organized, but the theory itself is narrowly closed, suspiciously misandric, and utterly divorced from men's experiences.

Cross-References

See chapter 8, "Feminism."

73. Amneus, Daniel. **The Garbage Generation** ....

883. Bakan, David. **And They Took Themselves Wives: The Emergence of Patriarchy in Western Civilization.**

885. Bloesch, Donald G. **Is the Bible Sexist? Beyond Feminism and Patriarchalism.**

597. Brittan, Arthur. **Masculinity and Power.**

396. Claridge, Laura, and Elizabeth Langland, eds. **Out of Bounds: Male Writers and Gender(ed) Criticism.**

96. Farrell, Warren. **The Myth of Male Power: Why Men Are the Disposable Sex.**

102. Gilder, George. **Men and Marriage.**

503. Hearn, Jeff. **Birth and Afterbirth: A Materialist Account.**

279. Hearn, Jeff. **Men in the Public Eye: The Construction and Deconstruction of Public Men and Public Patriarchies.**

702. Hopcke, Robert H. **Men's Dreams, Men's Healing.**

867a. Judy, Dwight H. **Healing the Male Soul: Christianity and the Mythic Journey.**

281. Keuls, Eva C. **The Reign of the Phallus: Sexual Politics in Ancient Athens.**

523. Louv, Richard. **FatherLove: What We Need, What We Seek, What We Must Create.**

526. Mackey, Wade C. **Fathering Behaviors: The Dynamics of the Man-Child Bond.**

122. Men Against Patriarchy. **Off Their Backs ... and on our own two feet.**

893. Miller, John W. **Biblical Faith and Fathering: Why We Call God "Father."**

711. Mitscherlich, Alexander. **Society Without the Father: A Contribution to Social Psychology.**

712. Monick, Eugene. **Phallos: Sacred Image of the Masculine.**

717. Pedersen, Loren E. **Dark Hearts: The Unconscious Forces That Shape Men's Lives.**

878. Perry, John Weir. **Lord of the Four Quarters: Myths of the Royal Father.**

291. Roper, Michael, and John Tosh, eds. **Manful Assertions: Masculinities in Britain Since 1800.**

421. Ruderman, Judith. **D. H. Lawrence and the Devouring Mother: The Search for a Patriarchal Ideal of Leadership.**

25. Sanday, Peggy Reeves. **Female Power and Male Dominance: On the Origins of Sexual Inequality.**

624. Tiger, Lionel. **Men in Groups.**

902. Visser't Hooft, W.A. **The Fatherhood of God in an Age of Emancipation.**

880. Vogt, Gregory Max. **Return to Father: Archetypal Dimensions of the Patriarch.**

439. Yaeger, Patricia, and Beth Kowaleski-Wallace, eds. **Refiguring the Father: New Feminist Readings of Patriarchy.**

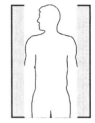

20

Psychology

Books in this chapter focus on the psychology and the counseling of males. Readers should also see chapter 15, "Masculinity," and chapter 23, "Spirituality."

683. Allen, Marvin, with Jo Robinson. **In the Company of Men: A New Approach to Healing for Husbands, Fathers, and Friends.** New York: Random House, 1993. xix, 236p. notes. appendix. Reprint, as *Angry Men, Passive Men: Understanding the Roots of Men's Anger and How to Move Beyond It.* New York: Fawcett Columbine, 1994. pa.

Beginning with his own experiences, Allen describes the personal and social blocks that keep men from psychological healing. Boys are socialized to repress emotion; the protector role, in particular, does not allow them to exhibit strong feelings. Dysfunctional fathers and mothers can produce sons who can express only destructive rage and not positive anger. Allen describes the price men often pay for love. In part 2, Allen narrates his dissatisfaction with traditional methods of counseling. These methods seemed only to alienate men. He recounts how he devised new methods of therapy that included group sessions and "rage work." As an adjunct to therapy, he created Wildman Gatherings. In contrast to some lurid media accounts of such sessions, Allen retells often-moving case histories of men transformed by them. He closes the book with chapters on healing male-female relationships, making peace between parents and children, and creative masculinity. The appendix contains a valuable listing of men's centers and organizations, men's publications, and men's retreats and seminars.

684. Baraff, Alvin. **Men Talk: How Men Really Feel About Women, Sex, Relationships, and Themselves.** New York: Plume, 1992. xiii, 269p. pa.

The founder of MenCenter in Washington, D.C., Baraff records 24 sessions of a men's therapy group. The reader is introduced to six men, listens in on their stories, and soon becomes absorbed in the drama of their lives and their interactions with each other. As the men talk about their fears, problems, and angers, they also exchange banter and insults with each other and with Baraff. After each session, Baraff supplies a brief interpretation, pointing out what is happening behind the men's words and indicating recurring themes in the sessions. Such themes include men's fear of therapy, avoiding feelings, the man's "biological clock," impotence, yearning for missed fathers, "shadow" mothers, and loneliness in a relationship. Baraff's book makes one feel personally close to the men, and his observations convey warmth and wisdom.

685. Bolen, Jean Shinoda. **Gods in Everyman: A New Psychology of Men's Lives and Loves.** San Francisco: Harper & Row, 1989. xiv, 338p. appendix. bibliography, 327-31. notes. index. pa.

A sequel to Bolen's *Goddesses in Everywoman*, this book employs images from the ancient Greek pantheon to describe recurring archetypes in men. Bolen envisions a new psychology of men aimed at overcoming the father-son hostility so prevalent in Greek and other ancient myths. For the book's central chapters, Bolen employs a "spiral" pattern that moves from a description of the god, to his corresponding masculine archetype, to problems surrounding the archetype, and to methods of growing with the archetype. Accounts of father-god archetypes—Zeus, Poseidon, and Hades—are followed by descriptions of son-god archetypes—Apollo, Hermes, Ares, Hephaestus, and Dionysus. All the archetypes have positive and negative potentials. The final section considers how men can "re-member" themselves by rediscovering parts of the self that they have lost or repressed. Only by reviving Metis, the lost Mother goddess, can men recover their feminine. The appendix offers a who's who of Greek mythology; a chart connecting gods and archetypes is also included. Bolen tends to see mostly the negative aspects of patriarchy, to overrate men's power in patriarchal societies, and to underrate women's advantages in them. Ultimately, she sees men achieving wholeness by discovering the feminine and not the deep masculine.

686. Bowskill, Derek, and Anthea Linacre. **Men: The Sensitive Sex.** London: Frederick Muller, 1977. vii, 150p. pa. Reprint, Los Angeles: Brooke House, 1977.

This exercise in popular psychology offers observations on such topics as impotence, the current battle of the sexes, fantasy and masturbating, gender role traps, and therapy. Discussion is sometimes marred by trendy misandry.

687. Chesler, Phyllis. **About Men.** New York: Simon and Schuster, 1978. xx, 283p. illus. bibliography, 265-81. Reprint, New York: Bantam Books, 1979. pa. Reprint, San Diego, CA: Harcourt, 1989. pa.

In this "multidimensional" approach to the psychosexual bases of male personality, part 1 presents mythopoetic interpretations of selected works of art. In stanzas of prose-poetry, Chesler touches upon infanticide and cannibalism as the masculine "original sin," uterus envy, the conflict between sons and mothers, phallic sexuality, and male-male violence. In part 2, the author provides vignettes from her relationships with men—with her Jewish father who drove a truck in Brooklyn; with her first husband, a Moslem, who took her home to a patriarchal family and society in central Asia, where their marriage deteriorated; with an assortment of lovers who were always imperfect in some way; and with various teachers, supervisors, and colleagues who usually exhibited some masculine psychic malady. In part 3, "An Essay About Men," Chesler reinterprets the oedipal drama to show the son learning how to placate a threatening, rejecting father through fear and performance. She discusses male sexuality as compulsive and egocentric, and she reverts to the topic of male-male and male-female violence. An epilogue contains horror stories of male violence gleaned from the newspapers. Chesler's professed compassion for humanity is belied by her animosity toward the male half of the human race and by her almost entirely negative assessment of masculine psychosexuality. Reader reaction to *About Men* is likely to range from those who regard the book as an imaginative descent into the lower depths of the male psyche, to those who regard the book as a slick example of anti-male hate literature welling up from the lower depths of Chesler's psyche.

688. Corey, Michael Anthony. **Male Fraud: Understanding Sexual Harassment, Date Rape, and Other Forms of Male Hostility towards Women.** Nashville, TN: Winston-Derek, 1992. xi, 119p. bibliography, 113-16. notes. index. pa.

In this exercise in pop psychology, Corey locates the source of male hostility towards women in the Macho Ideal, which he believes is the product of a patriarchal belief in male superiority. Dependence upon females and anger at being rejected by them also foster male hostility. Readers may find Corey's observations uneven, ranging from the simplistic to the perceptive. The book describes the negative Macho Ideal at length but lacks an effectively envisioned positive ideal to counteract it.

689. Dinnerstein, Dorothy. **The Mermaid and the Minotaur: Sexual Arrangements and Human Malaise.** New York: Harper & Row, 1976. xv, 288p. bibliography, 286-88. notes. pa.

Deliberately quirky and convoluted, this book argues that female domination of child rearing guarantees malaise in sexual arrangements. Because mother is the first denier of the infant's wishes, she bears the brunt of human disappointments with life. She becomes a "scapegoat goddess." The child must eventually react against her, the boy by bonding with his father and the girl by idealizing him. Male domination in society and the sexual double standard are accepted by both males and females because of a need to control female (i.e., mother's) will. But the flight from the female tyranny of childhood results in the acceptance of patriarchal tyranny later in life. By blocking male access to child rearing, mother domination deforms both sexes, shrinking the willful-executive propensities of women and the empathic-nurturant propensities in men. Only when both sexes participate in child rearing will the resulting imbalance in personality characteristics and social arrangements be remedied.

690. Drew, Jane Myers. **Where Were You When I Needed You Dad?: A Guide for Healing Your Father Wound.** Newport Beach, CA: Tiger Lily, 1992. vi, 202p. illus. bibliography, 194. pa.

The author, whose father died when she was 14-months old, has created a guide for healing the father wound. The guide is derived from her father-wound workshops. Those who experienced inadequate fathering or whose fathers were absent, distant, judgmental, or abusive are invited to mourn and release their pain. Through a series of exercises, Drew helps readers to reappraise their fathers, heal the child within, and become their own good father. Drew guides readers to find the wisdom in their wound, to reconnect with the father, and to build satisfying relationships. The illustrations are drawings made by participants in her father-wound workshops.

691. Earl, William L. **A Dancer Takes Flight: Psychological Concerns in the Development of the American Male Dancer.** Lanham, MD: University Press of America, 1988. xxvi, 143p. appendixes. bibliography after each chapter. notes. pa.

A former dancer, choreographer, and director, Earl is now a therapist. In this study, he raises questions about the link between male ballet dancers and neurosis. The image of Nijinsky has created a cliché of the male dancer as psychologically damaged "caged talent." Earl questions accounts of the madness that supposedly ended Nijinsky's career. He depicts the talented boy developing through symbolic, egocentric, sociocentric, and universalistic stages, and he concludes that male dancers are not significantly different from other self-driven male achievers. Addicted to excellence, these males do not come from a single type of family background, nor do they represent a single personality type.

692. Etheredge, Lloyd S. **A World of Men: The Private Sources of American Foreign Policy.** Cambridge: MIT Press, 1978. xv, 178p. illus. appendixes. bibliography, 157-67. notes.

Etheredge attempts to link mistakes in U.S. foreign policy to specific male personality characteristics. Because in the 1970s virtually all world political figures were male, he attempts to identify features of male psychology that contribute to such failures. Drawing upon a 1971-1972 State Department survey and other evidence, Etheredge finds that characteristics such as dominance, ambition, and competitiveness—all traits that assure male ascendancy—also produce a paranoid view of political "others." "Male narcissism syndromes" combine this paranoia with machismo to create a belief that one's country is a paternalistic benefactor of other nations. Etheredge presents a psychohistory of twentieth-century political decisions, linking historical particulars and personality types. He concludes that heroic ambition has its darker side and that the virtually all-male composition of world politics increases the likelihood of war.

693. Farmer, Steven. **The Wounded Male.** New York: Ballantine Books, 1991. xv, 223p. bibliography, 221-22. pa.

Farmer provides a self-help guide to a journey of healing for the wounded man. Weaving together autobiographical accounts and case histories, Farmer explores the various kinds of psychological and emotional wounds that males are likely to sustain. Wounding by father and mother is likely, and modern society wars against the expression of male emotion. With the aid of 34 exercises, Farmer suggests ways for men to open up emotionally, to find women as friends and lovers, and to cultivate male friendships.

694. Fine, George. **Sex Jokes and Male Chauvinism.** Secaucus, NJ: Citadel Press, 1981. 236p.

Long on examples and short on analysis, Fine's book stresses the misogynist character of many jokes. (Among the dozens of examples cited, however, many jokes ridicule males, many simply delight in being naughty, and many revel in women and sexuality.) Fine's indignation about an ill-defined group of "male chauvinists" is a trendy but threadbare response to the material he presents.

695. Fine, Reuben. **The Forgotten Man: Understanding the Male Psyche.** New York and London: Haworth Press, 1987. xvi, 423p. bibliography, 351-54. notes. pa.

"In the extensive literature on human and sexual liberation," Fine writes, "there is one startling omission: the psychology of the man." In psychoanalytic theory and practice, males are "the forgotten man." Fine argues that many dimensions of the male's psychic structure and psychology have been ignored. His discussion is divided into three parts: sexuality, aggression, and social role. In all three areas, he finds that many men are troubled. Sexual conflicts are ever present in male lives, from childhood to adulthood. The aggressive search for power can destroy males. Men who attain success in their social roles often experience a hollow victory that deforms them. Fine punctuates his discussion with vignettes of well-known men, ranging from Mozart to Gordon Liddy. His views are forthright, clearly presented, and sometimes so politically incorrect that they may offend some readers and delight others. As examples, he regards divorce proceedings as a legalized system for allowing vindictive wives to punish their ex-husbands, he regards homosexuality as a refuge from the demands of adult masculinity, and he sees women's liberation as heavily laced with misandry. In part 4 of the book, Fine argues that ours is a culture of hate (i.e., one in which hatred of others is cultivated as the norm); the solution is to foster a culture of love. Part 5 presents 10 discussion papers responding to Fine's views. The introduction by Herbert S. Strean emphasizes the failings of allegedly male-centered psychoanalysis to understand the male psyche and to grapple with male problems.

696. Fine, Reuben. **Troubled Men: The Psychology, Emotional Conflicts, and Therapy of Men.** San Francisco: Jossey-Bass, 1988. xv, 348p. (The Jossey-Bass Social and Behavioral Science Series). bibliography, 309-29. patient, name, and subject indexes.

Being regarded as the superior sex has left men with the dubious legacy of being regarded as the trouble-free sex. Fine argues that males experience at least as many psychological difficulties as females do. The primary audience for this book is therapists, and Fine's aims are to survey the problems that men present in psychotherapy and to suggest ways of handling those problems, to expound on the concept of the ideally normal man (an analytic ideal), and to provide examples of the working-through process that exemplifies Fine's psychodynamic perspective. Fine surveys the literature dealing with men's emotional problems and investigates the therapeutic principles of treating men. Two chapters devoted to men's problems of loving and sex include myths about harmful effects of masturbation, "premature" ejaculation, Don Juan behavior, difficulties caused by virgin-whore stereotyping, impotence, and overt homosexuality (which Fine believes departs from the analytic ideal for a man). Separate chapters discuss pleasure and pain (including self-destructive behaviors), the denial of feelings among men, men's roles in family (including childhood sexuality), social roles and the price that men pay for "success," self-image, work as a blessing or a curse, inexpressive men, and creative men, who often suffer from mental and emotional instability. The epilogue extols analytic-ideal therapy. Fine's discussion is often highly personal, opinionated, and thought provoking.

697. Fogel, Gerald I., Frederick M. Lane, and Robert S. Liebert, eds. **The Psychology of Men: New Psychoanalytic Perspectives.** New York: Basic Books, 1986. x, 310p. illus. bibliography after each chapter. index.

Freud left a rich but incomplete psychology of men, according to Gerald I. Fogel, and the aim of the 13 essays in this volume is to fill out that incomplete inheritance. Essays are divided into four sections. Part 1 essentially asks, what do men want from women? The answers vary. Male attraction to and fear of women is established wittily by George Stade in an essay on *Dracula*. John Munder Ross argues that the boy must recover both femininity and fatherliness to become a successful adult male, but Roy Schafer indicates that males feel compelled to struggle against sentimentality or "feminine" feelings. Ethel S. Person discusses the omni-available woman and lesbian sex in male fantasies. Part 2, on men's fears, introduces differences over homosexuality. In an essay offering a conceptual model of male perversion, Otto F. Kernberg concludes that "male homosexuality ... presents itself linked to significant character pathology." But, surveying the history of homosexuality from ancient Greece to the European Renaissance, Robert S. Liebert concludes that acceptance of homosexuality varies in different time periods. (In the book's final essay, Richard A. Isay argues that "efforts to change sexual orientation of gay patients is not clinically helpful.") Frederick M. Lane contends that both boys and girls can experience genital envy. Part 3, "Men Growing Up," contains Peter B. Neubauer's examination of the effects of fathering on both men and children. In an essay on adolescence, Eugene Mahon concludes that boys need to accept femininity to develop maturely. Part 4, on clinical treatment, contains articles on male-male and female-male analyst-patient dyads, as well as Isay's examination of homosexuality in homosexual and heterosexual men.

698. Freud, Sigmund. **The Standard Edition of the Complete Psychological Works of Sigmund Freud.** 24 vols. Edited by James Strachey, with Angela Richards. Translated by James Strachey, with Anna Freud, Alix Strachey, and Alan Tyson. London: Hogarth Press and Institute of Psychoanalysis, 1966-1974. illus. bibliography, notes, and indexes in vol. 24.

Freud's understanding of male psychology permeates nearly everything he wrote and has crucially shaped modern thinking about males, if only in some cases as a point of departure for disagreement. General readers may want to start with *An Autobiographical Study* (1925, 1935), in which Freud crystallizes his career and the history of psychoanalysis, thereby providing a concise introduction to both. Fuller understanding of Freud's view of the dynamics of the mind—including such matters as the Oedipus complex, repression, fixation, and the conscious and the unconscious—can be obtained from such shorter works as *Five Lectures on Psychoanalysis* (1910), *The Ego and the Id* (1923), and *An Outline of Psychoanalysis* (1940). This latter work shows Freud late in his career, rethinking the possibilities of his earlier formulations. For the larger implications of Freud's ideas, *Civilization and Its Discontents* (1930, 1931) provides a succinct statement of the cost that civilization exacts from the individual. Those interested in the ramifications of Freud's views of males may want to start with "The Most Prevalent Form of Degradation in Erotic Life" (1912), dealing with the boy's incestuous desires for his mother, and *Totem and Taboo* (1912, 1913), with its account of the "original sin" in the primal horde (the father is murdered by his sons who seek possession of females). Also, *Leonardo da Vinci and a Memory of His Childhood* (1910, 1919, 1923) shows Freud psychoanalyzing a famous man and "reading" several of his paintings. Individual paperback editions of many of Freud's works are published by W.W. Norton.

699. Gilmartin, Brian. **The Shy-Man Syndrome: Why Men Become Love Shy and How They Can Overcome It.** Lanham, MD: Madison Books, 1989. xi, 215p. appendixes. bibliography, 205-12. index.

Severe shyness is a major problem for millions of men, Gilmartin argues. Although many women also suffer from shyness, the trait is socially acceptable in a female and seldom prevents her from dating and marrying. The societal requirement that males must initiate and face rejection in social and sexual relationships creates momentous problems for shy men. Basing his conclusions on interviews with 500 love-shy men and 200 nonlove-shy men, Gilmartin examines the biological bases and cultural factors that induce shyness. Love shyness can be shaped by intrauterine antecedents, by family composition, and parenting practices. The all-male peer group can terrify and terrorize the shy boy. Some shy men become "male lesbians," heterosexual men who wish they were women. Gilmartin describes therapy for the love-shy and proposes solutions (e.g., society should encourage females to initiate socially; society should create co-ed scout groups) to reduce the problem.

700. Grinker, Roy R., and John P. Spiegel. **Men Under Stress.** 1945. Rev. ed. New York: McGraw-Hill, 1963. xii, 484p. bibliography, 461-63. index. pa.

In this classic study of the mental and emotional damage that combat can do to males, the authors present 65 case histories from their work with

World War II Army Air Force combat fliers. The concluding chapter examines implications for civilian psychiatry.

701. Hall, Nor. **Broodmales: A Psychological Essay on Men in Child-birth.** Introducing **The Custom of Couvade** (1929), by Warren R. Dawson. Dallas, TX: Spring Publications, 1989. ix, 173p. illus. appendix. bibliography, 151-61. index. pa.

Hall's 44-page introduction to Dawson's classic work on couvade updates analysis of the subject to recent times. Couvade, or practices of "male pregnancy," are worldwide and subject to numerous interpretations. Dawson collected a wealth of information about couvade from ancient, British, and American sources, but he regarded the practice as a curiosity from a bygone era of superstition. Hall, on the other hand, sees archetypal patterns in the various practices and invests them with multiple meanings, most positive but some negative. The concept of male brooding is a key image for warm, nurturing fatherhood. Fathers have been nursing infants for centuries, as archaeological evidence of "artificial" methods of milk feeding indicates. In some cultures, couvade is a ritual that prepares the male for fatherhood. In others, it is a means of invoking the "male mother." In some cases, couvade can become morbid, especially when males attempt to take over female pregnancy. Hall cites John Lennon's appropriation of Yoko Ono's pregnancy as his own. Hall concludes that modern attempts to deny or minimize female pregnancy in the name of sexual equality block males from a necessary understanding of and participation in pregnancy.

702. Hopcke, Robert H. **Men's Dreams, Men's Healing.** Boston and London: Shambhala, 1990. viii, 220p. bibliography, 207-10. notes. index. pa.

Distinguishing among dream work, dream analysis, and dream interpretation, Hopcke uses the dreams of two of his patients to illustrate current men's emotional and gender difficulties. The first patient, Pete, is homosexual; the second, Nick, is heterosexual. Influenced by radical feminist perspectives, Hopcke sees "patriarchy" and traditional gender roles as the principal problems facing modern men and women. Despite some feminist criticism of Jung's work, Hopcke finds great value in it. He links his patients' dreams with Greek mythology, and he often interprets them as political dramas in which patriarchy oppresses the feminine. For Nick, Hopcke urges the idea of liberating the feminine within. Pete's dreams, haunted by a Dark Young Man who develops into an Italian Father played by Al Pacino, point to the need for a redemptive father. Similarly, Nick's dream of unconventionally baptizing his daughter indicates the importance of fatherhood as a mode of physical and spiritual immortality. Given these interpretations, Hopcke's entirely negative view of "patriarchy" needs rethinking.

702a. Hudson, Liam, and Bernadine Jacot. **The Way Men Think: Intellect, Intimacy and the Erotic Imagination.** New Haven, CT, and London: Yale University Press, 1991. xii, 219p. illus. bibliography, 205-13. notes. index. pa.

The authors argue that there is a male-specific "wound" that predisposes males to think differently than females think. The tendency among some modern advocate-scholars to blur sexual differences has produced a "gender industry," culminating in what the authors call "Mead-plus-Marx." From this perspective, gender is largely determined by culture and can be re-engineered almost at will. Without subscribing to biological determinism, the authors argue that there is a gender-specific "male wound" created by the separation of the male from the feminine—and specifically from the mother. "Dis-identification" with the mother gives the male separateness; "counter-identification" gives him maleness. This male wound has costs and benefits. It can lead to personal insensitivity and misogny, but it also can energize males, give them a sense of freedom, and allow them to passionately pursue abstract reasoning, mathematics, science, and eroticized art. The authors elaborate on this idea, using biographies of famous men (e.g., Rilke, Ruskin, Newton, Skinner, Hardy, Degas, and Shakespeare). The discussion shines an intriguing—and controversial—light on numerous male tendencies, including superior mathematical skills and abstract thinking.

703. Johnson, Robert A. **He: Understanding Masculine Psychology.** Rev. ed. New York: Harper & Row, 1989. xi, 83p. bibliography, 83. pa.

Using the Holy Grail legend and the story of Parsifal as a starting point, Johnson examines masculine development in terms of Jungian psychology and religious meaning. The wounded Fisher King, for example, represents arrested male development that can adversely affect the whole community. Johnson extends his observations into everyday matters. He advises males not to be seduced by the inner feminine; rather, males are to serve the inner feminine. Parsifal is at first unable to heal the wounded king because Parsifal is still wrapped in the garment that his mother wove for him; in other words, he has not yet broken with the feminine as controlling mother. Johnson also comments on the current state of religion. For example, the Catholic doctrine of Mary's assumption into heaven completes the male-oriented Trinity with the feminine. Only after an arduous quest does Parsifal attain the knowledge that enables him to heal the wounded king and restore the kingdom. This revised edition fleshes out the story of Parsifal and updates the commentary. In this edition, healing the kingdom means healing the environment as well as renewing the psychological and spiritual life of the community.

704. Jung, C. G. **Aspects of the Masculine.** Translated by R. F. C. Hull. Edited by John Beebe. Princeton: Princeton University Press, 1989. xvii, 183p. (Bollingen Series). illus. appendix. notes. pa.

Jung's writings about men and the masculine are scattered throughout several volumes of his work, written at different times in his life. John Beebe has collected 19 works or excerpts that explore various aspects of the masculine. Section 1 contains two selections describing the Hero as an archetype of one stage of male development: Through initiation, the young Hero must break from the Mother's dominance. (Jung indicates elsewhere that the male must reconcile himself later in life with the feminine and thus return to the Mother.) The second section, dealing with initiation and the development of masculinity, contains four selections that range from a discussion of midlife transition to the *puer aeternus* as an infantile aspect of the self. Section 3, focused on the Father, contains excerpts from "The Significance of the Father in the Destiny of the Individual," as well as a study of the archetype of the Father. Section 4 attempts to identify Sol and Luna (sun and moon) as archetypes of the masculine and the feminine. The fifth section focuses on the masculine in women, and the sixth describes the anima as the feminine aspect of the male self. The final section contains Jung's reflections on Spirit, including his psychological readings of fairy tales and arcane alchemical symbolism. The figure of Mercurius, derived from ancient mythology and medieval alchemy, is especially important as an image of the archetypal masculine. Aimed at the educated lay reader, Beebe's introduction sets the selections within the larger context of Jung's work. The appendix lists the contents of 30 volumes of Jung's works published by the Princeton University Press. In Beebe's anthology, an index and clearer identification of the selections would have helped. "Though far from the only one possible," as Beebe himself admits, this selection provides a rich assortment of Jung's lifelong reflections on the masculine. The book is an important source, given the enormous influence of Jung's thought on the mythopoetic wing of the men's movement.

705. Jung, Carl G., M.-L. von Franz, Joseph L. Henderson, Jolande Jacobi, and Aniela Jaffé. **Man and His Symbols.** London: Aldus Books, Jupiter Books, 1964. 320p. illus. notes. index. pa. Reprint, New York: Dell, Laurel Books, 1968. pa.

For nonspecialists, this beautifully illustrated volume is perhaps the best introduction to Jung's psychology of men and women. It contains "Approaching the Unconscious," one of Jung's last and most clearly written summaries of his thought. Especially helpful for understanding Jung's concept of the female anima and the male animus is M.-L. von Franz's essay "The Process of Individuation." Readers should experience this exposition of Jung's vision in the Aldus edition, with its larger type and clear illustrations, many in color.

706. Kiley, Dan. **The Peter Pan Syndrome: Men Who Have Never Grown Up.** New York: Dodd, Mead, 1983. xxvii, 281p. bibliography, 275-81. Reprint, New York: Avon, 1984. pa.

Borrowing the name of James Barrie's "boy who would not grow up," this popular book defines the Peter Pan Syndrome as one that characterizes a large number of males who either cannot or will not assume adult responsibility. Sex role confusion, parental neglect, and social indifference often turn the oldest male child of a middle- or upper-class family into an irresponsible and irresolute charmer. "Girls have a license to actualize both the masculine and feminine sides of their personality," Kiley writes. "Boys don't have this same license." While girls have been given new scripts for their sex roles (sometimes with contradictory directives), boys are stuck with the same old script—or left without one to follow.

707. Lenfest, David. **Men Speak Out: In the Heart of Men's Recovery: Six Dialogues For, By, and About Conscious Men.** Deerfield, FL: Health Communications, 1991. xi, 196p. appendix. notes. pa.

Lenfest interviews six men who have taken a leading role in men's recovery efforts: John Lee, Ken Richardson, Robert J. Ackerman, Terry Kellogg, Mike Lew, and Pat Mellody. The discussion ranges over a wide number of topics, such as, wild-man weekends, hero roles, the mythopoetic men's movement, the spirituality of Southwestern Indians, 12-step recovery programs, co-dependency, alcoholism, males as victims of child abuse, Robert Bly, midlife crisis, and feminism. Yet a certain unanimity also occurs: each of the men believes that many males in the United States are severely damaged in the process of growing up and that these men need healing. "Men are abused," Terry Kellogg remarks. "We are taught about war, to play war, to be aggressive. . . . Then we get in trouble when we act it out."

708. Martel, Leslie F., and Henry B. Biller. **Stature and Stigma: The Biopsychosocial Development of Short Males.** Lexington, MA: Lexington Books, D. C. Heath, 1987. x, 117p. bibliography, 103-11. author and subject indexes.

Discrimination against the short male is, in John Kenneth Galbraith's words, "one of the most blatant and forgiven prejudices in our society." In this study of how stature (height) interacts with other factors to affect male behavior, Martel and Biller document the accuracy of Galbraith's observation. Being short can negatively affect the male's personality. Socially, the short male has greater difficulty with dating and fewer marriage choices. Both women and taller men negatively stereotype short men, a prejudice that appears to be universal. The authors describe their research and its results. Many college women in the project held strong negative views of short males, and short males had internalized the prevailing negative views. To compensate for shortness, many men adopt a defensive style. The authors offer advice to parents and clinicians on ways to offset the cultural prejudice. They speculate that shortness may be associated with childishness or lack of male maturity, and they urge an awareness of and resistance to the prejudice directed against short males.

709. May, Ronald J., and Murray Scher, eds. **Changing Roles for Men on Campus.** San Francisco: Jossey-Bass, 1988. 105p. (New Directions for Student Services, No. 42). bibliography after each chapter. index. pa.

An entry in the Jossey-Bass Higher Education series, this sourcebook presents eight articles discussing the counseling of male college students. Because most student affairs professionals have focused on female concerns, males are an "overlooked" and "at risk" population on campuses. In the lead article, Ronald J. May places male students' issues within a developmental framework. Other authors stress sex role strain as a source of college male discomfort about such matters as date rape, homophobia, and career choices. Gregg A. Eichenfield discusses "special populations" of men on campus, such as ethnic males, gay and bisexual males, international students, and adult male students. Fred Leafgren surveys developmental programs dealing with men's issues, and Beverly Prosser-Gelwick and Kenneth F. Garni discuss methods of counseling and psychotherapy that are likely to work with male students. The final chapter, dealing with resources, lists books, bibliographies, media resources, and organizations.

710. Meth, Richard L., and Robert S. Pasick, with Barry Gordon, Jo Ann Allen, Larry B. Feldman, and Sylvia Gordon. **Men in Therapy: The Challenge of Change.** New York and London: Guilford Press, 1990. xvi, 284p. notes. index. pa.

Psychology has been androcentric but gender blind, writes Ann Hartman in the foreword to this study of therapy and men's gender role changes in the United States. In the preface, the authors explain that Meth and Pasick began the book but, in a representative masculine bind, found themselves too busy to complete it satisfactorily. Calling in colleagues and friends, they produced a collaborative volume that is all the stronger for its collaboration. The writers are remarkably pro-male and sympathetic to masculine binds, an attitude that seems essential if therapy is to be helpful for men. In part 1, five chapters examine men in U.S. society, including hazards along the road to masculinity, work in men's lives, men as husbands, fathers and fathering, and male friendships. Unlike women who have large social support for voicing their dissatisfactions, U.S. men often lack a context to express theirs. Part 2 considers men and the process of change through therapy. Eight chapters are devoted to topics such as creating a framework for men's change, helping men understand themselves, men and mothers, men and fathers, and changing the nature of men's friendships. Barry Gordon and Jo Ann Allen contribute an outstanding chapter on helping men in couple relationships, capping a volume marked by superb insights into men and the nature of therapy.

711. Mitscherlich, Alexander. **Society Without the Father: A Contribution to Social Psychology.** Translated by Eric Mosbacher. New York: Harcourt, Brace, and World, 1969. xi, 329p. notes. name and subject indexes. Reprint, New York: Schocken Books, 1970. pa. Reprint, New York: Harper Perennial, 1992. pa. Original publication, published as *Auf dem Weg zur vaterlosen Gesellschaft* (Munich: R. Piper and Co. Verlag, 1963).

Aimed at an audience familiar with Freudian depth psychology, this influential study explores the breakdown of "paternal" and "paternalistic" authority in modern mass society, with the accompanying difficulties of maintaining individual freedom and responsibility in the restructuring of the social order. Mitscherlich touches on a wide range of topics, including the dynamics of adaptation, the need for human "re-education," roles and masks, and the concept of taboo. General readers will find most accessible chapter 7, "The Invisible Father," which discusses the effects upon modern society of father absence from the home, and chapter 12, "Two Kinds of Fatherlessness," which includes discussion of the mass leader as collective father figure: "surprising as it may seem, he is much more like the imago of a primitive mother-goddess . . . [who] demands a regressive obedience and the begging behavior that belongs to the behaviour pattern of a child in the pre-Oedipal stage." Indeed, terms like *paternal* and *paternalistic,* when applied to modern society, are misleading: "The nation is still referred to out of habit as *la patrie*, the fatherland, land of the fathers, etc., but the passive, demanding attitude to it betrays a deeper tie; it is nuzzled against as if it were a mother goddess with innumerable breasts." The 1992 edition contains a foreword by Robert Bly.

712. Monick, Eugene. **Phallos: Sacred Image of the Masculine.** Toronto: Inner Books, 1987. 141p. (Studies in Jungian Psychology by Jungian Analysts, No. 27). illus. bibliography, 133-35. notes. index. pa.

This brief, packed, thought-provoking, and influential study argues that both Freudian and Jungian theory and practice have been hampered by a failure to incorporate *phallos*, the archetypal masculine. As archetype, phallos must be distinguished from patriarchy, which Monick defines as male-dominated society. As the Present Consciousness of patriarchy disappears, masculinity itself is in danger of being atrophied. Although dominated by males, patriarchy has been no friend to phallos. The disjunction between religion and sex in the Western world has driven phallos underground. As Monick sees it, phallos is akin to a "god," a revelation and a religious experience that reveals itself to a man willy nilly. Phallos is autonomous and may not be fully controlled. Both Freud and Jung recognized the need for the young male to reject the Mother/Feminine, but both they and their followers over-emphasized the Mother as primal parent. It is time, Monick argues, for phallos to assume equal consideration as foundational psychic image in psychological theory and practice. Monick rejects the distinctions between lower and higher masculinity, although he recognizes a brutal shadow of phallos that expresses itself in sexual violence. He explores such images as the *axis mundi*, a key image of phallos, and he traces the phallic significance of such mythological figures as Hermes, Dionysus, Zeus and Ganymede, and (especially) Mercurius, Jung's protean image of phallos. In a closing chapter, Monick discusses two phallic dreams and the animus in women. The epilogue reemphasizes the importance of enthroning the archetypal masculine as a foundational component of psychotherapy and theory.

713. Mullahy, Patrick. **Oedipus, Myth and Complex: A Review of Psychoanalytic Theory.** New York: Hermitage Press, 1948. xix, 538p. bibliography, 532-38. notes. Reprint, New York: Grove Press, 1955. pa.

A crucial component in twentieth-century psychology of males, the Oedipus complex is surveyed in this volume. An extended review of the theories of Sigmund Freud, Alfred Adler, C. G. Jung, Otto Rank, Karen Horney, Erich Fromm, and Harry Stack Sullivan is followed by a complete translation of the three Oedipus plays by Sophocles.

714. Nowinski, Joseph. **Hungry Hearts: On Men, Intimacy, Self-Esteem, and Addiction.** New York: Lexington Books, 1993. x, 163p. notes. index.

Nowinski examines the topic of men and addiction. Defining addiction as an obsession that takes over one's life, he finds that more males than females become victims to such addictions as alcohol and drugs. The origins of addiction are not genetic but social: Over the past two centuries, Western society has imposed a hierarchical, rather than a relational, criterion of success upon men. Required to be tough and insensitive, men often split off emotions from their masculinity, leaving men insecure. To assuage this insecurity, many men become addicts. The tendency of some female psychologists to pathologize male behavior in general offers little help to men. Father absence in the modern home contributes to male insecurity. Nowinski introduces writing exercises to help male readers discover the origins of their low self-esteem. He examines the various ways in which men resist intimacy and explores means to break the pattern. He envisions a new, more androgynous man of the future who will be better able to express his emotions.

715. Osherson, Samuel. **Wrestling with Love: How Men Struggle with Intimacy with Women, Children, Parents and Each Other.** New York: Fawcett Columbine, 1992. 372p. notes. index. pa.

Men often have a conflicting desire for intimacy and a wish to avoid it. The current pressure on men to express their feelings is often fraught with mixed messages: the man may be punished for being vulnerable. Osherson examines the differences between guilt and shame: It is shame (i.e., failure to live up to one's ideals) that often leaves men tongue-tied. Using materials from his workshops, as well as extensive readings and his own experiences, Osherson indicates that the boy's need to separate from his mother may leave him with conflicted emotions. Bonding with the father, who may be a puzzle, can be difficult. Still, the "father hunger" of boys is powerful and can drive them on quests for substitutes for an absent father. Osherson examines the role of anger in men's lives and some men's need for autonomy even in interdependent relationships. In the latter half of the book, Osherson examines male relationships with various women in their lives (e.g., mothers and wives) and men's intimacy with their children and their own parents. He describes men's groups and the difficulties of intimate male-male sharing. The book closes with a portrait of the connected self. Osherson's warmth and understanding suffuse this compassionate study.

716. Pasick, Robert S. **Awakening from the Deep Sleep: A Powerful Guide for Courageous Men.** San Francisco: HarperSanFrancisco, 1992. x, 253p. bibliography, 252-53. pa.

Traditional masculine gender roles shut down men's feelings, leaving them in a "deep sleep" of emotional detachment. Noting that the worldwide roles for males are provider, protector, and procreator, Pasick describes how these roles work to separate men from their emotions. Drawing upon responses in a men's group, he explores how males can be affected by "deep sleep" fathers and the requirement that sons detach themselves from mothers. Noting that men have been raised to work and not to relate, he indicates that men are often distanced from female partners, their parents, friends, and even their own sexuality. In clear prose, Pasick offers guidelines for getting back in touch with feelings (especially grief and anger) and for healing alienated relationships.

717. Pedersen, Loren E. **Dark Hearts: The Unconscious Forces That Shape Men's Lives.** Boston and London: Shambhala, 1991. xiii, 247p. bibliography, 226-40. notes. index. pa.

In this intriguing work of Jungian psychology, Pedersen argues that if men are to become more positively individuated, they must encounter the anima—the dark heart, or substrate, of consciousness. Male fear of the feminine conflicts with the male need to encounter the feminine within. This anima is often a wounded woman held captive by the dark side of the masculine. To support this idea, Pedersen depicts a prehistory in which the Great Mother ruled. This matriarchal age is now often celebrated by some feminists who prefer to ignore its dark side. Males were often sacrificed to ensure the Great Mother's fertility. Pedersen reviews more recent initiation rituals, finding many of them to be painful manifestations of matriarchal sacrificial rites. Still, rituals and myths of initiation help to convey the male from childhood to adulthood, and the modern world is poorer without some rituals. Pedersen is critical of Freud's oedipal theories, which he regards as founded on erroneous anthropology and psychology. The patriarchal gods have negative aspects (e.g., the devouring gods like Ouranos and, to some extent, Zeus), and negative patterns of patriarchal behavior can be found in fathers who are authoritarian, passive, macho, incestuous, absent, and so on. The healthy father represents the positive aspects of patriarchy. Pedersen argues that the shadow side of the masculine is both collective and personal, and it can be fostered by culture. The positive side of the masculine is seen in the loving man who has integrated eros and phallos. Just as the ancient matriarchies were replaced by patriarchies, so now patriarchies are being replaced by a psychological androgyny that combines the masculine and feminine. Pedersen concludes by listing seven developmental issues that men now need to work on.

718. Pedersen, Loren E. **Sixteen Men: Understanding Masculine Personality Types.** Boston and London: Shambhala, 1993. x, 246p. appendix. glossary. bibliography, 233-37. notes. index. pa.

Drawing upon Jungian concepts of typology, Pedersen argues that an awareness of psychological types can provide benefits such as deeper understanding of the self, improved communication among different types, choice of appropriate therapy, and selection of suitable occupations. Pedersen defines the nature of psychological typology and constructs 16 "type profiles." Each of these types is examined and illustrated by a representative fictional character. Because men tend to be stronger in the thinking function, Pedersen provides suggestions for raising the feeling function. The appendix provides statistical information on the 16 types, and a glossary defines Jungian terms.

719. Rochlin, Gregory. **The Masculine Dilemma: A Psychology of Masculinity.** Boston: Little, Brown, 1980. xii, 310p. notes. index.

Rejecting the current trend of treating boys and girls alike, Rochlin presents a Freudian analysis of male psychology in which the boy's need to establish his masculine identity is prelude to the man's continuing effort to do so. "There are not only special difficulties in becoming masculine," Rochlin writes, "but also in maintaining it throughout life." In childhood, when the boy must differentiate himself from the feminine, his penis is a source of pride that lowers females in his estimate. Boys engage "naturally" in aggressive play, stimulated in part by mothers who live vicariously in their achievements. Drawing upon some of Freud's famous studies (e.g., those of Little Hans, Judge Schreber, and the Wolf Man), as well as case histories from his own practice, Rochlin examines the boy's fears of loss and abandonment, which are usually more severe than those of girls. He indicates the problems that can arise when boys and girls are naively regarded as possessing the same psychological makeup. In later chapters, Rochlin examines literary classics for example, *Gilgamesh* (entry 325), *The Iliad* (entry 327), *The Odyssey* (entry 328), *Tom Sawyer*, and *Lord Jim*. He also examines the phases of male youth and adulthood. Masculinity is depicted as "a precariously held, endlessly tested, unstable condition" that must be reaffirmed at each phase of a man's life.

720. Ross, John Munder. **The Male Paradox.** New York: Simon and Schuster, 1992. 350p. bibliography, 337-39. index.

The male paradox, Ross argues, is the male's attraction to the female and his need to differentiate from the feminine. Thus, women inspire conflicting responses from males. A clinical psychologist, Ross develops the premise with a series of imaginatively re-created case histories involving current male binds, sometimes with graphic sexual details. He shows men unwilling to examine male fears and resorting to womanizing as a form of running scared. He presents portraits of "men who love too much" being hurt by divorce and suffering as "ex-fathers." He sees gay men as suffering from father absence and a fear of losing their male selves in a woman. Other portraits include men facing failure (such as being fired), hindered by illness, or trying to cope with a "damaged" child. More than a dozen such cases are re-created. The penultimate section, "The Making of a Man," follows the development of Chuck Watson (perhaps an autobiographical pseudonym) from childhood to adulthood. The final section, "Men at Their Worst," examines cases of incest and child abuse.

721. Ruitenbeek, Henrik M., ed. **Psychoanalysis and Male Sexuality.** New Haven, CT: College and University Press, 1966. 268p. bibliographies after some chapters. notes. pa.

Although somewhat dated, the 14 articles in this collection also contain some thought-provoking observations. Contributions include Melanie Klein on early stages of the Oedipus complex, Karen Horney on the male dread of women, and Felix Boehm on the femininity complex in men. Other essays discuss such topics as initiation rites, the castration complex, phallic passivity in men, transvestism, and fetishism.

722. Sanford, John A., and George Lough. **What Men Are Like.** New York: Paulist Press, 1988. 315p. appendixes. bibliography after each chapter. notes. pa.

"In recent years there have been many books on feminine psychology, but few on masculine psychology," Sanford writes in the introduction. In clear prose, Sanford and Lough review the psychology of men from a Jungian and Christian perspective. After defining the concept of Jungian archetypes, the authors examine the role of play in boyhood. The tumultuous changes of adolescence in modern society are exaggerated by the lack of initiation rituals and spiritual values. They examine the problems of the egocentric Self. Employed work is described in terms of the senex and puer archetypes and the Olympian gods. Middle life is often a time of burnout in which individuation can renew the exhausted Ego. The authors stress the value of the feminine side of masculine psychology. Male-female and father-son relationships are explored. The final chapters examine the importance of symbolism in male fantasies, individuation in old age, and the anima as it appears in dreams, fairy tales, and myths (such as the story of Sir Gawain and the Green Knight). One appendix explains Jungian psychological typology; the other reads *Alice in Wonderland* as a symbolic account of adolescent development.

723. Scher, Murray, Mark Stevens, Glenn Good, and Gregg A. Eichenfield, eds. **Handbook of Counseling and Psychotherapy with Men.** Newbury Park, CA: Sage Publications, 1987. 400p. bibliography after each chapter.

An indispensable guide for mental health professionals, this volume brings together a wealth of information concerning the counseling of and psychotherapy with men. After an introductory survey of contemporary men by Joseph H. Pleck, the book presents 26 articles from distinguished experts exploring various aspects of men's counseling. Essays examine topics such as male counselors of men, female counselors of men, counseling men in groups, career counseling, counseling men about sexuality, griefwork with men, body-focused psychotherapy, training others to counsel men, counseling adolescent males, therapy with college men, and counseling aging men. Other articles consider counseling Asian men, African-American men, and Hispanic men. In a section on "special populations," separate articles examine counseling gay men, bisexual men, men in the AIDS crisis, single fathers, dual-career couples, men who batter, men in prisons, male substance abusers, veterans, physically challenged men, and men in health care settings. A final, brief essay pulls together themes in the book and indicates that men can benefit from counseling and therapy more than they have in the past.

724. Skovholt, Thomas M., Paul G. Schauble, and Richard Davis, eds. **Counseling Men.** Monterey, CA: Brooks/Cole, 1980. x, 213p. bibliography after each chapter. notes. index.

This book collects 18 articles about men's roles and their significance for the counselor. After an introductory overview of the men's movement and current men's issues by Thomas M. Skovholt and Art Hansen, the second section of the book assembles seven articles examining several aspects of men's awareness, including Joseph H. Pleck's discussion of men's power with women and other men and Robert A. Lewis's account of the roadblocks to emotional intimacy among men. Other essays examine what constitutes a definition of a competent male, the components of male heterosexual behavior, male homosexuality, and men's reluctance to undertake psychotherapy. The concluding section contains 10 essays on intervention: the problem of boys' behavior in "feminized" classrooms, special considerations in counseling black males, characteristics of and treatment of sex offenders, treatment of secondary impotence, healing the divided allegiance that men face between work and family ("The time has come to change the world outside the client," Michael Berger and Larry Wright conclude), the process of involving men in childbirth and bonding with children, a psychoeducational model for classes on fathering, fathers with child custody, helping men to cope with a child's death, and the male in marital and family therapy. Although compiled primarily for therapists and counselors, the material in this book is likely to impress other readers as both pertinent and enlightening.

725. Solomon, Kenneth, and Norman B. Levy, eds. **Men in Transition: Theory and Therapy.** New York and London: Plenum Press, 1982. xiv, 503p. notes. index.

An important distillation of current research and views on men's gender roles, the 20 essays in this volume provide insight and controversy. John Money's introduction makes significant distinctions among sex-irreducible roles, sex-derivative roles, sex-adjunctive roles, and sex-arbitrary roles. James

A. O'Neil surveys men's changes in the seventies and the relevant literature of men's awareness, and Kenneth Solomon analyzes the current characteristics of masculinity and their effects upon men. Reviewing such theorists as Freud, Jung, Sullivan, Mahler, Erikson, Levinson, and Vaillant, Martin R. Wong places men's gender identity within the context of psychoanalytical-developmental theory. Solomon discusses the process of altering male roles in psychotherapy, and Marvin R. Goldfried and Jerry M. Friedman describe the gender role behavior that brings men into therapy. Androgyny is explored by Jacqueline Boles and Charlotte Tatro. Jack O. Balswick examines the causes, effects, and possible treatment for male inexpressiveness, while David A. Dosser, Jr., provides an extensive exposition of behavioral intervention for inexpressiveness. A survey of recent gay awareness is provided by Joseph L. Norton, and Robert E. Gould argues that the tidal wave of impotence caused by women's liberation is largely fictional. Theodore Nadelson and Carol Nadelson explore the pitfalls and promises of dual-career families, and Ellen Halle describes the abandoned husband. Father also suffers from the empty-nest syndrome, argue Robert A. Lewis and Craig L. Roberts, and Solomon describes older men. Men's groups are analyzed by Terry S. Stein. Perhaps best of all are the rebuttals: Wolfgang Lederer's and Alexandra Botwin's call for male heroism, Richard L. Grant's questioning of the new roles described for men, and (above all) Lederer's ringing riposte to current shibboleths about male inexpressiveness, androgyny, the alleged oppression of women by men, and the value of the more "feminized" man. The capstone of a distinguished volume, Lederer's "Counterepilogue" is necessary reading for anyone interested in men's awareness.

726. Staudacher, Carol. **Men and Grief: A Guide for Men Surviving the Death of a Loved One: A Resource for Caregivers and Mental Health Professionals.** Oakland, CA: New Harbinger Publications, 1991. ix, 225p. bibliography, 217-25. pa.
     Written clearly and compassionately, Staudacher's book seeks to define what is common to the grief responses of men and to discover how men's grieving can be facilitated in order to enhance healing. Both men and women pass through three stages of grieving: retreating, working through, and resolving. For various reasons, however, men and women may have different modes of grieving. Men's grieving may be shaped by cultural expectations that males should be the strong ones, should remain silent, or should grieve in secret or in isolation. Masculine gender roles may urge men to feel anger, to take control during the grief process, to mask their fears, and to resort to risk taking. Staudacher examines the alcoholic survivor, boys and adolescent males who suffer death loss, adult males who lose a parent, a husband's loss of a wife, and fathers who lose children. She offers advice on releasing grief, sharing with a support group, writing as a form of grief therapy, and male companionship as an aid to grieving.

727. Theweleit, Klaus. **Male Fantasies.** Vol. 1: **Women, Floods, Bodies, History.** Translated by Stephen Conway, with Erica Carter and Chris Turner. Minneapolis: University of Minnesota Press, 1987. xxii, 517p. (Theory and History of Literature Series, no. 22). illus. bibliography, 489-501. notes. index. pa. Original publication, as *Männerphantasien*, Vol. 1: *Frauen, Fluten, Körper, Geschichte* (Frankfurt, Germany: Verlag Roter Stern, 1977).
     In this rambling, encyclopedic investigation, chapters resemble separate books. Chapter 1 (256 pages) focuses on the writings of seven members of the Freikorps that formed the vanguard of Nazism after World War I. As militant "soldier males," these men recorded in autobiographies and novels their fear and loathing of female fluidity and their preference for male rigidity. Rejecting Oedipal conflicts as the source of fascism, Theweleit concludes that misogyny

(which he sees as endemic to capitalist patriarchy) is the villain. Although fascinating, much of the material seems, by turns, undigested and overinterpreted. At times, texts are gratuitously trashed: When one of his Freikorps men reports his wife's enthusiasm for strong men, Theweleit (with no evidence) dismisses the report as a male lie. Chapter 2 (206 pages) exhaustively documents the association of women with chaotic water, floods, blood, and (in less healthy minds) with mud, muck, slime, excrement, and the Red tide of communism. As Theweleit ranges through history, literature, popular culture, and much else, evidence often seems mangled to fit a Procrustean bed of theory or ideology. Homer's Penelope is "one of literature's saddest figures, keeping herself busy for eons by fending off robust young men with a representation of Odysseus' phallus, so stiff only he can bend it." Marilyn Monroe's suicide represents her canceling of "the contract for patriarchal dominance." Adding to the uncertainty of the analysis, many of the illustrations have little or no apparent connection with the printed text. In contrast, the foreword by Barbara Ehrenreich is so clear, concise, organized, and balanced that some readers will wish she had written the book instead of Theweleit.

728. Theweleit, Klaus. **Male Fantasies.** Vol. 2: **Psychoanalyzing the White Terror.** Translated by Erica Carter and Chris Turner, with Stephen Conway. Minneapolis: University of Minnesota Press, 1989. xxv, 508p. illus. bibliography, 479-91. index. pa. Original publication, as *Männerphantasien*, vol. 2: *Männerkörper: Zur Psychoanalyse des weissen Terrors* (Frankfurt, Germany: Verlag Roter Stern, 1978).

In this second volume of "male fantasies," Theweleit again examines the writings of male soldiers of the German Freikorps and just about everything else that comes under his eye. The result is another encyclopedic fantasia describing the darker side of masculine psychology. Or does masculine psychology have nothing but a darker side? Theweleit is (deliberately?) not clear. He is as much concerned with the Nazis as with male soldiers of the post-World War I Freikorps. The digressive analysis periodically returns to the argument that males (German males? all males?) seek to structure a hard armor around an empty core of non-feeling. In this way, males resist the fluidity of the feminine, especially the feared feminine within. The sometimes strained analysis seems unduly influenced by 1970s feminist theorists like Luce Irigaray, who argues that males are boring because they are obsessed with phallic unity, while females are intriguingly dual (because their erotic awareness of the two lips of the vulva prevents them from being preoccupied with unity). Apparently intent upon exhibiting feminine duality and irresolution, Theweleit writes a text that wanders, turns on itself, digresses into psychoanalytic theory and social history, and ends with questions rather than a conclusion: Will feminine segmentedness triumph over male wholeness? And, if it does, will it too become a stifling orthodoxy? The foreword by Jessica Benjamin and Anson Rabinbach offers helpful hints to guide the reader through Theweleit's often-unchartered text. Reader reaction to the book is likely to vary widely.

729. von Franz, Marie-Louise. **The Problem of the Puer Aeternus.** New York: Spring Publications, 1970. (unpaged) ca. 300p. pa.

In this series of 12 lecture-discussions, von Franz examines the Jungian archetype of the *puer aeternus,* or eternal boy. In antiquity, he appears as a god child (e.g., Iacchus, Dionysus, Eros) associated with vegetation and resurrection, the counterpart of such oriental deities as Tammuz, Attis, and Adonis. In literature, the archetype appears in works like *The Little Prince*, which von Franz analyzes at length. Men who identify with the *puer aeternus* suffer from a "mother complex" that can result in the son's homosexuality or Don Juan-like promiscuity. *Puer aeternus* men can be charming and irresponsible, never wishing to assume an adult male role. Von Franz's wide-ranging analysis touches on such matters as the need for male initiation rites to be shielded from the mockery of the overprotective mother, as well as the frustrating relationships that can develop between *puer aeternus* men and their women. Later chapters extensively analyze Bruno Goetz's *The Kingdom Without Space* (1919, 1925). One cure for the *puer aeternus* problem, von Franz argues, lies in work—the day-in, day-out variety that requires self-discipline and self-motivation.

730. Wellisch, E. **Isaac and Oedipus: A Study in Biblical Psychology of the Sacrifice of Isaac in *The Akedah*.** London: Routledge and Kegan Paul, 1954. xi, 131p. illus. bibliography, 117-23. author and general indexes.

Although many kinds of infanticide have existed, Wellisch focuses on paternal sacrifice of sons. He presents evidence of such sacrifices in early societies, explicates the Oedipus complex as a partly successful attempt to reconcile paternal-filial tensions, and views *The Akedah* (the biblical story of Abraham and Isaac) as marking the resolution of the conflict.

Cross-References

See chapter 1, "Anthropology, Sociology," chapter 13, "Male Midlife Transition," chapter 15, "Masculinity," chapter 23, "Spirituality."

72a. Adams, Kathleen. **Mightier Than the Sword: The Journal as a Path to Men's Self-Discovery.**

148. American Association of Counseling and Development, Committee on Men. **Men's Issues: A Bibliography.**

154. Astin, Helen S., Allison Parelman, and Anne Fisher, comps. **Sex Roles: A Research Bibliography.**

319. Apuleius. **The Golden Ass.**

593. Balswick, Jack. **The Inexpressive Male.**

770. Barnhouse, Ruth Tiffany. **Homosexuality: A Symbolic Confusion.**

594. Betcher, R. William, and William S. Pollack. **In a Time of Fallen Heroes: The Re-creation of Masculinity.**

477. Biller, Henry B. **Fathers and Families: Paternal Factors in Child Development.**

478. Biller, Henry. **Paternal Deprivation: Family, School, Sexuality, and Society.**

479. Biller, Henry, and Dennis Meredith. **Father Power.**

907. Bolton, Frank G., Jr., Larry A. Morris, and Ann E. MacEachron. **Males at Risk: The Other Side of Sexual Abuse.**

484. Cath, Stanley H., Alan R. Gurwitt, and John Munder Ross, eds. **Father and Child: Developmental and Clinical Perspectives.**

485. Colman, Arthur, and Libby Colman. **Earth Father/Sky Father: The Changing Concept of Fathering.**

540. Robertson, Bryan E., and Robert L. Barret. **The Developing Father: Emerging Roles in Contemporary Society.**

830. Rofes, Eric E. **"I Thought People Like That Killed Themselves": Lesbians, Gay Men and Suicide.**

832. Ross, Michael W. **The Married Homosexual Man: A Psychological Study.**

1013. Rubin, Theodore Isaac, and David C. Berliner. **Understanding Your Man: A Woman's Guide.**

1020. Shapiro, Joan, with George Hartlaub. **Men: A Translation for Women.**

451. Sharp, Daryl. **The Survival Papers: Anatomy of a Midlife Crisis.**

139. Skjei, Eric, and Richard Rabkin. **The Male Ordeal: Role Crisis in a Changing World.**

841. Socarides, Charles W., and Vamik D. Volkan, eds. **The Homosexualities and the Therapeutic Process.**

930. Sonkin, Daniel Jay, Del Martin, and Lenore E. Auerbach Walker. **The Male Batterer: A Treatment Approach.**

621. Steinberg, Warren. **Masculinity: Identity, Conflict, and Transformation.**

966. Stouffer, Samuel A., and others. **The American Soldier.** 4 vols.

433. von Franz, Marie-Louise. **The Golden Ass of Apuleius: The Liberation of the Feminine in Man.**

591. Voth, Harold M. **The Castrated Family.**

1043. Weiss, Robert S. **Staying the Course: The Emotional and Social Lives of Men Who Do Well at Work.**

1028. Wetzler, Scott. **Living with the Passive-Aggressive Man.**

559. Yablonsky, Lewis. **Fathers and Sons.**

21

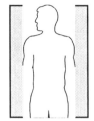

Sexuality

A. Heterosexuality: Heterosexualities, Impotence, Male Sexual Health

For additional books, readers should consult chapter 9, "Health and Related Topics."

731. Bennett, Alan H., ed. **Management of Male Impotence.** International Perspectives in Urology, vol. 5. Baltimore, MD, and London: Williams and Wilkins, 1982. xvi, 253p. (International Perspectives in Urology, vol. 5). illus. bibliography after each chapter. index.

This volume collects 19 scholarly papers on aspects of male sexual function, including impotence—its causes and possible correctives.

732. Berger, Richard E., and Deborah Berger. **Biopotency: A Guide to Sexual Success.** Emmaus, PA: Rodale Press, 1987. xiv, 225p. illus. notes. index.

In clear prose, the Bergers argue that over half of all impotence problems are biologically related and not the result of emotional disorders. After examining what impotence is and what it is not, they describe the normal erection, and how a healthy lifestyle can enhance sexual functioning. The female partner must be included in any impotence recovery plan. The Bergers offer advice on choosing a medical professional and review various medical solutions for physical problems. The authors examine sex therapy as an option, and they discuss women's problems with men's impotence. A final chapter lists guidelines for lifetime sexual success.

733. Brandes, David, ed. **Male Accessory Sex Organs: Structure and Function.** New York: Academic Press, 1974. xi, 527p. illus. bibliography after each chapter. author and subject indexes.

This collection consists of 19 scholarly articles on sex hormones, structure of accessory sex organs, hormone action, and immunology and systematic abnormalities.

734. Brooks, Marvin B., with Sally West Brooks. **Lifelong Sexual Vigor: How to Avoid and Overcome Impotence.** Garden City, NY: Doubleday, 1981. xii, 249p. bibliography, 225-35. index.

This clear and thorough guide for general readers points out that both partners are necessarily affected by erectile difficulties. After explaining the mechanics of normal erections and surveying historical views of impotence, the book examines possible causes. Physical causes include birth defects, diseases, surgery, hormonal problems, medications, smoking, alcohol, and chemicals. Among the psychological causes are performance anxiety, stress, parent-child problems stemming from the male's upbringing, homosexuality, marital discord, midlife crisis, personality characteristics, and aging. Possible treatments are surveyed, including aphrodisiacs, sexual aids, techniques for discovering whether the problem is physical or psychological, sex therapy, and penile prostheses. A final chapter explores the woman's role in coping with impotence.

735. Caprio, Frank S. **The Sexually Adequate Male.** New York: Citadel Press, 1952. ix, 213p. illus. index. pa.

As a period piece showing the kind of sexual advice men were given in the fifties, Caprio's book serves well. Some of the advice is still valid, but readers may be intrigued by the burdens imposed upon the honeymooning groom (he was expected to play Prince Charming and erotic expert to a sexually ignorant virgin). Similarly diverting are the views on oral sex, homosexuality, and "male menopause."

736. Carlton, Eric. **Sexual Anxiety: A Study of Male Impotence.** New York: Harper & Row, Barnes and Noble Imports, 1980. viii, 197p. bibliography, 187-93. notes. index. Original publication, Oxford, England: Martin Robertson, 1980.

Chatty, informed, and skeptical, Carlton surveys for the general reader what is known about impotence. Noting the difficulty of defining impotence, he settles upon "the conscious intention to attempt intercourse that fails for involuntary reasons," a definition he readily admits has its own problems. Equally slippery is the attempt to define "normal" sexual performance, which can vary from one culture to another, and can be influenced by such matters as age, illness, and drugs. Carlton provides an overview of impotence in primitive and ancient societies before sketching the contemporary scene. Seven case histories illustrate the range of impotence. After reviewing several theories of male sexual dysfunction (physiological, sensuality-deprivation, psychological, and sociological), Carlton evaluates prevailing forms of sex therapy, especially those of Masters and Johnson. Among the conclusions is a link between dominant fathers and impotent sons, and another between dominant mothers and premature ejaculation in sons.

737. Castleman, Michael. **Sexual Solutions: For Men and the Women Who Love Them.** Rev. ed. New York: Simon and Schuster, Touchstone Books, 1989. 302p. illus. appendixes. bibliography, 281-85. index. pa.

This book discusses a wide range of men's sexually related topics in informal, witty, jargon-free prose. Its basic message is that men should aspire to whole-body eroticism. They should be neither "cavemen" nor "delivery boys" (i.e., neither would-be "superstuds" nor "nice guys" who let women run the entire show). Castleman advocates sensitive sensuality, or mutually satisfying lovemaking, arguing that men and women are usually alike in their preferences. He rejects the term *foreplay* for "loveplay." Castleman explores male hang-ups (such as concern about penis size), suggests techniques for lasting longer, and describes ways of dealing with erection problems. (He avoids terms like *premature ejaculation* and *impotence*.) He distinguishes between orgasm and ejaculation, and describes what turns women on—and off. A chapter is devoted to how a man can cope with the situation when the woman he loves is raped or (the term he prefers) sexually assaulted. (Deploring some men's tendency to dismiss women's reports of sexual assault, Castleman commits the opposite error of suggesting that false rape accusations never occur.) He believes pornography saddles men with an unhealthy lovestyle. Castleman discusses male contraception, noting that because of health hazards, the condom has made a comeback. Various sexual infections are described, and the final chapter is devoted to sexual self-care for men. Appendix 1 describes male and female anatomies; appendix 2 reprints adulatory references to *Sexual Solutions* from "The *Playboy* Advisor." Telephone numbers for confidential advice on sexuality and for referral to certified sex therapists are included.

738. Ellis, Albert. **Sex and the Liberated Man.** Secaucus, NJ: Lyle Stuart, 1976. 347p. bibliography, 309-36. index.

An extensively rewritten version of Ellis's *Sex and the Single Man* (1963), this book attempts to bring the discussion of heterosexuality into the 1970s. A cheerleader for an "erotic revolution," Ellis jeers at those who associate sex with guilt. He summarizes feminist complaints about sex and offers men advice for making sex more mutually enjoyable.

739. Fanta, Robert D. **The Fanta Sex Report: Self-Help for Male Hang-Ups.** Los Alamitos, CA: Hwong, 1980. 48p. appendixes. bibliography, 44-47.

Although recognizing a variety of causes, this brief report focuses on how male impotence can be created and maintained by the female partner. After reviewing research on how the female can reinforce male impotence, Fanta provides a chapter of self-help suggestions for alleviating the situation. One appendix lists the reasons why a person may decline sex; the other describes the Masters and Johnson technique of sex therapy.

740. Fellman, Sheldon L., and Paul Neimark. **The Virile Man.** New York: Stein and Day, 1976. 228p.

A urologist and surgeon who believes that most sex therapy takes too long, Fellman presents a sampling of cases involving male sexual problems, including impotence, premature ejaculation, latent homosexuality, "castrating" women, and difficulties with attaining male ideals of performance. Fellman attempts to treat these problems in a 60-minute session or two.

741. Friday, Nancy. **Men in Love: Men's Sexual Fantasies: The Triumph of Love over Rage.** New York: Delacorte Press, 1980. xii, 528p. Reprint, New York: Dell, 1981. pa. Reprint, London: Hutchinson, 1993.

From approximately 3,000 male responses describing sexual fantasies, Friday has selected approximately 200 for publication, making no claims for the representativeness of the responses. The printed fantasies are divided into 21 groupings (including oral sex, anal sex, bisexuals, and sadomasochism), and, although sometimes abridged, the responses are not expurgated. Throughout the book, Friday comments understandingly upon the fantasies, relating them to psychological theory. The introductory chapter, "The Masculine Conflict," indicates that some fantasies may represent the triumph of men's love over their rage at women, especially the internalized female who proscribes sexual expression. Only a tiny minority of men, however, report fantasies of male rape of females; masochistic scenarios are far more common. Like the comments throughout the book, Friday's introduction reflects sympathetic insights into men's lives and roles. "Given the way the family and society are set up," Friday asks, "is the male role so enviable?"

742. Gilbaugh, James H. **Men's Private Parts: An Owner's Manual.** Rev. ed. New York: Crown Trade Paperbacks, 1993. 120p. illus. glossary. index. pa.
    In clear, no-nonsense prose, Gilbaugh surveys male reproductive anatomy, normal functions, and problems. Causes and treatments of impotence, prostate enlargement, cancer, and even bladder diseases are included. Gilbaugh concisely sums up the pros and cons of circumcision, concluding with a very slight nod in favor of the procedure. A final chapter contains hints to improve sexual enjoyment.

743. Goldstein, Irwin, and Larry Rothstein. **The Potent Male: Facts, Fiction, Future.** Los Angeles: The Body Press, 1990. xiv, 210p. illus. appendixes. glossary. bibliography, 193-206. index. notes. pa.
    This book describes medical techniques for restoring erections to men who are "impotent." The authors describe the biomechanics of erection and discuss causes for dysfunction. They describe treatments, listing advantages and disadvantages. Male readers are cautioned to consult a medical specialist and to understand that the techniques described carry no guarantees. Separate chapters are then devoted to four men whose sexual problems spring from different sources. Because the mind plays an important role in many cases of dysfunctioning, these chapters include sections by Dr. Alma Dell Smith, who provides a psychological assessment of the individual cases. Techniques include sex therapy, sensate focusing, injections, surgery, and implants. A chapter on special concerns deals with diabetes, Peyronie's Disease, spinal cord injuries and other neurological disorders, low testosterone and other hormonal disorders, priapism, cancer, impotence in teenagers and in the elderly, and medication-associated impotence. The appendixes include a glossary of terms and a list of support groups, as well as the notes and bibliography.

744. Hass, Aaron. **Love, Sex, and the Single Man.** New York: Franklin Watts, 1983. 238p. index.
    The sexual revolution has left problems in its wake by permitting physical intimacy to outdistance emotional closeness. Hass distinguishes among love, sex, and intimacy. The new sexual freedom that promised so much to single men has actually created pitfalls for them. The divorce of sex from caring makes casual sex disappointing; the increased pressures for performance and satisfaction leave single men with sexual problems. To truly enjoy sex, the man must like women in general and must love *this* woman in particular. The primacy of love (conveyed in the book's title) is stressed in a chapter on the need for recovering romance. Hass warns against pseudofeminists who want men to treat them as equals but cannot bring themselves to accept men who do so. Likewise, many men may be liberated in their heads but not in their hearts.

745. Hite, Shere. **The Hite Report on Male Sexuality.** New York: Alfred A. Knopf, 1981. xxxiii, 1129p. appendixes. index. Reprint, abridged and rev. ed., New York: Ballantine Books, 1982. pa.
    Drawing upon 7,239 responses to an essay questionnaire, this much-discussed survey provides a wealth of male opinion on a wide range of sex-related topics. In the preface, Hite explains and defends her methodology as scientific even if the results are not entirely representative, and she provides statistical information. The bulk

of the book is devoted to excerpts from the responses, interspersed with Hite's observations—which have a way of turning into feminist sermonettes. If the commentary is more political than perspicacious, the responses themselves provide an abundance of male experiences and viewpoints. The men discuss numerous matters, including relationships between fathers and sons (mostly aloof and unsatisfying, from the son's perspective); friendships between men (few respondents have close male friends); relationships with women; monogamy (most of the respondents have had extramarital sex); cohabitation arrangements; men's anger at being used by women for financial security; men's tendency to identify sex with intercourse and male sexuality with orgasm during intercourse; problems with intercourse (impotence, "premature ejaculation," pressures to provide partners with orgasms); men's complaints about women's inability to stimulate them effectively; men's resentment at always being the initiators of sexual activity; their uncertainty about women's orgasms; and their views on aging (many say sex gets better), homosexuality, rape, pornography, and masturbation (which some say produces more intense orgasms than intercourse). The varied and unexpurgated responses in this report provide a vivid montage of men and their sexuality.

746. Janus, Sam, Barbara Bess, and Carol Saltus. **A Sexual Profile of Men in Power.** Englewood Cliffs, NJ: Prentice-Hall, 1977. xxiii, 190p. bibliography, 183-87. index.

The authors examine the extramarital sex lives of men in politics. Using interviews with 68 elite call girls and 12 madams, as well as other materials, the authors conclude that political figures are more sexually active than other men, are more likely to frequent prostitutes, often seek "kinky" or deviant sex, and spend considerable amounts of money to satisfy their sexual needs. These political figures often retain adolescent attitudes into adulthood, many were closely bound to their mothers, and a few have homosexual tendencies. The authors suggest a link between the power drive and the sex drive. Discussing deviant behaviors, the authors note that many of these men seem to be proving their manhood by enduring pain. The authors also describe political figures from other countries, as well as the call girls themselves. For the typical political man pictured here, Henry Kissinger's aphorism holds true: "Power is the ultimate aphrodisiac."

747. Johnson, A. D., W. R. Gomes, and N. L. Vandemark, eds. **The Testis.** 3 vols. New York and London: Academic Press, 1970. xv, 684; xv, 468; xv, 596p. illus. bibliography after each chapter. author and subject indexes.

The 28 scholarly papers in these volumes deal with the development, anatomy, and physiology of the testis, biochemistry, and influencing factors.

748. Julty, Sam. **Male Sexual Performance.** New York: Grossett and Dunlap, 1975. 353p. illus. Reprint, as *MSP: Male Sexual Performance*, New York: Dell, 1976. pa.

Impotency is the subject of this book. Informal but informed, Julty uses taped interviews to assess how men and women feel about impotence. He then analyzes for laypeople the male sexual apparatus. Using interviews with professionals (e.g., urologists, diabetes specialists, psychiatrists), he explores possible causes and solutions—both physical and mental—to impotency. Julty has negative views of the American medical system and of the cultural pressures on males to define themselves in terms of sexual performance.

749. Kelly, Gary. **Good Sex: The Healthy Man's Guide to Sexual Fulfill-ment.** New York: Harcourt Brace Jovanovich, 1979. 244p. illus. bibliography, 235-38. index. Reprint, New York: New American Library, Signet, 1981. pa.

"Straight" male scripts often narrow men's sexual enjoyment, Kelly argues. Attempting to bring the whole man into sexual activity, he discusses communication with one's partner and getting beyond male myths to warmth and caring, equality, trust, and respect. Often, the penis is a barometer of a man's emotional life. Throughout the book, Kelly provides techniques of getting in touch with one's body, slowing ejaculation timing, impotence, and other sexual problems—including women's difficulties. A final chapter discusses brotherhood (feeling between men), fatherhood, and selfhood.

750. Kinsey, Alfred C., Wardell B. Pomeroy, and Clyde E. Martin. **Sexual Behavior in the Human Male.** Philadelphia and London: W. B. Saunders, 1948. 804p. illus. appendix. bibliography, 766-87. index.

A landmark study of male sexuality, this famous report continues to be a necessary reference tool for later researchers. Tracing the patterns revealed by 5,300 white males and utilizing information from a total of 12,000 persons, the study describes its methodology and findings in detail. With the aid of numerous charts and graphs, the authors examine such matters as the kinds of sexual outlets available to males; early sexual growth and activity; adolescence; and the effects of age, marital status, social level, rural-urban background, and religious persuasion upon sexual outlets. Also studied are the various outlets, including masturbation, nocturnal emissions, heterosexual petting, premarital intercourse, marital intercourse, intercourse with prostitutes, homosexual outlets, and animal contacts. Among the findings are the universality of masturbation, 37 percent of the total male population has some overt homosexual experience to orgasm, and 4 percent of white males are exclusively homosexual throughout their lives. As might be expected, some parts of the study have been criticized. In particular, recent writers have questioned the authors' belief that the rapidly ejaculating male is "superior" to the one who can prolong intercourse.

751. Levine, Linda, and Lonnie Barbach. **The Intimate Male: Candid Dis-cussions about Women, Sex, and Relationships.** Garden City, NY: Anchor Press/Doubleday, 1983. xiii, 364p. bibliography, 351-52. notes. index.

The 120 men interviewed for this frank account of sex are mostly professionals, 90 percent are white, and all are college graduates; the range of ages is 20 to more than 70. Middle-class heterosexuals who feel positively about sex, the men discuss their rejection of machismo for more intimate relationships. For good sex, a good relationship with the woman is primary. Other topics include masturbation, first encounters, role reversals, gourmet sex, communicating with one's partner, and sex in later years. As Bernie Zilbergeld notes in the introduction, these men are not the insensitive ignoramuses depicted in some sex surveys.

752. Llewellyn-Jones, Derek. **EveryMan.** New York: Peter Bedrick Books, 1983. viii, 303p. illus. appendix. bibliography, 292-98. Original publication, London: Oxford University Press, 1981.

For the general reader, Llewellyn-Jones discusses sex differentiation, gender, sexuality, and health. He describes the development of the male fetus, socialization into the masculine role, the dynamics of male sexual response, how to be a better lover, the decision to have children, contraception, expectant fathers, sexual problems (impotency, premature ejaculation, etc.), diseases, homosexuality, middle-age sexuality, heart trouble, and aging. The appendix is a glossary of terms.

753. MacKenzie, Bruce and Eileen, with Linda Christie. **It's *Not* All in Your Head: A Couple's Guide to Overcoming Impotence.** New York: E. P. Dutton, 1988. xiv, 192p. glossary. index.

The founders of Impotents Anonymous and I-Anon (support groups for impotent men and their female partners), the MacKenzies argue that more than half of the cases of impotence have physical rather than psychological causes and that impotence affects more than 10 million couples. Discussing their own situation, the authors report that Bruce's impotence was for a long time misdiagnosed; eventually, diabetes was discovered as the cause, and a penile implant helped solve the problem. Discussing 12 false myths about impotence, the MacKenzies urge sufferers to immediately see a urologist who understands impotence and can treat it. Taking the reader through the stages of dealing with impotence, the authors review tests to determine its causes and the medical procedures to correct it. They discuss diseases of the nervous system and offer advice on handling matters after medical treatment. They also discuss psychologically induced impotence and how to treat it. After a chapter about the need to deal with impotence as a couple's challenge, the authors print some of their correspondence on the subject of impotence.

754. McCarthy, Barry. **What You *Still* Don't Know about Male Sexuality.** New York: Thomas Y. Crowell, 1977. iv, 244p. appendix. bibliography, 230-33. index.

Pleasure, not performance, is the keynote of this book. McCarthy endorses sexual fantasies, masturbation, and a range of sexual practices that are mutually pleasurable. The benefits and costs of extramarital sex need to be weighed. Separate chapters are devoted to venereal diseases, father participation in pregnancy and childbirth, learning to increase arousal and potency, ways to perk up sex in the middle years, sex and the single-again man, and aging and sex. The appendix discusses how to find a reliable therapist.

755. Milsten, Richard. **Male Sexual Function: Myth, Fantasy and Reality.** New York: Avon Books, 1979. 205p. bibliography, 197-98. notes. index. pa.

Although covering a range of topics, this book for general readers focuses on impotence. After explaining the mechanics of erection, Milsten discusses 16 psychological and 8 physical causes of impotence. A lengthy chapter is devoted to treatment. Milsten also touches on fallacies surrounding male sexual performance (e.g., the effects of masturbation, vasectomy, and circumcision), aging in men, and the female partner. The final chapter presents a self-evaluation questionnaire for men concerning their sexual condition and attitudes.

756. Penney, Alexandra. **How to Make Love to a Man.** New York: Clarkson N. Potter, Publishers, 1981. 143p. Reprint, New York: Dell, 1982. pa.

For the woman mustering nerve to take the initiative, Penney provides the dos and don'ts. Similar popular advice can be found in Penney's *How to Make Love to a Woman* and *How to Make Love to Each Other*. (See also entry 1011.)

757. Pietropinto, Anthony, and Jacqueline Simenauer. **Beyond the Male Myth: What Women Want to Know About Men's Sexuality: A Nationwide Survey.** New York: Times Books, 1977. xi, 430p. appendix. index. Reprint, New York: New American Library, Signet, 1978. pa.

This survey is based upon more than 4,000 responses to a 40-item questionnaire, as well as essay responses. The men ranged in age form 18 to 65. The authors describe their methodology and print the entire questionnaire in the introduction; the appendix contains statistical breakdowns of the 40 non-essay questions. The survey was devised to elicit information about men that would be useful to women dealing with them. The authors debunk the "myth" of the insensitive male, and they maintain a running battle with the conclusions about men in *The Hite Report*. Among their survey conclusions are: half of the respondents regard marriage with their wife as the only sex partner as the ideal sex life; rather than feeling threatened, most men preferred a more aggressive or active sex partner; they like today's more liberated women; they were not threatened by women's ability to prevent pregnancy; the widespread acceptance of vasectomy indicated that they did not equate manliness with fertility; most men were interested in their partner's orgasms; they craved cuddling even when intercourse was not imminent; they enjoyed foreplay and sexual variations; and they did not fall asleep immediately after ejaculation. The authors summarize: "The notion that men only want to penetrate, thrust, and ejaculate is, as we have seen, outdated, if, indeed, it was ever true."

758. Roen, Philip R. **Male Sexual Health.** New York: William Morrow, 1974. 190p. illus. index.

In readable question-and-answer fashion, Roen addresses such matters as prostate troubles, impotence, sex in elderly men, venereal diseases, and vasectomy.

759. Rowan, Robert L. **Men and Their Sex.** New York: Avocation, 1979. 159p. illus. Reprint, New York: Irvington, 1982. pa.

In popular, light style, Rowan describes the physiology of the male reproductive system, with brief chapters on the penis, testicles, prostate gland, and the mechanics of ejaculation. The system's diseases (e.g., Peyronie's Disease, Priapism, Phimosis), congenital birth defects, and injuries are described, as well as their treatment. Rowan explains why he favors routine circumcision. Sections on venereal diseases and cancer of the penis are included. The book provides instructions for self-examination of the testicles, a procedure that Rowan urges men to follow regularly.

760. Shanor, Karen. **The Shanor Study: The Sexual Sensitivity of the American Male.** New York: Dial Press, 1978. 274p. appendix. bibliography, 271-74. Reprint, New York: Ballantine Books, 1978. pa.

"The American male is a more complete person than contemporary views of him allow," Shanor concludes from her study utilizing 4,062 questionnaire responses and 70 interviews. The author devotes separate chapters to orgasm (some men occasionally fake it), masturbation (it is performed more frequently since the time of Kinsey's study), and sexual fantasies. Shanor then offers profiles of men throughout the life cycle. Later chapters examine sexual activity of black men and homosexuals, impotence, sadomasochistic fantasies, and characteristic behavior during sex. The final chapter presents an overview, an attempt to fix a representative portrait of current male sexuality in transition. Numerous quotes from Shanor's respondents are incorporated into the text. The appendix provides the questionnaire and statistical information.

761. Silber, Sherman J. **The Male: From Infancy to Old Age.** New York: Charles Scribner's Sons, 1981. xii, 212p. illus. index. pa.

In readable style, Silber examines numerous facets of male sexuality. He describes how the male's organs work, what can go wrong (e.g., impotence, prostate trouble, venereal disease), the boy's problems, and gender identity and homosexuality. The discussion is aided by Scott Barrow's illustrations.

762. Stanway, Andrew. **A Woman's Guide to Men and Sex: How to Understand a Man's Sexual and Emotional Needs.** New York: Carroll and Graf, 1988. 239p. illus. bibliography 232-35. index.

In part 1 of this book, Stanway rapidly surveys such topics as myths about men, the stages of men's lives, work (often emotionally unrewarding), marriage (it suits men better than women), family, fear and hatred of women, homophobia, pornography, violence and aggression, and love (men are more romantic than women). Part 2 deals with sexuality, including men's concern with penis size, the basics of sex organs, foreplay, and intercourse. Stanway distinguishes between mechanical copulation and emotionally involved intercourse. Part 3 examines communicating with one's partner. Men often have difficulty conveying their needs; women often do not know how to please men. The final chapter deals with male sexual problems such as impotence and premature ejaculation. Some readers may be startled by a few of Stanway's more controversial generalizations about men and women; many will find his advice clear and helpful.

763. Swanson, Janice M., and Katherine A. Forrest, eds. **Men's Reproductive Health.** New York: Springer, 1984. xvii, 398p. (Focus on Men series, no. 3). illus. bibliography after each chapter, 377-84. index.

This collection contains 20 essays grouped under four categories: men's health and men's roles in society, the male reproductive system and its disorders, men and family planning, and male sexuality and sexual disorders. In the opening essays, the authors indicate that the modern health care system is not well geared to serve men's gender-specific needs. In particular, it cannot cope with the causes of early male death or high mortality among younger males. James B. Harrison's classic essay, "The Male Sex Role May Be Dangerous to Your Health," is included. In part 2, two essays describe the male reproductive anatomy and sexual development in adolescence. A lengthy article by Eliseo J. Pérez-Stable and Gary Slutkin discusses sexually transmitted diseases. Other essays explore disorders of the male reproductive system, male infertility, effects of drugs on sex and reproduction, and environmental and occupational hazards to male sexuality. Part 3 opens with Lawrence Diller's brief update on male contraceptives (there was no misogynist plot by male scientists to place the burden of contraception upon women, he concludes). Other articles examine condoms and withdrawal as contraceptive methods, shared contraception, and helping men ask for help in family planning. Part 4 focuses on male sexual problems, such as effects of male socialization on sexuality; organic male sexual malaise; taking men's sexual histories (especially if one is a woman); and counseling men on disability, illness, and aging. The essays are scholarly and clearly written; the collection contains a wealth of helpful information.

764. Taguchi, Yosh. **Private Parts: A Doctor's Guide to the Male Anatomy.** Edited by Merrily Weisbord. New York: Doubleday, 1988. iv, 172p. illus. index. pa.

A specialist in urology, Taguchi provides direct answers to many questions that male patients have asked him over the years. He describes the male sex organs and how they function normally. Separate chapters are devoted to impotence and its treatment, problems of the penis (circumcision apparently provides some benefits in preventing cancer of the penis), and problems of the prostate gland (enlargement, cancer, and infection). Taguchi discusses male and female infertility and vasectomy. Other chapters consider scrotal lumps, sexually transmitted diseases, sex changes, and some female urological problems. The final chapter discusses care of the genitals.

765. Williams, Warwick. **It's Up to You: Overcoming Erection Problems.** Balgowah, Australia: Williams and Wilkins, Adis Press, 1989. Reprint, Wellingborough, England: Thorsons, 1989. x, 165p. illus. appendixes. index. pa.

A doctor and sex therapist, the author argues that much impotence can be overcome through a rigorously pursued self-help program. Advising readers to follow his discourse step by step, Williams discusses normal erection processes, the effects of aging on a men's sex drive, and false myths about impotence. Impotence does not mean diminished sex drive but inability to have and retain an erection. Advising that the female partner must be included in the program, Williams reviews the various causes of impotence and how to evaluate them. Seventeen appendixes describe the author's self-help program for impotence that does not require medical intervention. Two additional appendixes contain recommended reading and a glossary of terms.

766. Zilbergeld, Bernie. **The New Male Sexuality.** New York: Bantam Books, 1992, 1993. viii, 645p. illus. appendix. notes. index. pa.

Much has changed since the first appearance in 1978 of Zilbergeld's popular guide to male sexuality. As a result, the new version is much expanded and updated. In addition to the lively counseling on sexual fulfillment, the present edition responds to current awareness (mostly from women) that sex takes place within a human relationship; much advice on enriching that relationship has been added. Zilbergeld also seeks to counter the current male bashing that permeates U.S. culture by including a section on the ways in which males get a raw deal in our society. Opening with the obstacles that U.S. society puts in the path of men's sexual enjoyment, Zilbergeld's first two chapters debunk familiar "myths" about male sexuality. The succeeding four chapters examine the "reality" of sexual experience and are followed by 12 chapters on improving sexual relations. Zilbergeld explores such matters as what constitutes "normal" behavior, how to be a better listener to your partner, the importance of touching, the dos and don'ts of initiation and seduction, sex and the single man, and keeping the spark in long-term relationships. Nine chapters cover ways to resolve problems, both sexual and relational. Zilbergeld discusses matters such as arousal and ejaculation problems, the merits of various forms of therapy, and how a man can develop positive sexual awareness in his son. Information on sexually transmitted diseases is included. The appendix examines the effects of drugs on male sexuality.

B. Homosexuality: Gay Men, Homosexualities

Given the large number of books published on the subject, homosexuality deserves a book-length bibliography unto itself. Below are listed a selection of books indicating the range of materials available on gay men and homosexuality.

767. Adams, Stephen. **The Homosexual as Hero in Contemporary Fiction.** New York: Barnes and Noble, 1980. 208p. notes. index.

In contrast to the homosexual as villain or foil, the homosexual as hero appears in many recent novels that examine changing sex roles and sexual politics. Adams examines the works of such writers as Gore Vidal, James Baldwin, James Purdy, John Rechy, E. M. Forster, Christopher Isherwood, Angus Wilson, and Jean Genet.

768. Altman, Dennis. **The Homosexualization of America: The Americanization of the Homosexual.** New York: St. Martin's Press, 1982. xiv, 242p. bibliography, 227-36. notes. index. Reprint, Boston: Beacon Press, 1983. pa.

Urbane and informed, Altman traces the influence of an increasingly visible and assertive gay culture upon American styles, fashions, cityscapes, psychological and historical thought, consumer capitalism, politics, and sexual freedom.

769. Bahnsen, Greg L. **Homosexuality: A Biblical View.** Grand Rapids, MI: Baker Book House, 1978. 152p. bibliography, 135-47. Scripture index. pa.

From a study of Scripture, Bahnsen concludes that homosexuality is sinful, that churches should deny membership and office to unrepentant homosexuals, and that homosexuality should be considered a civil offense. Bahnsen argues that although scholars are uncertain about the causes of homosexuality, the Bible is clear in condemning both homosexual orientation and acts. He warns, however, against "holier than thou" attitudes towards homosexuals and against indiscriminate state persecution of them. The churches should proclaim the good news of deliverance for homosexuals who repent.

770. Barnhouse, Ruth Tiffany. **Homosexuality: A Symbolic Confusion.** New York: Seabury Press, Crossroads Books, 1977. xiv, 190p. appendixes. notes. index.

Although she supports the decriminalization of homosexual acts and regards persecution of homosexuals as a great evil, Barnhouse has serious reservations about recent efforts to describe homosexuality as normal. She questions such events as the American Psychiatric Association's 1973 declaration that homosexuality is not a mental disorder. She is also skeptical of Christian apologists for gay love. As a theologian, Barnhouse concludes that heterosexuality is "a symbol of wholeness, of the reconciliation of opposites, of the loving at-one-ment of God and creation." Its primary goal is not satisfaction but wholeness. In this view, homosexuality is a failure in human adaptation, a symbolic confusion.

771. Berger, Raymond M. **Gay and Gray: The Older Homosexual Man.** Urbana: University of Illinois Press, 1982. 234p. appendixes. bibliography, 223-26. index.

Combining an interview study and a questionnaire study, Berger discredits stereotypes of the older homosexual. The interviews present the men as individuals; the questionnaire findings indicate that they are by no means the pathetic and promiscuous creatures of popular imagination.

772. Bérubé, Allan. **Coming Out Under Fire: The History of Gay Men and Women in World War II.** New York: Free Press, 1990. Reprint, New York: Penguin Books, Plume Books, 1991. xiii, 377p. illus. notes. index. pa.

During World War II, large numbers of gay men were drafted or volunteered for military service. Bérubé tells the stories of gay men and lesbian women during military induction and service. If the candidate passed enlistment screenings by doctors and mental health personnel, he or she faced the task of blending in with heterosexuals. For some men, GI drag was a way of acting out gayness. Although gay cliques formed, they were constantly threatened by military police intervention. Dishonorable discharges and denial of GI benefits were used to punish gays or suspected gays. Despite the danger of being relegated to "queer stockades," gay lovers were a part of military life. Psychiatrists who worked with gay personnel mounted the first challenges to the military's anti-homosexual policy. After the war, many gays and lesbians went on to fight another war—against homophobia and anti-gay bias.

773. Boswell, John. **Christianity, Social Tolerance, and Homosexuality: Gay People in Western Europe, from the Beginning of the Christian Era to the Fourteenth Century.** Chicago and London: University of Chicago Press, 1980. xviii, 424p. illus. appendixes. bibliography, 403-9. notes. index of Greek terms and general index. pa.

This scholarly study examines European attitudes toward gay people from the Roman empire through the High Middle Ages. Neither ancient Rome nor early Christianity appears to have stigmatized homosexual behavior. Boswell examines biblical texts and early Christian writings for allegedly anti-homosexual injunctions—and he finds none. During the disintegration of the Roman state, however, hostility toward gays became manifest, but from civil authorities rather than the church. During the Middle Ages, a gay subculture was tolerated, and by the eleventh century gays were prominent at many levels of society in Europe. But during the latter half of the twelfth century, hostility toward gays and homosexuality again reappeared as part of a rise of general intolerance throughout Western society. Embedded in theological, moral, and legal complications of the later Middle Ages, this hostility influenced Western thought through later centuries. In appendix 1, Boswell discusses St. Paul's epistles, and appendix 2 contains texts and translations of key works. Boswell's scholarship—erudite, lively, controversial—makes this a book to reckon with.

774. Brown, Howard. **Familiar Faces, Hidden Lives: The Story of Homosexual Men in America Today.** New York and London: Harcourt Brace Jovanovich, 1976. 246p. pa.

A well-known medical doctor who came out in the early seventies, Brown recounts with balance and sympathy the stories of numerous homosexuals, including himself, depicting what it has been like to be gay in the United States. Brown retells human stories rather than case histories. He examines such areas as the mistaken tendency to blame parents for their child's sexual preference, gays in small towns, married homosexuals, long-term relationships, and the ways in which religion, psychiatry, and the law have oppressed homosexuals. An epilogue looks forward to a brighter future for gays in the United States.

775. Browning, Frank. **The Culture of Desire: Paradox and Perversity in Gay Lives Today.** New York: Crown, 1993. vii, 243p. bibliography, 231-33. index.

Browning uses the motif of a journey to gay male sites (e.g., San Francisco, Washington, Miami, Palm Springs, Fire Island) as the starting point for a series of reflections on U.S. gay men today. He notes such matters as the emergence of queer rage in organizations that are sometimes torn apart by the rage of their own internal dissensions. He examines such topics as the gay redefinition of extended family. Browning profiles a number of colorful people (e.g., Bill Fotti, a gay artist and tobacco farmer). The ominous presence of AIDS is never far from the surface of Browning's account. He concludes that gay culture is at its best when embracing the paradoxes of its perversity—the desire to be recognized by mainstream U.S. society and the desire to be free from "normalcy."

776. Bullough, Vern L. **Homosexuality: A History.** New York: New American Library, Meridian Books, 1979. ix, 196p. bibliography, 163-64. notes. index. pa.

From a historical perspective, Bullough examines in concise style a number of topics including past definitions of homosexuality, religion, the law, schools, lesbianism, and coming out.

777. Burg, B. R. **Sodomy and the Perception of Evil: English Sea Rovers in the Seventeenth-Century Caribbean.** New York and London: New York University Press, 1983. xxiii, 215p. bibliography, 193-209. notes. index.

Against the background of homosexuality in seventeenth-century England, Burg focuses upon "sodomy" among pirates of the Caribbean.

778. Chester, Lewis, David Leitch, and Colin Simpson. **The Cleveland Street Affair.** London: Weidenfeld and Nicolson, 1976. 236p. illus. bibliography, 234-36. notes.

The most notorious of Victorian scandals—the subject of this study—involved a brothel employing telegraph boys, high-ranking patrons (including the Heir Presumptive Albert Victor and Lord Arthur Somerset), and a massive cover-up engineered by such people as the Prince of Wales (later Edward VII) and the prime minister, Lord Salisbury.

779. Cowan, Thomas. **Gay Men and Women Who Enriched the World.** New Canaan, CT: William Mulvey, Mulvey Books, 1988. xii, 257p.

After an introductory chapter that examines gay experience and explains his selection of subjects, Cowan provides brief sketches of 31 gay males and 9 gay females who made major contributions to the world. The men include Alexander the Great, Plato, Michelangelo, Frederick the Great, Walt Whitman, Peter Ilyich Tchaikovsky, Charles Laughton, Noël Coward, Tennessee Williams, Benjamin Britten, James Baldwin, Yukio Mishima, and Andy Warhol. Among the women are Sappho, Gertrude Stein, and Marguerite Yourçenar.

780. De Cecco, John P., ed. **Homophobia: An Overview.** New York: Haworth Press, 1984. ix, 198p. bibliography after each chapter. index. pa.

This special issue of *The Journal of Homosexuality* 10 (numbers 1/2) features 11 scholarly articles, plus a preface by the editor. The authors address various aspects of homophobia, usually from a psychological or sociological perspective. The final article contains a bibliographic guide to government hearings, reports, legislation, and speeches on homosexuality.

781. Delph, Edward William. **The Silent Community: Public Homosexual Encounters.** Beverly Hills, CA: Sage Publications, Sage Mark Editions, 1978. 187p. appendix. bibliography, 183-86. notes. pa.

Delph studies the ways in which gays in the 1970s communicated nonverbally while making sexual contacts in public places, such as restrooms, parks, bars, and steambaths. Because the problems of conducting such research were (to say the least) intriguing, readers may want to start with the appendix on methodology.

782. D'Emilio, John. **Sexual Politics, Sexual Communities: The Making of a Homosexual Minority in the United States, 1940-1970.** Chicago and London: University of Chicago Press, 1983. x, 257p. notes. index.

This scholarly and readable study portrays the forces and events in the United States between 1940 and 1970 that led to gay liberation. In the opening chapter, D'Emilio surveys homosexuality in the United States from its founding to the 1930s; in later chapters, he provides more detailed accounts of homosexual awareness during World War II, the formation of gay urban cultures, the crackdown on gays during the McCarthy period, and the uneven fortunes of gay organizations like the Mattachine Society. During the sixties, important legal decisions coincided with the rise of gay activism on both the east and west coasts, culminating in the Stonewall riots of 1969. In a concluding chapter, the author surveys the post-Stonewall scene.

783. Denneny, Michael, Charles Ortleb, and Thomas Steele, eds. **The Christopher Street Reader.** New York: Coward-McCann, 1983. 428p. pa.

Forty-six contributions from the *Christopher Street* magazine are divided into sections dealing with living the gay life, the conditions of gays in modern America, the situation of gays abroad (e.g., Moscow, Rio, Paris, London), aspects of gay history, and gay cultural politics in the United States. The contents include essays, reports, personal reminiscences, and interviews (with, e.g., Gore Vidal and Jean Paul Sartre).

784. Dover, K. J. **Greek Homosexuality.** 1978. Rev. ed., Cambridge: Harvard University Press, 1989. x, 246p. illus. bibliography, 228-34. notes. indexes. pa.

In this landmark study, Dover utilizes solid scholarship to depict homosexuality among ancient Athenian citizens. Acceptable eros (love) between males was always a matter of a "superior" and "inferior," usually between an older man or youth and a boy under the age of 18. Homosexuality between "equals" in age was frowned upon. The courtship of the boy could involve elaborate gift giving. Ordinarily, the boy and his family regarded this courtship unfavorably, at least at first. If the courtship was successful, intercourse was completed intercrurally, i.e., between the thighs. Athenian citizens censured anal penetration, and being a male prostitute could debar a man from citizenship privileges. Dover illuminates the subject with a wealth of information drawn from vase paintings, law proceedings, literature, and numerous artifacts from Greek life. The book includes a postscript updating the earlier edition and a list of vases discussed in the text. Three indexes list Greek texts and documents cited in the study, important Greek words, and general names and terms. Numerous illustrations, mostly of vase paintings, illustrate the study.

785. Duberman, Martin, Martha Vicinus, and George Chauncey, Jr., eds. **Hidden from History: Reclaiming the Gay and Lesbian Past.** New York: Meridian Books, 1989. xi, 579p. notes. pa.

Twenty-nine essays, plus an introduction, present a multicultural examination of aspects of gay and lesbian life throughout history. Authors focus on the ancient world, preindustrial societies, the nineteenth century in the United States and in England, and the twentieth century in Western societies and in South Africa. Contributors include David M. Halperin on pederasty in classical Athens, Vivien W. Ng on homosexuality in late-imperial China, James M. Saslow on homosexuality during the European Renaissance, Paul Gordon Schalow on literary depictions of male love in early modern Japan, Martha Vicinus on British boarding school friendships between 1870 and 1920, Eric Garber on lesbian and gay subculture in Jazz Age Harlem, and John D'Emilio on gay politics in San Francisco since World War II. Most of the essays focus on gay men.

786. Dynes, Wayne R., ed. **Encyclopedia of Homosexuality.** 2 vols. New York and London: Garland, 1990. xxxviii, 755; 757, 1485p. index.

Compiled in association with Warren Johansson and William A. Percy, and with the assistance of Stephen Donaldson, this comprehensive encyclopedia offers brief essays on an extensive list of categories, such as famous persons, terms, historical events, psychology, and so on. These two volumes are an indispensable source of basic information about innumerable facets of homosexuality.

787. Ebert, Alan. **The Homosexuals.** New York: Macmillan, 1977. xii, 332p.

Ebert presents interviews with 17 gay men; their stories provide a cross-section of gay experience in the 1970s.

788. Feinbloom, Deborah Heller. **Transvestites and Transsexuals: Mixed Views.** New York: Delacorte Press/Seymour Lawrence, A Merloyd Lawrence Book, 1976. ix, 303p. appendixes. bibliography, 283-96. index.

The overwhelming majority of transvestites and transsexuals are males. Transvestites are males who dress as the opposite sex. (Females who dress as men are seldom regarded as abnormal.) Transsexuals identify themselves as members of one sex but possess the body of the "wrong" sex. After defining terms, Feinbloom combines scholarly literature and "participant observation" to analyze the world of heterosexual transvestites, homosexual transvestites, and transsexuals. She follows the activities of a transvestite group, as well as the life of one person who undergoes a male-to-female sex change operation. Although some readers may be disappointed that the book sheds comparatively little light on the causes of male transvestism and transsexualism, Feinbloom is wisely cautious in her conclusions.

789. Galloway, David, and Christian Sabisch, eds. **Calamus: Male Homosexuality in Twentieth-Century Literature: An International Anthology.** New York: William Morrow, 1982. 503p. appendix. pa.

This anthology includes twentieth-century fiction and poetry by 35 international authors (not all of whom are gay) dealing with male homosexuality. In their foreword, the editors note the widespread violent persecution of gay men (a situation apparently not suffered by lesbians) that shapes much of the writing in this volume. They also note recurring themes and images (e.g., the handsome sailor) in literature dealing with homosexuality. Contributions include Robert Musil's "Young Törless," an account of initiation into gay sex; Constantin Cavafy's poetic hymns to male beauty; Sherwood Anderson's "Hands," a story of violent homophobia in a small U.S. town; stories by D. H. Lawrence and Ernest Hemingway of repressed homosexuality in the military; Federico García Lorca's "Ode to Walt Whitman"; selections from Allen Ginsberg's poetry; and Yukio Mishima's "Onnagata," a tale of smoldering homosexual jealousy. Biographical information about the authors is included.

790. Goodich, Michael. **The Unmentionable Vice: Homosexuality in the Later Medieval Period.** Santa Barbara, CA: American Bibliographical Center-Clio Press, 1979. xv, 165p. appendix. bibliography, 143-55. notes. index. Reprint, Santa Barbara, CA: Ross-Erikson, 1979. pa.

This scholarly study traces the growth of anti-gay attitudes in medieval Europe between the eleventh and the fourteenth centuries. At first, persecution of homosexuals was sporadic, although official disapproval of homosexuality was evident. Gradually, as homosexuality became linked with heresy, the Catholic hierarchy moved to impose stricter sanctions against it. Goodich traces the activities of Peter Damian and other moral reformers, the legislation concerning homosexuality issued by various councils, the development of scholastic thought on the subject, and the increasingly severe reprisals taken by secular law. The appendix provides testimony from the trial of Arnold Verniolle, a fourteenth-century French subdeacon accused of homosexual practices.

791. Gonsiorek, John C., ed. **Homosexuality and Psychotherapy: A Practitioner's Handbook of Affirmative Models.** New York: Haworth Press, 1982, 1985. 212p. index. notes. pa.
　　Notable for being an early affirmative approach to counseling for gay people, this collection of 16 articles focuses primarily on gay males. Although scholarly, the articles are written for a general audience. A range of perspectives is evident: contributors include David P. McWhirter and Andrew M. Mattison on psychotherapy for gay couples, Martin Rochlin on the sexual orientation of the therapist and therapeutic effectiveness with gay clients, and James B. Nelson on religious and moral issues in working with homosexual clients. No mention of AIDS occurs in this early-1980s collection. The contents were originally published in the *Journal of Homosexuality* 7 (numbers 2/3).

792. Goodwin, Joseph P. **More Man Than You'll Ever Be: Gay Folklore and Acculturation in Middle America.** Bloomington and Indianapolis: Indiana University Press, 1989. xv, 122p. bibliography, 111-20. notes. index.
　　Like other subcultures, gay subcultures develop their own folklore. Goodwin examines the gay folklore in Middle America, principally that around Bloomington and Indianapolis, Indiana. This folklore consists of stories, jokes, all sorts of word play, and other signs. The context in which this folklore appears is crucial to its meaning. The various signs can be used as coded communication, ice-breakers, forms of solicitation, and expressions of solidarity. Goodwin supplies plentiful examples of such folklore, ranging from anti-lesbian jokes to coming-out stories, from Tallulah Bankhead yarns to the ubiquitous "welcome to the wonderful world of AIDS" tale. Politically correct readers should be forewarned: Many of the stories and jokes are gross, sexist, heterophobic, anti-Semitic, racist, anti-Polish, and so on. Many are also hilarious and moving.

793. Greenberg, David F. **The Construction of Homosexuality.** Chicago and London: University of Chicago Press, 1988. x, 635p. bibliography, 501-613. notes. pa.
　　This encyclopedic volume presents nothing less than a connected, cross-cultural survey of how societies throughout history have "constructed" homosexuality—what people in these societies understood homosexuality to be and what homosexual practices they permitted and engaged in. To accomplish such a monumental task, Greenberg has digested vast amounts of research and assembled it into a readable overview of homosexuality throughout world history. Knowing that much evidence requires careful interpretation, the author exercises judicious skepticism when appropriate. Beginning in early kinship-structured societies, the survey moves through archaic and early civilizations, feudalism, the Renaissance and Reformation, and into the modern world. Here, the medicalization of homosexuality occurred, along with

bureaucratic record keeping of gay peoples. The study closes with an account of Gay Liberation and the outbreak of AIDS. Most of the information is about gay men, although (when evidence warrants) Greenberg explores the constructions of lesbianism. A colossal study in historical sociology, *The Construction of Homosexuality* is a veritable gold mine of information about homosexuality and humanity itself.

794. Halperin, David M. **One Hundred Years of Homosexuality, and Other Essays on Greek Love.** New York and London: Routledge, 1990. x, 230p. illus. bibliography, 213-14. notes. index. pa.

Paying tribute to K. J. Dover's *Greek Homosexuality* (entry 784), Halperin devotes six essays to clarifying aspects of ancient Greek homosexual love. The modern concept of "homosexual," however, is only a century old, Halperin argues, and this concept cannot define ancient practices. Indeed, a major theme of this volume is that sexual identity is not a biological given but a social construct. Sex among ancient Greek citizens was both personal and political; it involved both attraction and social status. In an exchange with Richard Schneider, Halperin defends his view (although he has difficulty arguing that modern homosexuality is a socially constructed antisocial construct). In other chapters, Halperin critiques the work of Harald Patzer and Michel Foucault, discusses heroes and companions (especially in *Gilgamesh*, entry 325, and in the Books of Samuel), and addresses the question of why male prostitutes in ancient Athens could not hold public office. A final essay asks why, in Plato's *Symposium*, the one who conveys wisdom to Socrates is a woman, Diotima. Halperin concludes that gender, as well as sexual identity, is a social fiction, thus making moot the question of Diotima's identity.

795. Harry, Joseph, and Man Singh Das, eds. **Homosexuality in International Perspective.** New Delhi, India: Vikas, 1980; distributed by Advent Books. xiii, 134p. bibliography after each chapter. index.

Nine essays explore such diverse topics as the link between homosexuality and the arts (apparently intrinsic), employment discrimination against gays, a Canadian gay community, the connection between gay culture and leisure culture, the gay ministry, why gays are disliked by heterosexuals (both effeminate behavior and sexual preference create dislike, but mainstream appearance and behavior help offset it), public attitudes towards gays in New Zealand, sexual identity problems of male prostitutes in West Germany, and homosexual practices in nineteenth-century English schools.

796. Hart, John, and Diane Richardson, with Kenneth Plummer, Charles Dodd, Glenys Parry and Ray Lightbrown, Rose Robertson, and Jeffrey Weeks. **The Theory and Practice of Homosexuality.** London, Boston, and Henley, England: Routledge and Kegan Paul, 1981. vii, 206p. illus. bibliography, 190-202. index. pa.

This scholarly work examines homosexuality in theory and in practice, raises the question of homosexual identity, and assesses the availability of professional help for those seeking it. A selected list of English and Irish groups and organizations is included.

797. Hinsch, Bret. **Passions of the Cut Sleeve: The Male Homosexual Tradition in China.** Berkeley: University of California Press, 1990. xvii, 232p. illus. appendix. bibliography, 205-15. notes. index.

Male homosexualities have a long and diversified history in China, reaching back to the Zhou Dynasty (1122-256 B.C.). Earliest evidence from court documents describes male favorites such as the almost legendary Mizi Xia. Such court lovers often came to a sorry end as they aged and fell from favor, a recurring theme in later stories of emperors' lovers. During the Han Dynasty (206 B.C.-A.D. 220) the cut sleeve became a symbol of male homosexuality, and a rich literature of court loves emerged. Some eunuchs also became court lovers. Although court society apparently accepted gay love among upper-class males during their youth, heterosexual marriage for more mature males was expected. During the Tang and Song Dynasties (618-1279), the first negative responses to male homosexuality appeared, and rape of males became a legal concern. Hinsch uses popular humor to glimpse the state of homosexuality outside the upper classes, and he describes master-servant relationships as well as boy prostitutes. In modern times, Western influences have helped to curb Chinese homosexual traditions, although, ironically, the Chinese government has denied the existence of those indigenous traditions and has insisted that homosexuality is an import from the decadent West. The appendix describes lesbianism in Imperial China, a topic about which comparatively little is known.

798. Hippler, Mike. **So Little Time: Essays on Gay Life.** Berkeley, CA: Celestial Arts, 1990. xii, 240p. pa.

A columnist for the *Bay Area Reporter*, Hippler gathers 50 essays covering personal and public gay matters. Among the topics are coming out to family, prosecuting gay-bashers, a gay wedding, the havoc of AIDS, and religion and gays. Whatever the topic, Hippler treats it with a combination of earnestness and good humor.

799. Humphrey, Mary Ann. **My Country, My Right to Serve: Experiences of Gay Men and Women in the Military, World War II to the Present.** New York: HarperCollins, 1990. xxxiii, 296p. illus. appendixes. bibliography, 270-85.

A former captain in the U.S. Army who was discharged for being a lesbian, Humphrey has collected 42 autobiographical accounts of gay people in the military. Most of the contributors are males. Some of the names are well known (Vernon Berg III, Leonard Matlovich, Joseph Steffan), and some use pseudonyms. Most are ordinary soldiers caught in the military's ban on homosexuality. Appendix A provides the U.S. Army regulation defining homosexuality/sodomy, appendix B contains the government document on "Nonconforming Sexual Orientation and Military Suitability," and appendix C lists gay and lesbian support organizations and other miscellaneous services.

800. Isay, Richard A. **Being Homosexual: Gay Men and Their Development.** New York: Farrar, Straus & Giroux, 1989. ix, 159p. notes. index.

Drawing from work with more than 40 gay men in analysis or therapy, the author concludes that homosexuality is "constitutional" and not "environmental" in origin. He also concludes that homosexual orientation is normal and not pathological. As a psychotherapist, however, Isay devotes most of this study to childhood and adolescent development of homosexuality, and not to its origins. He finds that early erotic attachment to the father, bonding with the mother, and alienation from peers are familiar manifestations of homosexuality. The homoerotic fantasies of heterosexual males are different from those of homosexual males, and psychotherapy that tries to "convert" the homosexual to heterosexuality is dangerous. Many of gays' problems derive from a society that overvalues the masculine and undervalues the feminine in males.

801. Isensee, Rik. **Love Between Men: Enhancing Intimacy and Keeping Your Relationship Alive.** New York: Prentice Hall Press, 1990. xiii, 223p. notes. index.

Because gay men face daunting difficulties in modern society, keeping a gay relationship alive can be arduous. A psychotherapist, Isensee provides practical advice, insights, and exercises for gay couples. Part 1 of the book discusses resolving conflicts between the men and others, part 2 offers suggestions on how to keep the relationship going, and part 3 discusses seeking help for severe problems. Isensee covers such matters as coping with family reactions, open and monogamous relationships, AIDS, losing a partner, breaking up, drugs, alcohol, and recovering from addictions.

802. Katz, Jonathan. **Gay American History: Lesbians and Gay Men in the U.S.A: A Documentary History.** Rev. ed., New York: Meridian, 1992. xvii, 702p. illus. bibliography and notes, 667-78. index. pa.

This massive documentary history covers the fortunes of gay men and women in the U.S. from the sixteenth century to the present. Topics include oppression of gays, treatments to "cure" homosexuality, passing as a member of the opposite sex, gays among Native Americans, resistance to persecution, and love.

803. Kleinberg, Seymour. **Alienated Affections: Being Gay in America.** New York: St. Martin's Press, 1980. xiii, 256p. Reprint, New York: Warner Books, 1982. pa.

In a series of graceful, thoughtful essays, Kleinberg uses his own experiences as a New York Jew coping with his homosexuality, informal interviews, and research to examine a number of personal and social concerns. Among the topics touched upon are homosexual concepts of glamor in Hollywood films, gays in ballet, the relationships between gay men and straight women, transsexuals and cross-dressing, the new macho style of homosexuals, sadomasochism, prison rape, the adjustments of aging gays, and psychoanalysis and homosexuality. Sometimes severely critical of gay culture, Kleinberg envies feminist solidarity and indulges in across-the-board references to heterosexual white males as "the enemy" and "the oppressor."

804. Koranyi, Erwin K. **Transsexuality in the Male: The Spectrum of Gender Dysphoria.** Springfield, IL: Charles C. Thomas, 1980. xv, 198p. (American Lecture Series). illus. appendix. glossary. bibliography, 177-91. index.

In clear but sometimes technical language, Koranyi defines a spectrum of disorders involving a male's maladaptation to his anatomical sex. Transsexuality may be related to, but is not identical with, transvestism and homosexuality. Probing biological theories and psychological etiologies, the author presents case histories representing good and bad prospects for sex change operations. A chapter by Selwyn M. Smith and Betty J. Lynch details the medical and legal tangles surrounding sex reassignment surgery, and a chapter by Norman B. Barwin describes, with numerous drawings, the operation itself. A glossary of terms is provided.

805. Kronemeyer, Robert. **Overcoming Homosexuality.** New York: Macmillan, 1980. viii, 220p.

Arguing that homosexuality is "a pathological adaptation" to a frustrating and nonnurturing mother-child relationship, Kronemeyer advances a holistic approach (Syntonic Therapy) to get at the roots of the problem. The author believes that fathers by themselves cannot create homosexuals if the mother-child relationship is sound. He regards homosexuals as neither evil nor a social threat but as suffering from a disease that is now curable in many.

806. Levine, Martin P., ed. **Gay Men: The Sociology of Male Homosexuality.** New York: Harper & Row, 1979. vi, 346p. bibliographies and notes after some chapters. index. pa.

This collection of 21 articles reflects sociology's understanding of gay males as of the late 1970s. The essays concern oppression of gays, gay identity, various homosexual "scenes," lifestyles (including gay couples, gay fathers, women among gay men, the aging homosexual, and the black homosexual), and the gay movement from liberation to "butch."

807. Lewes, Kenneth. **The Psychoanalytic Theory of Male Homosexuality.** New York: Simon & Schuster, 1988. 301p. bibliography, 259-85. notes. index.

Lewes casts a critical eye on psychoanalytic theories of homosexuality. He finds Freud to be limited in his understanding of homosexuality and ambiguous in his ideas about its connection with "normal" sexuality. Nevertheless, Freud was far more sympathetic to homosexuals than many of his followers who increasingly adopted a moralistic, condemnatory stance. Lewes argues that anti-gay sentiment flaws much of psychoanalytic theory right up until the 1970s.

808. Licata, Salvatore J., and Robert P. Petersen, eds. **Historical Perspectives on Homosexuality.** New York: Stein and Day, Haworth Press, 1981. 224p. bibliography, 191-210. notes. index.

In addition to 13 articles covering historical periods from the Middle Ages to the present, this volume also includes William Parker's annotated bibliography of homosexuality in history, as well as reviews of two books. This is the hard-cover edition of *Journal of Homosexuality* 6 (numbers 1/2).

809. Marotta, Toby. **The Politics of Homosexuality.** Boston: Houghton Mifflin, 1981. xiv, 369p. notes. index.

Describing "how lesbians and gay men have made themselves a political and social force in modern America," this history follows the homophile movement from the fifties to 1980.

810. Marotta, Toby. **Sons of Harvard: Gay Men from the Class of 1967.** New York: William Morrow, 1982. 288p. pa.

Among Harvard's best and brightest were a number of gay men, some of whom have come out of the closet. Through interviews Marotta chronicles the growing acceptance, both personal and social, of homosexuality, but the use of assumed names by nearly all the men in this book says much about persisting intolerance.

811. Masters, William H., and Virginia E. Johnson. **Homosexuality in Perspective.** Boston: Little, Brown, 1979. ix, 450p. bibliography, 413-36. index. Reprint, New York: Bantam Books, 1982. pa.

This study by two leading sex experts covers both the preclinical and clinical states of their 20-year investigation into homosexuality. Topics discussed include behavior patterns, physiology, ambisexuals, male and female homosexual dysfunctioning and dissatisfactions, and therapy.

812. McNaught, Brian. **A Disturbed Peace: Selected Writings of an Irish Catholic Homosexual.** Washington, DC: Dignity, 1981. vi, 125p. pa.

In a series of sensitive essays, McNaught reflects on the clash between his homosexuality and his Catholic upbringing, as well as the ways in which he has come to terms with both.

813. McNeill, John J. **The Church and the Homosexual.** Kansas City, KS: Sheed Andrews and McMeel, 1976. xiii, 211p. notes.

A Jesuit priest, McNeill questions Catholicism's traditional view of homosexuality in light of scriptural, theological, moral, and scientific considerations. "In the name of a mistaken understanding of the crime of Sodom and Gomorrah," McNeill writes, "the true crime of Sodom and Gomorrah [cruel injustice] has been and continues to be repeated every day."

814. McWhirter, David P., and Andrew M. Mattison. **The Male Couple: How Relationships Develop.** Englewood Cliffs, NJ: Prentice-Hall, 1984. xv, 341p. appendix. bibliography, 303-14. index.

Interviewing 156 male couples, the authors trace a recurring six-stage development: blending (first year), nesting (second and third years), maintaining (fourth and fifth years), building (years six through ten), releasing (years eleven through twenty), and renewing (beyond twenty years). The authors also examine such topics as male bonding, homophobia, coming out, and sexuality. The authors describe the history of their study; the interview format is contained in the appendix.

815. McWhirter, David P., Stephanie A. Sanders, and June Machover Reinisch, eds. **Homosexuality/Heterosexuality: Concepts of Sexual Orientation.** New York: Oxford University Press, 1990. xxviii, 423p. (The Kinsey Institute series). bibliography after each chapter. name and subject indexes.

This solid collection of 22 scholarly articles (plus a prologue, an overview, and an epilogue) examines sexual orientation from seven perspectives: historical and religious, psychobiological, evolutionary, cultural and sociological, identity development, relational, and conceptual and theoretical. Many contributors present their findings as extensions or critiques of the work of Alfred Kinsey. Among the highlights are the editors' overview of homosexual perspectives since Kinsey's time, John Boswell on sexual and ethical categories in premodern Europe, John Money's assessment of the Kinsey scale, Richard C. Pillard's examination of distant fathers and homosexual sons, Ronald D. Nadler's survey of literature on homosexual behavior in nonhuman primates, Richard A. Isay's discussion of psychoanalytic theory and the therapy of gay men, and Philip Blumstein and Pepper Schwartz's analysis of variabilities in intimate relationships. Common to all the essays is the rejection of a dichotomous view of sexual orientation and the formulation of more complex models.

816. Melton, J. Gordon. **The Churches Speak On: Homosexuality: Official Statements from Religious Bodies and Ecumenical Organizations.** Detroit: Gale Research, 1991. xxxi, 278p. index. pa.

Melton collects 100 documents from Catholic, Protestant, Eastern Orthodox, Jewish, American Humanist, Latter Day Saints, Gay and Lesbian Atheist, and Unitarian Universalist organizations. As might be expected, the range of responses to homosexuality varies greatly.

817. Mendola, Mary. **The Mendola Report: A New Look at Gay Couples.** New York: Crown, 1980. xiii, 269p. appendix. index.

Based upon more than 400 responses to questionnaires and on extended interviews with some of the couples, this report depicts life among gay couples, both male and female. Aside from the social pressures and legal disparities, homosexual couples experience many of the same joys and difficulties that heterosexual couples do. Choosing to concentrate on vignettes from the couples' experiences, Mendola touches upon such matters as sexual fidelity, gays as parents, life insurance and wills for gay couples, gay divorce, gays at work, gay widowerhood, and the new generation of gays. Despite some bitterness toward society for its discrimination against gays, Mendola's sympathies are extensive. Of heterosexual men she writes, "How does a man define himself if it is not in terms of his ability to 'take care of a woman.' Men are as shackled by society's role stereotyping as women are. And when can we expect a men's liberation movement? It is long overdue." The appendix contains the text of the questionnaire.

818. Mieli, Mario. **Homosexuality and Liberation: Elements of a Gay Critique.** Translated by David Fernbach. London: Gay Men's Press, 1980. 247p. notes. pa. Original publication Turin, Italy: Giulio Einaudi editori s.p.a., 1977.

From the Italian school of gay Marxism, Mieli denounces heterosexual capitalist society. Arguing that society warps children's undifferentiating sexual impulses into heterosexuality, Mieli suggests ways to foster polymorphous sexual behavior in the early years. He attacks "psycho-Nazis" (i.e., professional psychotherapists) for stigmatizing homosexuality as a pathology to be cured. Christianity comes under heavy fire for its repressiveness, and sports are criticized for submerging their homoerotic aspects. Mieli extols the superiority of homosexuals, arguing that only they know how to love women truly. These and other radical views make for arresting, if not always convincing, reading.

819. Murphy, Lawrence R. **Perverts by Official Order: The Campaign Against Homosexuals by the United States Navy.** New York and London: Harrington Park Press, 1988. xiii, 340p. illus. bibliography, 323-30. notes. index. pa.

Murphy examines a little-known witch-hunt conducted against homosexuals in 1919 in Newport, Rhode Island. Much of the alleged evidence was fervently collected by a Navy-authorized anti-gay squad created by Ervin Arnold. The hunt centered upon the Newport YMCA and its chaplain, Reverend Samuel Neal Kent. Before the investigations and hearings were over, Franklin D. Roosevelt (then assistant secretary of the Navy) and John R. Rathom (publisher of the *Providence Journal*) found themselves having to deal with the machinations that the Navy had created. Murphy's account has a prophetic ring to it, anticipating more recent events concerning gays and the military.

820. Murray, Stephen O., ed. **Male Homosexuality in Central and South America.** New York: GAU-NY, 1987. 201p. (Gai Saber Monograph, no. 5). pa.

Rather than an overview of male homosexuality in Latin America, this monograph provides a brief tour of several major locales. Beginning with a look at homosexuality in Precolumbian and Colonial Mexico (historical evidence was often destroyed by the conquistadors), this anthology moves on to explore such topics as gay life in São Paulo, male homosexuality in Afro-Brazilian possession cults, and differing attitudes towards homosexuals in Haiti during different phases of political and AIDS crises. Nearly all the articles describe contradictory responses to homosexuality: On the one hand, gayness is at times accepted and incorporated into social life, while on the other hand it is excoriated as perversion. One article contains a bibliography of homosexuality in Brazil.

821. Newton, Esther. **Mother Camp: Female Impersonators in America.** Rev. ed. Chicago and London: University of Chicago Press, Phoenix, 1979. xx, 136p. illus. appendix. notes. pa.

Distinguishing between street fairies and stage performers, Newton focuses on homosexuals who perform in drag. The author examines the conditions under which they work, describing several stage shows in detail. The appendix provides field methods, and the new preface deplores the rise of macho styles among homosexuals. This book first appeared in 1972.

822. Oraison, Marc. **The Homosexual Question.** Translated by Jane Zeni Flinn. New York: Harper & Row, 1977. 132p. notes. pa. Original publication, as *La question homosexuelle* (Paris: Éditions du Seuil, 1975).

A French priest, doctor, and psychiatrist, the author questions traditional Catholic moral teachings on homosexuality, finding them inhuman. Reviewing many aspects of homosexuality and drawing upon case histories, Oraison attempts to "open a window" to ventilate musty moral doctrines.

823. Pharr, Suzanne. **Homophobia: A Weapon of Sexism.** Inverness, CA: Chardon Press, 1988. xv, 95p. illus. pa.

Addressed to a lesbian audience, Pharr's book has a political agenda that denies that gay and straight men are negatively affected by homophobia. As Pharr tells it, homophobia oppresses lesbians and straight women only, while it reinforces the power of all males in society. To make this argument, Pharr engages in considerable special pleading, selective use of evidence, and negative stereotyping of males. Thus, while attempting to address homophobia, Pharr exhibits considerable misandry and heterophobia.

824. Plant, Richard. **The Pink Triangle: The Nazi War Against Homosexuals.** New York: Henry Holt, A New Republic Book, 1986. x, 259p. appendixes. bibliography, 236-48. notes. index.

As a fugitive from Hitler's Germany, Plant returned after the war to research Nazi persecution of homosexuals, a topic often ignored by historians. Beginning with the Nazi ideological assaults on homosexuality, Plant records the active persecution, beginning in the mid-1930s, of gay men. He names Heinrich Himmler as the Grand Inquisitor of the witch-hunt. Plant estimates that between 5,000 and 15,000 gay men perished in Nazi death camps. In the opening and closing sections of the book, Plant records his own poignant postwar search for his friend Eric. Eventually, he learns that Eric was executed by the Nazis.

825. Plummer, Kenneth, ed. **The Making of the Modern Homosexual.** Totowa, NJ: Barnes and Noble, 1981. 280p. appendixes. bibliographies, 231-39, 253-74. notes. index.

Eight essays consider homosexuals in a social context and explore the challenges of conducting sociological research into homosexuality.

826. Preston, John, ed. **Hometowns: Gay Men Write About Where They Belong.** New York: Dutton, 1991. xiv, 366p.

A hometown is where you feel you belong. But as gay youngsters become aware of their sexual orientation, their original hometown may be a place where they no longer feel they belong. The 29 essays in this collection describe hometowns from which the gay authors fled (e.g., Medfield, Massachusetts; Charleston, South Carolina; Oak Ridge, Tennessee) and hometowns where they found refuge (e.g., Key West, San Francisco, Provincetown, and Greenwich Village). Some surprises occur: Preston, for example, found his new hometown in Portland, Maine.

827. Rechy, John. **The Sexual Outlaw: A Documentary.** New York: Grove Press, 1977. 307p.

Described as a "non-fiction account, with commentaries, of three days and nights in the sexual underground," this book focuses on "Jim" as he cruises the Los Angeles world of impersonal gay sex in the pre-AIDS era. A series of graphic scenes form a montage depicting, and probably romanticizing, Jim as a sexual outlaw who defies conventional morality and its police enforcers.

828. Rector, Frank. **The Nazi Extermination of Homosexuals.** New York: Stein and Day, 1981. 189p. illus. bibliography, 179-82. notes. index.

Rector recounts Nazi persecution of gays from the initial crackdowns to the death camps. Contemporary photographs help document the horrors.

829. Rist, Darrell Yates. **Heartlands: A Gay Man's Odyssey Across America.** New York: Dutton, 1992. 486p.

In this vivid travel account, Rist explores gay lives and personalities off the beaten track in the heartland of America. His travels take him to the Southwest, the deep South, Alaska, and Pennsylvania Dutch country. The odyssey concludes with a gay-pride rally in Washington, D.C., and the death of a New York friend from AIDS. Although the account is punctuated by awareness of the AIDS tragedy, the characters whom Rist encounters are vibrantly alive (e.g., a crusty old cowboy at the Denver Gay Rodeo, a pair of visionaries in Santa Fe, a black female impersonator in Nashville). If AIDS deaths suggest that more men are gay than had been believed, Rist's portraits suggest that gay men are more diverse and resilient than is commonly believed.

830. Rofes, Eric E. **"I Thought People Like That Killed Themselves": Lesbians, Gay Men and Suicide.** San Francisco: Grey Fox Press, 1983. x, 163p. illus. appendix. notes. index. pa.

Because lesbians and gay men must sometimes make a choice between disgrace and self-destruction, suicide is a serious problem among gays. Similarly, social pressure on gays can lead to despair. Scandal, blackmail, and public exposure are still threats to gay people, and coming out is no guarantee of immunity from them. Rofes provides numerous cases of homosexuals driven to suicide, he outlines areas of needed research, and he discusses methods of intervention, therapy, and prevention. The appendixes examine the fiction of

Sappho's suicide, the dubious use of gay suicide statistics by some conservative Christian writers, common misconceptions about suicides, and techniques of counseling gays through hotlines.

831.   Roscoe, Will. **The Zuni Man-Woman.** Albuquerque: University of New Mexico Press, 1991. xxi, 302p. illus. appendixes. bibliography, 267-89. notes. index. pa.

Roscoe provides both a biography of the memorable Zuni berdache, We'wha, as well as background to the man-woman tradition among Southwestern tribes. Born in 1849, We'wha chose the path of the lhamana, the man who dresses as a woman and performs women's tasks. We'wha soon became well known for his skill as a potter, weaver, and female artisan. Taken to Washington, D.C., in 1885 by the formidable traveler-anthropologist Matilda Coxe Stevenson, We'wha fascinated high society, and almost no one realized that the Indian "princess" was a man. In 1892, We'wha took part in resistance against U.S. soldiers attempting to arrest a Zuni man, and he was briefly imprisoned. We'wha died in 1896. Roscoe recounts the role of man-woman as an alternate gender among the Zunis, the efforts of Westerners to suppress the tradition, and its rebirth among gay Native Americans. The appendixes provide a guide to pronunciation and a summary of the Zuni origin myth.

832.   Ross, Michael W. **The Married Homosexual Man: A Psychological Study.** London and Boston: Routledge and Kegan Paul, 1983. xvi, 184p. appendixes. bibliography, 178-82. index. pa.

Two surveys are the basis of this study. The first, done in 1975, involved 63 respondents in Australia and New Zealand. The second, conducted in 1978, involved 488 respondents in Sweden, Finland, and Australia. Ross discusses such topics as the homosexual's reasons for marrying (social hostility toward homosexuality is a major factor) and the unlikeliness that the marriage will alter the man's sexual orientation. Ross sketches a profile of the homosexual who is likely to marry and presents several case histories. The appendixes reprint the questionnaire and discuss methodology.

833.   Rowse, A. L. **Homosexuals in History: A Study of Ambivalence in Society, Literature and the Arts.** New York: Macmillan, 1977. xiii, 346p. illus. index.

Brilliant and bitter, Rowse provides a series of vignettes of famous homosexuals in Western history, from the Renaissance to the present. The book's epigram, "Homo homini lupus," strikes the keynote of anger at treatment of homosexuals through the ages. Among those portrayed are Leonardo da Vinci, Michelangelo, Christopher Marlowe, Henri III, Rudolf II, James I, Louis XIII, Lord Hervey, Frederick the Great, Walt Whitman, Oscar Wilde, T. E. Lawrence, Roger Casement, Ludwig Wittgenstein, and Yukio Mishima.

834.   Ruse, Michael. **Homosexuality: A Philosophical Inquiry.** Oxford and New York: Basil Blackwell, 1988. xi, 299p. illus. bibliography, 272-91. notes. index.

Mustering philosophic acuity, Ruse surveys various theories of the origins and morality of homosexuality. His inquiry is thus both epistemological and ethical. After defining terms, he groups theories of the causes of homosexuality into three categories: psychological, hormonal, and sociobiological. Reviewing classic Freudian views, Ruse concludes that, despite Freud's limitations, his descriptions of sexuality may yet form the basis for more adequate explanations. Ruse finds less value in "adaptational" or "phobic" positions (i.e., homosexuality is an adaptation to fear of the opposite sex). Reviewing studies of hormonal causes of homosexuality, Ruse finds them often methodologically suspect or limited; in any event, they indicate no simple connection between hormones and sexual orientation. Ruse discovers similar complications in sociobiological explanations; he finds no easy linking of homosexual behavior with a biological imperative. Determinism and reductionism come in many forms, he notes, thereby complicating our understanding of the causes of homosexuality. Moving on to the social and ethical implications of homosexuality, Ruse surveys ancient Greek society. Relying on K. J. Dover (entry 784), he finds less acceptance of homosexual behaviors than is popularly supposed. In Judeo-Christian views, homosexual orientation is not condemned, but homosexual behavior is proscribed as unnatural. Ruse finds little merit, however, in the "unnatural" argument and even less in the argument that homosexuality is a sickness. He concludes: "Homosexuality within a loving relationship is a morally good thing." A final chapter surveys the legal position of homosexuals. Ruse concludes: "Although justice requires that we not discriminate against homosexuals, justice forbids us to discriminate in their favour." Occasionally, Ruse mars the discussion with gratuitous insults directed against heterosexual males. (Sample: "Heterosexual males seem obsessed with the idea of dildos and other penis substitutes—no doubt they find it difficult to imagine that women could find sexual satisfaction without their own presence, at least by proxy.") Usually, however, Ruse pursues his inquiry with equitableness.

835. Sarotte, Georges-Michel. **Like a Brother, Like a Lover: Male Homosexuality in the American Novel and Theater, from Herman Melville to James Baldwin.** Translated by Richard Miller. Garden City, NY: Anchor Press/Doubleday, 1978. xv, 339p. bibliography, 306-27. index. Original publication as *Comme un frère, comme un amant* (Paris: Flammarion, 1976).

This literary and social study opens with an overview of intolerance in the United States and the emergence of the homosexual in novels and plays. Discussing numerous authors and works, Sarotte then examines four archetypes of the homosexual in literature (adolescents, teacher and pupil, captain and soldier, and white and black), as well as the circumstances in which the homosexual is depicted in novels and plays. Individual chapters are devoted to such major figures as playwrights Tennessee Williams, William Inge, Edward Albee, and novelist Henry James. More controversial are chapters on "latent" homosexuality in the works of Jack London, F. Scott Fitzgerald, Ernest Hemingway, and Norman Mailer.

836. Shilts, Randy. **Conduct Unbecoming: Lesbians and Gays in the U.S. Military, Vietnam to the Persian Gulf.** New York: St. Martin's Press, 1993. xiv, 784p. bibliography, 767-70. notes. index.

In a "narrative, non-fiction" style, Shilts tells the story of gay people in the U.S. military. The brief section devoted to the years between 1778 and 1954 focuses on a gay man, Baron Frederick von Steuben, as one of the founders of the American army. Most of the book is devoted to the period between 1954 and 1969. Tracking dozens of people and events, Shilts places these stories against the larger picture of the U.S. military's war on gays, usually through dishonorable discharges for "conduct unbecoming." Among the episodes of military heavy-handedness are the Ensign Berg story (entry 42), the Navy's attempt to attribute an explosion on board the *U.S.S. Iowa* to an allegedly gay man, and the panic over AIDS. Shilts frames his narrative with the moving story of Tom Dooley, well known as a humanitarian but less well known as a gay ex-serviceman.

837. Signorile, Michelangelo. **Queer in America: Sex, the Media, and the Closets of Power.** New York: Random House, 1993. xix, 379p. index.

A gay who bashes back at gay-bashers, Signorile advocates "outing" because gays who hide in the closet play into the hands of homophobes. The three sections of *Queer in America* focus on three sites: New York as site of media power, Washington as site of governmental power, and Hollywood as site of a gay-denying entertainment industry. In part 1, Signorile describes growing up gay in Italian Catholic Brooklyn, his outing of Malcolm Forbes posthumously, and the politics of ACT UP. In part 2, he discusses gays in the government, and in part 3, he describes Hollywood's silencing of gayness. The epilogue contrasts anti-gay ordinances in Oregon with gay openness in the Silicon Valley. A queer manifesto that rejects the closet closes the book.

838. Silverstein, Charles. **A Family Matter: A Parents' Guide to Homosexuality.** New York: McGraw-Hill, 1977. v, 214p. bibliography, 214. pa.

"This book," the author states, "is for families who want to learn how to deal with a homosexual son or daughter, and come to terms with their own feelings about homosexuality." Silverstein defines and clarifies terms, dissects stereotypes of homosexuals, and presents five case histories of families coping with a homosexual member. He discusses responsible therapy for homosexuals and their families.

839. Silverstein, Charles. **Man to Man: Gay Couples in America.** New York: William Morrow, 1981. 348p. appendix. name index. pa.

Using interviews with 190 men, Silverstein addresses numerous questions concerning gay couples, including the eroticized father-son relationship, peers in school, coming out, major issues confronting male couples (e.g., the search for excitement vs. the need to build a home), and varieties of gay couples. The appendix describes the interview technique.

840. Silverstein, Charles, and Felice Picano. **The New Joy of Gay Sex.** New York: HarperCollins, 1992. xvi, 223p. illus. index.

In alphabetical order—from AIDS to wrestling—the authors discuss the details of male gay sex and lifestyle. The numerous illustrations are by F. Ronald Fowler (black-and-white) and Deni Ponty (color). The preface is by Edmund White.

841. Socarides, Charles W., and Vamik D. Volkan, eds. **The Homosexualities and the Therapeutic Process.** Madison, CT: International Universities Press, 1991. xii, 315p. bibliography, 293-302. name and subject indexes.

In this companion volume to Socarides and Volkan's 1990 volume, *The Homosexualities: Reality, Fantasy, and the Arts* (Madison, CT: International University Press), 14 essays discuss various aspects of understanding and treating different forms of homosexuality. The use of "homosexualities" in the title indicates the authors' awareness that homosexuality occurs on "a spectrum at one end of which oedipal conflicts dominate, while at the other is evidence of an inability to differentiate the self-representation from the representation of the object." Most of the essays in the collection are primarily Freudian in orientation and focus on problems arising in the pre-oedipal stage, especially the task of separating from the mother. Most of the articles assume that the homosexual patient is suffering from a mental illness. In the final essay, Socarides urges psychoanalysts to discourage sexual contact among their homosexual patients because of the AIDS situation.

842. Whitam, Frederick L., and Robin M. Mathy. **Male Homosexuality in Four Societies: Brazil, Guatemala, the Philippines, and the United States.** New York: Praeger, 1986. xxxii, 209p. (Praeger Special Studies). bibliography, 183-97. index.

Whitam and Mathy argue that homosexuals are a biologically derived minority that appears in all societies at about the same rate. Because the majority of people are heterosexual, homosexuals cluster in subcultures that often exhibit cross-cultural similarities. To argue this thesis, the authors survey what is known about past homosexual subcultures and examine gay subcultures in greater detail in four societies. They describe similarities of psychosexual development among gay men: cross-gender behavior is an early and inevitable feature of homosexual development. Although there is a range of gay types, transvestic homosexuals are one type known to most societies. Gay men are drawn to certain social tasks and occupations (e.g., the arts of embellishment, house and home, and entertainment and the arts). Lesbians are more interested in athletics than heterosexual women are, while gay men are less interested in athletics than heterosexual men are. Reactions to gay people by different societies can range from repression to ·acceptance. Latin countries, for example, generally accept relations between *machos* and *pasivos* so long as the distinction is maintained. Among the Filipinos, relations between the gay *bayot* and the "callboys" who service them permit a less hostile interaction than is usually found in the United States. In the final chapter, the authors review various "causes" theories of homosexuality to strengthen their case that gays are a biologically derived minority, and thus a permanent one. Numerous tables, usually based upon the authors' studies, appear throughout the text and support the findings.

843. White, Edmund. **States of Desire: Travels in Gay America.** New York: E. P. Dutton, 1980. xi, 336p. pa. Reprint, New York: Bantam Books, 1981. pa. Reprint, New York: Plume, 1991. pa.

In this highly acclaimed and often-imitated book, interviews and reflections are woven together into a tapestry depicting the U.S. homosexual scene in nearly two dozen major cities.

844. Williams, Walter L. **The Spirit and the Flesh: Sexual Diversity in American Indian Culture.** Boston: Beacon Press, 1986, 1992. xx, 344p. illus. bibliography, 317-33. notes. index.

This study focuses on the berdache, a man who adopted feminine behaviors in Native American cultures. Because of the diversity among American Indian tribes, generalizations are difficult. In some cultures, the berdache was ridiculed; in others, he was exalted as an androgynous shaman with prophetic and healing powers. Many tribes respected such androgynes as mediators between male and female, spirit and body. Williams argues several controversial points. He contends that many Native Americans recognized the berdache as a third gender, although accounts of berdaches vary: Some peoples saw them as both man and woman, others as half-man and half-woman. Williams also argues that the berdache was almost always homosexual and almost always played the "passive" or "feminine" role with heterosexual males. Relationships between berdaches were unacceptable, but some berdaches married women. Williams negatively portrays Europeans, especially the Spanish, for penalizing homosexual behaviors among Latin American Indians. Homosexuality, however, was evident among "New World" settlers (e.g., Caribbean pirates and cowboys). In the face of European pressures, the berdache went underground, and Indians stopped talking about sexual practices. With the emergence of gay pride in the United States, however, berdache traditions are resurfacing.

845. Wolinsky, Marc, and Kenneth Sherrill, eds. **Gays and the Military: Joseph Steffan Versus the United States.** Princeton, NJ: Princeton University Press, 1993. xxli, 222p. notes. index. pa.

From the legal briefs prepared by the law firm of Wachtell, Lipton, Rosen, and Katz for Joseph Steffan's case against the U.S. military ban on homosexuals, the editors have compiled eight affidavits and other legal documents. The result is a book that explores numerous areas concerning matters such as the causes of sexual orientation, gays in military life, gay history, and legal concerns. In affidavit 1, for example, John Boswell surveys the history of social attitudes toward homosexuality from ancient Greece to the present. Richard Green discusses homosexual orientation as an immutable characteristic, and Robert Rankin argues the ability of gay people to perform well in the military. The final word, however, is Judge Oliver Gasch's opinion supporting the military ban on homosexuals as reasonable.

846. Woods, James D., with Jay H. Lucas. **The Corporate Closet: The Professional Lives of Gay Men in America.** New York: Free Press, Macmillan, 1993. xviii, 331p. bibliography, 315-26. notes. index.

Based on a study of seventy men, plus numerous additional interviews, this book examines the toll paid by gay men in professional life who either remain in the closet or attempt to come out. Although homophobia and the assumption of heterosexuality are widespread in the corporate world, that world is non-asexual. Everything from wedding bands to benefits packages indicate a presumption of heterosexuality as the norm. This situation leaves many gay men shuttling between two worlds, one straight and one gay. Some find the closet comfortable, others practice uncomfortable dodges to appear straight, and still others come out. The results of the latter decision vary: Some suffer discrimination, some are granted token status, and some are accepted as gay. The final chapter suggests strategies for dismantling the corporate closet. The appendix provides details of the study.

847. Zeeland, Steven. **Barrack Buddies and Soldier Lovers: Dialogues with Gay Young Men in the U.S. Military.** New York: Harrington Park Press, 1993. xii, 293p. pa.

A civilian employee of the U.S. Army, Zeeland lived in Frankfurt, Germany, from 1983 to 1991, where he taped the 16 interviews contained in this book. In frank discussions, the men tell of intense, sometimes disruptive, homosexual relationships among army men and of hostility from straights. Few of the men took precautions against AIDS and have since tested HIV-positive. The foreword is by Allan Bérubé.

848. Ziebold, Thomas O., and John E. Mongeon, eds. **Alcoholism and Homosexuality.** New York: Haworth Press, 1982. 107p. bibliography after each chapter. index.

Rejecting the idea of any necessary link between alcoholism and homosexuality, the 10 essays in this collection examine the causes and treatment of alcohol abuse among gays. This is the hardbound edition of the *Journal of Homosexuality* 7 (number 4).

Cross-References

See chapter 7, "Erotica and Pornography," and chapter 9, "Health and Related Topics."

71. Abbott, Franklin, ed. **Men and Intimacy: Personal Accounts Exploring the Dilemmas of Modern Male Sexuality.**

592. Bahr, Robert. **The Virility Factor: Masculinity Through Testosterone, the Male Sex Hormone.**

389. Balbert, Peter. **D. H. Lawrence and the Phallic Imagination: Essays on Sexual Identity and Feminist Misreading.**

475. Barret, Robert L., and Bryan E. Robinson. **Gay Fathers.**

478. Biller, Henry. **Paternal Deprivation: Family, School, Sexuality, and Society.**

480. Bozett, Frederick W., ed. **Gay and Lesbian Parents.**

909. Buffum, Peter C. **Homosexuality in Prisons.**

157. Bullough, Vern L., W. Dorr Legg, Barrett W. Elcano, and James Kepner, comps. **An Annotated Bibliography of Homosexuality.**

395. Butters, Ronald R., John M. Clum, and Michael Moon, eds. **Displacing Homophobia: Gay Male Perspectives in Literature and Culture.**

599. Cherfas, Jeremy, and John Gribbin. **The Redundant Male: Is Sex Irrelevant in the Modern World?**

863. Clark, J. Michael, with Bob McNeir. **Masculine Socialization and Gay Liberation: A Conversation on the Work of James Nelson and Other Wise Friends.**

397. Crompton, Louis. **Byron and Greek Love: Homophobia in 19th-Century England.**

271a. Darmon, Pierre. **Damning the Innocent: A History of the Persecution of the Impotent in Pre-Revolutionary France.**

158. Dynes, Wayne R., comp. **Homosexuality: A Research Guide.**

401. Fone, Byrne R.S. **Masculine Landscapes: Walt Whitman and the Homoerotic Text.**

42. Gibson, E. Lawrence. **Get Off My Ship: Ensign Berg vs. the U.S. Navy.**

986. Gochros, Jean Schaar. **When Husbands Come Out of the Closet.**

177. Green, Richard. **The "Sissy Boy Syndrome" and the Development of Homosexuality.**

43. Greenburg, Dan. **Scoring: A Sexual Memoir.**

606. Hapgood, Fred. **Why Males Exist: An Inquiry into the Evolution of Sex.**

160. Horner, Tom, comp. **Homosexuality and the Judeo-Christian Tradition: An Annotated Bibliography.**

329. Ihara Saikaku. **The Great Mirror of Male Love.**

917. Island, David, and Patrick Letellier. **Men Who Beat the Men Who Love Them: Battered Gay Men and Domestic Violence.**

47. Kantrowitz, Arnie. **Under the Rainbow: Growing Up Gay.**

411. Koestenbaum, Wayne. **Double Talk: The Erotics of Male Literary Collaboration.**

49. Kopay, David, and Perry Deane Young. **The David Kopay Story: An Extraordinary Self-Revelation.**

870. Lawlor, Robert. **Earth Honoring: The New Male Sexuality.**

359. Lawrence, D.H. **Lady Chatterley's Lover.**

52. Leiris, Michel. **Manhood: A Journey from Childhood into the Fierce Order of Virility.**

1003. Malone, John. **Straight Women/Gay Men: A Special Relationship.**

1046. Mitzel, John. **Sports and the Macho Male.**

610. Money, John, and Patricia Tucker. **Sexual Signatures: On Being a Man or a Woman.**

712. Monick, Eugene. **Phallos: Sacred Image of the Masculine.**

1008. Nahas, Rebecca, and Myra Turley. **The New Couple: Women and Gay Men.**

894. Nelson, James B. **The Intimate Connection: Male Sexuality, Masculine Spirituality.**

611. Ong, Walter J. **Fighting for Life: Contest, Sexuality, and Consciousness.**

163. Parker, William, comp. **Homosexuality: A Selective Bibliography of Over 3,000 Items.**

164. Parker, William, comp. **Homosexuality Bibliography: Supplement, 1970-1975.**

612. Petras, John W., ed. **Sex: Male/Gender: Masculine: Readings in Male Sexuality.**

185. Pomeroy, Wardell B. **Boys and Sex.**

1047. Pronger, Brian. **The Arena of Masculinity: Sports, Homosexuality, and the Meaning of Sex.**

61. Richards, Renée, with John Ames. **Second Serve: The Renée Richards Story.**

721. Ruitenbeek, Henrik M., ed. **Psychoanalysis and Male Sexuality.**

423. Savran, David. **Communists, Cowboys, and Queers: The Politics of Masculinity in the Work of Arthur Miller and Tennessee Williams.**

544. Schulenburg, Joy A. **Gay Parenting.**

26. Scott, George Ryley. **Phallic Worship.**

425. Sedgwick, Eve Kosofsky. **Between Men: English Literature and Male Homosocial Desire.**

22

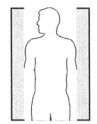

Single Men: Never Married, Divorced, Widowered

849. Anderson, Nels. **The Hobo: The Sociology of the Homeless Man.** Rev. ed. Chicago and London: University of Chicago Press, 1961. xxix, 296p. illus. appendixes. bibliography, 287-93. notes. index. pa.

First published in 1923, this study has become a classic that describes the homeless men in "Hobohemia." Its influence upon sociology has been considerable. In the new introduction, the author notes that the hobo has vanished with the world described in the book's pages.

850. Burgess, Jane K. **The Single-Again Man.** Lexington, MA: D. C. Heath, Lexington Books, 1988. xv, 173p. bibliography, 157-66. index.

According to the author, we need "to provide men in our society with the same sympathy, empathy, and emotional support offered women when they face a situation too traumatic to be handled alone." Using interviews, Burgess examines the problems faced by men who lose a spouse through divorce, death, or a physical or mental breakdown. Each year, 250,000 men become "single-again." The stereotype of the dashing single-again man blinds many people to the grief these men experience. In divorce, the man's reactions may vary depending upon whether he, his ex-wife, or both together initiated the divorce. Likewise, whether a wife's death was expected or sudden can greatly affect the husband's reaction to it. Burgess discusses such topics as coming to terms with loss, becoming a single-again parent, socializing and dating, men's need for love and sex, thoughts of remarriage, and methods for helping single-again men. The book exhibits the sympathetic understanding that Burgess preaches.

851. Campbell, Scott, with Phyllis R. Silverman. **Widower.** New York: Prentice Hall Press, 1987. 227p. appendix.

A quarter of a million men become widowers each year, and the experience hits most of them hard. To make matters worse, the myth that "women grieve, men replace" blocks sympathetic understanding of their pain. In this book, Campbell presents extended interviews with 20 widowers, followed by commentary informed by Silverman's expertise as a bereavement expert. Most widowers experienced shock, grief, anger, and loneliness. Drinking can be harmful; group sessions can be helpful. Professionals are often less beneficial than lay people with similar experiences. Perhaps the most interesting account is that of "Peter," whose bereavement included involving his children in the funeral rites and visionary experiences of his dead wife. The brief appendix lists self-help organizations and readings.

852. Gilder, George. **Naked Nomads: Unmarried Men in America.** New York: Quadrangle/New York Times Press, 1974. ix, 180p. notes. index.

In this controversial study, Gilder attempts to debunk the single life, especially for men. Rejecting the stereotype of the swinging bachelor, he depicts single men as unhappier, poorer, more criminal, more disturbed, and more suicidal than married men. Arguing that men need the stability of marriage and children more than women do, Gilder excoriates the sexual revolution for attempting to short-circuit marriage. He deplores competition between men and women fostered by the entrance of large numbers of women into corporate life. Males, Gilder concludes, are at their best when they are able to adjust to women's sexual and procreative rhythms in monogamous family life.

853. Gordon, William J., and Steven D. Price. **The Second-Time Single Man's Survival Handbook.** New York: Praeger, 1975. 175p. illus.

Maintaining a light touch, the authors consider the lot of the divorced male, offering suggestions for sharing living quarters with another male, checking out apartments, furnishings, housecleaning, operating in the kitchen, keeping oneself in clothes, dating again, and coping with kids. The humorous cartoons are by Roy Doty. (William J. Gordon is sometimes listed under the name William J. Goode.)

854. Kohn, Jane Burgess, and Willard K. Kohn. **The Widower.** Boston: Beacon Press, 1978. xvi, 169p. bibliography, 157-66. index.

Concerned by the few studies of widowers and by the casual assumption that widowers face few problems, the authors—both of whom had lost spouses before their marriage to each other—combine their efforts to present a personal and professional view of widowers. Each of the eight chapters follows the same pattern: Bill, a plant superintendent, recounts his experiences during and after his first wife's terminal illness. Commenting more broadly on bereavement, Jane, a professor of sociology, draws upon interviews with 35 widowers and 15 young persons who had lost parents. Topics covered include the immediate reaction to a loved one's death, acceptance of death, recovery from grief, and helping children to cope with the situation (when his first wife died, Bill had six daughters to raise). Noting that 550,000 widowers, half of whom have children to care for, are accounted for yearly, Jane examines the man's ability to function as a single parent (this chapter is titled "It's a Fact—Men Are Capable of Parenthood"), the widower's reentry into paired society, dating again, and deciding whether or not to remarry. The bibliography, although extensive on related matters, demonstrates how little has been written about widowers. Both authors write with exceptional sensitivity.

855. Rubinstein, Robert L. **Singular Paths: Old Men Living Alone.** New York: Columbia University Press, 1986. viii, 263p. appendixes. bibliography, 257-61. index.

Older men constitute a "forgotten" minority, overlooked by researchers and by social workers who tailor programs for women. In 1982, a million and a half elderly men lived alone. Drawing upon interviews with 47 such men in the Philadelphia area, Rubinstein defines some common themes in their experiences, while insisting upon each man's uniqueness. For widowered men, the loss of a spouse can be the most devastating experience of their lifetime. Even among never-married men, sources of grief are found. Many of the men desired the honor of "elder status," yet none had attained it. Loneliness, relationships with grown children, health, and structuring the day are among the elders' concerns. One appendix describes the research method; the other suggests ways for service providers to make men feel more comfortable with senior centers.

856. Witkin, Mildred Hope, with Burton Lehrenbaum. **45 and Single Again.** New York: Dembner Books, 1985. x, 198p. index.

Written for both women and men, this book offers compassionate and evenhanded advice for those who find themselves widowed or divorced after midlife. The book's three sections deal with the trauma of divorce or a spouse's death, sexuality in later life, and such matters as financial security and remarriage.

Cross-References

See chapter 14, "Males in Families," section C, "Divorced and Single Fathers, Stepfathers."

492. Elster, Arthur B., and Michael E. Lamb, eds. **Adolescent Fatherhood.**

305. Friedman, Bruce. **The Lonely Guy's Book of Life.**

362. Lopate, Phillip. **Bachelorhood: Tales of the Metropolis.**

539. Robinson, Bryan E. **Teenage Fathers.**

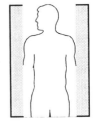

23

Spirituality

A. Archetypal and Mythic Studies, Mythopoetic (or Mythopoeic) Men's Movement, Religious Concepts of Masculinity

This section contains books that focus on masculine spirituality, often in terms of archetypes or myths. Other books on archetypes and masculinity can be found in chapter 15, "Masculinity," and in chapter 20, "Psychology."

857. Anderson, William. **Green Man: The Archetype of Our Oneness with the Earth.** London and San Francisco: HarperCollins, 1990. 176p. illus. bibliography, 169-73. notes. index. pa.

The male counterpart of Gaia, the Earth Goddess, Green Man has appeared in iconography and ritual since the earliest times. Anderson traces the history and meaning of Green Man in this richly illustrated volume. Most of the 136 illustrations are photographs (color and black-and-white) by Clive Hicks. Anderson finds three kinds of Green Man images: foliate heads (male heads formed out of a leaf mask), a male head disgorging vegetation from his mouth and (sometimes) eyes and ears, and a male head formed of flower or fruit. In classical times, Green Man was associated with dying-resurrecting vegetation gods. During the Dark Ages in Europe, Green Man images and folk ceremonies transferred from pagan to Christian belief. In the Middle Ages, imagery of Green Man triumphed in Gothic architecture. Reborn in Victorian times, Green Man has been given yet another lease on life in the twentieth century through ecological concerns and Green Man's affinity with the Wild Man. Anderson explores Green Man's multiple meanings—religious, social, psychological. Green man is the male image that links the individual with the natural world; he is the symbol of divine imagination. His words are leaves that speak of creation. Anderson concludes that ancients worshipped the earth and moderns have exploited it, but Green Man now reminds us that we and the natural universe are one.

858. Arnold, Patrick M. **Wildmen, Warriors, and Kings: Masculine Spirituality and the Bible.** New York: Crossroad, 1991. xii, 240p. notes. index. pa.

A Jesuit priest, Arnold meshes masculine archetypes with Judeo-Christian belief. Masculine spirituality, Arnold argues, now has an uphill battle against sexist stereotypes of males as unspiritual, against patriarchal restrictions that limit male experience, and against Christianity's tendency to separate body and spirit. While urging men to support the women's movement toward greater gender equality, Arnold attacks misandry, the hatred of men fostered by the dark side of feminism. Misandry has become dogma to many new goddess worshipers who designate men as the source of all evil and who exalt all women as immaculate conceptions, free of original sin. Masculine spirituality is deeply rooted in masculine traits such as competition, independence, vulnerability, and responsibility. It is fostered by rites of separation, initiation, and reintegration; it is directed by images of the hero. In men's current spiritual crisis, the Christian churches, increasingly feminized, have been driving men away from spirituality. Scanning the Bible, Arnold finds archetypal images in Abraham as Patriarch and Pilgrim, Moses as Warrior and Magician, Solomon as King and Lover, Elijah as Wild Man, Elisha as Healer, Jeremiah as Prophet, Jonah as Trickster, and David as Lover. He discusses Jesus as man and the masculine attributes of God. The book's foreword is by Robert Bly.

859. Becker, Verne. **The Real Man Inside: How Men Can Recover Their Identity and Why Women Can't Help.** Grand Rapids, MI: Zondervan Publishing House, 1992. 206p. bibliography, 203-4. notes.

A Christian, Becker finds important spiritual meaning in the mythopoetic men's movement. Hearing the "rattle" of something missing in their lives, many men are seeking the real man inside. Modern men suffer numerous wounds, including the techno wound of industrialized society that isolates them from the natural world. At the moment, neither the political left nor the political right offers genuine help to men, the media ridicule the men's movement without understanding it, and radical feminist reactions to it are defensive. More significantly for Becker, Christian responses are ambivalent. Seeking to alter this situation, Becker argues the value of myth and archetypes, especially the warrior archetype. Because he sees many men, including himself, as underfathered and overmothered, Becker agrees with Robert Bly's assessment of soft men in *Iron John* (entry 861): They are nice but sadly passive. Lacking masculine energy, they cannot set boundaries. In Jesus, Becker finds the consummate figure who embodies crucial archetypal meaning.

860. Black Elk. **Black Elk Speaks: Being the Life Story of a Holy Man of the Oglala Sioux.** As told through John G. Neihardt (Flaming Rainbow). New York: William Morrow, 1932. Rev. ed., Lincoln and London: University of Nebraska Press, Bison Books, 1961, 1988. xix, 298p. illus. appendixes. pa. Reprint, New York: Pocket Books, 1972. pa.

An indispensable document of Native American history, *Black Elk Speaks* also has become a classic of masculine spirituality. In May 1931, Black Elk's spoken narrative was interpreted into English by his son Ben, written down by Enid Neihardt, and reworked by her father, John G. Neihardt, into the present text. Black Elk's autobiography contains compelling accounts of the incursion of white settlers and soldiers into the Dakotas, the gruesome battles of Little Big Horn and Wounded Knee, the destruction of the bison herds, and Black Elk's travels to New York and Europe with Buffalo Bill Cody's Wild West show. Perhaps more important, the book tells of Black Elk's great religious visions and how he translated those visions into ceremonies that helped preserve his people's identity.

At a time when many people lament the lack of masculine spiritual ritual in modern U.S. life, Black Elk speaks powerfully to an ever-widening audience.

861. Bly, Robert. **Iron John: A Book About Men.** Reading, MA: Addison-Wesley, 1990. xi, 271p. notes. Reprint, New York: Random House-Vintage, 1992. pa.

Perhaps the most influential book about men in recent times, *Iron John* resonates in numerous ways. Retelling an ancient European tale of the Wild Man—Iron John—Bly reflects upon segments of the story, applying its insights to the situation of modern men. The story tells of a King's son who releases a captured Wild Man and then flees with him into the forest. There, Iron John provides wisdom that enables the boy to confront battle and to win a princess. Bly's commentary on the tale utilizes a rich array of literature, myth, and current events. Because Bly's poetic, prophetic text is designed to be experienced, it cannot be adequately summarized. Nevertheless, some recurring themes include the following: In modern society, the shortage of societal Fathers and Wild Men blocks the development of boys into adult men; modern society is no longer a patriarchy but an industrial-military wasteland that impoverishes the spirits of men and women; grief for the absent father characterizes most men nowadays; the remoteness of fathers leads to their being perceived as demons; women cannot provide the initiation into manhood that boys need; the initiation process is marked by a wounding of the boy that may be a blessing; the "soft male," who is overly sensitive to feminist concerns, is not a safe guide to genuine manhood, nor is the "naive male," who takes on women's suffering and ignores his own; the Wild Man is Nature itself and has been the object of persecution through much of Western history. In the final chapter, Bly retells the story of Iron John without interruption, letting the reader savor its meanings. Controversial and seminal, *Iron John* has become a force in many men's lives.

862. Campbell, Joseph. **The Hero with a Thousand Faces.** 1949. 2d ed. Princeton. NJ: Princeton University Press, 1968. xxiii, 416p. (Bollingen Series XVII). illus. notes. index. pa.

A central text in the men's mythopoeic movement, *The Hero with a Thousand Faces* is a classic study in which Campbell charts the monomyth, that is, the underlying pattern of countless myths, legends, tales, dreams, and rituals in numerous cultures through world history. The motif of a journey into strange realms is a near-universal element in this monomyth. The hero hears a call and ventures forth. He is guided by a mentor, often supernatural, crosses the first threshold, and reaches "the belly of the whale," the place from which rebirth occurs. He encounters the Goddess, sometimes in the threatening form of the Temptress or the Dark Mother. He reaches atonement with the Father, often through initiation rites. The hero returns to his place of departure, brings great blessings with him, and achieves apotheosis and immortality. Campbell also explores the "cosmogonic cycle," the Virgin Birth, the various manifestations of the hero (e.g., as warrior, lover, saint), and the multiple significances of the monomyth for modern society. Campbell's exposition remains infinitely rich in its psychological, religious, historical, and social meanings.

863. Clark, J. Michael, with Bob McNeir. **Masculine Socialization and Gay Liberation: A Conversation on the Work of James Nelson and Other Wise Friends.** Arlington, TX: Liberal Press, 1992. ix, 88p. bibliography, 87. notes. pa.

Drawing upon the work of James Nelson and others, Clark concludes that "heteropatriarchy" deforms both heterosexuality and homosexuality. By separating body and mind, prevailing Western belief blocks a truly sacramental understanding of sexuality, and it exalts performance over intimacy. Clark's discussion at times turns into a conversation between himself and his spouse, Bob McNeir. The final chapter considers the whole gay man, reconstructed and liberated.

864. Doty, William G. **Myths of Masculinity.** New York: Crossroad, 1993. ix, 243p. illus. bibliography, 227-39. notes. index.

Sensing an anti-feminist element in the mythopoetic men's movement, Doty attempts to align myth with an anti-sexist commitment. He also seeks to revision kinder, gentler masculinities from myth. Doty focuses on Gilgamesh and Enkidu as archetypes of male friendship and bonding (entry 325), Herakles as trickster who manages to act out his feminine side, Narcissus as the male preoccupied with his own beauty, Hermes as multifaceted masculinities, and Ares as the sometimes admirable warrior. Doty cites the Navajo story of "The Two Who Came to Their Father" (entry 881) as depicting the need for active and passive masculinities, and he argues for the importance of integrating Apollo and Dionysus, who are more complex than usually allowed. Doty is critical of Joseph Campbell's monomyth of the hero (entry 862), citing its lack of heroic diversity. Doty envisions new versions of the hero for a new age. Readers who have trouble with the author's pro-feminist perspective will note Doty's minimizing of misandry among radical feminists, his dismissal of the men's rights movement as a backlash to protect "male power," and his belief that males are a privileged class of oppressors.

865. Eliade, Mircea. **Rites and Symbols of Initiation: The Mysteries of Birth and Rebirth.** Translated by William R. Trask. New York: Harper & Row, Harper Torchbooks, 1958, 1975. xv, 175p. notes. index. pa. Reprint, Dallas, TX: Spring Publications, 1994. pa.

This influential study classifies three kinds of initiation rites: those that mark the passage from childhood to adolescence and adulthood, single-sex rites (usually male) that create bonding, and rites that induct a person into shamanistic offices. Eliade touches on numerous matters, including reasons for the predominance of rites for males, the meanings of circumcision, the spiritual subtexts of the rites, and the appearance of the rites in literature and modern religions. For anyone exploring the significance of initiation rites, Eliade's book is essential reading.

866. Gurian, Michael. **The Prince and the King: Healing the Father-Son Wound: A Guided Journey of Initiation.** New York: Jeremy P. Tarcher/Putnam Books, 1992. xv, 272p. appendix. bibliography, 268-71. pa.

Because wounding by the father afflicts many men, Gurian seeks, through myth and archetypes, to fashion a guide to healing the father-son rift. His principal archetype is the Sacred King who initiates the son/prince into responsible male adulthood. Among numerous folk stories, Gurian finds his principal tales in *The Odyssey* (entry 328), where prince Telemachus searches for his father Odysseus and in "Strong Hans," a tale from the Brothers Grimm in which a boy suffers under an abusive father, returns to a diminished father, and sets off in search of a sacred father. Using such mythopoeic materials, Gurian offers exercises for undertaking a vision quest by which a man can rediscover both his father and his own self. Steps in this quest include contacting elder men, freeing the lover within, and experiencing the warrior's descent into the dark cave. Eventually, sons must bid farewell to mentors, forgive fathers, and take their own place by standing in the sun. The foreword is by Douglas Gillette and Robert Moore; the appendix provides a brief guide to the principal archetypes. (See entry 353.)

867. Harding, Christopher, ed. **Wingspan: Inside the Men's Movement.** New York: St. Martin's Press, 1992. xxii, 265p. illus. bibliographies after many chapters. pa.

Wingspan has been among the most influential of men's movement journals, especially among mythopoetic men. For this anthology, Harding has collected nearly 50 essays and poems that exemplify the vitality of mythopoetic men. In the introduction, Harding describes *Wingspan* and defines four branches of the men's movement—mythopoetic, pro-feminist and gay-affirmative, men's rights, and addiction-recovery. The essays are divided into seven sections: issues that concern men, in search of male community, learning from mythology, living the male archetypes, ceremonies of body and soul work, challenges to the mythopoetic movement, and resources. Asa Baber leads off the collection recounting his discovery of the New Warrior Training Adventure. Many subsequent essays and poems are energized with a similar sense of renewal. Familiar names among the contributors include Douglas Gillette, Michael Meade, Jack Kammer, Shepherd Bliss, Robert Bly, Aaron R. Kipnis, and Bill Kauth. Among the nay-sayers to the movement are Harry Brod and Sam Keen. The concluding chapter on resources includes selected men's centers and councils, men's movement publications, bibliographies, and book and tape sources.

867a. Judy, Dwight H. **Healing the Male Soul: Christianity and the Mythic Journey.** New York: Crossroad, 1992. x, 188p. illus. bibliography, 184-88. pa.

Adapting mythopoetic insights to a Christian spirituality, Judy describes a man's spiritual development in terms of a mythic journey described by Joseph Campbell (entry 862) and others. Judy re-visions original sin as an historical and psychic event in which the young male breaks away from Mother. Prehistoric matriarchal societies, he argues, had little consciousness of male responsibility, and they accepted the sacrifice of disposable males to the Great Mother. In the story of Abraham and Isaac, the patriarchal God rejects the human sacrifice that was acceptable to matriarchal cultures. Judy explores three archetypes that mirror stages of male spiritual growth. The hero-warrior, exemplified by Hercules, labors to control male aggression so that it serves human life rather than destroys it. The hero-transcendent—exemplified by Dionysus, Augustine, and Christian contemplatives—seeks to nourish a spiritual life, sometimes in rebellion against a corrupted earthly existence. The hero-creative—exemplified by Parsifal—attempts to create both a new earth and a new heaven. Judy urges men to follow a quest like Parsifal's, one that will heal both the soul and society. Throughout the book, the discussion is enriched by numerous allusions to mythic figures and religious stories.

868. Keen, Sam. **Fire in the Belly: On Being a Man.** New York: Bantam Books, 1991. xv, 272p. notes. pa.

In this best-seller, Keen examines the current crisis in masculinity and charts a roadmap for a journey toward a masculinity of the future. First, men must separate themselves from WOMAN, the archetypal Mother, and must undergo the ancient processes of ritual—separation, initiation, and reintegration. Keen denounces rites that are violent, arguing a "violence in, violence out" theory (i.e., males become violent when they are subjected to violence). Achieving "success" in modern economic systems often involves spiritual violence to the male. Before men can find joy, they must explore the inner self and descend into grief. Modern men must then re-vision masculinity, making it more peaceable and ecologically sensitive. They must cultivate wonder, empathy, the "heartful mind," moral outrage, friendship, husbanding, and wildness. They must recognize the justice in many feminist complaints, as well as the injustice in much feminist male-blaming. Respecting and loving the differences between the sexes, men and women must journey together into a future that rediscovers the value of family, children, community, and reverence for the earth. Written in straightforward, readable prose, *Fire in the Belly* addresses both heart and mind.

869. Kipnis, Aaron R. **Knights Without Armor: A Practical Guide for Men in Quest of Masculine Soul**. New York: Jeremy P. Tarcher/Perigee Books, 1991. xv, 292p. notes. appendix. pa.

Into this one volume, Kipnis seems to have packed at least four books, each of them filled with insights. Part 1 examines, from a men's rights perspective, the negative attitudes and stereotypes about males that often cripple men in their everyday lives. Part 2 attempts to reclaim the masculine soul by avoiding the sky-god, hero-martyr models that predominate in patriarchal societies, as well as the misandric models of men that permeate current Earth Mother worship among some ecofeminists. Part 3 examines down-to-earth implications of the new masculinity, including the initiation of younger men into life-affirming masculine adulthood, the transformation of work into an exercise that realizes men's dreams, and the use of elder men as a resource of masculine wisdom. Part 4 argues that psychology, in both theory and practice, is skewed toward women; men's groups can help to supply the need for support. This outline merely suggests the book's richness, which ranges from an analysis of Hamlet as uninitiated male to an examination of drumming as a form of therapy particularly suitable for men. Many of the book's insights grew out of a seven-man recovery group in which Kipnis participated. The positive messages in the book are crystallized in 10 tasks and a "new male manifesto." The brief appendix lists resources; the foreword is by Robert A. Johnson. Many readers will want to give this book at least two readings.

870. Lawlor, Robert. **Earth Honoring: The New Male Sexuality.** Rochester, VT: Park Street Press, 1989. 194p. illus. appendix. bibliography, 188-89. notes. index. pa.

Lawlor seeks to restore the older sense of the sexual as sacred. Defining the spiritual as a recognition of unseen forces at work on the universe, he depicts human history as oscillating cycles of polar energies—in particular, the masculine and the feminine. The modern Western world is suffering from an overbalance of the patriarchal (i.e., dominant masculinity and repressed femininity). An increase of femininity would increase the honor paid to Mother Earth and the ecosystem. Lawlor recognizes, however, that the feminine does have its shadow side: The Great Mother vs. the Devouring Mother. (He does not seem to recognize that patriarchy has a light side.) Spiritual symmetry, he concludes, can be achieved through a fourfold reciprocity of opposites. Readers will have to decide whether Lawlor is a genuine visionary or a New Age guru. The book's large generalizations and sometimes questionable conclusions require a large leap of faith. Lawlor, for example, urges "spermatic retention" because too many seminal emissions can drain off a man's masculinity. His argument that use of the Pill led to increased homosexuality is less than persuasive. He does not always have his facts straight (e.g., he misunderstands the Immaculate Conception). In short, it sometimes takes a suspension of disbelief to follow Lawlor's train of thought.

871. Matthews, John, ed. **Choirs of God: Revisioning Masculinity.** London: Mandala, HarperCollins, 1991. 221p. illus. bibliography, 218-21. pa.

In the introduction to this collection of 10 essays on mythic spirituality, Matthews stresses the need for men to reclaim the God just as women are reclaiming the Goddess. The essays vary in topic, treatment, and plausibility. On the one hand, Robert Bly's lead-off essay on the structures and significance of initiation ceremonies is rich with insights. On the other hand, Robert Lawlor's account of the fall of ancient matriarchies and the rise of male power employs free-association history laced with misandry and anti-Catholicism. Ean Begg argues the importance of recovering the masculine animus, while John Rowan's account of his work with male groups is laden with shaming of the masculine. Other essays include an autobiographical account of a vision quest, an exploration of magical arts, a ritual to honor the God within, a poetic account of the God of Wicca, and a re-visioning of the God-Wanderer. In the final essay, Peter Lamborn Wilson rejects the polarity of God and Goddess for the androgyny of the Child God.

872. Meade, Michael. **Men and the Water of Life: Initiation and the Tempering of Men.** San Francisco: HarperSanFrancisco, 1993. 446p. bibliography, 439-42.

Meade retells eight folk tales from various countries, interpreting each in term of men's psychological and spiritual development. The African story, "The Hunter and His Son," illustrates male wounding and the need to heal those wounds so that men will not continue to wound others. Another African story, "The Boy and the Half-Giantess," symbolizes the boy's need to separate from the mother. Meade's reflections on the tales are enriched by autobiographical stories and accounts of reactions to his retelling of the folk tales to retreat groups. The Irish "Tale of Conn-Eda" is enlivened by Meade's narrative of his being drafted during the Vietnam War era. "The Water of Life" tale illustrates the continuing need for initiation, for a renewal of the self at each succeeding stage of life. The final story, "The Companions," becomes a parable of the need for male bonding that seeks positive social and personal goals.

873. Moore, Robert, and Douglas Gillette. **King Warrior Magician Lover: Rediscovering the Archetypes of the Mature Masculine.** New York: HarperCollins/HarperSanFrancisco, 1990. xix, 160p. illus. bibliography, 157-59. pa.

In the first of five volumes on masculine archetypes, Moore and Gillette argue that modern society lacks the rituals to move males from Boy Psychology to Man Psychology. Neither patriarchy nor feminist attacks on men nor pseudo-rituals that deform masculinity are helpful. The authors suggest that, by tapping into positive archetypes and avoiding negative ones, males can enhance their adult development. After describing The Divine Child archetype and related archetypes of Boy Psychology, the authors explore at length four positive images of Man Psychology—King, Warrior, Magician, and Lover, as well as their negative counterparts. In the conclusion, the authors offer methods for accessing these archetypes, and they urge men to reject the male shaming and guilt mongering that have been dumped on them in recent times.

874. Moore, Robert, and Douglas Gillette. **The King Within: Accessing the King in the Male Psyche.** New York: William Morrow, 1992. 336p. illus. appendixes. bibliography, 313-26. notes. index. pa.

Examining archetypes of the mature masculine, Moore and Gillette blend psychology, religion, myth, history, literature, and ritual to explore more fully the king archetype. In worldwide myths promising the arrival or return of the king, the authors find expression of male desire to access the king archetype. The ability to do so on a large scale would herald the arrival of a nobler society. Current forms of patriarchy, they argue, are not rule by males as a class but rule by a few immature males for their own benefit. The king archetype appears in numerous ancient beliefs, images, and rituals. Often, the idea of the king as the people's servant is paramount. Some societies identify the actual king with the archetype; others present the king as a mortal servant of a divine archetype. The archetypal king is characterized by fullness, centeredness, fertility, and the reconciliation of opposites. He fulfills the almost universal definitions of the masculine as procreator, provider, and protector. The shadow of the archetypal king can appear as the tyrant or the weakling abdicator. Although modern democracies are founded upon regicide, the king within is returning to an increasing number of men. Welcoming the king can be facilitated by rituals and male bonding.

875. Moore, Robert, and Douglas Gillette. **The Lover Within: Accessing the Lover in the Male Psyche.** New York: William Morrow, 1993. 288p. illus. appendixes. bibliography, 252-78. notes. index.

The final volume in Moore and Gillette's five-volume series, this book examines positive archetypes of the male lover, the negative shadow of the lover, and means of accessing the lover within. As in the previous four volumes, the first two chapters repeat the authors' account of gender identity and define their vocabulary for discussing the male psyche. Chapters three through six describe the archetypal lover, tracing his images in world cultures. Shiva with his creative lingam, Priapus with his enlarged phallus, and Dionysus in ecstasy are but a few of the divine images of the generative lover. Central to the lover is the garden of delights to which he seeks to return. The authors define eros as sexual love, storge as "family" love, philia as friendship, and agape as love of humanity. They discuss amor, or the blend of sexual and spiritual love that has emerged in Western societies since the Middle Ages. The lover archetype represents the drive toward incarnation, the desire to embody the spiritual in the sensual. Chapters seven and eight portray the shadow side of the lover. The impotent lover often has been unable to separate from the Mother, sometimes because of the absent Father. Vulnerability is not a virtue in love, the authors note; receptivity is. The addict commits the "sin of sensuality" with alcohol, drugs, or sex (e.g., Don Juan). The final chapter offers suggestions for accessing the lover within, such as learning to dance, finding pleasure time, and opening oneself to mystic experiences. The epilogue proclaims the joy to the world of returning to the garden through love. The three appendixes discuss concepts of the self that build upon but move beyond Jungian psychology.

876. Moore, Robert, and Douglas Gillette. **The Magician Within: Accessing the Shaman in the Male Psyche.** New York: William Morrow, 1993. 304p. illus. appendixes. bibliography, 267-91. notes. index.

The fourth installment in Moore and Gillette's five-volume series depicting archetypes of the mature masculine, this book (like others in the series) repeats the opening two chapters of earlier installments. Denying that masculinity is inherently deformed, the authors argue that society must foster and channel positive aspects of both the masculine and the feminine. After defining Jungian terms (especially *archetype*), the authors describe the magician's role as one of mediator between the spirit world and human communities. Allied to the King, the magician is often celibate or asexual. In history and myth, the magician is as old as humanity and can be seen in such figures as Jesus the miracle worker, Merlin, Black Elk the visionary (entry 860), and such modern magician-thinkers as Einstein, Freud, and Jung. The magician occupies sacred space and time, and he often travels the three-step process of initiation—the call, the passage through the belly of the whale, and the return. The magician must not be confused with the entertainer, who affects no permanent inner change. The shadows of the magician include the passive innocent who denies his deep knowledge and the trickster who is a detached manipulator of others. The authors depict the ideal magician and view Joseph Campbell as a flawed but powerful magician whose books and videos have guided millions to the world of myth. Providing suggestions on how to access the magician within, the authors conclude that men must now be "Earthshamans," no longer limited to a single tribe, but committed to the global community.

877. Moore, Robert, and Douglas Gillette. **The Warrior Within: Accessing the Knight in the Male Psyche.** New York: William Morrow, 1992. xvi, 302p. illus. appendixes. bibliography, 263-90. notes. index.
   "Often disparaged, seldom understood, the Warrior is the most controversial of the archetypes." In this third installment of a five-part series of books on mature masculine archetypes, Moore and Gillette define the positive aspects of male aggressiveness as embodied in the Warrior archetype. The first two chapters, which frame the discussion and define key terms of the male psyche, are repeated from the previous volume, *The King Within*. Readers familiar with that book can begin with chapter three in which Moore and Gillette argue that females as well as males possess aggressiveness. Unfortunately, modern society lacks an adequate supply of fathers, elders, and initiation rites to channel male aggressiveness into personally and socially positive directions. In later chapters, the authors review historical and mythic images of the Warrior, and describe "the way of the warrior" as one incorporating self-discipline, faithfulness, and "legitimate expressions of controlled aggression." Noting that the soldier is not necessarily the warrior, Moore and Gillette depict the Shadow Warrior as split into the masochist and the sadist. Later sections of the book link the sword and the phallus, the image of legitimate male aggressiveness and sexuality. The authors urge men to become "Earthknights" by harnessing—not eliminating—masculine energy.

878. Perry, John Weir. **Lord of the Four Quarters: Myths of the Royal Father.** New York: Braziller, 1966. xvi, 272p. (Patterns of Myth series). illus. bibliography, 251-53. notes. index. Reprint, New York: Collier Books, 1970. pa.
   For anyone interested in the manifestations of the archetypal king-father in ancient times, this volume is indispensable. In his introduction, Perry examines the connections between myth and ritual, as well as the development, function, and archetypal nature of kingship. The bulk of the book is devoted to records of the Royal Father from cultures of the Nile, the Near East, the Indo-European diffusion (India, Iran, the Hittites, Greece, Rome, and the Norse lands), the Americas (the Toltecs, the Aztecs), and China. Perry translates the texts, comments on their meaning, and illustrates them with photographs of ancient monuments.

879. Rohr, Richard, and Joseph Martos. **The Wild Man's Journey: Reflections on Male Spirituality.** Cincinnati, OH: St. Anthony Messenger Press, 1992. xii, 225p.
   A Franciscan retreat master, Rohr provided the reflections on male spirituality that Martos converted into a series of essays for this book. Borrowing from Robert Bly, Robert Moore, and others, Rohr and Martos argue that

Catholic Christianity needs to encourage, harness, and direct masculine energy into greater social activism. Deploring the "soft male" that Christianity has hitherto fostered (patterned on John the beloved disciple), the authors urge men to tap into the wild-man energies of saints like John the Baptist. The authors champion the men's mythopoeic movement as a search for masculine spirituality; they depict modern males as stunted by patriarchal capitalism. Whenever the authors write about greater social activism, they always speak in terms of the Third World or poverty in the United States. Many readers will applaud the authors' application of masculine archetypes to Christian practice, but some men's rights activists will be disappointed that the authors seem unaware of an agenda of men's issues.

879a. Upton, Charles. **Hammering Hot Iron: A Spiritual Critique of Bly's Iron John.** Wheaton, IL: Quest Books, 1993. xvi, 246p. bibliography, 231-32. notes. index. pa.

Upton critiques Robert Bly's *Iron John* (entry 861) and much of the mythopoetic men's movement for a failure to do justice to transcendental religions in general and Christianity in particular. "In the world of pop mythopoeia," Upton notes, "anyone who takes the Bible as orthodoxy and holy writ is in danger of being ridiculed, but if someone justifies a practice by saying 'the Sioux Indians do it' or the Yoruba or the Maoris or the Australian Aborigines, he or she is met with automatic and pious approval." The polytheism of some new mythopoetic paganism is a step backwards for men. Upton draws upon a wide variety of mythic, poetic, and religious sources (including William Blake, Jungian scholars, traditional and apocryphal religious texts, and his own poems) to provide a free-wheeling commentary on *Iron John*. The discussion reveals Upton's admiration for and disagreements with Bly's mythopoetic vision.

880. Vogt, Gregory Max. **Return to Father: Archetypal Dimensions of the Patriarch.** Dallas, TX: Spring Publications, 1991. vi, 179p. bibliography, 164-68. pa.

In a poetic prose that blends philosophy, myth, religion, folklore, etymology, and psychology, Vogt refashions positive archetypes of the patriarch for modern men. Patriarchy, according to Vogt, comes in two forms. Dualistic patriarchy, which insists on separation and conflict, is oppressive; homologous patriarchy, which insists on similarity and unity, is beneficial. Rather than side with the opponents of patriarchy, Vogt urges men to reconnect with the constructive patriarch who initiates boys into affirmative manhood. In many societies, father-rule both regulates and nurtures, and the family "house" is the extension of male care. Vogt examines the hunter, the builder, and the philosopher as "bodies," biosocial entities that males have inherited from the past.

881. **Where the Two Came to Their Father: A Navaho War Ceremonial Given by Jeff King.** Text and paintings recorded by Maud Oakes. Commentary by Joseph Campbell. 3d ed. Princeton, NJ: Princeton University Press, 1991. xiii, 133p. (Bollingen Series I).

Early in World War II, when young Navaho men were being inducted into the U.S. military, a traditional war ceremonial was revived to bless them. The ritual legend and sand paintings, as given by medicine man Jeff King, were recorded by Maud Oakes during an 11-day period. In its first edition (1943), this beautiful volume, complete with color reproductions of the paintings, was the first of the prestigious Bollingen series. The Navaho legend tells a familiar story: Two young men, Monster Slayer and Child Born of Water, must leave their mother (Changing Woman) and seek their father (the Sun) in order to learn how to destroy the monsters that threaten their world. The story recounts the familiar journey from Mother to Father that the young male seeking adulthood must make. Revived to protect young soldiers and often used as a healing rite, the ceremonial is a moving example of masculine spirituality, a Native American ritual that nurtures the manhood of the tribe's young men.

B. Religion: Traditional Religions

Although reference to archetypes and myth also appear in this section, the books listed below frame their discussion of males primarily within traditional religious structures, especially Judaism and Christianity.

882. Andelin, Aubrey P. **Man of Steel and Velvet.** Santa Barbara, CA: Pacific Press Santa Barbara, 1972. 316p. Reprint, New York: Bantam, 1983. pa.

"This is a book which teaches men to be men," Andelin declares in his introduction. Because men have failed to be men, women have been forced to take the lead in too many areas of life. The results can be seen in dominant mothers, frustrated women, unruly children, juvenile delinquency, increasing homosexuality, and the stridency of women's liberation. Andelin's ideal man combines strength and gentleness, steel and velvet. The discussion is presented from a conservative Christian viewpoint.

883. Bakan, David. **And They Took Themselves Wives: The Emergence of Patriarchy in Western Civilization.** New York: Harper & Row, 1979. 186p. illus. notes. index.

Working closely with biblical texts, Bakan explores the centrality of paternity in the Bible, along with its traces of matrocentrism. After fixing the frames for interpreting the Bible, the author touches on such matters as ideas of divine impregnation and the meanings of circumcision, animal sacrifice, and male involvement in warfare. Among his conclusions is the idea the Bible is associated with the reduction in gender role differences through its depiction of males "effeminized" toward greater child care.

884. Bianchi, Eugene C., and Rosemary R. Ruether. **From Machismo to Mutuality: Essays on Sexism and Woman-Man Liberation.** New York: Paulist Press, 1976. v, 142p. appendix. notes.

Bianchi and Ruether alternate essays in this volume. A theologian influenced by radical feminism, Ruether reduces history to a tale of male oppression and female subjugation. A former Jesuit, Bianchi deplores the anti-female sexism inculcated by his church. "Mutuality" in this book seems to consist of indiscriminate female denunciations of men as evil, accompanied by male recitations of mea culpa.

885. Bloesch, Donald G. **Is the Bible Sexist? Beyond Feminism and Patriarchalism.** Westchester, IL: Crossway Books, 1982. 139p. notes. Scripture, name, and subject indexes. pa.

Rejecting both patriarchalism (that subordinates women to men) and feminism (that declares women's independence of men), Bloesch argues for a biblical alternative stressing the interdependence of men and women. Denouncing sexism as a sin, Bloesch nevertheless has reservations about some feminist goals and attitudes. In particular, he questions feminist efforts to alter biblical language, contending that, in some cases, the proposed changes create distortions. Bloesch is critical of societies like modern Sweden where he sees neopaganism and feminism allied to create a situation that dignifies neither women nor men.

886. Carmody, John. **Toward a Male Spirituality**. Mystic, CT: Twenty-Third Publications, 1990. x, 117p. notes. pa.

From a traditional Catholic perspective, Carmody describes male spirituality, focusing on work, prayer, and love. Because he doubts the wisdom of replacing the traditional Christian focus on Christ with psychological-mythical archetypes, relatively little about archetypal masculinity enters into the discussion.

887. Dalbey, Gordon. **Healing the Masculine Soul: An Affirming Message for Men and the Women Who Love Them.** Dallas, TX: Word Publishing, 1988. 247p. appendix. notes. pa.

Modern men are caught between the misandric stereotypes proclaimed by many feminists and the macho heroes glorified by the entertainment industry. Dalbey combines the awareness of mythopoetic men with traditional biblical Christianity to forge a male-positive spirituality. Men, he says, must admit the wound they suffer from and find the lion within (actually, The Lion of Judah, a Biblical predecessor of Robert Bly's Wild Man). Men must separate themselves from the Feminine-Mother without denigrating women. Homosexuality, he believes, results from wounded masculinity. It is time for men to start healing themselves by coming to terms with their own fathers, by serving as responsible and loving fathers, and by connecting with God the Father. Church services, which now appeal more to women than men, need to be revised, and Christian men need to formulate ceremonies for "calling out" boys to adult manhood. The book contains an extensive study guide for use in classrooms or group sessions.

888. Dittes, James E. **The Male Predicament: On Being a Man Today.** San Francisco: Harper & Row, 1985. xiii, 223p.

Dittes's aim is to help liberate men from the constricting aspects of "being manly." He emphasizes that women are not the problem, nor are recent changes in women's roles. In a series of meditations, he explores how Christian society has often put males in the "frozen" nonsexual role of Joseph, husband of Mary. Nevertheless, Joseph is also actor and doer, as is the Joseph whose story is told in Genesis. Dittes discusses those who, like Aaron, are diverted into worshipping current idols. He reflects on such topics as shouldering masculine responsibility, the passive-aggressive yes-man who does not give of himself, and how men's and women's liberation can proceed in tandem. In the end, Dittes concludes that Joseph, the putative father of Jesus, is truly a father.

889. Eller, Vernard. **The Language of Canaan and the Grammar of Feminism.** Grand Rapids, MI: William B. Eerdmans, 1982. xiv, 56p. pa.

In this brief book, Eller takes issue with feminist critics who denounce biblical language as sexist. In particular, he argues that *man,* like most words, has several levels of meaning depending upon usage; its use as a generic term comes closer to biblical meanings than do modern substitutes like *humanity* or *humankind.* Likewise, the pronoun *he,* at one level, is "sexually ignorant" (i.e., it does not call attention to sexual differences). The modern "he or she," however, forces gender differences into grammatical situations where they are inappropriate. Eller argues that biblical imagery of God as masculine is not sexist, nor is the imagery designating God and Israel, Christ and Church, as lover and beloved. In their zeal to have women recognized in language, feminists have inadvertently distorted biblical meanings.

890. Hardenbrook, Weldon M. **Missing From Action.** Nashville, TN: Thomas Nelson, 1987. 192p. bibliography, 186-92. notes.
      Hardenbrook argues that men are now confused about their sexual identity and need to return to responsible manhood. Nowadays, men are likely to follow false icons of manhood created by the entertainment industry. Women are not to blame for the situation, because U.S. men have abandoned their earlier roles of spiritual and social leadership for an empty pursuit of freedom, power, and wealth. As women went from producers to consumers in U.S. society, they also became moral leaders, exercising excessive control over home, school, and church. Motherhood was elevated over fatherhood. The results can be seen in current father absence. Female-dominated schools have a negative effect on boys, and some feminists are now proclaiming that manhood itself is the source of all evil. Citing Job (29:1-20) as a primary description of the just adult man, Hardenbrook list nine traits of biblical masculinity. He urges a return to fatherhood and male friends, and offers other suggestions for men to reclaim their positive role in family, society, government, and the church.

891. Heller, David. **The Soul of a Man.** New York: Ballantine Books, 1990. xiii, 175p. bibliography, 175.
      Men's spirituality needs fuller exploration than it has hitherto received, Heller believes, comparing this exploration to a journey similar to Abraham's. Mothers convey many spiritual messages (positive as well as negative) to males, but boys must eventually separate from them. Their understanding of God may be linked, for better or for worse, with their fathers. Today's media heroes offer questionable images of manhood; men need a religious faith to sustain them through difficult times. Heller explores topics such as the nature of courage, problems posed by the work ethic, the good and bad sides of sports, the madonna-whore contrast that preoccupies many men, ways of keeping romance alive, and being better fathers. He concludes that the greatest manhood is a "sense of humanity conceived in the image of God."

892. Johnson, James L. **What Every Woman Should Know About a Man.** Grand Rapids, MI: Zondervan, 1977. 176p. bibliography, 176. notes. pa.
      For the more liberated Christian woman, Johnson attempts to explain what is often going on beneath the silent facade of the man—or men—in her life. Although many men find the armor of masculinity confining, they still wear it assiduously. The author cautions women to look beyond the "myths," or images of men perpetuated by society and fostered by the media. He urges women to avoid the manipulative "total woman" role recommended by some advocates of femininity; such a role he finds insulting to men and demeaning to women. Arguing for "equal but different" roles in the male-female relationship, Johnson discusses love, sex, striving, feelings, communication, the middle years, and the Christian man.

893. Miller, John W. **Biblical Faith and Fathering: Why We Call God "Father."** New York and Mahwah, NJ: Paulist Press, 1989. iv, 165p. appendix. notes. index. pa.

Rejecting the idea of patriarchy as male-dominated society, Miller argues that it refers to father-involved families and societies. Although one of humanity's greatest cultural achievements, the father-involved family is a fragile institution. If not cultivated by society, males will drift from responsible family behaviors, and families will revert to mother-child dyads. While mother involvement with a child is largely determined by biology, father involvement is largely determined by culture. The discovery of the male role in reproduction by early societies laid the foundations for enduring male-female and father-child relationships. But the mother had to give up exclusive rights to the child, and female virginity and sexual fidelity became imperative. Early societies enacted laws (e.g., the Code of Hammurabi) to guard against husband abuse of wives. Early restraints upon child abuse can be seen in the Hebrew proscription of child sacrifice: the abortion of Abraham's sacrifice of Isaac dramatizes the issue. In contrast to other Near Eastern religious systems, which are dominated by son-gods and populated with weak father-gods, Hebrew belief is dominated by a caring father-God. This belief allowed Hebrews to create a larger role for caring, human fatherhood. The Christian era marked a shift from human families and fathers to spiritual families and fathers, but Christianity spread the cult of the caring father throughout the world. In recent centuries, the father-involved family has been weakened by the industrial and sexual revolutions, creating the modern situation of father absence, father hunger, single-mother families, and unsocialized sons. Miller concludes that monotheistic father religion has optimal benefits for men and women. The appendix discusses the story of Abraham and Isaac as a charter of children's rights.

894. Nelson, James B. **The Intimate Connection: Male Sexuality, Masculine Spirituality.** Philadelphia: Westminster Press, 1988. 140p. notes. pa.

Although Nelson rejects the "sexist dualism" that has recurred in Christian history, he sees sexuality intricately linked with spirituality. The present time, however, is not a good one for either male sexual or male spiritual health. Many men, he believes, are "recovering sexists" struggling with a heritage of male dominance. Because humans are bodies, Nelson advocates "body theology" or "incarnational theology." He urges men to embrace sexuality, male friendships, their own mortality, and their masculinity. Like Robert Bly (entry 861), he sees "soft men" as producing "gentleness without strength, peacefulness without vitality, tranquillity without vibrancy." Nelson argues that, in contrast to Christian dualisms of the past, religion must incorporate sexuality into spirituality.

895. Olson, Richard P. **Changing Men's Roles in Today's World: A Christian Perspective for Men—and the Women Who Care About Them.** Valley Forge, PA: Judson Press, 1982. 159p. appendix. notes. pa.

Olson combines insights from men's awareness writers (especially Warren Farrell and Herb Goldberg) with a biblical Christian viewpoint. The Bible does not endorse macho behavior, and the freeing of men's feelings can bring personal and spiritual gain. Although skeptical of radical feminist critiques of men as oppressors, Olson garners insights from the women's liberation movement. He finds the Bible less sexist than some critics have argued, and he endorses egalitarian marriages. Men's liberation, he concludes, should be a conversion experience.

896. Pable, Martin W. **A Man and His God: Contemporary Male Spirituality.** Notre Dame, IN: Ave Maria Press, 1988. 143p. bibliography, 143. pa.

In the mode of devotional Catholicism, Pable explores a masculine theology designed to cure the emptiness resulting from the male pursuit of wealth, status, and power. Only a close relationship with God, Pable concludes, will satisfy male spiritual hunger.

897. Renich, Fred. **The Christian Husband.** Wheaton, IL: Tyndale House, 1976. 249p.

From a biblical Christian perspective, Renich argues that husbands are mandated to leadership in the family. Not to be confused with tyranny, this loving leadership requires husbands to reflect their sensitivity to God in their sensitivity to their wives. The mature husband is able to stop loving the idealized bride that he married and to begin loving the real woman who is his wife.

898. Smail, Thomas A. **The Forgotten Father.** London: Hodder and Stoughton, 1980. 189p. notes. index. pa.

An Anglican professor, Smail offers a corrective to recent Christian movements focusing on the Son and the Holy Spirit. The Jesus movement and the charismatic movements need to be complemented by a Father movement. In Christian scriptures and liturgy, God is revealed primarily as Abba, or Father. Smail traces the historical, charismatic, and doctrinal implications of Christian fatherhood imagery.

899. Tamez, Elsa. **Against Machismo: Rubem Alves, Leonardo Boff, Gustavo Gutiérrez, José Míguez Bonino, Juan Luis Segundo ... and Others Talk About the Struggle of Women.** Translated by Meyer-Stone Books. Oak Park, IL: Meyer-Stone Books, 1987. ix, 150p. pa.

The English title is misleading. Elsa Tamez interviews various Latin-American liberation theologians who focus exclusively on "the oppression of women" and have little to say about Latin-American males or machismo. Hugo Assmann is fairly typical of the interviewees' Marxist-based views: Males are an oppressor class. Even when they are oppressed themselves, "oppressed men are still oppressive men." Clearly, this liberation theology offers men little liberation from negative stereotyping.

900. Tennis, Diane. **Is God the Only Reliable Father?** Philadelphia: Westminster Press, 1985. 117p. bibliography, 115-17. pa.

"Do not abandon God the Father," Tennis argues. "There is danger in abandoning the Father image." A Protestant feminist, Tennis suspects both patriarchy and certain aspects of radical feminism. Because reliable fathers are in short supply in modern society, Tennis argues that the image of God as reliable father is desperately needed, especially by women. Although Mother Goddess religions promise women relief from patriarchy, they foster elitism, burden women with impossible responsibilities, and tempt them with spiritual hubris. Because the manhood of Jesus is linked with servantship, it too is a positive male image for women and men.

901. Vaughn, Joe, and Ron Klug. **New Life for Men: A Book for Men and the Women Who Care About Them.** Minneapolis, MN: Augsburg, 1984. 156p. bibliography, 155-56. pa.

Men are caught in the middle of gender role changes, the authors argue. The old roles do not fit comfortably, and the new ones are alien to many men. Combining psychology and biblical religious beliefs, Vaughn and Klug guide men into an inner journey of spiritual recovery. They offer practical advice on such matters as avoiding workaholism, discovering alternate ways of being masculine, learning to express feelings, finding male friends, reducing workplace frustrations, rediscovering play, dealing with women in their lives, honing fatherhood skills, maintaining bodily health, strengthening Christian spirituality, and starting a men's support group.

902. Visser't Hooft, W.A. **The Fatherhood of God in an Age of Emancipation.** Philadelphia: Westminster Press, 1982. xi, 163p. notes. pa.

The history of the modern world records the emancipation of people from authority, usually represented in patriarchal form. Many peoples have overthrown patriarchal rulers (i.e., kings) and colonialism. Workers are emancipating themselves from masters, women from men, youth from elders, and the laity from hierarchical clergy. Some people have revolted against "paternal" morals, and many believers are rebelling against the fatherhood of God. Although Visser't Hooft supports the trend toward greater freedom, he argues that emancipation is not always good, nor is patriarchy always bad. Revolutionary emancipation often ends in an "all is permitted" mentality that can destroy the individual and society. The fatherhood of God, as revealed by Jesus, is not oppressive but liberating, and Mother Goddess worship holds pitfalls for women. The author urges a liberation that will result in responsible action.

Cross-References

See chapter 15, "Masculinity," and chapter 20, "Psychology."

388. Absher, Tom. **Men and the Goddess: Feminine Archetypes in Western Literature.**

72a. Adams, Kathleen. **Mightier Than the Sword: The Journal as a Path to Men's Self-Discovery.**

319. Apuleius. **The Golden Ass.**

769. Bahnsen, Greg L. **Homosexuality: A Biblical View.**

770. Barnhouse, Ruth Tiffany. **Homosexuality: A Symbolic Confusion.**

582. Benson, Dan. **The Total Man.**

685. Bolen, Jean Shinoda. **Gods in Everyman: A New Psychology of Men's Lives and Loves.**

773. Boswell, John. **Christianity, Social Tolerance, and Homosexuality: Gay People in Western Europe from the Beginning of the Christian Era to the Fourteenth Century.**

651. Brod, Harry, ed. **A Mensch Among Men: Explorations in Jewish Masculinity.**

979. Carmody, John. **What Women Don't Understand About Men: And Vice Versa.**

485. Colman, Arthur, and Libby Colman. **Earth Father/Sky Father: The Changing Concept of Fathering.**

486. Corneau, Guy. **Absent Fathers, Lost Sons: The Search for Masculine Identity.**

489. Dobson, James C. **Straight Talk to Men and Their Wives.**

211. Melton, J. Gordon. **The Churches Speak On: Pornography: Official Statements from Religious Bodies and Ecumenical Organizations.**

530. Miller, Ted, ed. **The Christian Reader Book on Being a Caring Father.**

125. Murphey, Cecil. **Mantalk: Resources for Exploring Male Issues.**

822. Oraison, Marc. **The Homosexual Question.**

129a. Ornstein, Yevrah, ed. **From the Hearts of Men.**

231. Rowan, John. **The Horned God: Feminism and Men as Wounding and Healing.**

722. Sanford, John A., and George Lough. **What Men Are Like.**

549. Shedd, Charlie. **The Best Dad Is a Good Lover.**

589. Shedd, Charlie W. **Letters to Philip: On How to Treat a Woman.**

1021. Stapleton, Jean, and Richard Bright. **Equal Dating.**

1022. Stapleton, Jean, and Richard Bright. **Equal Marriage.**

144. Thompson, Keith, ed. **To Be a Man: In Search of the Deep Masculine.**

590. Vernon, Bob, and C. C. Carlson. **The Married Man.**

433. von Franz, Marie-Louise. **The Golden Ass of Apuleius: The Liberation of the Feminine in Man.**

189. Weiner, Bernard, et al. **Boy into Man: A Father's Guide to Initiation of Teenage Sons.**

730. Wellisch, E. **Isaac and Oedipus: A Study in Biblical Psychology of the Sacrifice of Isaac in *The Akedah*.**

438. Wren, Brian. **What Language Shall I Borrow? God-Talk in Worship: A Male Response to Feminist Theology.**

24

Victims and Violence: Crime, Domestic Violence, False Accusations of Wrongdoing, Physical and Sexual Abuse, Prisons, Rape, Sexual Harassment

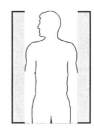

903. Bartollas, Clemens, Stuart J. Miller, and Simon Dinitz. **Juvenile Victimization: The Institutionalization Paradox.** New York: John Wiley, Sage Publications, 1976. xv, 324p. illus. appendixes. bibliography, 275-85. name and subject indexes.

"This is not the first, nor is it likely to be the last, in a long series of books, monographs, and articles which indict the juvenile correctional system as anti-therapeutic, anti-rehabilitative, and exploitive and demeaning to keepers and kept alike," the authors write. Focusing upon a Columbus, Ohio, correctional institution for boys, the authors find widespread sexual and nonsexual exploitation, with a definite and vicious pecking order among inmates. Toughness and the ability to fight are essential if a boy is not to be victimized. Racial overtones of exploitation are obvious: Blacks outnumber and dominate whites. The staff offers little help, is sometimes victimized itself by wily inmates, and occasionally exploits some inmates. The study makes it abundantly clear why some people are urging the dissolution of such institutions.

904. Beneke, Timothy. **Men on Rape.** New York: St. Martin's Press, 1982. xiv, 174p. appendix. notes. pa.

Part I of this book attempts to sensitize male readers to what rape does to women, both individual victims and women collectively. Beneke sees rape mentality evidenced in U.S. society by "rape signs" in cartoons, humor, and other popular expressions. The metaphors of sex and violence constitute "rape language." Under the rubric "she asked for it," he considers rationalizations offered for rape. Part 2—the longest and most interesting section—consists of statements about rape from a variety of men, including an angry rapist who was abused by his stepmother; husbands, lovers, and friends of women who have been raped; and lawyers, doctors, and policemen involved in rape cases. The range of sensitivities and viewpoints is considerable. Some of the men are remarkably hostile and callous toward women, others offer legitimate considerations that complicate discussion of what constitutes rape, and still others demonstrate considerable compassion for victims and disgust for perpetrators. In the final section, Andrea Rechtin, a rape victims advocate, responds to assumptions underlying some of the statements from interviewees. Beneke concludes that rape is a male problem that men must solve collectively. Neither

Rechtin nor Beneke, however, has listened carefully to what some of the men said: in particular, Rechtin's wholesale anger at the interviewees fails to discriminate among them. Any deviation from a simplistic party-line view of rape is condemned as insensitivity or as another form of "blaming the victim." The book considers only female victims of rape. "I wanted to interview a man who had been raped," Beneke writes, "but was unable to find a man who would consent to an interview. That fact alone may say more than the interview would have." The appendix lists men-against-rape groups in the United States and Canada.

905. Biller, Henry B., and Richard S. Solomon. **Child Maltreatment and Paternal Deprivation: A Manifesto for Research, Prevention, and Treatment.** Lexington, MA: Lexington Books, 1986. xii, 307p. bibliography, 233-87. author and subject indexes.

Taking an extensive survey of the literature, Biller and Solomon conclude that a clear but complex connection exists between child abuse and father deprivation. Child abuse is more likely to occur when the child's father is absent or ineffective. The authors define terms like "child abuse" and "paternal deprivation," noting that no single definition now exists and that the concepts have evolved throughout history. They find a continuum exists, ranging from paternal neglect to abuse. Most child abuse, however, occurs in the single-parent family, which is usually headed by a mother. This abuse is linked to the absence of the father. Younger boys and adolescent girls are more often the targets of abuse. In cases of sexual abuse, two-thirds of the abuse is perpetrated by males, often in the absence of the biological father. Both boys and girls benefit from a positive father presence in the family, thus creating a special risk factor in single-parent families. The authors explore methods of preventing and intervention, and they offer extensive guidelines for effective fathering. They conclude: "The single most detrimental factor damaging family functioning is the lack of sufficient positive involvement of fathers."

906. Blumenthal, Monica D., Robert L. Kahn, Frank M. Andrews, and Kendra B. Head. **Justifying Violence: Attitudes of American Men.** Ann Arbor: Institute for Social Research, University of Michigan, 1972. xii, 367p. illus. appendixes. bibliography, 355-58. index.

Based upon a survey conducted in the summer of 1969 of 1,374 men between the ages of 16 and 64, this study explores reasons given for justifying violence in urban racial disturbances, student campus protests, and police responses. The study examines how respondents justify violence for or against social change, and how identification with the perpetrators or victims of violence can alter one's definition and perception of violence. It is a sign of the times that 58 percent of the respondents defined burning a draft card as an act of violence, while only 56 percent felt that police beating of students constituted violence. In this survey, taken before the turmoil at Kent State and Jackson State, almost 50 percent of the respondents felt that shooting was a good way to handle campus disturbances "almost always" or at least "sometimes."

907. Bolton, Frank G., Jr., Larry A. Morris, and Ann E. MacEachron. **Males at Risk: The Other Side of Sexual Abuse.** Newbury Park, CA: Sage Publications, 1989. 222p. bibliography, 198-220. pa.

This review of literature attempts to summarize what is known about sexual abuse of boys. The task is difficult because U.S. society often overlooks male victimization. Growing up male is easier said than done, the authors argue, and a double standard regarding boys complicates the process of defining and identifying sexual abuse. It is difficult to locate reliable information on matters such as pedophilia. Most perpetrators of boy abuse are males, although some women abuse boys. The authors review the literature on the sexual, emotional, and behavioral consequences of sexual abuse. Boys usually experience anger and betrayal, and they are likely to question their gender identity. There is a great need for treatment programs for abused boys. The authors examine matters such as whether the gender of a therapist is significant, the setting for treatment, whether individual or group therapy is preferable, whether the abuse survivor is likely to become a perpetrator as an adult, and whether the survivor should confront the abuser. The kind of systematic multi-remedial treatment that is needed is described in the final chapter.

908. Brownmiller, Susan. **Against Our Will: Men, Women and Rape.** New York: Simon and Schuster, 1975. 472p. notes. index. Reprint, New York: Bantam Books, 1976. pa. Reprint, New York: Fawcett Columbine, 1993. pa.

An influential book, *Against Our Will* examines numerous aspects of rape. Brownmiller explores the legal view of rape from biblical times to the present, and the incidence of rape during wars, revolutions, riots, and pogroms. She examines the fate of white women among Indians and Indian women among whites. She depicts the racial and sexual politics of rape during slavery as an institutionalized means of destroying black women's integrity. The fear of black men raping white women is traced as an element of American racial tensions, and the rape of males, especially in prisons, is depicted as an exercise in male dominance. Brownmiller argues that women are trained to be victims. She questions the prevailing Freudian views of rape, even as elaborated by Helene Deutsch and Karen Horney, which posit an inherent masochism in women. Brownmiller is scornful of current attitudes toward the rape victim, particularly among police and attorneys. While illuminating many aspects of rape in history, law, and psychology, Brownmiller is so busy scoring polemical points that she often sheds more heat than light on the subject. Brownmiller uses rape as a brush to tar all men. A principal thesis of the book—"from prehistoric times to the present, I believe, rape ... is nothing more or less than a conscious process of intimidation by which *all men* keep *all women* in a state of fear"—has become notorious as a sexist absurdity. A related passage insists that rapists are the "shock troops" who do the dirty work for the entire male sex in its war against women. Brownmiller suggests that all men secretly celebrate and admire the likes of Jack the Ripper, the Boston Strangler, Richard Speck, and Charles Manson. For many readers, the venomous misandry that permeates Brownmiller's book corrodes much of its credibility.

909. Buffum, Peter C. **Homosexuality in Prisons.** Washington, DC: U.S. Department of Justice, Law Enforcement Assistance Administration, National Institute of Law Enforcement and Criminal Justice, 1972. 48p. bibliography, 43-48. notes. pa.

Dispassionately, this monograph reviews the literature and examines sexual conditions in prisons. It considers the various sex roles that prisoners assume, racial factors, the different problems involved, and the means of intervention.

910. Drew, Dennis, and Jonathan Drake. **Boys for Sale: A Sociological Study of Boy Prostitution.** New York: Brown Book, 1969. 223p.

Informal rather than scholarly, this account of boy prostitution surveys historical and geographic instances. The book hints at an appalling amount of misery inflicted upon boys over the centuries, but the authors regard man-boy sex as inevitable and rather casually suggest that society adjust to the practice.

911. Dziech, Billie Wright, and Linda Weiner. **The Lecherous Professor: Sexual Harassment on Campus.** Boston: Beacon Press, 1984. vi, 219p. appendixes. bibliography, 210-14. notes. pa.

Examining sexual harassment on campus, the authors betray the seriousness of the subject by reducing it to an exercise in male-shaming. Sample cases of harassment are cited to indicate an "epidemic" of campus harassment. The authors ignore female harassment of males and same-sex harassment because such cases do not fit their misandric agenda. Overgeneralizations about male professors, card-stacking, and failure to listen to the males quoted in the book are among the book's lapses. Typical of the authors' sexism is the claim that male professors are almost uniformly unattractive: "If there is a star who most resembles the typical accounting, art history, or seventeenth-century literature professor, it would have to be Woody Allen." The quote indicates the level at which the discussion is pitched in this book.

912. Eberle, Paul and Shirley. **The Abuse of Innocence: The McMartin Preschool Trial.** Buffalo: Prometheus Books, 1993. 416p. illustrations. bibliography, 415-16.

The Eberles retell the terrifying story of how an unlikely accusation of child molestation at the McMartin preschool in California touched off community hysteria and led to the longest trial in U.S. history. As the story proceeds, the horrors mount: rumors of satanic rituals and animal sacrifices, children being coaxed and coached into lurid accusations by overzealous and underqualified staff personnel, vigilantes seeking revenge, distorted and sensationalized media coverage, tenacious and vindictive prosecuting attorneys, and interminable legal proceedings. At the center of the story is Ray Buckey, who spent nine years under arrest before being acquitted of child molestation charges. Significantly, the whole Kafkaesque scenario was set in motion by irrational fears of a male working with young children. When one mother asked if she noticed anything out of the ordinary at the preschool, she replied, "I noticed that he was a male.... It seemed strange someone his age would want to be working with children."

913. Groth, A. Nicholas, with H. Jean Birnbaum. **Men Who Rape: The Psychology of the Offender.** New York and London: Plenum Press, 1979. xviii, 227p. notes. index.

Based on data from five hundred offenders, this study examines the "myths" and realities of rape and the men (and women) who commit it. Groth defines rape as a "pseudo-sexual act," indicating that, from a clinical viewpoint, any form of sexual assault should be included. Among the "myths" surrounding rape is the idea that pornography causes it. The author distinguishes among anger rape, power rape, and sadistic rape; discusses possible methods of resistance; and examines the multiple motives underlying rape. He notes sexual dysfunctioning of offenders, their subjective responses to their crime, and the effects of intoxication on them. Remarking that the majority of men are not rapists, Groth indicates that rape "appears to be the result of a core group of highly repetitive or chronic offenders." Many of these offenders had suffered sexual trauma in childhood, often some form of sexual abuse. Patterns of rape, including gang rape, are discussed. Using information from 20 offenders and seven victims, Groth explores rape of males, noting the likely underreporting of such offenses. "Women victims do not report that they feel less of a woman for having been raped," he writes, "but men victims do often state that they feel the offender took their manhood." The underreporting of sexual assaults upon boys is also indicated, with Groth estimating that boys and girls are probably equally the victims of such assaults. The female offender, he notes after discussing one such case, "remains an incompletely studied and insufficiently understood subject." Groth's account of rape is a much needed antidote to the many political and misandric discussions of the topic.

914. Grubman-Black, Stephen D. **Broken Boys/Mending Men: Recovery from Childhood Sexual Abuse.** Blue Ridge Summit, PA: TAB Books, 1990. xiii, 168p. bibliography, 163-68. pa. Reprint, New York: Ballantine Books, 1992. pa.

Boys are victims of sexual abuse, and they often lack family and social support. Because the perpetrators are usually male, homophobia contributes to people's unwillingness to confront boy abuse. The perpetrators can count on society's silence and denial. Furthermore, Grubman-Black argues, current definitions of masculinity create problems for victimized boys. Males are supposed to endure suffering in silence. Real men should neither permit themselves to be victimized nor be "turned on" by sexual activity with another male. Throughout this book, discussion of recovery from sexual abuse is interspersed with autobiographical excerpts from survivors, including Grubman-Black. Sexual abuse can leave boys confused about their gender identity, can generate feelings of despair and abandonment, and can produce numerous psychosexual difficulties. Because recovery requires the survivor to talk about the abuse, good listeners are essential. Healing may also require spiritual renewal as well as psychological adjustment. Grubman-Black lists the circumstances that may lead to sexual abuse, and he closes the book with an account of his own continuing process of recovery.

915. Herman, Judith Lewis, with Lisa Hirschman. **Father-Daughter Incest.** Cambridge: Harvard University Press, 1981. xi, 282p. appendix. notes. index. pa.

Using survey data, clinical material, anthropological literature, popular literature, and pornography, Herman explores father-daughter incest. She then draws upon interviews with 40 victims of incest, and 20 daughters of "seductive fathers." The book's final section deals with problems of disclosing and prosecuting incest, and with remedies for healing victims and restoring families. The book's "feminist perspective" includes considerable animosity toward males in general. Herman does not interview the fathers, nor does she try to get at the roots of their behavior. Instead, she blames father-daughter incest on all-purpose villains (male perverseness and patriarchal society) and uses incest as another stick for beating males.

916. Hunter, Mic. **Abused Boys: The Neglected Victims of Sexual Abuse.** Lexington, MA: Lexington Books, 1990. xii, 340p. appendixes. bibliography, 319-34. notes. index.

"Girls are raped and hate it, but boys are seduced and love it": This prevailing myth blocks public attention to sexual abuse of boys. Tens of thousands of boys are abused each year in the United States, Hunter argues, yet attention, sympathy, and resources are almost always directed to female victims. Hunter defines various forms of sexual abuse and indicates that the frequency of abuse may be staggering. Americans do not take claims of sexual abuse of boys seriously, especially if it is committed by a woman. U.S. society rates sexual offenses by women as less serious than those by men, films glamorizing the "seduction" of boys by older women are readily available at videostores (listed under "Comedy"), and social workers tend to focus primarily on girl victims. Hunter examines the factors that can affect the impact of sexual abuse (e.g., whether coercion was used, age of victim, duration and frequency of abuse), and he lists the victim's life areas that can be affected by abuse (e.g., physical and mental problems, dissociation from reality, emotional trauma, guilt and shame, loneliness, anger, addictive disorders, entering into abusive relationships, sexual difficulties, and spiritual confusion). Recovery for victims includes issues such as working through grief, denial, anger, and sadness, as well as reaching acceptance and forgiveness, deciding whether to tell others, whether to confront the offender, and whether to go public. The second half of this book is devoted to 11 autobiographical accounts by abuse victims. The circumstances of the abuse vary. Some victims were abused by males, some by females. A final chapter lists resources for abuse victims. The appendix includes the author's questionnaire for readers, especially those who were victims of childhood abuse.

917. Island, David, and Patrick Letellier. **Men Who Beat the Men Who Love Them: Battered Gay Men and Domestic Violence.** New York: Harrington Park Press, 1991. xxiii, 301p. Haworth Gay and Lesbian Studies. appendix. bibliography, 287-89. index. pa.

For a variety of reasons, little attention has been paid to gay and lesbian domestic violence. The myth that only males batter and only females are battered dies hard. Using Letellier's experience in an abusive gay relationship as an entrance into the subject, the authors examine such matters as defining domestic violence among gay couples, reasons why the battering may occur more than once, determining who is the victim, the characteristics of a batterer, how the victim can get out and stay out of an abusive situation, and how someone can help a battered friend. Island and Letellier discuss therapists and intervention programs, the complex and unusual psychology of domestic violence, and ways to stop the violence. The appendix presents gender-inclusive legal definitions of domestic violence. The study reveals that misconceptions about domestic violence, especially the belief that only females are victims, do not fit reality. These misconceptions compound the difficulties faced by non-stereotypical victims.

918. Kivel, Paul. **Men's Work: How to Stop the Violence That Tears Our Lives Apart.** New York: Ballantine Books, 1992. xxxiii, 294p. appendix. bibliography, 282-93. pa.

The cofounder of the Oakland Men's Project, Kivel addresses the sources of male violence and offers guidelines for eradicating it. He attempts to understand how socialization of males can lead them to become violent, how men can overcome this training, and how they can learn to take responsibility for their actions. Most boys, he states, have been boxed into "Act Like a Man" behavior that includes occasional violence. Kivel offers exercises designed to uncover assumptions that men use to justify violence. Drugs are often part of the violence problem, he finds, but anger need not be: Legitimate expression of anger can be non-abusive. Kivel describes his work in prisons and with teenagers. In an epilogue, he describes the current mythopoetic men's movement as a backlash against feminism. The appendix recounts the goals and assumptions of the Oakland Men's Project. The book's focus on male violence toward women and minorities tends to downplay male violence directed toward other males. Some readers may question how deeply Kivel sees into the roots of violence.

919. Lew, Mike. **Victims No Longer: Men Recovering from Incest and Other Sexual Child Abuse.** New York: Nevraumont, 1988. Rev. ed., New York: Harper & Row, Perennial Library, 1990. xxiv, 326p. bibliography, 310-15. index. pa.

According to Lew, "our culture provides no room for a man as a victim." Consequently, male victims of child sexual abuse are a hidden topic, although evidence suggests that nearly as many boys are sexually abused as girls. Our society tends to overlook male victimization, to stereotype adult males as the sole perpetrators of all childhood abuse, to deny that women ever abuse children, to romanticize seduction of boys by older women as sexual initiation, and sometimes to profit from child pornography involving boys. The male victim may hide his "shame," question his masculine identity, be troubled by sexual excitement, and try to overcome his victimization by a variety of means (some beneficial, some harmful). Lew is a therapist who focuses on recovery of victims. Each chapter is built on the same pattern: a discussion of a particular aspect of sexual abuse is followed by a personal statement from an abuse survivor. (Lew discusses the merits of replacing the term *victim* with *survivor*.) Chapters discuss topics such as breaking secrecy, counseling, group therapy, and moving on. The final chapter lists resources. The foreword is by Ellen Bass, author of *I Never Told Anyone: Writings by Women Survivors of Child Sexual Abuse*.

920. Lloyd, Robin. **For Money or Love: Boy Prostitution in America.** New York: Vanguard Press, 1976. xx, 236p.

After his two sons were approached by a photographer who sells photos of nude boys, journalist Lloyd found himself increasingly interested in the topic of boy prostitution. In this account, he constructs composite pictures of typical "chickens" (boy prostitutes), and he offers a verbatim account from a "chicken hawk" (a man who patronizes boy prostitutes). Estimating the extent of such prostitution in the United States is difficult, Lloyd says, but part 1 of the book offers glimpses of the situation with accounts of mass rape and murder of boys in Houston and scandals in Boise, Idaho, and Waukesha, Wisconsin. Part 2 surveys the history of boy prostitution and briefly describes the present situation in several key cities around the world. Lloyd provides an overview of the boy pornography business, and he examines the exploitation of boys in correctional facilities. Part 3 suggests some possible cures, including a federal department of education and youth. Lloyd raises questions about juvenile justice and the incarceration of minors, cites the potential of group homes, and stresses the need for more humane supervisors. Lloyd suggest that boy prostitutes are likely to become bisexual. The book's introduction is by Senator Birch Bayh, whose senate subcommittee findings corroborated the extent of boy prostitution in the United States.

921. Miles, Rosalind. **Love, Sex, Death, and the Making of the Male.** London: Grafton Books; New York: Summit Books, 1991. 274p. bibliography, 258-62. notes. index.

Modern society breeds violent males, Miles argues. Or, perhaps, males are a messed-up sex that is given to mayhem in a way that females are not. Both theses seem to be at work in Miles's book, depending on where one opens it. Miles discusses how males must struggle to become male in the womb and how the struggle goes on after birth. Society at large, schools, parents, and peers subject boys to often brutal treatment as they grow up. It is little wonder, then, that some males turn to violence. To correct the situation, we must overhaul the socialization of boys, stop glamorizing violence, and allow boys' emotional expression. Unexplained contradictions mar the discussion: Boys are a favored sex, Miles argues, but are treated worse than girls. Male genitalia in male infants is unduly prized but is often subjected to the mutilation of circumcision. More baffling is Miles's attitude toward men. At times she adopts the hectoring tone of radical feminists depicting males as moral scum; at other times, she regards males sympathetically as the victims of inhumane socialization. After pages of misandric ranting about males as tainted by dark desires that females are morally superior to, Miles suddenly offers, on the book's last two pages, a list of thoughtful, compassionate suggestions for improving the male lot.

922. Porter, Eugene. **Treating the Young Male Victim of Sexual Assault: Issues and Intervention.** Syracuse, NY: Safer Society Press, 1986. 85p. illus. appendixes. bibliography, 67-71. pa.

In the 23-page introduction, Fay Honey Knopp argues that American society's preoccupation with female rape and incest victims has hidden boys as sexual abuse victims. Evidence indicates that boys are nearly equally at risk with girls as child victims. One survey indicated that 98% of boys abused by women did not report the abuse. Sexual abuse of boys by females is not recognized by many people as abuse at all. A high rate of adult male abusers were themselves victims of abuse. In the main body of the book, Porter reports that boys are in fact harmed by sexual molestation, although U.S. society seems blind to the fact. He describes various strategies for therapists. The male may go through a three-stage progression in therapy: rage, identification, and choosing options. Identification can be problematic. If the victim regards his molester as a model of the masculine, the victim may in turn become a victimizer. The male victim may question his sexual identity and may engage in self-blame. Porter describes means of terminating counseling. Four appendixes provide additional material, including a brief list of male-victim treatment providers interviewed by the author. The foreword is by A. Nicholas Groth.

923. Russell, Diana E.H. **Rape in Marriage.** Rev ed., Bloomington: Indiana University Press, 1990. xxxviii, 421p. appendixes. bibliography, 403-12. notes. index.

In this study based upon interviews with eighty-seven women, Russell examines rape in marriage, exploring its legal aspects, the difficulties of defining it, and its connection with family violence and larger social structures. Russell's approach to the subject is decidedly partisan; her anger with men stems from a belief that "the oppression of women as a class by men as a class has been ... universal" and that men regard women as property. In this study, only the wives were interviewed. Russell justifies her failure to interview husbands on the grounds that ours is a "patriarchal culture" and that it is time for women to be heard. Men are "heard" here only through carefully selected snippets culled from such sources as *The Hite Report on Male Sexuality* (entry 745) and the pornographic *My Secret Life.* Using such tactics, Russell is able to minimize the number of battered men, justify wifely violence as self-defense, and create a caricature of husbands as unfeeling oppressors.

924. Sanday, Peggy Reeves. **Fraternity Gang Rape: Sex, Brotherhood and Privilege on Campus.** New York and London: New York University Press, 1990. xxv, 203p. bibliography, 197-201. pa.

In February 1983, a university student named Laurel had sex with five or six fraternity members. Because Laurel was both drunk and high on four hits of LSD, Sanday argues that she was unable to consent to sex; thus, the incident was an example of fraternity gang rape. As this conclusion illustrates, Sanday's treatment of the episode is not exactly evenhanded. She exempts Laurel from responsibility because of her alcohol and drug "problem"; she does not excuse the fraternity brothers, who also drank excessively, because of their alcohol "problem." Evidence that Laurel invited sex is quickly swept under the carpet. Sanday blurs the facts of the case with dubious psychoanalyzing; she argues, for example, that the fraternity brothers engaged in serial sex with a woman in order to conceal their homoerotic desires for each other. When Sanday uses anthropological materials to attack male bonding, it is noticeable that she stresses the mother's family role and entirely ignores fathers as parents. Uncritical use of biased sources such as Susan Brownmiller (entry 908) and Mary Koss further damages the book's conclusion that patriarchy and phallocentrism are the sources of all human woe.

925. Scacco, Anthony M., Jr., ed. **Male Rape: A Casebook of Sexual Aggressions.** New York: AMS Press, 1982. xxi, 326p. AMS Studies in Modern Society: Political and Social Issues, no. 15. bibliographies and notes after many essays. index. pa.

Most of the 26 essays in this collection are concerned with sexual violence in which males are victims, especially in prison. As Scacco notes in the preface: "In today's world the judge who sentences a young person to reform school or prison passes male rape on him as surely as the sentence." The anthology contains both previously printed and original articles. Wilbert Rideau and Billy Sinclair's opening essay describing prison as a sexual jungle is followed by a harrowing account of the 1973 prison gang rape of peace activist Donald Tucker—which is followed by Tucker's even more harrowing essay written nearly a decade later and revealing all too clearly the psychosexual damage that he sustained. Later essays analyze racial factors involved in such attacks (often the victim is white, the aggressor black). Also studied is sexual violence in other institutions. such as juvenile correctional facilities, mental wards, military prisons, and women's prisons (Dorothy West's terrifying account of rape by female inmates matches Tucker's story.) The book's later sections present psychological profiles of sexual offenders, and suggest treatment and methods of reducing sexual violence in U.S. society.

926. Scacco, Anthony M., Jr. **Rape in Prison.** Springfield, IL: Charles C. Thomas, 1975. xi, 127p. bibliography, 117-22. notes. index.

One of the first to examine extensively sexual exploitation of males, Scacco here depicts victimization in juvenile correctional facilities and prisons. The victim is nearly always white, Scacco points out, indicating that black rapists are revenging themselves upon white society. Rape is a means of validating one masculinity, especially to males raised in female-dominated families. Scacco connects sex and violence (relying perhaps too confidently upon Kate Millett's *Sexual Politics*, entry 680) and discusses what can be done to alleviate the situation in prisons.

927. Schechter, Susan. **Women and Male Violence: The Visions and Struggles of the Battered Women's Movement.** Boston: South End Press, 1982. illus. appendixes. bibliography, 349-54. index. pa.

A socialist feminist, Schechter recounts the history of the battered women's movement in impassioned prose, depicting it as a feminist grassroots revolution against capitalist-patriarchal tyranny. The author's socialist theorizing reduces the causes of domestic violence to a question of power, that is, patriarchy and capitalism empower men as a class and victimize women as a class. In order to reach this conclusion, Schechter dismisses psychological and sociological accounts of domestic violence, dismisses evidence for the existence of battered husbands, and skates around the fact that some lesbians also batter their partners. By turning the issue of domestic violence into a gender-class power struggle, Schechter necessarily turns it into a misandric exercise. Battered men will find no shelter in Schechter's ideology.

928. Shupe, Anson, William A. Stacey, and Lonnie R. Hazelwood. **Violent Men, Violent Couples: The Dynamics of Domestic Violence.** Lexington, MA: Lexington Books, 1987. xi, 153p. appendixes. bibliography, 143-50. notes. index.

This is one of the few studies to face honestly and courageously the fact that domestic violence is not simply a matter of male violence against females. The information that significant numbers of women batter men and that couples can engage in mutual violence has infuriated some feminist activists, who have tried to silence researchers attempting to discuss such matters publicly. Apparently motivated by anti-male animosity and by an unquestioning faith in the stereotype of women as victims, these activists may also fear that scarce funds for battered women's shelters will be further diminished. The authors of this book, however, have not been thrown off balance by misandric politics. In part 1 they discuss the dynamics of domestic violence and the characteristics of violent males and violent females. Chapter 3, "The Violent Woman," is necessary reading for anyone who still imagines that only men commit domestic violence. In part 2 the authors examine the culture of violence in the United States, noting how military life and fundamentalist religion can foster a context for domestic violence. Part 3 presents an agenda for dealing with violence, specifically programs that address family violence and with antiviolence strategies at the community level. Appendix A presents a life-endangerment index, and appendix B prints the survey instrument used in a follow-up study of violent men.

929. Sonkin, Daniel Jay. **Wounded Boys, Heroic Men: A Man's Guide to Recovering from Child Abuse.** Stamford, CT: Longmeadow Press, 1992. xiv, 226p. appendixes. bibliography, 217-23. pa.

"If you were physically, sexually, or psychologically abused as a boy, this book is for you," Sonkin announces. This self-help guide for abused males utilizes Jungian psychology and Joseph Campbell's account of the hero's journey (entry 862) to aid awareness and healing. Avoiding overgeneralization, Sonkin indicates that boys are more often victims of physical abuse, girls of sexual abuse. The author provides methods for breaking denial and for healing oneself through expressing feelings, fostering helpful attitudes, practicing self-affirming behaviors, and encouraging positive sexuality. Sonkin discusses the advisability of making peace with the abuser, and he examines the importance of spirituality in the process of making peace with oneself. The appendixes provide advice on how to start a self-help wounded men's group, a bibliography, and a list of national and local resources.

930. Sonkin, Daniel Jay, Del Martin, and Lenore E. Auerbach Walker. **The Male Batterer: A Treatment Approach.** New York: Springer, 1985. xv, 256p. appendix. bibliography after each chapter, 239-48 and notes. index.

All but two chapters of this study are written by Sonkin, who describes the male batterer and the methods of counseling him. The remaining two chapters, one each by Martin and Auerbach Walker, present a misandric agenda strongly suggesting that *only* males batter. Taking an overview of batterers, Sonkin finds them frequently to be dependent men suffering from low self-esteem. Often they were victims of childhood physical or sexual abuse. Sometimes, alcohol and drugs exacerbate a domestic quarrel. Sonkin examines the treatment of male batterers, including the technique of bolstering the man's masculine self-esteem. This method enlists masculinity itself against battering. Sonkin also explores legal, professional, and ethical issues in counseling male batterers. The two chapters by Martin and Auerbach Walker provide radical feminist analyses of domestic violence: It is the result of patriarchal oppression that sanctions male violence against females. Martin is defensive about anyone's even noticing the existence of battered husbands. The radical feminist framework of the discussion also renders certain other topics off limits, such as statistical evidence that women initiate domestic violence more often than men do, some domestic violence as mutual behavior, some male "battering" as a defense against an abusive woman, and the apparently high level of battering among lesbian couples. In this study, everyone treads gingerly around such politically incorrect topics. An epilogue by "Nik" is a personal account of a reformed batterer. The appendixes contain a number of forms used in Sonkin's treatment program and a list of San Francisco domestic violence men's programs.

931. Spiegel, Lawrence D. **A Question of Innocence: A True Story of False Accusation.** Parsippany, NJ: Unicorn, 1986. 276p. illus. appendixes.

On 9 December 1983, Spiegel, a clinical psychologist, was arrested on charges that he had sexually molested his two-and-a-half-year-old daughter. The charges had been made by Spiegel's angry ex-wife. For more than two years, while the courts dithered and various agencies maneuvered, Spiegel was not permitted to see his daughter. His reputation was in tatters, his career in shambles. One of his business partners deserted him and then tried to seize the institute that Spiegel headed. His finances were wiped out. When he was at last acquitted, Spiegel successfully sought custody of his daughter. The afterword by Douglas J. Besharov discusses how unfounded reports pose a threat to children. Spiegel's story illustrates how false allegations of child molestation (currently the weapon of choice in many custody cases) can easily put a man—and a child—through hell.

932. Straus, Murray A., Richard J. Gelles, and Suzanne K. Steinmetz. **Behind Closed Doors: Violence in the American Family.** New York: Anchor Press/Doubleday, 1980. ix, 301p. appendixes. bibliography, 273-84. notes. index. pa.

This important study of domestic violence based upon 2,143 interviews is relevant to men's studies for several reasons. It is one of the first studies to demonstrate the amount of violence directed against males in the family. Indeed, the authors note that violence against husbands is slightly more frequent than violence against wives—although they are quick to point out that these statistics do not mean that there are more battered husbands than battered wives. Furthermore, the study points out that mothers, not fathers, are more often child abusers and that boys, not girls, are more likely to be victims of parental violence. Such violence, the authors state, "may be approved of and used as a 'character builder' for boys." Moreover, they question the pure genetic theories of male predisposition toward violence: "If men have a genetic predisposition to be violent, one would expect them to be more violent at home than their wives. Yet, an examination of violence between couples and violence by parents toward children reveals that women are as violent or more violent in the home than are men." The authors argue cogently for regarding much domestic violence as cases of mutual violence among family members, in contrast to the theory that most domestic violence is perpetrated by one family member (the husband is usually suspected). *Behind Closed Doors* has demonstrated that the issue of battered husbands deserves not to be swept under the rug. It also points to the need for greater understanding of how violence inflicted upon children, especially boys, produces additional family violence when these children become parents.

933. Straus, Murray A., and Gerald T. Hotaling, eds. **The Social Causes of Husband-Wife Violence.** Minneapolis: University of Minnesota Press, 1980. x, 272p. bibliography, 235-53. notes. author and subject indexes. pa.

Unwilling to settle for "single cause" answers, the authors of the thirteen essays in this volume examine the interweaving of cultural norms and social organization that fosters domestic violence. Such violence grows out of the nature of social arrangements, it is argued; it is not due to mental illness but is the result of learned and socially patterned behavior. Among the findings are: men with low "resources" in a marriage find it difficult to maintain the dominance which society expects of them and may resort to violence to regain their sense of masculinity; while wife-beating is the more serious problem, evidence of considerable violence against husbands has been found; until society convinces men of the benefits to them of a more "egalitarian" marriage, many men will feel antagonistic toward such marriages; and domestic violence may be related to the general level of acceptable violence in the larger society. The final essay suggests ways to reduce domestic violence in the United States.

934. Sussman, Les, and Sally Bordwell. **The Rapist File.** New York: Chelsea House, 1981. 215p. appendix.

This book presents interviews with 15 rapists in correctional institutions in New York, Louisiana, and Illinois. The rapists' comments are both baffling and disturbing. Often, the men's grasp of reality is strangely shaky. It is difficult to know whether they are telling the truth, putting on the interviewers, fantasizing, or simply unable to understand reality. Wild contradictions abound in their statements, as do peculiar discrepancies between thought and feeling. Some are convinced they did no wrong; others know they did. Some believe that their victims enjoyed being raped despite glaringly obvious evidence that they did not. A few got ideas from pornography, some did not, and one sees Dolly Parton as a pornographic turn-on. Many exhibit hostility toward women, sometimes because of their mother's abuse—or alleged abuse. One man says he was raped by a prostitute at age nine. Sal, a sadistic rapist-murderer, is chillingly psychopathic. Quentin, a Joe College type, breezily believes that most other men are rapists like him; he also believe that many women want to be raped. Nearly all agree that rapists are regarded as scum by fellow prisoners and are primary targets for rape in prison. Few of the men seem to have had psychological counseling or to have benefitted from what they did have. The news that some of them would soon be released is unlikely to cheer many readers. Given the bewildering diversity of the men, the authors in their opening comments wisely counsel against pat generalizations about rapists. Unfortunately, Ellen Frankfort's introduction trots out nearly every pat generalization from the all-men-are-rapists-at-heart school of thought. The appendix consists of letters from rapists which are, if possible, even less reassuring than the interviews.

935. Toch, Hans, with John J. Gibbs, Robert Johnson, and James G. Fox. **Men in Crisis: Human Breakdowns in Prison.** Chicago: Aldine, 1975. vii, 340p. notes. index.

Based upon interviews with 175 prisoners and information gathered about four suicides, Toch's study analyzes the elements of breakdowns and self-injury in prisons. A chapter is devoted to women in crisis, but the bulk of the study is concerned with male prisoners.

936. Tong, Dean. **Don't Blame Me, Daddy: False Accusations of Child Sexual Abuse.** Norfolk, VA: Hampton Roads, 1992. vi, 217p. appendixes. bibliography, 213-15. pa.

Tong recounts four case histories of false sexual abuse allegations (including his own case). He then discusses such allegations as the weapon of choice in bitter custody hearings. Almost always, men are the targets of such accusations. Once accused, the man will find himself in a Kafkaesque situation where he is presumed guilty even after he has been proven innocent. Such accusations provide the accuser (usually a vindictive ex-wife) with an easy, instant win in custody battles. Few attorneys, judges, or social workers are aware of the SAID (Sexual Allegations in Divorce) Syndrome. Tong criticizes the use of "anatomically correct" dolls to determine the truth, because for most children doll play is automatically "make believe." He cites evidence to show how social workers lead children to the "right" answers. Social agencies often conduct dubious interviews without the father's knowledge, and because of heavy case loads, many courts take the easy way out and credit flawed evidence. Tong provides cautionary advice for divorcing fathers. The book also contains addresses of organizations fighting false accusations and checklists of characteristics of false charges. The foreword is by Ralph Underwager.

937. Webb, Cathleen Crowell, and Marie Chapian. **Forgive Me.** Old Tappan, NJ: Fleming H. Revell, 1985. 220p. illus. appendixes. Reprint, New York: Berkley Books, 1986. pa.

In 1977 Cathleen Crowell was a scared teenager who feared that sex with her boyfriend had made her pregnant. To cover herself, Crowell claimed that she had been raped. Following prescribed rules that female "victims" must be believed and treated sensitively, neither her foster family nor the police questioned Crowell closely about discrepancies in her story. Pressured to finger someone as the rapist, Crowell at random selected Gary Dotson from police mug shots. Despite testimony that exonerated him, Dotson was convicted of rape and sentenced to prison. In 1985 Crowell Webb, now a wife, mother, and born-again Christian, recanted her testimony against Dotson, who had spent six years in prison. With stunning inflexibility, Judge Richard Samuels rejected her testimony and sent Dotson back to prison. Public outrage, however, prompted Illinois Governor James Thompson to release Dotson, although Dotson was still officially a felon. In *Forgive Me* Crowell Webb, retelling her story with the help of Marie Chapian, makes no excuses for herself; her determination to right a wrong she did is admirable. Of the three appendixes, the second contains an Air Force model listing characteristics of a false rape accusation.

938. Weiss, Carl, and David James Friar. **Terror in the Prisons: Homosexual Rape and Why Society Condones It.** Indianapolis, IN: Bobbs-Merrill, 1974. xiv, 247p.

According to the dust jacket of this book, more men than women are raped every year in the United States—in prisons. Piecing together information from official reports, congressional hearings, investigative reporting, interviews, and other sources, the authors construct a mosaic of rape in the prisons. Despite numerous exposés of prison rape, this sexual violence remains one of America's best-kept secrets. The public prefers to ignore it; the system condones—and even encourages—it. The conspiracy of silence includes the victims (who are too helpless and ashamed to report it), the media, and the prison officials (who prefer silence on the subject). Nevertheless, the price of prison rape is high. The male victim's sexual identity is often shattered, and he leaves prison seeking revenge upon a society that quietly condoned the outrages done to him. One need not actually be convicted of a crime to suffer prison rape; assaults upon males waiting for trial or being held on suspicion of a misdemeanor can occur. Making radical solutions, the experts betray their desperation with the set-up: One expert suggests that "the failure of the prison system to protect young men from sexual abuse rendered illegal the confinement of those young men." The authors agree that the public is amply repaid for its indifference to the prison situation by those released prisoners who are eager to avenge the abuse inflicted upon them by institutionalized sexual violence.

939. Weiss, Karel, ed. **The Prison Experience: An Anthology.** New York: Delacorte Press, 1976. xxx, 366p. notes. index.

This collection of over 100 excerpts from the famous and unknown criticizes the prison system and what it does to people. Among the nineteen sections in the anthology, separate ones are devoted to such topics as slave labor, sex in prison, the keepers, and the military dissident. The editor and many of the writers note that prisons often reflect society's class and caste prejudices, but no one raises the question of whether they also reflect society's gender prejudices.

940. Wooden, Wayne S., and Jay Parker. **Men Behind Bars: Sexual Exploitation in Prison**. New York and London: Plenum Press, 1982. x, 264p. illus. appendixes. notes. index.

Sexual exploitation of men in prisons is a recognized but unacknowledged and inadequately addressed problem. Based upon more than 200 interviews and questionnaire responses from a California prison, the study examines the prison setting, the dynamics of sexual exploitation, and the factors contributing to it. Among such factors are race or ethnic group (black, white, Chicano) and sexual orientation (heterosexual, bisexual, homosexual). The authors describe the sexual roles (jockers, punks, sissies) and the situation of homosexuals in prison. Nine percent of the heterosexual males were sexually assaulted in prison; 41 percent of the homosexuals were pressured into sex. Some solutions to alleviate the problem are offered by the authors, including policy changes in placement of prisoners, personnel requirements, and protection for inmates who complain of abuse. The appendixes contain the questionnaire and statistical tables.

Cross-References

See chapter 25, "War and Peace."

71. Abbott, Franklin, ed. **Men and Intimacy: Personal Accounts Exploring the Dilemmas of Modern Male Sexuality.**

942. Barker, A. J. **Prisoners of War**.

156. Bowker, Lee H., comp. **Prison and Prisoners: A Bibliographic Guide**.

339. Conroy, Pat. **The Prince of Tides**.

688. Corey, Michael Anthony. Male Fraud: **Understanding Sexual Harassment, Date Rape, and Other Forms of Male Hostility Towards Women**.

341. Dickey, James. **Deliverance**.

96. Farrell, Warren. **The Myth of Male Power: Why Men Are the Disposable Sex.**

346. Forster, E. M. **A Passage to India**.

159. Franklin, H. Bruce, comp. **American Prisoners and Ex-Prisoners: Their Writings: An Annotated Bibliography of Published Works, 1798-1981**.

402. Franklin, H. Bruce. **Prison Literature in America: The Victim as Criminal and Artist**.

948. Gaylin, Willard. **In the Service of Their Country: War Resisters in Prison**.

349. Golding, William. **Lord of the Flies**.

1043. Gorn, Elliott J. **The Manly Art: Bare-Knuckle Prize Fighting in America**.

952. Habenstreit, Barbara. **Men Against War**.

607. Holliday, Laurel. **The Violent Sex: Male Psychobiology and the Evolution of Consciousness**.

161. Johnson, Carolyn, John Ferry, and Marjorie Kravitz, comps. **Spouse Abuse: A Selected Bibliography**.

958. Kasinsky, Renée G. **Refugees from Militarism: Draft-Age Americans in Canada**.

868. Keen, Sam. **Fire in the Belly: On Being a Man**.

364. Mamet, David. **Oleanna**.

417. Massey, Daniel. **Doing Time in American Prisons: A Study of Modern Novels**.

1005. McEvoy, Alan W., and Jeff B. Brookings. **If She Is Raped: A Book for Husbands, Fathers and Male Friends**.

182. Miedzian, Myriam. **Boys Will Be Boys: Breaking the Link Between Masculinity and Violence**.

611. Ong, Walter J. **Fighting for Life: Contest, Sexuality, and Consciousness**.

633. Rudovsky, David. **The Rights of Prisoners: The Basic ACLU Guide to a Prisoner's Rights**.

168. Suvak, Daniel, comp. **Memoirs of American Prisons: An Annotated Bibliography**.

624. Tiger, Lionel. **Men in Groups**.

969. Uhl, Michael, and Tod Ensign. **GI Guinea Pigs: How the Pentagon Exposed Our Troops to Dangers More Deadly than War: Agent Orange and Atomic Radiation**.

25

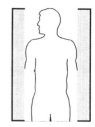

War and Peace: The Military,
Military Conscription,
Resistance to War, Combat

941. Anderson, Martin, ed. **Registration and the Draft: Proceedings of the Hoover-Rochester Conference on the All-Volunteer Force.** Stanford, CA: Hoover Institution Press, Stanford University Press, 1982. xi, 417p. notes. index.

This volume contains 26 presentations (papers, summaries, rebuttals, discussions) from the Hoover-Rochester Conference on the All-Volunteer Force held December 13-14, 1979. The legality and advisability of national service are considered, as well as numerous issues connected with it. Significantly, the issue of inequality to males is never raised.

942. Barker, A. J. **Prisoners of War.** New York: Universe Books, 1975. 249p. illus. appendixes. bibliography, 236-42. index. Original publication, as *Behind Barbed Wire* (London: Beresford, 1974).

The fate of men captured during war has always been miserable and precarious, but in the twentieth century the numbers of military prisoners and the barbarities inflicted upon them have risen alarmingly. (In World War II alone, an estimated 6 to 10 million men perished in prison camps.) Even those who survive and are repatriated can often expect lifelong aftereffects from their ordeal. Without sensationalizing, Barker provides a historical overview of military prisoners, and he describes the shock of capture and the first ordeals of prison life. He then explores numerous facets of military prison life, the effects of indoctrination, and the results of repatriation. A concluding chapter offers a code for survival in prison camps. One appendix discusses the 1949 Geneva Conference rules of prisoner treatment, the other the roles of "protective powers" and humanitarian agencies in alleviating the prisoner's lot. A useful bibliography is included.

943. Bradley, Jeff. **A Young Person's Guide to Military Service.** Rev. ed., Harvard and Boston: Harvard Common Press, 1987. xi, 227p. bibliography, 167-70. notes. index. pa.

Impartially examining the advantages and disadvantages of military service, Bradley offers high school students (and, to some extent, college students) balanced information to help them assess military life intelligently. He provides questions to ask recruiters, a brief history of each branch of

service, and information about basic training, job opportunities, and requirements for admission to service. Separate chapters on women and blacks in the
military precede a final discussion of the male-only draft, draft counseling, and
conscientious objector status. The foreword is by Edward M. Kennedy.

944.   Bressler, Marion A., and Leo A. Bressler, eds. **Country, Conscience, and
Conscription: Can They Be Reconciled?** Englewood Cliffs, NJ: Prentice-Hall,
1970. iv, 121p. (Inquiry into Crucial American Problems). bibliography, 116-21.
notes. pa.
      This selection of 29 essays and excerpts covers the pros and cons of the
military draft, the reasons why some men oppose it, and what alternatives to
it exist. Included is an abridged version of Margaret Mead's "The Case for
Drafting All Boys—and Girls."

945.   Elshtain, Jean Bethke. **Women and War.** New York: Basic Books, 1987.
xvi, 288p. illus. notes. index.
      Despite the title, this book also has much of interest to say about men and
war. A feminist, Elshtain disagrees with feminists who blame men for making
wars and who portray women as the life-affirming sex. Rather, war seduces men
and women alike. Men adopt the role of Just Warriors, while women play the role
of Beautiful Souls—the succoring mothers and healing nurses (who are "rightly"
protected from the risks and guilt of warfare). In reality, both sexes contribute to
the war effort. After surveying her own intellectual development during the 1950s
and 1960s, Elshtain examines ideas about warfare from ancient to modern times,
in particular the idea of a "just war." Stereotypes of men as brutal life-takers and
women as peace-loving life-givers only muddle our thinking about war. Throughout history, a ferocious minority of women have engaged in warfare, and a minority
of male pacifists have dedicated their lives to seeking peace. Many women
recruited into noncombatant roles find themselves energized by wartime opportunities. Many male combatants sacrifice their lives to save others and thus hardly
qualify as vicious warriors. Feminists as a whole are divided about war; they
cannot decide whether to protest it or to join it. To bring about peace, both men
and women must act as individuals who can see beyond stereotypes of the sexes.

946.   Fields, Rick. **The Code of the Warrior: In History, Myth, and Everyday
Life.** New York: HarperCollins, Harper Perennial, 1991. xii, 340p. illus. bibliography, 321-26. notes. index. pa.
      This gracefully written history traces the origins and history of the
warrior as imaginative and historical figure. Fields argues that hunting gave
rise to the warrior mentality. Eventually, the realization that good warriors
get both meat and women created war. Fields traces various manifestations of
the warrior through early kings of Sumer (including the legendary Gilgamesh,
entry 325), Indo-European bands of warriors, ancient Greek warriors from
Achilles to Alexander the Great, ancient Indian warriors such as those depicted
in the *Mahabharata*, the Taoist demoting of military warriorhood and the rise
of martial arts in China, medieval knighthood, the Japanese samurai warriors,
Native American warriors like Crazy Horse, and the rise of the lone warrior in
U.S. mythology (e.g., the Lone Ranger, The Virginian, and John Wayne west-
erns). Fields devotes a chapter to women warriors of the past, the corporate
warriors of modern Japan, and the rise of eco-warriors who fight to save the
earth. These latter, according to Fields, demonstrate the positive side of the
warrior code, the side that seeks to protect someone or something valuable from
depredation.

947. Friedman, Leon. **The Wise Minority.** New York: Dial Press, 1971. xvii, 228p. appendixes. notes. index.

"We are a nation of ... *conscientious* lawbreakers," writes Friedman in this study that places resistance to military draft into the historical context of U.S. civil disobedience. Discussion covers such matters as the intellectual background for conscientious lawbreaking, the Whiskey Rebellion, the Alien and Sedition Acts, abolitionists, labor and farm revolts, minority groups, as well as resistance to the draft from the Civil War to the Vietnam War. The author concludes: "Draft resistance is nothing new in American history."

948. Gaylin, Willard. **In the Service of Their Country: War Resisters in Prison.** New York: Viking Press, 1970. vi, 344p.

A psychoanalyst, Gaylin explores the effects of prisons upon conscientious objectors during the Vietnam War, offering critical reflections upon a society that perpetrates such dehumanization upon its young men.

949. Goldman, Peter, and Tony Fuller, with Richard Manning, Stryker McGuire, Wally McNamee, and Vern E. Smith. **Charlie Company: What Vietnam Did to Us.** New York: William Morrow, A Newsweek Book, 1983. 358p. illus. appendixes. bibliography, 351. index.

This emotionally powerful account of 65 men from Charlie Company tells how they were swept up at the age of 18 or 19, placed amid the carnage of the Vietnam War, and then returned home to face indifference or hostility from a nation that wanted to forget them. The authors also include accounts of those men who were killed in Vietnam. A final section of the book tells of the men's reunion in 1981. Expanded from a *Newsweek* special report that was one of the earliest reassessments of the Vietnam experience, *Charlie Company* provides vivid evidence of what Vietnam and its aftermath did to the men who served there.

950. Gray, J. Glenn. **The Warriors: Reflections on Men in Battle.** 3d ed. New York: Harper & Row, Torchbooks, 1970. xxiv, 242p. pa.

In this classic series of reflections on men and war, Gray draws upon his experiences as a soldier in World War II to consider the appeals of war, love as an ally and foe of war, the soldier's relation to death, images of the enemy, the ache of guilt, and the future of war. First published in 1959, the book now contains an introduction by Hannah Arendt (1967) and a new foreword by Gray (1970).

951. Greene, Bob. **Homecoming: When the Soldiers Returned from Vietnam.** G. P. Putnam's Sons, 1989. 269p. Reprint. New York: Ballantine Books, 1990. pa.

When syndicated columnist Bob Greene asked his readers about stories of homecoming Vietnam soldiers being spit upon at airports by anti-war "hippies," the request triggered an emotional outpouring from Vietnam veterans. Drawing upon more than a thousand responses, Greene lets the veterans (most of them young males) tell their own, usually painful, stories. Many of the veterans were literally spit upon, at airports and elsewhere. The veterans usually just "took it" for a variety of reasons: most were taken by surprise, some did not want to risk a fight while in uniform, and some could not strike back at a female heckler. Other forms of harassment occurred elsewhere—in college classrooms, in bars, at home. It would be comforting to think that the "spitters" were protesting the war, but most of the attacks upon the soldiers were personal, mean-spirited, and cowardly. Some of Greene's respondents, however, deny that any such incidents occurred, and others report acts of kindliness and compassion. Still, the over-all effect of Greene's book is one of shame that national division over the Vietnam War could have resulted in acts that targeted the young men who were among the war's chief victims.

952. Habenstreit, Barbara. **Men Against War.** Garden City, NY: Doubleday, 1973. iv, 210p. bibliography, 203-4. index.

"There has never been a war when no one came," Habenstreit notes, "but in every war some men have always stood up against their governments and refused to serve." This survey aimed primarily at high school readers focuses upon pacifists who rejected all violence, opponents of particular wars, and draft resisters in U.S. history. Beginning with the Shakers and Quakers in colonial times, Habenstreit follows, chronologically, the Revolutionary War, the Mexican War, the anti-draft riots during the Civil War, the war hysteria and persecutions of World War I, the nonresistant methods of the civil rights movement, and opposition to the Vietnam War. Among the men touched upon are David Low Dodge, Noah Worcester, William Ladd, William Lloyd Garrison, Henry David Thoreau, James Russell Lowell, Samuel J. May, Elihu Burritt, George C. Beckwith, the unlikely combination of Clarence Darrow and William Jennings Bryan (who were both temporarily disciples of Russia's Leo Tolstoy), Oswald Garrison Villard, Norman Thomas, Roger Baldwin, Eugene V. Debs, Martin Luther King, and Philip and Daniel Berrigan. The "men" against war include some women as well, notably Angelina and Sarah Grimké, Jane Addams, and Fanny Garrison Villard. Habenstreit also notes the existence of peace organization in U.S. history, the influence of non-Americans such as Gandhi, and the unknown men who stood their ground, often at great personal cost, against violence and war.

953. Helmer, John. **Bringing the War Home: The American Soldier in Vietnam and After.** New York: Free Press, 1974. xv, 346p. illus. appendixes. notes. index.

Characterizing Vietnam soldiers as "the poor man's army," Helmer assesses the war's impact upon working-class veterans. Using interviews with 90 subjects, Helmer describes how the men enlisted or were inducted into military service, their experiences in Vietnam, and their homecomings. Noting the frequency with which the military equates combat suitability with masculinity, the author uses Marxist class-consciousness theories to describe the alienation and rebellion among veterans, and to suggest why the U.S. working class failed to mobilize against Vietnam era injustices.

954. Hicken, Victor. **The American Fighting Man.** New York: Macmillan Co., 1969. ix, 496p. illus. bibliography, 457-74. notes.

Although sometimes critical, Hicken's readable study remains a tribute to the U.S. soldiers, sailors, and marines who fought from pre-Revolutionary days to the Vietnam conflict. The "average" U.S. soldier represents a bewildering variety of ethnic and racial groups, and despite his universal love of griping, he has demonstrated enormous *esprit* and awesome courage. (For a less enthusiastic view of the U.S. soldier, see John Laffin's *Americans in Battle*, entry 962.)

955. Jacobs, Clyde E., and John F. Gallagher. **The Selective Service Act: A Case Study of the Governmental Process.** New York: Dodd, Mead, 1967. xi, 209p. illus. index.

The authors provide a brief history of wartime conscription of males in the U.S., from colonial times through the Civil War and into the twentieth century. Peacetime conscription of men became a reality in 1948 when Congress enacted a Selective Service bill. The authors describe the administration of the act and focus on the tortured case of Daniel Seeger, who in 1959 claimed conscientious objector status even though he did not believe in a "Supreme Being" as the law required. That it finally took the Supreme Court to find in Seeger's favor indicates the U.S. government's tenacity in holding young men to conscripted military service. Published in 1967, the book shows no awareness of sexism in a male-only draft, nor does it deal with the strain that the Vietnam War put on large numbers of young men facing the draft.

956. Jeffords, Susan. **The Remasculinization of America: Gender and the Vietnam War.** Bloomington and London: Indiana University Press, 1989. xv, 215p. (Theories of Contemporary Culture series). bibliography, 206-12. notes. index. pa.

The thesis of this androphobic study is that the Vietnam War and its representations in fiction, films, and memoirs represent a patriarchal backlash against women's liberation. To borrow one of the author's favorite verbs, the study "(con)fuses" the war and its representations, jumping from Ron Kovic (entry 961) to Rambo without a blink. Jeffords sees patriarchy as a male plot to subjugate women and feminize subordinate men. (In the absence of specific evidence, Jefford's prose relies heavily on the passive voice to suggest an aura of masculine conspiracy.) Masculinity represents a heterosexual evil opposed to androgynous or bisexual femininity. Many of the Vietnam War "texts" portray male bonding that transcends racial and class differences, a practice that the author sees as a rejection of the feminine. Jeffords is upset with sympathetic treatment and depiction of Vietnam veterans because this sympathy challenges women's status as the official victims of modern society. Because some war writers use metaphors of pregnancy and birth, the author fears that men are trying to appropriate reproduction. Jeffords quarrels with feminists like Jean Bethke Elshtain (*Women and War*, entry 945) who refuse to blame war entirely on masculinity. The study offers readings of books like *Armies of the Night*, films like *The Deer Hunter*, and memoirs like *Born on the Fourth of July* (entry 961). Many Vietnam veterans, male and female alike, are likely to resent Jefford's reducing their sufferings and sacrifices to grist for the radical feminist mill.

957. Johnson, R. Charles. **Draft, Registration and the Law: A Guidebook.** 2d ed. Occidental, CA: Nolo Press, 1985. 250p. illus. appendixes. notes. pa.

Johnson's guidebook is a reminder of what young men faced during and after the Vietnam War era and may face in the future. In clear prose (and with a sense of humor), the author explains in part 1 how the draft system works, how enlisting is one way to beat the draft, and how to go about registration and resistance. The lengthy second part examines how to claim deferment as a conscientious objector, as a man with dependents, as a sole-surviving son, as a minister or theological student, and so on. Johnson provides advice on how to take the medical examination, and he discusses gays and the draft. In part 3, Johnson examines how to handle legal appeals. Three appendixes discuss aliens and the draft, counseling agencies, and medical standards. The fourth contains the notes.

958. Kasinsky, Renée G. **Refugees from Militarism: Draft-Age Americans in Canada.** New Brunswick, NJ: Transaction Books, 1976. 301p. appendixes. notes. index. Reprint, Littlefield, NJ: Adams Quality Paperbacks, 1978. pa.

Drawing upon six years (1969-1975) as a participant observer, more than 600 questionnaire responses, and 30 in-depth interviews, Kasinsky reconstructs events that led thousands of young men to leave the United States for Canada during the Vietnam era.

959. Keegan, John. **The Face of Battle.** New York: Viking Press, 1976. 354p. illus. bibliography, 337-43. index. Reprint, New York: Penguin Books, 1983. pa.

In this highly acclaimed book, Keegan recreates what combat is like for the ordinary fighting man. Citing the limitations of traditional military history with its "decisive battle" mentality and set-piece language, Keegan tries to answer questions seldom raised in these accounts. He shifts his focus away from the generals and their strategy to such matters as the motivations for the men to engage in battle, the conditions under which the men in the ranks fought, how they were wounded and how they were treated, how they died, how prisoners were taken, the relationship between junior officers and fighting men, and the use of compulsion to get men to hold their ground. With these and similar concerns in mind, Keegan describes three famous battles: Agincourt (October 25, 1415), Waterloo (June 18, 1815), and The Somme (July 1, 1916). In a final chapter, he concludes—perhaps too sanguinely—that the young men who are increasingly unwilling to be forced into warfare have already spelled the doom of battle as a historical event.

960. Klein, Robert. **Wounded Men, Broken Promises.** New York: Macmillan Co., 1981. xv, 278p.

In this account of "how the Veterans Administration betrays yesterday's heroes," Klein reports horror stories of red tape, insensitivity, medical bungling, and psychiatric mistreatment. For young men contemplating a military stint, Klein offers sobering food for thought.

961. Kovic, Ron. **Born on the Fourth of July.** New York: McGraw-Hill, 1976. 208p. Reprint, New York: Pocket Books, 1977. pa.

One of the most searing accounts to come out of the Vietnam War, Kovic's biography painfully crystallizes the story of thousands of young U.S. men of the Vietnam era. Raised in a working-class family on Long Island, Kovic was a natural athlete whose patriotic dreams, fed by war films and a marine recruiter, helped propel him into the Vietnam conflict. In a series of nightmare incidents, Kovic accidentally killed a corporal from Georgia, was involved in an attack that wounded and killed Vietnamese children, and was cut down by bullets. Paralyzed from the waist down, Kovic was returned to the United States to be rehabilitated in a rat-infested veterans' hospital. Kovic's disillusionment with the war, the U.S. government, and the treatment of veterans led to bouts of alcoholism and eventually to anti-war activism. Kovic's scrappiness is evident in this pounding autobiography, but so too are the miseries that are his daily legacy of war.

962. Laffin, John. **Americans in Battle.** New York: Crown Publishers, 1973. x, 213p. illus. bibliography, 195-204. index.

Viewing the U.S. fighting man with an admiring but critical eye, Laffin finds him generous, charitable, resourceful, but possessing a "rowdy strain" that make him oversexed, given to drink and drugs, and lacking in discipline. The author traces the history of the ordinary U.S. soldier from the Revolution to Vietnam, finding the United States a war-loving nation. (This book is intended as something of a corrective to Victor Hicken's *The American Fighting Man*, entry 954.)

963. Norman, Michael. **These Good Men: Friendships Forged from War.** New York: Crown, 1989. 310p. illus. index.

One of the most moving accounts to come out of the Vietnam War, Norman's story begins with a bloody battle at Bridge 38 on 19 April 1968. During the skirmish, several men are killed and several are wounded. Many years later, Norman is impelled to reestablish contact with the survivors and with the families of those who were killed. He tells of how the survivors' later lives were shaped by their war experiences, and he reconstructs the lives of those who were killed. Gradually, the men begin a touching process of re-bonding. Their story climaxes at a reunion in Montclair, New Jersey, during August 1985. Although battered by their experiences in the war, the survivors have gained deep friendships because of it. As one of the men says, "There's just something about us that I'll never have with another man." Photographs show the men during and after the war.

964. O'Sullivan, John, and Alan M. Meckler. **The Draft and Its Enemies: A Documentary History.** Urbana: University of Illinois Press, 1974. xx, 280p. bibliography, 281-85. notes. index.

Utilizing pertinent documents, the authors plot the stormy history of U.S. conscription, from colonial times to the 1970s. The account raises questions about the legal and political legitimacy of the military draft in a democracy; certainly, such conscription goes against the grain of U.S. ideals of free choice and individualism. The preface is by Russell F. Weigley; the introduction is by Senator Mark O. Hatfield, who describes the draft as "inherently inequitable, inefficient, and unjust—a form of involuntary servitude striking at the heart of the principles which have made this country strong, vital, and creative." Whatever one's views on male-only military obligations, this book is essential reading.

965. Starr, Paul, with James F. Henry and Raymond P. Bonner. **The Discarded Army: Veterans after Vietnam.** New York: Charterhouse, 1973. xiii, 304p. (The Nader Report on Vietnam Veterans and the Veterans Administration). notes. index.

Based on considerable research, this study of veterans after the Vietnam conflict examines such problems as Veterans Administration hospitals, drug treatment programs, "bad" discharges, veteran unemployment, and education. The introduction by Ralph Nader indicates that the Veterans Administration itself is central to the men's postwar problems.

966. Stouffer, Samuel A., and others. Vol. 1: **The American Soldier: Adjusting During Army Life.** Vol. 2: **The American Soldier: Combat and Its Aftermath.** Vol. 3: **Experiments on Mass Communications.** Vol. 4: **Measurement and Prediction.** Princeton, NJ: Princeton University Press, 1949-1950. ix, 600; 676; x, 346; x, 758p. (Studies in Social Psychology in World War II). illus. appendixes. notes. indexes.

The result of massive studies conducted over a four-year period by the Research Branch of the Army Information and Education Division, these four volumes provide an enormous body of information about U.S. fighting men during World War II. General readers are likely to be most interested in the first two volumes. After exploring the differences between the "old" army of World War I and the "new" army of the 1940s, volume 1 examines how men adjusted to the authoritarian nature of the military, its sharply defined class system, and other elements of army life. The authors explore such matters as social mobility in the army, job assignment and job satisfaction, attitudes toward leadership and social control, and the soldiers' orientation toward the war. A separate chapter is devoted to Negro soldiers. Volume 2 utilizes responses from 12,295 men to explore such matters as the soldiers' attitudes toward combat before and after their experience of it, the general conditions of ground combat in Europe and the Pacific, the stressful nature of combat, and the relationships among the men engaged in combat duty. Also examined are the soldiers' motivations for going into combat and their attitudes toward replacement policy, rear echelons, and those on the homefront. Of special importance is a section describing the relation between masculinity and the role of the combat soldier. Other chapters are devoted to men engaged in flying combat missions and aerial combat. Psychoneurotic symptoms in the army are also described. Later chapters consider the rotation of soldiers, the end of the war, and the soldier as veteran. Volume 3 is concerned with the effects upon soldiers of mass communication such as films, radio broadcasts, filmstrips, and so on. Volume 4 examines theoretical and empirical analysis of problems of measurement, and problems of predicting the soldiers' postwar plans.

966a. Surrey, David S. **Choice of Conscience: Vietnam Era Military and Draft Registers in Canada.** New York: Praeger, 1982. xi, 207p. (A J. F. Bergin Publishers Book). bibliography, 189-97. notes. index.

From structured interviews and the author's work with over 1,000 men during and after the Vietnam War era, this book surveys the history of conscription and resistance in the United States, the lives of the young U.S. men who fled to Canada during the Vietnam era, their reception in Canada, their assimilation into Canadian life, the effects of amnesty, and the lingering legacies of the Vietnam War.

967. Tax, Sol, ed. **The Draft: A Handbook of Facts and Alternatives.** Chicago and London: University of Chicago Press, 1967. ix, 497p. appendix. notes. index of persons and subject index. pa.

Although dated, this collection of papers and discussions still contains valuable insights into the military draft. Part 1 consists of 25 papers contributed to a conference on the draft held December 4-7, 1966, at the University of Chicago. Authors discuss problems with the draft system, the possibilities of broadening the draft to a form of "universal" national service ("universal" usually means male-only), different perspectives on the draft (from history, other cultures, and a survey of high school students), and alternatives to the draft, especially voluntary service schemes. Part 2 contains discussions of the papers and pursues numerous themes introduced by them. Part 3, an epilogue, consists of four postconference documents indicating that, in formulating the Selective Service Act of 1967, Congress by and large rejected reform innovations and stayed with the status quo. Two signs of the dated nature of the materials are, first, no discussion of homosexuals in the military occurs, and, second, the sexist nature of the male-only draft is challenged only by Margaret Mead, who, interestingly, argues that women should be conscripted but not allowed into combat because they are likely to be more savage fighters than men.

968. Taylor, L.B., Jr. **The Draft: A Necessary Evil?** New York: Franklin Watts, 1981. 85p. bibliography, 77-79. index.

An excellent text for high school and college study, this book reviews clearly and evenhandedly the history of conscription, the draft situation in the early 1980s, the arguments for and against drafting women, and the pros and cons of a nonvoluntary military obligation.

969. Uhl, Michael, and Tod Ensign. **GI Guinea Pigs: How the Pentagon Exposed Our Troops to Dangers More Deadly than War: Agent Orange and Atomic Radiation.** Chicago: Playboy Press, 1980; distributed by Harper & Row. xv, 256p. illus. appendixes. bibliography, 251-56. Reprint, New York: Wideview Books, 1980. pa.

The controversy still rages over the military's exposing soldiers to radiation and Agent Orange. The authors provide a damaging account of government and military complicity in endangering the health and lives of soldiers by knowingly subjecting them to radiation and deadly chemicals.

970. Williams, Roger Neville. **The New Exiles: American War Resisters in Canada.** New York: Liveright, 1971. xiii, 401p.

During the Vietnam War, thousands of young U.S. men were caught in the bind of having to disobey their country's conscription laws or become part of a war they could not support in conscience. As William Sloane Coffin, Jr., says in this book's foreword, they had the choice of being either criminals or killers. Using extended interviews and other methods, Williams charts the history of about 40,000 to 100,000 young men who sought refuge in Canada. The author provides an overview of the war resistance movement and the flight to Canada, as well as individual stories of draft resisters and military deserters.

971. Young, Peter. **The Fighting Man: From Alexander the Great's Army to the Present Day.** New York: Rutledge Press, 1981. 240p. illus. index.

With the aid of over 100 illustrations, many in color, this oversized book focuses upon the ordinary soldiers who have done the killing and the dying in major battles and campaigns. Subjects include Roman legions, Vikings, Normans of the First Crusade, the army of Frederick the Great, Napoleon's army, Billy Yank and Johnny Reb, the U.S. Marines, the Viet Minh, the French Foreign Legion, and the Israeli army.

Cross-References

54. Mathias, Frank F. **G.I. Jive: An Army Bandsman in World War II.**

877. Moore, Robert, and Douglas Gillette. **The Warrior Within: Accessing the Knight in the Male Psyche.**

819. Murphy, Lawrence R. **Perverts by Official Order: The Campaign Against Homosexuals by the United States Navy.**

370. Remarque, Erich Maria. **All Quiet on the Western Front.**

631. Rivkin, Robert S. **GI Rights and Army Justice: The Draftee's Guide to Military Life and Law.**

632. Rivkin, Robert S., and Barton F. Stichman. **The Rights of Military Personnel: The Basic ACLU Guide for Military Personnel.**

332. Shaw, George Bernard. **Arms and the Man.**

634. Sherrill, Robert. **Military Justice Is to Justice as Military Music Is to Music.**

836. Shilts, Randy. **Conduct Unbecoming: Lesbians and Gays in the U.S. Military, Vietnam to the Persian Gulf.**

376. Trumbo, Dalton. **Johnny Got His Gun.**

881. **Where the Two Came to Their Father: A Navaho War Ceremonial Given by Jeff King.**

845. Wolinsky, Marc, and Kenneth Sherrill, eds. **Gays and the Military: Joseph Steffan Versus the United States.**

847. Zeeland, Steven. **Barrack Buddies and Soldier Lovers: Dialogues with Gay Young Men in the U.S. Military.**

26

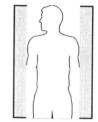

Women and Men

This chapter includes a selection of scholarly and popular books dealing with both sexes and with current gender issues.

972. Annechild, Annette. **Your Man and His Mother**. Stamford, CT: Longmeadow Press, 1992. 207p.

For an audience of women, Annechild explains that, when something goes wrong in a relationship, a man's behavior can often be traced to his mother's upbringing. Listing 15 types of negative mothers, ranging from the distant to the abusive, Annechild profiles cases of relationship breakdown and examines how the man's actions are linked to his mother's behavior. The author provides dos and don'ts for a woman in each situation. Annechild treats men fairly, but some mothers may be unduly blamed.

973. Barnes, Bonnie, and Tisha Clarke. **How to Get a Man to Make a Commitment: Or Know When He Never Will.** New York: St. Martin's Press, 1985. 149p.

It's a jungle of confusion on the dating scene with liberated women and wary men, but this book confounds confusion. The authors' advice makes no logical sense whatsoever (e.g., they insist upon sexual equality while also insisting that the man do the driving and pay for the date). Nevertheless, the authors tell women readers about current practices on the bar scene, acceptable ways of getting a man's attention, how to behave on the initial dates, and a two-week program to get him to commit or to break up the relationship.

974. Bird, Caroline. **The Two Paycheck Marriage: How Women at Work Are Changing Life in America**. New York: Rawson, Wade, 1979. xiv, 305p. notes. index. Reprint, Pocket Books, 1980. pa.

Bird presents the two-paycheck marriage as the triumph of the women's movement, but many readers will question how adequately she understands men's viewpoints on the issues she raises. Certainly, the sexist generalizations about men ("Fathers do what they like doing with children, mothers what has to be done for them") do not inspire confidence.

975. Botwin, Carol. **Men Who Can't Be Faithful: How to Pick Up the Pieces When He's Breaking Your Heart.** New York: Warner Books, 1988. x, 291p. appendixes. bibliography, 281-85. index. pa.

Although the subject of this book lends itself to male bashing, Botwin discusses "unfaithful" men without rancor toward men in general. Writing for a female audience, she explores such topics as the indicators of male "unfaithfulness," biological and cultural theories of why some men stray, ways of coping with an "unfaithful" man, and advice for women enduring a breakup. With admirable fairness, she explores ways in which some women collude in their man's affairs. She also advises women who have had bad experiences with some men: "Don't decide that all men are like that."

976. Brothers, Joyce. **What Every Woman Should Know About Men.** New York: Simon and Schuster, 1981. 268p. Reprint, New York: Ballantine Books, 1983. pa.

For an audience of middle-class white women, Brothers summarizes in readable fashion what current studies reveal about men. Among the topics she surveys are the biological bases for maleness, the stages of the male life cycle, men and work, sexual concerns, and love and marriage. Brothers offers advice on how women can live with men as equals and lovers without being subservient or hostile. Some readers may find Brothers's discussions lucid and helpful; others may find them simplistic and occasionally condescending to men.

977. Browne, Joy. **Why They Don't Call When They Say They Will ... and Other Mixed Signals.** New York: Simon and Schuster, 1989. 203p.

Browne presents standard scenarios of mixed signals between the sexes, the way women and men blame each other, her own explanation of what is going on in each case, and ways to resolve the misunderstanding.

978. Campbell, Bebe Moore. **Successful Women, Angry Men: Backlash in the Two-Career Marriage.** New York: Random House, 1986. xvii, 237p. bibliography, 233-36.

"All is not well with the two-career couple," the author writes. Divorce is especially high among women and men who had committed themselves to "egalitarian" marriages. Feminists were often naive about the difficulties of maintaining such a marriage. Being gender pioneers, two-career couples experience unforeseen problems. Some men wonder what are the payoffs for them; some women are torn between careers and family demands. Making matters worse for these couples, a 1980s "backlash" against feminism exalted the feminine. The author describes how two-career marriages break down and offers advice for sustaining them. Men will perhaps be most interested in chapter 11, "The Free Men of the Eighties." The author concludes, "It isn't likely that female anger and male guilt will be the catalyst for permanent change in society."

979. Carmody, John. **What Women Don't Understand About Men: And Vice Versa.** Mystic, CT: Twenty-Third Publications, 1992. v, 106p. pa.

From a Catholic-Christian standpoint, Carmody examines current gender issues, both secular and sacred. Using a dialogue between "Tom" and "Sue" (interspersed with his own observations), Carmody explores a variety of issues, including men's uneasiness with condemnations of masculinity by the churches and women's sense of being ignored by the churches they support. The wandering discussion also touches on feelings, the men's mythopoetic movement, sin, guilt, language and communication, and the sexuality and gender images of God.

980. Carter, Steven, with Julia Sokol. **Men Who Can't Love: When a Man's Fear Makes Him Run from Commitment (and What a Smart Woman Can Do About It).** New York: M. Evans, 1987. xii, 235p. appendix.

Aimed at a female market, this book examines what it calls "commitmentphobia," or alleged male fear of making a commitment. Repeatedly assuring women that any problems in this area are *his* fault, the book depicts men as unreliable, elusive, and immature. That such clichés will benefit either sex is extremely unlikely.

981. Cline, Sally, and Dale Spender. **Reflecting Men at Twice Their Natural Size.** New York: Henry Holt, Seaver Books, 1987. 193p. illus. bibliography, 187-93.

"Men have egos; women do not" is this book's opening line. The rest of the book is an extended exercise in special pleading, depicting men as callous egotists and women as oppressed creatures who wear themselves out trying to please men. The book's (almost) hidden agenda is a lesbian separatist one, urging women to leave those dreadful, demanding males and find repose in sisterhood. Having interviewed more than 280 women, the authors deplore female wiles to make men feel good about themselves, insisting that women do so only because they have been brainwashed and need men's money. The premise that only men have egos would seem to be belied, however, by Cline's account of her second wedding (before she moved on to lesbianism). To attract attention, she wore "an outrageous orange leather trouser suit with tall black boots," but the press noticed only her husband's "purple and black regency gear." Cline's outrage over the slight hardly squares with a lack of female ego.

982. Ehrenreich, Barbara. **The Hearts of Men: American Dreams and the Flight from Commitment.** Garden City, NY: Anchor Press/Doubleday, 1983. vii, 206p. notes. index. pa.

Taking an original, thought-provoking look at what happened to American men between the fifties and the eighties, Ehrenreich depicts the decline and fall of the "breadwinner ethic." During the fifties, pressure upon men to marry and support families was intense; those who did not were "irresponsible," "immature," or (worse yet) homosexual. But rebellion against gray-flannel conformity was led by such forces as *Playboy*, which promoted a single-life sexuality; the Beat Generation, which rejected job and marriage; and medical writers, who emphasized male biological vulnerability as demonstrated by men's greater susceptibility to heart disease and the lethal aspects of Type A behavior. In short, the breadwinner trap was deadly to men. Despite some hostility to men, the feminist movement promised them relief once women shared the breadwinning. The men's movement of the seventies publicized the hazards of being male and the ways in which women's liberation could mean men's liberation. But, fearful that freeing men from the breadwinner ethic would ruin the family, the New Right (the same people who defeated the ERA) created a backlash against men's liberation. Ehrenreich is admittedly uncertain whether the "male revolt" was a perfidious abandonment of responsibilities, another step toward the liberal humanistic ideal of greater freedom, or a revolt against an exploitive social system. Unsure whether it was a revolt at all, she argues that men freed themselves from economic responsibilities before women gained economic parity. In any event, family support by a single breadwinner has virtually disappeared, partly because of corporate failure to provide adequate wages. Drastic solutions—including the creation of a welfare state—are the only workable ones. Ehrenreich ponders whether men and women can work together as rebels to create a more humane society.

983. Eno, Susan. **The Truth About What Women Want in Men.** New York: William Morrow, 1980. 312p. index.

After interviewing "hundreds" of women, ages 17-40, mostly single or divorced, Eno offers advice to men who want to succeed with women. Appearance, assurance, assertiveness, and aliveness are the four key elements of male attractiveness. Eno advises men on such concerns as hairstyles, facial hair, clothes, body language, conversation, breaking up, and sex. Her advice is fairly traditional: women prefer gentlemanly men who take the lead, who pay for dates (at least until a closer relationship develops), and who respect them— while taking the initiative in sexual matters. Eno does not consider why some men find these roles contradictory and distasteful and why they are reluctant to perform them.

984. Fishel, Elizabeth. **The Men in Our Lives: Fathers, Lovers, Husbands, Mentors.** New York: William Morrow, 1985. 382p. bibliography, 375-82. notes.

Utilizing interviews from about seventy women, as well as biographical writings and scholarly research, Fishel draws composite portraits of the men in women's lives. Part 1 examines various types of fathers: the Patriarch, the Pal, the Bystander, the Charmer, the Absent Father. Part 2 is devoted to Mr. Wrong and Mr. Right, the Mentor, and a woman's Inner Man. Some of the women are well known (e.g., Jane Fonda and Georgia O'Keefe); some are daughters of famous men (e.g., Holly Heston and Susan Cheever). Once regarded by social scientists as the negligible parent, the father looms large in these women's lives, often overshadowing the lovers, husbands, and mentors.

985. Gilbert, Lucia Albino. **Men in Dual-Career Families: Current Realities and Future Prospects.** Hillsdale, NJ: Lawrence Erlbaum, 1985. xv, 185p. appendix. bibliography, 166-75. author and subject indexes.

A study of 51 professional couples (nearly all of them white) indicates that the two-career family has both benefits and problems. In particular, it suffers from tensions between traditional expectations and new roles. The author considers such topics as whether men pay a price in two-career families, whether their career aspirations are affected by their wives' employment, the husband-wife relationship, parenting, stress, and techniques of coping with it. The largest payoff for men seems to come in their closer relationships with children. The second part of the book considers counseling for men who are changing roles, the organizational behavior of the work world, and the future of dual-career lifestyle. The appendix contains a guide to the interview used in the study. Some readers will feel that the discussion in the book suffers from simplistic notions of power (men have it, women don't), uncritical use of terms like "patriarchy" and "male-dominated society," and the belief that traditional roles are simply social conventions capable of being easily altered.

986. Gochros, Jean Schaar. **When Husbands Come Out of the Closet.** New York: Haworth Press, 1989. xv, 267p. (The Haworth Series on Women, no. 1). appendix. bibliography, 257-61. index.

A therapist, Gochros estimates that the number of married gays runs into the millions. Based upon a study of 103 wives whose husbands came out of the closet, this book is addressed primarily to women, offering them insights and advice on coping and surviving the disclosure of their husbands' homosexuality or bisexuality. She provides background information on the wives, discusses gay-straight marriages, and describes how disclosure occurs (voluntary disclosure by the husband is usually best). After disclosure, wives must face numerous crises, as well as stress, damage to self-esteem, and anger. In some cases, the marriage can survive. Gochros lists sources of help for women, offers advice for husbands and wives, and discusses AIDS and family problems. The appendix contains the bibliography, a list of resources, and information on methodology.

987. Goldberg, Herb. **The New Male-Female Relationship.** New York: William Morrow, 1983. 274p. notes. index. Reprint, New York: New American Library, Signet, 1984. pa.

Goldberg examines current gender roles and elaborates an ideal toward which both sexes can strive. Refusing to blame one sex for the other's troubles, he argues that both sexes have been victims of restrictive gender roles. Such roles—male machine and female child, actor and reactor, success object and sex object—had failure built into them, because they converted romance into disillusionment, love into hostility, and sex into a battleground. But liberation philosophy itself can also disguise hostility towards the opposite sex. The newly sensitized male and the militant feminist can sometimes be "more liberated than thou" hatemongers. Most women, however, need training in asserting themselves; most men need training in learning to let go, relax, and stop feeling responsible for everything. Both sexes need to rediscover playfulness, to recognize that opposition to sexism is not so much a matter of role reversals but of achieving a more open ideal of the other person as a whole human being. Goldberg inveighs against obsession with sexual technique and standards of performance; he labels too-early parenthood as the source of much family discord. Looking toward a better future, he believes that the battle of the sexes will become anachronistic as men and women outgrow traditional gender roles with their built-in failures.

988. Halas, Celia. **Why Can't a Woman Be More Like a Man? The 20 Questions Men Ask Most Frequently About Women.** New York: Macmillan, 1981. ix, 243p.

In this book about women written for men, Halas argues that social conditioning has damaged many women. She offers insights designed to help men understand and cope with women's difficulties, especially a sense of powerlessness and inferiority. The author, a psychotherapist, draws upon case histories to answer 20 questions about women that puzzle men (e.g., why does she feel so misunderstood? why does she act so helpless? why does she cling so close and act so jealous?). Perhaps inevitably, the book implies that only women have gender difficulties. It skirts the questions of whether men's social conditioning has also been damaging to men and whether women have a corresponding obligation to understand and cope with men's difficulties.

989. Hanson, Dian. **How to Pick Up a Man.** New York: G. P. Putnam's Sons, 1982. 187p.

A managing editor of *Oui*, Hanson argues that the days of waiting for a man to make the first move are over (if indeed they ever existed). For women readers, Hanson provides guidelines for breaking out of passivity, meeting men, and getting a man's attention. The foreword comments are by Eric Weber, whose *How to Pick Up Girls*, written a decade earlier, sold over 1 million copies.

990. Hart, Lois B., and J. David Dalke. **The Sexes at Work: Improving Work Relationships Between Men and Women.** Englewood Cliffs, NJ: Prentice-Hall, Spectrum Books, 1983. xii, 180p. appendixes. index. pa.

In this popular guide, the authors isolate problem areas in the modern professional workplace and offer suggestions on such matters as sexual harassment, sexual attraction, sex-biased language, expressing emotions, etiquette, and related matters. The discussion shows a lively sense of women's viewpoints but skims men's feelings and concerns.

991. Hoffman, Susanna M. **The Classified Man: Twenty-two Types of Men (and What to do About Them).** New York: Coward, McCann, and Geoghegan, 1980. 309p. appendixes. Reprint, New York: G. P. Putnam's Sons, Perigee Books, 1980. pa.

For a general audience of women, the author categorizes 22 types of men, providing each with a catchy description (e.g., The Gender Ascender, the Disaster Broker). Designating each type's identifying signs, sex signals, money matters, and family aspects, the author offers advice on dealing with each group. Hoffman appears friendly toward, but wary of, men.

992. Jeffers, Susan. **Opening Our Hearts to Men.** New York: Fawcett Columbine, 1989. x, 303p. appendixes. bibliography, 301-3. notes. pa.

Jeffers argues that anger against men in general hurts women and locks them into futile bitterness. Women are entitled to express legitimate anger, but they must release it at legitimate targets. Also, women must look at themselves honestly with a mirror and not with a magnifying glass. Some women project their own least attractive qualities onto men. Women also need to re-vision their hidden and sexist expectations of what men are expected to be and do. Too many women are inconsistent in what they say they want from a man and in what their behavior demonstrates they want from a man. Indiscriminate blaming of men prevents women from seeing how their own behavior traps them in unhealthy relationships. Only when women take responsibility for their own happiness will they empower themselves to create that happiness. Jeffers advises women on how to break the passive woman/active man syndrome that leaves women victims. She debunks current assumptions about male privilege and power, about which some women are so angry. Jeffers urges women to celebrate their own femininity and that of other women, and she advocates awareness of a spiritual higher self. Jeffers's book glows with her own self confidence and openness to men and women.

993. Kammer, Jack. **Good Will Toward Men: Women Talk About Fairness and Respect as a Two-Way Street.** New York: St. Martin's Press, 1994. xvii, 247p. appendix. bibliography, 224-25.

Kammer interviews 22 women, ranging from liberal feminists to conservatives, about men's issues. The women are uniformly savvy, articulate, and independent-minded in their views on gender topics. A committed feminist, Barbara Dority strongly opposes censorship of erotica as "pornography." Women's Studies coordinator Gayle Kimball explains the value of joint custody, while sociologist Suzanne Steinmetz discusses battered husbands (and the sexual politics of those who deny their existence). Karen DeCrow, former president of NOW, explains how she got diapering facilities into men's public rest rooms. Sportscaster Jane Chastain takes a dim view of sportswriter Lisa Olson's visits to the Boston Patriots' locker room, and Naval Reserve officer Sandra Rippey has similar doubts about media coverage of the alleged Tailhook scandal. Carol Iannone discusses the negative impact of some feminist scholars on academic freedom, while Ruth Shalit recounts how a false rape accusation against a male college student took on a life of its own. Doris Caldwell and Audrey Chapman discuss hostility against black men, and several interviewees examine discrimination against divorced fathers. Elizabeth Herron closes the volume, protesting that the misandric one-note in which public discourse of gender is pitched does not represent the majority of women, even feminist women. Kammer's questions are often consciousness-raising exercises in their own right. The lists of resources include books, periodicals, men's organizations, institutes, videos, and computer networks.

994. Kelley, Susan Curtin. **Why Men Commit: Men Explain What It Takes to Turn a Casual Relationship into the Love of a Lifetime.** Holbrook, MA: Bob Adams, 1991. 188p. appendixes. bibliography, 173-77. index.

This exercise in popular advice for women draws upon men's responses to over 1,000 questionnaires. The average age of the male respondents was 39.2 years. Kelley suggests that women may be misled by stereotypes about men. She surveys the reasons why men commit to relationships, contrasts committers with noncommitters, and offers advice on such matters as the dos and don'ts of seduction, strategic planning to get him to commit, and ways to "make it happen." In the final chapter, several men explain their reasons for making a commitment.

995. Kimball, Gayle. **The 50-50 Marriage.** Boston: Beacon Press, 1983. xiii, 312p. appendixes. bibliography, 225-26. notes. index.

Drawing upon extended interviews with 150 egalitarian couples, the feminist author draws a profile of the perils and payoffs of shared moneymaking, child care, housework, and decision making. In this analysis, the pluses outweigh the minuses.

996. Kimball, Gayle. **50-50 Parenting: Sharing Family Rewards and Responsibilities.** Lexington, MA: Lexington Books, D. C. Heath, 1988. xxiii, 337p. appendixes. bibliography, 283-313. notes. index.

Kimball expounds on the benefits of shared parenting for parents and for children. Fathers are brought into closer contact with family members, mothers are freed up to pursue additional options, and children are allowed greater input into family decisions. Although discussing democratic discipline, Kimball nevertheless recommends authoritative parenting. For male readers, chapter 7, "Involving Fathers," is central to understanding Kimball's proposals. After divorce, she urges that some form of joint custody be the primary consideration. Kimball also addresses stepparents, communal parenting, and ways in which the workplace can be made more responsive to parents' needs. The four appendixes contain a general description of her study of 291 co-parents, information on the children's responses, a bibliography on role sharing, and a resource guide for co-parents.

997. Kingma, Daphne Rose. **The Men We Never Knew: Women's Role in the Evolution of a Gender.** Berkeley, CA: Conari Press, 1993. xi, 275p.

Repelled by the current battle of sexes, Kingma argues that both sexes must mature emotionally. Men have had their feelings "hazed out" of them by social demands that they conform to the masculine role of protector and provider. Women need to stop complaining about men, they need to understand how they collude in male inexpressiveness, and they must help men reclaim their inner feminine. Misandry is common among U.S. women, who often say they want men to express feelings but are unreceptive when they do. Most women have little feeling for the difficulties of the male role. Romance and commitment still mean that the man must assume responsibility for the woman. Rather than unfeeling monsters, men act out their emotions; verbal expressiveness is a feminine mode that many men feel uncomfortable with. The warrior men's movement has helped men to reestablish bonding with other men and to heal the father wound, but it has not helped men with women nor with their own inner feminine. Kingma argues that women must take on the "holy work" of initiating men into the feminine. She offers 26 steps and 22 conversational questions for women seeking to help men find expressiveness. It is time for women to move beyond the "men are oppressors" and "women are victims" stereotypes, Kingma concludes; women and men together must be the architects of a more humane future.

997a. Kipnis, Aaron, and Elizabeth Herron. **Gender War, Gender Peace: The Quest for Love and Justice Between Women and Men.** New York: William Morrow, 1994. 301p. bibliography, 275-84. notes. index.

When Kipnis and Herron take a group of men and women on a week-long camping trip, everyone brings along considerable sex-hate baggage. The narrative, written in turns by the two authors, shows the women and men rehashing the gender antagonisms that have become current coin in modern U.S. society. Gradually, however, anger begins to fade into understanding and reconciliation. The account benefits greatly from Kipnis's unusually savvy awareness of men's issues and Herron's unusually sensitive understanding of women's concerns.

998. Korda, Michael. **Male Chauvinism! How It Works.** New York: Random House, 1973. 243p. notes.

Focusing on the office, Korda analyzes how male chauvinism obstructs women's advancement at work. Indoctrinated by society to be submissive, women are handicapped in competing with men who have been taught to be aggressive. Despite such problems as office politics, unequal pay, sexual harassment of women, and the stigma of success for women, Korda notes that the modern office is nevertheless a fairly civilized workplace in which equality between men and women can emerge. Women, Korda says, are coming to grips with their problems and concerns; it is time for men to do likewise. Some readers will find Korda's analysis of male bias in the executive suite enlightening; others will be alienated by the hectoring tone that echoes radical feminist denunciations of the early seventies.

999. Kozmetsky, Ronya and George. **Making It Together: A Survival Manual for the Executive Family.** New York: Free Press, 1981. xii, 155p.

The authors, an executive couple, offer strategies for management of dual-career families, including how to keep together, handle children, balance leadership, cope with crises, and get started and move ahead in business.

1000. Kurtz, Irma. **Mantalk: A Book for Women Only.** New York: William Morrow, Beech Tree Books, 1986. 192p.

Ostensibly a look at the way men talk, Kurtz's book is really a series of personal essays on men and women. Witty, acerbic, disillusioned, Kurtz is equally critical (and fond) of both sexes. Noting the male fear of failure, for example, Kurtz observes how much all humanity has gained from this anxiety: "When men fail, everyone fails." Kurtz concludes: "It is difference, not likeness or equality, that produces progress, and it is friction that produces excitement." Though the book is labeled "for women only," many men will find it amusing and enlightening.

1001. Lewan, Lloyd S., with Roger G. Billingsley. **Women in the Workplace: A Man's Perspective.** Denver, CO: Remington Press, 1988. 103p. bibliography, 96-100. pa.

A successful businessman, Lewan argues that tensions in the workplace result because males "objectify women" and women emphasize relationships. Lewan urges both sexes to be more tolerant of each other. Lewan's gallantry towards women sometimes results in misandric clichés. For example, if child custody were routinely awarded to men, he argues, mothers would pay support diligently. (Statistics indicating a higher percentage of deadbeat moms than dads, however, suggest otherwise.) Lewan is apparently unaware that some women commit rape, and his belief that having female political leaders would ensure world peace is quaintly Victorian.

1002. Maine, Margo. **Father Hunger: Fathers, Daughters and Food.** Carlsbad, CA: Gürze Books, 1991. xv, 254p. appendixes. notes. index. pa.

Maine does not blame fathers for women's eating disorders. Rather, she argues that U.S. society regards fathers as second-class citizens and places many roadblocks in the way of greater father involvement in the family. As a result, father absence can be a major source of a daughter's low self-esteem and thus can be connected with such eating disorders as bulimia and anorexia. Maine charts the potential links between a father's behavior and a daughter's desire to achieve acceptance through body image. In the closing chapters of this study, Maine provides practical advice for fathers to achieve greater and more beneficial involvement with their children and for daughters to overcome the negative effects of father hunger. The preface is by Craig Johnson. The four appendixes provide strategies for educators, physicians, therapists, and other professionals and adults.

1003. Malone, John. **Straight Women/Gay Men: A Special Relationship.** New York: Dial Press, 1980. xi, 207p. bibliography, 205-7. notes.

Drawing upon interviews with 150 people, Malone depicts the special relationships that can exist between straight women and gay men. After describing the women's and the men's viewpoints, Malone explores sexual complications and indecisions. He reports on marriages broken by the husband's coming out and on enduring marriages between a gay man and a straight woman (e.g., Charles Laughton and Elsa Lanchester). After discussing the ambiguities of bisexuality, Malone concludes with a chapter assessing the current state of this kind of relationship.

1004. McEvoy, Alan W., and Jeff B. Brookings. **If She Is Raped: A Book for Husbands, Fathers and Male Friends.** Holmes Beach, FL: Learning Publications, 1984. 133p. appendixes. bibliography, 129-31. index. pa.

The authors offer advice for men coping with the rape of a woman close to them (e.g., wife, lover, friend, or daughter). Examining misunderstandings about rape, they reprove the tendency to doubt the victim or to believe that she "asked for it." They enumerate immediate and long-term concerns, advising men that the woman needs support and must herself make such decisions as whether or not to prosecute (if she knows her attacker). At no time should the man's anger set the agenda. If appropriate, the man should help the woman overcome her fears about sex after rape. Because interracial rape can lead to racist fear and hatred, the man must guard against racial overgeneralizations. If the rape is reported and if the case goes to trial, the woman will have to relive the attack when she would rather heal; once again, the man's understanding and patience can provide needed support. While men must avoid taking responsibility for another's happiness, their sympathetic understanding can demonstrate their unconditioned love. The three appendixes contain illustrative case histories, a listing of rape crisis centers by state, and suggested readings.

1005. Mooney, Elizabeth C. **Men and Marriage: The Changing Role of Husbands.** New York: Franklin Watts, 1985. 212p. index.

Married in 1946 and now a widow, Mooney finds that gender roles of wives and husbands have altered greatly in the past 40 years. Wives' new freedoms are balanced by insecurities. Husbands do not behave in the old, expected ways either. With chatty good humor, Mooney surveys the new gender landscape, wreckages and all. She sees POSSLQs (Persons of the Opposite Sex Sharing Living Quarters) adapting to new sexual moralities that bring greater liberation and confusions. Many fathers, she finds, are more involved with children, but there also seem to be more men who want to get out of long-term marriages. Divorced fathers and mothers need to piece together new lives, and remarriages can produce mixed results. Most middle-aged women have lost their beauty power and are devalued; successful middle-aged men seem to be more attractive than when they were younger. For both men and women, retirement brings its own rewards and stresses. Despite all the changes, however, Mooney concludes that husbands are nice to have around.

1006. Mornell, Pierre. **Passive Men, Wild Women.** New York: Simon and Schuster, 1979. 192p. bibliography, 191-92. notes. Reprint, New York: Ballantine Books, 1980. pa.

In this informal study, Mornell depicts a familiar pattern in modern man-woman relationships: *he* is emotionally withdrawn and uncommunicative, while *she* tries to be emotionally involved and communicative. For the divorced, a similar pattern merges: *He* is wary of becoming committed to a relationship, while *she* seeks to establish a close relationship with a "good" man. Mornell sees much of the male's passivity deriving from father absence in the modern family, a situation that leaves males uncertain with and chary of women. In the closing sections of the book, Mornell provides suggestions for escaping the passive man/wild woman impasse.

1007. Nahas, Rebecca, and Myra Turley. **The New Couple: Women and Gay Men.** New York: Seaview Books, 1979. ix, 291p. bibliography, 285-91. notes.

Through interviews and research, the authors informally explore three types of female-gay relationships. In the first type, the gay man is married to the woman; such relationships usually involve serious problems. In the second, the relationship is primarily a nonsexual friendship between people with similar professional interests; these relationships usually work smoothly. In the third, sex is a part of the relationship although the male is not wholly committed to heterosexuality; these relationships can also involve tensions and misunderstandings. The authors speculate on how the conjunction of the women's liberation movement and gay liberation has fostered these new couples.

1008. Nin, Anaïs. **In Favor of the Sensitive Man, and Other Essays.** New York and London: Harcourt Brace Jovanovich, Harvest/HBJ Books, 1976. 169p. pa.

In the essay "In Favor of the Sensitive Man," Nin fears that some women miss the old male dominance, feel bewildered by their new freedom, mistake male gentleness for weakness, and construe male flexibility toward women as indifference. She exhorts women to welcome the kind of man they say they have been looking for, and to reject the success-driven male that so many women in the past have found attractive.

1009. Nir, Yehuda, and Bonnie Maslin. **Loving Men for All the Right Reasons.** New York: Dial Press, 1982. 275p. Reprint, New York: Dell, 1983. pa.

Writing for women, a husband and wife team of therapists recount a series of no-win "lovestyles" illustrating self-defeating patterns of relating to men. The authors provide four ways for women to recognize and unlearn these patterns. In a final chapter, the authors recognize that men too can be victimized by similarly defeating patterns of relating to women and that men are often less successful than women in recognizing and breaking out of them.

1010. Novak, William. **The Great American Man Shortage and Other Roadblocks to Romance (and What to Do About It).** New York: Rawson, 1983. 210p. notes. index.

Puzzled by complaints that "all the good ones are either married or gay," Novak investigates the alleged man shortage. For women 30 and over, a shortage of eligible males does exist: Larger numbers of women survive at each age level, males die younger than females, gay men outnumber gay women, and some divorcés marry much younger women. Also, the baby boom generation has created a shortage of males for women who traditionally marry slightly older men. Though real, the man shortage does not create impossible odds. Between the ages of 25 and 29, a "surplus" of males already exists, and (as the baby boomers age) a "surplus" of slightly older men will exist for younger women to marry. Novak devotes the second half of his book to the situation of the single, over-30 woman. He finds that romance has been subverted by hostility between the sexes fostered by "Me Decade" selfishness, and by the fact that the women's movement has not been balanced by a men's movement to articulate men's issues. Novak devotes an interesting chapter to male "talking back" to female demands and complaints. Among men's grievances are "selective equality" (the tendency of some women to demand equality when it benefits them and to reject equality when it doesn't), the general failure of women to take greater initiative in relationships and to pay their fair share, and the conflicting demands of some women: "They're looking for somebody who's John D. Rockefeller at the office and Dr. Benjamin Spock at the dinner table.... I'm sorry, but I'm only one person, not two."

1011. Penney, Alexandra. **How to Keep Your Man Monogamous.** New York: Bantam Books, 1989. x, 192p.

For a popular audience, Penney surveys men's diverse attitudes toward monogamy and the various threats to it. She indicates when men are vulnerable to temptation, and she offers women advice on how to prevent their men from straying. (See also entry 756.)

1012. Pleck, Joseph H. **Working Wives/Working Husbands.** Beverly Hills, CA: Sage Publications, 1985. 168p. bibliography, 160-67. notes. pa.

Criticizing the "exchange theory" of earlier studies of family work, Pleck formulates a new approach that utilizes feminist critiques of women's role-overload in family work and outside employment. The technical analysis of numerous family work studies in this book underlines how easily flawed and difficult to interpret most such studies are. Thus, although Pleck concludes that wives' overload is decreasing and husbands' participation in family work is increasing, nothing less than a careful reading of the book can do justice to the many nuances that necessarily qualify any bald summary of its findings.

1013. Rubin, Theodore Isaac, and David C. Berliner. **Understanding Your Man: A Woman's Guide.** New York: Ballantine Books, 1977. 186p. pa.

In this popularly written guide for women, Rubin surveys a wide range of topics about male psychology and sexuality, including machismo, men's fear of intimacy and rejection, male dependency on women, oedipal feelings, male anxiety and guilt feelings, heterosexual relations, the importance of the penis, fantasies, masturbation, pornography, infidelity, and the male climacteric. Because some topics are controversial, readers may find themselves disagreeing occasionally with Rubin. This guide heeds various messages from the women's liberation movement without being overwhelmed by them.

1014. Ryan, Andrew. **The REAL Romantic Marketplace: Know Good Women?** New York: Vantage Press, 1991. 139p. illus. notes.

When *Newsweek* announced on June 2, 1986, that the marriage opportunities for a single woman over 30 were virtually nil, the cover story was but the latest in a media blitz insisting that there were "no good men" available. Ryan takes satiric aim at this myth and finds it largely the result of "reverse sexism" directed against men. He questions popular ideas about what constitutes a "good" man, notices the pervasive misandry that informs such laments for the unmarried woman, looks closely at the statistics involved, and asks women to examine their own consciences about their behaviors toward men.

1015. Ryglewicz, Hilary, and Pat Koch Thaler. **Working Couples: How to Cope with Two Jobs and One Home.** New York: Sovereign Books, 1980. 181p. index.

Presented as an exploration and guide, the popularly written book offers practical advice on allocating household chores, sustaining a loving relationship between husband and wife, raising children, handling money, using leisure, creating special lifestyles (e.g., working at home), and coping with pressures and pitfalls in two-career relationships. Although more attuned to women's issues and views, the authors treat men's concerns sympathetically.

1016. Seskin, Jane, and Bette Ziegler. **Older Women/Younger Men.** Garden City, NY: Anchor Press/Doubleday, 1979. xix, 143p. appendixes. bibliography, 142-43. notes.

From interviews and research, the authors examine the apparent increase in the number of older women/younger men relationships. In separate chapters, these relationships are discussed by the couples, by the men alone, and by the women alone. The concluding two chapters consider "expert" opinions on such romances and the authors' positive afterthoughts about them. For the younger men (who were more reluctant to speak with the authors) the advantages of such relationships include initiation into sex by an experienced partner, the unlikelihood of having children, the lowered demand for performance, and the lack of competition with the woman. The book does not pretend to be an exhaustive study, and readers should expect to find some questions unanswered.

1017. Shaevitz, Marjorie Hansen, and Morton H. Shaevitz. **Making It Together as a Two-Career Couple.** Boston: Houghton Mifflin, 1980. xiii, 282p.
bibliography, 269-72. notes. index.

A couple working in family and career counseling, the authors have
distilled their insights and experiences into practical advice on such matters
as housework, parenting, child care, money decisions, finding the right employer, coping with overload, and maintaining the couple's relationship.

1018. Shaevitz, Morton H. **Sexual Static: How Men Are Confusing the
Women They Love.** Boston: Little, Brown, 1987. xii, 175p. bibliography,
170-75.

"A book for women about men," *Sexual Static* argues that women have
changed but men are still dragging their feet. Like the book's title, Shaevitz
usually implies that men are the problem while women have their act together.
The analysis of men's behavior seldom rises above TV-talk-show clichés. The
final chapter, "The Last Word," is by Marjorie Hansen Shaevitz.

1019. Shain, Merle. **Some Men Are More Perfect Than Others: A Book
About Men, and Hence About Women, and Love and Dreams.** Philadel-
phia and New York: J.B. Lippincott, 1973. ix, 117p. Reprint, New York: Bantam
Books, 1974.

In witty, informal essays on such matters as loving (as opposed to romantic
ego-tripping and casual sex), marriages (both good and bad), the battle of the sexes,
affairs, rejection, divorce, and the single life (both good and bad), Shain touches
upon what "the best men" are like. "Much of women's resentment toward men at
the moment," she writes in a representative passage, "is related to their notion
that men, since they are supposed to be superior, should meet all their needs, and
that is a pretty heavy trip to lay on anyone and generally leaves men feeling they've
been charged with the national debt."

1020. Shapiro, Joan, with George Hartlaub. **Men: A Translation for
Women.** New York: Dutton, 1992. 245p. bibliography, 237-38. index.

A psychiatrist, Shapiro utilizes her knowledge of psychological theory
and of men in therapy to "translate" men's behaviors for women. Our society
trains men to be soldiers, to do painful and dangerous things without question.
Thus, men learn early to repress feelings. As boys, males learn they must
differentiate from Mother, and as men they continue to resist being too
domesticated by women. Men create structures to keep things in order and
under control in case of a crisis. Whereas women talk things out to establish
relationships, men tend to be in a trance, that is, they filter out talk and
feelings to keep focused on their task. Men need other men to validate their
sense of masculinity, and work is often a way of winning other men's approval
and of showing their love for women. For men, sex is a route to feelings; for
women, feelings are a route to sex. Men tend to be fascinated with numbers,
and sports serves many male needs. Throughout the book, Shapiro writes in
clear prose for a lay audience. Although she sometimes accepts too uncritically
the notion that U.S. society devalues women and values men, her goodwill
toward men and women makes this a healing, rather than a divisive, book.

1021. Stapleton, Jean, and Richard Bright. **Equal Dating.** Nashville, TN:
Abingdon Press, 1979. 127p.

Within a framework of traditional ideas about sexual morality, the authors
argue for greater equality in dating. Current patterns push males and females

into roles that neither sex is comfortable with. Both sexes must take mutual responsibility in dating. Women must take the initiative more often and must pay their fair share. Men must learn that dating is not a proving ground for their masculinity: They must learn to say no to women, politely and clearly. "Chivalry is out," the authors write, "kindness is in." Casual and premarital sex, they argue, subverts a close, long-term relationship. They debunk the idea that chastity is harmful to anyone. Chapters are devoted to relating to each other's family, breaking up, and getting engaged. The diamond ring for women reinforces sexist roles; it needs to be replaced by an exchange of gifts between the couple. The penultimate chapter on getting married raises questions about who pays for what, who does the planning, and how the ceremony can be more egalitarian. A brief final chapter recognizes value in the unmarried life.

1022. Stapleton, Jean, and Richard Bright. **Equal Marriage.** Nashville, TN: Abingdon Press, 1976. 144p. bibliography, 141-44.
    As widowed spouses now married to each other, the authors describe the gains and losses both partners can expect in an equitable marriage. Extramarital affairs, as suggested in books like *Open Marriage*, strike "a blow to the heart of marriage." The authors also reject a relationship of child-wives to fatherly husbands, as advocated in some conservative marriage manuals. Instead, Stapleton and Bright affirm equity in marriage, arguing that each partner must learn the other's skills (he must learn housekeeping, she repair and maintenance work). Each must contribute financially to the marriage. The authors describe the benefits of having two parents available to children, argue that sexual equality leads to greater sexual satisfaction, and offer suggestions on how to promote non-sexist attitudes in children.

1023. Sterling, A. Justin. **What *Really* Works with Men: Solve 95% of Your Relationship Problems (and Cope with the Rest).** New York: Warner Books, 1992. xii, 209p.
    Sterling offers hard-nosed advice (primarily to upscale women) about how to establish a relationship with a worthwhile man. He warns that what attracted the woman to the man will probably be what she later most dislikes about him. Women must be the architects of relationships (because men do not know how to do the job), and such relationships require sacrifice and discipline. Women need to accept themselves first; they should never get close to a man they do not trust. Women should regard men as aliens from another planet and attend to what men do and not to what men say. Men want to please women, Sterling argues, and the woman who massages a man's ego for pleasing her has discovered the major policy of long-lasting relationships.

1024. Sunila, Joyce. **The New Lovers: Younger Men/Older Women.** New York: Fawcett Gold Medal Books, 1980. 254p. pa.
    Given the raw deal older women get in our society, Sunila argues, the older woman/younger man relationship is the preferred option for truly liberated women. Contrasting the taboo against such relationships in modern America with numerous examples of them from the past, Sunila denies that these younger men are seeking mothers in older lovers. She takes a cross-cultural look at such relationships, assesses current cultural depictions of them, and considers the practical issues involved. Sunila's humane egalitarianism would be more convincing if she were less angry with and contemptuous of older men and if she were more comfortable with the idea of women financially supporting men.

1025. Wagenvoord, James, Peyton Bailey, et al. **Men: A Book for Women.** New York: Avon Books, 1978. 383p. illus. bibliography, 370-76. index. pa.

A popular attempt to unravel the mysteries of men for an audience of women, this pleasantly designed book explores such topics as the genetic basis of maleness, men's bodies, reproducing and aging, sensuality and sexuality, men and work, marriage and separations, and fathering.

1026. Wagenvoord, James, Peyton Bailey, et al. **Women: A Book for Men.** New York: Avon Books, 1979. 384p. illus. bibliography, 370-76. index. pa.

A companion piece to *Men: A Book for Women* (entry 1025), this popularly written book explains for the general male reader such matters as the genetics of femininity, women's bodies, sexuality, working women, and motherhood.

1027. Walczak, Yvette. **He and She: Men in the Eighties.** London and New York: Routledge, 1988. 166p. bibliography, 159-63. index. pa.

Drawing upon interviews with 51 British men ranging in age from 17 to 90, Walczak attempts to understand how males have responded to social changes and gender issues. After presenting her questionnaire, she argues that biological differences do not determine behavioral differences. She reports the men's views on topics such as gender differences, educational opportunities, employment, relationships, finances and housework, and child rearing. The men's reactions are mixed. Some favor the more egalitarian views that Walczak espouses; others believe in greater sexual differentiation than Walczak does. The final chapter presents fuller portraits of three men: Tom (who believes in sharp sexual differences), Graham (who has mixed beliefs about gender equality), and Nigel (who believes in absolute equality between the sexes). The study's major shortcoming is its narrow focus on feminist topics. Walczak ignores men's issues such as male-only military obligations and combat duty, male health and longevity, and fathers' rights. When one man remarks that "justice is not always done when fathers are deprived of custody," Walczak does not pursue the issue but quickly changes the topic to a feminist one. Her next sentence is: "Opinions were split on whether mothers should go out to work."

1028. Wetzler, Scott. **Living with the Passive-Aggressive Man.** New York: Simon and Schuster, 1992. 207p. index.

Aimed at the women's "self help" market, this exercise in popular psychology attempts to aid women in coping with men who send mixed messages of non-involvement and animosity. Wetzler describes "passive-aggressive" conduct and advises women on how to handle such behavior in male lovers, relatives, and coworkers. The author recognizes that women can also be passive-aggressive but avoids dealing with such an unmarketable topic.

1029. Yablonsky, Lewis. **The Extra-Sex Factor: Why Over Half of America's Married Men Play Around.** New York: Times Books, 1979. 239p. notes.

On the basis of in-depth interviews with over 50 men and 16 women, as well as 771 responses from married men to a brief, general-survey questionnaire, Yablonsky concludes that more than half of American married men engage in extramarital sex (or "extra-sex," in the author's terminology). Allowing that the men's motives are complex, Yablonsky nevertheless concludes that marital fidelity is not the norm in America, that most married men engaging in extra-sex do not intend to leave their home situation, that most affairs are brief, and that most men engage in extra-sex for the companionship of other women and not simply for sex. Excerpts from the interviews, which form the bulk of the book's content, indicate that extra-sex grows out of and creates considerable emotional turmoil.

1030. Zola, Marion. **All the Good Ones Are Married: Married Men and the Women Who Love Them.** New York: Times Books, 1981. xviii, 257p. Reprint, as *All the Good Ones Are Married: Women Talk Frankly about Men and Love Today*, New York: Berkley, 1982. pa.

    Zola explores extramarital affairs from the viewpoints of "the other woman," "the man in the middle," and "the woman at home." Using interviews with 200 women and 100 men, she constructs scenarios of typical affairs and recounts particular intrigues, replete with soap-opera complications.

Cross-References

See chapter 8, "Feminism."

648. Ali, Shahrazad. **The Blackman's Guide to Understanding the Black-woman.**

474. Appleton, William S. **Fathers and Daughters: A Father's Powerful Influence on a Woman's Life.**

580. Arcana, Judith. **Every Mother's Son.**

74. Astrachan, Anthony. **How Men Feel: Their Responses to Women's Demands for Equality and Power.**

77. Baker, Mark. **What Men *Really* Think: About Women, Love, Sex, and Themselves.**

82. Berkowitz, Bob, with Roger Gittines. **What Men Won't Tell You: But What Women Need to Know.**

393. Boose, Lynda E., and Betty S. Flowers, eds. **Fathers and Daughters.**

689. Dinnerstein, Dorothy. **The Mermaid and the Minotaur: Sexual Arrangements and Human Malaise.**

690. Drew, Jane Myers. **Where Were You When I Needed You Dad?: A Guide for Healing Your Father Wound.**

945. Elshtain, Jean Bethke. **Women and War.**

97. Farrell, Warren. **Why Men Are the Way They Are: The Male-Female Dynamic.**

493. Fields, Suzanne. **Like Father, Like Daughter: How Father Shapes the Woman His Daughter Becomes.**

274a. Filene, Peter G. **Him/Her/Self: Sex Roles in Modern America.**

104. Goldberg, Herb. **The Inner Male: Overcoming Roadblocks to Intimacy.**

105. Goldberg, Herb. **The New Male: From Self-Destruction to Self-Care.**

496. Goulter, Barbara, and Joan Minninger. **The Father-Daughter Dance: Insight, Inspiration, and Understanding for Every Woman and Her Father.**

501. Hammer, Signe. **Passionate Attachments: Fathers and Daughters in America Today.**

915. Herman, Judith Lewis, with Lisa Hirschman. **Father-Daughter Incest.**

111. Hornstein, Harvey A. **A Knight in Shining Armor: Understanding Men's Romantic Illusions.**

892. Johnson, James L. **What Every Woman Should Know About a Man.**

309. King, Florence. **He: An Irreverent Look at the American Male.**

585. Klein, Carole. **Mothers and Sons.**

516. Leonard, Linda Schierse. **The Wounded Woman: Healing the Father-Daughter Relationship.**

226. Levine, Judith. **My Enemy, My Love: Man-Hating and Ambivalence in Women's Lives.**

162. Loeb, Catherine R., Susan E. Searing, and Esther Stineman, comps., with Meredith J. Ross. **Women's Studies: A Recommended Core Bibliography, 1980-1985.**

527. Marone, Nicky. **How to Father a Successful Daughter.**

23. McGill, Michael E. **The McGill Report on Male Intimacy.**

609. Mead, Margaret. **Male and Female: A Study of the Sexes in a Changing World.**

1038a. Milwid, Beth. **Working with Men: Women in the Workplace Talk About Sexuality, Success, and Their Male Coworkers.**

126. Naifeh, Steven, and Gregory White Smith. **Why Can't Men Open Up? Overcoming Men's Fears of Intimacy.**

587. Olsen, Paul. **Sons and Mothers: Why Men Behave As They Do.**

715. Osherson, Samuel. **Wrestling with Love: How Men Struggle with Intimacy with Women, Children, Parents, and Each Other.**

532a. Owen, Ursala, ed. **Fathers: Reflections by Daughters.**

756. Penney, Alexandra. **How to Make Love to a Man.**

757. Pietropinto, Anthony, and Jacqueline Simenauer. **Beyond the Male Myth: What Women Want to Know About Men's Sexuality: A Nationwide Survey.**

923. Russell, Diana E.H. **Rape in Marriage.**

547. Secunda, Victoria. **Women and Their Fathers: The Sexual and Romantic Impact of the First Man in Your Life.**

762. Stanway, Andrew. **A Woman's Guide to Men and Sex: How to Understand a Man's Sexual and Emotional Needs.**

141. Steinmann, Anne, and David J. Fox. **The Male Dilemma: How to Survive the Sexual Revolution.**

167. Stineman, Esther, comp., with Catherine Loeb. **Women's Studies: A Recommended Core Bibliography.**

429. Tannen, Deborah. **You Just Don't Understand: Women and Men in Conversation.**

431. Todd, Janet, ed. **Men by Women.**

558. Woolfolk, William, with Donna Woolfolk Cross. **Daddy's Little Girl: The Unspoken Bargain Between Fathers and Their Daughters.**

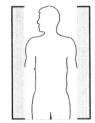

27

Work and Play

A. Careers, Employment, Unemployment

1031. Cockburn, Cynthia. **In the Way of Women: Men's Resistance to Sex Equality in Organizations.** London: Macmillan Education, 1991. Reprint, Ithaca, NY: ILR Press, 1991. 260p. (Cornell International Industrial and Labor Relations Report, no. 18). bibliography, 242-45. index. pa.

A socialist feminist, Cockburn immediately lays down the party-line theory: Men are an oppressor class, women are an oppressed class. Having thus stacked the theoretical deck, Cockburn then distorts everything to fit neo-Marxist doctrine. (Cockburn's glossy new term for the threadbare theory is "historical materialist feminist tradition.") She investigates four British organizations: "High Street Retail," "The Service," "The Council" (or the Local Authority), and a national trade union. Although she confesses that her research is neither large nor representative, she asserts that it is "qualitative research" (i.e., she "spent a couple of months in and around" each organization's office). Cockburn, however, did interview more than 200 people, two-thirds of whom are male (although the men are given precious little chance to have their say in Cockburn's report). Insisting that equality of opportunity is not enough, Cockburn champions social engineering that will produce equality of outcomes. Translation: Women need special favors from the state. She faults the British 1975 Sex Discrimination Act for offering equal protection to both sexes, not to women alone. Why, she asks, has none of the four organizations achieved gender equality of outcome? The answer, of course, is men—whom Cockburn caricatures as an evilhearted class of power-mad jerks desiring nothing more than to keep women in subjection. The grammatical give-away of this male conspiracy theory (i.e., the heavy use of the passive voice to suggest a conspiracy where no evidence exists) is everywhere evident in Cockburn's prose. Black men get no sympathy from Cockburn; after all, they are men and they oppress black women. She castigates gay men for their misogyny but admires them slightly because she believes they weaken male power structures. Cockburn concludes with "strategies" for achieving equality of outcomes by subverting democratic processes and implementing socialist engineering.

1032. Glasstone, Richard. **Dancing as a Career for Men.** New York: Sterling, 1981. 114p. illus. index. Original publication, as *Male Dancing as a Career* (Tadworth, Surrey: Kaye and Ward, 1980).

Although this crisply written guide to male careers in dancing is aimed at boys and their parents, others may find it an illuminating discussion of contemporary attitudes towards male dancers. The second chapter, raising the question of whether male dancing is effeminate or homosexual, points out that males have been dancing throughout human history. The current association of dance with effeminacy derives from the way in which nineteenth-century classical ballet was taken over by ethereal females dancing *sur les pointes* and representing delicate or dying creatures. The male dancer was reduced to second-class lifter and was branded with the overwhelmingly "feminine" nature of most ballet performances. Glasstone puts this aberration in the history of dance into perspective, presenting a survey of the male dancer through time. The opening chapter provides an overall view of dancing as a career for males, and other chapters describe the ballet scene, modern (or contemporary) dance, and dancing in show business. The final chapter contains a directory of practical information and useful addresses concerning professional schools, associations of dancing teachers, dance publications, bookstores, and so on. Simon Rae-Scott's photographs enhance the text.

1033. Halle, David. **America's Working Man: Work, Home, and Politics among Blue-Collar Property Owners.** Chicago and London: University of Chicago Press, 1984. xviii, 360p. illus. appendix. bibliography, 339-51. index. pa.

In this six-year study begun in 1974, Halle examines the lives of working men in a large oil refinery in Elizabeth and Linden, New Jersey. While recognizing distinctions, Halle also stresses the overlaps between blue- and white-collar lives of men. He notes that dull jobs lead the men to male-bonding leisure pursuits. These friendships can conflict with the demands of marriage, although after the children leave home, many blue-collar couples experience something of a second honeymoon. The work itself is highly automated, dull, and sometimes dangerous. Working shifts can cause problems and lack of education prevents the men from moving upward socially. Nevertheless, the men do have some control over their work. Unions and joking affirm masculine solidarity. Politically, the men are "classical democrats" who are often critical of politicians, corporate influence, and Jews (whom many believe to have inordinate power in U.S. society.) The men often dislike Blacks and Hispanics for a variety of reasons (e.g., allegedly bringing down property values). The lives of the men, Halle concludes, reflect "the sociology of the mediocre": Their religion is flat, their ethnicity is a secondary matter, and their celebration of national holidays lacks vitality. America's working men, Halle concludes, will have great influence (for good or ill) upon the nation's future.

1034. Halper, Jan. **Quiet Desperation: The Truth About Successful Men.** New York: Warner Books, 1988. x, 279p. notes.

"The mass of men lead lives of quiet desperation": Henry D. Thoreau's famous observation is applied by Halper to successful male executives, mostly from Fortune 500 companies. Her study is based upon 1,426 interviews with male executives, plus 43 in-depth interviews. While many of these men enjoy their work, Halper examines an undertow of discontent among some of them. The troubled men feel that they have sold their souls for success: they feel stifled and repressed in the corporate atmosphere, and they feel unappreciated and unloved at home. Committing emotional suicide, the men repress feelings, have no close male friends, and believe that they have been reduced to their job. Many of these men, however, are "unharnessing" themselves. Halper encourages this practice, offering suggestions to workaholics, perfectionists, and low self-esteem men. Many working men present a secure facade, but are inwardly unsettled: some play "nice guy" and cannot confront other workers, some become tyrants, and others are puzzled by women's changes and mixed signals. Many men see women's entry into the workplace as upsetting the old rules, introducing double standards, and creating new rules that do not quite work. In their personal lives, even men who have mistresses tend to stay monogamous. Sometimes, however, men will leave "the perfect wife" (who wasn't really perfect), and sometimes their wives will leave them. Both situations cause emotional stress. Halper remains hopeful, however, that men are making necessary changes, and she concludes with accounts of relationships that work well.

1035. Komarovsky, Mirra. **The Unemployed Man and His Family: The Effect of Unemployment upon the Status of the Man in Fifty-nine Families.** New York: Dryden Press, 1940. xii, 163p. appendix. bibliography, 163. index. Reprint, New York: Arno Press and New York Times, 1971.

This classic study, based upon case histories of 59 families from 1935 to 1936, indicates that in 13 families, the husband's status declined because of his unemployment. In such cases, the man was sometimes brutally blamed for being out of work and was rejected by family members. Regarded primarily as a breadwinner, these men suffered loss of authority, although the loss of self-esteem was felt by other men in the study too. Komarovsky also examines the men's tendency to blame themselves for their "failure," their altered relationships with younger and adolescent children, their social and political views, and the decline in sexual relations between husband and wife. The appendix discusses methodology.

1036. La Velle, Michael. **Red, White and Blue-Collar Views: A Steel-worker Speaks His Mind About America.** New York: Saturday Review Press/E. P. Dutton, 1975, xi, 212p.

This collection of La Velle articles from the *Chicago Tribune* provides a working-man's view of big business, big unions, right to work laws (which he calls "right to scab laws"), the ERA (which he supports, while chivalrously hoping to retain protective legislation favoring women), higher education, the news media (which, he says, ignore blue-collar workers), worker safety, and much more. La Velle writes a "tough" prose style, and his anger is real and often justified—although, as Studs Terkel points out in his introduction, La Velle sometimes seems to take aim at the wrong targets.

1037. LeMasters, E. E. **Blue-Collar Aristocrats: Life-Styles at a Work-ing-Class Tavern.** Madison: University of Wisconsin Press, 1975. ix, 218p. notes. index. pa.

Between 1967 and 1972, sociologist LeMasters frequented a blue-collar tavern that he calls the Oasis. From his interaction with approximately 50 regular patrons, he constructs a portrait of blue-collar people and argues that the theory of class homogenization in America has been overemphasized. The tavern men held such jobs as carpenter, plumber, bricklayer, roofer, sheet-metal worker, and so on. Among his findings are that the men in general liked their work; that it paid well; that blue-collar marriages had both problems and rewards (the latter include stability and longevity); that marital failure often adversely affected blue-collar men and women; that the battle of the sexes was alive and well at the Oasis; that virginity was out—for girls as well as for boys; that hostility towards homosexuals, feminists, and radical blacks was in; that raising "unspoiled" children was the big problem of parenting; that social life and blue-collar humor flourished at the Oasis; that the men drank more heavily than the women; and that political views were conservative or middle-of-the-road. In a final chapter, LeMasters assesses the new generation of male workers and Vietnam veterans who were beginning to frequent the Oasis.

1038. Matthiessen, Peter. **Men's Lives.** New York: Random House, Vintage Books, 1986. xvi, 336p. notes. pa.

This elegantly written portrait of a disappearing way of life focuses on the fishermen of Long Island's South Fork. Using vividly told anecdotes, the author reconstructs the history of fishing in the area, from colonial times to the 1980s. The book focuses principally upon fishermen whom Matthiessen has known from the 1950s. The politics of the rivalry between commercial and sport fishermen often points to shameful environmental abuse. Rather than a formal sociological study, Matthiessen has written a personal and moving elegy for hardy men whose lives were shaped by daily encounters with the sea.

1038a. Milwid, Beth. **Working with Men: Women in the Workplace Talk About Sexuality, Success, and Their Male Coworkers.** Hillsboro, OR: Beyond Words, 1990. 271p. Reprint, New York: Berkley Books, 1992. pa. Original publication, as *What You Get When You Go for It*, New York: Dodd, Mead, 1987.

After interviewing 125 women in the corporate workplace, Milwid finds both success and tensions. Some of the tensions are gender-specific to women, others are not. Many of the women feel uncomfortable with the nature of the workplace as well as with their male coworkers. Unfortunately, Milwid interviewed no men, and because readers cannot hear their side of the story, the book inevitably creates a "women versus men" effect. It is something of a surprise to learn in Milwid's epilogue that many male workers share the women's discontent with work and the workplace and that Milwid believes these men will join with women to transform the working world.

1039. Mitchell, Joyce Slayton. **Choices and Changes: A Career Book for Men.** New York: College Entrance Examination Board, 1982. ix, 309p. illus. pa.

For the male high school student, Mitchell surveys 14 clusters of related careers: art, architecture, and design; business: administration and management; business: adverting and marketing; business: computer operations; business: money management; business: sales; communications; education; government; health; science and technology; social service; social science; and transportation. In the introduction, Mitchell advises males to avoid the "success object" trap by which a man is valued according to his income; she describes a "new age" for men in which they can be more flexible about sharing obligations and rewards—on the job and in the family—and can strive toward being "a whole person with many choices."

1040. Mitchell, Joyce Slayton. **Free to Choose: Decision Making for Young Men.** New York: Delacorte Press, 1976. xii, 263p.

Written for high school males, this collection of essays is designed to raise the male consciousness about sexual decisions (in the pre-AIDS era), male-female relationships, drug use, spirituality, athletics, education, and careers. Mitchell has written many sections of the book; other contributors include Marc Feigen Fasteau, Richard V. Lee, Warren Farrell, Leonard Swidler, Marnin Kligfeld, Natalie M. Shepard, and Betty M. Vetter. Mitchell's misandric assumptions are sometimes grating, and the book's concept of male liberation is often guilt-ridden.

1041. Parnes, Herbert S., Joan E. Crowley, R. Jean Haurin, Lawrence J. Less, William R. Morgan, Frank L. Mott, and Gilbert Nestel. **Retirement Among American Men.** Lexington, MA: Lexington Books, D. C. Heath, 1985. xviii, 236p. appendix. bibliographies after each chapter. notes. index.
The six authors draw upon a 15-year study of men begun in 1966. Of the 4,938 men involved at the start of the study, 2,794 men were still living in 1981. At this time, the surviving men were all between the ages of 61 and 74. The authors devote separate chapters to topics such as the factors affecting mortality (e.g., race, education, market skills), the patterns and reasons for taking retirement, and the men's economic well-being in retirement. Other chapters examine the leisure activities and social networks of retired men, the psychological and physical effects of retirement on the men, and some men's reasons for avoiding retirement. The concluding chapter by Parnes succinctly summarizes the study's findings.

1042. Swados, Harvey, ed. **The American Writer and the Great Depression.** Indianapolis, IN: Bobbs-Merrill, 1966. xli, 521p. (The American Heritage Series). illus. bibliography, xxxvi-xli. notes. index. pa.
The two purposes of this anthology are "to convey the impact of the depression of the 1930's on the life and thought of the American people and to present what Harvey Swados calls 'a cross section of good writing of the period.' " Many of the 35 short stories, poems, and excerpts from longer works focus on the working man, providing vivid recreations of male experiences during this period of American hardship. Stark photographs abet the writing of such authors as Sherwood Anderson, John Steinbeck, Erskine Caldwell, James T. Farrell, Nelson Algren, Richard Wright, John Dos Passos, and Thomas Wolfe.

B. Athletics, Sports

1043. Gorn, Elliott J. **The Manly Art: Bare-Knuckle Prize Fighting in America.** Ithaca, NY, and London: Cornell University Press, 1986. 317p. illus. notes. index.
This history of bare-knuckle fighting in the United States combines gender, social, and labor history. After a prologue describing the origins of prize fighting in England, Gorn recounts its transplanting to the United States. He recounts the exploits of Tom Molineaux, a black fighter, and John Morrissey, an Irishman, as early U.S. boxing stars. Fear of working-class disorder and of male depravity led the middle class to reject bare-knuckle prize fighting as a sport, but it throve among working men. In the latter part of the nineteenth century, prize fighting declined as rowdiness grew, but it was reprised as a sport around the turn of the century, when athleticism and the outdoor life were being celebrated as manly. After the glory days of John L. Sullivan and James J. Corbett, the era of bare-knuckle boxing was over. For men's studies scholars, chapter 4, "The Meanings of Prize Fighting," will be most illuminating. Gorn argues that working men took to boxing to supplement their income and that prize fighting provided forms of male bonding, class solidarity, and ethnic identity. Prize fighting represented a working-class version of the

American dream, a way of defying the niceties of middle-class "civilization." Work undermined the masculinity of nineteenth-century male laborers, but boxing reinforced a masculinity that was not responsible and upright, but tough and resilient. As a manly sport, it served to differentiate men from the feminine. The sport of the "bachelor culture," prize fighting was a rejection of domesticity, and it reinforced the male concept of honor. Moreover, for centuries, males had been subjected to violence; prize fighting transformed that violence into an art form. The boxer embraced the violence of life and toughed it out.

1044. Messner, Michael A. **Power at Play: Sports and the Problem of Masculinity.** Boston: Beacon Press, 1992. xi, 240p. (Men and Masculinity Series). appendixes. bibliography, 217-33. index.

Conducting a feminist inquiry, Messner finds that sports often encourage some of the less desirable traits of masculinity. Drawing upon his own experiences and interviews with 30 male former athletes, he sees sports as a "gendered institution" constructed by society. Among boys, the competitiveness of sports often enforces male separateness and homophobia. The boy's desire to win can make defeat painful, and the lure of sports can lead some young men (especially black men) to devalue academics. As currently constructed, sports encourage males to separate mind from body. Male athletes are driven to play when injured and to resort to drugs to enhance performance. Team spirit often involves sexist views of women, and disengaging from sports can cause some men to experience a crisis of masculine identity. Messner welcomes the entrance of more females into sports but is unclear about whether sports will harm femininity as he believes it has harmed masculinity. He does not advocate doing away with sports altogether; rather, he urges a more egalitarian society in which the problem of sports and masculinity will diminish.

1045. Messner, Michael A., and Donald F. Sabo, eds. **Sport, Men, and the Gender Order: Critical Feminist Perspectives.** Champaign, IL: Human Kinetics Books, 1990. vii, 288p. bibliography, 257-80. notes. index.

Because most contributors to this volume employ a radical feminist perspective, the book's prevailing view is that sports reinforces men's power over women, a dominating mode of masculinity, heterosexism, racism, ageism, and other social evils. This reductive view of athletics ensures that most of the essays in the collection will be narrowly politicized. The editors' introduction lays out the theoretical groundwork for the volume, undercutting liberal feminism and supporting radical, socialist feminism. Essays in part 1 consider theoretical and historical foundations, those in part 2 consider contemporary research, and those in part 3 examine challenges, changes, and alternatives to masculinity-dominated sports. Some essays transcend ideological posturing, most notably Michael Kimmel's account of baseball's role in defining U.S. masculinity from 1880-1920 and Richard Majors's analysis of sports as black male "cool pose." Other essays become mired in thinly veiled misandry. Bruce Kidd denounces sports as "the men's cultural centre" that excludes women, Donald F. Sabo and Joe Panepinto deplore the way in which football reproduces male roles, and Lois Bryson condemns athletics as a tool of dominant masculinity and capitalism. Some essays are marred by moral smugness. R. W. Connell's portrait of Steve Donoghue, a young Australian "iron man," looks suspiciously like a put-down motivated by envy. In the epilogue, Carole Oglesby invokes Mary Daly and Adrienne Rich to lament that contributors to the volume have insufficiently exalted the Radical Feminine.

1046. Mitzel, John. **Sports and the Macho Male.** 2d ed. Boston: Fag Rag Books, 1976. 32p. illus. pa.

Mitzel berates organized sports in the United States for fostering "straight macho" values of aggressiveness, militancy, and repressiveness, and for downplaying of the affectional, homoerotic aspects of male bonding.

1047. Pronger, Brian. **The Arena of Masculinity: Sports, Homosexuality, and the Meaning of Sex.** New York: St. Martin's Press, 1990. xii, 305p. illus. bibliography, 277-88. notes. index. pa.

Reflecting on male sports, Pronger comments on a variety of matters connected with homosexuality. He argues that the gay male often is alienated from sports because of their role in developing heterosexual masculinity through contest. The paradox of gay interest in sports is that homosexuality simultaneously embraces and violates the norms of heterosexual masculinity. Gay sensibility is "fluid," he argues, shifting from de-emphasis (downplaying gayness) to irony (a conscious discrepancy between appearance and reality) to change (altering social constructions of sexuality.) Pronger examines matters such as jock pornography, locker-room erotics, and gay athletics. Pronger's reflections are sometimes propped by dubious arguments such as: heterosexuality is hopelessly corrupted because it replicates "patriarchy's" oppression of women, homosexuality represents gender equality because members of the same sex practice it, "pornography" depicts males as objects whereas gay "homoerotic materials" present the male as a partner in an erotic world, and the violence in homoerotic materials is merely playful.

1048. Sabo, Donald F., and Ross Runfola, eds. **Jock: Sports and Male Identity.** Englewood Cliffs, NJ: Prentice-Hall, 1980. xvii, 365p. bibliography, 339-52. notes. index. pa.

"All the selections in this book," the editors note, "share the critical assumption that sports shape many undesirable elements of the male role and perpetuate sexist institutions and values." Twenty-seven essays, plus an editorial introduction and a conclusion, stress the negative aspects of sports in fostering such characters as sexism, authoritarianism, negative forms of aggression, paramilitary mentality, and patriotic imperialism. Among the selections are Warren Farrell's 1974 description of the Super Bowl as machismo ritual, Peter J. Stein and Steven Hoffman's analysis of sports and male role strain, Ross J. Pudaloff's discussion of sports in U.S. literature, and Edgar Z. Friedenberg's analysis of homoerotic fantasy in spectator sports. Three essays discuss women in sports, and the concluding seven essays suggest alternatives to current attitudes and practices in sports. In the final selection, the editors trace the development of the men's liberation movement and the dissatisfaction of some men with traditional sports.

1049. Will, George F. **Men at Work: The Craft of Baseball.** New York: Macmillan, 1990. 353p. illus. index. Reprint, New York: HarperPerennial, 1991. pa.

"Winning is not everything," Will writes. "Baseball—its beauty, its craftsmanship, its exactingness—is an *activity* to be loved, as much as ballet or fishing or politics, and loving it is a form of participation." Now that sports are increasingly the target of sometimes heavy-handed analyses that reduce them to a source of gender, race, and class evils, Will's lovingly detailed look at men who play professional baseball provides a refreshing corrective, although he refuses to romanticize the game. Will speaks of the "hard blue glow" of the male athlete who achieves mastery in his sport. Will's chapters ostensibly focus on manager Tony La Russa, pitcher Orel Hershiser, batter Tony Gwynn, and fielder Cal Ripken. These men, however, are often the starting point for a series of observations and anecdotes about the game and the professional players who experience "the sweet exaltation of work."

Cross-References

974. Bird, Caroline. **The Two Paycheck Marriage: How Women at Work Are Changing Life in America.**

3. Blotnik, Srully. **Ambitious Men: Their Drives, Dreams, and Delusions.**

36. Bouton, Jim. **Ball Four, Plus Ball Five.**

978. Campbell, Bebe Moore. **Successful Women, Angry Men: Backlash in the Two-Career Marriage.**

691. Earl, William L. **A Dancer Takes Flight: Psychological Concerns of the American Male Dancer.**

982. Ehrenreich, Barbara. **The Hearts of Men: American Dreams and the Flight from Commitment.**

99. Filene, Peter, ed. **Men in the Middle: Coping with the Problems of Work and Family in the Lives of Middle-aged Men.**

176. Fine, Gary Alan. **With the Boys: Little League Baseball and Preadolescent Culture.**

101. Gerson, Kathleen. **No Man's Land: Men's Changing Commitments to Family and Work.**

985. Gilbert, Lucia Albino. **Men in Dual-Career Families: Current Realities and Future Prospects.**

990. Hart, Lois B., and J. David Dalke. **The Sexes at Work: Improving Work Relationships Between Men and Women.**

112. Hunter, Mark. **The Passions of Men: Work and Love in the Age of Stress.**

49. Kopay, David, and Perry Deane Young. **The David Kopay Story: An Extraordinary Self-Revelation.**

998. Korda, Michael. **Male Chauvinism! How It Works.**

999. Kozmetsky, Ronya and George. **Making It Together: A Survival Manual for the Executive Family.**

1001. Lewan, Lloyd S., with Roger G. Billingsley. **Women in the Workplace: A Man's Perspective.**

659. Liebow, Elliot. **Tally's Corner: A Study of Negro Streetcorner Men.**

630. Lynch, Frederick R. **Invisible Victims: White Males and the Crisis of Affirmative Action.**

57. Meggyesy, Dave. **Out of Their League.**

366. Miller, Arthur. **Death of a Salesman.**

1012. Pleck, Joseph H. **Working Wives/Working Husbands.**

665. Rogosin, Donn. **Invisible Men: Life in Baseball's Negro Leagues.**

1015. Ryglewicz, Hilary, and Pat Koch Thaler. **Working Couples: How to Cope with Two Jobs and One Home.**

1017. Shaevitz, Marjorie Hansen, and Morton H. Shaevitz. **Making It Together as a Two-Career Couple.**

31. Weiss, Robert S. **Staying the Course: The Emotional and Social Lives of Men Who Do Well at Work.**

32. Wheelock, Jane. **Husbands at Home: The Domestic Economy in a Post-Industrial Society.**

33. Whyte, William H., Jr. **The Organization Man.**

846. Woods, James D., with Jay H. Lucas. **The Corporate Closet: The Professional Lives of Gay Men in America.**

Author/Title Index

Numbers cited in index are entry numbers. Titles of books, films, etc., followed by an *n* are citations in annotations.

Subject Index

Numbers cited in index are entry numbers.